# PERSPECTIVES ON DISABILITY

# Text and Readings on Disability

## Mark Nagler, Ph.d.
### University of Waterloo

## Foreword by Evan J. Kemp, Jr.
### Former Chairman, U.S. Equal Employment Opportunity Commission

# PERSPECTIVES ON DISABILITY

## SECOND EDITION

HEALTH MARKETS RESEARCH
PALO ALTO, CALIFORNIA

Published by HEALTH MARKETS RESEARCH
851 Moana Court
Palo Alto, CA 94306

Printed in the United States of America

*Library of Congress Cataloging-in-Publication Data*

Editor, Mark Nagler, Ph.D.

Perspectives on Disability
Text and Readings on Disability
Second Edition

Library of Congress Catalog Card Number 93-079106

1. Disability  2. Social Interaction

ISBN 0-9627640-3-5 (hardcover)

# TABLE OF CONTENTS

# FOREWORD

July 26, 1990, will ever remain an historic day for people with disabilities and all concerned with civil rights, as President George Bush signed the Emancipation Proclamation for people with disabilities, the "Americans with Disabilities Act" (ADA). As I said when I shared the platform with the President~without whom that day would not have been possible~the ADA is "the most important civil rights legislation of the last quarter of a century" for Americans. Embodying the world-wide activism of people with disabilities and their representatives, the ADA proclaims that "the Nation's proper goals regarding individuals with disabilities are to assure equality of opportunity, full participation, independent living, and economic self-sufficiency for such individuals."

While affirming the principle of equality of access and opportunity for millions of disabled Americans, the ADA, moreover, represents a critical shift in Federal policy toward mainstreaming and integration, and away from dependency and segregation. Independence, freedom of choice, and involvement in the social and economic mainstream, whether in the workplace or in public accommodations and public transportation, are now fostered by this revolutionary legislation.

The ADA's five titles prohibit discrimination in employment, public accommodations, public services, public transportation, and telecommunications. The law will thus require that all new public accommodations be designed and constructed to be fully accessible. Likewise, new buses and trains, and new transportation facilities will have to be accessible. In addition, the ADA mandates the creation of a national telecommunications relay system so that, at long last, several million speech-and hearing-impaired citizens will be able to use the telephone.

But the crux of the ADA is its employment provisions, for joblessness is the truly disabling condition. A staggering 58 percent of all men with disabilities and 80 percent of all women with disabilities are unemployed. So long as two-thirds of disabled Americans are unemployed, we will be unable to break the terrible cycle of dependency and segregation. And, if people with disabilities cannot break the grip of economic dependence, our society is doomed to spend more than $100 billion dollars a year on benefits that most recipients would willingly trade for a good job.

Hence the significance of Title I of the ADA, dealing with employment discrimination~who is covered and how the law is to be enforced. For the most part, the law adopts the three-part definition of "individual with handicaps' used in the Rehabilitation Act of 1973: an individual with a physical or mental impairment that substantially limits at least one of that person's major life activities; an individual with a record of such an impairment; and an individual regarded as having such an impairment.

The first part of the definition is intended to include only those persons with substantial disabilities "in a major life activity" such as walking, seeing, hearing, speaking, and breathing. Thus, for example, an individual with epilepsy, paralysis, blindness, or a hearing impairment would be covered by this definition. Minor impairments, however, such as faulty vision which can be corrected with glasses or a broken leg which will heal in a few months, are not included in this definition of disability.

Secondly, individuals with a *record* of a substantially limiting impairment are covered. This includes, for example, an individual with a history of cancer that has been in remission for a number of years.

Lastly, the definition includes those persons who are regarded as having a substantially limiting disability, regardless of whether the disability exists in fact. To illustrate, a person with a limp may actually have no physical impairment which would hinder his or her ability to perform the job duties in question. But if an employer, reacting out of bias against the person's limp, refuses to hire that individual, that employer will be violating the ADA.

The core nondiscrimination requirement provides that no employer shall discriminate against any qualified individual because of such individual's disability in regard to job application procedures, hiring or discharge, compensation, advancement, job training, or other terms, conditions, and privileges of employment. A "qualified individual with a disability" means an individual with a disability who, with or without reasonable accommodation, can perform the essential functions of the employment position that the individual holds or desires.

The law provides several important exemptions from the definition of disability. Disabilities do not include: homosexuality, bisexuality, transvestism, transsexualism, pedophilia, exhibitionism, voyeurism, or other gender identity or sexual behavior disorders; compulsive gambling, pyromania, kleptomania; and psychoactive substance abuse disorders resulting from current use of illegal drugs. Much concern had been raised about the ADA's application to persons using illegal drugs, but the definition of disability explicitly excludes them. Employers may, if they wish, conduct drug testing to detect the use of illegal drugs by applicants and employees and may make employment decisions based on the results so long as the test accurately detects the presence of illegal drugs. Moreover, the bill specifically provides that employers may prohibit employees in the workplace from using or being under the influence of illegal drugs or alcohol as well. And employers may require employees to follow the Drug Free Workplace Act of 1988 as well as applicable government regulations covering sensitive jobs.

An employer's refusal to make a *reasonable accommodation* that would not impose an undue hardship is also considered discriminatory under the ADA. In brief, a reasonable accommodation is a provision for a person with a disability to perform the essential duties of the position. But an employer's reasonable accommodation responsibility is not limitless. First, the employer must know about the physical or mental limitations of the disabled person. If a disability is hidden and the disabled person does not request an accommodation, an employer is not required by the ADA to intuit whether an accommodation is needed.

Second, the obligation to make a reasonable accommodation only extends to "otherwise qualified" individuals with disabilities. Thus, the ADA does not require an employer looking for someone with a degree or experience in marketing to handle its advertising department to hire or accommodate a disabled person with a degree in philosophy and no experience in advertising.

Third, if an employer can show that the accommodation would impose an undue hardship on the operation of its business, it is relieved of the obligation to provide that accommodation. The ADA defines "undue hardship" as "an action requiring significant difficulty or expense" according to several factors the bill lists to assist EEOC and the courts. EEOC and the courts may look at site-specific resources as well as the resources of the employer as a whole. The site-specific factors require an examination of the relationship between the employer and the site providing the accommodation to determine whether resources from the employer generally are available to the site or not. Exactly when the resources of the employer or the resources of the site alone will be controlling for undue hardship purposes will be decided on a case by case basis. The guiding principle remains that larger employers have a greater duty to make accommodations than do smaller employers.

In addition to requiring an employer to make a reasonable accommodation, the ADA would make it illegal for an employer to deny an employment opportunity to a disabled applicant or employee *if* the basis for the denial is the individual's need for reasonable accommodation. This provision is intended to cover a situation in which an eligible and qualified employee is denied a promotion because his new position would require the employer to purchase equipment needed to accommodate his disability. It also responds to instances where employees or applicants themselves offer to provide a necessary accommodation (say, an expensive talking computer) that would otherwise impose an undue hardship on the employer.

With respect to employee selection criteria, the ADA prohibits the use of qualification tests or selection criteria that screen out or tend to screen out a qualified disabled individual or a class of qualified disabled individuals. Employers cannot rely on standards, tests, or criteria that arbitrarily exclude disabled people. An employer may, however, use standards or criteria that are not arbitrary but are job-related and consistent with business necessity. If a disabled applicant cannot meet a job-related standard and there is no accommodation that would enable the applicant to satisfy the standard, the applicant is not qualified for the job. It is not unlawful to refuse to hire him.

In addition, an employer may not make pre-employment inquiries as to the existence, nature, or severity of an applicant's disability, but it may ask questions as to an applicant's ability to perform job-related duties. Also consistent with section 504 regulations, implementing the Rehabilitation Act of 1973, an employer may require a pre-employment medical examination only after a conditional offer of employment and only if a medical examination is required of all applicants for a particular position. Information obtained through such examinations must be kept confidential and must be used in a manner consistent with the requirements of the ADA. This means that if a medical examination reveals that an applicant cannot perform essential job functions, an employer must consider a reasonable accommodation which would permit the applicant to perform the job.

The employment title of the ADA took effect on July 26, 1992~two years after the date of the law's enactment. During the first year following enactment, the US. Equal Employment Opportunity Commission (EEOC) has issued implementing regulations, and, working with the Attorney General, developed and implemented a plan for technical assistance to employers, employer organizations, persons with disabilities and disability organizations, directly, as well as through grants and contracts. A technical assistance manual has also been issued. For the two years after the effective date of July 26, 1992, the law covers only employers with 25 or more employees. Then, two years later (July 26, 1994) the law's jurisdiction will extend to employers with 15 or more employees, the same standard currently imposed by Title VII of the Civil Rights Act of 1964. This will result in coverage of approximately 15 percent of all employers and 87 percent of all employees.

The ADA incorporates Title VII's charge-processing procedures. Thus, an individual claiming employment discrimination on the basis of disability must first file a charge with the EEOC. After 180 days, the individual may request a right-to-sue notice from the EEOC and may then file a lawsuit in court, if he or she wishes to proceed independently. Alternatively, the individual can await the EEOC administrative process of investigating, determining whether there is cause to believe discrimination has occurred, and, if cause has been found, conciliating, and when that fails, determining whether the EEOC itself will bring suit.

Hence, EEOC has a critical role to play in implementing the ADA. Established by Title VII of the Civil Rights Act of 1964, this agency has 25 years of experience in breaking down barriers to employment opportunity in the private sector caused by race, color, sex, national origin, and religion. Since 1978 the Commission also has been enforcing the Equal Pay Act, the Age Discrimination in Employment Act, and section 501 of the Rehabilitation Act of 1973, as amended. The latter law requires that the Federal Government take affirmative action to employ and promote qualified individuals with disabilities. Each Federal agency is required to prepare an affirmative action plan to report to the Commission its progress in hiring and promoting disabled persons. In addition, Federal Government workers and applicants for Federal employment may file complaints of employment discrimination based on disability with their agencies and may make administrative appeals to EEOC if a Federal agency rules against them. In its capacity as an administrative appellate body, EEOC has grappled with many difficult issues under the Rehabilitation Act that will arise under the ADA as well. These include questions concerning the definition of disability as well as the scope of an agency's duty to provide reasonable accommodation. Although this experience with disability discrimination law had been limited to government employment, it provided EEOC with a solid foundation for implementing the ADA employment provisions in the private sector.

EEOC is a small Federal law enforcement agency with approximately 3,000 employees and a Fiscal Year 1993 appropriation of $222 million. The agency has 50 District, Area and Local offices throughout the United States. During Fiscal Year 1992, EEOC received over 70,000 charges of employment discrimination in private sector employment. With the Civil Rights Act of 1991 the EEOC received the power to sue employers for damages in cases of discrimination, a powerful addition to securing hiring, promotion, or back pay. The increased powers will also apply to the enforcement of the ADA.

In November 1992, EEOC received an astounding total of 1,706 new charges under ADA, for a total of 2,461 in the three months Title I was in effect. Thus the ADA could increase the agency's workload by over twenty percent beyond the Fiscal Year 1992 charges. The success of the EEOC in enforcing the ADA as well as its other mandates is dependent on its budget, which enables it to acquire the human capital of investigators and attorneys.

The EEOC is ready to help make the promise of the Americans with Disabilities Act a reality. But government alone, even with the newly crafted tool of the ADA, cannot make this happen. It will take the persistent efforts of informed people with disabilities to ferret out discrimination, expose it to the light of day, and eradicate it. The contributions to this volume exemplify such educational efforts. We need more of them like these as the EEOC seeks to inform, conciliate, and litigate, to eradicate barriers and bring persons with disabilities into the mainstream. Moreover, the ADA should be looked upon as model civil rights legislation generally, which can remind all who fall under the civil rights laws of the importance of empowerment, education, and mainstreaming.

Evan J. Kemp, Jr.
Chairman
United States Equal Employment Opportunity Commission
Washington, D.C.

January 19, 1993

# Acknowledgments

As in the first edition, I would like to thank those fellow academics and fellow people with disabilities who prompted this work. The selected articles reflect a spectrum of interest that they have conscientiously identified.

I am indebted to my publisher, Martin Rosner and his wife Judy, of Health Markets Research, Palo Alto, California, for having the courage to undertake the publication of an in depth work such as this.

I would also like to thank Wendy Brillinger for her conscientious commitment to this project. This second edition could not have been accomplished in its present form without her insight and commitment for which I am truly appreciative. I would also like to thank Craig Bryson, Kelly Hannah, Joan Elvy, Judith McAdam and Rhea Brillinger for their assistance in typing the final draft. I would also like to acknowledge my parents, Ann and Leo Nagler, and to Sabine Helman ~ important people who have always been there for me.

I am grateful to my colleagues at Renison College and the University of Waterloo who have been responsible for providing a rich intellectual environment and the facilities for this work.

Again, and most importantly, I want to express my ongoing appreciation to Sharon, Adam and David for a life that makes everything worthwhile and important. Their observations on a daily basis have been my inspiration.

Mark Nagler, Editor

# About the Author

Dr. Nagler was born with Cerebral Palsy which was not diagnosed until he was five years old. His parents, relatives and friends provided him with support which allowed him to progress through the education system to receive a Doctoral degree in Sociology from the University of Sterling in Scotland. The author specializes in the study of disability related issues, deviance, and race and ethnic relations. He is immediate past president of the Advocacy Resource Center for the Handicapped (ARCH) in Toronto, Ontario, Canada. ARCH is the umbrella legal clinic which covers forty-one organizations for people with disabilities and whose people defend the rights of people with disabilities. Dr. Nagler has also chaired a committee for people with disabilities on behalf of the Canadian Jewish Congress. Given the experience and contributions of Dr. Nagler to disability related issues, it is evident that he possesses a unique and personal understanding of the concerns addressed in this book.

Dr. Nagler is presently an Associate Professor in the Department of Sociology at Renison College, University of Waterloo, Waterloo, Ontario, Canada N2L 3G4

*Preparation of the second edition of* **Perspectives** on **Disability** *was gratefully supported in part by a grant from the University of Waterloo, Social Sciences and Humanities Grant Fund (UW/SSHRC).*

# Introduction to the Second Edition
## *A Positive Perspective*

The social and philosophical advancement generated in the last twenty years has been a powerful thrust producing positive changes that have emancipated a number of groups as we approach the year 2000. People with disabilities, like other minority groups, entered the twentieth century lacking power, acceptance and legitimacy. The "proper way" of doing things illustrated that it was normal to insulate and isolate minority groups from mainstream society. Fortunately, this tradition has undergone dynamic change. The philosophical perspective that envelops this publication emanates from the tradition of labeling theory and symbolic interaction.

People with disabilities have been a significant part of this social change which is affecting almost all segments of western life. Specifically for people with disabilities, the significant patterns of social change have involved de institutionalization, integration, empowerment, advocacy, and acceptance. In many social spheres the advent of the Americans with Disabilities Act (ADA) (1990) signified that people with disabilities had become a recognized minority group who were capable of exercising power and autonomy in their lives. Former United States President, George Bush, recognized this powerful constituency and thus promised people with disabilities the ADA. The majority of people with disabilities in the United States supported George Bush's initial Presidential thrust in return for the ADA. The ADA mandated to all Americans with disabilities the legal establishment of their legitimate rights as people. Traditionally, people with disabilities were usually at the bottom of the socioeconomic ladder and were a part of a disenfranchised minority who were the last to be hired and the first to be fired.

The prevailing philosophy governing people with disabilities' roles in most societies stemmed from a Judaeo-Christian tradition of charity, welfare and pity. Although many of these people were cared for, they were often labeled as contemporary societal lepers and seldom, if ever, were they included in all realms of society. Many people with disabilities throughout history distinguished themselves as a consequence of their unique drives and intellectual capacity. The Old Testament illustrated that Moses had a speech impairment (stuttering). Franklin D. Roosevelt, Helen Keller and Steven Hawking have astounded society by the depths of their intellectual accomplishments in spite of apparent severe physical afflictions. What these people demonstrate is that many people with disabilities, given the opportunity, are able not only to be self-sufficient but also have the capacity and ability to make significant contributions. The majority of people with disabilities, especially up until the 1950's, mirrored the plight of many other disadvantaged groups. They were often labeled, isolated, alienated and institutionalized. One wonders how many individuals with the capacities of Helen Keller are languishing in institutions because their potential is not recognized.

Thus, the prevailing philosophy mandated by the ADA creates a generalized environment receptive to the legitimate acceptance and integration of people with disabilities. Children with disabilities sometimes with the support of teachers aids, are now being integrated into most school systems and this allows them the opportunities to become legitimate societal participants. However, many people with disabilities continue to be affected by the stigma, discrimination and prejudice that have affected this group in the past. People with disabilities are not only entering all realms of societal life, but they are also entering the criminal system and are often victims of all forms of family violence and abuse. But this major pattern of dynamic social change which is integrating them into society has also at times exposed them to the deviant side of society. People with disabilities are now in the process of adjusting to all aspects of their respective societies. They continue to encounter significant barriers, but they are able to amass the support systems and the power to overcome these obstacles. As Even Kemp, former chairman of the Equal Employment Opportunity Commission in Washington, D.C., and the authors of the articles in this text attest, people with disabilities are now making significant strides in all realms of society with the support they have garnered from legislative dictums, changes in philosophy, and their own "exercise of power". They are in the process of achieving the legitimacy that they and other minority groups are entitled to.

The 1954 United States Supreme Court decision mandating the integration of Black Americans into mainstream society heralded the emergence of a new philosophy which mandated acceptance, integration, and inclusion of minority groups in western life in general and North American life in particular. Data in all branches of disability research illustrate that people with disabilities are now viewed in a positive way and the philosophy of acceptance of this group of people is associated with normalcy, integration, and legitimacy. As such, people with disabilities are expected to be given the same opportunities as other minority groups.

The reader will note that there are articles in this second edition which appeared in the first edition of *Perspectives on Disability*. The article by Balcazar, et. al. *Common Concerns of Disabled Americans: Issues and Options* outlines the "disabled universe" in terms of needs, goals and obstacles that form the significant world for people with disabilities. It is interesting to note that the ADA which mandates most of this powerful change forms a significant part of the philosophical and legal codes being adopted in Canada and other countries to enshrine and establish the rights of people with disabilities in their respective societies. Likewise, the other articles reproduced in this volume must be regarded as seminal reports which illustrate significant perspectives with regard to the interests and concerns related to disability.

This volume, like its predecessor, is addressed to medical and paramedical personnel, social workers, rehabilitation specialists, educators, social scientists, the clergy, employers, peers of people with disabilities, families of people with disabilities, and all those who in their specialized capacities interact with the disabled population, and most importantly, those people with disabilities. The articles address the spectrums of concerns which are crucial in understanding the issues related to the study of disability and people with disabilities. This work has been enriched by the constant feedback I have received from the first edition of *Perspectives on Disabilities*.

I wish to thank my publisher and the contributors to this text, other experts, and many of my fellow colleagues who are disabled and who have encouraged me to produce the second edition of this textbook. The philosophy governing this edition of *Perspectives on Disability* reflects the positive thrusts achieved by people with disabilities in recent decades. I am indebted to all these people for their observations, insights and intellectual stimulation.

Mark Nagler
Department of Sociology
Renison College,
University of Waterloo,
Waterloo, Ontario, CANADA
N2L 3G4

July 1993.

# 1 What It Means to Be Disabled

Disability is evolving into a positive term. The trend to this positive orientation reflects the fact that twenty-five per cent of the North American population is classified as being disabled. Most disabled people desire normalization and integration in all spheres. Although traditionally the disabled have been the objects of prejudice and discrimination, the majority of disabled people desire to achieve acceptance and integration and to participate fully with their able-bodied counterparts. One significant factor important to the acquisition of legitimacy for all minorities is self-esteem~both at individual and group levels. Self-esteem allows people to *believe* they are included as members of society and therefore strive for the achievement of integration. The consequences of the disabled population acquiring self esteem is that significant social change is taking place after decades of deferential treatment that stemmed from ancient and biblical traditions.

The leper, a biblical term for people with disabilities, was traditionally separated, isolated and segregated from society. Legitimate integration recognizes that people with disabilities have equal, or occasionally superior, qualifications and skills to their able-bodied counterparts. Overcoming traditions of negativity is not an easy social process as in addition to overcoming the problems posed by traditional prejudice and discrimination, people with disabilities are also victimized by downturns in the economic sector. They, like other minorities, are often counseled to wait until the 'time is right'. If minorities waited until the time was right, they would probably wait forever.

The weaknesses illustrated by the disabled were, in part, a consequence of an organizational factor. Various groups of people with disabilities, (e.g., diabetics, Cerebral Palsied and paraplegics), focused on their own individual concerns. Disabled citizens began to realize the advantages to be gained by acting in concert. Perhaps the most renowned consequence of the advantages of group action for the disabled was the Americans with Disabilities Act (ADA). President George Bush realized that twenty-five per cent of the American population represented a significant political power base and by promising Americans with disabilities the ADA he was able to attract the largest segment of this population constituency. In evolving the ADA, President Bush gave legislative and legal reality to the rights of disabled people. This legislation was a most significant first step towards mandating inclusion for the disabled in American society. Hopefully, this type of legislation will become instrumental as a forerunner for people with disabilities in other societies. However, the mandating of legislation is not the only requirement for empowering disadvantaged groups. There needs to be not only the enactment of the legislation, but the eventual full acceptance of the legislation by mainstream society.

The empowerment of people with disabilities is enhanced not only by legislation such as the ADA, but by the organization and amalgamation of allied groups of people with disabilities into mainstream society and by the changing of societal attitudes. In many instances society is realizing that it is more economically efficient and more cost effective to integrate people with disabilities as opposed to the traditional patterns of treatment which served to isolate and segregate them from societal participation. Thus, people with disabilities are beginning to take their rightful place in society as illustrated by Balcazar, et al, in their article, *"Common Concerns of Disabled Americans: Issues and Options"*. This group is endeavoring to be integrated at all levels. The route to integration is through empowerment. Indeed, research in social science has discovered in many realms that integration through empowerment is much cheaper and more cost efficient than segregation and traditional disabled apartheid.

Advocacy is an important constituency of social change. Minorities often benefit from the support of others who are committed to the establishment and maintenance of democratic

2

ideals. People such as Max and Colleen Starkloff, *Matters of Control: An Oral History*, have learned from personal experience the necessity of taking control in an environment that is patronizing and dehumanizing; and to strive to develop "...a strong and expansive network of grassroots advocates for change."

In a society which is now concerned with issues of 'political correctness', it becomes vital to delineate the legitimate terms which ought to be used to describe specific minorities. As Zola illustrates in, *"Self, Identity and the Naming Question: Reflections on the Language of Disability"*, "naming" is a powerful and effective tool to "keep people in their place". Therefore, language ought to be recontextualized in order to present a factual description of specific people and who and what they represent. Joan Blaska in her article, *"The Power of Language: Speak and Write Using 'Person First' "*, augments this perspective by illustrating that attitudes are shaped by the words people hear or read about themselves and others. The mass media has a powerful influence on the attitudes developed and exercised by large segments of the population. In many instances it is obligatory that these traditional images be modified, if not erased, in order to portray individuals as 'people first'. This process is inhibited because traditional prejudice and discrimination are often deeply embedded in the social system. As Blaska maintains, "We can help people with disabilities develop positive self-esteem by referring to them in words that acknowledge ability, merit and dignity".

The fourth article addresses the constituent of power - an important constituent for any group in society concerned with establishing its rightful position The editor, in his article, *"The Disabled: The Acquisition of Power"*, illustrates that power, used in a legitimate way, is necessary because traditionally, democratic society has been reluctant to grant equality to disadvantaged minorities.

Harlan Hahn in his article, *Politics of Physical Differences: Disability and Discrimination*, illustrates the significant effects of appearance in terms of how people are labeled and treated. As Hahn illustrates, socio-political understanding of disability requires that attention be paid to both existential and esthetic sources of discrimination. Until the passing of the ADA legislators and the judiciary were reluctant to implement the principle of equality by ensuring environmental modifications in response to people's clinically demonstrable organic defects or deficiencies. For instance, prior to the ADA, employers were slow to modify their washroom facilities and therefore people who use wheelchairs were denied access to working environments.

In the article, *Further Thoughts on a Sociology of Acceptance for Disabled People,* Schwartz conveys the ideology that society is becoming more accepting and more committed to including not only the disabled, but indeed all minorities. The importance of social science research in promoting further public awareness, acceptance and integration of minority groups is a critical component to the achievement of inclusivity for marginalized groups. As Schwartz conveys, the public support of a hearing-impaired individual to the position of the Presidency of Gallaudet University illustrates the legitimacy that the public is now attaching to the occupancy of important positions by these individuals. (Note: Gallaudet University in Washington, D.C. is an educational institution for hearing-impaired people which had traditionally been administered by people with no hearing impairments ).

Further, the term 'disability' has been associated with aspects of stigma. Those labeled with disabled status were assumed to be less qualified to perform a variety of societal tasks and functions. Fine and Asch in, *Disability Beyond Stigma: Social Interaction, Discrimination and Activism,* illustrate that there are many individuals who are labeled as disabled and who, if given the opportunity, can perform as well or better than their able-bodied counterparts. The authors illustrate the consequences of social evolution as they state, "As laws, institutional arrangements, and social relationships begin to change, so too must the social psychology of disability change to reflect the altered experience of people with disabilities~and of persons without disabilities~as members of a common moral community".

The medical profession, because of its status, has traditionally been one of the most influential groups in defining disability. This status group defines and legitimizes a condition involving physical and/or psychological impairment as the first part of the definitional process. Conveyed to individuals is the diagnosis and prognosis of their conditions as well as therapeutical strategies which are vital in structuring the person with a disability's view of her or his past, present, and future potential. The medical model of disability has limitations in that there are a multitude of other groups who define disability in terms of their unique focuses.

Physiotherapists and occupational therapists as well as those in the legal, political, economic and social work professions have their own valid perspectives and definitions of disability. Rehabilitation therapists define the condition and utilize whatever techniques are available to maximize habilitative and/or rehabilitative potential. To a large extent their efforts are not only dependent on their own particular skills, but on the motivation of their clients. The legal profession attempts to measure the consequences of disability in terms of the impediments in a person's life. When possible, legal experts attempt to gain redress for injuries that may affect a client's future life.

Psychologists and psychiatrists and the nursing profession endeavor to motivate people with disabilities to accept their conditions but to also attempt to achieve maximum rehabilitation. Those in the political arena and those in the social work profession are interested in matters of social policy, pensions and the establishment and maintenance of facilities designed to house, employ, and protect segments of the disabled population requiring this type of support. Economists, politicians, educators, and allied professionals are now focusing on endeavors to effectively educate various segments of the disabled community so that they can live as self-supporting contributors to society. Society is beginning to realize the social and economic advantages to be achieved by utilizing policy to mainstream people with disabilities whenever possible. In establishing policies to accomplish these goals, society is now beginning to encounter issues related to employment equity, advocacy, and empowerment. Social scientists have looked at disability in terms of deviance, stigma, identity formation and the maintenance and restructuring of identity as a consequence of the onset of, or exposure to, disability. The clergy, often allied with members of the social work profession, are involved on an intimate basis with individuals and families experiencing the reality and consequences of disability. As well, the legal, political, economic, and social segments of society evolve their particular views of disability and what it means to them. Once disabilities are defined and probable strategies categorized, there are a variety of adaptations that can be adopted by the person who is experiencing disability.

World renowned scientist and intellectual, Stephen Hawking, a victim of amyotrophic lateral sclerosis, also known as Lou Gehrigs Disease, has refused to allow the severest handicapping condition to impede his personal, economic, social, and scientific goals. On the other hand, there are instances where individuals with minimal disabling conditions abdicate their positions in society. The fact remains that society is becoming more open to all minorities with the axiom, "We are interested in your abilities, not your disabilities". The important ramification of this orientation is that more and more people with disabilities are being presented with opportunities to develop and maintain their corporate lives. While barriers still exist because of traditional folkways, mores and laws which inhibit people with disabilities in many spheres, it remains that public awareness and education are paramount factors in alleviating these barriers.

4

# Common Concerns of Disabled Americans: Issues and Options

Yolanda Suarez De Balcazar, Barbara Bradford, Stephen B. Fawcett

The hallmark value of the disabilities rights and independent living movements is the assurance of equal access to all activities society offers, both work and leisure-related. Over 30 million people with disabilities accept responsibility for their work, family, and individual lives. Their substantial contribution to society can be attributed both to personal competence and to the strength of those communities that foster and support attempts to live independently. However, there are still many physical and social barriers that limit adequate jobs, housing, accessible transportation, and other needed services. These community problems thwart even the most heroic personal attempts to pursue a full life. This article outlines the major problems in communities that limit independence. It also provides alternatives for action from the perspective of people with disabilities. It summarizes quantitative data from nearly 13,000 people with disabilities in 319 communities in 10 states and provides qualitative information about the issues and options they identified during local town meetings and public forums. This compendium presents common concerns of people with disabilities and their insights into what actions would help assure equality of opportunity.

Questionnaires were administered to all identified citizens with disabilities in the local community or state. Sponsoring organizations included independent living centers, state vocational rehabilitation agencies, and consumer advisory committees. Average scores for importance and satisfaction were used to identify relative strength (i.e., items of high importance and high satisfaction) and possible problems (i.e., items of high importance and low satisfaction). Finally, qualitative information was obtained when the results of each survey were discussed in town meetings. Disabled citizens discussed major issues, identifying specific dimensions of issues and generating possible solutions.

## MAJOR PROBLEMS IDENTIFIED BY DISABLED AMERICANS

This section provides a summary of 18 issues identified as major problems, which are organized alphabetically by category headings. Under each category, problematic aspects are noted as well as the total number of participants who responded to surveys in which that issue was chosen as a top problem. The overall average importance and satisfaction ratings for all respondents are also presented.

### Assistive Devices: Affordability and Availability

The issue of assistive devices (e.g., wheelchairs) involves aspects such as affordability, availability of financial assistance, cost of services and repair, cost of rental, and price. Six related survey items were chosen by consumers and responded to by 6,355 people with disabilities in 6 different surveys. The issues received consistently high importance ratings, an average of 80 percent, and relatively low satisfaction ratings, an average of 42 percent.

*Consumer-Identified Dimensions:*
- Assistive devices, such as wheelchairs, are very expensive. Most people with disabilities do not have enough money to purchase devices.
- Rental of assistive devices is almost nonexistent. If rental is possible, consumers don't know where to go or get needed information.
- Medicaid and Medicare do not cover all assistive devices.

*Consumer-Generated Alternatives:*
- Change legislation regarding Medicaid and Medicare to cover purchase and repair of assistive devices.

## Commercial Services: Accessibility

The issue of accessibility of businesses, particularly public restrooms, has been selected as a problem in three different surveys. Two related survey items were responded to by 299 consumers. The issues were rated with an average importance of 87 percent and an average satisfaction rating of 47 percent.

*Consumer-Identified Dimensions:*
- In many businesses and restaurants, the restrooms are inaccessible.
- Survey businesses and provide feedback and suggestions.
- Write letters to local businesses about upgrading facilities.
- Consumers should keep informed about and review access plans and permits for new construction in the community.

## Commercial Services: Availability of Discounts

A second issue related to commercial services and identified as a problem is the availability of special rates for disabled consumers. This issue was selected in one survey involving 1,185 respondents, with an importance rating of 82 percent and a satisfaction rating of 35 percent.

*Consumer-Identified Dimensions:*
- Disabled people do not get the same discounts and shopping privileges as senior citizens. Most disabled people are on a very low fixed income.

*Consumer-Generated Alternatives:*
- Independent living centers can sell discount cards to consumers for use with participating merchants, as was done by Westside CIL in Los Angeles.
- Have a group of disabled people discuss a proposal with local merchants.

## Community Support and Responsiveness

This category includes issues related to family, community, and government support in meeting the needs of persons with disabilities. Five somewhat related items were chosen by 1,914 consumers in six surveys. They received consistently high importance ratings, with an average of 86 percent, and relatively low satisfaction ratings, with an average of 46 percent.

*Consumer-Identified Dimensions:*
- Families and communities do not encourage disabled members to be independent.
- The community does not provide opportunities or assistance for disabled people to live independently.
- There are not enough support groups available for people with disabilities and their families.
- Sexuality counseling for people with disabilities is not available.
- Local governments are unresponsive to disability issues, especially if solutions cost money. For example, disabled citizens are discouraged from registering and voting by inaccessible registration sites, polling places, and lack of transportation.

*Consumer-Generated Alternatives:*
- Encourage community groups to organize support groups and events to involve disabled people and their families.
- Encourage churches to work with support groups, and include disabled people and their families in church activities.
- Use local media to feature stories about including people with disabilities in community activities.
- Ask city councils for help in organizing programs that will encourage independence for disabled people and their families.
- Independent living centers should provide training for their staff counselors in sexuality counseling or bring in professional counselors for a workshop and provide materials.
- Consumer groups should represent themselves at city council and county court meetings, become familiar with city budgets, and advocate for funds for access improvements and disability programs.
- Consumer groups should encourage and assist disabled citizens to register to vote.
- Use the American Civil Liberties Union to enforce existing access and registration laws.

## Disability Rights and Advocacy

Issues related to involving disabled citizens in advocacy activities, increasing their knowledge about their rights, and training in self-advocacy were selected in four different surveys. Three related questions were chosen by 2,430 people with disabilities. They received an average importance rating of 88 percent and an average satisfaction rating of 45 percent.

*Consumer~Identified Dimensions:*

• People with disabilities are unaware of their legal rights.

• Most people with disabilities are unaware of what pending legislation at state and national levels they should support or oppose.

• People with disabilities need training in forming advocacy organizations.

*Consumer~Generated Alternatives:*

• Professionals and independent living centers can foster local and state leadership within the disabled community.

• People with disabilities need to inform themselves and attend advocacy meetings at all levels, get on mailing lists for disability groups involved in legislation, and obtain names, addresses, and numbers of elected officials.

• Disabled consumers should organize locally around identified issues and connect with state and national groups.

• Training in advocacy skills should be provided.

## Employment Accommodations, Disincentives, and Training

Five survey items related to job accommodations in the workplace, work disincentives, and quality of job assistance and training programs were identified by 9,118 consumers as relative problems in six surveys. They received an average importance rating of 83 percent and an average satisfaction rating of 42 percent.

*Consumer~Identified Dimensions:*

• Many businesses do not provide reasonable accommodations in the workplace.

• Work disincentives still exist within the social security system. In addition to loss of economic benefits are losses or reductions in medical benefits, housing subsidies, food stamps, attendant services, etc.

• Disabled job hunters lack basic job seeking skills and are unaware of incentives to employers and laws prohibiting discrimination.

• Blind people have lost their tax credit; other disability groups were never eligible.

• People with disabilities do not know where to go for job training or assistance in finding a job.

*Consumer~Generated Alternatives:*

• Consumer groups need to form a coalition to lobby legislators at federal and state levels for tax credits.

• VR could offer training in job-seeking skills.

• Consumer groups should develop guidelines on what constitutes reasonable accommodation in the workplace.

• Disseminate information about where to go for job training skills and job~related assistance.

## Employment Discrimination

Two survey items related to job discrimination were identified by 9,314 consumers as top problems in eight surveys. They received an average importance rating of 86 percent and an average satisfaction rating of 41 percent.

*Consumer~Identified Dimensions:*

• People with disabilities are discriminated against because of their disability.

Qualified disabled individuals are not given the same opportunity as non-disabled people.

*Consumer~Generated Alternatives:*

Consumers need to teach disabled job seekers about proper attitudes and how to develop a businesslike demeanor when dealing with a potential employer. Disabled people must sell an employer on their abilities and not rely on sympathy.

If a specific employer is perceived as insensitive, invite a representative of that company to speak to a disability group about employment.

Independent living centers and advocacy groups need to encourage and assist disabled job applicants and employees to enforce laws and regulations prohibiting discrimination.

Disabled individuals can contact the Job Accommodations Network or similar resources for help in locating jobs and training, marketing themselves to prospective employers, and obtaining reasonable accommodation.

## Employment Opportunities

Two survey items related to employment opportunities were identified by 9,412 consumers as relative problems in 11 surveys. They received an average importance rating of 84 percent and an average satisfaction rating of 40 percent.

*Consumer~Identified Dimensions:*
- Job opportunities for people with disabilities are very limited.
- If there is a nondisabled person and a disabled individual applying for a job, employers prefer to hire the non-disabled person.

*Consumer-Generated Alternatives:*
- Consumers should educate employers in tax credits, reasonable accommodation, and advantages of hiring disabled employees.
- Disability groups must keep a coalition going at the national level to lobby for reduction of work disincentives.
- Job placement people should know which employers routinely hire disabled applicants.
- Use publicity to inform the community about job needs, interests, and capacities of disabled people, similar to TV spots from Job Service on specific jobs.
- Talk with industries to design programs for people with disabilities similar to programs designed for immigrants.

## Handicapped Parking

One survey item related to the issue of enforcement of parking ordinances was identified as a major problem by 8,607 people in 13 surveys. The item received an average importance rating of 83 percent and an average satisfaction rating of 41 percent.

*Consumer~Identified Dimensions:*
- There are not enough handicapped parking places close to shopping and workplaces.
- Many spaces are not wide enough to unload wheelchairs or put down van lifts.
- Some spaces are not well-marked with an upright sign.
- Police do not ticket violators as often as they should.
- Courts are lax in enforcing handicapped parking laws.

*Consumer~Generated Alternatives:*
- Review local statutes;  seek state uniformity.  Include private as well as public zones.
- Ask local mayors to publicize local ordinances.
- Consumer groups can conduct public awareness campaigns and letter-writing campaigns to local officials.
- Develop rapport with several police officers to assure better enforcement.
- Conduct study session with police, courts, and consumer groups to promote enforcement.
- Consumers can monitor violations and use data to advocate for compliance.
- Consumers can discuss parking problems with merchants where they shop.
- Consumer groups can distribute stickers to violators.
- Consumers can attend city council meetings and voice concerns to get adequate legislation.
- Consumers can advise businesses about adequate  spaces and upright signs.
- Consumer groups can patronize businesses who provide and enforce handicapped spaces.
- Publicize how to get parking IDs.
- Increase fines to over $25 to put teeth into the law.
- Form coalitions among groups needing access and parking.
- Provide consumer consultation in design of spaces.
- Put parking places on end of row for van lifts.  In Anderson, IN, violators get a "candid camera" treatment.  In a cooperative effort between local consumers and the town's newspaper, a photo and brief statement by violators appeared on the front page of the local section.
- Some police departments have deputized local disabled consumers to ticket handicapped parking violators, paying their salaries from fines.

## Health Care:  Affordability and Availability

Six survey items were selected relevant to the availability and affordability of health care, including whether hospitals accept Medicaid and Medicare, regulations for Medicaid and Medicare, and sensitivity of health care providers to consumers.  Items were identified as relative problems by 3,485 consumers in seven surveys.  They received an average importance rating of 88 percent and an average satisfaction rating of 48 percent.

*Consumer~Identified Dimensions:*

- Increasing numbers of doctors are refusing to take Medicaid or Medicare, because payment is very late and inconsistent.
- There is no respite care for families caring for disabled and elderly family members.
- People with disabilities often cannot afford regular, nonemergency medical care and medications.
- Transportation to medical appointments is difficult, especially regular long~distance transportation, and transportation for rural citizens who go to large cities for dialysis or cancer treatment.
- Medical professionals are often insensitive in dealing with disabled patients, preferring to deal with family members rather than communicate directly with the disabled patient as a responsible adult.
- Medical professionals are often unaware of special medical or physical assistance needs imposed by a disability. Thus, discomfort and temporary setbacks can result or even life~threatening situations.
- The general public is unaware that existing programs do not provide adequate medical care for people with disabilities.
- Disabled consumers are often unaware of medical aspects of their own disabilities or good self-care habits. This occurs because they accept the public's definition of themselves as sick and needing to be cared for rather than healthy human beings responsible for their own well-being.
- Another problem is attendant care. If no state attendant care program is available (Wyoming has no Medicaid waiver or state-funded program), there is no paid attendant care for low-income disabled consumers. They must depend on family and friends or live in nursing homes.

*Consumer-Generated Alternatives:*

- Use local media to describe health problems of people with disabilities and solicit suggestions to solve these problems.
- Organize local volunteers, church, and civic groups for medical transportation.

- Consumer groups should educate medical professionals about the special needs of disabled patients. The Association for Retarded Citizens does this for people with developmental disabilities.
- Invite medical professionals to speak to meetings of consumers to increase their own sensitivity and educate consumers at the same time.
- Provide inservice training for medical professionals in the dignified, courteous treatment of persons with disabilities. This should be conducted by consumer groups and consumer-run agencies.
- Provide education to consumers in how they can advocate for themselves with health care providers.
- Form coalitions with other consumer groups to work on common health care objectives.
- Form a protection and advocacy organization to help disabled patients in cases of unfair treatment by health care providers.
- Educate medical professionals about treating different disabilities as part of medical and nursing school curricula.
- Use mutual support groups, counselors, and self-education to encourage good medical habits, nutrition, exercise, and prevention of illness.
- Locate sources of health care for persons with disabilities; make a directory of these resources.
- Arrange local medical fitness centers for people with disabilities. Provide outreach to commercial fitness centers and provide transportation to them for people with disabilities.
- Place people with disabilities as employees of health care providers (i.e., as social workers and patient advocates).
- Involve independent living centers in training and advocacy.
- Consumer groups at the state level could conduct a survey of health care facilities that covers disabilities served, access to offices and parking, acceptance of Medicaid and Medicare, and sources for financial assistance. This could be conducted through state medical and dental societies and updated periodically.

- Educate consumers about medical aspects of their own disabilities.  Train them to advocate for themselves with medical professionals, and teach them to take personal responsibility for educating health care providers about their own appropriate treatment and needs.
- Write government and elected officials about health care issues.
- Attend city council meetings, and petition for city funds to help with medical expenses.
- Seek establishment of adult day care and home health services.  Develop directory of doctors who accept Medicaid and Medicare payments for treatment of people with disabilities;.
- Provide toll-free legal advice about legal matters relating to nonacceptance of Medicaid and Medicare or refusal of treatment to disabled consumers.
- Advocate for program changes to facilitate more timely and consistent payment of Medicaid and Medicare.
- Advocate for cooperative living arrangements with shared attendant care for those who need help.
- Consumer groups need to present need for attendant care and cost effectiveness data to state legislature.
- Support national groups lobbying for national attendant care programs.

## Housing Affordability, Availability, and Accessibility

Six survey items related to the affordability, availability, and accessibility of housing have been identified as major problems by 4,127 consumers in 12 surveys. They received an average importance rating of 86 percent and an average satisfaction rating of 37 percent.

*Consumer-Identified Dimensions:*
- There is an extreme shortage of accessible, affordable housing for people with disabilities.
- Eligibility requirements and regulations keep some disabled consumers, especially the nonelderly who live with family members or attendants, from living in public or subsidized housing.
- Builders do not comply with existing laws, where laws exist, that require a certain percentage of accessible units.

- Managers and directors of public housing are unaware of, and often indifferent to, the needs of disabled tenants.

*Consumer-Generated Alternatives;*
- Talk to owners if the manager is uncooperative.
- Disabled and low-income people should lobby social service agencies for housing assistance.
- Disabled consumers should educate city officials on housing needs of people with disabilities.
- Local consumer groups can bring complaints to local housing authorities.
- Consumers can be educated to be aware of tenant rights and raise money to finance suits when necessary.
- Disabled residents should become familiar with codes, where to file complaints where codes don't exist, and how to introduce legislation.
- Groups can obtain 202 and other HUD loans for accessible housing and manage the housing units themselves.
- Examine eligibility requirements for subsidized housing; use net, not gross income.
- A consumer group in Los Angeles located two HUD projects in good neighborhoods; the Telephone Pioneers donated money and labor to upgrade the structure.
- Establish subsidized housing administered by occupants.  Provide income subsidy within housing cooperatives.
- Some communities in Minnesota provide vouchers to subsidize rent for housing anywhere in the community.
- Establish a referral network for accessible, affordable housing.
- Enforce existing laws setting aside a certain number of units for people with disabilities.
- Consumers need to educate building professionals and make information available.
- Advocate for statewide legislation to encourage adaptability of units.
- Consumers need to lobby elected officials on lack of accessible housing.
- Disabled community members need to get on housing boards.
- Educate disabled homeowners about programs to help modify their homes for access and safety.

### Insurance for Auto, Life, and Liability

This issue refers to the availability and affordability of auto, life, and liability insurance for people with disabilities. This item was selected as a major problem by 2,355 people completing two surveys. It received an average importance rating of 89 percent and an average satisfaction rating of 35 percent.

*Consumer-Identified Dimensions:*
- Insurance premiums are more expensive for people with disabilities.
- Insurance companies discriminate based on disability.

*Consumer-Generated Alternatives:*
- Have a group of disabled people discuss possible solutions with insurance companies regarding adequate prices.

### Insurance for Health Care

One survey question related to the affordability of health insurance was identified as a problem by 5,624 consumers in two surveys. It received an average importance rating of 86 percent and an average satisfaction rating of 38 percent.

*Consumer-Identified Dimensions:*
- Disabled consumers cannot buy health insurance because of their disability and/or pre-existing conditions.
- Disabled consumers cannot afford health insurance.
- Health insurance often does not cover supplies, equipment, regular medications, or therapies used by disabled consumers.
- Inability to purchase individual health insurance and exclusion from some group policies are serious disincentives to individuals with disabilities looking for work.

*Consumer-Generated Alternatives:*
- Consumer groups can advocate for national health insurance.
- Disabled consumers can set up health insurance cooperatives as they did in Los Angeles.
- Shared risk insurance is an option so consumers with disabilities and pre-existing conditions can get group insurance.
- Educate consumers about supplemental insurance available through groups such as

AARP, professional associations, and credit card holders.
- Independent living centers can train and assist consumers in filling out forms, challenge actions and policies of Medicaid, Medicare, and insurance companies, and assist in advocacy, complaints, and appeals processes.
- Get information from and make use of the state insurance commissioner's office.

### Media Portrayal and Public Information

Three survey items related to media portrayal of people with disabilities and their access to information about services, benefits, and programs were selected as problems by 7,547 consumers in three surveys. The items received an average importance rating of 81 percent and an average satisfaction rating of 39 percent.

*Consumer~Identified Dimensions:*
- The media do not provide enough information about what is available for disabled citizens.
- The media portray people with disabilities in a negative and unrealistic way, preferring the sensational or pitiful to the everyday and human side of disability.

*Consumer~Generated Alternatives*
- Consumer groups should bring accessibility and independent-living issues to the attention of the press.
- Consumers should monitor coverage of disability issues.
- Consumers should educate the media to correct negative portrayals and terminology.
- Consumer groups should meet with service providers about developing a directory of services and programs for people with disabilities that could be disseminated through the media.

### Public Access

Issues related to safe access to public places, including availability of curb cuts, accessible entrances, and snow removal, have been selected as major problems. Two related survey items were chosen by 204 consumers in two different surveys, with an average importance rating of 81 percent and an average satisfaction rating of 48 percent.

*Consumer~Identified Dimensions:*
● Disabled citizens are forced to stay home or use the street, because curb cuts and sidewalks are absent or inadequate, or in some instances, snow is not removed promptly.
● Many public buildings are totally inaccessible or technically accessible with inadequate or unsafe access.

*Consumer~Generated Alternatives:*
● Discuss among disabled consumers key areas that need to be made accessible.
● Make up an annual priority list of access and safety issues.
● Describe problems in newsletters and solicit opinions from other disabled community members.
● Offer modification assistance to owners of inaccessible buildings and appropriate government and social agencies.
● Offer assistance to government agencies on ways to increase the safety of streets and sidewalks.

## Social Services

Four survey items related to information social agencies provide to consumers about services and legal issues were selected as major problems in six surveys. A total of 3,581 consumers responded to these questions, with an average importance rating of 88 percent and an average satisfaction rating of 51 percent.

*Consumer~Identified Dimensions:*
● Social service agencies fail to inform disabled consumers about all services available to them through their own agency, other agencies, or the community.
● Benefits or services from one agency can limit benefits or services from another agency.
● Most social service agencies are unaware of services available at other agencies.
● Disabled people are referred from one agency to another, often encountering agencies unable to serve them or refusing services.
● Forms and policies of social service agencies are confusing.

*Consumer~Generated Alternatives:*
● Organize a consumer group to review forms used by social service agencies.
● Form a consumer network for information and referral.

● Create more support groups for mutual assistance.
● Provide corrective feedback and information to social service agencies that fail to inform clients about benefits to disabled consumers.
● Provide social service agencies with training on benefits available to disabled consumers.
● Consumers should demand that VR cases be reopened. If they have not been fully informed about all benefits available.
● Independent living centers should train consumers in what benefits are available and how to access them effectively.
● Independent living centers or consumer groups could organize regular cooperative meetings involving representatives of all social service agencies in the community, or if such an organization exists, become active and advocate for services to people with disabilities.
● If consumers are referred to an agency unable to serve them, they should contact the referring agency and tell them the referral was inappropriate and why.
● Educate consumers to use the state CAP agency, Legal Aid, and other available legal help when services are unjustly refused.
● Set up courses in self-reliance that teach consumers to use social services such as the one used by the CIL in Anaheim, Calif.

## Transportation: Availability and Affordability

Three survey items related to the availability and affordability of accessible transportation services were identified as major problems by 4,008 consumers in nine surveys. They received an average importance rating of 83 percent and an average satisfaction rating of 40 percent.

*Consumer~Identified Dimensions:*
● Disabled citizens are segregated from the rest of the community and forced to remain at home because of lack of transportation.
● In most areas, public transportation is not wheelchair-accessible, and paratransit is expensive or nonexistent. In rural areas, accessible transportation is available infrequently.

- Lack of transportation is the primary barrier to community participation, education, employment, recreation, adequate medical care, and independent living for people with disabilities.
- Weekend and evening transportation is a problem.
- Transportation between neighboring cities and from rural areas to cities is a problem.
- Ideally, a city should have accessible mainline transportation for those who can use it and paratransit for those who need it.
- Recreational events and facilities are sometimes inaccessible. Transportation to recreational events is unavailable.

*Consumer~Generated Alternatives:*
- Consumer groups need to work with existing community recreational facilities to make them accessible and usable for people with disabilities.
- Contact organizers of recreational events for transportation for disabled participants.
- People with disabilities need to become involved in the planning of community recreational events and active in interest groups.
- Form a local task force on transportation, decide what local consumers need and want, then fight for it.
- It is against federal law for paratransit to cost more than mainline transportation. Educate consumers about this law, how to make complaints, and how to ensure its enforcement.
- Develop a share-a-fare system as they did in Kansas City, Mo. where 900 wheelchair users a month participate.
- Give testimony to state legislatures on transportation funding.
- Have life buses operate at fixed rates and schedules as they do in Denver, a city with almost 100 percent accessible buses.
- Slow transit schedules to accommodate disabled riders. Drivers should call out stops ahead of time.
- Include disabled drivers in existing driver training programs.
- Develop car pools.
- Conduct public education on varied modes of transportation needed by disabled citizens.

- Submit formal complaints to transportation authorities concerning mainline wheelchair~accessible buses.
- Develop creative rural and small city alternatives. Examples include merging existing systems serving disabled riders (Morgantown, W.V.), ownership of a lift van by a consumer group or cooperative (Cuba, MO), and use of idle church or school life-equipped buses.

## Utility Bills

One survey question related to the affordability of utility bills was identified as a major problem in four surveys. A total of 1,611 consumers answered this survey item, with an average importance rating of 89 percent and an average satisfaction rating of 34 percent.

*Consumer~Identified Dimensions:*
- Disabled consumers on a fixed income cannot afford inconsistent and high utility bills.
- Because of their medical needs, many disabled consumers cannot survive without water, gas for heat, and electricity to operate their equipment.

*Consumer~Generated Alternatives:*
- Obtain help to establish programs for weatherization.
- Encourage landlords to weatherize units.
- Educate landlords and disabled homeowners about tax credits for weatherizing and solar installation.
- Encourage consumers to join annualized level payment plans.
- Consumer groups should maintain a list of agencies that help pay utility bills.
- Call local consumer affairs office for help if utilities are shut off.
- Consult local phone company about discounts for disabled consumers.
- Write elected officials describing problems with utility bills and ask for legislative solutions and assistance programs.

This report represents the comments and suggestions of thousands of Americans with disabilities. They have identified specific community features that inhibit independent living, including inadequate job opportunities, job discrimination, insufficient accessible and affordable service options. These community problems are counterproductive to achieving society's goal of independence.

The common concerns outlined here frame an agenda for public, private, and self-help initiatives. These consumer-generated alternatives feature many practical steps that can be taken at local, state, and national levels. Taken together, these issues and options pose a challenge to all who believe that justice requires equal opportunities to achieve independence.

********

**Source:**  Reprinted with permission from *Social Policy,* Fall 1988, pp. 29-35. Published by Social Policy Corporation, New York, NY.

# Self, Identity and the Naming Question: Reflections on the Language of Disability
## Irving Kenneth Zola

**Abstract** ~ *With all the emphasis on 'political correctness', it is especially important to delineate the functions of naming. People with disabilities are facing issues quite similar to minority groups which have preceded them in attempting to enter 'mainstream' America. Their similarities and differences with these groups are traced as well as their own unique path (with all its implications) and some possible analytic and political solutions.*
**Key Words** ~ self, identity, language, disability

"When I use the word, it means just what I choose it to mean~neither more nor less"

Humpty
Dumpty

## I. THE POWER OF NAMING

*Language...has as much to do with the philosophical and political conditioning of a society as geography or climate...people do not realize the extent to which their attitudes have been conditioned to ennoble or condemn, augment or detract, glorify or demean. Negative language inflicts the subconscious of most...people from the time they first learn to speak. Prejudice is not merely imparted or superimposed. It is metabolized in the bloodstream of society. What is needed is not so much a change in language as an awareness of the power of words to condition attitudes.*[1]

A step in this awareness is the recognition of how deep is the power of naming in Western culture. According to the Old Testament, God's first act after saying "Let there be light" was to call the light "Day" and the darkness "Night". Moreover, God's first act after the creation of Adam was to bring in every beast of the field so that Adam could give them names; and "whatsoever Adam called every living creature, that was

the name thereof" (Genesis 2:20). Thus what one is called tends 'to stick' and any unnaming process is not without its difficulties and consequences.[2] While a name has always connoted some aspect of one's status (e.g. job, location, gender, social class, ethnicity, kinship), the mid-twentieth century seems to be a time when the issue of naming has assumed a certain primacy [3,4]. In the post-World War II era Erik Erikson [5] and Alan Wheelis [6] noted that "Who am I" or the issue of identity had became a major psychological concern of the U.S. population. The writings of C. Wright Mills [7] as well as the Women's Movement [8], however, called attention to the danger of individualizing any issue as only a "personal problem".

The power of naming was thus recognized not only as a personal issue but a political one as well. While social scientists focused more on the general 'labelling' process [9-13] and the measurement of attitudes toward people with various chronic diseases and disabilities [14,15], a number of 'liberation' or 'rights' movements focused on the practical implications. They claimed that language was one of the mechanisms by which dominant groups kept others 'in place' [16,17]. Thus, as minority groups sought to gain more control over their lives, the issue of naming~what they are called~was one of the first battlegrounds. The resolution of this was not always clear-cut. For some, the original stigmas became the banner: Negroes and coloreds become Blacks. For others, only a completely new designation would suffice~a 'Ms" has caught on as a form of address but 'womyn', 'wimmin' have not been so successful in severing the vocabulary connection to 'men'.

People with disabilities are in the midst of a similar struggle. The struggle is confounded by some special circumstances which mitigate against the easy development of either a disability pride or culture [18,19]. While most minority group members grow up in a recognized subculture and thus develop certain norms and expectations, people with chronic diseases and disabilities are not similarly prepared. The nature of their experience has been toward isolation. The vast majority of people who are born with or acquire such conditions do so within families who neither have these conditions nor associate with others who do. They are socialized into the world of the 'normal' with all its values, prejudices, and vocabulary. As one generally attempts to rise out of one's status. there is always an attempt to put this status in some perspective. The statements that one is more than just a Black or a woman, etc., are commonplace. On the other hand, where chronic illness and disability are concerned, this negation is almost total and is tantamount to denial. Proof of successful integration is embodied in such statements as "I *never* think of myself as handicapped' or the supreme compliment, "I *never* think of you as handicapped".

What then of the institutions where too many spend too much of their time~the long-term hospitals, sanitoria, convalescent and nursing homes? These are aptly labelled 'total institutions' [20], but 'total' refers to their control over our lives, not to the potential fullness they offer. The subcultures formed within such places are largely defensive and designed to make life viable within the institution. Often this viability is achieved at such a cost that it cannot be transferred to the non-institutional world.

For most of their history, organizations of people with disabilities were not much more successful in their efforts to produce a viable subculture. their memberships have been small in comparison to the potential disabled population, and they have been regarded more as social groups rather than serious places to gain technical knowledge or emotional support. And though there are some self-help groups which are becoming increasingly visible, militant and independent of medical influence, the movement is still in its infancy [21]. Long ago, Talcott Parsons articulated the basic dilemma facing such groups:

The sick role is...a mechanism which...channels deviance so that the two

most dangerous potentialities, namely group formation and successful establishment of the claim of legitimacy, are avoided. The sick are tied up, not with other deviants to form a 'subculture' of the sick but each with a group of nonsick, his personal circle, and, above all, physicians. The sick thus become a statistical status and are deprived of the possibility of forming a solid collectivity. Furthermore, to be sick is by definition to be in an undesirable state, so that it simply does not 'make sense' to assert a claim that the way to deal with the frustrating aspects of the social system is for everyone to get sick [22,p.477].

A mundane but dramatic way of characterizing this phenomenon can be seen in the rallying cries of current liberation movements. As the 'melting pot' theory of America was finally buried, people could once again say, even though they were three generations removed from the immigrants, that they were proud to be Greek, Italian, Hungarian, or Polish. With the rise of black power, a derogatory label became a rallying cry, "Black is beautiful". And when women saw their strength in numbers, they shouted "Sisterhood is powerful". But what about those with a chronic illness or disability? Could they yell, "Long live cancer" "Up with multiple sclerosis" "I'm glad I had polio!" "Don't you wish you were blind?" Thus, the traditional reversing of the stigma will not so easily provide a basis for a common positive identity.

## 2. SOME NEGATIVE FUNCTIONS OF LABELLING

The struggle over labels often follows a pattern. It is far easier to agree on terms that should *not* be used than the designations that should replace them [23-25]. As with the racial, ethnic [26] and gender groups [27,28] before them, many had begun to note the negative qualities of certain 'disability references' [29,30]. Others created quite useful glossaries [31].

Since, as Phillips [32] notes, the names one calls oneself reflect differing political strategies, we must go beyond a list of 'do's' and 'don'ts' to an analysis of the functions of such labelling [33-36]. As long ago as

1651, Thomas Hobbes~in setting his own social agenda~saw the importance of such clarifications, "seeing then that truth consists in the right ordering of names in our affirmations, a man that seeks precise truth has need to remember what every name he uses stands for; and to place it accordingly; or else he will find himself entangled in words as a bird in lime twigs; the more he struggles the more belimed" [37, p.26].

There are at least two separate implications of such naming which have practical and political consequences. The first is connotational and associational. As Kenneth Burke [38, p.4] wrote "Call a man a villain and you have the choice of either attacking or avenging. Call him mistaken and you invite yourself to attempt to set him right". I would add, "Call a person sick or crazy and all their behavior becomes dismissable". Because someone has been labelled ill, all their activity and beliefs~past, present, and future~ become related to and explainable in terms of their illness [20,39]. Once this occurs, society can deny the validity of anything which they might say, do, or stand for. Being seen as the object of medical treatment evokes the image of many ascribed traits, such as weakness, helplessness, dependency, regressiveness, abnormality of appearance and depreciation of every mode of physical and mental functioning [17,40,41]. In the case of a person with a chronic illness and/or a permanent disability, these traits, once perceived to be temporary accompaniments of an illness, become indelible characteristics. "The individual is trapped in a state of suspended animation socially, is perpetually a patient, is chronically viewed as helpless and dependent, in need of cure but incurable" [17, p.420}.

A second function of labelling is its potential for spread, pervasiveness, generalization. An example of such inappropriate generalizing was provided in a study by Conant and Budoff [42]. They found that a group of sighted children and adults interpreted the labels 'blind' and 'legally blind' as meaning that the person was totally without vision~something which is true for only a small segment of people with that designation. What was problematic became a given. Another example of this process occurs when

disability and person are equated. While it is commonplace to hear of doctors referring to people as 'the appendicitis in Room 306" or " the amputee down the hall", such labelling is more common in popular culture than one might believe. My own analysis of the crime-mystery genre [43], noted that after an introductory description of characters with a disability, they are often referred to by their disability~e.g. 'the dwarf', 'the blind man', 'the one-armed', 'the one-legged'. This is usually done by some third person observer or where the person with the disability is the speaker. The disability is empahsized~e.g. "said the blind man". No other physical or social descriptor appears with such frequency.

Perhaps not unexpectedly, such stand-in appellations are most commonly applied to villains. They were commonplace during the heyday of the pulp magazines, where the disability was incorporated into their names~"One-Eyed Joe", "Scarface Kelly" a tradition enshrined in the Dick Tracy comic strips. It is a tradition that continues, though with more subtlety. Today we may no longer have "Clubfoot the Avenger", a mad German master-criminal who crossed swords for 25 years with the British Secret Service [44-51], but we do have "The Deaf Man", the recurring thorn in the side of Ed McBain's long-running (over 30 years) 87th Precinct novels [52-54]. All such instances can reinforce an association between disability, evil, and abnormality [55].

A very old joke illustrates the pervasiveness of such labelling:

> A man is changing a flat tyre{sic} outside a mental hospital when the bolts from his wheel roll down a nearby sewer. Distraught, he is confronted by a patient watching him who suggests, "Why don't you take one bolt off each of the other wheels, and place it on the spare?" Surprised when it works, the driver says, "How come you of all people would think of that?" Replies the patient, "I may be crazy, but I'm not stupid".

This anecdote demonstrates the flaw in thinking that a person who is mad is therefore stupid or incapable of being insightful. As the social psychological literature has long noted, this is how stigma comes about~from a process of generalizing from a single experience, people are treated categorically rather than individually and are devalued in the process, [56-58]. As Longmore so eloquently concludes, a "spoiling process" [59} results whereby "they obscure all other characteristics behind that one and swallow up the social identity of the individual within that restrictive category" [17, p.419]. Peters puts it most concretely: "The label that's used to describe us is often far more important in shaping our view of ourselves~and the way others view us~than whether we sign, use a cane, sit in a wheelchair, or use a communication board" [23, p.25].

While many have offered vocabulary suggestions to combat the above problems of connotation and pervasiveness, few have analytically delineated what is at stake in such name changes [l7, 60, 6l]. The most provocative and historically-rooted analysis is an unpublished paper by Phillips [32] who delineates four distinct strategies which underly the renaming. While she carefully notes that further investigation may change or expand her categorization, the very idea of her schema and the historical data describing the genesis of each 'recoding' remain timely.

'Cripple' and 'handicapped', as nouns or adjectives, she sees as primarily 'names of acquiescence and accommodation', reflecting an acceptance of society's oppressive institutions. Terms such as 'physically challenged' by so personalizing the disability run the risk of fostering a 'blaming the victim' stance [62]. Such terms, as well as 'physically different', 'physically inconvenienced', not only may be so euphemistic that they confound the public as to who is being discussed but also contribute strongly to the denial of existing realities [33]. Two other strategies represent a more activist philosophy. 'Handicapper' and 'differently-abled' are 'names of reaction and reflection' whose purpose is to emphasize 'the can-do' aspects of having a disability. To the group of Michigan advocates who coined the term [63], a 'Handicapper' determines the degree to which one's own physical or mental characteristics direct life's activities. Anger, says Phillips, is basic to "names of renegotiation and inversion" where the context sets the meaning. Perhaps the best examples occur when disability activists, in the privacy of their own circles, 'talk dirty', referring to themselves as 'blinks', 'gimps', or telling 'crip' jokes and expounding on the intricacies of 'crip' time. More controversy arises, however, when people publicly proclaim such terms as a matter of pride. Recently, for example, many have written about the positive aspects of 'being deaf' [64, 65] or, even more dramatically of being a 'cripple' [66]. Kriegel [60, 61] says that 'cripple' describes "an essential reality", a way of keeping what needs to be dealt with socially and politically in full view. Nancy Mairs [67], a prize-winning poet who has multiple sclerosis, clearly agrees; and in the opening remarks of her essay, "On Being a Cripple", states it most vividly:

The other day I was thinking of writing an essay on being a cripple. I was thinking hard in one of the stalls of the women's room in my office building, as I was shoving my shirt into my jeans and tugging up my zipper. Preoccupied, I flushed, picked up my book bag, took my cane down from the hook, and unlatched the door. So many movements unbalanced me, and as I pulled the door open, I fell over backwards, landing fully clothed on the toilet seat with legs splayed in front of me: the old beetle-on-its-back- routine. Saturday afternoon, the building deserted, I was free to laugh aloud as I wriggled back to my feet, my voice bouncing off the yellowish tiles from all directions. Had anyone been there with me, I'd have been still and faint and hot with chagrin.

I decided that it was high time to write the essay. First, the matter of semantics. I am a cripple. I choose this word to name me. I choose from among several possibilities, the most common of which are handicapped and disabled. I made the choice a number of years ago, without thinking, unaware of my motives for doing so. Even now, I'm not sure what those motives are, but I recognize that they are complex and not entirely flattering. People~crippled or not~wince at the word cripple, as they do not at handicapped or disabled. Perhaps I want them to wince. I want them to see me as a tough customer, one to whom the fates/gods/viruses have not been kind, but who can face the brutal truth of her existence squarely. As a cripple, I swagger [67, p.9].

While Phillips' very titles may imply an evaluation of the particular strategies, it is clear from her own caveats that while many may try to impose their terminology as "the correct language", "None feel really right" [23, p.25].

## 3. RECONTEXTUALIZING NAMES

The ultimate question, of course, is whether any of these renaming procedures, singly and alone, can deal with the connotational and generalization issues discussed previously. I would argue that the context of usage may be every bit as important (as Phillips implies) as the specific terminology. Thus one of the reasons for all the negative associations to many terms is a result of such contexts. Here social scientists, researchers and clinicians are particularly at fault in the medicalizing of disability [55, 68, 69]. In their writings and in the transmission of these writings by the popular press and media, people with varying diseases and disabilities are inevitably referred to as 'patients', a term which describes a role, a relationship and a location (i.e. an institution or hospital) from which many connotations, as previously noted, flow. For the 43 million people now designated as having a physical, mental or biological disability, only a tiny proportion are continually resident in and under medical supervision and are thus truly patients. Similarly, the terms 'suffering from', 'afflicted with' are projections and evaluations of an outside world. No person with a disability is automatically 'suffering' or 'afflicted' except in specific situations where they do indeed 'hurt', are 'in pain', or 'feel victimized'.

I am not arguing, however, for the complete elimination of medical or physical terminology. As DeFerlice cautions, "The disabled movement has purchased political visibility at the price of physical invisibility. The crippled and lame had bodies, but the handicapped, or so the social workers say, are just a little late at the starting gate. I don't like that: it's banal. When we speak in metaphorical terms, we deny physical reality. The farther we get from our bodies, the more removed we are from the body politic..." [70].

One meaning I derive from his caution is that we must seek a change in the connotations and the pervasiveness of our names without denying the essential reality of our conditions. Thus biology may not determine our destiny, but, as with women, our physical, mental and biological differences are certainly part of that destiny [71, 72].

A way of contextualizing our relationship to our bodies and our disabilities may not be in changing terms but in changing grammars. Our continual use of nouns and adjectives can only perpetuate the equation of the individual equaling the disability. No matter what noun we use, it substitutes one categorical definition for another. An adjective colors and thus connotes the essential quality of the noun it modifies. Such adjectives as 'misshapen', 'deformed', 'defective', 'invalid'~far from connoting a specific quality of the individual~tend to taint the whole person.

The same is true with less charged terms. Thus 'a disabled car' is one which has totally broken down. Could 'a disabled person' be perceived as anything less? Prepositions, on the other hand, imply both 'a relationship to' and ' 'a separation from'. At this historical juncture the awkwardness in phrasing that often results may be all to the good, for it makes both user and hearer stop and think about what is meant, as in the phrases 'people *of* color' and 'persons *with* disabilities'.

Distance and relationship are also at the heart of some very common verb usages. The first is between the active and passive tense. Note the two dictionary meanings:

**Active**—*asserting that the person or thing represented by the grammatical subjects performs the action represented by the verb [73, p.12]*

**Passive**—*asserting that the grammatical subject to a verb is subjected to or affected by the action represented by that verb [73, p. 838].*

Thus in describing an individual's relationship to an assistive device such as a wheelchair, the difference between 'being confined to a wheelchair' and 'using' one is a difference not only of terminology but of control. Medical language has long perpetuated this 'disabled passivity' by its emphasis on what medicine continually *does to* its 'patients' rather than *with* them [74, 75].

Similarly the issues of 'connotation' and 'pervasiveness' may be perpetuated by the differential use of the verbs 'be' and 'have'. The French language makes careful distinctions between when to use 'etre' (be) and when to use 'avoir' (have). English daily usage is blurry, but another look at Webster's does show the possibilities:

**be** ~ *to equal in meaning; to have same connotation as; to have identity with; to constitute the same class as [73, p. 96].*

**have** ~ *to hold in possession; to hold in one's use; to consist of; to stand in relationship to; to be marked or characterized by; to experience; SYN~to keep, control, retain, or experience [73, p. 526].*

Like the issue of nouns vs prepositions, verbs can also code people in terms of categories (e.g. X is a redhead) instead of specific attributes (e.g., X has red hair), allowing people to feel that the stigmatized persons are fundamentally different and establishing greater psychological and social distance [76]. Thus, as between the active and passive tense, so it is between 'I am...' Both specify a difference in distance and control in relation to whatever it is one 'is' or 'has'. And since renaming relates to alternative images of distance and control, grammar, which tends to be normative, concise, shared and long-lasting, may serve us better than sheer name change. Though I personally may have a generic preference (e.g., for 'disability' over 'handicap'), I am not arguing for any 'politically correct' usage but rather examining the political advantages and disadvantages of each [36].

For example, there may be stages in the coping with a particular condition or in the perceived efficacy of a particular 'therapy' (e.g., the 12 steps in Alcoholics Anonymous) when 'ownership' and thus the use of 'I am' is deemed essential. Those old enough to remember President Kennedy's words at the Berlin Wall, *"Ich bin ein Berliner"* (I am a Berliner), will recall the power of its message of kinship. Similarly, when we politically strategize as a minority group [77] and seek a kinship across disease and disability groups [78], the political coming-out may require a personal ownership best conveyed in terms of 'I am...'.

On the other hand, there are times when the political goals involve groups for whom disease and disability is not a permanent or central issue. On my university campus, for a myriad of reasons, people with mobility impairments are virtually non-existent. Yet we are gradually retrofitting old buildings and guaranteeing accessibility in new ones. The alliance here is among women who are or may become pregnant, parents with small children, people with injuries or time-limited diseases, and others who perceive themselves at risk, such as aging staff or faculty. They rarely see themselves as disabled but often admit to having a temporary disability or sharing a part of 'the disabled experience' (e.g., "Now I know what it's like to try to climb all those stairs"). Thus where coalition politics is needed, the concept of 'having' vs 'being' may be a more effective way of acknowledging multiple identities and kinship, as in our use of hyphenated personal and social lineages~e.g., Afro-American.

## 4. A FINAL CAVEAT

One of the sad findings in Phillips' study [32] is how divisive this struggle over names has become. People thus begin to chastise 'non true-believers' and emphasize to others 'politically correct' usage. In so doing, we may not only damage the unity so necessary to the cause of disability rights but also fail to see the forest for the trees. Our struggle is necessary because we live in a society which devalues, discriminates against and disparages people with disabilities [77, 79]. It is not our task to prove that we are worthy of the full resources and integration of our society. The fault is not in us, not in our diseases and disabilities [41, 62, 80, 81] but in mythical denials, social arrangement, political priorities and prejudices [82].

Here too, a renaming can be of service not of us but of our oppressors [83]. As Hughes and Hughes [84] note, when we turn the tables and create epithets for our oppressors, this may be a sign of a beginning cohesiveness. Thus the growing popularity of terms like TAB's and MAB's (temporarily or momentarily able-bodied) to describe the general population breaks down the separateness of 'us' and 'them' and emphasizes the continuity and inevitability of 'the disability experience'. Thus, too, those who have created the terms 'handicappism' [85] and 'healthism' [68, 86, 87] equate these with all the structural '-isms' in a society which operates to continue segregation and discrimination. To return finally to the issue of naming, the words of Philip Dunne reflect well the choices and consequences of language:

> If we hope to survive in this terrifying age, we must choose our words as we choose our actions. We should think how what we say might sound to other ears as well as to our own. Above all, we should strive for clarity...if clarity {is} the essence of style, it is also the heart and soul of truth, and it is for want of truth that human freedom could perish [88, p.14].

********

## REFERENCES

1. Saturday Review, Editorial, April 8, 1967.
2. LeGuin U. K. She unnames them. *New Yorker,* January 21, p.27, 1985.
3. Friedrich O. What's In a Name? *Time.* August 18, p. 16, 1986.
4. Vickery H. Finding the right name for brand X. *Insight,* pp. 54-55, January 27, 1986.
5. Erikson H. *Childhood and Society.* Norton, New York, 1950.
6. Wheelis A. *The Quest for Identity.* Norton, New York, 1958.
7. Mills D. W. *The Sociological Imagination.* Oxford University Press, Oxford, 1959.
8. Boston Women's Health Book Collective. *Women and Our Bodies* (In later revised versions, *Our Bodies Ourselves*). New England Free Press, Boston, 1970.
9. Becker H. *Outsiders.* The Free Press, Glencoe, IL., 1963.
10. Becker H. (Ed.) *The Other Side~Perspectives on Deviance.* The Free Press, Glencoe, IL., 1964.
11. Erikson K., Notes on the sociology of deviance. *Soc. Problems* 9, 307-314, 1962.
12. Erikson K. *Wayward Puritans: A Study in the Sociology of Deviance.* Wiley, New York. 1966.
13. Schur E. *Crimes Without Victims.* Prentice-Hall, Englewood Cliffs, N.J. 1965.
14. Siller J. The measurement of attitudes toward physically disabled persons. In *Physical Appearance, Stigma, and Social Behavior: The Ontario Symposium* Edited by Herman P. D., Zanna M. P., and Higgins E. T.), Vol. 3, pp. 245-288. Lawrence Eribaum Associates, Hillsdale, NJ. 1986.
15. Yuker H., Block J.Z. and Young J. H. *The Measurement of Attitudes Toward Disabled Persons.* Human Resources Center, Albertson, NY. 1966.
16. Gumperz J. J. (Ed.) *Language and Social Identity.* Cambridge University Press, Cambridge, 1982.
17. Longmore P. K. A Note on language and the social identity of disabled people. *Am. Behav. Scient.* **28,** (3). 419-423, 1985.
18. Johnson M. Emotion and pride: the search for a disability culture. *Disability Rag,* January/February, p. 1, 4-10, 1987.
19. Zola I. K. 'Whose voice is this anyway? A commentary on recent collections about the experience of disability'. *Med. Human Rev.* **2,** (1), 6-15, 1988.
20. Goffman E., *Asylums,* Anchor, New York, 1961.
21. Crew N. and Zola I. K. *et al. Independent Living for Physically Disabled People.* Jossey-Bass, San Francisco, 1983.
22. Parsons T. *The Social System.* The Free Press, Glencoe, 1951.
23. Peters A. Developing a language. *Disability Rag,* March-April, p. 25, 1986.
24. Peters A. The problem with 'Gimp'. *Disability Rag,* July/August, p. 22, 1986.
25. Peters A. Do we have to be named? *Disability Rag,* November/December, p. 31, 35, 1986.
26. Moore R. B. *Racism in the English Language~A Lesson Plan and Study Essay,* The Council of Interracial Books for Children, New York, 1976.
27. Shear M. Equal writes. *Womens Rev. Book 1,* (11), 12-13, 1984.
28. Shear M. Solving the great pronoun debate. *Ms.* pp. 106, 108-109, 1985.
29. Biklen D. and Bogdan R. Disabled~yes; handicapped~no: the language of disability, p. 5, insert in "Media Portrayals of Disabled People: A Study in Stereotypes". *Interracial Books Children Bull.* **8,** (3, 6 & 7), 4-9, 1977.
30. Corcoran P. J. Pejorative terms and attitudinal barriers--editorial. *Arch Phys. Med. Rehabil.* **58,** 500, 1977.
31. Shear M. No more supercrip. *New Directions for Women,* P. 10, November-December, 1986.

32. Phillips M. J. What we call ourselves: self-referential naming among the disabled. *Seventh Annual Ethnography in Research Forum,* University of Pennsylvania, Philadelphia, 4-6, April 1986.

33. Chaffee N. L. Disabled...handicapped...and in the image of God?~~Our language reflects societal attitudes and influences theological perception. Unpublished paper, 1987.

34. Gill C. J. The disability name game. *New World for Persons with Disabilities,* **13**,(8), 2, 1987.

35. Gillett P. The power of words~~can they make you feel better or worse? *Accent on Living,* pp. 38-39, 1987.

36. Lindsey K. The pitfalls of politically correct language. *Sojourner,* p. 16, 1985.

37. Hobbes T. *Leviathan,* Dutton, New York, 1950.

38. Burke K. *Attitudes Toward History,* , revised edn. Hermes, Oakland, CA, 1959.

39. Link B. G., Cullen F. T., Frank J. and Wozniak J. F. The social rejection of former mental patients: understanding why labels matter. *Am. J. Sociol. 1987,* **92,** (6), 1461-1500, 1987.

40. Goodwin D. Language: perpetualizing the myths. *Impact, Inc.* (Newsletter of Center for Independent Living, Alton, IL.). Vol. l, No. 2, pp. 1-2, 1986.

41. Zola I. K. *Missing Pieces: A Chronicle of Living with a Disability.* Temple University Press. Philadelphia, 1982.

42. Conant, S. and Budoff M. The development of sighted people's understanding of blindness. *J. Vis. Impairment Blindness* **76**, 86-96-, 1982.

43. Zola I. K. Any distinguishing features: portrayal of disability in the crime-mystery genre. *Policy Stud. J.* **15,** (3), 485-513, 1987.

44. Williams V. *The Man With the Clubfoot.* Jenkins, London, 1918.

45. Williams V. *The Secret Hand.* Jenkins, London, 1918.

46. Williams V. *Return of Clubfoot.* Jenkins, London, 1918.

47. Williams V. *Clubfoot the Avenger,* Jenkins, London, 1924.

48. Williams V. *The Crouching Beast.* Hodder & Stoughton, London, 1928.

49. Williams V. *The Gold Comfit Box.* Hodder & Stoughton, London, 1932.

50. Williams V. *The Spider's Touch.* Hodder and Stoughton, London, 1936.

51. Williams V. *Courier to Marrakesh.* Hodder 7 Stoughton, London, 1944.

52. McBain E. *Fuzz.* Doubleday, New York, 1968.

53. McBain E. *Let's Hear It for the Deaf Man.* Random House, New York, 1973.

54. McBain E. *Eight Black Horses.* Avon, New York, 1985.

55. Conrad P. and Schneider J. W. *Deviance and Medicalization: From Badness to Sickness.* C. V. Mosby, St. Louis, 1980.

56. Ainlay S. C., Becker G. and Coleman L. M. (Eds) *The Dilemma of Difference; A Multidisciplinary View of Stigma,* Plenum, New York, 1986.

57. Jones E. E., Farina A., Hastorf A. H., Markus H., Miller D. and Scott R. *Social Sitgma: The Psychology of Marked Relationships.* W. H. Freeman, New York, 1984.

58. Katz I. *Stigma: A Social Psychological Analysis.* Lawrence Eribaum Associates, Hillsdale, NJ, 1981.

59. Goffman E. *Stigma: Notes on the Management of Spoiled Identity.* Prentice-Hall, Englewood Cliffs, NJ, 1963.

60. Kriegel L. Uncle Tom and Tiny Tim: reflection on the cripple as Negro. *Am. Scholar* **38,** 412-430, 1969.

61. Kriegel L. Coming through manhood, disease and the authentic self. In: *Rudely Stamp'd: Imaginal Disability and Prejudice* (edited by Bicklen D. and Bailey L.), pp. 49-63. University Press of America, Washington, DC, 1981.

62. Ryan W. *Blaming the Victim.* Pantheon, New York, 1970.

63. Gentile E. and Taylor J. K. Images, words and identity. Handicapper Programs, Michigan State University, East Lansing, MI, 1976.

64. *Disability Rag.* Cochlear implants: the final put-down. March/April, pp. 1, 4-8, 1987.

65. Innerst C. A. Will to preserve deaf culture. *Insight,* November 24, pp. 50-51, 1986.

66. Milam L. *The Crippled Liberation Front Marching Band Blues.* MHO and MHO Works, San Diego, CA, 1984.

67. Mairs N. On being a cripple. In *Plaintest: Essays,* pp. 9-20. University of Arizona Press, Tucson, AZ, 1986.

68. Zola I. K. Medicine as an institution of social control. *Social Rev.* **20,** 487-504, 1972.

69. Illich I. *Medical Nemesis: The Expropriation of Health.* Calder & Boyars, London, 1975.

70. DeFelice R. J. A crippled child grows up. *Newsweek,* November 3, p. 13, 1986.

71. Fine M. and Asch A. Disabled women: sexism without the pedstal. *J. Social Soc. Welfare* **8,** (2), 233-248, 1981.

72. Fine M. and Asch A. (Eds) *Women with Disabilities~~Essays in Psychology, Culture, and Politics.* Temple University Press, Philadelphia, 1988.

73. *Webster's New Collegiate Dictionary.* Merriam, Springfield, MA, 1973.

74. Edelman M. The political language of the helping professions. In *Political Language,* pp. 59-68. Academic, New York, 1977.

75. Szasz T. S. and Hollender M. H. A contribution to the philosophy of medicine: the basic models of the doctor-patient relationship. *AMA Arch Internal Med.* **97,** 585-592, 1956.

76. Crocker J. and Lutsky N. Stigma and the dynamics of social cognition. In *The Dilemma of Difference: A Multidisciplinary View of Stigma* (Edited by Ainlay S. C.), pp. 95-121. Plenum, New York, 1986.

77. Hahn H. Disability policy and the problem of discrimination. *Am. Behav. Scient.* **28,** 293-318, 1985.

78. Harris L. *et al. Disabled Americans' Self Perceptions: Bringing Disabled Americans into the Mainstream,* Study No. 854009, International Center for the Disabled, New York, 1986.

79. Scotch R. K. *From Goodwill to Civil Rights: Transforming Federal Disability Policy.* Temple University Press. Philadelphia, 1984.

80 Crawford R. You are dangerous to you health: the ideology of politics of victim blaming. *Int. J. Hlth Services* **7,** 663-680, 1977.

81. Crawford R. Individual responsibility and health politics. In *Health Care in America: Essays in Social History* (Edited by Reverby S. and Rosner D.), pp. 247-268. Temple University Press, Philadelphia. 1979.

82. Gleidman J. and Roth W. *The Unexpected Minority: Handicapped Children in America.* Harcourt, Brace, Jovanovich, New York. 1980.

83. Saxton M. A peer counseling training program for disabled women. *J. Social Soc. Welfare* **8,** 334-346, 1981.

84. Hughes E. and Hughes H. M. "What's in a name". In *Where People Meet~~Racial and Ethnic Frontiers,* p. 130-144. The Free Press, Glencoe, IL, 1952.

85. Bogdan R. and Biklen D. "Handicappism", *Soc. Policy, pp.* 14-19, March/April, 1977.

86. Crawford R. Healthism and the medicalization of everyday life. *Int. J. Hlth Services,* **10,** 365-388, 1980.

87. Zola I. K. Healthism and disabling medicalization. In *Disabling Professions* (Edited by Illich I., Zola I. K., McKnight J., Caplan J. and Shaiken H.), pp. 41-69. Marion Boyars, London, 1977.

88. Dunne P. Faith, hope, and clarity. *Harvard Mag.* **88,** (4), 10-14, 1986.

**About the Author:** Irving Kenneth Zola is affiliated with the Department of Sociology, Brandeis University, Waltham, MA. 02254, USA.

**Source:** Reprinted with permission from *Social Science & Medicine,* Vol. 36, No. 2, pp. 167-173, 1993. Published by Pergamon Press Ltd. Oxford, England.

# The Power of Language: Speak and Write Using "Person First"

Joan Blaska, Ph.D.

The words or phrases people speak and write plus the order in which they are sequenced greatly affects the images that are formed about individuals with disabilities and the negative or positive impressions that result.

> A group of children on a school outing entered the department store with excitement. One young man worked his way through an aisle of clothing. While the going was slow, he mastered the challenge and found the football jerseys. His teacher gave him a "high-five" for his accomplishments of maneuvering his wheelchair and locating the "sporting goods" department. This student who has cerebral palsy had a successful outing with his classmates.

The language used in this scenario promotes a positive image of a young man who is on an outing with classmates trying to find the football jerseys. Oh yes, he happens to have a disability! Compare this to the following scene:

> A group of handicapped children on a field trip with their normal classmates entered the department store with excitement. One wheelchair-bound young man who suffers from cerebral palsy struggled as he maneuvered his wheelchair through the clothes. His teacher praised his efforts in finding the football jerseys in the sporting goods department.

The language describing this scenario produces an immediate image of a young man sitting in a wheelchair with a disability. By using the word handicapped early in the narrative to describe the children, the reader conjures up an immediate image, based on his or her past experiences, of someone who is "handicapped". The remaining words allude to his limited capabilities because of his disability. With this choice of language, it is difficult to get past the disability and recognize the abilities that are evident. This scenario creates a negative image by the very choice of words and confuses the person with a condition.

Over 500 million people in the world have disabilities because of mental, physical, or sensory impairments (Strand, 1992). According to the National Organization of Disability, more than 40 million Americans have disabilities that interfere with the major tasks of daily life (Tyler, 1990). People with disabilities are included into society more than at any other time in history. What language do you use when you speak about a person with a disability? In the past, a variety of terms, labels, and descriptors have been used which often were derogatory and tended to perpetuate negative attitudes and false stereotypes. Too often language has been used that portrayed people with disabilities in "stereotypical, imprecise or devaluing ways" (Hadley & Martin, 1988, p. 147).

Language is a reflection of how people in a society see each other. Historically, persons with disabilities were viewed with sympathy, sometimes as pathetic, and occasionally even with horror. Individuals with disabilities were often hidden from society which meant the rest of the people did not have the opportunity to understand the disabilities and more importantly to see them as people first and recognize the abilities of this population. With little education available to children with disabilities, they did not have the opportunity to develop to their fullest capabilities.

In the United States, Public Law 94-142, The Education for all Handicapped Act (EHA) was passed in 1975. This law ensured a free, appropriate, public education to people with disabilities ages 3 to 21 years (Federal Register, 1975). For the first time, individuals with disabilities had the opportunity for an appropriate education with some of this training occurring in mainstream classrooms.

It became apparent that students with disabilities had the capabilities to develop skills that could be utilized in society. We are now becoming more aware of the contributions that people with disabilities have given to society. Respect for these individuals is steadily increasing.

Stereotyping sex, race, and disability through language usage is very pervasive and can have a negative effect on society's perceptions of persons with disabilities as well as affect the self-image of individuals with disabilities (Froschel, Colon, Rubin, & Sprung, 1984). Stereotypic language can send a negative message of alienation and apartness and can limit the aspirations of persons with disabilities and lead them to doubt their self-worth (Slapin, 1990). Whereas, in a positive verbal environment the words used by adults can make the children feel like valued members of society (Kosteinik, Stein, & Whiren, 1988). The language used to describe someone with a disability may be particularly influential to individuals who have had no exposure or experiences with people with disabilities.

The words that are utilized to describe individuals convey individual and/or societal prejudices toward a specific group of people. Stereotyping persons with disabilities occurs when using words such as "handicapped" which originated from a begging term meaning "cap-in-hand" or the word "cripple" which is derived from the term "creep". Using words such as "confined" to a wheelchair becomes inappropriate as in reality the wheelchair is a liberating vehicle which allows the person to move around independently (Foschl, et al., 1984). Words such as these conjure up feelings of pity and uselessness and perpetuate stereotypes.

In recent years, there has been a strong movement toward emphasizing the need to accept diversity of all people as the demographics around the world are changing. While the concept of diversity includes persons with and without disability (Derman-Sparks, 1989), the emphasis of this movement has been diversity of culture. This is evidenced through growing numbers of recently published adult and children's books with multicultural themes, antibias curricula

emerging in the classrooms, and numerous attempts of language changes in reference to minority groups (i.e. Blacks as African American; Indians as Native Americans). These same revisions and additions need to be made in relationship to individuals with disabilities including language changes that demonstrate respect.

According to the results of a study by Foschl et al. (1984), many teachers have become aware of racial and ethnic slurs and do not allow children to use them. However, these teachers admitted they were less aware of sex and disability bias in language and indicated a need to become more aware of the words they use which may be promoting disability bias. According to Steer (1979), attitudes of school staff toward persons with disabilities are translated primarily through the language used. Also, the degree to which children are able to perceive themselves as competent and worthy, or the opposite, is heavily influenced by the verbalizations used by their teachers (Kosteinik, et al., 1988). Studies have found that labeling of students does affect teacher expectations which in turn affects student progress (Gillung & Rucker, 1977). While labeling is often needed to access services, with these findings it makes it very important that we be respectful and cautious in their use.

Children's attitudes can be shaped by the words they hear or read (Byrnes, 1987). Because of the influence of print media on society, children with disabilities need to hear and see themselves referred to in a positive way, in order to see themselves as important individuals in society. It is the responsibility of all caring adults to select materials that portray persons with disabilities in a realistic manner. This then becomes the message that will be sent to all children and can help end the stereotype of persons with disabilities not being productive citizens. It is with information such as this that stereotyping can be stopped.

In this media-influenced society, the press can have an enormous impact on society's knowledge, attitudes, and public policies regarding individuals with disabilities. "This influence can, at its best, enhance knowledge and promote social awareness of disabilities. At its worst, it can promulgate misinformation and reinforce negative stereotypes (Keller, Hallahan, McShane, Crowley, & Blandford, 1990, p. 217).

Keller, et al (1990) conducted a national study of American newspapers to check the premise that the press's coverage has provided a less than ideal picture of individuals with disabilities and disability issues. The results of their study indicated that 48% of the references that described disabilities had a negative impact with only 1% of the references having a positive impact. When the newspaper's portrayal was negative, the focus was on the person's general, physical, and social-emotional well-being. Whereas, positive dimensions which relate the individual who has the disability to his or her family or to society received very little coverage. Unbalanced coverage such as this reinforces stereotypic images of people who have disabilities. Their strengths and contributions to society go unseen. Negative portrayals are offensive to persons who have disabilities and have the potential to affect the reader's perceptions, and possible actions, toward individuals with disabilities.

## THE POWER OF LANGUAGE

The use of words or expressions when referring to persons with disabilities is very subtle and might seem unimportant. However, "when one considers that language is a primary means of communicating attitudes, thoughts, and feelings...the elimination of words and expressions that stereotype becomes an essential part of creating an inclusive environment" (Froschl, et al., 1984, p.20).

## "PERSON FIRST' LANGUAGE

The philosophy of using person first language demonstrates respect for people with disabilities by referring to them first as individuals, and then referring to their disability when it is needed. This philosophy demonstrates respect by emphasizing what people can do by focusing on their ability rather than their disability and by distinguishing the person from the disability.

This philosophy was first adopted by TASH, The Association for Persons with Severe Handicaps (Bailey, 1992). Since that time, many disability groups and advocacy organizations have published similar information in an attempt to educate the public regarding "person first" language. People with disabilities have also been vocal about this issue. Perske (1988) tells of a woman who stood up at a meeting and said, "We are tired of being seen first as handicapped, or retarded, or developmentally disabled. We want to be seen as people first." It is important to avoid giving a disability more prominence than it deserves. "Most people who have disabilities forget about them much of the time" (Hadley & Brodwin, 1988, p. 147).

Using the expression "the blind child" makes the disability the most important attribute about the child, while saying, "the child who is blind" takes the focus away from the disability, making the disability but one descriptor. While this order of reference is more awkward, it is more respectful of persons with disabilities. According to Kailes (1985), this order is preferred as a "psychologically sounder expression" (p.68).

Individuals who have disabilities, their families and friends are particularly aware of words and phrases that convey stereotyping attitudes (Hanft, 1989). Support groups and advocacy coalitions (i.e. United Cerebral Palsy, National Easter Seal Society, Parent Advocacy Coalition of Educational Rights {PACER}) are educating families about the philosophy of "person first" language and are encouraging its use. A college student shared with her classmates the following story which had happened to her while making a home visit. Without thinking, the teacher referred to the child with whom she was working as a "handicapped" child. A teenage sister happened to be home and heard the teacher's language. The teenager challenged the teacher and asked, "Why did you call my sister a handicapped child when really she is a little girl who happens to have a handicap?" Somewhere this teenager had heard or read about "person first" language. Families like the respect this philosophy affords their family member who has the disability and are likely to challenge professionals who are not changing their language (Blaska, 1991).

To keep the "person first" philosophy in perspective, consider how you might introduce one of your friends who does not have a disability. You would use that person's name first and then perhaps tell where he or she lives, works, and so forth. Why should it be any different for someone who has a disability? Everyone is made up of many attributes and most people do not want to be identified by any one characteristic (Pacesetter, 1989). While a disability may create challenges, the need for information or assistance, it does not define a person's entire existence (Hanft, 1989). A disability should be represented in its proper perspective. If the disability is totally irrelevant, reference to it may be omitted entirely (Hadley & Brodwin, 1988).

### Examples of "Person First" Language:

| *Use This:* | *Instead of This:* |
| --- | --- |
| • child with a disability | disabled child |
| • man who is blind | the blind man |
| • child with Down syndrome | Down Syndrome Child |
| • boy with a physical disability | crippled boy |
| • girl who is deaf and cannot speak | deaf and dumb girl |
| • babies addicted to crack | crack babies |
| • person with epilepsy | epileptic |
| • child with retardation | retarded child |
| • man who has quadri- plegia or paralysis of both arms and legs | quadriplegic |

### DISABILITY VS HANDICAPPED

Whether to use "disability" or "handicap" has been an on-going controversy. A disability is defined as a condition of the person, either emotional or physical. Whereas, a handicap is the cumulative result of the barriers imposed by society which come between an individual and the environment of an activity which the person wants to do (Hadley & Brodwin, 1988: Kailes, 1985; Wright, 1960).

A disability does not have to be a handicap!  A disability may mean "that a person may do something a little bit differently from a person who does not have a disability, but with equal participation and equal results" (Kailes, 1985, p. 68).

| *Use This:* | *Instead of This:* |
| --- | --- |
| • the boy with a disability | handicapped boy |
| • children with disabilities | handicapped children |
| • peers without disabilities | non handicapped peers |
| • disabling conditions | handicapping conditions |

### NORMAL CHILD OR PERSON

The difficulty with using the term "normal" to refer to a person without a disability is the inference that a person with a disability is "abnormal" or "not normal". While a person with a disability may have some abnormal development, he or she is not an "abnormal" person. When referring to what is "normal" or inferring what is "abnormal", be careful to indicate you are talking or writing about development and not a person or program.

| *Use This:* | *Instead of This:* |
| --- | --- |
| • normal development | normal child |
| • normally developing | normal child |
| • child without a disability | normal child |
| • refer to specific development: i.e., normal eyesight, normal hearing | |
| • mainstream classroom | normal classroom |
| • refer to specific classroom i.e., first-grade classroom | |
| • children without disabilities | normal children or normal peers |

## WORDS TO AVOID

Avoid words that have negative or judgmental connotations (Tyler, 1990). Words such as these fail to demonstrate respect and do not recognize the person's strengths and abilities. The following words should be avoided as they create images of people who are less abled and are to be pitied. Words such as these perpetuate negative stereotypes of people with disabilities (United Cerebral Palsy: Hanft, 1989).

*Avoid using words such as these:*

| | |
|---|---|
| afflicted | confined |
| crippled | drain or burden |
| stricken | poor |
| suffers from | unfortunate |
| victim | disease |

## DISABILITY OR DISEASE

A disability is not a disease. Often individuals with disabilities are very healthy. Words such as patients, cases or symptoms should be avoided unless talking or writing about someone's health or medical condition.

## PORTRAYAL

People with disabilities should "be portrayed as actively going about the business of living as other people do, *not* as passive victims, tragic figures, or super-heroes" (Hadley & Brodwin, 1988).

## CATEGORIZING PEOPLE

Avoid grouping people with disabilities into categories such as "the retarded", "the handicapped" (Hanft, 1989). "Do we really see children as individuals, or do we say, for example, that all children with Down syndrome are warm, friendly, happy and will never be able to read?" (Steer, 1979, p.40).

| *Use This* | *Instead of This:* |
|---|---|
| • people with disabilities | the disabled |
| • people with retardation | the retarded |
| • people with disabilities | the handicapped |
| • individuals with hearing impairments | the deaf |
| • children with visual impairments | the blind |

## ADDITIONAL SUGGESTIONS

Usually a form of the verb "to have" is the most effective way of expressing the link between a person and a disability (Hadley & Brodwin, 1988). "A person is a human being and should not be confused with a condition" (Tyler, 1990, p.65).

| *Use This:* | *Instead of This:* |
|---|---|
| • has autism | is autistic |
| • had cerebral palsy | is cerebral palsied or is CP |
| • has spastic muscles | is spastic |
| • has epilepsy | is an epileptic |
| • has retardation | is retarded |

Assistive devices, prostheses, and wheelchairs are examples of equipment and devices that people use to assist them in their life activities (i.e., wheelchairs enable individuals to escape confinement) (Hadley & Brodwin, 1988; RTC/IL, 1990).

| *Use This:* | *Instead of:* |
|---|---|
| • uses a wheelchair | confined to a wheelchair |
| • walks with crutches | is on or has to use crutches |
| • walks with braces | uses braces |

Some thoughts about using the word "special": "Special" is a word actively utilized in regards to persons with disabilities (i.e., special education, special buses, special needs). About using this word, "Pershe (1988) stresses: "Being seen as special might not be so bad, if you're a top celebrity or the national champion" (p.59). But, if you've been singled out as not...normal, given a label, excluded from full participation, exist in out of the way residences, or attend "out of the real world programs" when you felt you wanted to live "in the middle of things", "calling you special might only add to the wound you already feel" (p. 59). While all persons with disabilities may not be offended by the use of "special", Pershe's comments serve as a reminder to choose your words carefully and always speak with respect to all people.

## MOVEMENTS TOWARD 'PERSON FIRST' LANGUAGE

### Business Communication:

Tyler (1990) advocates incorporating "people first" language into business communication courses. Tyler emphasizes that the number of Americans with disabilities entering the workplace continues to increase. Yet, few textbooks used in business communication even mention the subject of how to communicate appropriately about people with disabilities. According to Tyler, "people first" language could fit in with the discussions of linguistic sexism and how to avoid it, racism, and other possible biases which are already included. Tyler indicated that the book, *Without Bias: A Guidebook for Nondiscriminatory Communication* might be a helpful resource in courses such as this as it provides suggestions for avoiding bias with regard to race, ethnicity, gender, age and does include disability. The focus of this guidebook is on-the-job situations and provides illustrations and sample sentences which could be used.

### Professional Journals:

Some professional journals are now requiring that authors use "person first" language in order for their articles to be considered for publication. For example, in the *Journal of Early Intervention,* the Guidelines for Authors instruct authors accordingly: "In describing the subjects of studies or in referring to infants, children, and other individuals with disabilities, authors must place the disability descriptor after the child or adult descriptor. This policy follows the precedent established by the Association for Persons with Severe Handicaps in placing

the child before the handicap in sentence structure" (Bailey, 1992).

### Laws and Statutes:

While the United States legal and political systems had favored the word "handicapped" and had not demonstrated a sensitivity toward person first language, some changes have recently occurred. On October 30, 1990 the president signed into law The Education of the Handicapped Act Amendments of 1990. One of the significant changes was to give the law a new title to reflect "person first" language: Individuals with Disabilities Education Act (IDEA). At that time, the legislation instructed that the entire statute be amended to make the language changes which utilized the word "disability" and "person first" language (Walsh, 1990).

Some states have followed the federal government's lead. For example, in 1991 the Minnesota legislature passed a bill to make all MN statues reflect "person first" language and "disability" was to replace all reference to "handicap". The directive concluded with, "It is extremely important that we not only build in respect and dignity toward people with disabilities in our statutes, but that these attitudes become second nature within our everyday language" (Henry, 1991). Another example is that new "Handicapped Parking" signs will now use the term "disability" (Minnesota State Council on Disabilities, Personal Communication, December, 1992). While this does not make the language "person first", it does make a change in utilizing more respectful language and is a step in the right direction.

### Preservice Training:

In preservice training, some professors are training professionals who will be working with individuals with disabilities and their families to use the preferred "person first" language. For example, at a state university in the midwest in an undergraduate class of 32 special education teachers and speech/language clinicians, the professor began the ten-week course with a discussion of "person first" language. Activities about "person first" language were done in class, handouts were provided, and the professor modeled this philosophy throughout the quarter. The students were told that the expectations for the class would be that everyone would try and use "person first" language when speaking in class. The professor and classmates would remind each other in a non threatening manner and reinforce one another. "Person first" language was also required in all written work. After ten weeks of class, the final written projects displayed 100% success using "person first" language. At the conclusion of the course, some students were still forgetting to reverse the referent when speaking. However, in most cases the students were self-correcting. They were actually hearing the miscue and correcting their expression to make it "person first". The changes demonstrated by the students in this class clearly indicate that preservice training can be effective in promoting "person first" language and changing old habits.

### SUMMARY

The utilization of "person first" language demonstrates acceptance and respect for differences among people as we speak and write and in turn can have a positive effect upon society. While it is not easy to change old habits, it can be done. Professionals who work with individuals with disabilities should ask themselves: How do I refer to the children or students with whom I work? When I speak to parents, how do I refer to their child and his or her disability? When I speak to colleagues how do I refer to the children? When I write, what order do I place my words in when referring to a person with a disability? When the wording becomes cumbersome, do I persevere and refuse to use hasty short cuts that lack respect? Have you made the change? (Blaska, 1991). We can help individuals with disabilities develop positive self-esteem by referring to them in words that acknowledge ability, merit and dignity (United Cerebral Palsy).

What image do you have of the new family that just moved into the neighborhood?~

"Hi, Mom! I called to tell you about the new family that just moved in next door! We're so lucky to have a family with young children about the ages of Tommy and Mindy. They will all be going to the same school in the fall. Won't that be neat for the children to have friends while waiting for the bus? Yes, they have three children all two years apart. The boys will probably play ball with Tommy and their Sara might go to Brownies with Mindy. As you can tell, I'm really excited about the new neighbors".

Mindy has Down syndrome, but the disability wasn't mentioned in this telephone conversation! The essence of a "person first" philosophy has been achieved when the disability is not the first characteristic identified and is mentioned only when the disability is or becomes a significant factor.

Words are "powerful tools by which a civilization perpetuates its values~~both its proudest achievements and its most crippling prejudices (Radloff, 1974, p. 8). Words and phrases and the attitudes they perpetuate are often the greatest handicap an individual must overcome (Maine D.D. Council, 1990). We have a choice to continue to send negative messages which will be harmful to persons with and without disabilities or we can accept the challenge and CHANGE OUR LANGUAGE, which has the potential to positively impact society.

\*\*\*\*\*\*\*\*

### REFERENCES

Bailey, D. (1991). Guidelines for authors. *Journal of Early Intervention*, **15** (1), pp 118-119.
Blaska, J. K. (1991, June), President's message. DEC Network, p. 5.
Bubar, J. (1990). *Jargon and Acronyms*. (Available from the Main Developmental Disabilities Council, State House Station #139, Augusta, Min).
Byrnes, D. A. (1987). *Teacher, they called me a --- -------! Prejudice and discrimination in the*

*classroom.* New York: Anti-Defamation League of B'nai Brith.

**Derman-Sparks, L. (1989).** *Anti-bias curriculum: Tools for empowering young children.* Washington, DC: National Association for the Education of Young Children.

**Federal Register. (1975).** Public Law 94-142, Education of the Handicapped Act. Washington, DE: United States Department of Health, Education and Welfare.

**Froschl, M., Colon, L., Rubin, E., & Sprung, B. (1984).** *Including all of us: An early childhood curriculum about disability.* New York: Educational Equity Concepts, Inc.

**Gillung, T. B., & Rucker, C.N. (1977).** Labels and teacher expectations. *Exceptional Children,* **43,** 464-465.

**Hadley, R. G., & Brodwin, M.G. (1988).** Language about people with disabilities. *Journal of Counseling and Development,* **67,** 147-149.

**Hanft, B. (1989).** How words create images. In B. E. Hanft (Ed.) *Family-Centered care: An early intervention resource manual* (pp. 277-278). Rockville, Maryland: American Occupational Therapy Association, Inc.

**Henry, A. (1991).** *Education statues to reflect "people first" language.* (Available from the Minnesota State Legislature, St. Paul, Minnesota).

**Horne, M. D. (1988).** Handicapped, disabled, or exceptional: Terminological issues. *Psychology in the Schools,* **25,**, 419-421.

**Kailes, J. (1985).** Watch your language, please! *Journal of Rehabilitation,* **51,** (1), 68-69.

**Keller, C. E., Hallahan, D. P., McShane, E. A., Crowley, E. P., & Blandford, B. J. (1990).** *The Journal of Special Education,* **24,** (3), 272-282.

**Kosteinik, M. J., Stein, L. C., & Whiren, A. P. (1988).** Children's self-esteem: The verbal environment. *Childhood Education,* Fall, 29-32.

**National Easter Seal Society.** *Portraying people with disabilities in the media.* (Available from The National Easter Seal Society, 2023 West Ogden Avenue, Chicago, Illinois 60612).

**PACER. (1989, September).** It's the 'person first' - Then the disability. *Pacesetter.* Minneapolis, MN: Parent Advocacy Coalition of Educational Rights.

**Perske, R. (1988).** *Circle of friends.* Nashville, TN: The Parthenon Press.

**Radloff, B. (1974).** Racism and sexism in children's books. *Carnegie Quarterly,* **22,** (4), 1.

**RTC/IL.** *Guidelines for reporting and writing about people with disabilities.* (Available from the Research and Training Center on Independent Living, Bureau of Child Research, University of Kansas, Lawrence, KS 66045).

**Slapin, B. (1990).** *Books without bias: A guide to evaluating children's literature for handicapism.* Berkeley, CA: Squeaky Wheels Press.

**Steer, M. (1979).** Fostering positive attitudes toward the handicapped. *Education Canada,* Winter, 36-41.

**Strand, R. (Ed.). (1992, December).** United Nations recommends 'full participation' of people with disabilities. Futurity, p. 2.

**Tyler, L. (1990).** Communicating about people with disabilities: Does the language we use make a difference? *The Bulletin of the Association for Business Communication,* **53,** (3), 65-67.

**United Cerebral Palsy.** *Watch your language - fact sheet.* (Available from the United Cerebral Palsy Association, inc., 66 East 34th Street, New York, NY 10016).

**Walsh, S. (Ed.) (1990, December).** Education of the handicapped act. *Early Childhood Reporter: Children with Special Needs and Their Families, p. 5.*

**\*\*\*\*\*\*\*\*\*\***

**About the Author: Joan Blaska** is an Associate Professor in the College of Education at St. Cloud State University in St. Cloud, Minnesota, where she coordinates the early childhood special education program. Her research interests are student teaching supervision, issues of grieving for parents who have children with disabilities, early literacy and children's literature, and transition. She possesses a Ph.D. in Education Administration with a minor field of special education and a collateral field of Family of Social Science.

**Source:** Reprinted with permission from the author. Article on "Person First" Language was written specifically for this edition of *Perspectives on Disability.* Copyright held by Health Markets Research, Palo Alto, CA.

# The Disabled: The Acquisition of Power
Mark Nagler, Ph.D.

## Introduction:

Any group striving for equality must achieve power. With the acquisition of power, minorities can lobby for legislation which empowers them with the means to achieve measures of integration. However, laws do not necessarily translate into policy. Legislation which mandates significant social change may not become a reality for decades. People with disabilities are discovering that significant legislation such as the Americans with Disabilities Act (ADA) [1] does not achieve the immediate social justice which translates into acceptance and integration. While the ADA conveys for some a mandate that a 'mecca' has been achieved for people with disabilities, the reality is that attitudinal and socioeconomic change takes much longer than the signing of a document.

Although people with disabilities have witnessed significant positive changes in quality of life and integration, they still find themselves victimized by long-standing and traditional social, psychological, physical, fiscal, architectural and political barriers~all of which are inhibitors to the acceptance and participation by the disabled in mainstream society. The most significant barrier is the concept of cost-effectiveness or fiscal responsibility. People with disabilities are often counselled to wait until the "time is politically right". If disadvantaged groups waited for balanced budgets and ideal economic climates, no social change would ever take place. The ethic and goal for all minorities is equality, integration, and social justice. However, the social justice advances made in the last few decades for people with disabilities have spawned many myths concerning the degree to which integration of the disabled population has been achieved. There is still much to be fought for, and there are still many barriers and myths to overcome.

The social disadvantages arising from the isolation, segregation and discrimination of minority groups have perpetuated the inequality and the sense of powerlessness of these groups.

The successful orientation towards equality has been open only to the less disadvantaged groups. Disadvantaged minorities with limited power often discover that the social justice and equality which they seek are difficult to achieve. This discussion will analyze the significant factors associated with the aceptance and integration of the disabled population during the last four decades. In many instances, it is the accepted and uninformed opinion that granting equality to the disabled population group is not justifiable because of the cost, because of opposing values, or because of the inconvenience to mainstream society.

## People With Disablities as a Minority Group

Disadvantaged minorities must become aware of the significance of power. Individuals or groups who have power are in a position to control their own destinies. Those who are powerless through physical or environmental circumstance have no control over their destinies. The disabled do not constitute a 'group' in the sociological sense, but they do possess some group attributes. They share similar difficulties and barriers in their corporate lives with other minority groups~barriers and difficulties which prevent them from achieving a significant measure of autonomy. Differing in a sociological sense from other groups, the disabled do not have constituents such as a common culture, mores, folkways, laws, and a sense of 'peoplehood'. In addition, they differ from other sociological groups because they do not experience a consciousness of a kind, or an 'esprit de corps'. Many ethnic minority groups like the Irish or the Dutch, for instance, experience this esprit de corps along with an ethnocentrism which magnifies the positive characteristics of group identity and disparages outsiders. People with disabilities come from all walks of life, from differing cultural backgrounds, and from varying degrees of circumstance and experience.

The disabled, therefore, have not been very successful in establishing themselves as a sociological group. Segments of the disabled population such as the sight and hearing impaired have focused on their unique concerns and have commanded public attention for their particular disabilities, but these people have been unable to form a voice of their own without outside advocacy. In spite of their unique and common impairments, as groups these people still remain isolated, compartmentalized, shielded and closeted by society, professionals, families and institutions. As well, large segments of the disabled population continue to be socialized to believe they should be 'grateful' for what is done for them. As a result, and tragically so, it has become the norm for this vulnerable group to seldom question or protest injustices.

The disabled have become classic subjects of victimology. Powerless groups are vulnerable to oppression and as such are victims of economic, social, psychological, political and sexual exploitation. So it is with many disabled people who constitute a loosely connected amalgamation of individuals. Because people with disablties lack a group perspective and an overall group identity, they consequently lack the power to fight for and obtain their rights. As well, educational and economic opportunities are often frustrated for these individuals as counsellors and advisors do not encourage them to pursue challenges in these areas of endeavour. Paralleled to the situation of African Americans who have yet to obtain full equality in the 1990's, in spite of significant civil rights legislation, the situation of people with disabilities has a similar status.

Traditionally the value system of North American society has perpetuated the notion of the disabled as a weak and semi-competent segment of the population~a segment which must be 'looked after and tolerated'. In some views, this perspective is considered as more humanitarian than the former situations in Greece and the more recent past Nazi era when the physically and psychologically disabled people were removed from society. Yet large numbers of people with disabilities feel removed from society in more subtle ways, through the social and economic systems, and through the physical barriers that confront them on an ongoing basis. To overcome these biases and barriers, the disabled must find a means to unite and bind together as a strong, sociological group if they are to make an impact on society and effect change in their status.

### Towards the Acquisition of Power

In spite of the past and prevailing attitudes towards marginalizing this significant number of individuals, there is slowly growing evidence that people with disabilities are beginning to emerge from decades of isolation and institutionalization. The United Nations Charter of Human Rights specifies a "...universal respect for human rights and and fundamental freedoms for all...." [2]. As David Baker analyzes, "The subsequent passage of the declaration of rights for mentally retarded persons (1971) and the declaration of rights of disabled persons (1975) and the appointment of the U.N. sub-committee on the protection of minorities (which was specifically to consider the rights of disabled persons) further substantiates this position" [3]. This declaration has served as an impetus for the disabled to seek legislation which will enshrine their positions as equals in mainstream society. A significant step towards the attainment of power as a group was evidenced during the last presidential election as the disabled people in the U.S. shifted their votes to George Bush when he announced his intention to draft the Americans with Disabilities Act. It has been estimated that three million disabled Americans supported Bush because this policy would constitute a positive directive towards the achievement of legitimate integration in society. In other words, three million votes represented *power*. As promised, in July of 1990 the ADA became law. The ADA proclaims, "...the Nation's proper goals regarding individuals with disabilities are to assure equality of opportunity, full participation, independent living, and economic self-sufficiency for such individuals" [4].

## Societal Barriers for the Disabled

In spite of the U.N.'s Declaration of Human Rights, the Bill of Rights and other significant Charters throughout the world, societies have not enjoyed an exemplary image in the treatment of disadvantaged minoritiy groups. For instance, in Canada and the U.S., Japanese citizens lost their possessions and rights during World War II and legitimate restitution has yet to be made to these people in spite of the fact that they were loyal citizens. As well, hundreds of individuals were dispossessed during the McCarthy era. Only now are North Americans beginning to see the human destructiveness and degradation that these injustices imposed on innocent individuals. More recently, the disadvantaged Native communities of Watts and Wounded Knee in the U.S. and the community of Oka in Canada have not received the benefits of the promises and legislation which were enacted on their behalf.

Similarly, the disabled community is being integrated into the mainstream of North American society at a 'snail's pace'. While educational awareness programs and legislation are creating a foundation for acceptance and integration, there is resistance to implementing and facilitating these changes. Not only does a general attitude of acceptance towards the disabled have to be changed from one of exclusion to inclusion, but society's institutions, geared as they are to budgets and cost effectiveness, must find the financial means for implementing physical changes and providing access to the disabled in all areas of the social environment.

Basic to the right of the individual to achieve autonomy and freedom of choice in making decisions for his or her own life is the right to obtain an education. Barriers to the exercising of this right by the person with a disability are slow to overcome. Some educational institutions remain inaccessible to people with all types of disabilities because of prejudice, discrimination, and lack of physical accessibility to buildings. Although much is being done to provide adequate training and life-skills education for the mentally and intellectually disadvantaged~perhaps because this is the more visibly disadvantaged segment of the disabled group~progress is slow in efforts to overcome obstacles for the physically disabled who are intellectually normal or superior. Students with physical disabilities who have intellectual ability are often advised to compromise their goals for achieving higher education by taking general level programs. It would seem that educational authorities are reluctant to provide the necessities which would allow the person to flourish and develop his or her full potential. As well, situations exist where some educators are reluctant to give oral exams or extra assistance to a physically disabled person because "it is not a condition of their contract". While this type of prejudice is difficult to prove, it does exist. Not surprisingly, it is also 'felt' by the disabled person as the discriminatory means for excluding him or her from opportunities for personal achievement.

While segregated educational institutions are in place for many segments of the disabled population, it still seems to be overlooked that the inclusion of these people in mainstream educational institutions has proven to be the most productive strategy in allowing people with disabilities to be fully integrated into North American society. As well, while segregated facilities are designed to accommodate the physical barriers faced by the disabled, public educational institutions are slow to re-design or alter structures to suit these needs. Some institutions remain inaccessible for the mobility-impaired population because construction of these buildings took place during times when accessibility issues were not considered. The costs required to restructure older buildings are either prohibitive or it is structurally unfeasible to do so. With all these barriers still to overcome, it continues to be difficult for those disadvantaged by physical disability to obtain access to higher education.

********

## REFERENCES

1. Americans with Disabilities Act, enacted July 1, 1990.

2. The foundation document for International Protection of Human Rights (1948) which states

that everyone is entitled to all rights and freedoms without discrimination of any kind.

3. Baker, David. (1993) Human Rights for Disabled People. In *Perspectives on Disability*. 2nd Edition, M. Nagler (Ed.) Health Markets Research, Palo Alto, CA.

4. Kemp, Evan. (1990) From the Foreward in *Perspectives on Disability,* p. vii. M. Nagler (Ed.). Health Markets Research, Palo Alto, CA.

**About the Author:** Mark Nagler is an Associate Professor in the Sociology Department of Renison College, University of Waterloo, Waterloo, Ontario, CANADA. He received his Ph.D. in Sociology from the University of Sterling in Scotland. He is the Editor of the first and second editions of *Perspectives on Disability*, and specializes in the study of disability-related issues, deviance, and race and ethnic relations.

**Source:** Reprinted with permission by the author and editor of this book. From a paper delivered at the annual meeting of the Society for Disability Studies, June 1990.

# The Politics of Physical Differences:
# Disability and Discrimination
Harlan Hahn

**Abstract~**_Although a "minority group" model has emerged to challenge the traditional dominance of the "functional-limitations" paradigm for the study of disability, research on attitudes toward disabled people has not produced a theoretical orientation that reflects these developments. This paper proposes a new conceptual framework, based on the fundamental values of personal appearance and individual autonomy, for assessing the "aesthetic" and "existential" anxiety aroused by persons with disabilities. Investigations using this perspective might contribute to determining the attitudinal foundations of the competing models that are dividing research on disability._

In recent years, a growing social and political movement of disabled citizens has had a major impact on the study of disability. Inspired in part by the passage of major legislation, such as Section 504 of the Rehabilitation Act of 1973 and P.L. 94-142, the Education of All Handicapped Children Act of 1975, many persons with disabilities have begun to feel that their problems stem primarily from prejudice and discrimination rather than from their functional impairments. This trend has promoted a corresponding interest by researchers in a new theoretical approach to issues confronting this segment of the population--namely, a minority-group" model of disability, in contrast to the earlier "functional-limitations" model (Hahn, 1985a).

Much of the impetus for this change can be traced to a significant shift in the definition of disability. While disability traditionally has been examined from a _medical_ approach that focuses on functional impairments or from an _economic_ approach that emphasizes vocational limitations, a new _socio-political_ approach has emerged that regards disability as a product of interactions between individual and environment (Hahn, 1982). The latter viewpoint avoids the limitations of the clinical model (Stubbins, 1982) by recognizing that the fundamental restrictions of a disability may be located in the surroundings that people encounter rather than within the disabled individual. From a socio-political vantage point, the difficulties confronted by disabled persons are viewed as largely the result of a disabling environment instead of personal defects or deficiencies. The extent to which environmental modifications could ameliorate the functional constraints of a disability may eventually be determined by technology and by the limits of human imagination in designing a world adapted to the needs of everyone. Just as important, this perspective can guide research viewing disabled citizens as an oppressed minority. Whereas the medical and economic definitions have tended to concentrate on methods of improving the disabled individual's capabilities, the socio-political approach indicates the need for strengthened laws to combat discrimination against persons with disabilities.

There are at least two additional corollaries that follow from a socio-political view of the problems of disabled persons. First, this approach emphasizes that the functional demands exerted on human beings by the environment are fundamentally determined by public policy. The present forms of architectural structures and social institutions exist because statutes, ordinances, and codes either required or permitted them to be constructed in that manner. These public policies imply values, expectations, and assumptions about the physical and behavioral attributes that people ought to possess in order to survive or to participate in community life. Many everyday activities, such as the distance people walk, the steps they climb, the materials they read, and the messages they receive, impose stringent requirements on persons with different levels of functional skills. These characteristics of the environment that have a discriminatory effect on disabled citizens cannot be considered simply coincidental. Rather than reflecting immutable aspects of an environment decreed by natural law, they represent the consequences of prior policy decisions.

Second, awareness that the environment is basically molded by past and present public policy suggests *public attitudes* as a crucial component of the surroundings with which disabled people must contend. From a minority-group perspective many of their difficulties can be traced to the attitudinal environment of society (Hahn, 1985b). In a culture that places a high premium on the physical and behavioral capabilities for mastering the environment, the effort to disentangle attitudinal factors from functional standards is obviously a complex endeavor. Yet this task seems crucial to the evaluation of people with disabilities as a minority group.

Although many nondisabled observers are reluctant to openly acknowledge their aversion to persons with disabilities, there is a strong possibility that both the prevalent emphasis on disabled people's functional limitations and the pervasive features of an unaccommodating environment disguise widespread feelings of bias or prejudice. As Siller (1976) has noted, "typical 'gut' reactors frequently express queasy feelings aroused by the sight of disability and vehemently resist working or socializing with severely handicapped individuals"( p.67).

Although many early studies (Baker, Wright, Meyerson, & Gonick, 1953: Safilios-Rothschild, 1970; Wright, 1960) acknowledged that disabled people constituted a minority group, this approach was overshadowed by the predominant focus on functional limitations. The relative lack of a theory identifying disabled persons as an oppressed minority seems to have been perpetuated in studies of attitudes toward disability. Two recent surveys of the literature on this subject (Altman, 1981; Livneh, 1982), for example, offered impressive evidence of burgeoning research on attitudes toward disability, but neither developed a framework that would facilitate investigation of the empirical foundations of the functional-limitations and the minority-group models. Since existing social-psychological theories on attitudes and attributions do not seem clearly adaptable to consideration of the role of disabled citizens in modern society (Hahn, 1985c) there appears a pressing need to develop a new conceptual framework for appraisal of attitudes toward people with disabilities.

## Attitudes and Discrimination

Minority groups have been subjected to various forms of exploitation and oppression, and the sources of their treatment may be traced to pervasive social values of the dominant majority. A principal problem in establishing the concept of disabled persons as an oppressed group has been the prevalent assumptions of their biological inferiority. Whereas a major thrust of social science research on other minorities during the past century has been to refute such assumptions and to demonstrate that their unequal status stems primarily from prejudicial attitudes, many professional as well as popular images of disabled individuals continue to harbor presuppositions of inferiority based on their functional incapacities. Consequently, it has been commonly overlooked that the origins of prejudice are based on widespread perceptions that disabled individuals violate important cultural norms and values, and that this fact permits them to be set apart from the remainder of the population.

Two critical values in 20th-century Western society that especially influence the treatment of disabled people are personal appearance and individual autonomy. The crucial importance of these values is revealed by sources that range from the mundane to the philosophical. Persons who fail to meet prescribed standards of physical attractiveness and functional independence not only are assumed biologically inferior, but they are also exposed to a stigma that depicts them as "not quite human" (Goffman, 1963, p.5).

These ideas can provide the basis for a major reconceptualization of the structure of attitudes about disability. Like other minorities who have been victims of discrimination, disabled persons have characteristics that permit them to be differentiated from the rest of the population. These characteristics, which may be identified by physical or behavioral cues or by verbal labels, are likely to arouse strong feelings in nondisabled observers about their own appearance or autonomy. Moreover, these responses of observers are clearly related to the theoretical underpinnings of the competing models for the study of disability. Whereas responses to disability elicited by worries about individual autonomy are closely related to the functional-limitations model, reactions evoked by concerns about personal appearance are closely associated with the minority-group model. Thus, a new approach to the examination of attitudes toward disabled persons based on the concepts of autonomy and appearance may have important practical as well as theoretical utility for further research on disability.

The need for such a framework is underscored by the relative paucity of studies founded on the minority-group model of disability. Although surveys indicate that 45% of disabled Americans believe people with disabilities are a minority group in the same sense as are blacks and Hispanics (Harris & Associates, 1986), academic investigations of the problems of disabled persons as a minority group are comparatively recent and rare (Gliedman & Roth, 1980; Hahn, 1985c). The purpose of this paper is to propose a new and still speculative conceptual framework for research on attitudes toward disabled persons that encompasses the minority-group as well as the functional-limitations models of disability.

## Components of Attitudes Toward Disability

The concepts of "aesthetic" and "existential" anxiety occupied a prominent position in the propositional inventory developed by Livneh (1982), and they seem to constitute a valuable means of assessing the attitudinal foundations of the minority-group and the functional-limitations paradigms for the study of disability (Hahn, 1983). Both of these concepts represent deep and powerful apprehensions.

The term *aesthetic anxiety* refers to the fears engendered by persons whose appearance deviates markedly from the usual human form or includes physical traits regarded as unappealing. These fears are reflected in both the propensity to shun those with unattractive bodily attributes and the extraordinary stress that modern society devotes to its quest for supernormal standards of bodily perfection.

*Existential anxiety* refers to the threat of potential loss of functional capabilities by the nondisabled. The existential anxiety triggered by disabilities occasionally may become the subject of conscious attention. Sometimes these concerns are evident in the silent thought that "there, but for the grace of God (or luck or fate or other fundamental beliefs) go I." At other times, these worries may be verbalized in statements such as, "I would rather be dead than live as a paraplegic (or as blind, deaf, or immobilized)." In fact, the threat of a permanent and debilitating disability, with its resulting problems, can even outrank the fear of death, which is, after all, inevitable.

***Existential Anxiety.*** Probably the most common threat from disabled individuals is summed up in the concept of existential anxiety: the perceived threat that a disability could interfere with functional capacities deemed necessary to the pursuit of a satisfactory life. The expectation that everyone ought to achieve modal levels of functional proficiency - or perhaps the fear that many might lose these abilities - seems so strong that, for hundreds of years of modern history, almost no thought was given to the possibility that human capabilities could be increased by altering the environment in which people lived. Individuals who failed to attain the mobility, sensory, or communications skills to master the existing environment were consigned to being recipients of disability benefits from whatever social welfare programs existed in a society. The principal effects of existential anxiety have been to relegate disabled individuals to the role of helpless or dependent nonparticipants in community life, and to exacerbate nondisabled persons' worries about the potential loss of physical or behavioral capabilities that could result from a disability. In a society that appears to prize liberty more than equality, and that tends to equate freedom with personal autonomy rather than with the opportunity to exercise meaningful choice, the apprehensions aroused by functional restrictions resulting from a disability often seem overwhelming.

In general, empirical studies based on the functional-limitations model of disability have not identified existential anxiety as a single component of attitudes toward disabled persons. Jones et al. (1984), for example, described five dimensions of attitudes toward stigmatized groups in addition to aesthetic qualities. Yet all of the specified characteristics of visible human difference including their origin, peril, disruptiveness, and the course or prognosis of the disability, would have little importance unless respondents had some understanding of the personal consequences of these characteristics. In other words, the social stigma of a disability fundamentally derives from the fact that the resulting functional impairments may interfere with important life activities. Hence, there appears ample justification for using existential anxiety as a comprehensive concept to describe unfavorable perceptions of disabled people stemming from the functional-limitations model of disability.

Existential anxiety seems to involve a sense of personal identification with the position of a disabled person. Therefore, the presence or absence of this type of identification could be investigated to determine whether or not a propensity to project existential fears onto disabled people is a primary source of unfavorable perceptions of individuals with disabilities.

*Aesthetic Anxiety*. The aesthetic anxiety aroused by the appearance of people with visible disabilities has at least two major aspects. First, the discrimination directed at disabled individuals is partly due to their being devalued because they do not present conventional images of human physique or behavior. After an extensive review of research on body images, Fisher (1973) concluded,

> *Despite all the efforts invested by our society in an attempt to rally sympathy for the crippled, they still elicit serious discomfort. It is well documented that the*

> *disfigured person makes others feel anxious and he becomes an object to be warded off. He is viewed as simultaneously inferior and threatening. He becomes associated with the special class of monster images that haunt each culture. (p.73)*

These worries may well reflect a prevalent preoccupation by men and women about their own appearance.

Second, aesthetic anxiety may result in a tendency to place those who are perceived as different or strange in a subordinate role. Throughout history, perceptible features such as racial or ethnic characteristics, gender, and aging have formed an important basis for prejudice toward minority groups. Little research has been conducted on the extent to which people with disabilities are regarded as failing to meet commonly accepted standards of personal appearance. However, studies have shown that perceptions of physical appearance affect the evaluation of writing talent (Landy & Sigall, 1974) and employment decisions (Schuler & Berger, 1979). On the basis of numerous studies, Saxe (1979) concluded that attractiveness...

> *...seems to be more insidious than previously suggested, as it affects and, in some cases, pervades our relationships with others. It causes discomfort, both to the unattractive (who are denied justice) and to the attractive (who may be expected to perform at levels higher than they are capable of). (p.12)*

Other research has shown that unattractive physical characteristics can lead to the attribution that their bearer has a disability such as epilepsy (Hansson & Duffield, 1976). By similar logic, there is reason to believe that the perceived unattractiveness of a disability could be a significant source of unfavorable attitudes toward the disabled person, as in the findings of Bull (1979). Also, disabled men and women possess limited choices in the formation of personal relationships as a result of an "aesthetic-sexual aversion" to disability that permeates society (Hahn, 1981; Safilios-Rothschild, 1970). Thus, in a society that places extraordinary stress on beauty and attractiveness, aesthetic anxieties may be an important component of perceptions of disabled people.

***Relationship of Existential and Aesthetic Anxiety.*** One of the major problems that has plagued prior studies of attitudes toward disabled persons can be traced to the traditional ascendancy of the functional-limitations model in research on disability. Most investigators who have defined and understood disability primarily as a problem of physical or behavioral impairments have tended to assume that reactions to disabled individuals can be explained solely in terms of existential concerns. However, both existential anxiety and aesthetic anxiety are involved in unfavorable perceptions of people with disabilities. An important task for future research is to determine how existential and aesthetic feelings, either separately or in combination, affect the treatment of persons with disabilities in a wide variety of circumstances.

Given the traditional prevalence of the functional-limitations model, relatively few nondisabled people may be prepared to understand disability as a problem that revolves largely around aesthetic considerations. The effort to disentangle existential and aesthetic elements of attitudes toward disabled people could provide an important contribution to resolving the conflict between the functional-limitations model and the minority-group model for research on disability.

Whereas aesthetic concerns are aroused by the pervasive cultural emphasis on personal attractiveness, existential worries seem based on a process of identification between a disabled individual and the nondisabled observer. Hence, attempts to assess the amount of identification that occurs between disabled and nondisabled persons could provide a means of unraveling responses to disability. If nondisabled individuals were found to have a strong capacity to internalize the threat posed by a disability and to project those feelings onto a disabled individual, such a finding would suggest support for the primacy of existential anxiety. In contrast, if most nondisabled observers lack the capability to form a close or accurate identification with

the circumstances of a disabled person, their unfavorable perceptions may simply indicate a desire not to associate or interact with others considered alien or strange. The former results would be most consistent with the functional-limitations model, while the latter outcome would highlight the discrimination identified as a major problem by the minority-group paradigm. Some support for the latter interpretation seems indicated by the fact that predominant attitudes toward persons with disabilities reflect aversion rather than more intense manifestations of anxiety (Altman, 1981; Livneh, 1982).

**Policy Implications**

A socio-political understanding of disability requires that attention must be paid to both existential and aesthetic sources of discrimination. From a functional-limitations perspective, existential anxiety seems primary; that is, non-disabled persons are presumed to focus on the alleged biological inferiority of people with disabilities, thus arousing fears about the potential mutability and deterioration of their own bodies. Yet policy makers and courts usually have been reluctant to implement the principle of equality by mandating environmental modifications in response to people's clinically demonstrable organic defects or deficiencies. On the other hand, the minority-group model may compel observers to consider the manner in which aesthetic anxieties operate to distance and disparage disabled individuals. Precisely because these worries are relatively trivial and difficult to rationalize, research assessing them could form a firm foundation for constitutional challenges to the unequal treatment of the disabled minority.

The two components of attitudes toward persons with disabilities seem to yield different policy implications. Both types of anxiety can be discriminatory. For example, many job qualifications that bar disabled individuals from employment may reflect existential worries. However, in an environment not yet adapted to the needs of disabled people, aesthetic anxiety is clearly more difficult to justify than existential anxiety. Hence. a finding that aesthetic considerations form a major source of unfavorable assessments of disabled persons could lend strong support to the argument that citizens with disabilities should be considered a "suspect class" within the meaning of the equal protection clause of the Fourteenth Amendment to the U.S. Constitution.

In addition, the results of empirical research utilizing this conceptual framework might have an important impact on strategies for achieving attitude change. For example, the relative lack of success of past efforts to persuade employers to hire disabled workers may be due to the possibility that aesthetic anxiety is less susceptible to influence by cognitive appeals than is existential anxiety. An increased emphasis on the aesthetic component of attitudes toward people with disabilities could fruitfully shift the emphasis in advocacy efforts to the affective dimension of attitude change.

*******

## REFERENCES

Altman, B.M. (1981). Studies of attitudes toward the handicapped: The need for a new direction. *Social Problems*, 28, 321-337

Barker, R.G., Wright, B.A., Meyerson, L., & Gonick, M.R. (1953) *Adjustment to physical handicap and illness: A survey of the social psychology of physique and disability.* New York: Social Science Research Council.

Bull, R. (1979) The psychological significance of facial deformity. In M. Cook & G. Wilson (Eds.), *Love and attraction: An international conference* (pp.21-25) Oxford: Pergamon.

Fisher, S. (1973) *Body consciousness: You are what you feel.* Englewood Cliffs, NJ: Prentice-Hall.

Gliedman, J., & Roth, W. (1980).*The unexpected minority: Handicapped children in America.* New York: Harcourt Brace Jovanovich.

Goffman, E. (1963) *Stigma: Notes on the management of spoiled identity.* Englewood Cliffs, NJ: Prentice-Hall.

Hahn, H. (1981). The social component of sexuality and disability: Some problems and proposals. *Sexuality and Disability, 4, 220-233.*

Hahn. H. (1982). Disability and rehabilitation policy: Is paternalistic neglect really benign? *Public Administration Review, 43, 385-389*

Hahn. H. (1983, March-April) Paternalism and public policy. *Society, pp. 36-46.*

Hahn, H. (1985a). Changing perceptions of disability and the future of rehabilitation. In L.G. Perlman & G.F.Austin (eds.), *Societal influences in rehabilitation planning: A blueprint for the 21st century* (pp.53-64). Alexandria, VA: National Rehabilitation Association.

Hahn, H. (1985b). Disability policy and the problem of discrimination. *American Behavioral Scientist, 28. 293-318.*

Hahn, H. (1985c). Toward a politics of disability: Definitions, disciplines, and policies. *Social Science Journal, 22, 87-105.*

Hansson, R.O. & Duffield, B.J. (1976). Physical attractiveness and the attribution of epilepsy. *Journal of Social Psychology, 99, 233-240.*

Harris, L. & Associates (1986). *The ICD survey of disabled Americans: Bringing disabled Americans into the mainstream.* New York: Author

Jones, E.E., Farina, A., Hastorf, A.H., Markus, H., Miller, D.T., Scott, R.A. & French R. de S. (1984). *Social stigma: The psychology of marked relationships.* New York: Freemen.

Landy, D., Sigall, . 1974). Beauty is talent: Task evaluation as a function of the performer's physical attractiveness. *Journal of Personality and Social Psychology. 29, 299-304*

Livneh, H. 1982). On the origins of negative attitudes toward people with disabilities. Rehabilitation Literature, 43, 338-347.

Safilios-Rothschild, C. (1970)The sociology and social psychology of disability and rehabilitation. New York: Random House.

Saxe, L. (1979). The ubiquity of physical appearance as a determinant of social relationships. In M. Cook & G. Wilson (Eds.), *Love and attractiveness: An international conference (pp.9-13)* Oxford: Pergamon.

Schuler, H., & Berger, W. (1979). The impact of physical attractiveness on an employment decision. In M. Cook & G. Wilson (Eds.) *Love and attraction: An international conference (pp.33-36)* Oxford: Pergamon.

Stubbins, J. (1982). *The clinical attitude in rehabilitation.* New York: World Rehabilitation Fund.

Wright, B. (1960) *Physical disability: A psychological approach.* New York: Harper & Row.

*******

**Source:** Reprinted from *Journal of Social Issues*, Vol. 44, No. l, 1988, pp. 39-47. Published by the Society for the Psychological Study of Social Issues.

# Further Thoughts on a "Sociology of Acceptance" for Disabled People
## Howard D. Schwartz

**Introduction:** Social scientists studying the relationship between people with disabilities and the larger society, in recent years and with increasing intensity, have been waging a frontal assault against the dominant conceptual model of disability as deviance perspective leads to a predetermined view of people with disabilities as negatively valued by, and socially isolated from, the rest of society.

To be found among the growing number of critical voices are Robert Bogdan and Steven Taylor (1987) who call for the development of "sociology of acceptance" through which to view people with disabilities. In proposing this, Bogdan and Taylor do not totally reject the deviance approach. Rather, they point to the need for adding a complementary perspective to accommodate those instances when the disabled person is accepted rather than rejected by others. While this contention seems legitimate and important, the informality of their presentation makes their argument less persuasive than it might be.

In the first place, and Bogdan and Taylor recognize this, the supporting data they present are less than satisfactory. Drawn ad hoc from their 15 years of clinical work in human services, the evidence is more suggestive than confirmatory regarding societal acceptance of people with disabilities.

Second, the authors talk about two different accepting public postures without, unfortunately, providing anything more than a preliminary discussion of either posture or the difference between them. On the one hand, they speak of the kind of acceptance found in the seminal work of Nora Groce's *Everyone Here Spoke Sign Language* (1958). Analyzing the position of the deaf in the community of Martha's Vineyard up to the first part of this century, Groce concludes that "they were just like everyone else" (which is, in fact, the title of the first chapter). In a community where everyone was bilingual in English and sign language, the deaf were simply seen as equal to the hearing, no better, no worse.

On the other hand, Bogdan and Taylor consider acceptance in terms of disabled persons being viewed by others as "special, more interesting, more stimulating, more challenging, more appreciative". The example of a caseworker and his mentally retarded client is used to show the disabled person in this favored-status role. After a while, the caseworker came to value as special his disabled friend's candor, which included the ability to express feelings and show emotions.

For conceptual clarity, the *acceptance* will be used here to define relationships between disabled and ablebodied persons in which all participants are viewed as equals. The term *advocacy* will be employed where those with disabilities are given favored status. It thus becomes the positive counterpart of rejection in a continuum of public postures that includes rejection, acceptance, and advocacy.

With these comments about the Bogdan and Taylor argument in mind, what emerges for the recent empirical research, including my own, is admittedly limited, but clear evidence of a change toward a far more favorable public opinion of disabled persons.

## Evidence for a "Sociology of Acceptance"

In 1986, in a paper that received considerable attention, Katz, Kravetz, and Karlinsky reported the results of a study comparing the attitudes of high school seniors in Berkeley, Calif., toward disabled and nondisabled people. According to the authors, what was notable about the study results was that they were not consistent with those of many earlier research results, since they seemed "to imply that the disabled person is viewed more positively than the nondisabled one in the United States".

The students had been presented with video-tapes of a man who was variously identified as being a civilian or in the military, disabled or ablebodied. The respondents rated, on intelligence, vocational (work) competence, morality, and sociability, the individual that they viewed. After an overall rating score was calculated for each student, it was found that the average score for the disabled person was significantly higher than the average score for the able bodied one.

The researchers speculate that an explanation of their results might be found in the unique nature of Berkeley. As an archetypical academic environment, it contains a substantial disabled population affected by mainstreaming and other educational innovations aimed at changing public attitudes toward persons with a disability. Consequently, "the nondisabled population is exposed to persons with disabilities who cope and live within the community and "get to know them and their abilities beyond the disability."

In one study, Siegfried and Toner (1981) asked college students to rate two target subjects: a potential co-worker and a potential supervisor. One-half of the students thought these people were disabled due to an automobile accident, the other half were presented with the identical description except that there was no mention of a disability. For 11 of the 16 dependent measures, covering a wide range of work-related behaviors (e.g. professional competence, missing work, successful performance, and ability to travel), the disabled and ablebodied target subjects were rated equally. On those five factors for which significant differences were found, the disabled person was rated higher. He or she was seen as more likely to be approached with a personal problem, more likely to be asked a favor of, less likely to upset co-workers, and less likely to need special assistance.

In a similar vein, in a study published earlier by Krefting and Brief (1976), college students rated a disabled person (a paraplegic using a wheelchair) equal to an ablebodied person on most job-related measures, but higher on work motivation and likelihood of being a long-term employee.

## The Playboy Study

My own research, carried out in the fall of 1987, can now be added to this body of literature (Schwartz, 1988). While similar to the aforementioned studies in its use of student respondents, a wheelchair-user target subject, and the same kind of experimental technique, it differed in an important way. The target subject was neither a military man nor a potential employee, but Ellen Stohl, the first disabled woman to be the subject of a *Playboy* (1987) photo layout.

As explained in the story accompanying the pictures, Ms. Stohl, who had a spinal-cord injury, offered to pose for *Playboy* as a way of demonstrating that people with disabilities can also be sexy. In the letter in which she asked the magazine for the opportunity to pose, she wrote, "Sexuality is the hardest thing for disabled persons to hold onto," and that she wanted "to teach society that being disabled does not make a difference."

Irving Kenneth Zola (1987) a sociologist writing about disability in America, views "the right to be sexy" as a central item on the agenda related to the psychological and social liberation of people with disabilities. Harlan Hahn (1988) has touched on the same issue in his article, "Can Disability Be Beautiful?". Nevertheless, there seem to be limited opportunities for disabled people to assert their claim to sexuality, particularly through the media of popular culture. The *Playboy* article is unique in providing such a forum. It also offered the possibility of research to ascertain how, in a sexual context, the public evaluates the disabled person compared to the ablebodied one, and the disabled versus the ablebodied person's "right to be sexy."

The study was carried out at a medium-sized state university in Virginia, with a total enrollment of about 8,000. The majority of students came from urban centers within a 500-mile radius of the university such as Washington, D.C., with about one-third coming from more rural areas in the general vicinity of the university. Ten percent are from out of state.

The respondents were all of the students taking introductory sociology. Each student was shown one of two pictures of Ellen Stohl that had appeared in *Playboy*: One showed Stohl's face in closeup and shoulder partially bare; the other, providing a higher level of sexual display, had a partially-nude Stohl sitting on a couch with her legs tucked under her and wearing a negligee open in the front exposing a breast and her midriff. An additional aspect for the research design was that each student was given only one of two versions of whichever picture he or she received. An ablebodied version included, along with the picture, a biographical sketch which noted that Stohl was a college student and that the pictures had appeared in a national magazine with a readership of over 3 million. A second, disabled version had the identical biography except that Stohl was identified as spinal-cord injured, and a smaller picture of her fully clothed in a wheelchair was presented along with the larger picture. The analysis centered on comparing, for each picture, the responses of the students receiving the two versions.

The almost 700 respondents (80 students who had seen the pictures in *Playboy* or had heard about them were excluded) were asked to look at the photo of Stohl and rate her on six personal characteristics and on six factors concerned with conjectured success-failure or satisfaction-dissatisfaction in present or future life situations.

Regardless of the picture seen (the specific picture viewed had no effect in any of the comparisons), the disabled Stohl was rated equal to the ablebodied Stohl on sociability, intelligence, physical attractiveness, and the likelihood of having a fulfilling life.

Most interestingly, for five of the eight dependent measures for which a significant difference was found, Stohl was rated higher when presented as disabled than when presented as ablebodied. When identified as spinal-cord injured , she was seen as having greater strength of character, sensitivity to others, and competence at work, more likelihood of being a good parent, and less likelihood of getting divorced. The disabled Stohl's perceived relative superiority on these factors seems to confirm the finding

of the previously cited studies which used the same or similar dependent measures that a disabled person is seen as better than one who is not disabled. Put another way, there is the strong hint of the disabled person's being viewed as a "paragon of virtue".

For two of the three measures on which the disabled Stohl was rated lower - the likelihood of getting married and satisfaction with life - the differences, while statistically significant, were so small as to be negligible. On the third, sexual appeal (the only measure to show a gender difference), the women saw no difference between the disabled and ablebodied Stohl while the men favored the latter. Yet as far as the response of the male students is concerned, this is somewhat misleading. In fact, while both the men and women rated the disabled Stohl's sexual appeal as very high, the men rated it higher than the women did. In absolute terms, the men rated Stohl when disabled as "very sexually appealing," the second highest response on the 6-point Likert item.

Taken together, the ratings on sexual appeal and the equal ratings on physical attractiveness lead us to conclude that disability did very little, if anything, to diminish Stohl's physical appeal in the eyes of the respondents.

In addition to rating Stohl on this array of measures, respondents were asked, "In your opinion, was it appropriate for this women to pose for this picture?" (The respondents could answer "yes" , "no", or "undecided"). The results show unequivocally that it was deemed more appropriate for the disabled Stohl to pose.

In all but one group comparison (over 80 percent of the men who viewed Stohl's face in closeup approved of her posing), a significantly higher percentage of those who saw the disabled Stohl approved of her posing. For example, of those shown the partially-nude picture, 55 percent with the disabled version approved compared to 36.4 percent with the ablebodied version. For men alone, the corresponding percentages were 75 percent versus 52.1 percent, and for women, 43.2 percent to 30.6 percent.

## The Right to Be Sexy

Analysis of the open-ended responses of those who, upon viewing the disabled Stohl, approved of her posing can better help us to understand the distinction between acceptance and advocacy of the disabled person's "right to be sexy." Grouping respondents according to the reasons given for approval allows us to differentiate those reasons in terms of whether they are likely to lead to one or the other positive postures.

Acceptance would seem to be a logical outcome of the responses of two groups. The first group gave whether they are likely to lead to one or the other positive postures. what might be called "disabled-blind" explanations ("Why not?  An honest way to make a dollar"). The common factor here was the absence of any recognition of the disability. A second group did take account of Stohl's disability, couching their approval in terms of the very basic theme of equal rights ("She has as much right as anyone to pose for this picture").

Advocacy would likely follow from the responses of three other groups. A good number of respondents saw Stohl as an example of role model representing to the public and/or other disabled people the ability of the disabled to succeed in endeavors in which they have not, historically, had the opportunity to participate ("Maybe her doing so will show other handicapped people that they are beautiful and show the general public the same. Good for her"). The responses of a second group expressed admiration for the disabled person having to overcome much more than others to achieve a goal ("With her disability it is a great step and very courageous.  She is doing things in her life.") The underlying theme in the responses of the third group was the unique social-psychological benefits that a disabled person would derive from this experience ("If it makes her feel more 'complete' or happier why not?)".

Assuming that the above speculation about the link between response type and the two positive public postures has validity, the difference between acceptance and advocacy is that in the case of advocacy there exists the perception of a greater urgency, salience, or merit related to the disabled person's "right to be sexy." This is most evident in the statements of those students who held a double standard resulting in a type of "reverse discrimination" on behalf of the disabled. As one respondent put it, "Normally, I'm *very* against people posing in these pornographic pictures, but in this case I feel she had a statement that she is comfortable with, and I can't but help admire her reasons for it.  She's trying to convey that handicapped people can be human, they are sexually attractive, and they are in control of their lives."

## Disabled Persons in Society

The data presented provide support, and the beginnings of an empirical database, for social scientists like Bogdan and Taylor, who insist that there is a need to augment the conceptual and theoretical arsenal used in assessing the role of disability and disabled people in society. The finding of overwhelmingly favorable student attitudes toward an individual who uses a wheelchair raises doubts about the relevance of the deviance perspective to specific instances of disability. Maybe most striking is the absence in my research of any evidence of what Hahn has argued is discrimination toward disabled people based on aesthetic criteria. Not only was the disabled Stohl seen as physically attractive as her ablebodied counterpart, but also her disability did not lead to the imputation of "sexlessness," a causal sequence taken as a given in the literature. Quite to the contrary, the disabled Stohl was perceived as a woman with considerable sexual appeal.

Exploration of the origins and implications of the view of the disabled individual as a "paragon of virtue" is called for. Bogdan and Taylor see this perception as arising from the particular character of a specific one-to-one relationship between a disabled and nondisabled individual. While they may be correct on this score, the new research points to the existence of a more generalized notion that may involve a cultural stereotyping of disabled people in this way. Future research can provide important answers as to why they are seen as more likely to fulfill normatively-defined role obligations in circumstances ranging from friend to parent, spouse to employee. It is worth cautioning, that although obviously there is nothing inherently wrong with being viewed as a good person, there is always the possibility that this kind of stereotype could lead to unrealistic and unfair expectations concerning what disabled people are like and how they are likely to behave.

The limited purview of the studies presented precludes any grandiose claims about how far society has come in the way it perceives and treats people with disabilities. For example, the target subjects were all physically-disabled wheelchair users. And the literature shows that, in general, the physically disabled evoke more positive reactions from ablebodied people that do those with emotional and cognitive impairments (Bordieri and Drehmer, 1987). Despite this, the data presented do underscore the need to refrain from viewing all disabled people as occupying a unitary social status. One would hope that a new generation of writers will avoid describing all those with disabilities as "stigmatized" (Goffman 1963) or as "outsiders" inhabiting the "other side" (Becker, 1963, 1964). It is time for works of quality that deal with how the various public reaction-that is, rejection acceptance, and advocacy - are distributed over the broad range of disabled persons.

A theoretical perspective that needs to be exploited in the future is one implied by Bogdan and Taylor and explicated most clearly by those taking a "minority group" approach to disabled people. It would replace the focus on disabled versus nondisabled individuals with one on disabling and enabling environments. The research cited here suggests that, as with the contexts of family and friends discussed by Bogdan and Taylor, educational institutions may now constitute enabling environments. This was a position taken by Katz and his colleagues to explain the Berkeley high school students' favorable perception of disabled people. It is also compatible with my impression of the social milieu at the sight of my study. There, over the last decade, disabled people have become an increasingly visible and prominent segment of the campus community.

Student attitudes in the studies discussed may also be a consequence of a more favorable climate toward disabled people in the society at large. In this regard, I cannot help but make mention of the recent, and very striking, events that took place at Gallaudet University in the spring of 1988. The unexpected force of public support - both immediate and seemingly unanimous - for the student body seeking deaf leadership may have been the critical factor in the swift capitulation of the powers-that-were. As the board of trustees' choice for the presidency of the university declared when she resigned, "I was swayed by the ground swell across the nation that it is time for a deaf president."

Finally, something must be said about the relevance of what has been discussed to the very practical issue of the employment of the disabled. When *Playboy* decided to publish pictures of Ellen Stohl, the mass media reported that the editorial staff was strongly divided on the wisdom of that decision and that those who held the negative opinion felt that the public was not ready for it. As my data show, they needn't have worried. Moreover, insofar as employers are reluctant to hire disabled people for fear of an unaccepting public, the data from all four studies show that they may be misreading public opinion. The dissemination of social scientific research and perspectives relating to the acceptance and advocacy of people with disabilities would seem an important step in any process that is to have the capability of leading to their full integration into the larger society.

*********

### REFERENCES

**Becker, Howard S.,** *Outsiders: Studies in the Sociology of Deviance* (New York: The Free Press, 1963)

----*The Other Side: Perspectives on Deviance* (New York: The Free Press, 1964).

**Bogdan, Robert and Steven Taylor**, "Toward a Sociology of Acceptance: The Other Side of the Study of Deviance," *Social Policy* (Fall 1987), pp. 34-39.

**Bordieri, James W. and David E. Drehmer**, "Attribution of Responsibility and Predicted Social Acceptance of Disabled Workers," *Rehabilitation and Counseling Bulletin* (June 1987), pp. 219-26.

**Grace, Nora**, *Everyone Here Spoke Sign Language: Hereditary Deafness on Martha's Vineyard* (Cambridge: Harvard University Press, 1985).

**Goffman, Erving**, *Stigma: Notes on the Management of Spoiled Identity* (Englewood Cliffs, NJ: Prentice-Hall, 1963).

**Hahn, Harlan**, "Can Disability be Beautiful?" Social Policy *(Winter 1988), pp.26-31*

*Kratz, Shlomo, Schlomo Dravetz, and Mickey Karlinsky*, "Attitudes of High School Students in the United States Regarding Disability: A Replication of an Israeli Study, *Rehabilitation Counseling Bulletin* (December 1986), pp.102-9.

**Krefting, Linda A. and Arthur P. Brief**, "The Impact of Applicant Disability on Evaluative Judgments in the Selection Process" *Academy of Management Journal* December 1976, pp.675-80.

"Meet Ellen Stohl," *Playboy* (July 1987), pp. 16-18.

**Schwartz, Howard D.**, "Disability and Sexual Display. Empirical Evidence of Public Advocacy for Disabled People and the Disabled Person's Right to be 'Sexy.'" Paper presented at the annual meeting of the American Sociological Association, Atlanta, August 28, 1988.

**Siegfried, William D. and Ignatius J. Toner**, "'Students' Attitudes toward Physical Disability in Prospective Co-Workers and Supervisors." *Rehabilitation Counseling Bulletin* September 1987, pp.20-25.

**Zola, Irving, Kenneth**, "Neither Defiant nor Cheering", *Disability Rag* (September/October 1987), pp. 16-18.

******

**Source:** Reprinted with permission from *Journal of Social Policy*, Fall 1988, pp. 36-39. Published by Social Policy, New York, New York 10036.

# Disability Beyond Stigma: Social Interaction, Discrimination, and Activism

Michelle Fine

Adrienne Asch

**Introduction:** Between 1981 and 1984, the Eastern Paralysed Veterans Association, Disabled in Action of New York City, and other organizations of people with disabilities fought a court battle with the New York City Metropolitan Transit Authority to gain architectural access to the city's mass transit system. The MTA opposed modifying the system, claiming that the expense would never be made up by rider fares of those mobility-impaired people then denied transit access. The *New York Times* ("Editorial," 1983; "The $2,000 Subway Token," 1984), along with most other sectors of the community, generally favoring progressive social change, supported the Transit Authority in the fight it eventually lost (Katzmann, 1986).

In 1982 and 1983, the national media described two cases where the parents and doctors of infants with disabilities denied the infants medical treatment based on their impairments. In the first case, an infant with Down syndrome died of starvation six days after birth; in the second case, the parents finally consented to the surgery. The impairments of the infants were used as the basis for denying them treatment that could have alleviated certain of their medical problems but left them with permanent disabilities that no treatment would cure. Virtually the only supports of the infants' right to treatment over parental objections were those commonly associated with the right-win and right-to-life sectors of society, and perhaps also people with disabilities themselves *(Disability Rag,* 1984). (For a discussion of these cases and their meaning for notions of "community," see Sarason, 1986; and for a civil libertarian supporter of Baby Doe, see Hentoff, 1987).

In 1983 and 1984, and again in 1986, Elizabeth Bouvia, a young woman whose cerebral palsy made it impossible for her to control any of her limbs save some functions

of one hand, sought to get California hospitals to allow her to die by starvation. The American Civil Liberties Union (ACLU), generally regarded as championing the progress of many social causes, wrote a brief in her behalf describing her disability as causing her "pitiful existence," referring to her "affliction" as "incurable and ... intolerable",and commenting on the "indignity and humiliation of requiring someone to attend to her every bodily need" (ACLU Foundation of Southern California, 1983, pp.14,17,35). The entire tone of the brief implied that it was not at all surprising that someone with her level of disability would wish to end her life. The ACLU was not dissuaded from its line of argument by testimony of the Disability Rights Coordinating Council (DRCC), including a psychologist who was also quadriplegic, suggesting that Ms. Bouvia's situation was complicated by a host of stresses apart from her disability: "death of a sibling, marriage, pregnancy, multiple changes in residence, financial hardship, miscarriage, increased physical pain, terminal illness of a parent, and dissolution of marriage" (DRCC, 1983, p.3). The DRCC did not dispute that people had the right to take their own lives. It disputed the unquestioned assumption that disability was a reason to end life.

The Superior Court of California, unmoved by those who sought to disentangle Ms. Bouvia's request from the situation of people with disabilities generally, endorsed her request, saying among other things: "She, as the patient, lying helplessly in bed, unable to care for herself, may consider her existence meaningless. She cannot be faulted for so concluding." Later, in describing her, it stated: "Her mind and spirit may be free to take great flights, but she herself is imprisoned, and must lie physically helpless, subject to the ignominy, embarrassment, humili-ation, and dehumanizing aspects created by her helplessness" (*Bouvia v. Superior Court of California*, 1986, pp. 19,21).

In this issue of *JSI*, we wish to resurrect the challenge to social psychology posed by Meyerson, Barker, and others in their 1948 *JSI* issue on disability. In this first article, we review the ways that disability has been viewed by social psychology over the past decades, trying to do for the study of disability what Sampson (1983) has done for the view of justice: namely to offer some challenges to the assumptions that have guided theory and research, to speculate on the bases for these assumptions, and to suggest how alternative assumptions would alter the study of disability. We conclude by previewing the remaining articles in this issue as they reflect theory and research grounded in both old and new assumptions about the social nature of physical and mental disabilities.

**Defining the Population of Interest**

Although other articles in this issue elaborate upon the problem of accurately defining and describing the current situation of people with disabilities in 1987, it is essential to specify briefly whom this issue is about. In 1980 Bowe estimated the total population of people with disabilities in the United States to be 36 million or perhaps 15% of the nation's people. In 1986 ("Census Study"), the *New York Times* reported some 37 million people over 15 years of age with disabling conditions. As Asch (1984) has discussed elsewhere, the mere attempt to define and enumerate the population shows that disability is a social construct. The Rehabilitation Act of 1973, as amended in 1978, defines a handicapped individual as "any person who (i) has a physical or mental impairment which substantially limits one or more of such person's major life activities, (ii) has a record of such an impairment, or (iii) is regarded as having such an impairment" (Section 7B).

We can say the following with assurance: The nation's population includes some 10% of school-aged children classified as handicapped for the purposes of receipt of special educational services (Biklen, this issue); somewhere between 9 and 17% of those between 16 and 64 years of age report disabilities that influence their employment situation (Haber & McNeil, 1983); nearly half of those over 65 indicate having one or more disabilities that interfere with their life activities or are regarded by others as doing so (DeJong & Lifchez, 1983).

Laws governing the provision of educational and rehabilitation services, and prohibiting discrimination in education, employment, and access to public programs, all stress the similarities in needs and in problems of people with a wide variety of physical, psychological, and intellectual impairments. (Scotch, this issue, discusses the benefits to the disability rights movement of such a legislative approach). In this space, however, it is important to acknowledge the *differences* among disabling conditions and their varied impact on the lives of people in this group.

First, different conditions cause different types of functional impairment. Deafness, mental retardation, paralysis, blindness, congenital limb deficiencies, and epilepsy (all taken up in greater detail in this issue) may pose common social problems of stigma, marginality, and discrimination, but they also produce quite different functional difficulties. Several of these disabilities obviously interfere with functions of daily life, but the last, epilepsy, may not. Some persons with epilepsy have no inherent limitations whatever. Nevertheless, they are likely to be regarded as having an impairment.

Furthermore, people with disabilities have different degrees of impairment: Amounts of hearing and visual loss differ; some people with impairment of mobility can walk in some situations while others cannot. Mental retardation ranges from profound to mild--so mild that many out of school never get the label. In addition, some disabilities are static, while others are progressive. Multiple sclerosis, muscular dystrophy, cystic fibrosis, some vision and hearing impairments, some types of cancer and heart conditions present progressive disabilities that cause ever-changing health and life situations. Some conditions are congenital, others are acquired.

All of these factors that distinguish the origin, experience, and effects of disability must be kept in mind in social science research on disability.

Researchers (Davis, 1961; Goffman, 1963; Ladieu, Adler, & Dembo, 1948) have long been aware that the degree of visibility of impairment or the age at which it was acquired (Barker, 1948; von Hentig, 1948) may influence the psychological consequences and the social situation of people with disabilities. More recently, scholars have addressed the impact of ethnicity, class and gender upon the experience of disability (Fine & Asch, 1981, 1988). In this issue, Schneider focuses on the social-psychological situation of people with a relatively invisible condition (epilepsy), and Mest analyzes the ways in which living and work contexts affect persons with retardation. Most of the other authors discuss the situations of people whose conditions are manifested by appearance or behavior. Ainlay and Frank (both in this issue) consider the different social-psychological impact of age of onset, and their conclusions contrast with the prevailing clinical and social-psychological views that acquiring a disability later is less damaging to the self and to social interaction than is growing up with an impairment. (See Asch and Rousso, 1985, for a review of psychoanalytic literature on disability.

## Disabled People as a Minority

Having acknowledged differences among these more than 36 million people in terms of their diagnoses, their social contexts, and their experiences of disability, it is important to return to the analysis that informs this article and this issue as a whole: disabled people comprise a minority group and most of their problems can and must be understood in a minority-group framework. This view is neither novel nor exclusively a post-Civil Rights Era position. Roger Baker in 1948 advanced thinking about disability in minority-group terms. Lee Meyerson, in his introduction to the 1948 *JSI*, opened by commenting, "There is general agreement in the literature on physical disability that the

problems of the handicapped are not physical, but social and psychological" (p.2). Our own analysis owes much to the Lewinian person-in-environment thinking of the 1948 *JSI* contributors, and to the thoughtful work of Wright (1960, 1983), herself a frequent collaborator with Barker, Meyerson, and Dembo. These authors acknowledged that people with disabilities must be understood as having psychological responses to their impairments themselves, but they went on to point out the following: environmental factors posed many barriers of discrimination, marginality, and uncertain social acceptance; people with disabilities faced ambiguous, if not rejecting, social responses; and these people responded psychologically and socially to such situations..

Our analysis expands on this significant work and the 40 intervening years of social and legislative change. In the last 15 years, the movement for disability rights has embraced a minority-group perspective. Scholars of disability outside of social psychology such as Gliedman and Roth (1980), Hahn (1983, this issue), and Scotch (1984, this issue) have attempted to elaborate a minority-group analysis of disability issues and the disability experience. Unfortunately, as seen from the ensuing discussion, much of the frequently cited social-psychological work on disability has not learned all it could from the 1948 *JSI* contributors, nor from others in the emerging field of disability studies.

The minority-group perspective that frames this volume accepts Dworkin and Dworkin's (1976) definition of a minority group, applying it to people with disabilities. The criteria include "identifiability, differential power, differential and pejorative treatment, and group awareness" (p.viii).

While disabled people as a group may fit these criteria, they nevertheless face many obstacles in developing a minority-group consciousness, as Hahn (this issue) and Scotch (this issue) discuss in some detail. Not the least of these obstacles is the inaccessibility of the built environment, rendering transportation and public facilities unusable for people with any impairment, and disrupting potential efforts at organizing. While many people with disabilities have not developed a minority-group consciousness, a recent Louis Harris survey of disabled Americans reported that 74% of people with disabilities feel some common identity with one another and that 45% see themselves as a minority in the same sense as people who are black or Hispanic (Hill, Mehnert, Taylor, Kagey, Leizhenko et al., 1986). As a footnote to Dworkin and Dworkin, we begin with the premise that a lack of shared consciousness *by some* does not negate the importance of understanding the social, structural, and psychological situation of people with disabilities in minority-group terms. As Hahn (1983, this issue) argues, the consequences of any impairment cannot be understood or appreciated without giving due weight to the environment -- physical, structural, social, economic, psychological, and political--of the person with the disability. Just how disabling would deafness be if 20th-century urbanites, like Groce's (1985) rural villagers of Martha's Vineyard in the 19th century, all practice sign language? How disabling would paraplegia be if all cities were barrier free? (See Scheer & Groce, this issue). How limiting would mental retardation be if nearly all labeled children received their educations in settings with the nonlabelled, as Biklen (this issue) discusses?

Barker (1948) was right when he reminded us that not all of the disabled person's situation can be explained by prejudice and discrimination. It is true that some activities are foreclosed merely because of the biological impairment itself. But the articles in this volume expand upon his thinking by demanding that we cease considering the environment--whether physical or attitudinal--as given. The *JSI* contributors of 1948 and this issue contrast sharply with much of the social-psychological writing about disability in the intervening decades, which assumes that the issues of disability reside in the person and tends to minimize or neglect the environment.

## Assumptions About Disability

Considered below are a set of common assumptions about what disability means. For each, there have been important methodological and theoretical consequences:

1. *It is often assumed that disability is located solely in biology, and thus disability is accepted uncritically as an independent variable.* The disability and the person are assumed synonymous, and the cause of others' behaviors and attitudes. Several experimental social psychologists (Katz, 1981; Kleck, 1969; Kleck, Ono, & Hastorf, 1966) have simulated disability in the laboratory to verify Goffman's reports that handicapped people arouse anxiety and discomfort in others and are socially stigmatized. In these experiments, researchers have simulated disability by using a confederate who in one experimental condition appeared disabled and in another appeared nondisabled. The experiments did support the hypothesis that nondisabled people react differently to people with disabilities than they do to people without them. Nevertheless, it should be remembered that the confederate, whose only experience of having disability may have been simulating it by sitting in a wheelchair, employed none of the strategies commonly used by disabled people to ease the discomfort of strangers in first meetings (David 1961; Goffman, 1963). By focusing on initial encounters with strangers and by using a confederate whose only experience with disability might be simulating it, these experiments tell us nothing about how disabled people *actually* negotiate meaningful social interactions. Reports by David (1961) and Goffman (1963) acknowledge that obvious disability is generally prominent in initial social encounters. However, the extent to which an experimental confederate's naiveté about living with a disability can contribute to the prominence and the awkwardness of disability has not been recognized as an intervening variable. In these experiments, disability is viewed as an independent variable, much as gender had been considered prior to the early 1970's (Under & Denmark, 1975). Disability is portrayed as the variable that predicts the outcome of social interaction when, in fact, social contexts shape the meaning of a disability in a person's life.

Most social-psychological work using disability to examine the concept of stigma takes the experience as equivalent, regardless of such factors as the disabled person's race, culture, class and gender. Scheer and Groce (this issue), Becker and Arnold (1986) provide valuable correctives by viewing the situation of disabled people through the disciplines of anthropology and history.

2.  *When a disabled person faces problems, it is assumed that the impairment causes them.* In a very thoughtful expansion of Goffman's notion of stigma, Jones et al. (1984) elaborate on the consequences for the "marked" person of being singled out by others. Throughout their discussion of marking and its social-psychological consequences for disabled and nondisabled alike, however, these authors never question the extent to which disability per se poses difficulties in social participation, as contrasted with difficulties caused by the environment--architectural, social, economic, legal, and cultural. For example, in their discussion of changes in the life situations of people who became disabled, the authors never question that *the disability* keeps the person from continuing the employment or from going to restaurants or other recreational facilities. The entire discussion of stigma and marked relationships assumes as "natural" what Hahn aptly terms as *disabling environment;* it views obstacles as being solely the person's biological limitations rather than the human-made barriers of architecture or discriminatory work practices.

Even Barker's (1948) early work went only part way to indicting the environment as an obstacle to the disabled person's participation. Far ahead of his time, he called for antidiscrimination laws in education and employment, although he failed to challenge the architecture, the transportation, and the communication methods that confronted people with disabilities and hampered full participation. Barker's concluding comments took social arrangements as given, urging counseling and psychotherapy for people with disabilities, so that they could come to accept "the fact that the world in which [they live] presents serious restrictions and frustrations." He went on to say that education and antidiscrimination laws cannot "remove all restrictions on the physically deviant in a world constructed for

the physically normal. The ultimate adjustment must involve changes in the values of the physically normal. The ultimate adjustment must involve changes in the values of the physically disabled person" (p.37).

Barker's (1948) view is understandable 25 years before the passage of federal legislation to modify public-sector physical environments. Jones' and his colleagues' (1948) obliviousness to environmental issues is not. Their otherwise valuable work on the social-psychological consequences of disability and stigma suffers seriously from such omissions. We can contrast these omissions of attention to environmental effects with Sampson's (1983) work on justice. Sampson urges students of justice and of resource allocation to attend to and be critical of current systems rather than merely to accept them and their consequences. We urge the same for students of disability.

3.  *It is assumed that the disabled person is a "victim."* In a great deal of social-psychological research on attribution, the disabled person is seen as a victim who copes with suffering by self-blame (Bulman & Wortman, 1977), by reinterpreting the suffering to find positive meaning (Taylor, Wood, & Lichtman, 1983), or by denying that he or she is really suffering (Taylor et al., 1983). Bulman and Wortman studied 29 people paralysed in accidents. Lerner (1980) describes these people as "young people who had been recently condemned to spend the rest of their lives crippled" (p.161). In order for Lerner to make sense of why Bulman and Wortman's respondents were not displaying a sense of victimization, he posits their belief in a just world and suggests that their interpretations of the disabling events are constructed so as to retain a strong belief that the world is a just place and that bad things only happen to people for reasons. The psychological experiences of the persons with disabilities are thus examined *not* on their own terms, but instead as a form of denial. Disability is used as a synonym for victimization in this theoretical analysis.

Taylor et al.'s (1983) article, "It Could Be Worse," also illustrated the unchecked presumption of disabled-person-as-victim. The researchers examined the responses of people with cancer shortly after the onset of their condition and discovered that the interviewees consistently maintained that their situations "could be worse." To explain this finding, five "strategies" used by these "victims" to make sense of their situations were described. It is disturbing to us that these authors, who were interested in the rich qualitative ways that people describe their coping experiences, minimized informants' consistently expressed view that the trauma was not as severe as it could have been.

As Taylor et al. argued, people diagnosed as having cancer are surely traumatized, and they actively generate coping strategies. However, our concerns arise with respect to the authors' a priori assumptions. First, it should be noted that Bulman and Wortman, and Taylor and her colleagues, studied people quite shortly after the onset of disability, before they had a chance to discover what would or would not be problematic about their lives. Their findings that self-blame (Bulman & Wortman, 1977) and making downward comparisons (Taylor et al., 1983) occurred within the first months or years after disability differ dramatically from those of Schulz and Decker (1985) in their study of people with spinal cord injuries 5-20 years after disability. The former authors can be read as suggesting, if inadvertently, that the experience of disability is static in a person's life and that "coping" is the same at any point in time or in one's life situation. The work of Schulz and Deckwer (1985), and Ainlay (this issue), correct this prevailing assumption and enrich our understanding of disability by demonstrating that responses at a specific time may not be the ones people retain after living with a disability for several years.

There are two more problems with the interpretations of disabled-person-as-victim put forward by Bulman and Wortman (1977), Janoff-Bulman and Frieze (1983), Lerner (1980), and Taylor et al. (1983). First, in contrast to Ladieu et al.'s (1948) report on the reactions of disabled veterans after World War II, these later researchers seem to discount the experiences described by the people they interviewed. Taylor et al., for example, view their respondents as having

strategies for managing or camouflaging what must be truly tragic. To the "outsider," the researcher, the "objective situation" is that a diagnosis of cancer is primarily a tragedy. That "insiders", those with cancer, overwhelmingly state that they had fared better than they would have expected is not used self-reflectively by the researchers to reframe their notions about how people think about traumatic life events (cf. Frank, this issue). Rather, the statement is interpreted to illustrate psychological defenses that disabled people mobilize in order to manage what researchers feel is not really manageable. What needs to be stated is that disability--while never wished for--may simply not be as wholly disastrous as imagined.

Second, these authors presume that the disability itself constitutes the victimizing experience. None of them emphasize the subsequent reactions or deprivations that people experience because of social responses to their disability or environmentally imposed constraints. While Janoff-Bulman and Frieze (1983) recognize discrimination based on sex or gender to be a societal injustice, disability is assumed a biological injustice and the injustices that lie in its social treatment are ignored.

4. *It is assumed that disability is central to the disabled person's self-concept, self-definition, social comparison, and reference groups.* Taylor and her colleagues (1983) describe their respondents as having to make downward social comparisons, lest they come face to face with how bad their situations really are. Jones et al. (1984), in their discussion of stigma, assume that the recently disabled paraplegic compares herself to others who are also paralysed. She may, but perhaps only when it comes to assessing her capacity to perform certain activities from a wheelchair. Gibbons (1986) claims that while such severely stigmatized people as those labeled retarded must make only downward social comparison to preserve self-esteem, more "mildly stigmatized" people such as those using wheelchairs seek out similarly disabled people with whom to compare themselves, and avoid social interactions and social comparisons with nondisabled people. Because disability is clearly salient for the nondisabled, it is assumed that the marked

person incorporates the mark as central to self-definition.

The above authors forget that the woman who is paralysed may be as likely to compare herself with other women her age, others of her occupation, others of her family, class, race, or a host of other people and groups who function as reference groups and social comparison groups for her. Disability may be more salient to the researchers studying it than to the people being studied, who may define themselves as "similar to" or worthy of comparison with people without disabilities. Gurin (1984) reminds researchers in social comparison and relative deprivation to pay more attention to the conditions under which people choose particular groups with whom to compare themselves, and she stresses that social comparison may have nothing to do with gender, race, or disability.

Clearly contrasting with the above discussions of social comparison, Mest (this issue) demonstrates that their "mark" or stigma may be irrelevant to how mentally retarded persons define themselves and each other, particularly if they work and live in supportive contexts.

5. *It is assumed that having a disability is synonymous with needing help and social support.* People with disabilities are perceived to be examples of those ever in need of help and social support (Brickman et al., 1982; Deutsch, 1985; Dunkel-Schetter, 1984; Jones et al., 1984; Katz, 1981, Krebs, 1970; Sarason, 1986). Such an assumption is sustained both by what researchers study and write about those with disabilities and by their omission of disabled people in their discussions as providers of support.

The assumption that disability is synonymous with helplessness is not surprising when we remember that "the handicapped role" in the United States has been seen as one of helplessness, dependence, and passivity (Gliedman & Roth 1980; Goffman, 1963). Brickman et al. (1982), in their excellent discussion of different models of helping and coping, review the essence of the medical model: The person is responsible for neither the problem encountered nor the solution required. The handicapped role, like

the sick role of which it is an extension, compels the occupant to suspend other activities until recovered, to concentrate on getting expert therapy, to follow instructions, to get well, and only then to resume normal life. The nonhandicapped person equates having a disability with a *bad and eternal flu,* toothache, or broken leg. When such conditions are temporary, it may be acceptable to entrust oneself to helpers and to forego decision making briefly; but when forced to confront a moment of weakness, unsteadiness, or limitations in the capacity to see, hear, or move, people experience grave difficulty in adjusting. However, it is erroneous to conclude that their difficulties mirror those of the person who has a long-term disability and who has learned to use alternative methods to accomplish tasks of daily living and working.

The disability is assumed tantamount to incompetence and helplessness has been investigated, and supported in laboratory research. Unfortunately, the writing that has been generated *accepts* rather than *challenges* this stereotype. Katz (1981), who found that whites gave more help to competent blacks than to ones they perceived to be less competent and enterprising, expected that the same help-giving pattern would be true for nondisabled subjects when confronting a person with a disability. Contrary to his hypothesis, however, he found that nondisabled people gave *less* help to disabled persons perceived as competent and friendly than to those perceived as incompetent and unfriendly. They also gave less help to the "disabled person" (simulated) than to the nondisabled persons. To explain this, Katz relied on Goffman (1963) and Gliedman and Roth (1980) in asserting that nondisabled persons are relatively offended or uncomfortable when confronting a person with an impairment who manages life competently. As Jones and his colleagues (1984) remind us, the able-bodied deny the reality of successful adaptation by the disabled person. They perceive it as the disabled person "making the best of a bad job," and this view supports their conviction that their own health and capacities are as important, and infallible, as they think (p.87).

Even while we wonder whether Katz would have gotten the same finding had he used a person who actually had a disability rather than one who had simulated an impairment, it is valuable to have this experimental support for what Goffman, Gliedman and Roth, and untold numbers of people with disabilities have described. Unfortunately, Jones et al. (1984) fall prey to their own unchallenged assumptions in thinking about ongoing relationships between people with and without disabilities: Throughout their book, and especially in the chapter by French (1984), it is assumed that the person with the disability is in constant need of help and support, rather than being a victim of nondisabled persons' projections or fantasies. Thereby, three problems arise: first, that the person with a disability may need assistance with certain acts is generalized to all aspects of the relationship between a person with a disability and one without. Second, if the person does need assistance, it is assumed that a previous reciprocal relationship will change, rather than that new methods or relationships will develop to provide it. Concurrently, it is assumed that the biological condition rather than the environment and social context makes one-way assistance inevitable. Third, it perpetuates the idea that the impaired person is forever the recipient, rather than ever the provider, of help and support. If disabled people are mentioned, they are mentioned as only on the receiving end of a helping transaction.

In French's (1984) chapter on marriages between disabled and nondisabled people, the assumptions are never challenged that the disability causes marital roles to change fundamentally, that blindness or quadriplegia per se will make resuming a work role difficult or impossible, that recreation will have to be curtailed. The spouse who performs certain amounts of physical caretaking is seen not only as a physical caretaker but as a generous intellectual and emotional caretaker as well. Physical incapacities are perceived as leading inevitably to incapacities in other spheres of life. Wright's (1983) notion that disability "spreads" throughout a relationship is embedded unchallenged in this entire discussion.

Moreover, it is the disability, not the institutional, physical, or attitudinal environment, that is blamed for role changes that may occur. The person with a disability may (initially, or always) need physical caretaking, such as help in dressing, household chores, or reading. It must be asked, however, whether such assistance would be necessary if environments were adapted to the needs of people with disabilities--if , for example, more homes were built to accommodate those who used wheelchairs, if technological aids could be developed to assist in performing manual tasks, if existing technology to convert the printed word into speech or Braille were affordable to all who needed it. Thus, again, the physical environment as an obstruction remains an unchallenged given. In addition, the author is assuming that the role of human assistant for all these tasks will automatically fall to the "significant other" rather than considering whether such activities could be performed by others, including public sector employees, thus permitting the primary relationship to function in its primary spheres of intimacy, sharing, and emotional nurturance for both participants. If the partners reorganize their roles after the impairment of one member, such reorganizations may result from a variety of factors: the way they think about disability, their relational obligations, the way that health care professionals inform them about the implications of disability, or the difficulties faced in affording appropriate assistance in the United States. These are consequences of how people think about disability and of current national disability policy, not of disability per se. As with all too mich of this literature, as Wright (1983) points out, researchers who are outsiders make attributions to persons and thus neglect the powerful role of the environment.

The third problem mentioned above-- that disabled people are always seen as recipients--may stem not only from distortions about people with disabilities but also from using disability as a metaphor to illustrate theory rather than to reveal more about the lives of people with impairments. Deutsch (1985) may be correct in speculating that, at least temporarily, resources would or should go to a sick child rather than to a well one; Dunkel-Schetter (1984) may plausibly learn about the mechanisms of social support by studying what people with cancer find valuable and supportive from others after such a diagnosis; Krebs (1970) makes an important point in discussing how assumptions of legitimacy of others' dependency influence the helping process. Nonetheless, by staying with questions about theories of distributive systems (Deutsch, 1985,) social support (Dunkel-Schetter 1984), or altruism (Krebs, 1970) and by not focusing on ongoing reciprocal transactions, the person with a disability is never imagined or shown to be a provider of support. As Schumaker and Brownell (1984) remind us, those who receive support also commonly seek to provide it, if not to those who gave it to them, then to others. It is regrettable that people with disabilities, when studied or considered at all in most social-psychological literature, are examined only in ways that reinforce and perpetuate existing stereotypes rather than in ways that question and challenge them. In this manner, the literature fails to enrich our understanding of the lives of people with handicapping conditions.

Particularly disturbing, as an illustration of disability-as-metaphor, is Sarason's (1986) discussion of the Baby Jane Doe case. Unfortunately, his laudable effort to call for a renewed commitment to the "public interest" and a lessening of individualism is flawed by uncritically accepting the assumption that the infant with a disability can never be expected to make a valuable contribution to family or society. He consistently refers to the existence of the severely disabled child as a problem to both family and society. Sarason's examination of the public interest and of the search for community continues in this "disabled-as-helpless" vein. He refers only to "afflicted children"; finds that families who adopt disabled children were "managing their situations in surprisingly adaptive, stable, and inspiring ways" (p.903); and describes the child only as a "problem", without any consideration of the possible contributions,

benefits, or pleasures the infant born with a disability might bring to its family and society.

## The Role of These Assumptions for Society and for Social Science

It is worth speculating on how these assumptions get made, why they persist, and what functions they serve for researchers and society. It remains a task for future research to discover the plausibility of these speculations.

Jones and his colleagues (1984) contend that the thought or awareness of disability evokes feelings of vulnerability and death. They suggest that the nondisabled person almost wants the one with the disability to suffer so as to confirm that the "normal" state is as good and as important as the "normal" thinks it is. Because disability can be equated with vulnerability to the controllable, observing someone with a disability forces all of us to wonder about the consequences of what one cannot control. In a society seeking to control ever more of life, is there a leap to the assumption that one cannot live with the consequences of what one cannot control? Social researchers are in the business of expanding knowledge of the world and trying to optimize prediction and control. As researchers, we highly prize knowledge and the control it can provide. Does such a commitment to control suggest that social scientists may view disability as fearful, unacceptable, and different because the person with the disability is a reminder that we cannot control all life events?

As discussed earlier, perceptions of disability have been the repository and projection of human needs. How much do the social and psychological problems that many people associate with disability actually pervade all of human life? If one can think of a person with a disability as needy, in contrast, one can view those without impairments as strong and as not having needs. By thinking of the disabled person as dependent in a given situation, and the one without disabilities as independent and autonomous, one can avoid considering how extensively people without disabilities too are dependent and sometimes not. Rather than the world being divided into givers and receivers of help, we are all actually interdependent. Attributing neediness and lack of control to people with disabilities permits those who are not disabled to view themselves as having more control and more strength in their lives than may be the case.

Last, perceiving a person with a disability as a suffering victim, as a stimulus object, as in need, or as different and strange, all reinforce what Goffman (1963) describes as perception of the stigmatized as "not quite human"(p.6). In discussing the scope of justice, Deutsch (1985) comments, "Justice is not involved in relations with others ...The narrower one's concept of community, the narrower will be the scope of situations in which one's actions will be governed by considerations of justice" (pp.36-37). Deutsch goes on to contend that it has been a

> too-common assumption of victimizers, even those of good will, as well as of many social scientists, that the social pathology has been in the ghetto rather than in those who have built the walls to surround it, that the disadvantaged are the ones who need to be changed rather than the people and institutions who have kept the disadvantaged in a submerged position ...It is more important to change educational institutions and economic and political systems so that they will permit those groups who are now largely excluded from important positions of decision-making to share power than to try to inculcate new attitudes and skills in those who are excluded (p.61).

These words apply as much to the situation of people with disabilities as to that of people with economic disadvantages whom Deutsch considered. By concentrating on cure or on psychological and physical restoration of the impaired person, society and the discipline of psychology have avoided the need to focus on essential changes in the environmental side of the "person-in-environment" situation. If the person with a disability is "not quite human," then that person can remain outside the community of those who must receive just distributions of rewards and resources (Deutsch, 1985). In contrast, if people with

disabilities were perceived as having the same rights to mobility and life's opportunities as people without impairments, we would inevitably be compelled to rethink the view that transportation for people with mobility impairments, or access to treatment for infants or adults with disabilities, are gifts or charities that can be withdrawn when times are tight. Once people with disabilities are admitted inside the human and moral community, the task becomes one of creating an environment where all humans--including those with impairments--can truly flourish.

## Aims of This Issue

We conclude by discussing what research might look like without the five assumptions described above and by posing questions for future study.

Although we do not see the influence of the 1948 *JSL* issue on disability in much of contemporary research, we believe it has influenced social policy in the intervening decades and has informed much of the research found in the present volume. Many of the 1948 policy recommendations have been realized: children with disabilities are now entitled to a free, appropriate public education alongside their nondisabled counterparts (Cain, 1948). Many state civil rights laws now provide people with disabilities the same protection against discrimination in employment, housing, and public accommodations as is afforded to other minority groups. Federal law now mandates that disabled people have equal access to employment and services in all programs that receive federal money (Barker, 1948; Meyerson, 1948b,c,). As laws, institutional arrangements, and social relationships begin to change, so too must the social psychology of disability change to reflect the altered experience of people with disabilities--and of persons without disabilities--as members of a common moral society.

Having been critical of the picture of disability portrayed in much of the social-psychological research previously discussed, we must ask what has kept so much research locked into the narrow assumption about people with disabilities. As Asch (1984) has described, the focus of much social-psychological research on disability has been to determine the impact of contact with disability upon people without impairments. Such a question, particularly when framed by a researcher outside the disability experience, makes the person with the disability the object, not the subject, of study and distances the research from the disabled person's life experience. Furthermore, much of this research was undertaken primarily to bolster particular theoretical notions about stigma, victimization, social comparison processes, justice, altruism, or social support. Not surprisingly, but regrettably, the authors have used notions of disability as a metaphor to advance social theories rather than to advance our knowledge of the experience of disability.

We wonder what keeps researchers from imagining a context in which disability would not be handicapping. Major reasons may be that most research has not focused on the lives and experiences of people with disabilities, and it has often been conducted without substantial contact with people with disabilities. By contrast, the research presented in the following pages, like that of the 1948 *JSI.* stems from the authors' interest in people with disabilities. The articles adopt varying disciplinary perspectives, and they demonstrate that disability often functions as an independent variable, but that reactions to and consequences of disability are dependent upon multiple variables in the social and psychological contexts of disabled and nondisabled persons. (Similarly, several essays in the collection Ainlay, Becker, and Coleman (1986) demonstrate how much historical and cultural variation exists in just who is stigmatized, who becomes a deprived minority.)

In this issue, both Hahn and Biklen examine the ways in which having a disability contributes to minority status. As Dworkin and Dworkin (1976, p.18) have pointed out, "selection of the relevant characteristics upon which identifiability is based is neither fixed or self-evident; rather, it is variable and socially defined and interpreted." Hahn looks at what he classifies as nondisabled persons'

"existential" and "aesthetic" anxieties as the basis for labeling, and Biklen focuses on educational finances as the primary *raison d'être* for classifying schoolchildren into categories--disabled or not.

The paper by Ainlay examines the experience of becoming disabled, for elderly men and women, while Schneider discusses the experience of persons with disabilities in their interpersonal relationships over time. These two articles demonstrate how time with an impairment modifies its lived experience. In the spirit of Schulz and Decker (1985), they challenge the notions of Bulman and Wortman (1977) and Taylor et al. (1983).

The articles by Frank and Mest examine interactions among disabled people, and between disabled people and the nondisabled who are in their intimate worlds, to discover how both members of any transaction are influenced by the presence of a known impairment in one or both of them. These reports lead us to question the way disability has been viewed in the stigma and social support literatures. Makas contributes to this analysis by advancing a methodology that distinguishes between "good" and "bad" disability attitudes.

Scheer and Groce, Darling, and Scotch all portray how different cultures and different political climates reshape the experience of having a disability. Impairment may be an ubiquitous "human constant," but response to it is not. Scheer and Groce carry on in the tradition of Hanks and Hanks (1948) to examine how different cultures, eras, institutions, and social structures influence the social integration of people with disabilities in 19th-century rural and 20th-century urban U.S. society.

Darling and Scotch each address the political responses generated by persons with disabilities and/or their advocates. Darling traces how families of disabled people have transformed a medical view of disability into a minority-group and political one. Scotch similarly analyzes the disability rights movement of the 1970s, focusing on the experience of disabled people themselves. These papers demonstrate that while the biological fact of disability may be a given, the environment need not be.

As a collection, these articles reframe disability as a minority-group issue in which a set of socially negotiated meanings of the body are played out psychologically, socially, and politically. They force reanalyses along several dimensions, pointing out the following:

1. How the experience of disability is influenced by professionals (Biklen), and how it can be studied by non-disabled researchers (Hahn; Frank; Makas).

2. That disability needs to be studied over time and in context, as a socially transforming and changing process, not a static characteristic of an individual (Ainlay; Becker; Mast; Schneider).

3. That a social-constructivist view of disabilty (Gergen, 1985) enables a reassessment of previously taken-for-granted views of the nature and consequences of life with impairment (Darling; Scheer & Groce; Scotch).

4. That accepting a minority-group perspective on disability and attending to all the aspects of the life space that extend beyond the person with the impairment causes social psychologists to raise new questions for research. Examples of such questions include the following: What sustains the belief that having a child with a disability is predominantly burdensome and tragic? What would make possible a different outcome? What does the experience of being close to someone with a disability do to broaden one's sense of moral community or to shrink it? What are the consequences and costs, of both disabled and nondisabled people, of an increasingly integrated society? Under what conditions, and with what consequences, does the independent-living movement promote notions of individualism over notions of community? What are the psychological barriers to a person with a disability getting involved in the disability-rights movement? What barriers keep progressives without disabilities from involving themselves in the disability-rights movement?

5. That quality-of-life judgments underpinning public and professional views of individuals like Baby Doe and Elizabeth Bouvia deserve serious re-evaluation. Similarly, accepting the powerful role of environment as a mediating variable in outcomes for people with disabilities forces us to re-examine what a just allocation of resources would be.

This *JSI* volume is presented as an interdisciplinary, provocative exploration of an already existing literature on disability and a rapidly emerging transformed perspective on the topic. The 1948 *JSI* issue influenced social policy and the field of rehabilitation psychology. We hope that the ensuing pages will stimulate further development in social psychology and social policy.

********

## REFERENCES

**ACLU** Foundation of Southern California. (1983).*Elizabeth Bouvia v. County of Riverside* (Memorandum of points and authorities in support of application for temporary restraining order and permanent injunction). Los Angeles: Author

**Ainlay, S., Becker, G., & Coleman, L.** (Eds,) (1986). *The dilemma of difference: A multi-disciplinary view of stigma.* New York: Plenum.

**Asch, A.** (1984). The experience of disability: A challenge for psychology. *American Psychologist, 39, 529-536.*

**Asch, A/. & Rousso, H.** (1985). Therapists with disabilities: Theoretical and clinical issues. *Psychiatry, 48,* 1-12

**Barker, R.B.** (1948). The social psychology of physical disability. *Journal of Social Issues, 4* (4), 28-37.

**Becker, G., & Arnold, R.** Stigma as a social and cultural construct. In S. Ainlay, G.Becker, & L. Coleman (Eds.), *The dilemma of difference: A multi-disciplinary view of stigma* (pp.39-58). New York: Plenum

**Bouvia v. Superior Court of the State of California.** Court of Appeals of the State of California. Second Appelate District, Division Two, 2nd Cir. No.B019134 (1986, April 16)

**Bowe, F.** (1980) *Rehabilitating America.* New York: Harper & Row.

**Brickman P., Rabinowitz, V.C., Karuza, J., Coats, D., Cohn, E., & Kidder, L.** (1982) Models of helping and coping. *American Psychologist, 37,* 368-384.

Bulman, R., & Wortman, C. (1977). Attributions of blame and coping with the "real world": Severe accident victims react to their lot. *Journal of Personality and Social Psychology, 35,* 351-363.

Cain, L. F. (1948). The disabled child in school. *Journal of Social Issues, 4* (4), 90-93.

Census study reports one in five adults suffers from disability. (1986, December 23). *New York Times,* p.67.

Davis, F. (1961) Deviance disavowal: The management of strained interaction by the visibly handicapped. *Social Problems, 9,* 120-132.

DeJong, G. & Lifchez, R. (1983). Physical disability and public policy. *Scientific American, 48,* 240-249.

Deutsch, M. (1985). *Distributive justice.* New Haven, CT: Yale University Press.

*Disability Rag.* (1984, February-March). Entire issue.

Disability Rights Coordinating Council (1983). *Elizabeth Bouvia v. County of Riverside* Declaration of Carol Gill. Los Angeles: Author.

Dunkel-Schetter, C. 1984). Social support and cancer: Findings based on patient interviews and their implications. *Journal of Social Issues, 40*(4), 77-98.

Dworkin, A. & Dworkin, R. (Eds.) (1976) *The minority report.* New York: Praeger.

Editorial, *New York Times,* (1983, June 17).

Fine, M. & Asch, A.(Eds.) (1981). *Women with disabilities: Essays in psychology, culture and politics.* Phildelphia: Temple University Press.

French, R. De S.(1984). The long-term relationships of marked people. In E. E. Jones et al., *Social stigma: The psychology of marked relationships* (pp.254-295). New York: Freeman.

Gergen, K. (1985). The social constructivist movement in modern psychology. *American Psychologist, 40,* 266-275.

Gibbons, F.X. 1986). Stigma and interpersonal relations. IN S.Ainlay, G.Becker, & L. Coleman (Eds.) *The dilemma of difference: A multi-disciplinary view of stigma* (pp.123-144). New York: Plenum.

Gliedman, J. & Roth, W. (1980). *The unexpected minority: Handicapped children in America.* New York: Harcourt, Brace, Jovanovich.

Goffman, E. (1963. *Stigma: Notes on the management of spoiled identity.* Englewood Cliffs, NJ: Prentice-Hall.

Groce, N. (1985). *Everyone here spoke sign language: Hereditary deafness on Martha's Vineyard.* Cambridge, MA: Harvard University Press.

Gurin, P. (1984) Review of *Relative deprivation and working men. Contemporary Psychology, 29,* 209-210.

Haber, L. & McNeil, J. (1983) *Methodological questions in the estimation of disability prevalence.* Washington, DC: Population Division, U.S. Bureau of the Census.

Hahn, H. (1983, March-April). Paternalism and public policy. *Society,* pp. 36-46.

Hanks, J. Re., & Hanks, L.M. (1948). The physically handicapped in certain non-Occidential societies. *Journal of Social Issues, 4* (4), 11-19.

Hentoff, N. (1987). The awful privacy of Baby Doe. In a. Gardner & T. Joe (Eds.). *Images of the disabled: Disabling images* (pp. 161-180). New York: Praeger.

Hill, N., Mehnert, T., Taylor, T., Kagey, M., Leizhenko, S. et al. (1986) *The ICD survey of disabled Americans: Bringing disabled Americans into the mainstream.* New York: International Center for the Disabled.

Janoff-Bulman, R., & Frieze, I.H. (1983). A theoretical perspective for understanding reactions to victimization. *Journal of Social Issues, 39* (2) 1-17.

Jones, E.E., Farina. A., Hastorf, A.H., Markus, H., Miller, D.T., Scott, R.A. & French, R. de S.(1984) *Social stigma: The psychology of marked relationships.* New York: Freeman.

Katz, I. (1981). *Stigma: A social-psychological analysis.* Hillsdale, NJ: Erlbaum.

Katzmann, R.A. (1986). *Institutional disability: The saga of transportation policy for the disabled.* Washington, D.C.: Brookings Institute.

Kleck, R., Ono, H., & Hastorf, A. (1966). The effects of physical deviance upon face-to-face interaction. *Human Relations, 19,* 425-436.

Krebs, D.L. (1970) Altruism: An examination of the concept and review of the literature. *Psychological Bulletin, 73,* 258-302.

Ladieu, G., Adler, D.L., Dembo, T. (1948). Studies in adjustment to visible injuries: Social acceptance of the injured. *Journal of Social Issues, 4* (4) 55-61.

Lerner, M.J. (1980) *The belief in a just world: A fundamental delusion.* New York: Plenum.

Myerson, L. (1948a). Physical disability as a social psychological problem. *Journal of Social Issues, 4* (4), 107-109.

Rehabilitation Act of 1973, Pub. L. No. 93-112, 87 Stat. 357 (1973).

Roth, W. (1983, March-April). Handicap as a social construct. *Society.* pp. 56-61.

Sampson, E. (1983) *Justice and the critique of pure psychology.* New York: Plenum.

Sarason, S.B. (1986) And what is the public interest? *American Psychologist, 41,* 899-906.

Schultz, R., Decker, S. (1985). Long-term adjustment to physical disability: The role of social support, perceived control, and self-blame. *Journal*

*of Personality and Social Psychology, 48,* 1162-
1172.

**Scotch, R.K.** (1984) *From good will to civil rights:
Transforming federal disability policy.* Phildelphia:
Temple University Press.

**Shumaker: S., & Brownell, A.** (1984).  Toward a
theory of social support:  Closing conceptual gaps.
*Journal of Social Issues, 40* (4), 11-36.

**Soloman, H.M.**   (1986).    Stigma and Eastern
culture:  A historical approach.  In S. Ainlay, G.
Becker, & L. Coleman (Eds.), *The dilemma of
difference:  A multi-disciplinary view of stigma*
(pp.59-76). New York: Plenum.

**Taylor, S.E., Wood, J.V., & Lichtman, R.R.**
(1983) "It could be worse":  Selective evaluation as
a response to victimization.    *Journal of Social
Issues 39*(2), 19-40.

The $2,000 subway token, *New York Times,* (1984,
June 23).

**Unger, R.K. & Denmark, F.L.** (1975).  *Woman:
Dependent or independent variable?*  New York:
Psychological Dimensions.

**von Hentig, H.** (1948).     Physical desirability,
mental conflict and social crisis. *Journal of Social
Issues, 4* (4), 21-27.

**Wight, B.A.** (1960) *Physical disability: A psychosocial approach.* New York: Harper & Row.

**Wright, B.A.** (1983).  *Physical disability:    A
psycho-social approach.*      New York:   Harper
Row.

********

**Source:**  Reprinted with permission from *Journal
of Social Issues,* Vol. 44, No. 1, 1988, pp. 3-21.
Published by The Society for the Psychological
Study of Social Issues, Ann Arbor, MI.   48106-
1248.

# Matters of Control: An Oral History
Max and Colleen Starkloff

**Abstract** ~ *Max Starkloff became a C3-5 quadriplegic in 1959. He was given the rudimentary rehabilitation of the day, then sent home to live with his mother. After four years at home, the physical, emotional and financial hardships became too much, and the family started looking for alternatives. At the age of 25, Max entered a nursing home.*

We found a very fine, very high quality nursing home run by Jesuits about an hour outside of St. Louis. It had rolling hills, a lake and beautiful country, and I said to myself that this is really a very nice place. But I was covering up a lot of worries, like the probability that I'd spend the rest of my life there, that I'd probably die there with a lot of old people. The average age at this place was 82 years.

They didn't understand what was going through a young man's mind - it was the same negative stereotypical view of anybody with a disability that's still around now - that you're asexual and pathetic so now they must take care of you. I fought it from the very beginning, to the point that I became that bitter young man, unfriendly and unreachable. I withdrew from them completely.

I got very serious about painting and really considered it my career. A couple of prominent St. Louis artists took me under their wing, but the nursing home's attitude was very condescending toward my work. They couldn't afford to lose control, so they controlled by intimidation or threat or through their paternalistic attitudes.

They'd say things like "It's nice that you have something to do," or "Considering how you paint, it's pretty good."

## Losing Control

Control was something I kept thinking about - you want to maintain your dignity, at least on the surface, and for me it was very important not to look depressed. So I'd act like this is where I wanted to be. My whole rationale was, "I'm an artist living out in the country. I've got a studio right in my bedroom."

There was a guy at the home who had been a regional opera star in his day, and of course he loved to hear opera and had stacks and stacks of records. They told him that he was disturbing the other patients and they took his radio and records away. Here's a man who spent his whole life in music and all of a sudden they take it away from him. But that was the way they did things. They'd threaten people to maintain control. They'd lay down strict rules: no visitors on the floor after 5 o'clock. Not family, not anybody.

We had this really terrible meal once, meat loaf and mashed potatoes floating in this watery stewed tomato sauce, so I complained to Brother Damian. He looked at me and said, "Max, after all we've done for you, you think you have the right to complain?" That really intimidated me, so I backed off and went up to my room and cried.

*You're in an environment that is not designed to promote independence. They don't understand in nursing homes why anybody would want to struggle for dignity and independence. Their attitude is, "I'm taking care of you so why aren't you grateful?" And if you seem to be discontent with the fact that your dignity is not respected, then you are, in fact, ungrateful. All they can see is that you have a safe place to live and a roof over your head and three meals a day and people who cater to your needs - so what's the matter with you?*

*~ Colleen Starkloff*

They see they're losing control of a patient out there, and they don't want to lose that control. If they lose it with me, they've got a real problem. I got to a point where I started to feel very angry about it and realized that I really didn't have to take this anymore.

*When you lose your dignity and self-control, the best way to rationalize where you are at this point in time is to say that this is the best you can do, that this is really a good option. I learned that from Max, that it's a way of protecting yourself. And until you reach out and grab the brass ring, find something better, you have to rationalize that it's wonderful.*

*~ Colleen Starkloff*

## Taking Control

I had piles of books on my book shelves and in the window, but the Jesuits didn't like the way they looked from outside. They said I had to clean out my window. I said that I couldn't move my books, that they're important to my work, but they said I'd have to. I left the room for a while, and when I came back the books were gone from the window.

I blew up. I told them to keep their goddamn hands off my fucking books. And they did - somebody put them back in the window. They didn't know quite how to handle me, and things started to get better. So I started to break more rules.

There was a young woman about 24 years old - I was about 30 - and her name was Bobbi. She had a pretty questionable reputation, but she was very friendly. After her first day of work, she came to my room and we talked for hours about things I'd never discussed with a woman before. Very point blank, very direct, and I knew what she was interested in. She had a fascination - she'd never done it with a quad, so why not give it a try? When she left, she gave me a very passionate kiss. It was great and it was scary, but it was scariness you could enjoy, like driving a fast car. It was risky and thrilling, and it turned into a whirlwind relationship for about four months.

Once Bobbi and I were going out to dinner, and I was sitting in my coat and tie all ready to go and waiting for her to pick me up. Brother Mark walked over, very nervous: "Who are you going out with?" I said I was going out with Bobbi. And he says, "I don't know if we can allow that." What do you mean? He says, "Who's your guardian?" My guardian? I'm 30 years old. I don't have a guardian! "Well, I think you need a legal guardian because I cannot allow you to go with anybody other than your legal guardian."

You could see he was carrying the message from the administration. I put two and two together and told him he wasn't going to stop me. Bobbi arrived - and gave me a big kiss, which was the icing on the cake - and we left and I never heard another word about it.

By this time, the nursing home had totally lost control over me. They couldn't control my hours or anything else. I got a phone put in my room, and my uncle and my mother bought me an old VW van and had some ramps built for it. Some of the aides at the nursing home would drive me around, usually for the promise of a hamburger.

I met Colleen when she came to work at the nursing home in 1973, and we dated for two years. I had a little red popcorn popper, and we used to fix everything in this popcorn popper. We had sautéed mushrooms, corn on the cob, beef stew - all these aromas would come out of my room. They just didn't know how to handle it, so they left us pretty much alone.

We wanted to get married. By that time the brothers were overwhelmed by all this - that someone could come to their nursing home and eventually get out and get married and start a new life. They'd ask people who knew me if I really thought I could pull this off, because they didn't want to see me get hurt. "He's starting to really believe that he can do it," they'd say. By that time I was 38 years old.

*If your nursing home doesn't fit your criteria for independence, then one of the finest things you can do is declare your independence and celebrate the day you leave. We did. We got married. It was a celebration of beginning our lives together, but in a bigger sense, it was a grand celebration of independence. I was real aware of that at the altar. It was emancipation.*

*~ Colleen Starkloff*

And this was a very good nursing home. It never smelled, it was clean, the care was good, the setting was magnificent. But it's the whole concept that's bad. They believed that the only way to run it was to control people. That is so devastating. It's worse than if they abused you or withheld care.

It's so tragic, such a waste; why should we let it happen in the first place? The only way we can stop it is to get to young people before the whole thing sets in, get to the families and parents and let them know that you don't have to go through all this pain and suffering. You don't have to waste lives like that.

\*\*\*\*\*\*\*\*

## ABOUT MAX STARKLOFF

Max Starkloff has resided in St. Louis since his birth in 1937. When he was 21 years old, Max was involved in a disabling automobile accident. After an extended hospital stay and a subsequent stay with his mother for four years, the physical and financial strain became overwhelming. At the time, the only option for someone with a severe disability was to move into a nursing home, where he resided for 12 years.

During this period, when his young contemporaries were beginning their careers, getting married, having children and buying houses, Max became frustrated with his desire to do more than merely survive his accident. He wanted to "live" a full and productive life and was not willing to accept the prognosis of a life of dependence for people with injuries like his. His frustrations mounted as he discovered firsthand society's patronizing and negative attitudes towards people with disabilities and the lack of access and opportunity for an independent life.

Regardless, Max was not about to relinquish his dignity. He used this time of confinement to create a plan to escape the bondage of institutional captivity. He learned to release his frustrations by expressing his anxiety on canvas with a paintbrush clenched between his teeth. Having discovered the joy and satisfaction of this new skill, he recognized his ability to create and envision new possibilities.

Max set out to make the necessary changes for a more fulfilling life, so that he, as well as others with disabilities, could live independently. From the nursing home in which he lived, Max founded a privately funded independent living center he called Paraquad. Max finally left the nursing home and ran Paraquad as a mom and pop organization with his wife, Colleen. Today, Paraquad is a permanent institution serving and influencing thousands of people with disabilities, their families and employers.

Through Max's accomplishments, people with disabilities in St. Louis have gained the opportunity to live independently. Below are a few of his achievements.

- Founded Paraquad in 1979 as a privately funded Independent Living Center.
- Secured first ever state-wide, barrier-free legislation for local and state curb cuts.
- Acquired disabled parking legislation.
- Established Paraquad as one of the original 10 federally funded Independent Living Centers in the nation.
- In 1970, founded the St. Louis Chapter of the National Paraplegia Foundation.
- Labored for access to public buildings and schools.
- Acquired wheelchair lifts on public buses to set a nationwide precedent for public transportation.
- Received a commitment from the local transportation authority to adopt a policy that all new buses will be wheelchair lift-equipped.
- Organized and spearheaded a large support group of people with disabilities, volunteers and community leaders to support the above transportation policy.

- Influenced St. Louis' new light rail system to endorse total accessibility.
- Developed and implemented fee-for-service contractual relationships with area hospitals and rehabilitation centers, whereby people with disabilities, with Parquad's assistance, could achieve a lifestyle of independence upon discharge from the institution.
- Co-founder of the National Council on Independent Living.
- Serves on the board of directors of the World Institute on Disability, Berkeley, California; Blue Cross/Blue Shield of Missouri; Gazette International Networking Institute, Citizens for Modern Transit and Confluence, St. Louis, MO.
- Appointed to the Advisory Committee, Research & Training Center on Independent Living and Public Policy, World Institute on Disability, Berkeley, CA; Blue Ribbon Panel, National Project for Telecommunications Policy, World Institute on Disability, Berkeley, CA; Recruitment Selection Committee of Leadership, St. Louis; SSM Rehabilitation Institute Advisory Board, St. Louis; Committee for National Agenda for Prevention of Disability, American Institute of Medicine, Washington, DC; Research & Training Center Advisory Committee on Secondary Disabilities, Rehabilitation Institute of Chicago, Chicago, IL; National Advisory Panel for evaluation of standards for Independent Living, Rehabilitation Services Administration, Washington, DC.
- Appointed Chair of the Fourth Japan/USA Conference for People with Disabilities, US Delegation, 1991, St. Louis, MO; Official Advisor to the National Council on the Handicapped, Washington, DC.
- Received the President's Distinguished Service Award; Community Leadership Award, Leadership St. Louis; Commissioner's Distinguished Service Award, Rehabilitation Services Administration, Washington, DC; Mayor's Arch Award for leadership in disability rights, St. Louis, MO; Annual Civic Service Award from Maryville College, St. Louis, MO; Human Rights Award from United Nations Association, St. Louis, MO; Humanitarian Award, Human Development Corporation, St. Louis, MO and the St. Louis Award.
- Received Honorary Doctor of Humane Letters from Webster University, St. Louis, MO and Honorary Doctoral Degree, Doctor of Humane Letters, University of Missouri, St. Louis, MO.
- Recognized by National Council on the Handicapped and St. Louis Unit of NASW.

The single most outstanding aspect of Max Starkloff's contribution to the needs of people with disabilities is his record of achievement to develop such a strong and expansive network of grassroots advocates for change. Max has made it a point to attend and participate in all activities, meetings and events that may have consequential potential. Through his direct contact with a wide spectrum of institutions and people who make the St. Louis metropolitan area a vital, accessible and growing community, he has become the community's single most important resource and authority on disability issues. Although he recognizes the value of connecting with those of fame and position, Max has remained equally interested in and accessible to Paraquad's participants.

**Source:**  Reprinted with permission from the authors Max and Colleen Starkloff.  This article, *Matters of Control:  An Oral History* appeared in the magazine *New Mobility,* Fall 1992.  Copyright Max Starkloff, 4475 Castleman, St. Louis, MO. 63110.

# 2 Society and Disability

Fortunately, social images are not irrevocable. Society is now beginning to encounter people with disabilities as an integral part of its functioning because of the major changes in identity that have occurred in this population during the last two decades. The efforts of many people have slowly changed societal attitudes toward the disabled from ones of exclusion to inclusion. One major factor accounting for the acceptance of people with disabilities is the constant exposure they are beginning to have in all realms. During the early decades of this century, the disabled were isolated, separated, and alienated and were viewed as strangers. People seldom understand strangers. In fact, there is a tendency to conceive of strangers in terms of stereotypical ideology. However, exposure to people representing various groups induces us to evaluate people in terms of the qualities and abilities they possess rather than evaluating them in terms of their 'differentness'.

The building of relationships with people form the disabled community at all levels illustrates to mainstream society that people with disabilities usually have the same potential, the same goals, and the same needs for contributing to society and enjoying the same quality of life as non-disabled groups. Helen Keller illustrated to the world that people with the severest of disabilities are not only able to enjoy a satisfactory quality of life, but are also able to make significant contributions to society.

Psychologically and socially, people with disabilities are now participating at all levels in education, employment and society in general. This ideology of inclusion creates social norms of anticipating involvement and interaction with all segments of the disabled community. Perhaps the most positive illustration is the transition in image which people with disabilities have experienced in the mass media. For instance, in contemporary films such as *Elephant Man, Mask* and *Rainman*, the sensitivity, humanity and idealism of people with disabilities comes to the fore. Different from past portrayals in the movies, people with disabilities are no longer insensitively portrayed as people to be pitied, isolated and excluded. Indeed, it appears that there has been the establishment of norms motivating the social inclusion of not only the disabled, but all minorities. People with disabilities, like other minority groups, have established a social movement focused on achieving acceptance and involvement and, therefore, legitimate inclusion. To be sure, they still encounter social, psychological and economic barriers, but like all other minorities, they are involved in a process directed at alleviating the barriers which inhibit their participation in society.

Robert Bogdan and Douglas Biklen, in the classic article, *Handicapism*, cite renowned authors such as Erving Goffman, Thomas Scheff, Robert Scott and Dorothea and Benjamin Braginsky as laying the "groundwork for thinking about so-called handicapped people as societally created rather than as a natural or objective condition." Their article addresses the need for researchers and practitioners to scrutinize and reassess "assumptions concerning segregated service, differential treatment, the real source of the disability problem, labeling and language patterns, and funding mechanisms tied to labeling." As the first article in this chapter, it would appear that this challenge is being met as the subsequent articles cover a wide range of new research and reevaluation of old stereotypical views of disability.

Caroline Wang, *Culture, Meaning and Disability: Injury Prevention Campaigns and the Production of Stigma* illustrates the potential production of stigma through health promotion campaigns. As she points out, the notorious Jerry Lewis Telethon for the Muscular Dystrophy Association portrays people with disabilities as dependent and helpless. This investigator notes that the manner in which people are portrayed becomes instrumental in the way people are evaluated and treated.

M. Darrol Bryant outlines how Western religious traditions have spawned attitudes toward people with disabilities that perpetuated the notion of disability as "sin" or a punishment from God. However, he notes how the philosophy of the L'Arche Movement, founded by Jean Vanier, is creating an environment of acceptance and genuine respect as people with disabilities are being viewed as 'people first'.

In keeping with this positive and inclusive trend, Robert Bogdan and Stephen Taylor illustrate in their article, *Relationships with Severely Disabled People: The Social Construction of Humanness,* that able-bodied people do not necessarily stigmatize, stereotype and reject people with disabilities. In fact, they found that so-called 'normal' people viewed disability as secondary to a person's humanness; that disability appears to be on the road to becoming less of an issue in normal everyday interaction; and that the people who are not prone to these stereotypical attitudes toward people with disabilities should not be exposed to the 'telethon image' of this group.

However, challenges and barriers still exist, as pointed out by William Hanna and Betsy Rogovsky for women, and for women who are African-American with disabilities. As these authors reveal, women with disabilities are at a substantial disadvantage to their male counterparts because in addition to their disabilities, they must confront sexism, able-ism, and racism along with the problems posed by being handicapped *and* female.

Elaine Makas, *Getting in Touch: The Relationship between Contact with and Attitudes toward People with Disabilities,* examines the ways in which interpersonal contact with people with disabilities by those who do not have disabilities can lead to positive attitudinal change. She concludes that it is important to investigate further ways in which the barriers that separate these two groups of people can be broken down so that "...all people, regardless of their ability/disability status, can participate equally in mainstream society."

Finally, *Living with the Stigma of AIDS,* by Rose Weitz, is a reality that must be faced by all members of society as this newest and most dreaded disabling disease becomes more prevalent. Each one of us is touched in some way by its insidious presence in our families, in our communities, in our working world, in our private lives. It is important that we understand, not only our own reactions to the disease, but how the powerful stigma affects the social relationships of people with AIDS in all environments.

People without disabilities are now encountering people with disabilities in almost all realms of society. As a consequence of this process, both groups are achieving common understandings. While both groups continue to be victimized by long-standing stereotypes, attitudes and values emanating from traditions of exclusion, it appears that these traditions are now being challenged in a positive way because of contact, education, integration policies, employment and constant interaction between the groups.

# Handicapism
Robert Bogdan
Douglas Biklen

Thomas Szasz (1961), Erving Goffman (1963), Thomas Scheff (1966), Robert Scott (1969) and Dorothea and Benjamin Braginsky (1971) taught us to understand "handicap" categories as well as the term "handicap" itself as metaphors. They laid the groundwork for thinking about so-called handicapped people as societally created rather than as a natural or objective condition. These same authors and their associates in the interactionist or labeling school pointed to the importance of the quality and nature of how labelers interact with the labeled as a prerequisite for understanding handicap (see Lemert, 1967; Goffman, 1961; Davis, 1963; Wiseman, 1970). The interface of human service agencies and clients became an area in which social researchers could develop theoretical perspectives on how labels and definitions were applied (also see Gubrium, 1975; Bogdan, 1974).

While these researchers worked, parallel events occurred in the social action and political arenas. It is not clear who borrowed from whom, but the social construct/labeling school approach to handicap was manifested in a concern for issues of legal and human rights of those labeled handicapped (Kittrie, 1973; Gilhool, 1973). Now a strong "total institution" abolition movement is afoot and various peoples have formed handicap liberation groups. These include Disabled in Action, Mental Patients' Liberation, National Federation of the Blind, The Center on Human Policy, The Mental Health Law Project, and the National Center for Law and the Handicapped (Biklen, 1974; Mental Health Law Project, 1973; National Committee for Citizens in Education, 1976).

In the field of human services, consumer activism and a new professional consciousness have spawned moral and legal imperatives such as due process, "least restrictive environments," the right to treatment, delabeling, and normalization

(Wolfensberger, 1972; Wolfensberger and Zauha, 1973; Abeson, 1974). At present, however, neither the social researchers/theorists nor the social activists have developed an adequate conceptual scheme by which to examine collectively labeling, the moral and legal developments, and the structural and cultural aspects of differential treatment of people defined as handicapped.

Our purpose is to introduce the concept of *handicapism* as a paradigm through which to understand the social experience of those who have previously been known as mentally ill, mentally retarded, deaf, crippled, alcoholic, addicted, elderly, deformed, deviant, abnormal, disabled, and handicapped. Handicapism has many parallels to racism and sexism. We define it as a set of assumptions and practices that promote the differential and unequal treatment of people because of apparent or assumed physical, mental, or behavioral differences[1] Three terms~*prejudice, stereotype,* and *discrimination*~are inherent in our analysis.[2]

*Prejudice* is any oversimplified and overgeneralized belief about the characteristics of a group or category of people. Prejudice toward the so-called handicapped is indicated by such indicting assumptions as: they are innately incapable; they are naturally inferior (the mind set is "Thank God, I'm not you"); they have unique personalities, different senses, and different tolerances than the run-of-the-mill citizen; they have more in common with each other than with nonhandicapped persons and, therefore, they like to be with their own kind (see Goffman,

[1] Authors who have discussed handicapped categories as minority groups include: Dexter, 1964; Wright, 1960; Yuker, 1965, and Gellman, 1959.
[2] See Yinger, 1965 and Allport, 1954 for a discussion of the use of these terms in the study of ethnic relations.

1963; Wright, 1960). These beliefs provide the background assumptions for our action toward people labeled handicapped; they are the essence of handicapism.

Whereas "prejudice" is the general disposition, *stereotype* refers to the specific content of the prejudice directed toward specific groups. The mentally retarded, for example, are believed to be childlike, to enjoy boring routine work, and to be oversexed (Wolfensberger, 1975). The elderly are said to have deteriorated intelligence and are presumed to be unhappy and undersexed. The mentally ill are expected to be erratic in their behavior, are considered dangerous and bizarre, especially during the full moon (see Scheff, 1966; Biklen, 1976). The deaf are supposed to be melancholy (see Scott, 1969; Jernigan, 1975); and supposedly, once an alcoholic always an alcoholic. While sets of stereotypes are often contradictory, they are nevertheless seriously regarded by a number of people and are used to justify particular modes of treatment. Thus the retarded can be treated like children, the elderly ignored, and the mentally ill locked up.

Although inaccurate, a stereotype is often steadfastly maintained. The maintaining processes are themselves part of handicapism. First peers and culture support the transmission of stereotypes and therefore constantly reinforce them. Second, groups like the handicapped are isolated, have few opportunities for intimate relations to develop between themselves and the so-called normal people, and consequently have little chance of disproving the stereotypes. Last, and perhaps most important, handicapped people are treated in ways that correspond to their stereotypes and are rewarded for living up to others' image of them (see Lemert, 1951). Thus they learn the role of the handicapped and fall victim to the self-fulfilling prophecies (Merton, 1957).

"Prejudice" and "stereotype" point to the cognitive and ideological substance of handicapism. The concept of *discrimination* provides the structural and behavioral aspect. Unfair and unequal treatment of individuals or groups on the basis of prejudice and stereotypes translates into discrimination. Standards of fairness and unfairness vary from

society to society and from time to time as the social criteria for equality or discrimination change in accordance with social values. At one time it was considered the natural state of slaves to labor in the fields for the economic benefit of others, and for married women to serve their husbands; the treatment they received was not thought to be unfair. Similarly, handicapped people are generally thought to experience relative equality in this society especially since the advent of various categorical social service programs. They are considered to occupy their rightful place and to receive deserved treatment. For example, few people question the practice of rescinding drivers' licenses, fingerprinting, and taking mug shots of people admitted to state mental institutions despite the fact that there is no evidence that former patients of state mental hospitals are involved in any more accidents or commit more crimes than typical citizens (Scheff, 1966; Ramadas, 1975). It is equally common for public school districts to segregate handicapped children into special classes and even separate "special " schools although there is no empirical evidence to support any benefit, either educational or social, that results from segregated services. These kinds of policies and practices discriminate against people with disabilities. They are part of handicapism.

In the remaining pages we will demonstrate how handicapism manifests itself in personal interaction, in the organizational structure of the larger society, and in human service policy and practices. Our purpose is to identify and illustrate handicapism in these spheres, and to demonstrate the usefulness of the concept as a paradigm for social scientists. We have based our discussion largely on current lawsuits, studies reported in the professional literature, and our own research and experiences in the area of social policy and disability.

## HANDICAPISM IN INTERPERSONAL RELATIONS

Handicapism arises in the contacts between handicapped and so-called typical people as well as in the private conversations of typical people when the handicapped are not present. In face-to-face contacts, labeled and nonlabeled persons characteristically display anxiety and strain about how each will be perceived by the other (see Davis, 1961; Goffman, 1963; Wright, 1960). "The stigmatized individual may find that he feels unsure of how we normals will identify him and receive him" (Goffman, 1963). And the so-called normals feel that the stigmatized individual is too ready to read unintended meaning into our action. This self-conscious uneasiness results in a number of handicapist practices. For example, nonhandicapped persons avoid contact with "nonnormals." When they are forced into contact they tend to seek the earliest possible conclusion. When there is contact there is also the tendency for the disability (the alleged difference) to take on tremendous significance in the nonhandicapped person's mind: it becomes the master status (Davis, 1961). This often results in the nonhandicapped person either being overly gracious and overly sympathetic ("It must be hell to go through what you go through") or patronizing ("What a lovely belt, did you make that all by yourself?") or in some other ways be insensitive or ignore people with disabilities. One such behavior is to treat them like what Goffman (1960, 1963) calls "nonpersons."

In casual contacts with the handicapped, normals tend to measure them against the stereotype and such contacts reinforce common stereotypes. An example may help to demonstrate this process. Recently a number of typical skiers observed a blind skier coming down the slope. They spoke about him and his "amazing feat." They commented on how "truly remarkable" that he could have the courage and fortitude to do what must be exceptionally difficult for a person with no eyesight. From the tone of their comments it was clear that they did not perceive this person as any *ordinary* blind person. The sighted skiers did not question their stereotypes of the blind as physically inept. Instead, they confirmed the stereotype by classifying this skier as an exception to the rule - as "amazing." If he were not skiing but sitting in the lodge next to the fire, one might expect to hear passers-by whispering to each other something to this effect: "It's a shame that blind people have to miss out on so much fun."

## HANDICAPISM AT THE SOCIETAL LEVEL

To understand handicapism at the societal level one must analyze the culture and structure of basic institutions for manifestations of prejudice, stereotypes, and discrimination. Further, one must examine the legally sanctioned and illegal systematic mistreatment of people because of alleged physical, mental, and behavioral differences. And, as in personal interaction, one must study how major societal institutions routinely reinforce and perpetuate prejudice and stereotypes. Since this brief article can only introduce the handicapism paradigm and not exhaustively elaborate it, societal level handicapism is portrayed in only four of the many possible areas: (1) images of the handicapped in the media; (2) physical and literacy barriers to participation; (3) discriminatory laws, rules, and regulations; and (4) exclusion from basic organizations.

### Media Images

To what extent does the mass media present prejudicial and stereotypic images of the handicapped? What is the specific content of that imagery? What effect does it have on those who look at it? Impression and data suggest as starting hypotheses that mass media present prejudicial and stereotypic images of the handicapped. After reviewing images of mental illness in the media, Scheff (1966) concludes that mental patients appear stereotypically as bizarre and dangerous. Needleman and Weiner, (1974) two researchers who examined the relationship between physical attractiveness and crime in various media, found that physical ugliness and physical differences are often associated with violence and other forms of crime, as shown in the media. Our own study of horror movies, which are experiencing renewed popularity on the American scene, reveals a clear association of physical and mental handicap with acts of violence and hate. In children's stories there are inevitably hunchbacks, trolls, and other deformed and therefore supposedly frightening people hiding under bridges and in forests to grab pretty children who might be passing by. Disney, for example, frequently promoted handicapist imagery. The wicked witch who gives the beautiful Snow White the poison apple has to change from a beautiful woman to a hunchbacked, wart-nosed old lady to accomplish her terror. Dopey has Down's syndrome-like features and lives with the other childlike dwarfs in the forest. Then there is evil Captain Hook with the patched-eye pirates of *Peter Pan* fame.

In addition to movies and children's stories, cartoons appear to be important carriers of handicapist images. "Stupid idiot", "moron", "dumb" and "crazy" dot the landscape of comic strip captions. Key offenders include prestigious syndicated strips such as "Beetle Bailey" and "Archie". These comics not only confirm prejudicial and stereotypic attitudes toward people with disabilities, they also reveal that everyday words that refer to specific groups have become general curse words.

Handicapism is also manifested and perpetuated between normals when not in the presence of disabled people. Stereotypes and prejudice abound in daily conversation: "*Poor Aunt Jane is going blind.*" "I'd kill myself if I were as disabled as Luke." Our casual interpersonal conversation is heavy with handicapist phrases: "Did you hear the one about the *moron* who threw the clock out the window?" "It's like the *blind* leading the *blind*." "You babbling *idiot*." "What are you, *deaf*?" "Some of the students are real *retards*."

Handicapism takes more direct forms in the media as well. Often newspaper articles link crimes with various disabilities as if the disability was the cause of the crime. For example, in an Associated Press release published across the country a murderer who was scheduled for execution was referred to as "an alcoholic and mentally incompetent psychotic who was mentally retarded." Further, the media promote images of the handicapped as helpless by selectively covering certain events and refusing to cover others. For example, when Kenneth Jernigan, president of the National Federation of the Blind, called a press conference for one of his group's highly political conferences, newspaper and television reporters ignored the political organizational content, for they wanted, instead, to view corporate exhibits of walking aids, lead dogs , and other stereotyping symbols of blindness (Jernigan, 1975). The media promote images of the helpless handicapped by reporting regularly on charity drives that feature posters of crippled children. Telethons promote the same imagery. Their human interest features more often than not proclaim that the handicapped can be helped by charity, thus really reinforcing an image of dependence.. One public service advertisement on mental retardation that appeared nationally in newspapers and magazines carried the headline: "He'll be eight years old the rest of his life." The picture was of a child in front of a birthday cake with eight candles. The message was direct and stereotyped; it portrayed the retarded as childlike.

The effect of images of the handicapped in media on audiences has not been studied, perhaps because of the difficulty in isolating such influences. One can hypothesize, however, that it is an important part of handicapism.

**Physical and Literacy Barriers**

If you were told that because of your race or sex you were not allowed to enter buildings and to use public toilets, sidewalks, and mass transit, you would claim discrimination. People in wheelchairs are denied such access. The degree to which society's constructions and accessways unnecessarily impede participation for a significant segment of our population can be regarded as a primary indicator of handicapism. Recently cities have begun to establish access ordinances, but that did not save the New York City police from an embarrassing handicapist situation. There was a demonstration launched by Disabled In Action in which many of the protesters, who incidentally were in wheelchairs, blocked a road and refused to move. The demonstrators were about to be arrested when the police realized that the jails were not accessible to wheelchairs - a clear violation of state law.

In much the same debilitating fashion that architectural barriers deny access to the physically disabled, written directions (i.e. for tests, applications, forms, and signs) can provide untold obstacles for the person who cannot read and write. Some people leaving state schools for the mentally retarded, for example, report that their inability to read and write creates obvious barriers for their mobility in a society that relies so heavily on written communication. Most bus signs, maps, and street signs require the ability to read. People who cannot learn or simply were never taught to read and write have an extremely difficult time with the many forms such as income tax, employment applications, credit applications, and registration for school (see Dexter, 1964, for a complete discussion). Because it is generally assumed that everyone can and should read, it is terribly embarrassing as well as difficult for people who don't have such abilities to live independently.

## Discriminatory and Exclusionary Laws, Rules, Etc.

For many years it has been common practice for business employers, insurance companies, colleges and universities, and similar organizations to require applicants to identify their disability. The result was discrimination, so much so that the 1973 Vocational Rehabilitation Act mandated no discrimination against disabled workers by agencies that are federally funded. Similarly, some states have passed legislation to end discrimination by all employers and educational institutions (e.g., The 1974 Flynn Act, otherwise known as the Disability Amendments to the Human Rights Law in New York State). Also, the 1973 Vocational Rehabilitation Act established affirmative action requirements for federally funded employers. All of these developments do not suggest that discrimination has ended, merely that widespread discrimination is now acknowledged. Jobs often require physical examinations which automatically exclude disabled people from passing; however, the courts have ruled that all special requirements must reflect the actual nature of the job.

Barriers may not be perpetuated simply for the purpose of arbitrarily excluding people with disabilities.

Education, another basic institution in most people's lives, also practices exclusion. Until the 1971 *PARC v Commonwealth of Pennsylvania* case (Lippman and Goldberg, 1973), the various states freely excluded many handicapped children from public education. While federal legislation has since mandated the right to public education for all children with disabilities (P.L. 94-142, the Education for All Handicapped Children Act), a private research/action group (The Children's Defense Fund, 1974) reported that over one million disabled children still remain out of school altogether, ostensibly because of their disability or, more accurately, because of exclusionary policies.

Still another area rife with exclusionary policies is transportation. Clearly physical barriers create the greatest impediment to disabled people's use of mass transport, but certain modes of transportation have excluded disabled people unless accompanied by an aide. This was the case for several air carriers until a recent challenge by Judy Heumann, a member of the Senate Labor and Welfare Committee and, incidentally, a person whose physical disability requires that she use a wheelchair.

## Service Delivery

Ironically, handicapism manifests itself even in the organizations and institutions which have as their official duty the rehabilitation, care, and processing of people who are allegedly handicapped. It seems that most systems that are operating today for the handicapped are based on handicapist principles. Even those that serve clients' specific clinical needs often perpetuate handicapism. First, although the Supreme Court has ruled that separate is inherently unequal, most programs for the handicapped are segregated from the mainstream of society. Not only has society provided state institutions for the retarded, deaf, blind, and emotionally disturbed, governments have financed segregated schools, recreation programs, and sheltered workshops. The large residential institutions and smaller day-service facilities bring together large numbers of labeled people. Alternative integrated placements are usually unavailable. While this separation of the handicapped from the typical population has been recommended by some professionals to facilitate the delivery of services and thus improve the quality of life, research observations contradict this handicapist assertion. Research on the efficacy of separate classes for handicapped children, for example, does not show that children in separate classes achieve any better than children in regular classes (Blatt, 1956; Gennett, 1932; Cain and Levine, 1963; Cassidy and Stanton, 1959; Goldstein et al., 1965; Hottel, 1958; Pertsch,1936; and Wrightstone et al., 1959). On the other extreme, testimony in recent court cases involving state schools for the mentally retarded {e.g., Willowbrook (NY), Partlow (Ala.), Pennhurst (Penn.), Belchertown, Fernald (Mass.)} gives vivid and definitive evidence of the dramatic regression of skills among people who have been institutionalized.

The culture and structure of service systems for the disabled often work to support handicapism. People are herded, kept waiting, and regimented in barren surroundings designed and maintained to facilitate custodial concerns of cleanliness and efficiency of plant operation (Blatt, 1973; Wolfensberger, 1975; Goffman, 1961; Bogdan et al., 2974; Biklen, 1976; Gubrium, 1975). The handicapped are forced to take endless numbers of examinations. The residential treatment centers including nursing homes, state mental hospitals, and state schools exaggerate handicapist patterns in that residents are often denied personal possessions, have few rights, few opportunities for sexual and other expression, are dressed in ill-fitting clothing, and are often addressed by their diagnosis (i.e. mongoloid, senile, schizoid, low grade).

A cornerstone to the handicapism of professional systems is that services to the disabled people are considered a gift or privilege rather than a right. The American public gives billions of dollars each year to charity, much of which is solicited in the name of helping the handicapped. This system of collecting funds demeans its recipients by supporting the prejudice that the handicapped

are inferior people. Moreover, professionals who require charitable contributions to support their programs tend to distort the image of the handicapped in order to play on the public's pity. Thus, the crippled child becomes a poor soul whose disability evokes pity and guilt and the spirit of giving, but also lessens the possibility that disabled people can be regarded as people with personalities, with individual aspirations, and with an interest in being perceived as ordinary people.

The other major funding source for special services is the federal and state governments. But here too the money system promotes handicapism. In order to be eligible for state and federal funds, schools and other human services personnel must label children according to clinical disability categories for which there is reimbursement. They must list the name and diagnosis of the handicap and thereby begin people in their careers of being labeled mentally retarded, learning disabled, autistic, etc. (see Bogdan, 1976; Schrag and Divoky, 1975). In that kind of system the disabled become commodities and agencies become headhunters. In every instance where funds become available for a particular disability group, the number of people so labeled soars geometrically (see Schrag and Divoky). People whose disability might not ordinarily be thought of as a handicap suddenly find themselves labeled; they are pawns in the struggle for agency survival and growth, for they are the essential requisite by which agencies receive government funds. Not too long ago side shows were popular. Deviants were sought out and paraded for a price. While the system we have evolved does not parade its clients, except perhaps during telethons, it does promote labeling and it does thrive on the segregation and exaggeration of the nature and extent of the problem.

## NEW STARTING POINTS FOR DISABILITY RESEARCH AND POLICY

Civilizations have always created such categories as "handicapped" and "race" and, along with them, fostered prejudices, stereotypes, and discrimination. Some theorists have suggested that these serve real functions such as allowing us to find targets for our hostility, to find excuses for what goes wrong, to pinpoint people's fear, and to enjoy self-approval in the knowledge that we do not belong to the disapproved of groups (see Erikson, 1966; Barzun, 1965). Barzun suggests that the urge to classify and categorize people is reinforced in modern societies by the belief that scientific theories and systems of facts can account for and explain distinctions between people, differences in temperament and ability, and variation in bodily features and mental habits. By conducting research and formulating theory on commonsense notions of differences between preconceived categories, and by emphasizing statistically significant differences rather than the range within populations and overlapping of characteristics between categories, social science has done much to deify categories and therefore to entrench prejudice, stereotypes, and discrimination (see Bogdan and Taylor, 1976). Professionals and disability-related fields have followed a research tradition which has hindered the questioning of basic concepts in disability research. A disturbing number of handicapist assumptions have been taken as givens, as starting points for research.

We hope that the handicapism paradigm will enable researchers and practitioners to begin to reassess their assumptions concerning segregated service, differential treatment, the real source of the disability problem, labeling and language patterns, and funding mechanisms tied to labeling. Moreover, the concept of handicapism can facilitate research that will result in policy-related data. While we have not yet explored the full ramifications of handicapism, we have attempted to provide the foundation for conceptualizing the experience of handicaps in a way that will not perpetuate prejudicial notions, but rather will help reveal and eradicate injustice.

********

## REFERENCES

Abeson, Alan. 1974. "movement and Momentum: Government and the Education of Handicapped Children--ll."*Exceptional Children* 41:109-115

Aliport, Gordon W. 1954. *The Nature of Prejudice.*Boston: Beacon Press.

Barzun, Jacques. 1965. *Race: A Study in Superstition.* New York: Harper & Row.

Bennett, A. 1932. *A Comparative Study of Sub-Normal Children in the Elementary Grades.* New York: Teachers College Press.

Bilken, Douglas. 1974. *Let Our Children Go.* Syracuse: Human Policy Press.

----,1976. *Behavior Modification in State Mental Hospital: A Participant Observer's Critique."American Journal of Orthopsychiatry. 46, no.1.*

Blatt. Burton. 1956. *The Physical, Personality, and Academic Status of Children Who Are Mentally Retarded Attending Special Classes as Compared with Children Who Are Mentally Retarded Attending Regular Classes.* Unpublished Ph.D. thesis, The Pennsylvania State University.

----.1973. *Souls in Extremis.* Boston: Allyn and Bacon.

Bogdan, Robert. 1974. *Being Different: The Autobiography of Jane Fry.* New York: John Wiley.

----.1976. *National Policy and Situated Meaning."* American Journal of Orthopsychiatry 46, no.2: 229-235.

Bogdan, Robert and Taylor, Steven. 1976. The Judged Not Judges: An Insider's View of Retardation. *"The American Psychologist* 31, no.1.

Bogdan, Robert et al. 1974. "Let Them Eat Programs: Attendants' Perspectives and Programming in State Schools for the Mentally Retarded. *"Journal of Health and Social Behavior* 15, no.2.

Braginsky, D. and Braginsky, B. 1971, *Hansels and Gretels.* New York: Holt, Rinehart and Winston.

Cain, L. and Levine S. 1963. *Effects of Community and Institution Programs on Trainable Mentally Retarded Children.* Washington, D.C.: Council for Exceptional Children.

Cassidy, V.M. and Stanton, J.E. 1959. *An Investigation of Factors Involved in the Education of Mentally Retarded Children.* Columbus: Ohio University Press.

Children's Defense Fund. 1974. *Children Out of School in America.* Cambridge, Mass.: Children's Defense Fund.

Davis, Fred. 1961. "Deviance Disavowal: The Management of Strained Interaction by the Visibly Handicapped". *Social Problems* 9.

----. 1963. *Passage Through Crisis.* Indianapolis: Bobbs Merrill.

Dexter, Lewis. 1964. *The Tyranny of Schooling.* New York: Basic Books.

Erikson, Kai. 1966 . *The Wayward Puritans.* New York: John Wiley.

Gellman, W. 1959. "Roots of Prejudice Against the Handicapped. "*Journal of Rehabilitation* 25: 4-6.

Gilhool, Thomas K. 1973. "Education: An Inalienable Right." *Exceptional Children* 39: 597-609.

Goffman, Erving. 1961. *Asylums: Essays on the Social Situation of Mental Patients and Other Inmates.* Garden City: Doubleday & Co., Anchor Books.

----. 1963. *Stigma.* Englewood Cliffs N.J.: Prentice-Hall

Goldstein, H. Moss, J.W., and Jordan, L.J. 1965. *The Efficacy of Special Class Training on the Development of Mentally Retarded Children..* Cooperative Research Project No. 619. New York: Yeshiva University.

Gordon, Gerald. 1966. *Role Theory and Illness.* New Haven: College and University Press.

Gubrium, Jaber. 1975. *Living and Dying at Murray Manor.* New York: St. Martin's Press.

Hottel, J.V. 1958. *An evaluation of Tennessee's day class program for severely mentally retarded children.* Nashville: George Peabody College for Teachers.

Jermigan, Kenneth. 1975. "Blindness: Is the Public Against Us?" An address at the Annual Banquet of the National Federation of the Blind, July 3

Kittrie, Nicholas. 1973. *The Right to Be Different.* Baltimore: Penguin Books.

Lemert, Edwin. 1951. *Social Pathology.* New York: McGraw-Hill.

----. 1967. *Human Deviance, Social Problems and Social Control.* Englewood Cliffs, N.J.: Prentice-Hall

Lippman, Leopold and Goldberg, Ignacy I. 1973 *Right for Education.* New York: Teachers College Press

Mental Health Law Project (MHLP) 1973. *Basic Rights of the Mentally Handicapped.* Washington, D.C.

Merton, Robert. 1957. *Social Theory and Social Structure..* New York: Free Press.

National Committee for Citizens in Education (NCCE). 1976 *Network* (periodical) Maryland: Columbia.

Needleman, Burt and Weiner, Norman. 1974. "Faces of Evil: The Good, The Bad and The Ugly." Mimeographed. Dept. of Sociology, Oswego State College, New York. Presented at the Conference on Sociology and the Arts, Oswego, New York.

Pertsch, C.F. 1936. *A Comparative Study of the Progress of Subnormal Pupils in the Wards and in Special Classes.* New York: Teachers College, Columbia University Contributions to Education.

Ramadas, K.L. 1975. "Traffic Violation Frequencies of State Hospital Psychiatric Patients. "*American Journal of Orthopsychiatry* 45, No.5.

Scheff, Thomas J. 1966. *Being Mentally Ill: A sociological Theory.* Chicago: Aldine Publishing Co.

Schrag, Peter and Diane Divoky. 1975. *The Myth of the Hyperactive Child.* New York: Pantheon.

Scott, Robert. 1969 *The Making of Blind Men* New York: Russell Sage Foundation.

Szasz, T.S. 1961. *The Myth of Mental Illness.* New York: Hoeber-Harper.

Wiseman, Jacqueline. 1970. *Stations of the Lost.* Englewood Cliffs, N.J.: Prentice-Hall.

Wolfensberger, Wolf. 1972. *Normalization.* National Institute on Mental Retardation, Toronto, Canada.

----. 1975. *The Origin and Nature of Our Institutional Models.* Syracuse: Human Policy Press

Wolfensberger, Wolf and Zauha, Helen. 1973. *Citizen Advocacy.* National Institute on Mental Retardation, Toronto, Canada.

Wright, B. 1960. *Physical Disability: A Psychological Approach.* New York: Harper

Wrightstone, J.W.; Forlano, G.; Lepkowski, J.R., Santag, M.; and Edelstein, J.D. 1959. *A Comparison of Educational Outcomes Under Single-Track and Two-Track Plans for Educable Mentally Retarded Children.* Cooperative Research Project No.144 Brooklyn, N.Y.: New York City Board of Education.

Yinger, Milton. 1965. *A Minority Group in American Society.* New York: McGraw-Hill.

Yuker, H. 1965. "*Attitudes as Determinants of Behavior.*" Journal of Rehabilitation 31: 15-16.

******

About the Authors: Robert Bogdan is with the School of Education, Special Education Program, Syracuse University, 805 S. Crouse Avenue, Syracuse, New York 13244-2280

Source: Reprinted with permission from *Social Policy,* March/April 1977, pp. 14-19. Published by Social Policy Corporation, New York, New York 10036. Copyright 1977 by Social Policy Corporation.

# Culture, Meaning and Disability: Injury Prevention Campaigns and the Production of Stigma

## Caroline Wang

**Abstract~**_The potential production of stigma through health promotion campaigns is a problem that has not received attention in the current literature on the sociology of health promotion. Cultural production studies can shed light onto the ways in which injury prevention campaigns, and public health campaigns more generally, may call for life-saving interventions at the social expense of people with disabilities or other stigmatized conditions. Questioned here are not only the presumed benefits of health promotion campaigns, but also our conventional understandings of 'health' and 'disability'._

_This paper examines the way in which cultural production studies can contribute to a theory of the production of stigma by public health professionals. One view of cultural production views culture as a reflection of economic relationships between the dominant and the dominated. A second approach emphasizes the 'reception' of cultural works, or how audiences experience culture. Third, cultural production is sometimes analyzed in terms of texts, or the content of cultural artifacts. Insight into the dilemmas of health promotion can be provided by analyzing health promotion strategies in terms of their production, reception, and content as cultural works. Focusing on the case study of injury control and disability rights, health promotion campaigns are seen as potentially contributing to the production of stigma for people who already possess the attributes targeted for prevention. This analysis moves toward a broader theoretical foundation with which to grasp the unintended, even harmful consequences of prevention strategies, and the shared and oppositional interests of people with stigmatized conditions, targeted audiences of prevention, and public health advocates._

**Key Words:** cultural production, health promotion, injury, disability.

## INTRODUCTION

The political struggles in the U.S. for gun control, mandatory motorcycle helmet laws, seat belt laws, air bag regulations, and fire-safe cigarette legislation have been fueled by the travails of survivors of disabling injuries. The public health perspective contends that becoming disabled through injury is an unacceptable~and preventable~risk in our society. Long overdue, such legislation is consistent with a public health approach that locates problems within the built or (un)regulated environment rather than within the individual. Yet the explicit political claim about the need for injury control, however inadvertently, also makes a political claim about disability.

Progressive political agendas do not guarantee an understanding of the discrimination experienced by people with disabilities; nor does goodwill prevent the exploitation of the disabled. Rather, such efforts may unwittingly promote the stigmatization of people with disabilities. If the public health perspective rightly contends that _becoming_ disabled is an unacceptable risk in our society, it paradoxically often fails to acknowledge the stigmatizing notion that _being_ disabled in an unacceptable status in our society.

In order to analyze how injury prevention campaigns may reinforce social stigmatization of people with disabilities, it is useful to consider theoretical approaches developed in several disciplines for the study of cultural production. One view of cultural production views culture as a reflection of economic relationships between the dominant and the dominated. A second approach emphasizes the 'reception' of cultural works, or how audiences experience culture. Third, cultural production is sometimes analyzed in terms of texts, or the content of cultural artifacts. This paper explains the potential application of these theoretical methods to public health concerns. Focusing on the case study of injury control, it describes how these approaches can contribute to a theory of the production of stigma as perpetuated by health professionals. A critical summary that examines the conceptualization of prevention campaigns will point to promising directions for future research.

### The anthropological lens, the sociological eye:

The anthropological approach to cultural production examines how people live. A more traditionally sociological approach looks at the emergence of artifacts that exist within a culture. The disciplinary boundaries overlap, however, since each borrows from the other for methodological and theoretical support. To frame the distinction in its broadest sense, anthropologists embrace a theoretical and methodological approach that demands immersion in a culture to understand the 'other' as a route to understanding the 'self'. In contrast, sociologists tend to emphasize the emergence of cultural artifacts within determining social and economic structures, rather than exploring the internal structure of a whole culture. Drawing on the seminal framework developed by Stuart Hall, we might say that an anthropological approach investigates how communicative texts are 'decoded' within people's lives, while a sociological approach reveals how cultural texts are 'encoded' or produced with social structures [1].

Cultural production research ideally should draw on both sociological and anthropological, as well as historical and literary methods in order to create a multi-disciplinary approach offering a comprehensiveness and complexity that no single view could create. Such a multi-disciplinary approach is proposed here as a map for critical inquiry into how public health contributes to cultural production. Let me first briefly define 'the production of culture'.*

---

* Superb critical reviews of cultural production studies are offered by Ortner S. B. Anthropology since the sixties, *Comp. Stud. Society History* **25,** 1984; Schudson M. The new validation of popular

## THE PRODUCTION OF CULTURE

Stuart Hall [1] and Chandra Mukerji and Michael Schudson [2] have articulated a macro-sociological framework for studying the production of culture that analyzes three theoretical strategies: (1) the production of cultural objects; (2) the reception of the objects and the meanings attributed to them by audiences: and (3) the content of the objects themselves [3]. In other words, as Hall has pointed out, we want to understand the process by which culture as text is "encoded" (production); the process by which culture as text is "decoded" (audiences' reception); and the texts themselves (content) [1].

This paper emphasizes a theoretical inquiry into the production of popular culture, defined by Mukerji and Schudson as "the beliefs and practices, and the objects through which they are organized, that are widely shared among a population" [2].

By popular culture I adopt their definition which includes both 'folk' or 'popular' beliefs, behaviors, or objects, as well as class' beliefs, behaviors, or objects produced from state or commercial sources [2]. What is especially interesting is an inquiry that takes media-related artifacts as critical 'reflections' on the institution and profession of public health.

## THE PRODUCTION OF CULTURE AND PUBLIC HEALTH

Cultural texts include the immense array of visual, written, or auditory materials that audiences consume, including, for example, magazines, billboards, rap songs, advertisements, and cultural styles. Studies that have gathered sociological and anthropological as well as historical and literary views illustrate the unparalleled

---

culture; sense and sentimentality in academia. *Critical Stud. Mass Communication* **4,** 1987; and Mukerji C. and Schudson M. (Eds) *Rethinking Popular Culture: Contemporary Perspectives in Cultural Studies.* University of California Press, Berkeley, 1991.

complexity that multi-disciplinary approaches bring to the study of cultural production. Drawing on all of these perspectives, I examine the way in which cultural production studies can contribute to a theory of the production of stigma by public health professionals. I focus on the case study of injury control and disability rights, but will make parallels to other health issues such as AIDS, aging, alcohol problems, and Alzheimer's disease.

Before discussing how health promotion efforts may increase the stigmatization of people with disabilities and other groups, I borrow a caveat from Robertson's critique [4] of approaches to Alzheimer's disease. This analysis is in no way intended to romanticize disability nor to dismiss the efforts of health professionals and trauma survivors committed to preventing disabling injuries. It is offered as a contribution toward making those efforts more effective and more humane. At the same time, it seeks to explore the unintended, potentially negative effects of prevention campaigns~effects virtually ignored in research on public health and the sociology of health promotion.

### The injury control perspective

Injury is the leading cause of death among people ages 1-44. It kills more people ages 1-34 than all diseases combined. More than 140,000 people die from injuries every year [5]. In 1985, injuries to approx. 57 million persons cost the nation $156.7 bill [6]**

Because injuries are the number one cause of death among children and young adults, it greatly exceeds all major disease groups as the cause of prematurely lost years of life[5]. Many injury control advocates believe that powerful corporate interests and

the vulnerability of young people (those who are most severely affected by injuries) have delayed the response to community needs regarding injury control. The nonsmokers' rights movement has argued that we all have a right to breathe clean air. Injury control advocates contend that children ought not to be maimed and that citizens should be able to expect to live a full and productive life. The injury prevention movement seeks to transform the built environment and institutions, to increase the probability that each person survives to maturity.

### The disability rights perspective

The incidence of disability is often assessed by the criterion of employment. According to the 1980 census, 12,320,000 citizens between the ages of 16-46 had disabilities that limited or prevented employment. That figure represents 8.5% of the total labour force [7].*/*

The biomedical approach with Western science and clinical medicine most commonly views disability as the diagnosis of a motor or cognitive deficit. The limitation of this model is its implication that impairment is inherent in the individual and independent of social barriers to integration. By contrast, disability rights and independent living activists observe that functional limitations, such as the inability to walk, hear, learn, or lift, are but a few of the characteristics that make up a person's identity. One man who uses 24-hr attendant care told me:***

Some of us have a lot of trouble, but you can look out on any street and you can say, 'that

---

** The lifetime costs are the direct cost for medical treatment and the rehabilitation of patients injured that year and the indirect costs from loss of earnings associated with short and long-term disability and premature death (Rice, MacKenzie et al., 1989).

---

*/* It is more difficult to determine how many people acquire disability through injury each year. The present limitations of comprehensive national databases hinder accurate appraisal (Rice, MacKenzie et al., 1989). The National Research Council estimates, however, that each year more than 80,000 people will acquire a permanently disabling injury of the brain or spinal cord (1985).

*** Unless otherwise indicated, quotations are taken from the author's transcribed field notes from ongoing participant observation among people with mobility disabilities and among young adults enrolled in a health promotion course.

person's more disabled than I am. They're walking around and their head's so paralyzed, or they're *stuck* in some heavy place, or all they care about is money'. There's lots of ways to be screwed up.

Disability rights workers disdain the programs of health and social agencies that pathologize individuals as helpless, defective, and incapable of meeting their own needs. They champion programs that support personal autonomy. They struggle against discrimination in the public provision of transportation services, building access, and employment opportunities.

The psychosocial consequences of stigma heighten the stakes for millions of people with disability who must contend with the mythology of helplessness. This is relevant to personal identity [8-11], employment [12], social interaction [13,14], and policy outcomes [15,16].

## TOWARD A THEORY OF THE PRODUCTION OF STIGMA

Theories about the production of culture offer a vantage point from which one can understand the production of the meaning of disability. Second, they offer a theoretical plane from which to examine how artifacts in the culture may stigmatize, and how those artifacts are produced and consumed. Finally, they offer a perspective from which to analyze how the definition of deviance is influenced by class. This section will highlight the theoretical and methodological implications of the three approaches identified by Hall, Mukerji and Schudson, applying them to the question of the production of stigma within public health.

### The encoding process (the production of culture)

Using Hall's typology, the study of the 'encoding' process views cultural practices as evidence of specific political and economic relationships within society. The encoding paradigm is a lens through which one clearly locates class formations, relationships of dominance and opposition, social control, and ownership. This cultural critique is rooted in a Marxist tradition which places economic analysis at the heart of inquiry into mass communications and social structures.

### Health professionals and the production of stigmatizing artifacts

Andrew McGuire [17], director of the Trauma Foundation, has analyzed barriers to injury prevention by asking, "Who makes money off injuries?" Examining who profits from the production of stigma is a question worthy of an epidemiologist's shoe-leather and a sociologist's imagination. Who makes money from portraying people with disabilities or other conditions as incompetent? Who benefits from provoking public fear that they or someone they love might acquire a debilitating disease?

Most economic analyses of the health care industry focus on the biomedical sector. The non-profit public health sector typically is not associated with lucrative finances. Public health professionals**** who advocate prevention have traditionally been an oppositional voice in their struggle against a biomedical hegemony. But the production of materials for health promotion and prevention is an industry deserving of an economic interpretation in its own right.

What follows is not an exhaustive list of those whose livelihood depends on the afflictions of others. But several groups emerge as worthy of scrutiny because of their enormous potential to influence the portrayal of people with disabilities. Charitable organizations such as the March of Dimes and the Muscular Dystrophy Association curiously combine the public health intent for prevention and the medical intent for cure. They enjoy

---

**** Before further reflecting on this approach, it is useful to identify the imprecision of the term 'health professionals'. Groups as diverse as physicians, public health advocates, social workers, pharmaceutical conglomerates, hospital administrators, government workers, educational film suppliers, nutritionists, sanitarians, nurses, lab technicians, and voluntary agencies are self-described health professionals. Their approaches to health are as varied as their status in the eyes of one another and the public.

the legitimacy and goodwill of organizations that are viewed as representing the best interests of people with polio, mental illness, or other conditions. Yet one man who had polio as a teenager said:

The March of Dimes is a classic in terms of prevention of polio, and the charities, I think, are a good group of people to talk about. Jerry Lewis, that guy's a real jerk: what they do is portray disability in incredibly negative ways to get people to feel guilty enough to give their money. But that does irreparable damage to what we are, who we are, and our cause. And yet their bottom line is, well let's prevent polio, or let's prevent muscular dystrophy. But in that process you have to create so much fear. If you just think about it yourself, about the charities you've watched, or telethons, the process of creating fear is one that creates really awfully, negative attitudes toward us, which then hang around for generations. We have lots of ways we teach people to have prejudices and one of the ways we do is through our charities. They try to raise money and the money becomes the object, not the attitude of people towards people with disability, or not even a realistic view. The object is the money, get the money. You've got to make people feel bad or guilty or totally glad that they don't have a disability.

Another man related:

There's a huge charity industry that feeds off our suffering. Human interest stories, there's drawers full of them, you know about brave people who have gone out and done something tremendous like get across the street or something. And these kind of stories produce money. You don't want to be like that person even if they are very brave. So you better give to this charity. Or you better do this or that. It's a weird kind of stigma to be stuck with. Don't be like this person. And all this money is raised off of people, and a lot of people who have some self-respect don't want to be part of that anymore. It's really demeaning.

That the mentality of health professionals perhaps reflected, and shaped, the broader culture's view of disability was perceived by a third person who uses a wheelchair. He felt these professionals had an attitude that acquiring a disability

is such a terrible thing. And their underlying message is, 'You need our support. And our professional intervention. We are highly trained experts. We've spent years studying this. This is our life's work."

A woman with a disability summarized the implications: "So you'd *better* feel bad for six months." As she put it:

Disability has to be talked about in many of the same ways that racism is talked about. Why it's institutionalized, its relationship to capitalism, why people make money off of you needing professionalized services which people wouldn't need were disability more accepted in our society~so then, who would need to go to a psychologist for three years after you were disabled? Or if things were accessible then I wouldn't have to adjust to how it felt to be limited in where I go.

Arguing in this tradition, Irving Zola, John McKnight and others have drawn attention to the economic interests that drive the perceived beneficence of the health and medical professions. They probed the way in which professionalized service providers locate deficiency in the individual rather than address broader social needs and changes [18].

Finally, the contexts in which health professionals train and work should be examined, including social interactions and the extent to which broader class stratification is reproduced in the hierarchy of their organizations and the people who are served. Invoking Franco Basaglia, Scheper-Hughes has viewed physicians "as often unknowing 'agents of the social consensus' who are trained so as to fail to see the secret indignation of the sick expressed in ambiguous and 'subversive' symptoms" [19]. Prevention materials and programs should be considered in the context of their production, distribution, costs, advertising, the social structure of the outlets that make them and the class backgrounds of the people who produce them. Stone [20] has expressed concern that the country's national agenda for disability prevention emphasizes "more bureaucracy, more training programs, and more jobs for educated, middle-class, mostly nondisabled people."

Estes [21] makes relevant this framework in her analysis of the 'aging enterprise'. She examines the conglomerations of programs, bureaucracies, providers, interest groups and industries that serve the aging population, but most of all serve the needs of the business market of which they are a part [22]. Reproducing the worst aspects of our culture, the exploitation of fears of aging has perpetuated a geriatric 'social industrial complex' [23], or the discovery of gold in gray [22]. Gerontophobia has contributed to the body-as-temple oxymoron 'premature aging', from which advertisers selling 'anti-aging supplements' and other products benefit [24].

The strength of this application has been its macro-sociological emphasis on economic relationships within society. Since World War II, however, what Todd Gitlin has called the 'dominant paradigm' [25] in media sociology has been 'media effects' research that decodes audiences' experiences. The next section discusses how different audiences experience and decode both their own realities and the mass culture in which they live, and the implications for understanding health and disability.

### The decoding process (audiences)

The biomedical view of disease seeks to localize and then treat pathology within the individual. By contrast, public health is committed to the active promotion of health in population groups [26-28]. Dan Beauchamp, one of the leading ethicists in public health, elaborates the meaning of public health as social justice [26]. A key principle is *to identify and control the hazards* of the environment rather than focus on the behavioral limitations of those individuals damaged by the hazards. *Prevention* is a second principle. Preventing death and injury is contingent upon creating an environment through planned, organized, and *collective action,* a third priority. Beauchamp offers a final principle: that all persons are responsible for a *fair sharing of the burdens* of protection.

The approach of Beauchamp [26] and other prominent proponents of public health implicitly supports the minimization of disability through prevention [27]. The injury control movement claims a particular responsibility for this goal. Although medical and public health professionals are often at odds with each other over their respective approaches and use of resources, both ascribe to a hegemonic view of disability as deficit, as preventable tragedy. Yet the meaning of disability is changing.

Clifford Geertz has argued that culture as experience is a production of meaning [29]. As Mukerji and Schudson [30] have noted, Geertz views culture as an expression of human experience, which must be understood from the native's point of view. the study of culture constitutes interpretations of interpretations. Geertz admonishes the anthropologist to be ironically self-conscious of his or her own prejudices in the production of meaning.

The theoretical implication of this view is that all social practices are legitimate 'texts' inviting interpretation. The methodological implication is a commitment to 'thick description,' which involves

> setting down the meaning particular social actions have for the actors whose actions they are, and stating, as explicitly as we can manage, what the knowledge thus attained demonstrates about the society in which it is found, and beyond that, about social life as such [29].

Geertz argues that the greatest challenge of thick description, "how (to) tell a better account from a worse one" [29}, is also its greatest virtue. The anti-reductionist, interpretive approach rejects the 'thin description' usually associated with scientific explanation; it also rejects a radical relativism which suggests that all interpretations are equally faithful. As Mukerji and Schudson point out, description aspiring to a certain high level of intensity and reliability should yield "a high concentration of insight into social relations" [30] beyond the myths, for example, of tourist impressions. Geertz believes that one grasps the point of view of the other through interpreting social events and public acts. Thick description is the method embraced by sociologist Todd Gitlin for his analysis of the television industry's prime time players, content, and social organization [31].

It provides a social and cultural context within which to understand how reality and meaning are created. The decoding process embodies the theoretical and practical exploration of how audiences experience mass culture. Decoding invites inquiry into the production of the meaning of disability, both hegemonic and oppositional.

The anthropological distinction between self and other may offer a parallel for how health professionals view themselves and their clients. Anthropologist Gelya Frank presents the case of Diane DeVries, a young woman without limbs who thinks of herself as lovely, a Venus de Milo. DeVries experiences her body and herself as whole and beautiful, contrary to the medical profession's view of her body as dysfunctional and deviant [32]. Or again, disability rights activists and scholars insist that the biological condition of disability be conceptually distinguished from the handicap, which is the social consequence of the condition [33]. Handicap is a barrier imposed by society, the physical environment, or one's own self.

To what extent do health professionals understand this crucial distinction? The School of Public Health at the University of California at Berkeley until recently offered a course called "Programs and Services for Handicapped Children and Youth". That this professional school has managed to ignore the distinction, while situated in a geographical setting where disability activists flourish, suggests that the oppositional meaning of disability has not been widely adopted.

As Raymond Williams suggests, the history of language is a metaphor for consciousness [34]. Grassroots AIDS activists long ago recognized the significance of dehumanizing labels, rejecting the sensational term "AIDS victim' for "person with AIDS". The Alzheimer's Disease Association avoids using the stigmatizing term, "Alzheimer's victim". And as one individual said to me, "I'm a person with a disability. But I'm a person first".

People with disabilities have to deal with the words 'cripple' and 'invalid'. On the one hand, they are subject to the dominant discourse about the 'handicapped' and 'disabled'. At the same time, they contest that discourse. "Don't use that word", says one man. They are engaged in a negotiation over the meaning of disability. Negotiation takes place within their own selves, too; at times "you can't help but be frustrated and angry".

Yet a person with a disability can be much healthier in the broader sense of the term than many able-bodied people. The World Health Organization [35] currently defines health as "a state of complete physical, mental and social well-being, and not merely the absence of disease or infirmity". The WHO canon suggests that 'disability' and 'health' are mutually exclusive. They are not; the lives of Diane DeVries and many others bear witness. Oliver Sacks writes that the contradiction of illness that presents as wellness is one of the "chimeras, tricks and ironies of nature" [36]. DeVries and others embody the paradox of wellness that presents as disability.

An anthropologically informed approach that examines the emerging meaning of disability in the context of how people live their lives and experience their bodies may offer a more sophisticated meaning of health itself. Such a concept of health would negotiate among biomedicine's definition of disease, people's lived experience of illness, and the social relations that produce suffering. Murdock and Golding have stated, "In a sense, what needs explaining is how oppositional values ever emerge" [37]. I argue that the dominant approach to health promotion stigmatizes people with disabilities who are 'healthily' embodied [19].

Scheper-Hughes and Lock observe that the new forms of consciousness that emerge in the context of collective groups "are used in direct social and political action, as well as in the practice of group therapy" [38]. Anspach described how people with disabilities and former mental patients may become politically active in response to being stigmatized [39]. To extend the sociological comparison, for some people with disabilities the transformation of private troubles into public issues allows them to create a deeper connotation to the term 'community', a unit of social structure that, as Gottlieb notes, gives our lives meaning [40].

To comparatively highlight how different audiences might experience the meanings of a health promotion advertisement, college students enrolled in a health education course and people with mobility disabilities were presented examples of injury prevention advertisements, shown opposite. One, part of a statewide campaign to promote the use of seat belts, simply reads, "If you think seat belts are confining, think about a wheelchair". A young woman enrolled in a health education course related, "To me it still sends that same shiver, like, 'God, if I was in a wheelchair'". Her comment conveys the existential scariness and fear evoked by such images. Yet, as a woman with a mobility disability said:

You know, frankly, I'll look at an advertisement like this and say, what's so bad about using a wheelchair. And here we go getting the message again that we're not okay as wheelchair users, or people who are blind, or who use American Sign Language, or who use crutches, or whatever it is. (It might be effective) for people who buy into the whole idea that disability is negative and significantly diminishes one's quality of life. It's devaluing to the rest of us who know better.

The second advertisement, for a campaign against drunk driving, pairs a stark depiction of a wheelchair with the words, "Last year, 1057 teenagers got so drunk they couldn't stand up. Ever!" One man with an acquired disability said, "It's holding us up as someone to avoid". Or, as another man put it, "I feel it's an attack on my self esteem and dignity".

A critical anthropology of the conceptualization of health promotion campaigns might examine to what extent health professionals paradoxically reproduce the notion of people with disabilities as 'the stigmatized other'—people whom one should not become—by stressing that a transition to that category of 'other' is undesirable and unwanted. Greater phenomenological knowledge is needed about how people not previously viewed as stakeholders, such as people with disabilities, experience their illnesses and the popular culture's interpretation of their conditions. There are two major implications of this type of research.

First, the production of stigma through prevention is relevant to the way in which public health workers conceptualize other health conditions. Minkler [41] observes, for example, that the emphasis on the prevention of chronic illness and disability among the old may paradoxically suggest that the elderly are to blame for their conditions. A second, related importance of this paradigm is its contribution to our understanding of whose interests are at stake in the emerging debate over the effects of health education at this historical moment. Many researchers, for example, have paid great attention to how *intended* audiences (e.g., teenagers at high risk for motor vehicle injury) interpret health education efforts. No study to date has examined the paradox that a health education approach that warns that disability must be prevented may exert the greatest impact, directly and indirectly, on people with disabilities.

Choosing to include one of the most neglected yet consequential audiences, however unintended, is an exciting undertaking in itself. By implication, it also argues for the viability of applying a macro-sociology to future research on the effects of health education and broadening the definition of whose interests are at stake. This framework will expand the model for identifying distinct stakeholders, such as people with stigmatized conditions, risk groups, and health educators, involved in education undertaken to improve health. By recognizing the emergence of diverse communities affected by the formation of health education (including groups not traditionally viewed as stakeholders), this approach will begin to analyze the roles of culture, power, and professionalization in shaping what happens in a variety of contexts related to learning about health.

### The text (content)

What is a text? Within the model proposed by Clifford Geertz, culture itself became an ensemble of texts. Discourse, literary content, linguistic styles, and mass media are suitable for analysis as texts. To fully understand the process of stigmatization, we can turn to cultural production studies for a powerful vantage point from which to critically examine public health prevention campaigns. As an example of a charity appeal for which textual analysis is useful, an advertisement by the National Alliance for Research on Schizophrenia and Depression in *Time* [42] is worth analyzing. Beneath a large photograph of an infant, a headline states, "Odds are 1 in 5 she'll grow up to be mentally ill'. The text explains that tax-deductible donations are needed for researchers who want to "solve the mystery of mental illness", stating that it may even be "curable". People with schizophrenia and depression, as well as their family members and friends can attest to the great pain and suffering that such conditions produce. Because the mentally ill in this country are so stigmatized already, however, such appeals paradoxically may serve to heap more stigma on people with mental illness in the name of searching for treatment or cure. "Odds are 1 in 5 she'll grow up to be mentally ill" is suggestive of a curse, an omen, a terrible fate that stalks anyone. Yet one of the virtues of the advertisement is that it promotes increased awareness that mental illness can affect anyone; the advertisement democratizes the risk of mental illness.

Another example illustrates the potential relationship between prevention efforts and the production of stigma. An advertisement produced by Mothers Against Drunk Driving shows the universal symbol for wheelchair access at a parking spot for people with disabilities. The ad's headline reads: "Drink and drive and you could have the choicest parking spot at school". Below, the copy says: "But who cares? You'll lose your spot on the football team. The marching band. The prom dance floor. You'll sure be giving up a lot just because you didn't give up your keys". Texts provide the prototypes from which we can begin to theorize about the relationship between prevention efforts and the negation of social identity for people with disabilities or other stigmatized conditions.

Producers of educational films and other prevention materials have a nationwide audience of school administrators and corporations to which to sell educational materials. The Film Library of the National Safety Council, for example, offers more than 1800 "training safety and motivational films and videos" for rental at $75 per week. popular local pilot programs are sometimes reproduced for statewide or national audiences. One such pilot is the Prevent Alcohol and Risk Related to Trauma and Youth (PARTY) Program, developed by a nurse in response to the fatalities of young intoxicated drivers. The 3-hour program includes "a documentary video portraying three teenagers and their tragic stories. The students are then divided into small groups and whisked away to the Emergency Unit, the Intensive Care Unit, and the Rehabilitation Area" of a general hospital. A news photograph for the PARTY Program shows teenagers being strapped into cervical collars worn by quadriplegics. In an article lauding the 'scary' and 'explicit' PARTY Program, one teenager is quoted: "I would rather have to die than live that way" [43]. How the texts are viewed by vast captive audiences of schoolchildren and by people with disabilities will shed light on their cultural significance. The research would offer a descriptive and analytic study of the different ideological orientations of people with injury-acquired disabilities and the campaigns used to prevent injury.

The wide range of health promotion materials that can be analyzed may offer insight into the production of stigma. A television promotion advertisement for a program that opposes drunk driving depicts a drawing of a young woman in a varsity letter jacket sitting in a wheelchair, with the accompanying text, "The drunk driver got one year. She was sentenced to life". The advertisement implies that it will be to the viewer's own health benefit to watch the program about a basketball star. "She was sentenced to life" emphasizes that the metaphor for wheelchair is imprisonment. In however unintentional and ironic a fashion, it links disability to criminality.

In late 1990 and early 1991, the *New York Times* carried a full-page advertisement showing a photograph of James Brady, President Reagan's press secretary, shot on 30 March, 1981 [44]. Offering a more subtle model for cultural production analysis, the copy said:

Add your voice to mine. Help me beat the gun lobby. The gun lobbyists say a seven-day wait is 'inconvenient.' I'd like to see one of them try spending a day in my wheelchair.

The large photo of James Brady sitting in his wheelchair is emblematic of injury prevention ads that imply, "Don't let this happen to you!" One advocate with Handgun Control's Center to Prevent Handgun Violence observed that the James Brady advertisement, which also appeared in *The Washington Post,* generated a deluge of calls to the 1-900 telephone number listed.

The utility of the advertisement to Handgun Control, contrasted with a textual reading of the advertisement from a cultural production perspective, highlights the tension between the goals of injury control activists and disability rights activists. The oppressive significance of such an image for the social identity of people with disabilities may seem obvious at first. The advertisement may be interpreted as an embodiment of the stereotypical view of people with disabilities as helpless and passive victims. Yet it might also be viewed as offering a depiction of a trauma survivor as a powerful and dignified individual~~a public advocate who uses the authenticity of his experience to rivet attention to legislative change. Materials such as these provide grist for research into the commodification of stigma and fear related to health conditions, and the strengths~~and previously unquestioned costs~~of such approaches.

### Transcending the boundaries between three temptations

Social deviance is the dominant paradigm through which sociologists have studied physical disability. Erving Goffman's classic, *Stigma: Notes on the Management of Spoiled Identity,* highlights the parallels between the social position of the physically disabled and that of other socially marginal groups. Devalued groups are partly blamed for their perceived flaws, and society views them less as victim than as culprit [45, 13]. Levine and Perkins cite the well-known sociological

analysis that discrimination is "at least as pathological within the society as medical illness", and reflects power relationships with society [46].

### Deviance and distinction

The proposed line of investigation examines to what extent prevention materials produce what Basaglia calls "the double disease" [47]. As Scheper-Hughes and Lock [38] note, the social production of stigma creates a second affliction in addition to the original condition. Some scholars of cultural production have attempted to transcend the territory between the temptation to focus exclusively on the processes of 'encoding', 'decoding', or content, and to take care that their work is informed by more than one approach.

For example, the cultural stratification approach embodied by Pierre Bourdieu suggests that taste leaders manifest their aesthetic preferences as "the product of the conditions associated with a particular class of conditions of existence, [uniting] all those who are the product of similar conditions while distinguishing them from all others" [48]. Taste is thereby a representation of one's social class; taste accentuates the ways in which people are separate and unequal. Tastes establish who belongs to a group, serving to affirm one's own preferences and position in one's own social class, and to delegitimize the preferences of others. The term 'habitus', perhaps Bourdieu's best known contribution to anthropology, describes the "principles of the generation and structuring of practice" [49], which may be viewed as culture. He focuses on the scenes of everyday life, on the routine practices surrounding work, food, sleep, play and social interaction.

An important implication of Bourdieu's work is that what gets defined as deviant behavior reproduces class distinctions. Behavior interpreted as harmlessly eccentric for a wealthy, elderly executive might instead be diagnosed as Alzheimer's disease, with its accompanying stigma and incrimination, for a truck driver. Physicians typically suspect that poor people are more likely to fake a seizure than rich people, although there is no evidence that this is the case. In a more common example, intoxicated white fraternity brothers are much less likely to be arrested by police than intoxicated black teens. Bourdieu's analysis suggests that whether behavior is viewed as pathologically and dangerously deviant or as merely socially inappropriate is a function of the social class of the observed and the observer.

Bourdieu's work provides a theoretical basis for an analysis that recognizes that the definition of diseases differ by culture, region, and era. What is more, it can offer insight into how the profession and ideology of public health contributes, however unwittingly, to a notion of difference as deviance. How do systems that classify states of health serve to naturalize systems of hierarchy? How do public health campaigns that present people with disabilities as 'the other' paradoxically reinforce a stigmatized view of disability?

**SUMMARY**

Anthropological and sociological theories of the production of culture offer a unique contribution to public health. The hypothesized relationship between prevention and stigma, and the proposed research, depart in several important ways from traditional medical anthropology, medical sociology, and public health literature. The model I am developing extends the critique of largely ignored assumptions about prevention strategies. The dearth of disciplined and empirical studies of the unintended, negative consequences of health promotion campaigns underscores the need for this research. Analysis that is grounded in theories of cultural production can guide a critical theory of preventive health education.

Community participation is a fundamental principle of health promotion practice. The basis of this strategy is both ethical and practical: health strategies that reflect the community's own values and priorities are more likely to be culturally relevant [50], less alienating [51], and more effective overall [52-54]. As participants in the struggle to reduce injuries, trauma survivors can be powerful spokespersons for prevention. Having survived months and years

of acute care followed by rehabilitation and having achieved independence, trauma survivors challenge society to transcend the powerlessness of apathy, inertia, and ignorance [55].

Yet the notorious Jerry Lewis Muscular Dystrophy Association campaigns include people with disabilities, who 'participate ' in telethons as dependent and helpless people. Although future research may affirm the potential contribution of trauma survivors in injury prevention, it might also suggest community participation with a subtle distinction: the participation of trauma survivors who are sensitive to the political implications of public health campaigns that portray people with disabilities as tragic victims. A person with a disability possesses an indisputable right to claim their own fate as tragic. But a public health ethic that readily capitalizes on that person's suffering, even in the name of injury prevention, deserves scrutiny. By suspending our conventional wisdom about the unequivocal value of prevention, we may acquire a key to understanding the way in which certain prevention strategies serve to intensify "the double disease".

Far from viewing the stigmatization of the disabled as inevitable, Bogdan and Taylor presented the perspective of nondisabled people who do not stigmatize or stereotype people with severe disabilities, and argued that humanness is itself socially constructed [56]. And as Volinn's study noted, while physicians and nurses may act to stigmatize conditions, they also can serve as 'destigmatizers' of feared conditions [57]. Future research should evaluate not only the stigmatizing effects of prevention campaigns, but the extent to which public health advocates and the texts that they produce can decrease the stigma attached to health conditions.

Public health workers have an ethical mandate to 'do no harm'. This analysis aims to critically assess how prevention strategies may inadvertently contribute to the production of stigma. A second goal is to contribute to a more sophisticated perspective within public health for the design, implementation, and evaluation of the consequences of preventive interventions. Moving toward a broader theoretical foundation offers a vantage from which to self-consciously assess the unintended, even harmful, consequences of injury prevention strategies, and the shared and divergent interests of people with disabilities, intended audiences, and public health educators. Finally, this critique can contribute to the development of a new epistemology of prevention, one that will offer insight into the social production of stigma for a variety of health conditions.

*Acknowledgements*~~I am very grateful to Todd Gitlin for his teaching and for comments on an earlier version of this article. My heartfelt thanks to Meredith Minkler, S. Leonard Syme, Eugene Hammel and Nancy Chen, and especially to Seth Moglen and to Lawrence Wallack for encouragement and exacting criticism. My gratitude also to Andrew McGuire and to Elizabeth McLoughlin for invaluable support, and to my informants for time and ideas.

********

# REFERENCES

1. Hall S. Encoding and decoding in the television discourse. Center for Contemporary Cultural Studies, University of Birmingham, 1973. *Culture and Education.* Council of Europe, Strasbourg, 1974.

2. Mukerji C. and Schudson M. Popular culture. *Ann. Rev. Sociol.* **12**, 47-66, 1986.

3. Schudson M. The new validation of popular culture: sense and sentimentality in academia. *Critical Stud. Mass Commun.* **4**, 1987.

4. Robertson A. The politics of Alzheimer's disease: a case study in apocalyptic demography. *Int. J. Hlth Services* **20**, 429-442, 1990.

5. National Research Council, 1985. Committee on Trauma Research, National Research Council. *Injury in America.* National Academy Press, Washington, DC, 1985.

6. Rice D. P. and MacKenzie E. J. *et al. Cost of Injury in the United States: A Report to Congress.* The Johns Hopkins University, San Francisco, CA. 1989.

7. U.S. Bureau of the Census. *Untied States Population Estimates by Age, Sex, and Race~~1980 to 1987*, Series P-25, No. 1022, U.S. Department of Commerce, Washington, DC, 1988.

8. Leonard B. D. Impaired view: television portrayal of handicapped people. Ph.D. Dissertation, Boston University School of Education, 1978.

9. Fiedler L. A. Pity and fear: images of the disabled in literature and the popular arts. *Proc. Literary Symp.* sponsored by the International Center for the Disabled in collaboration with the United Nations, 1981.

10. Zola I. K. *Missing Pieces: A Chronicle of Living with a Disability.* Temple University Press, Philadelphia, 1983.

11. Murphy R. *The Body Silent.* Henry Holt, New York, 1987.

12. Saxton M. and Howe F. *With Wings: An Anthology.* The Feminist Press, New York, 1987.

13. Murphy R. F. *et al.* Physical disability and social liminality: a study in the rituals of adversity. *Soc. Sci. Med.* **26,**j, 235-242, 1988.

14. Bogdan R. and Taylor S. Relationships with severely disabled people: the social construction of humanness. *Soc. Problems* **36**, 135-148, 1989.

15. Zola I. K. *Ordinary Lives: Voices of Disability and Disease.* Applewood Books, Cambridge, MA, 1982.

16. Kaufman S. Long-term impact of injury on individuals, families, and society: personal narratives and policy implications. *Cost of Injury in the United States: A Report to Congress*, Chap. 6 (Edited by Rice D. and Mackenzie E. *et al.*). The Johns Hopkins University, San Francisco, CA. 1989.

17. McGuire A. Falls and firearms. Unpublished manuscript..

18. Illich I., Zola I. K., McKnight J. *et al. Disabling Professions.* Marion Boyars, London, 1977.

19. Scheper-Hughes N. Embodied knowledge: the message in the bottle. Paper presented at the American Anthropological Association Meetings, Washington, DC, 1989.

20. Stone D. A. Dissent from the report of the committee. In *Disability in America: Toward a National Agenda for Prevention* (Edited by Pope A. and Tarlov A.). National Academy Press, Washington, DC, 1991.

21. Estes C. *The Aging Enterprise.* Jossey-Bass, San Francisco, 1979.

22. Minkler M. Gold in gray: reflections on business' discovery of the elderly market. *The Gerontologist* **29**, 17-23, 1989.

23. O'Connor J. *The Fiscal Crisis of the State.* St. Martins, New York, 1973.

24. Wang C. *LEAR'S* magazine "for the woman who wasn't born yesterday": a critical review. *The Gerontologist* **28**, (5), 600-601, 1988.

25. Gitlin T. Media sociology: the dominant paradigm. *Theory and Society* **6**, 205-253, 1978.

26. Beauchamp D. E. Public health as social justice. In *Patients, Physicians, and Illness* (Edited by Jaco E.). Free Press, New York, 1979.

27. Blum H. L. *Planning for Health.* Human Sciences Press, New York, 1974.

28. Terris M. The public health profession. *J. Publ. Hlth Policy* **6,** 7-14, 1985.

29. Geertz C. *The Interpretation of Culture.* Basic Books, New York, 1973.

30. Mukerji C. and Schudson M. (Eds) *Rethinking Popular Culture: Contemporary Perspectives in Cultural Studies.* University of California Press, Berkeley, 1991.

31. Gitlin T. *Inside Prime Time.* Pantheon Books, 1983.

32. Frank G. On embodiment: a case study of congenital limb deficiency in American culture. *Culture, Med. Psychiat.* **10,** 189-219, 1986.

33. Fine M. and Asch A. (Eds) *Women with Disabilities: Essays in Psychology, Culture, and Politics.* Temple University Press, Philadelphia, 1988.

34. Williams R. *Marxism and Literature.* Oxford University Press, New York, 1977.

35. World Health Organization. *Constitution of the World Health Organization.* World Health Organization, Geneva, 1946.

36. Sacks O. *The Man Who Mistook His Wife for a Hat.* Harper and Row, New York, 1970.

37. Murdock G. and Golding P. Capitalism, communication and class relations. *Mass Communication and Society* (Edited by Curran J. *et al.*). Chap. 1. Sage London, 1977.

38. Scheper-Hughes N. and Lock M. Speaking "truth to illness: metaphors, reification, and a pedagogy for patients. *Med. Anthropol. Q.* **17,** 137-140, 1986.

39. Anspach R. From stigma to identity politics: political activism among the physically disabled and former mental patients. *Soc. Sci. Med.* **13A,** 765-773, 1979.

40. Gottlieb B. Social networks and social support: an overview of research, practice, and policy implications. *Hlth Educ. Q.* **12,** (1), 5-22, 1985.

41. Minkler M. Aging and disability: behind and beyond the stereotypes. *J. Aging Stud.* **4,** 245-260, 1990.

42. *Time,* 14 May 1990.

43. *Injury Awareness and Prevention Centre News* **4,** ll, 1990.

44. *New York Times,* 10 December 1991.

45. Goffman E. *Stigma: Notes on the Management of Spoiled Identity.* Prentice Hall, Englewood Cliffs, NJ. 1963.

46. Levine M. and Perkins D. *Principles of Community Psychology: Perspectives and Applications.* Oxford University Press, New York, 1987.

47. Basaglia F. *The Deviant Majority.* Torino, 1971.

48. Bourdieu P. *Distinction: A Social Critique of the Judgement of Taste* (Translated by Nice R.). Harvard University Press, Cambridge, MA 1984.

49. Bourdieu P. *Outline of a Theory of Practice.* Cambridge University Press, Cambridge, 1977.

50. U.S. Department of Health and Human Services. *Report of the Secretary's Task Force on Black and Minority Health.* U.S. Government Printing Office, Washington, DC. 1985.

51. Hatch J. W. and Eng E. Community participation and control: or control of community participation. In *Reforming Medicine: Lessons of the last Quarter Century* (Edited by Sidel V. W. and Sidel R.). Pantheon, New York, 1984.

52. Alinsky S. *Rules for Radicals.* Random House, New York, 1971.

53. Minkler M. Ethical issues in community organization. *Hlth Educ Monographs* **6,** 198-210, 1978.

54. Macrina D. M. and O'Rourke T. W. Citizen participation in health planning in the U.S. and U.K. *Int. Q. Community Hlth Educ.* **7,** 25-239, 1986-87.

55. McLoughlin E. *Passage of a Motorcycle Helmet Law for All Riders.* The Trauma Foundation, San Francisco, 1989.

56. Bogdan R. and Taylor S. Relationships with severely disabled people: the social construction of humanness. *Soc. Problems* **36,** 135-148, 1989.

57. Volinn I. Health Professionals as stigmatizers and destigmatizers of diseases: alcoholism and leprosy as examples. *Soc. Sci. Med.* **17,** 385-393, 1983.

********

**About the author:** Caroline Wang received her BA in Art, Media, and Politics from Duke University, and her doctorate in public health from the University of California, Berkeley. Her dissertation examined a serious gap in the theory, practice, and ethics of the health field: the paradox of health education's potential to stigmatize people with disabilities, and those affected by other health conditions, even as the goal is to reduce suffering. She also currently works with the comprehensive, community-based Women's Reproductive Health and Development Program, the aim of which is to improve rural Chinese women's health and social status. Her major research interests include

international primary health care, empowerment
education, disability, injury control, mass
communication, and the sociology of health
promotion. Correspondence to: 1835-B Addison
Street, Berkeley, CA 94703-1503 USA.

**Source:** Reprinted with permission from *Social
Science & Medicine,* Vol. 35, No. 9, pp. 1093-1102,
1992. Published by Pergamon Press Ltd., New
York, NY.

# Religion and Disability:
# Some Notes on Religious Attitudes and Views
M. Darrol Bryant

**Introduction**: The social scientific literature on disability is relatively new and growing rapidly. Sociologists, social workers, social scientists of every discipline have done much in recent years to extend our understanding and awareness of disability. But one area that has yet to receive extensive treatment is religion and disability. It is not, for example, an entry that makes it into dictionaries of Christianity, Judaism, the Bible or World Religions.[1] Yet there are many points of contact between religion and disability, most importantly within religious communities themselves and the attitudes and practices of those communities in relation to the disabled. How do believers in different religious communities regard the disabled? Do religious communities and institutions ensure full participation of the disabled in the rites of the community and its life? Are the disabled fully integrated into the religious life of the community or are they marginalized and excluded? The questions are many.

There is much that has been written about religious views of illness and health. Ari Kiev even claims that among primal religious communities attitudes and views "of illness have a universal pattern." [2] In those early views, Kiev argues, all illness is attributed to "'soul loss,' 'spirit intrusion,' violation of taboos or witchcraft."[3] The extent to which these early views of illness carry over into the great world religious traditions -- Buddhist, Confucian, Christian, Hindu, Jewish, Moslem, Taoist, etc. -- is not clear. We do know that the great traditions often developed medical and treatment traditions that reflected the worldviews of the respective traditions. Thus Tibetan medicine reflects Buddhist convictions and Ayurvedic medicine grows out of Hindu sources -- to name but two examples.[4]         However, the issue of disability, as it has come to be understood in the social scientific literature, has had only limited attention. The theme of

"religion and disability" could be explored in various ways. Historical studies could chart the attitudes and views that the various religious traditions expounded and encouraged in relation to the disabled. Textual studies could examine the sacred scriptures of the different traditions to see what, if anything, is taught in different scriptures concerning the disabled. Sociological studies could look at various religious institutions and the ways that they related -- or failed to relate -- to the disabled. Other studies could survey contemporary attitudes among religious adherents to see if there is any correlation of official teachings and current attitudes, or the responses there have been by religious institutions to the more recent awareness of disability issues. Hopefully, such valuable studies will be undertaken, but they exceed what will be undertaken here.

The intention here is modest: it is a series of notes on some of the attitudes and views of the disabled found in world religious sources, especially Jewish and Christian ones. It does not pretend to be either comprehensive or exhaustive; it intends only to open an area of inquiry and to raise some questions. It then concludes with the story of L'Arche, an attempt at Christian community explicitly related to persons with disabilities.

**Understanding Disability**: Disability has been defined in diverse ways. In his book, *Perspectives on Disability*, Mark Nagler identifies four types of disabilities: 1. disabilities arising from congenital disorders, 2. developmental disabilities, 3. instantaneous impediments, and 4. psychological disability.[5] His summary makes clear the wide range of cases and conditions covered by the term disability and the need to specify which aspect of disability one is addressing. More significant than issues of definition are issues of understanding that affect the way in which the people with disabilities are regarded within religious communities. Thus while we will attempt to keep these different aspects of disability before us, our attention will focus on understanding disability within the context of the religious traditions. Many of our comments will focus on the issue of disability arising from congenital disorders. We begin here since, we believe, it is often attitudes towards illness and disease found within religious communities that shape perceptions and views of the disabled. The further assumption is that it is imperative for contemporary religious communities across the planet to examine their own traditions for explicit and hidden biases towards the disabled and to discover those attitudes and practices that are fitting both to the disabled and to the deepest convictions and wisdom of the religions.

**Religious Attitudes to Illness & Disease:** As already indicated, there is often a tendency to regard disability arising from congenital disorders as part of the issue of religious attitudes towards disease and illness in general.[6]

Religious attitudes towards disease and illness vary widely. It is a popular Buddhist tradition that illness is "one of the messengers (duta) from the heavenly beings (devas) reminding humanity of its mortal condition."[6] There is a widespread belief in Jewish and Christian circles that sees illness as punishment for sins. This has some Biblical warrant, since as R. K. Harrison observes, "in the Pentateuch, illness is sent by God to punish the transgressor or to make clear divine displeasure."[7] According to Lawrence Sullivan, some Muslims believe that ". . .*jinn* (demonic spirits) insert disease and confusion into human life . . ."[8] On the other hand, Taoists because of their "reverential attitude towards humility" were often led to "honor hunchbacks and cripples because of the way they typified meekness and self-effacement."[9]

The question we must pose is whether or not these attitudes towards illness and disease often carry over into attitudes towards the disabled. When they do, the consequence is that persons with disabilities are regarded as either responsible for their own disabilities or deserving of such disabilities.

Biblical scholars, however, question whether such views have significant textual warrant. "Disabled" is a word that only occurs once in the Jewish and Christian scripture (Lev. 22:22). Even the term "disease" occurs only 58 times in the Hebrew Bible and Christian Old Testament and 64 times in the Christian scriptures (or an additional 6 times in the Christian New Testament). And 50 of those entries are in the book of Leviticus, most commonly in relation to "a leperous disease." It is from these texts that there emerges the image of the leper as one that must be excluded from the wider community, segregated and removed as "unclean." Something of this attitude may carry over to how people regard the disabled when the ritual and moral command to be a "holy people" is confused with degrees of natural wellness and illness in the community.

Moreover, biblical scholars point out that the Bible ". . . repudiated entirely any magical or demonic etiology of disease."[10] It is also clear that religious attitudes towards illness have developed and changed. Such changes of attitude and view are to be found even within scripture. The book of Job, for example, departs from the earlier tradition of seeing illness as sent by God to punish or to express divine displeasure. Harrison points out that Job ascribes disease not to God, "but to the activity of the adversary."[11]. Though this is a change one must ask if it is really an improvement? It seems clear that there is a great distance between Biblical sources and more contemporary understandings of illness. This is reflected in the fact that in the *New Catholic Encyclopedia*, R.A. Osbourn simply defines disease as "any deviation from normal structure or functioning of the body or mind, i.e., any departure from a state of health."[12] Such contemporary understandings are often vastly different from those found in Biblical sources. R. K. Harrison points out that Jesus "gave no support to the view that sickness and disease were punitive in character"[13] but this has not prevented countless Christians of holding precisely that view.

Nonetheless, the point here is attitudes towards those that are afflicted, for shorter, longer or even life long periods of time, by illnesses that affect their physical or emotional well-being.

**Religious Institutions and the Disabled:** Robert Goodman in an article on "The Disabled in the Jewish Community" makes an observation about the Jewish community that is probably accurate across the religious spectrum: "thousands of disabled receive no services; thousands more cannot participate fully within the Jewish community."[14]. Access is an essential issue for the disabled. It is not just a matter of religiously based or encouraged attitudes, but it is also a matter of access. Persons with disabilities are beginning to make us aware of the fact that often they are not present within religious communities and institutions simply because it is difficult, if not impossible, simply to enter the physical premises where religious rites and activities take place.

**Religious Ideals and Practice:** Another factor that is present in relation to persons with disabilities and religious communities is the gap between religious ideals and practices. It seems that there is often a gap, if not a yawning abyss, between the ideals and the practice of a given tradition. This gap can be found in every tradition, but I will illustrate the point in relation to two traditions, one eastern and one western. It is difficult to imagine a tradition more ideally suited to accord full dignity to the disabled then that of Buddhism. With its noble ideals of compassion, especially in the Mahayana strands of Buddhism, one would expect exemplary practice. Given, for example, the ideal of compassion within Buddhism coupled with its view of the interdependence of all things, it is difficult to understand its failure in practice to adequately address the issue of disability. Similarly, the Christian doctrine of agape or self-sacrificing love seems to imply an attitude and practice towards persons with disabilities that would be exemplary. Yet such ideals are seldom, if ever, fulfilled in practice. The point is not to suggest that contemporary secular society is exemplary in its attitudes towards persons with disabilities -- far from it. Rather, the point is that the gap between religious ideals and practices is a further factor that affects persons with disabilities within religious communities.[15]

**The Ambiguity of Religion:** When one looks across the broad spectrum of religious life one sees the deep ambivalence of the religious traditions to disability. While religions often fail to live up to their own professed ideals, or sanction erroneous perceptions of the disabled, they also often motivate and inspire the most profound regard for persons with disabilities. Instances of a profound regard for persons with disabilities could be found in all traditions, but here we will briefly focus our attention on a movement growing out of Christian sources: L'Arche. Here we see how persons inspired by the Christian faith were led into deep and abiding relationships with communities of persons with disabilities.

**The Story of L'Arche:** A quite remarkable story of the attempt to create a community that incorporates the disabled is that of L'Arche, the French work for "ark." Founded in 1964 by Jean Vanier, a remarkable Canadian and son of a former Governor General of Canada, L'Arche explicitly set out to create a christain community around people with disabilities. Initially, it took the form of "a home for mentally handicapped men,"[16] Nagler's fourth category of disability. But over time many of the L'Arche communities addressed themselves to many kinds of disability. Often Vanier speaks of "wounded people" when speaking of the handicapped or persons with disabilities. In what has become the L'Arche movement, Vanier speaks of what living with the disabled has meant for him:

"I have discovered that to live with the poor and the weak is very demanding, precisely because they are asking me to change, to grow and to be more compassionate and wise. I have learned how much I must die to my own ideas and self in order to listen to them and live with them. . . Above all, I have discovered how handicapped people can be a source of peace and unity in our terribly divided world, provided we are willing to listen to them, to follow them and to share our lives with them."[17].

Here, disability is seen not in a conventional way, or in a way which seeks merely to integrate people with disabilities into contemporary technological society. Instead, the emphasis falls here on the dignity of all persons, including and especially the disabled --

whether mentally or physcially. The concern is to create a community that takes the disabled seriously as they are.

For Jean Vanier, the problem that must be addressed in relation to persons with disabilities is that they have been rejected, isolated, and often abandoned. Consequently, Vanier argues that for the

". . . person who has felt abandoned, there is only one reality that will bring him back to life: an authentic, tender and faithful relationship. He must discover that he is loved and important to someone. Only then will he discover that he is worthwhile; only then will his confusion turn into peace. And to love is not to do something for someone; it is **to be with** him. It is to rejoice in his presence; it is to give him confidence in the value of his being. It is to listen to him and to his needs and desires. It is to help him find confidence in himself and in his capacities to please, to do, to serve, to be useful."[18]

Though his language is gender specific and speaks only of men, his point is obvious. For Vanier, it is the wound of abandonment and of rejection that is often at the heart of the experience of persons with disabilities that must be healed. It is the conviction of the L'Arche movement that this healing is finally divine since Vanier believes that we have all, to varying degrees, been wounded. Vanier writes that

"learning to love takes a lifetime, since the Holy Spirit must penetrate even the smallest corners of our being where there are fears, defenses and envy. Community begins to form when each person tries to welcome and love the others as they are. 'Welcome one another, therefore, as Christ has welcomed you' (Romans 15.7)."[19]

Thus the L'Arche movement has profound christian roots, but the communities are not exclusively composed of christians. L'Arche communities are open to persons of other faiths and in India this often means that the vast majority are not christian.[20]

In L'Arche communities, persons with disabilities are not the recipients of pity, nor are they treated in a condescending way.

Rather, it is the dignity of all persons, including and especially persons with disabilities, that is central to their life. As Vanier remarks, "the struggle of L'Arche is a struggle for liberation, the liberation on the one hand of handicapped people who are oppressed by the rejection of society and, on the other, of those who live with them."[21] In the L'Arche movement we see a remarkable example of how a religious faith can provide the inspiration for a profound response to persons with disabilities.

\*\*\*\*\*\*\*\*

## NOTES

[1] Among the more than twenty dictionaries and encyclopedias that I consulted are: Paul J. Achtemeier, General Editor, Harper's Bible Dictionary, San Francisco: Harper & Row, 1985, G. W. Bromiley, General Editor, The International Standard Bible Encyclopedia, Grand Rapids: Eerdmans Publishing Co., 1979, F. L. Cross, Editor, The Oxford Dictionary of the Christian Church, London: Oxford University Press, Macmillan, 1987, Ingrid Fischer-Schreiber, et. al., eds. The Encyclopedia of Eastern Philosophy and Religion, Boston: Shambhala, 1989, T. O. Ling, Editor, A Dictionary of Buddhism, New York: Chas. Scribner's Sons, 1972, Geoffrey Parrinder, A Dictionary of non-Christian Religions, Raans Road, UK: Hulton Education Publishing Ltd., 1971, and R. J. Zwi Werblowsky and G. Wigoder, Editors, The Encyclopedia of the Jewish Religion, London: Phoenix House, 1965.

[2] Ari Kiev, ed., Magic, Faith, & Healing, Studies in Primitive Psychiatry Today, New York: The Free Press, 1964, p.12. It is an interesting collection of essays that focus on psychiatric illness and mental disabilities among primal peoples.

[3] Ibid., p.12.

[4] See, for example, Dr. Yeshi Donden, Health Through Balance, An Introduction to Tibetan Medicine, translated and edited by Jeffrey Hopkins, Ithaca, NY: Snow Lion Publications, 1986. In speaking of the basic cause of disease, Dr. Donden writes that "the root is beginningless ignorance. Due to its force we are caught in cyclic existence, in the round of repeated birth, aging, sickness, and death. Ignorance is with us like our own shadow...we have had the basic cause of illness since beginningless time." p.26.

[5] Mark Nagler, Perspectives on Disability, Palo Alto, CA: Health Markets Research, 1990.

[6] For a study of states of health and illness that see both as an expression of the success or failure of the organism to adapt to its environment see Rene Dubos, Man Adapting, New Haven: Yale University Press, 1973 (19th printing), especially those sections on causation, pp. 323-330, patterns, pp. 231-253, and social acceptance, pp. 277-279.

[7] T. O. Ling, op.cit., p.104. The same point is made in an entry under "divine messengers" in The Encyclopedia of Eastern Philosophy and Religion, op.cit., where we read that "Old age, sickness and death are called 'divine messengers' in Buddhism. Their role is to make people aware of the suffering and impermanence of existence and urge them onto the path to liberation." p.92.

[8] R. K. Harrison, "Disease", The International Standard Bible Encyclopedia, op.cit., p.955. For an example of how the Jewish tradition is interpreted in relation to AIDS see Lord Jakobovits, "Aids: A Jewish Perspective," in Encyclopedia Judaic Year Book, 1990-1991, Jerusalem: Encyclopedia Judaica, 1992, pp. 77-81. Here Jakobovits distinguishes between "punishment: and "consequences." He denies the appropriateness of claiming that AIDS is a "divine punishment" but insists that it is a "consequence of a form of life that is morally unacceptable and utterly repugnant to Jewish tradition." p.7.

[9] Lawrence Sullivan, "Diseases and Cures" pp. 366-371 in M. Eliade, ed., Encyclopedia of Religion, NY: Macmillan, 1987, Vol. 4, p. 367. For an alternative approach to illness, one that emphasizes a holistic or psycho-somatic understanding of humanity see Gotthard Booth, The Cancer Epidemic: Shadow of the Conquest of Nature, Lewiston, NY: The Edwin Mellen Press, 1979, especially on the "Anthropological Aspects of the Cancer Epidemic," p. 131.

[10] Huston Smith, The World's Religions, San Francisco: Harper & Row, 1991.

[11] See R. K. Harrison, op. cit., p.9.

[12] Ibid., p.955. For an important comparative study see T. M. Manickam, Dharma According to Manu and Moses, Bangalore, India: Dharmaram Publications, 1977, which examines "the social and moral ideas of Dharmasastras and the Old Testament."

[13] R. A. Osbourn, "Disease" in the New Catholic Encyclopedia, New York: McGraw-Hill, 1967, Vol. IV, pp. 897-899.

[14] R. K. Harrison, op.cit., p.9.

[15] Robert Goodman, "The Disabled in the Jewish Community," New York: Task Force on the Disabled, Union of American Hebrew Congregations.

[16] I am not intending to suggest that there has been no response within either Buddhist or Christian communities to the situation of disabled persons. For something of that longer history see Whalen Lai, "Chinese Buddhist and Christian Charities: A Comparative History," Buddhist-Christian Studies, Vol. 12, 1992, p.5.

[17] See The Challenge of L"Arche, with an introduction and conclusion by Jean Vanier, Ottawa: Novalis, 1981, p.5. See also Jean Vanier, Community and Growth, London: Darton, Longman, and Todd, 1979, especially pp. 1-4, where he describes the beginning of L'Arche.

[18] The Challenge of L'Arche, op.cit., p.1.

[19] Jean Vanier, Community and Growth.

[20] Ibid.,

[21] See The Challenge of L'Arche where the communities in India, Asha Niketan in Bangalore, Calcutta, and Kerala are described.

[22] The Challenge of L'Arche,

******

**About the Author: M. Darrol Bryant** is the former chair of the Department of Religious Studies, Renison College, University of Waterloo, Waterloo, Ontario Canada. N2L 3G4. He has authored and edited thirteen books in the study of religion, lived in India with his family, and traveled extensively in the Far East and Latin America.

**Source:** Reprinted with permission from the author, M. Darrol Bryant, who wrote the article specifically for the second edition of *Perspectives on Disability*.

# Relationships with Severely Disabled People:
# The Social Construction of Humanness

Robert Bogdan,
Steven J. Taylor

**Abstract** ~ *This paper presents the perspective of nondisabled people who do not stigmatize, stereotype, and reject those with obvious disabilities. We look at how nondisabled people who are in caring and accepting relationships with severely disabled others define them. Although the disabled people in these relationships sometimes drool, soil themselves, and do not talk or walk~traits that most would consider highly undesirable~they are accepted by the nondisabled people as valued and loved human beings. We look at four dimensions of the nondisabled people's perspective that helps maintain the humanness of the other in their minds: (1) attributing thinking to the other, (2) seeing individuality in the other, (3) viewing the other as reciprocating, and (4) defining social place for the other. The paper illustrates a less deterministic approach to the study of deviance, suggests that people with what are conventionally thought of as extremely negatively valued characteristics can have moral careers that lead to inclusion rather than exclusion, and argues that the study of acceptance needs to be added to the more common focus on rejection.*

While no one can dispute the fact that people with obvious disabilities often have been cast into deviant roles in society, an exclusive focus on rejection has led many sociologists to ignore or explain away instances in which rejection and exclusion do not occur. Symbolic interactionism and labelling theory, though not by nature deterministic, often have been presented in terms of the inevitability of labeling, stereotyping, stigmatization, rejection, and exclusion of people defined as deviant, including those with recognizable disabilities. According to Goffman (1963:5), people with demonstrable stigma are seen as "not quite human" and "reduced in our minds from a whole and usual person to a tainted, discounted

one." Scott (1969:24) emphasizes how blindness is "a trait that discredits a man by spoiling both his identity and his respectability." The rejection and exclusion of deviant groups are so taken for granted that when labeled deviants are not stigmatized and rejected, such reaction is often described as "denial" and the "cult of the stigmatized" (Davis 1961; Goffman 1963).

This paper presents and seeks to understand the perspectives on nondisabled people who do not stigmatize, stereotype, and reject those with obvious disabilities. We look at how nondisabled people who are in caring and accepting relationships with severely disabled others (people with severe and profound mental retardation or multiple disabilities) define them. Although the disabled people in these relationships sometimes drool, soil themselves, do not talk or walk~traits that most would consider highly undesirable `they are accepted by the nondisabled people as valued and loved human beings.

We argue in this paper that the definition of a person is to be found in the relationship between the definer and the defined, not determined either by personal characteristics or the abstract meanings attached to the group of which the person is a part. This position illustrates a less deterministic approach to the study of deviance and suggests that people with what are conventionally thought of as extremely negatively valued characteristics can have moral careers that lead to inclusion rather than exclusion (Goffman 1961; Vail 1966) and that a sociology of acceptance needs to be added to the more common focus on rejection (Bogdan and Taylor 1987; Taylor and Bogdan 1989).

In what follows, we describe our research methods and data, discuss accepting relationships between those with severe disabilities and nondisabled people, and examine the latter's definitions of their disabled partners[1] and how they sustain their beliefs in the humanness of the disabled people.  At the end of the paper, we suggest how the relationships and perspectives described in this study might be interpreted.

## Data and Methods

For over 15 years we have conducted qualitative studies among people defined as mentally retarded and their family members, various medical and rehabilitative staff members, and others who work with or relate to people so defined (Taylor and Bogdan 1984).  Our earliest research was conducted at "state schools" and "hospitals" or developmental centers for people labeled mentally retarded, in other words, total institutions (Goffman 1961).  Ironically, in that research we studied the dehumanizing aspects of institutions, specifically, how staff defined the mentally retarded persons under their care as less than human (Bogdan et al. 1974: Taylor 1977, 1987; Taylor and Bogdan 1980).  We also constructed life histories of ex-residents of institutions to look at the experiences and perspectives of people who had been labeled "mental retarded" (Bogdan and Taylor 1982).  This research supported many of the arguments and conclusions in the literature on the stigma, stereotyping, and societal rejection of people with obvious differences.

More recently, we have studied people with disabilities in a broad range of school (Bogdan 1983; Taylor 1982) and community settings (Bogdan and Taylor 1987; Taylor, Biklen, and Knoll 1987).  As part of a team of researchers for the past four years, we have been conducting site visits to agencies

and programs that support people with severe disabilities in the community.  To date, we have visited over 20 sites throughout the country, and we continue to make visits.  Each site is selected because it has a reputation in the field of severe disabilities for providing innovative and exemplary services.  We have been especially interested in visiting agencies that support children with severe disabilities in natural, foster, and adoptive families and adults in their own homes or in small community settings.  The visits have lasted from two to four days and involve observations of homes and community settings and interviews with agency administrators and staff, family members, and, if possible, the people with disabilities themselves.  Our research design calls for us to focus on at least two people with disabilities at each site.  However, we have studied the situations of six to eight individuals at most sites.  During the visits, we often are escorted by a "tour guide," typically an agency administrator or social worker.  At several sites we have gotten the names and addresses of people served by the agency and subsequently visited them without these "guides."

Our methods are qualitative (Taylor and Bogdan 1984).  Interviews are open-ended to encourage people to talk about what is important to them:  we have thus far made roughly 1,000 pages of detailed fieldnotes, transcribed interviews, and observations.  Our analysis is inductive.  The perspectives and definitions described in this paper emerged as themes in the data.

Over the course of our visits, we have learned about aspects of the lives and situations of over 100 people with disabilities, mainly through the perspectives of the various nondisabled people who are involved with them.  This paper focuses on a subset of these relationships.  We are especially concerned here to examine the nondisabled who are in relationships with those labeled "severely disabled,"  those who cannot talk and whose humanness is often considered problematic.  We report on nondisabled people who have formed humanizing definitions or constructions of these severely disabled people.  Not all of the family members, staff members, and others who we have met and

---

[1] Throughout this paper, we use the term "partners" (as well as "person" or "people") to refer to the severely disabled people with whom nondisabled people have formed relationships.  This is our term, rather than a folk or member's term, and we use it to underscore the fact that these disabled people are members of caring and accepting relationships.  The nondisabled people refer to the disabled people in friendship ("friend"), kinship ("son", "daughter"), or pseudo-kinship ("foster son," "foster daughter") terms.  In the remainder of this paper, we describe the perspectives of nondisabled people that underlie their relationships with disabled people and sustain their belief in the other's essential humanness.  While these nondisabled people seldom use the word "humanness" in describing their partners, we use it because it captures their taken for granted view.

interviewed hold the perspectives described in this paper. Those involved with people who have severe disabilities use a broad range of characterizations and labels to define them, from clinical perspectives (Good 1984) to dehumanizing perspectives (Taylor 1977); Vail 1966) to the humanizing perspectives described here.

Our research methods do, of course, have their limitations. For instance, we spent relatively little time (from one to three hours) interviewing each of the people included in this study. This length of time does not afford the opportunity to develop a deep rapport with people or to probe many topics that emerge. However, we have spent enough time in institutions, schools, and service settings, and in interviewing people with disabilities and their families to help us recognize responses in which people simply tell us what they think we want to hear. Further, most of our data are generated from interviews and consist of verbal accounts. While we occasionally observed interactions between disabled and nondisabled people, this paper is primarily based on what people said to us and not what we observed them do.

This then is a study of how nondisabled people have presented their disabled partners to outsiders, in particular, to us. Depending upon theoretical perspective, one can view the object of this study in terms of either "accounts"~~how people "do" humanness in interaction with an outsider~~or "social meanings"~~how people define others in their lives as revealed by what they say in interviews. Our preference for a symbolic interactionism (Blumer 1969: Mean 1934) leads us toward the latter view.

## Accepting Relationships

The nondisabled described in this paper have developed accepting relationships with those who have severe and multiple disabilities. An accepting relationship is one that is longstanding and characterized by closeness and affection. In our case, those involved are people with severe and obvious disabilities and ostensibly nondisabled others. In such relationships, the deviant attribute, the disability, does not bring stigma or discredit. The humanness of the person with a disability

is maintained. The difference is not denied, but neither does it bring disgrace.

It is when these relationships are compared with staff-to-client relationships in formal organizations designed to deal with deviant populations (Higgins 1980; Mercer 1973; Scheff 1966; Schneider and Conrad 1983; Scott 1969) that they become especially interesting sociologically and important in human terms. People who have similar characteristics can be defined and interacted with quite differently from one situation to another. As Goode (1983, 1984) points out, identities are socially produced and depend upon the context in which people are viewed. The same group of people who were viewed as "not like you and me"~~essentially as nonpersons~~by institutional staff (Taylor 1977, 1987) were seen by the nondisabled in this study as "people, like us." Notwithstanding cultural definitions of mental retardation and the treatment in institutional settings of those so labeled, nondisabled people can and do form accepting relationships with those who have the most severe disabilities, and they construct positive definitions of them as human beings. While we do not claim that accepting relationships of the kind described in this study are common or that our data are statistically representative, we do claim that such alliances exist and need to be understood as one way to complicate overly deterministic conceptualizations of labeling, stigma, and rejection.

## Defining Humanness

Twenty year old Jean cannot walk or talk. Her clinical records describe her as having cerebral palsy and being profoundly retarded. Her thin, short, four- feet long, forty-pound body, atrophied legs, and disproportionately large head make her a very unusual sight. Her behavior is equally strange. She drools, rolls her head, and makes seemingly incomprehensible high pitched sounds. But this is the way an outsider would describe her, the way we described her as sociologists encountering her for the first time.

Some scholars and professionals would argue that Jean and others like her lack the characteristics of a human being (see Frohock 1986). Jean and the other severely and profoundly retarded people in our study have often been called "vegetables." People like those in the relationships we studied have been routinely excluded from the mainstream of our society and subjected to the worst kinds of treatment in institutional settings (Blatt 1970, 1973: Blatt and Kaplan 1966; Blatt, Ozolins, and McNally 1979; Taylor 1987).

To Mike and Penny Brown (these and the other names in the paper are pseudonyms), Jean's surrogate parents for the past six years, she is their loving and lovable daughter, fully part of the family and fully human. Their sentiments are similar to those expressed by the other nondisabled people in our study when discussing their disabled partners. In the remainder of this paper, we describe the perspectives of nondisabled people that underlie their relationships with disabled people and sustain their belief in the other's essential humanness. While these nondisabled people seldom use the word "humanness" in describing their partners, we use it because it captures their taken for granted view.[2] The nondisabled view the disabled people as full-fledged human beings. This stands in contrast to the dehumanizing perspectives often held by institutional staff and others in which people with severe disabilities are viewed as non-persons or sub-human (Bogdan et al. 1974: Taylor 1977, 1987). We look at four dimensions: (1) attributing thinking to the other, (2) seeing individuality in the other, (3) viewing the other as reciprocating, and (4) defining social place for the other. These perspectives enable the nondisabled people to define the disabled people as "like us" despite their behavioral and/or physical differences.

Our analysis has parallels to and builds on a small number of interactionist and

ethnomethodological studies of how people "do" normalcy or deviance (Goode 1983, 1984, 1986, forthcoming: Gubrium 1986: Lynch 2983; Pollner and McDonald-Wilker 1985). In contrast to some of these studies, we focus not on interactional practices that produce normalcy or humanness, but on the perspectives (Becker et al, 1961) associated with defining the other as human. Thus, we are interested in how these nondisabled intimates "construct" their severely disabled others.

## Attributing Thinking to the Other

The ability to think~to reason, understand, and remember~has sometimes been presented as defining humanness (Fletcher 1979). Intelligence is what separates people from animals. Many of the disabled people in the relationships we studied have been diagnosed as severely or profoundly retarded and were unable to talk. A few accomplished minimal communication through communication boards~boards with pictures or symbols on them that the person can point to as a method of communicating. In the conventions of psychological testing, many have extremely low IQs (below 20), so low in some cases that they are considered untestable. Many give few or no obvious signs of experiencing the stimuli presented to them. Most people would say that they lack the ability to think.

The assumption that people with severe and profound mental retardation and multiple disabilities cannot think initially seems plausible. Upon closer examination, whether or not these severely disabled people think is a much more complex question. The nondisabled people in this study believe and cited evidence that their disabled partners can and do think. Some people stated emphatically that they know exactly what the disabled person thinks. Others reported that, although it is impossible to tell for sure what is going on in the other person's mind, they grant them the benefit of the doubt.

What a person thinks is always subjective and never totally accessible to others (Schutz 1967). We know what other people think or experience by observing the symbols of speech, writing, gestures, or body language that are meaningful to us. The

---

[2] The nondisabled view the disabled people as full-fledged human beings. This stands in contrast to the de humanizing perspectives often held by institutional staff and others, in which people with severe disabilities are viewed as non-persons or sub-human (Bogdan et al, 1974; Taylor 1977, 1987). We are interested in perspectives and social definitions in this paper. The term "humanness" captures the underlying perspective on severely disabled people held by the nondisabled people described in this study. Whether or not people with severe disabilities "really are" human is not a matter of social definition. This is a moral and philosophical question and not a sociological one.

severely disabled people in this study were extremely limited in their abilities to move or make sounds and, hence, to produce symbols. Yet this inability did not prevent their nondisabled partners from attributing thinking to them.

According to the nondisabled people, thinking is different from communicating thought. From their perspective, a person can have full thinking capacity, be "intelligent" and reflective, but be locked in a body that is incapable of or severely limited in its capacity for communication. They hold the view that their severely disabled partners are more intelligent than they appear and that their physiology keeps them from revealing their intelligence more fully. As Gubrium (1986:40) writes of people with Alzheimer's disease, "Yet, while the victim's outward gestures and expressions may hardly provide a clue to an underlying humanity, the question remains whether the disease has stolen it all or only the capacity to express it, leaving an unmanifested, hidden mind."

Attributing thinking to a person, with or without severe disabilities is a matter of reading meaning into the gestures or movements the person makes. That people with severe disabilities may have a limited repertoire of gestures or movements does not prevent the nondisabled people described in this study from recognizing meaning in the gestures and movements they make. In a case study of communication between a deaf-blind child with severe mental retardation and her parents., Goode (forthcoming) describes how the mother, in particular, made use of nonlanguage resources and gestures to figure out what the young girl was thinking. Similarly, Gubrium (1986:45) reports how family members or caregivers around people diagnosed as having Alzheimer's disease "sharpen their perception so that whatever clues there are to the patient's inner intentions can be captured."

In our study, nondisabled people similarly emphasize the significance of minor sounds and movements in attributing intelligence and understanding to the disabled partner. One three-year-old boy we observed is completely paralyzed. The only movements

Mike makes, ones professionals consider involuntary, are slight in and out movements with his tongue and slow back and forth rolling of his blind eyes. The boy's foster parents have been told by doctors and social workers that the boy is not able to understand or communicate, that he has no intelligence. But the parents see in him movements and signs that refute this diagnosis. They describe how they can observe, when certain people come into his room, slight alterations in the speed of the tongue movements. They also claim that Mike, on occasion, moves his eyes toward the person in the room who is talking, an indication to them that he can hear and recognize others.

Many of the nondisabled people not only claimed that their disabled partners can think, but that they can understand the partners and know what they are thinking. With the limited range of gestures and sounds that many severely disabled people have, one might think such understanding would be extremely difficult. But these nondisabled people said this is not the case for them. While they all acknowledged that sometimes it was difficult to know what their partners thought, they maintained that most of the time they are able to understand them. They said they can read gestures and decipher signs of the inner state of the other that strangers cannot see. For instance, some claimed that they can understand their partners by reading their eyes.

Other nondisabled people said intuition is the source of understanding people with severe disabilities and what they think. As the parent of a profoundly retarded young woman explained when asked how she knows her daughter understands: "It's just something inside me....I really believe that deep in my soul." Goode (forthcoming) reports that parents and others in intimate relationships with those having severe disabilities often "just know" what the other is thinking or feeling.

Finally, some nondisabled people understand their severely disabled partners by putting themselves in their position or "taking the role of the other." That is, they imagine what they would feel in the same particular situations. One foster mother said that she makes decisions about how to treat her foster daughter by pretending she is the daughter and experiencing her actions. She reported experiencing, vicariously, the pleasure of being taken care of by looking at what she is doing for her foster child from her perspective. While people acknowledged the likelihood that their assessments of the other's inner life often may be flawed, they believed that the process brings them closer to their partners and leads them to a better understanding of what they are experiencing.

The nondisabled's belief in the capacity of their severely retarded friends and loved ones' ability to think often runs counter to professional and clinical assessments (Goode 1983: Pollner and McDonald-Wikler 1985). In some cases, doctors have told them that their partners are brain dead. The nondisabled people reported that they have often been bombarded with specialists' judgments that, in their eyes, underestimate their partners' capabilities. They argue that the specialists are not privy to the long day-by-day, hour-by-hour observation of the person. Behaviors that they cite as indicating understanding do not occur with such frequency that the professional is likely to see them. Further, unlike the nondisabled partners in these relationships, professionals are not intimately familiar with their clients and therefore are not attuned to the subtleties of their sounds and gestures.

What also bolsters nondisabled people's belief that the professionals are wrong in their assessments of intelligence are numerous examples of past professional judgments that are wrong. Some have watched their disabled companions live through predictions of early death. Others have cared for their disabled partners at home in spite of advice that such living arrangements would not be possible and that the person was destined to live his or her life in an institution. As a foster parent of a person who was profoundly retarded told us, "They [the physicians] said she'd have to be in an institution. I said to myself 'that's all I need to hear. We'll see about that,' I knew I could take care of Amy and I have." In one family with one profoundly retarded and two severely retarded adolescents, the parents told us that their foster children have been excluded from school because professionals had judged them

incapable of attending. Immediately after they were released from an institution and came to live with the family, they began attending regular school.

Whether or not people with such severe disabilities can understand and think as other people, professional assessments stand no greater claim to truth than the assessments of the nondisabled people reported in this study. While professional assessments may carry more authority or political weight in determining the life circumstances of people with disabilities, we do not consider them more accurate in an absolute sense or any less a reflection of social definitions and perspectives. Goode (forthcoming) critiques Pollner and McDonald-Wikler's (1985) account of a family's "delusional" beliefs in the competence of a severely retarded child—what they refer to as the "social construction of unreality"—and argues that clinical and medical bodies of knowledge cannot be used to provide a standard by which to judge the legitimacy of family belief systems. Clinical perspectives are based on different ways of knowing and seeing than the perspectives of people involved in intimate relationships with those who have disabilities. Further, clinical diagnoses are often proven wrong based on their own criteria. For example, case histories have come to light of people diagnosed at an early age as having no mental capacity who later are found to have normal intelligence when provided with communication devices (Crossley and McDonald 1980: Hay 1982).

### Seeing Individuality in the Other

Sitting in the living room of a foster home for a severely retarded young woman who had spent the majority of her life in an institution, the father described her as having very pretty hair and a great sense of humor and as being a very appreciative person. When this young woman arrived home from school she was dressed in a new stylish outfit complete with Reebok running shoes. The father told us how the girl, Monica, loved to get dressed in new clothes and how the color she had on was her favorite. He told us how her hairstyle had changed since coming to live with his family from an institutional bowl cut to its present high fashion form. Monica had a communication board on her lap. She moved her hand, placing it in the vicinity of the picture of a radio. He said, "OK, I have to start dinner and then I'll get the radio. We are having your favorite, chicken." As an aside he said, "Monica loves to listen to music and she gets very excited when she can smell something that she likes cooking."

A second way the nondisabled people in our study constructed their severely disabled companions as persons was to see them as individuals. The people we have been studying use perspectives toward their disabled others that define them as distinct, unique individuals with particular and specific characteristics that set them apart from others. Monica's foster father, for instance, saw her as having a distinct personality, particular likes and dislikes, normal feelings and motives, a distinct background—in short a clear identity. He and others we interviewed managed the disabled person's appearances to conform to such definitions.

*Personality.* The nondisabled people used a large variety of words to describe these distinctive qualities. Adjectives such as silly, fun, shy, live-wire, bright, appreciative, nice, likable, calm, active, kind, gentle, wonderful, amusing, pleasant, and good company fall under the broad category of "personality." Most of the words are resoundingly positive. Occasionally one might hear phrases like "He's a handful" or "She gave me a lot of trouble yesterday," indicating a more critical evaluation but not precluding the attribution of a distinctive personal quality.

Many nondisabled people in our study have nicknames for their disabled partners. Often the nicknames are given to capture something unique about the individual's personality. One man who has developed a close relationship with an elderly disabled man who had spent over 50 years of his life in an institution calls the older man "Mr. Rudy." Mr. Rudy is blind, unable to talk, and only walks by leaning on a wall. The nondisabled man said he couldn't explain how he came up with the nickname but believes that "Mr. Rudy" seems to go with the man's personality. He says that Mr. Rudy has been through a lot in his life, but "He made it and still has it together." For him the nickname conveys a sense of dignity.

None of these people use technical phrases like "profoundly retarded" or "developmentally disabled" to refer to their friend or loved one. Some feel that clinical designations are too impersonal and do not tell much about the person's character and personality. They said they believe that clinical labels define the person in terms of deficits rather than positive characteristics, a vantage point they prefer not to take. Such labels can strip the person of his or her unique personality. By using a rich repertoire of adjectives and defining the person in specific personal terms, these people maintain the humanness of their severely disabled partner.

*Likes  and  Dislikes.*  Another dimension of individuality involves being discriminating, having tastes and preferences. As illustrated in the remarks Monica's father made in describing her, the nondisabled people in this study know their partner's specific likes and dislikes and discuss them willingly. While people with severe disabilities may be severely limited in their activities and hence have few areas in which they can express preferences, the nondisabled people present them as having definite preferences about the things they do experience (Goode forthcoming). Music, food, colors, and certain other people are commonly cited as areas in which people with severe disabilities have preferences. Monica loves to listen to music, has a favorite color, and prefers to eat chicken. In one home with three disabled young people, two young men and a young woman, nondisabled family members explained that one person prefers classical music, a second likes rock, and a third does not like music. In another case, a woman who has a caring relationship with a 43-year old severely retarded woman described the woman as enjoying camping, sailing, and canoeing.

By viewing the disabled person as having likes and dislikes, the nondisabled partner not only confirms the other's individuality, but often reinforces the bonds between them as well. Comments such as "She likes to eat everything we do!" and "He loves the banana bread I make" indicate that the nondisabled people see themselves sharing things in common with these disabled others.

*Feelings and Motives.* In everyday interaction, we attribute feelings and motives to other people's words and acts. Rather than defining the actions of the disabled people as symptomatic of an underlying pathological state (Taylor 1977), the nondisabled people in our study define them in terms of normal motives and feelings. A foster mother told the following story about her foster child, Mike:

> Wednesday night he started to cry continuously. I got real upset and called my husband and told him to come right back. As soon as he got here he talked to Mike like he only can: "Hey bubba, what's wrong with you." Mike stopped crying and I held him but then he started up again. My husband told me to give him back and he sat in the rocker and talked with Mike and he stopped again. But the minute he got ready to lay him down he started up again...so he [Mike] has got to know something. How would he know to cry again, that we were going to lay him down?

As the above quotation illustrates, Mike's foster mother, as did the others we have studied, takes outward signs~crying, laughing, sighing~as indicators that the severely disabled person has the same feelings and motives as other people. When crying, laughing, and sighing are in conjunction with particular events, the events are said to have provoked them, thus revealing to the interpreters that the person is in touch with his or her surroundings and is expressing human emotion in familiar, shared-in-common ways.

*Life Histories.* One aspect of seeing another person as an individual is constructing a biography of the person that explains who he or she is today. In interviews, nondisabled people told stories of the background experiences of the disabled person. The individuality and the humanness of the disabled people are communicated through biographies that are often unique and detailed.

Life histories are sometimes told in two parts. The first has to do with the disabled person's experiences prior to the formation of the relationship. Especially when the person has been institutionalized, the nondisabled person described the associated suffering and deprivation. In recounting these experiences, the nondisabled person often put himself or herself in the disabled person's position and imagined what such experiences would have been like. In some cases, the people with disabilities are presented as survivors or even heroes for having undergone such experiences. The second part of the life history relates to improvement in the lives of the disabled people, especially when they are living with the nondisabled person telling the story. For example, the nondisabled partners often pointed to changes in weight, behavior, skills, personality, and appearance.

*Managing Appearances.* The nondisabled people in this study not only see individuality in the disabled partner, but actively create it by managing the other's physical appearance to downplay visible differences and accentuate individual identities. They sought to present the person to outsiders and to themselves as normal. By paying attention to clothing style and color and being attentive to other aspects of the person's appearance (hair style, nails, makeup, cleanliness, beards for men), they helped construct an identity consistent with their definitions of the person. In the case of Monica, described earlier, her foster parents selected clothes and a hair style that made her look attractive. The management of the disabled person's appearance often conforms to gender stereotypes. Many foster parents of young girls dress them in frilly, feminine dresses, complete with bows in their hair. Thus, the person is given not only an identity as an "individual," but also as a "little girl," "teenage boy," "middle-aged woman," "elderly man," and so on.

To an outsider, many of the disabled people in this study have obvious physical abnormalities, including large heads, frail bodies, bent limbs, and curved spines. However, the nondisabled people seldom mention these characteristics except when a particular condition is causing the disabled person difficulties or when recounting negative reactions to the person's abnormalities by an outsider.

Nondisabled people often expressed pride in the disabled person's appearance. For disabled people who have been institutionalized, many of their partners commented on the significant changes in their looks since leaving an institution. The change had been from institutional clothing, unstyled haircuts, dirty skin, and sloppiness to a physical self more nearly like that of other people. The transformation is symbolic of the disabled person's metamorphosis from dehumanized institutional inmate to family member or friend.

In dramatic contrast to total institutions that strip people of their identities (Goffman 1961), the nondisabled people in this study see and assist in the accomplishment of individual identities for the people with disabilities with whom they are involved. Personality, likes and dislikes, feelings and motives, a biography, and appearance are all individualized aspects of a person. By highlighting the severely disabled person's personal attributes, the nondisabled people in our study accept and include their partners rather than rejecting and excluding them from the mundane rounds of normal, everyday life.

**Viewing the Other as Reciprocating**

In order for somebody to be thought of as a fully competent participant in a relationship, they have to be seen as contributing something to the partnership. Exchange theorists (Blau 1964) have pointed to the tendency for close relationships to be reciprocal with both parties defining the relationship as receiving as much as they give. According to exchange theorists, people with equal resources (some combination of, for instance, social worth, talent, material resources) tend to form enduring relationships. When one person does not have much to offer, the relationship suffers from disequilibrium, which is experienced as stressful. Under these conditions the weaker partner is diminished in the other's eyes. Such formulations narrowly define the nature of the commodities exchanged and exclude the type of alliances discussed in this paper.

From the outside it might appear that the relationships in our study are one-sided (the nondisabled person giving all and receiving nothing) and, using the logic of exchange theory, doomed to stress and disintegration. After all, severely disabled people appear to have so few resources, so

little of social value, talent, and material resources to exchange. This is not the way the nondisabled people in our study saw their relationships or their disabled others. They defined the person with a disability as reciprocating or giving back something important.

Joe Bain, who, along with his wife and two children, shares his home with three severely disabled young men and a young woman, told why he lives with disabled people: "I am not doing what I'm doing for their benefit. They may benefit from it but I like it. It's fun. I see them as just people I enjoy to be with."

While not all of the people in this study are so exuberant, most mentioned deriving pleasure from their relationships because they like the disabled people and enjoy being with them. For some the disabled person is an important source of companionship. One person said that she does not know what she would do if she did not have her disabled loved one to take care of and to keep her company. A number of people mentioned how disabled people expanded their lives by causing them to meet new people and learn about aspects of their communities they had not been in touch with previously.

Companionship and new social relations are perhaps the most concrete of the benefits discussed. Some nondisabled people were philosophical about what the person with a disability gives them. A few said they believe that the relationships with severely disabled others have made them better people. A mother of a six-year-old boy who is severely retarded and was hydrocephalic said, "He has taught me to accept people for how they are. No matter how limited you are, that everyone has within them a quality that makes them special." Another parent, this time a father whose son is severely retarded and has spina bifida, stated, "He made all of our children and ourselves much more caring, much more at ease with all handicapped people."

Clearly the nondisabled we spoke to felt that they know their severely disabled partners intimately. They said they understand them and know their particular likes and dislikes. Intimately knowing the individual disabled person gives the nondisabled person a feeling of being "special." According to one person who has a caring relationship with a profoundly retarded child, "I think we have a very special relationship in that very often we're together alone. I feel like I'm the one person who knows him better than anyone else. I feel like I can tell if he's sick or what he needs better than anybody else."

Another benefit that some nondisabled people reported from their relationships is a sense of accomplishment in contributing to the disabled other's well-being and personal growth. As with personal appearance, the nondisabled people saw positive changes occurring in their disabled loved one or friend. Although the progress might be considered minor by outsiders, something they would not notice or understand, for the nondisabled person in the relationship it is significant. For example, one person who is in a relationship with a nonverbal severely retarded woman described how she had told the woman, Susan, to brush her teeth. Commenting on how, when Susan came out of the bathroom she was holding a toothbrush and tooth paste with the cap stuck, she explained. "That is asking for help: that is communication. She never would have done that five years ago: she wouldn't have even gone for the toothbrush and toothpaste!" Regarding a severely disabled woman, another woman said, "She laughs, she didn't do that before. People might think it's minor, but with Jane progress is slow."

## Defining Social Place for the Other

People belong to groups and are part of social networks, organizations, and institutions. Within these social groups, individuals are given and assume particular social places. The concept of role is often used to describe a person's social place. But social place is not merely a matter of playing a role. It is also a matter of being defined as an integral part of the group or social unit. Roles are particularized for each social unit and personalized by each occupant; there is a personal dimension to roles. Through playing particular social roles, social actors are defined as being part of the human community, "one of us."

The nondisabled in this study defined their disabled partners as full and important members of their social units; hence, they create a social place for them. First of all, they incorporate the disabled people in their definitions of their groups or social networks. While some of the relationships discussed in this paper involve two people, one disabled and one not, most involve people who have disabilities within families. In families, in particular, the disabled person is likely to be viewed as a central member. The person is not simply son or daughter, but "my son" or "my daughter." A foster parent of several children with severe disabilities, who could not have children of his own, said, "This gives us our family." In another foster family, the mother described how her natural son sees the foster child: "He's the little brother he never had." In short, the family would not be the same family without the disabled person.

Second, the nondisabled people defined a part for the disabled people in the rituals and routines of the social unit. In any group, members develop intertwined patterns of living. For instance, members of a family coordinate getting up, taking showers, getting breakfast, accompanying each other on important occasions, preparing for holidays, going on vacation, having birthday parties, and many other joint activities. The inclusion of a severely disabled person in a family's or primary group's routines and rituals, in its private times and public displays, acknowledges to the members and to others that he or she is one of them. As a foster parent of two people with severe disabilities explained, "We bring them to all family gatherings. My sister said we could hire a babysitter and leave all of the foster children home. We said that where we go, they go.... The family accepts them as part of the family." When, because of hospitalization or other reasons, people with disabilities are missing from the social unit, other members talk about how they are missed and how things are not the same without them. The person's absence interferes with normal family routines.

Primary groups belong to larger networks of human relations. When severely disabled people are integrated into primary groups, they have a vehicle to be included in the social web that defines community membership.  The mother of a profoundly retarded six-year-old girl who had spent most of her life in an institution said, "We take her to church, the grocery store, and everywhere we go."

## Conclusion

The humanizing sentiments underlying the relationships described in this paper are not unique to unions between nondisabled and severely disabled people. They are the same sentiments described in the phenomenological literature as sustaining the perception of the social world as intersubjective (Husserl 1961; Psathas 1973; Schutz 1967).  As Jehensen (1973:221) writes, "As an actor on the social scene, I can recognize my fellow-man not as 'something,' but as 'someone,' a 'someone like me'."  So, too, do the nondisabled people in this study recognize people with severe disabilities as "someone like me," that is, as having the essential qualities to be defined as a fellow human being.  Disability is viewed as secondary to the person's humanness.  What makes the perspectives described in this paper striking is that they are directed toward people who have often been denied their humanity by being defined as non-persons (Fletcher 1979).

An understanding of how nondisabled people construct the humanness of severely disabled people can inform ethical debates surrounding the treatment of infants, children, and adults with severe disabilities (The Association for Persons with Severe Handicaps 1984).  Whether or not people with severe disabilities will be treated as human beings or persons is not a matter of their physical or mental condition.  It is a matter of definition.  We can show that they, and we, are human by including, by accepting them rather than separating them out.

It is easy to dismiss the perspectives described in this paper.  One might argue that the nondisabled people are deceiving or deluding themselves when they attribute these qualities and characteristics to people with severe and profound mental retardation and other disabilities.  For example, some might consider the belief that such people can and do think as outlandish.  Yet it is just as likely that those who dehumanize people with severe disabilities, dispute their human agency, and define them an non-persons are deceiving themselves.  After all, no one can ever prove that anyone else is "someone like me" or that the assumption of common experience is anything but an illusion.  What and who others, as well as we, are depends upon our relationships with them and what we choose to make of us.

********

## REFERENCES

**The Association for Persons with Severe Handicaps**        1984 Legal, Economic, Psychological, and Moral Considerations on the Practice of Withholding Medical Treatment from Infants with Congenital Defects. Seattle, WA: The Association for Persons with Severe Handicaps.

**A.Becker, Howard S., Blanche Geer, Everett C. Hughes, and Anselm Strauss**        1961 Boys in White:  Student Culture in Medical School. Chicago: University of Chicago Press.

**Blatt, Burton.**        1973        Souls in Extremis. Boston, MA: Allyn and Bacon.
                1970        Exodus from Pandemonium. Boston, MA: Allyn and Bacon.

**Blatt, Burton, Andrejs Ozolins, and Joe McNally** 1979 The Family Papers. New York:  Longman.

**Blatt, Burton and Fred Kaplan** 1966  Christmas in Purgatory, Boston, MA: Allyn and Bacon.

**Blau, Peter** 1964 Exchange and Power in Social Life. New York: Wiley.

**Blumer, Herbert** 1969 Symbolic Interactionism. Englewood Cliffs, NJ: Prentice-Hall.

**Bogdan, Robert** 1983        "Does mainstreaming work? is a silly question."   Phi Delta Kappa 64:427:28.

**Bogdan, Robert and Steven J. Taylor** 1982 Inside Out: The Social Meaning of Mental Retardation. Toronto, Ont.: University of Toronto Press.
                1987 "Toward a sociology of acceptance: the other side of the study of deviance."  Social Policy, 18:34-39.

**Bogdan, Robert, Steven Taylor, Bernard deGrandpre, and Sandra Haynes**        1974        "Let them eat programs:  attendants' perspectives and programming on wards in state schools." Journal of Health and Social Behavior 15:142-51.

**Crossley, Rosemary and Ann McDonald** 1980 Annie's Coming Out. New York: Penguin

**Davis, Fred**        1961        "Deviance disavowal: the management of strained interaction by the visibly handicapped." Social Problems 9:120-32.

**Edgerton, Robert** 1967 The Cloak of Competence. Berkeley, CA: University of California Press.

**Fletcher, Joseph F.** 1979 Humanhood: Essays in Biomedical Ethics. lBuffalo, NY: Prometheus Books.

**Frohock, Fred M.** 1986 Sepcial Care. Chicago: University of Chicago Press.

**Goffman, Erving** 1963 Stigma. Englewood Cliffs, NJ: Prentice Hall.

1961 Asylums. Garden City, NY: Doubleday.

**Goode, David A.** 1983 "Who is Bobby? Ideology and method in the discovery of a Down's Syndrome person's competence." Pp. 237-55 in Gary Kielhofner (ed.), Health through Occupation. Philadelphia, PA: Davis.

1984 "Socially produced identities, intimacy and the problem of competence among the retarded." Pp. 228-48 in Sally Timlinson and Len Barton (eds), Special Education and Social Interests. London: Croom-Helm.

1986 "Kids, culture and innocents." Human Studies 9:83-106.

Forthcoming "On understanding without words: communication between a deaf-blind child and her coming parents." Human Studies.

Gubrium, Jaber F.

1986 "The social preservation of mind: the Alzheimer's Disease experience." Symbolic Interaction 9:37-51.

**Hay, David** 1982 "My story." Mental Retardation 32:ll-16.

**Higgins, Paul** 1980 Outsiders in a Hearing World. Berkeley, CA: Sage.

**Husserl, Edmund** 1962 Ideas. New York: Collier.

**Jehenson, Roger** 1973 "A phenomenological approach to the study of the formal organization." Pp. 219-50 in George Psathas (ed.). Phenomenological Sociology. New York: John Wiley.

**Lemert, Edwin** 1951 Social Pathology. New York: McGraw Hill.

**Lynch, Michael** 1983 "Accommodation practices: vernacular treatments of madness." Social Problems 31:152-64.

**Mead, George Herbvert** 1934 Mind, Self and Society. Chicago: University of Chicago Press.

**Mercer, Jane** 1973 Labeling the Mentally Retarded. Berkeley, CA: University of California Press.

**Pollner, Melvin and Lynn McDonald-Wikler** 1985 "The social construction of unreality: a case study of a family's attribution of competence to a severely retarded child." Family Process 24:241-54.

**Psathas. George, ed.** 1973 Phenomenological Sociology. New York: John Wiley.

**Scheff, Thomas** 1966 Being Mentally Ill. Chicago: Aldine.

**Schneider, Joseph W. and Peter Conrad** 1983 Having Epilepsy: The Experience and Control of Illness. Philadelphia, PA: Temple University Press.

**Schur, Edwin** 1971 Labeling Deviant Behavior. New York: Harper & Row.

**Schutz, Alfred** 1967 The Phenomenology of the Social World. Evnston, IL: Northwestern University Press.

**Scott, Robert** 1969 The Making of Blind Men. New York: Russell Sage Foundation.

**Taylor, Steven J.** 1977 The Custodians: Attendants and Their Work at State Institutions for the Mentally Retarded. An Arbor, MI: University Microfilms.

1982 "From segregation to integration." The Journal of The Association for the Severely Handicapped 8:42-49.

1987 "Observing abuse: professional ethics and personal morality in field research." Qualitative Sociology 10:288-302.

**Taylor, Steven J., Doublas Biklen, and James Knoll, eds.** 1987 Community Integration for People with Severe Disabilities. New York: Teachers College Press.

**Taylor, Steven J. and Robert Bogdan** 1980 Defending illusions: the institution's struggle for survival." Human Organization 39:209-18.

1984 Introduction to Qualitative Research Methods. 2nd ed. New York: John Wiley.

1989 "On accepting relationships between people with mental retardation and non-disabled people: towards an understanding of acceptance." Disability, Handicap & Society 4:21-36.

**Vail, Dvid** 1986 Dehumnization and the Institutional Career. Springfield, IL: Charles C. Thomas.

******

**Source:** Reprinted with permission from *Social Problems,* Vol. 36, No. 2, April 1989. Published by the Society for the Study of Social Problems, Inc.

# Women with Disabilities:  Two Handicaps Plus

William John Hanna
Betsy Rogovsky

**Abstract~~**In the USA, women with disabilities participate less in social relations, educational institutions, and the labor force than expected on the basis of male/female and male non-disabled/disabled disparities.  The resulting isolation appears to be linked with attributional, nurturance and attractiveness norms within the American socio-cultural system as well as to self-image and role selection components of the women's self-concepts.  Participation, the socio-cultural system, and the self-concepts are viewed schematically as elements in a triangular relationship of circular causation.

## INTRODUCTION

I'm a disabled woman now.  Two strikes.  I'm almost out?

You have to find the able parts of the disabled woman. [1]

Some years ago, we happened to be casually talking about the situation of women with long-term physical impairments.  The conversation led us to look for literature on the subject, but to our surprise most of the scholarly and popular literature on disability did not differentiate between men and women.  Furthermore, much of this literature was based upon studies of men.  Yet it seemed to us, on the basis of our personal observations, that there were differences between males and females who were disabled.  As but one example, in public situations we noticed more men with visible disabilities; yet we knew that there were at least as many women who were disabled.  We decided to explore this matter further.

We found that the approximately 20 million American women with visual, hearing, mobility and other physical impairments have been of relatively little policy concern or scholarly interest.  Policy in the USA pertaining to disability has recently gained

attention as the result of the Fair Housing Act of 1988 and the Disability Act of 1990.  Scholarly and other writing about women with disabilities only began to appear with any frequency in the 1980's.  Despite several recent scholarly publications (e.g. Fine & Asch, 1988; Deegan & Brooks, 1985) and participant observer anthologies (e.g. Saxton & Howe, 1987; Browne et al., 1985), Ellien's 1984 assessment still largely holds: "...the needs of disabled women have been largely unidentified and unexplored..." (1983-84, p. 10).

We decided to embark upon a program of research.  Our first agenda item was determining the extent to which the situations of disabled males and females were in fact different.  There are, of course, many approaches to this question; our choice was to focus on participation in the socio-economic system.  Our evidence indicates that women are more isolated from the larger system than men.  Our candidate explanations came from two further personal observations; the rather negative or unflattering views people often express about women (and people generally) with disabilities, and the seemingly passive, accepting poor self-concept held by many of these women.  Our research suggests that the low average participation rate of disabled women is linked with the broader socio-cultural system (and, derivatively, with the women's self-concept).  Three characteristics of our subject population are relevant: (1) they are women, (2) they have a physical disability, *plus* (3) they are women with a disability, that is, there are special consequences of the intersection of being female and disabled.

The framework guiding our study is in the form of a triangle, including 'participation,' 'socio-culture,' and 'self-concept.' (Needless to say, this simplifying framework excludes many other factors that must eventually be included if a full understanding of the situation of women with disabilities is to be achieved.)  Initially, we saw socio-culture as the driving force that led to low participation and poor self-concept. However, our revised view is that each of these three factors contributes to, sustains, and is influenced by the others. Thus we believe that a schematic portrayal of these factors should connect each to the other with bi-directional arrows.

## METHODS

We proceed as follows. First, we look at participation drawing upon two US national survey samples. Second, we focus on the socio-cultural system and the self-concepts of women with disabilities using a series of specially conducted in-depth interviews and survey questionnaires.

To study participation, we draw upon a US Census Bureau's (1984) special survey that included a series of questions (a module ) about health and disability, and a Louis Harris and Associates (1986) survey of disabled Americans. The Census Bureau's survey included 18,733 people, of whom 1748 were women with at least some long-term limitation. Harris interviewed 1000 people, 553 of them female.

We focus especially upon the responses of 40-49 year olds because people in this age category are less impacted on a gender-specific basis by childbirth and longevity. It should be noted that the relationship between social class and disability is especially strong among people of middle age (Heyman et al.,1990, p. 169). The numbers in our focal age category are: for the Census Bureau survey, 1877, of whom 219 are women with disabilities, and for the Harris disability survey, 126, including 61 females.

Using the Census data, we compare women who have disabilities with the three other age/disability categories:  non-disabled men, non-disabled women and men with disabilities. To judge whether gender and disability fully account for the situation of women with disabilities, we calculate an expected figure for women with disabilities in the following way: first, we judge the gender factor by calculating a female/male ratio drawing only upon data for those who are non-disabled; and second, we establish a disability norm by calculating a disabled/non-disabled

ratio drawing upon data for men. Our presumption is that if the actual figure for women with disabilities is lower than the expected one (i.e. less participatory), then the gap between the actual and the expected figures are not fully explained by gender and disability~and therefore need further exploration.

To learn about community and individual attitudes, we draw especially upon our studies of accessibility in Montgomery County, Maryland that included 30 non-random interviews with disabled adults and 102 telephone interviews with providers (Hanna et al., 1980), a set of 40 interviews lasting one to two hours we conducted with disabled women who volunteered to be interviewed (half with at least some college education, giving us some exposure to women with different life courses) in the Washington, DC metropolitan area, and questionnaire-based studies of University of Maryland undergraduate students' disability-focused free associations (N=181) and attributions (N=130) (Hanna, 1986).

Some of the contrasts we discover are statistically significant, whereas others are not. However, the *direction* of the results is consistent. It is the overall pattern which we find impressive~and suggestive of the situation of women with disabilities. Because the emphasis at this stage of our work is on general patterns, we cannot consider the undoubtedly rich variations based upon such factors as degree and visibility of impairment, social class, ethnic group membership and sexual orientation.

### Socio-economic Participation

Most women with disabilities are clearly *not* full or equitable participants in American society. Saxton & Howe (1987, p. 2) refer to "isolation" as one of the serious aspects of "the oppression of disability." In this section, we review some of our survey evidence.

### Social relations.  Women with disabilities appear to be relatively isolated at various levels of the social system. This may in part be due to 'shunning' by others, and it may reflect a general tendency of women with

health problems to withdraw more than men do. Morris (1989, p. 106) writes, "There can often be barriers to forming new friendships, mainly stemming from people's ignorance and fear of disability but also from our own feelings and lack of confidence."

Our exploration begins by looking at marriage. Consider first whether a person has ever been married. The Census data reveal that women with disabilities constitute the categoric group most likely to have remained single. These are the figures: male non-disabled, 4%; female non-disabled, 3%; male disabled, 4%; and female disabled, 7% (the expected figure is 3%, less than half the actual one). Suggestively, Harris reports that about half of the unmarried female respondents in his sample considered their disability to be an obstacle to "opportunities to marry." Turning now to those people who were or are married but not widowed, there is another indication of isolation. Disabled women are more likely to be divorced, separated, or married living apart than are those in the comparison groups. The figures are as follows: Male non-disabled, 12%; female non-disabled 15%; disabled male, 11%; female disabled, 25% (expected, 14%). Thus women with disabilities are less likely to marry and more likely to have a marriage effectively end than are their counterparts.

A wide variety of other evidence lends support to this picture of greater social isolation. For instance, women with disabilities are less likely to have children and to have intimate relationships. Suggestively, marriage and other social ties have repeatedly been found to be associated with good health. Thus disability may lead to isolation, but isolation may also contribute to disability.

Social isolation is reinforced by the lack of spatial mobility due to one's impairment, the handicapping deficiencies of the public transportation system, and the lack of funds to overcome private transportation barriers. Of course, people with mobility impairments are challenged by this problem; but it is equally challenging for those with a variety of other disabilities.

*Education.* Data on educational achievement reveal that people with a disability face severe handicaps created by educational institutions.

Among non-disabled males, only 16% did not graduate high school; 47% attended college for at least some period of time. For able bodied females, the figures are 18% and 38%. However, for males with disabilities, 33% did not graduate high school, and only 34% attended college. And for females with disabilities, the figures are 42% and 25%. The expected figures for women with disabilities are 37% and 28%, again suggesting that gender and disability alone do not fully account for the situation of women with disabilities.

These statistics are about years of formal education; they do not begin to reveal the differences in the educational experiences (or payoffs) due to the special needs and challenges faced by those with disabilities, combined with the discrimination practiced by some educational service providers. A satisfactory understanding of the impact of education on women with disabilities should compare the content of education offered to non-disabled and disabled males and females. Here, we can only suggest that differences exist which may have an important impact upon knowledge, skills, and self-esteem. One example: sex education for women with disabilities is vital, and it should include information about sexuality in relationship to the disability. Yet special education students are not always included in hygiene (Hannaford, 1985, p. 78) or sex education classes, and the material in the classes rarely incorporates information about disabilities (Ellien, 1983-84, p. 10).

*Labor force.* The above contrasts are reinforced by an examination of labor force data. The Census Bureau's survey reveals that 40-49 year old women with disabilities have a less-than-expected rate of labor force participation. Among the non-disabled, fully 91% of our males had a job compared with 65% of the females; for those with disabilities, the figures are 73% and 43% (expected, 52%). The disparity across gender and disability is further revealed by an examination of full-time employment. Here, the figures are as follows: male non-disabled, 88%; female non-disabled, 49%; male disabled, 69%; and female disabled, 33% (expected, 38%). Education does not overcome the job gap. At every level of education, including the highest, we find that women with disabilities have unexpectedly low participation rates.

Disabled men begin with some programmatic (and even nationalistic) advantages. 'Hire a vet' campaigns may help disabled veterans and other disabled males, but they are *not* likely to help disabled females (even though some are veterans). In addition, job related disabilities (more common among men) increase the chances of satisfactory rehabilitation and *re*-employment (see Altman, 1985).

Many impairment-related factors impact employment. For instance, some employers do not want to have a disabled employee because of the tangible costs (e.g. building entry ramps) and symbolic ones (e.g. thinking that disabled woman equals disabled business). Also, employers might not understand an impairment and consequently magnify or erroneously view its impact upon performance.

Not surprisingly, differences in employment are reflected in income. For people in their forties, the mean monthly income of non-disabled males is $2,330; and for non-disabled females, it is $1,744. But for those with disabilities, the figures are $843 for males and $578 for females (expected, $631). A similar pattern is revealed when only looking at full-time workers.

### Socio~culture

What's going on here? Why is the participation of disabled women, on the average, so low compared with their non-disabled and male counterparts? To borrow a Parsons (1951, p. 431) duality, disability is defined physically *and* socio-culturally. Disabled women and men are, of course, limited physically and handicapped by such barriers as curbs and meetings not interpreted. Said a campus student, "I don't have too much to do with campus life. When I think of the energy it takes to get to the Student Union, I usually opt out. It's physically draining." Extra time and energy is also required in many interpersonal relationships involving one or more people with physical limitations.

Socio-cultural factors are also important. Saxton & Howe (1987, p. 2) observe, "it is not possible to separate the cold facts, the day-to-day reality of living with a disability from the cultural and social obstacles disabled women must face, including outright and indirect discrimination in education and employment." Our focus here is upon the socio-cultural factors.

We suggest that three aspects of the prevailing socio-cultural system are especially relevant to an understanding of the situation of women with disabilities: sexism, able-ism (disabilityism), and a third (our 'plus factor') that appears to relate in particular to women with disabilities. We think that these three factors impact social, educational and labor force participation (and are in turn impacted by low levels of participation).

The consequences of these factors is stigma (Goffman, 1963)), that "special and insidious kind of social categorization" (Coleman, 1986, p. 219) carrying with it "devalued status" (Becker & Arnold, 1986, p. 49). Of course, stigma shapes the behavior of non-stigmatized *and* stigmatized people, and it gives each a reason to avoid the other.

Women in the USA (and elsewhere) have devalued status, and the same is true of people with physical disabilities. Indeed, there are similarities between the tow. As Saxton & Howe (1987, P. xii) write, "there are many parallels between the oppression of women and of disabled people. Both groups are seen by others as passive, dependent, and childlike; their skills are minimized and their contributions to society undervalued." Our surveys of university students clearly reveal that women with disabilities are in general viewed negatively, e.g. as passive and socially isolated. They are said to be sick and feeble, old and gray, childless and sexless. The comparisons with non-disabled women and disabled men are dramatic.

To explore why disabled *women* are apparently more stigmatized than disabled men~~even more than sexism and able-ism would lead one to predict~~we turn to the female/disabled 'plus factor.' We suggest that three elements may be involved: the social inappropriateness of the disability's cause, impaired nurturance, and despoiled beauty.

*Disability attributions.* When a disability is observed, it is common for the observer to wonder about its cause. In general, there tends to be a negative tone to disability attributions. Clearly, the eighteenth century view that "the wages of sin were disease and death" (Turner, 1985, p. 219) still influences our own perspectives. And in particular, there are gender differences in these attributions. Our evidence suggests that observers tend to attribute the disabilities of males to external situational factors, whereas attributions with regard to the disabilities of females are more likely to focus on the person herself. There may be a link between this pattern and 'just world' thinking, i.e. that some people (especially women?) get what they deserve (see Lerner, 1970).

In one study, we asked 130 undergraduate students to provide an explanation for the condition of an imagined 45 year old man who uses a wheel chair. The responses often dealt with injuries at war, and sometimes work was mentioned. Accident associations were either general or concerned automobiles or sports. By contrast, no student provided military or job explanations for a similarly aged female, and only one mentioned a sports accident. (Men under 50 do suffer more injuries than do women).

One explanation was offered for female wheelchair-users significantly more frequently that it was for their male counterparts: disease (or illness). This is especially important because some diseases are contagious, and degree of contagiousness is associated with negative reactions and avoidance behavior (Safilios-Rothschild, 1970; Sontag, 1978). As for accidents, general and automobile-related ones were frequently mentioned. But in contrast to the attributions for males, seemingly careless accidents (e.g. 'falling down stairs') were mentioned by a number of respondents as causes of females' accidents.

*Nurturance.* One component of sexism in American society is the expectation that women will be social caretakers, whereas men will do the 'work' (implicitly, paid work outside the home). In other words, women nurture~e.g. as 'mother,' 'wife' and 'sexual partner.' These are the same roles identified by Duffy (1981, p. 135) as reported by her disabled respondents that make them "feel most womanly."

What are society's images and expectations for a woman who is disabled? With a sad expression on her face, one of our respondents said, "Disabled women are seen as children." Another woman talked about an elderly image. That is, women with disabilities are seen as dependent and in need of caretaking; they cannot be the caretaker. Browne *et al* (1985, p. 13) write, "Dependence and childishness are presumed to be the totality of our existence." (See also Hannaford, 1985).

An important element in the discrimination is that many people treat women with disabilities (and to a lesser degree, disabled men) as if they were incapable of independence. Even parents sometimes talk about the disabled woman as if she were not present or responsible enough to participate.

Our study of the free associations of undergraduate students, added to the work of others, supports the view that these discriminatory images remain strong in the USA. In our study, we asked each student to write down three verbal associations with 'disabled woman' and, earlier or later, 'woman' (in addition to other concepts). The contrast between the responses is sharp. Among the associations with 'woman' are sexuality (e.g., soft, lovable, orgasm), work (e.g., intelligent, leader, career), or the mother or wife roles (e.g., married, mom, child bearer). But for 'disabled woman,' there are rarely such associations. Rather, these women lead respondents to have such associations as old and feeble. Let us look further at three nurturing roles.

*Being a mother:* "If a woman cannot have children," said one of our respondents, "that makes her less than a woman." The role of mother "is at the heart of women's lives" (Thompson, 1988, p. 4); it incorporates positive social recognition, and it is one of the few such roles available to young, poor women. In our interviews with disabled women, we often heard reports that physicians, parents and others told the women that they should not become pregnant. Some were told to have a tubal ligation. There was little or no preparation in special education classes or rehabilitation programs for the role of mother. Said one respondent, "Many people don't accept the idea of a disabled woman having a child." And another: "Even my family would be appalled if I had children." Some courts agree: in a well-publicized recent case, Californian Tiffany Callo, who uses a wheelchair because of cerebral palsy, was forced to give up her two sons to adoption. Many of our respondents were college educated women; yet some of their relatives and friends could not envision these women as mothers.

Of course, there is a powerful positive side to motherhood for most women, certainly including women with disabilities. There are challenges and adjustments, and the special feeling of achievement. (See Shaul *et al.*, 1985, pp. 139-140). Said one respondent, "My mothering worries everybody else. Even my own mother thinks I should never have children. But it sure doesn't worry me. It'll take me longer to do things, but I'll do it."

*Being a wife:* What is a 'wife'? In western society, it is often seen as a helping role that combines, among other things, being a domestic servant, nurse maid, social secretary, and provider of sexual services. Perhaps everyone could use a 'wife' (including, that is to say, women). But it may be hard for some women with disabilities to meet the expectations of the stereotypical 'wife.' After all, some may not be able to clean the house or talk over a regular telephone. A respondent commented: "There is a big difference between a disabled husband and a disabled wife. A disabled husband needs a wife to nurture him, but a disabled wife is not seen by society as capable of nurturing a husband who is not disabled." Furthermore, a husband is not expected to be the care giver. "Until recently, I was engaged," said a respondent. She continued: "His family had a difficult time seeing me being able to take care of him. ... They saw him in a constant state of doing for me." That is perhaps why so many women who become disabled have their marriages end in divorce or separation.

The challenge of mutual understanding is why some women with disabilities develop relationships with males who are disabled. "When you date someone else with a disability," a student commented, "that person understands the struggles. ...It's easier to have a relationship."

*Being a sexual partner:* Many men dream of a *Playboy*-type sexual partner: a beautiful body performing a variety of sexual services. However, few men think of a visibly disabled woman as a sex object. Indeed, there may for many people be a taboo against such an intimate relationship (see Hahn, 1981, p. 224). The July 1987 issue of *Playboy* did feature Ellen Stohl, a mobility impaired woman; but the nude photographs did not reveal her disability.

For the woman with a disability, sexuality is too often denied. "Indeed, there is often the assumption that she does not have a sex life, or in fact does not want one" (Hannaford, 1985, p. 78; see also Hahn, 1981, and Morris, 1989). Many parents think this way too (see Rousso, 1988). Even if a woman had been sexually active before impairment, that aspect of her person is thought to be lost. Said a respondent, "It is sad that part of your womanhood is supposed to end with a disability." Referring to the boyfriend she had before an impairing accident, Anderson (1985, p.276) writes, "I had to give him up. ...I felt I could not give him what he needed. I felt that my sex life was over."

Duffy (1981, p. 95) put it well: "Hormones know no handicap." Of course, a physical disability may well impair some aspects of sexual functioning (see Morris, 1989, pp. 89-92) and require adjustments. Commented a respondent with cerebral palsy, "There's nothing at all unusual about my sexuality. I really enjoy it."

*Physical attractiveness.* Beauty, writes Banner (1983, p. 9), is "a special category of women's experience." "To be worthy," write Sanford & Donovan (1981, p. 371), "we are supposed to be tall and extremely thin, with large womanly breasts but boyish hips, and flawless in our facial features." And Bogle & Shaul (1981, p. 92) write: "The media sex symbol of the day is an impossible standard for any woman to live up to, but disability places you at an even greater disadvantage. If you spend most of your time in a wheelchair, and if you wear braces, and if you have a scoliosis, no matter what you do, you're not going to look like Cheryl Tiegs or Marilyn Monroe."

Unattractiveness and disability are equated in the minds of some observers as well as some women with a disability. In one of our surveys, we found that the concept 'woman' is often linked with associations of beauty, whereas 'disabled woman' evokes such associations as 'ugly' and 'unpleasant.' The woman with a disability may well have a poor body image, and that in turn has been linked with a fear of rejection that leads to avoiding social encounters, intimate relationships, and employment opportunities. Reflecting on her own experience, Joyce (1990, p. 9) comments: "Amputees, especially adolescents and women, may feel mutilated and unattractive." (See also Hutchinson, 1988).

The social and economic consequences of physical attractiveness or unattractiveness are profound. A major summary of research (Patzer, 1985, p. 1) observes:

> Physical attractiveness is the most visible and most easily accessible trait of a person. Physical attractiveness is also a constantly and frequently used informational cue. ...Generally, the more physically attractive an individual is, the more positively the person is perceived, the more favorably the person is responded to, and the more successful is the person's personal and professional life.

The less physically attractive person is perceived to be relatively unintelligent, insensitive, uninteresting, unsociable, lacking in poise, unexciting, sexually cold, sad, passive, aloof and rigid, and is less likely to be preferred for a working, dating, or marriage relationship. (The unattractiveness even 'radiates' to a companion). Suggestive of the impact is that physical changes can have a significant impact. "Some parents, who gave their children with Down Syndrome cosmetic surgery," reports Asch (1984, p. 53), "have found that their children's social and intellectual skills improved once they no longer carried the stigma of the 'Mongoloid appearance.'"

*Self Concept*   "I don't have any regrets at all about being disabled," one of our respondents asserted. We think her attitude is an exception to the rule. More typical is Johnson's (1986, p. 28) reflection, "It has not felt good to be disabled and a woman." Low levels of participation and a culture embedded with sexism, able-ism, and the female/disabled 'plus factor' obviously are likely to have a powerful impact upon the self-concept of many disabled women. And for those impaired after birth, there is the added impact from the experience of becoming disabled and the sense of relative deprivation. Saxton & Howe (1987, p. 1) write, "The loss of body function becomes a loss of sense of self...." Poems in their edited volume refer to the body as "going away" and "changing into a stranger."

*Self-image.* Women with disabilities learn about, and too often accept, the image held of them by members of the larger society. As Saxton & Howe (1987, p. 105) put it, "...being targets of incorrect assumptions, stereotyped notions, and invalidating messages about who we are, sometimes even from our closest family and beloved friends, we begin to believe they are true; we internalize the oppression."

Beginning in early childhood, the person with a disability may be subjected to comments and behaviors that are damaging to their self-image. "I was always made fun of in school," a respondent recalled. Browne *et al*, (1986, p. 129) write, "As disabled children, we often become the scapegoats for an already exhausted and strained family system, bearing the burdens of the family's frustrations and resentments. ...We may come to believe that we are guilty for being disabled and for causing the family trouble." Alternatively, the guilt may be felt by family members who think they are to blame for the physical impairment; such guilt often leads to overprotection and consequently a denial of opportunities for independence. "Mothers of disabled kids are definitely overprotective," said a respondent in a rueful tone.

Self-esteem is obviously affected. Alas, "Our level of self-esteem affects virtually everything we think, say and do. It affects how we see the world and our place in it..."

(Sanford & Donovan, 1984, p. 3). Self-esteem is comparatively low among women, and it appears to be especially low among women with disabilities. A respondent commented,

> Disabled women have a self-image that accepts the image the rest of the world has: that they cannot do, and they shouldn't even attempt to do. So they don't try or only try half-heartedly to battle the obstacles....They say, 'well, okay.'...And it is so hard to fight the prejudices in the job market or even those of your family. So she passively sits back.

The prevailing social image of the disabled woman is transmitted to her by the most important people in her life: her teachers, medical professionals, and parents (see Duffy, 1981; Yuker, 1988). We often heard from our respondents that these significant others sent verbal and non-verbal messages fully compatible with the sexism and able-ism of the larger society. Wagner (1985, p. 60) writes that people were too quick to help. "They rushed in to complete tasks I had begun, or started others before I had a chance. I felt like it wasn't acceptable for me to proceed my own way~~that somehow I wasn't competent or whole any more." Note that the psychological impact of such behavior may be magnified (or the behavior even imagined) by the disabled woman who tends to find confirming evidence of her expectations (see Kleck & Strenta, 1980, p. 864).

Teachers from pre-school through higher education may transmit stigma-linked views of women with disabilities. A professor told one of our graduate student respondents, "All you can be is a beautician. Don't expect anything more...you don't have any possibility for success." This student is now completing her Ph.D. work. As for medical professionals, their differential behavior towards males and females has often been observed. For instance, Wallen *et al* (1979) found that physicians working with female patients tend to provide them with inappropriate information, to emphasize psychological compared with physical diagnoses, and to be pessimistic about recovery. Such behavior has obvious implications for the well-being of disabled women.

The parental message, in the words of one respondent, is that "we want you to stay here [at home] until you're old and gray." She continued, "I'm glad I was able to break out." Borsay (1900, p. 115) argues that "the delivery of care to all relatives is strongly allied to the motherhood model. Consequently, assistance is framed in terms of the immature child." She continues, "However inadvertently, therefore, the motherhood model turns family care into a form of social control, in which disabled adults are stigmatized by being treated as children."

Of course, these circumstances represent potential challenges. "We cope on a very basic level that gives us pride in our being. We confront issues of helplessness, autonomy and control daily and our struggle helps us grow" (Wagner, 1985, p. 61).

***Self-selected role(s).*** Because of the prevailing low levels of participation, the low expectations on the part of others, and poor self-concepts, some observers have characterized women with disabilities by using terms such as 'social indefinition' and 'rolelessness.' We think that this is far from accurate. A useful starting point is the suggestion by Parsons (1951) that there is a "sick role." Among the aspects of this role are exemption from normal responsibilities and the need to be taken care of. Clearly, the prevailing view of women with disabilities is based in part on an imposition of the idea of 'sick' upon people who are 'disabled.' After all, we have seen that women with disabilities are thought not to be able to function as wife, mother, or sexual partner, and to be in need of nurturing.

Given the socio-cultural situation that directs sick role expectations at women with disabilities, our observations lead us to conclude that there are two modal responses: acceptance or rejection of this role. Acceptance minimizes socio-cultural participation, and dependency may become the woman's culturally acceptable life style (DuBrow, 1965). If one is exempted from normal social roles, the stigmatized condition gains greater predominance. Coleman (1986, p. 223) argues that the negative identity "inhibits the stigmatized person from developing other parts of the self."

Acceptance of the sick role may be more common among women with disabilities. Fine & Asch (1985, pp. 8-9) suggest that women, compared with men, are more likely to internalize social rejection and to identify themselves as 'disabled.' In our interviews, respondents often referred to differences between disabled men and women. "It's easier for a man to push someone out of his path," said one. By not pushing, said another, many disabled women commit "mental suicide." And from another: "Males are tougher. They don't want the disability to get to them. They want it, and they want it now.... I have trouble making demands." Responses from community residents and university students indicate that weakness, passivity, and dependence are expected of women with disabilities.

Rejection of the sick role, by contrast, leads to efforts to accept responsibility and achieve independence as well as to a greater variety of roles in the social, educational and economic systems. Perhaps such women can be said to have the self-selected role of 'challenged' disabled woman~~or even challenged *woman*. Wienberg (1988, p. 151) writes, "Some people who embraced their disability saw the disability as a challenge, and meeting that challenge provided them with an extra feeling of satisfaction and confidence."

A sizeable minority of our respondents were challenged women. Said one, "I am very conscious of my role as a disabled woman." For her, it is not a matter of women's roles or disabled roles; the two are now fused. "It is my role to show what a 'disabled woman' can do. ...Aren't disabled women amazing!" Clearly, being disabled was energizing to her. Another respondent reflected, "Maybe I would be an ordinary girl, married. But because of my impairment, I want to compensate for it."

## CONCLUSION

All women with disabilities, challenged or accepting, appear to be faced with two handicaps plus: they confront sexism, able-ism, and the handicapping female/disabled 'plus factor' that is uniquely theirs. This socio-cultural situation is obviously not without consequences; our research provides strong warrant for the view that, on average, women with disabilities have relatively low levels of participation as well as relatively poor or limiting self-concepts.

The relationships among each pair of the three factors (participation, socio-cultural system, and self-concept) are, we think, bidirectional; that is, circular causation exists. However, the research methods that we have employed at this stage of our work makes our views no more than suggestive working hypotheses for the future. Clearly, these are promising lines of inquiry in need of multi-factor longitudinal research.

Although our work has been guided by a triangular view that includes participation, socio-culture, and self-concept, we believe that this triangle is really part of a more complex set of relationships involving both the individual and the community. The primary individual-level clusters of factors include resources (e.g., money and information), physical condition (e.g., degree of impairment), participatory behavior, and attitudes towards self and community; and at the community level, they include resources (e.g. the health care system), the physical environment (e.g. access barriers), cultures and subcultures, and patterns of behavior.

Each factor, we think, impacts upon all of the others in a complex network of circular causation. To take but one example that goes beyond our reported work, it appears that poverty leads to poor health and poor health care, poor health care contributes to poor health, poor health increases the chance of physical disability, and disabilities make poverty more likely. Thus Heyman *et al.* (1990, p. 182) write: "The class/handicap relationship is probably due to both handicapped people achieving lower socio-economic status and lower status being associated with conditions which cause handicapping conditions."

Clearly, there are powerful forces of circular causation at work. And just as clearly, the agenda for scholars working in the field of sex and disability is complex, demanding, and challenging to us all. Of course, the most important item on the agenda must be to make much of the research of no more than historical interest by eliminating the socio-cultural and other barriers to equitable participation and empowering self-concepts.

\*\*\*\*\*\*\*\*

*Acknowledgments.* We wish to thank Jack McNeil of the US Census Bureau for facilitating our acquisition and use of the special SIPP survey, Nina M. Hill for providing us with the Harris data tape, Alicia Seegrist for SAS help, Robin Miller for expert library and other assistance, and the many women in the disability community whose cooperation and support made our efforts possible. Thanks also to Adrienne Asch, whose ideas on nurturance have been especially helpful; and to the provocative comments of our anonymous journal reviewers. This project is in part supported by grants form the Graduate School and the College of Human Ecology of the University of Maryland at College Park.

**NOTE:** [1] The quotations are from the transcriptions of interviews the authors conducted with disabled women.

\*\*\*\*\*\*\*\*

## REFERENCES

Altman, Barbara (1985 L Disabled women in the social structure, in: Susan E. Brown, Debra Connors & Nanci Stern (Eds) *With the Power of Each Breath: a disabled women's anthology* (Pittsburgh, PA, Cleis Press).

Anderson, Lois (1985) The Lois Anderson story, in: Susan E. Brown, Debra Connors & Nanci Stern (Eds) *With the Power of Each Breath: a disabled women's anthology* (Pittsburgh, PA, Cleis Press).

Banner, Lois W. (1983) *American Beauty* (New York, Knopf).

Becker, Gaylene & Arnold, Regina (1986) Stigma as a social and cultural construct, in: Stephen C. Ainlay, Gaylene Becker and Lerita M. Coleman (Eds) *The Dilemma of Difference: a multidisciplinary view of stigma* (New York, Plenum).

Bogle, Jane Elder & Shaul, Susan L., (1981) Body image and the woman with a disability, in: David G. Bullard & Susan E. Knight (Eds) *Sexuality and Physical Disability: personal perspectives* St. Louis, MO, C.V. Mosby).

Borsay, Anne (1990) Disability and attitudes to family care in Britain: towards a sociological perspective, *Disability, Handicap & Society,* 5, pp. 107-122.

Brown, Susan E., Connors, Debra & Stern, Nanci (1985) *With the Power of Each Breath: a disabled women's anthology (Pittsburgh, PA, Cleis Press).*

Bureau of the Census (1984) *Survey of Income and Program Participation,* SIPP84-R3 (Washington, DC, US Department of Commerce).

Coleman, Lerita M. (1986) Stigma: an enigma demystified, in: Stephen C. Ainlay, Gaylene Baker & Lerita M. Coleman (Eds) *The Dilemma of Difference: a multidisciplinary view of stigma* (New York, Plenum).

Deegan, Mary Jo and & Brooks, Nancy A. (Eds) (1985) *Women and Disability: the double handicap (*New Brunswick, NJ, Transaction).

Durrow, Arthur L. (1965) Attitudes towards disability, *Journal of Rehabilitation,* 31(4), pp. 25-26.

Duffy, Yvonne (1981) *All Things Are Possible* (Ann Arbor, MI, A. J. Garvin).

Ellien, Valerie (1983-84) Women and disability: an international perspective, *Rehabilitation World,* 7(4), pp. 9-13.

Fine, Michelle & Asch, Adrienne (Eds) (1985) Disabled women: sexism without the pedestal, in: Mary Jo Deegan & Nancy A. Brooks (Eds) *Women and Disability: the double handicap* (New Brunswick, NJ, Transaction).

Fine, Michelle & Asch, Adrienne (Eds) (1988) *Women with Disabilities: essays in psychology, culture, and politics* (Philadelphia, PA, Temple University Press).

Goffman, Erving (1963) *Stigma: notes on the management of spoiled identity* (Englewood Cliffs, NJ, Prentice Hall).

Hahn, Harlan (1981) The social component of sexuality and disability: some problems and proposals, *Sexuality & Disability,* 4, pp. 220-223.

Hanna, William (1986) Women with disabilities: free associations and attributions (unpublished manuscript).

Hanna, William *et al* (1980) *Equity for the Disabled* (Bethesda, MD, H&HA).

Hannaford, Susan (1985) *Living Outside Inside: a disabled woman's experience* (Berkeley, CA, Canterbury).

Heyman, Bob *et al* (1990) Social class and the prevalence of handicapping conditions, *Disability, Handicap & Society,* 5, 167-184.

Hutchinson, Marcia Germain (1989) *Transforming Body Image: learning to love the body you have* (Freedom, CA, Crossing Press).

Johnson, Mary (1986) Ending the aloneness, *Disability Rag,* March-April, pp. 28-29.

Joyce, Stephanie (1990) My lost foot: adjusting after an amputation, *Washington Post Health,* October 23, p. 9.

Kleck, Robert E. & Strenta, Angelo (1980) Perceptions of the impact of negatively valued physical characteristics on social interaction, *Journal of Personality and Social Psychology,* (39(5), pp. 861-873.

Lerner, M. J. (1970) The desire for justice and reactions to victims, in J. Macauley & L. Berkowitz (Eds) *Altruism and Helping Behavior* (New York, Academic Press).

Louis Harris & Associates (1986) *The ICD Survey of Disabled Americans* (New York, International Center for the Handicapped).

Morris, Jenny (1989) *Able Lives: women's experience of paralysis* (London, Women's Press).

Parsons, Talcott (1951) *The Social System* (Glencoe, IL, Free Press).

Patzer, Gordon L. (1985) *The Physical Attractiveness Phenomena* (New York, Plenum).

Rousso, Marilyn (1985) *Daughters with Disabilities: defective women or minority women, in:* Michelle Fine & Adrienne Asch (Eds) *Women with Disabilities: essays in psychology, culture, and politics* (Philadelphia, PA, Temple University Press).

Safilios-Rothschild, Constantina (1970) *The Sociology and Social Psychology of Disability and Rehabilitation* (New York, Random House).

Sanford, Linda T. & Donovan, Mary E. (1984) *Women and Self-esteem: understanding and improving the way we think and feel about ourselves* (Garden City, NY, Anchor/Doubleday).

Saxton, Marsha & Howe, Florence Eds) *With Wings: an anthology of literature by and about women with disabilities* (New York, Feminist Press).

Shaul, Susan, Dowling, Pamela & Laden, Bernice F. (1985) Like other women: perspectives of mothers with physical disabilities, in: Mary Jo Deegan & Nancy A. Brooks (Eds) *Women and Disability: the double handicap* (New Brunswick, NJ, Transaction).

Sherr, Rose Lynn & Write, Beatrice A. (1985) Foreword, in Mary Jo Deegan & Nancy A. Brooks (Eds) *Women and Disability: the double handicap* (New Brunswick, NJ, Transaction).

Siller, Jerome *et al.* (1967) *Studies in Reactions to Disability, II: attitudes of the non-disabled toward the physical disabled* (New York, New York University School of Education).

Thompson, Linda (1988) Feminist resources for applied family studies, *Family Relations,* 37, pp. 1-6.

Turner, Bryan S. (1985) *The Body and Society: explorations in social theory*(Oxford, Basil Blackwell).

Wagner, Marjorie (1985) A four-Wheeled journey, in: Susan E. Brown, Debra Connors & Nanci Stern (Eds) (1985) *With the Power of Each Breath: a disabled women's anthology* (Pittsburg, PA, Cleis Press).

Wallen, Jacqueline *et al.* (1979) Physician stereotypes about female health and illness: a study of patient's sex and the informative process during medical interviews, *Women & Health,* 4(2), pp. 135-146.

Wienberg, Nancy (1988) Another persepctive: Attitudes of people with disabilities, in: Harold E. Yuker (Ed.) *Attitudes toward Persons with Disabilities* (New York, Springer-Verlag).

Yuker, Harold E. (1988) *Attitudes toward Persons with Disabilities (New York, Springer-Verlag).*

******

**About the Authors:** William John Hanna is a Professor in the Program of Urban Studies and Planning at the College Park campus of the University of Maryland.
Elizabeth Rogovsky is an Assistant Professor in the Department of Social Work at Gallaudet University, Washington, DC.

**Source:** Reprinted with permission from *Disability, Handicap & Society,* Vol. 6, No. 1, 1991, pp. 49-63. Published by University of Sheffield, Sheffield, UK.

# Getting in Touch: The Relationship between Contact with and Attitudes toward People with Disabilities
Elaine Makas, Ph.D.

The 1950's and 1960's were a time of great social change in the United States. An increase in civil rights activities and resultant legislation led to large-scale desegregation of schools, neighborhoods, and work places. Encouragement and financial support were given to social scientists in the hope that their increasingly scientific research could suggest ways to facilitate a peaceful transition from a primarily segregated society to a fully integrated one. The contact hypothesis, attributable to the work of many researchers including Allport (1954), Cook (1962, 1963; Cook & Selltiz, 1955), and Amir (1969), emerged as the theoretical basis for much of this work. In its infant state, the contact hypothesis suggested simply that interracial/interethnic contact could reduce stereotyping and discrimination. Intense theoretical and empirical efforts during the 1950's and 1960's, however, constructed a more precise hypothesis which specified the types of interracial/interethnic contact which would facilitate more harmonious intergroup relations.

During the time in which the contact hypothesis was being developed and refined, one minority group received little or no attention: people with disabilities. This is not surprising due to the fact that, during the 1950's and 1960's, most people with disabilities remained segregated from mainstream society. (The first two major laws related to disability rights were enacted in 1973 and 1975.) By the time that persons with disabilities were beginning to be acknowledged as a legitimate minority group, and large numbers of individuals with disabilities began to appear in mainstream society, contact hypothesis-related research was rarely being generated. A few researchers attempted to assess the relationship between contact with individuals who have disabilities and attitudes toward people with disabilities, but, with few exceptions (e.g., Yuker, Block, & Younng, 1970), these researchers paid little attention to the fine-tuning of the contact hypothesis which had occurred during the previous two decades.

The failure of most researchers to apply the contact hypothesis appropriately to disability studies persists to this day. Three methodological problems are particularly evident: 1) the lack of a clear and consistent definition of "contact"; 2) simplistic and/or vague measures of contact; and 3) inattentiveness to factors associated with the nature of the contact. These flaws have sometimes resulted in ill-advised programs designed to improve attitudes toward people with disabilities that have either had no impact on attitudes or have actually reinforced negative stereotypes. In addition, these flaws can lead to the erroneous conclusion that the contact hypothesis is simply not applicable to research on attitudes toward people with disabilities. This, in turn, can cause a decrease in further research on the important link between contact and attitudes.

## The Definition of "Contact"

In order to accurately assess the relationship between contact and attitudes, it is necessary to clearly define "contact." As Altman (1981) suggests, "'Contact'...has as many conceptualizations as there are studies that use it" (p. 330). Disability researchers need to acknowledge the differences in "contact" possibilities pointed out by Cook and Selltiz (1955) and supported by race relations research decades ago. Cook and Selltiz make an initial distinction between a "contact situation," which refers to proximity that makes interaction more likely, and "contact," which refers to actual interaction between people. They differentiate further by discriminating among types of "contact," ranging from observation of out-group members without communication to direct, prolonged, and intimate interaction. These graduated degrees of contact, however, have been uniformly referred to as "contact" in much of the research on attitudes toward people with disabilities, with the result that the link between contact and attitudes has been confounded. In general, the closer a study's operationalization of "contact" has been to Cook and Selltiz's strict definition of the term, the more supportive the study has been of the contact hypothesis.

At one extreme are studies that have been viewed as being tests of the contact hypothesis, either by the researchers themselves or by others citing their work, even though these studies do not even include a "contact situation." One example of such research is the disability simulation study. Wilson and Alcorn (1969), for example, gave some of their subjects "experience with the disabled" (p. 303) by having them simulate disabilities (e.g., simulating blindness by wearing bandages over their eyes). Although the researchers themselves do not refer to this experimental manipulation as "contact" per se, Altman (1981), somewhat surprisingly, cites Wilson and Alcorn's (1969) research as "actual contact with handicapped experiences" (Altman, 1981, p. 329). Other studies provide "contact situations," but not "contact" (according to the definitions offered by Cook & Selltiz, 1955). In these instances, the researchers have categorized people on the basis of proximity. Nondisabled subjects who are in situations in which interactions with persons with disabilities are more likely to occur have been classified as "contact" subjects, in contrast to "no contact" subjects who lack such proximity. Weinberg (1978) and Rowlett (1982), for example, identify college students as having had contact if they lived on the same floor in a dormitory with a student who had a disability. Gilfoyle and Gliner (1985-1986) use an even less strict criterion by categorizing children as "contact" or "no contact" subjects based on whether the school they attended had special education students, even if the two groups of students did not share any class activities at all. McFarlin, Song, and Sonntag (1991), on the other hand, use the more accurate terms high and low "exposure" to differentiate between companies on the basis of the number of persons with disabilities employed by each company.

Some studies, though including conditions which marginally satisfy Cook and Selltiz's (1955) definition of "contact," clearly represent one of the least interactive forms of contact (observation of out-group members without two-way communication). Donaldson (1980), for example, classifies subjects as having had "indirect (media) contact" (p. 505) if they had watched a videotape or had heard an audiotape of a panel presentation by individuals with disabilities. Potvin, Leduc, and Voyeur (1984) also used a videotaped presentation by people with disabilities to provide the "contact" condition for their subjects, confounding the situation further by using the same presentation by people without disabilities to provide the "information" condition. This imprecise labeling of the experimental conditions by Potvin et al. is very surprising, since the researchers themselves point out in their review of the literature that one of the major problems in research examining the relationship between contact and attitudes is the vague operationalization of "contact."

Some researchers have either produced situations or reported on naturally-occurring events which meet Cook and Selltiz's (1955) definition of interactive contact. Several, for example, have created an experimental situation in which interactions occur (e.g., Stewart, 1988). Others (e.g., Anderson, 1980; Elliott, Frank, Corcoran, Beardon, & Byrd, 1990; Fichten, Tagalakis, & Amsel, 1989b; Makas, 1989; Seifert & Bergmann, 1983) have investigated interactions which had occurred naturally (e.g., friends, relatives, classmates). Although "contact," even by a strict definition of the term, has certainly taken place in all of these instances, it is worth noting that most studies involving experimentally-generated contact do not take into consideration the naturally-occurring interactions which subjects may have already had with persons who have disabilities. As a result, these studies must be viewed as tests of the impact of specific experimental manipulations on attitudes rather than as tests of contact per se. Similarly, it is important to acknowledge that even some studies which request subjects' recall of naturally-occurring interactions as a measure of contact may only solicit information on interactions within certain settings (e.g., in school, in work), thus neglecting contact which has occurred in other facets of the individual's experience.

Although the majority of the studies referred to above are empirically sound, it must be noted that those which fail to meet the standards set by race relations researchers (e.g., Cook & Selltiz, 1955) for "contact" cannot be seen as being either supportive or nonsupportive of the contact hypothesis. Rowlett (1982), Weinberg (1978), and Gilfoyle and Gliner (1985-1986), for example, found that nondisabled students who had been in proximity to peers with disabilities, compared to those who had not, expressed significantly more positive attitudes. These results support the value of "contact situations" in producing more positive attitudes; however, they do not address the relationship between contact and attitudes.

It should also be acknowledged that, even though Donaldson's (1980) and Potvin et al.'s (1984) taped presentations appear to have had a positive impact on attitudes toward people with disabilities, this change must be attributed to the message and the mode of presentation rather than to true interaction. In the Potvin et al. study, for example, subjects who received information on disability, compared to those who did not, scored significantly higher on a measure of attitudes toward people with disabilities, regardless of whether the information was provided by actors/actresses with disabilities or by ones without disabilities. Since interaction did not occur in the Potvin et al. study, their failure to find a difference between these two groups also should not be seen as a contradiction of the contact hypothesis.

The problem of overgeneralizing the term "contact" is apparent in a study by King, Rosenbaum, Armstrong, and Milner (1989) in which a measure of interaction and the presence or absence of contact situations are treated equally as tests of the contact hypothesis. King et al. found that nondisabled children's attitudes were significantly and postively related to the amount of interaction they had had with friends and relatives who have disabilities, thus supporting the link between contact and attitudes. The children's

attitudes were not related, however, to their "school exposure," a measure of the amount of mainstreaming in the schools which they attended, thus not supporting the relationship between contact situations and attitudes. Despite the fact that only one of these measures actually assesses contact, King et al. conclude that their results only "modestly support the notion that contact between able-bodied and disabled children is associated with more positive attitudes and has the potential to promote relationships" (p. 243).

A potentially more damaging overgeneralization of "contact" occurs if the contact hypothesis is misapplied to justify disability simulation studies. Despite the fact that many of Wilson and Alcorn's (1969) subjects reported great stress as a result of their simulations (although not sufficient to produce significant negative attitude change), this experiential approach is still being advocated (e.g., Donaldson, 1980; Fichten & Amsel, 1986; Fix & Rohrbacher, 1977; Shapiro & Margolis, 1988). (These advocates, themselves, do not attempt to justify these "experiences" on the basis of contact hypothesis research, and some of them, most notably Shapiro and Margolis, warn that great care must be taken to avoid negative attitudinal consequences. Precedence suggests, however, that some reviewers of the literature will continue to recommend simulation as a means of experimentally generating "contact," and may justify its use on that basis.)

**The Measurement of Contact**

Even when "contact" is narrowly defined as situations in which interaction has actually taken place, the quantitative measurement of contact is often so imprecise that its predictive value is lost. Some researchers have used one dichotomous item to assess contact (e.g., Curtis, 1985; Experiment One in Elliott et al., 1990; Fichten & Amsel, 1986). Others have used a single item multiple-point continuum to measure the amount of contact (e.g., Experiment Two in Elliott et al., 1990; Semmel & Dickson, 1966). Still others have used multidimensional scales which encourage subjects to scan their memories for specific individuals with whom they have had contact, rather than simply summarizing their overall amount of contact (e.g., Anderson, 1980; Louis Harris and Associates, Inc., 1991; Makas, 1989). Further confounding has been caused by variations in the terminology used to indicate contact: "contact" versus "no contact" (Semmel & Dickson, 1966); "ever known" versus "never known" (Gaier, Linkowski, & Jaques, 1968); "ever personally seen" (yes/no), and "personally knew by name" (yes/no) (Thomas, Foreman, & Remenyi, 1985); and "ever met or heard of anyone" (yes/no) (Abrams, Jackson, & St. Claire, 1990). It is not surprising that such diverse methods of data collection and such diversity in terminology have resulted in great variability in the amount of contact reported by similar groups of subjects. In six studies conducted during the 1980's, for example, the number of nondisabled undergraduate students reported to have had any contact at all with persons with disabilities has ranged from "only a few" (Curtis, 1985, p. 290) to 34% (Study I in Fichten & Amsel, 1986) to 50% (Study II in Fichten & Amsel, 1986) to 66% (Amsel & Fichten, 1988) to 88% (Anderson, 1980) and 90% (Makas, 1989).

Yuker and Hurley (1987) summarize the problem concisely:

> Almost every study of the effect of prior contact on attitudes toward disabled persons utilized a measure constructed for and used only in that study... Most questions about contact tended to be primitive, based on a priori assumptions, and lacking psychometric evidence of reliability or validity... Although it would be desirable to have a multidimensional measure that could assess many different types of contact, a first step might involve the development of a unidimensional measure that is psychometrically adequate" (pp. 147-148).

Makas (1989) reviewed studies which attempted to assess the relationship between contact with and attitudes toward people with disabilities. She found a clear pattern among the 21 studies in which the complexity of the contact measure was deducible: the more detailed the assessment of contact, the more likely the study was to find a significant relationship between contact and attitudes.

While none of the five studies which used a dichotomous measure produced significant results, three of the five which used a three- or four-point contact continuum measure did. Of the eleven studies which used a more detailed assessment of contact (requesting either contact by setting or further information on the specific contacts), nine studies resulted in significant findings.

## Factors Associated with the Nature of the Contact

As race relations researchers discovered, however, even a clear definition and an accurate measure of contact are not sufficient to predict the impact of contact on attitudes. This fact was acknowledged nearly fifty years ago by Drake and Cayton (1945), who criticized "this almost mystical faith in 'getting to know one another' as a solvent of racial tensions" (p. 281). Yuker et al. (1970) report the same problem in disability research and readily admit that they failed to take other factors into consideration in one of their own studies. In their assessment of possible differences in attitudes between nondisabled students who had taken a course taught by an instructor with a disability and those who had taken the same course taught by a nondisabled instructor, "type of relationship between student and instructor was not controlled; no attempt was made to determine whether the change score was related to the grade that the student obtained in the course" (p. 83).

Allport (1954) began the long process of delineating the specific conditions under which contact between groups is most likely to result in positive attitude change. Although later researchers (e.g., Cook, 1962, 1963; Cook & Selltiz, 1955) added a few factors to Allport's (1954) list of more than 30 contact variables and somewhat refined his theory, the present contact hypothesis remains substantially the same as that which Allport detailed in his 1954 book. Among the contact variables found to be most predictive of attitudes are the relative status of the interactants, the degree of intimacy within the relationship, the frequency of contact, the length of the relationship, and the pleasantness of the interaction. Makas (1989) found a significant relationship among undergraduate students between attitudes toward people with disabilities and four of these five variables; she found a marginally significant relationship for the fifth variable, frequency of contact. In addition, she found the number of individuals with whom subjects had had contact to be significantly and positively related to attitudes. It is disconcerting to note, however, that few researchers (e.g., Anderson, 1980; Donaldson, 1980; Furnham & Gibbs, 1984; Furnham & Pendred, 1983; Palmerton & Frumkin, 1969b; Strohmer et al., 1984) have tested any of these variables in their studies of attitudes toward people with disabilities.

Yuker (1983) stresses the importance of these variables and concludes, "We should no longer waste time studying and discussing the effects of experience or contact in general. The precise nature and duration of the contact and the nature of the interpersonal relationships involved must be specified before conclusions can be drawn" (p. 100). Yuker's (1988) summarization of 274 studies which attempted to investigate the relationship between contact and attitudes demonstrates the importance of taking these other contact factors into consideration. Unspecified "contact" was found to produce positive attitude change in only 51% of the studies; in 10%, it produced negative attitude change; and in 39%, it failed to produce any significant change. In light of Yuker's (1983, 1988; Yuker & Hurley, 1987) strong advocacy of "delineating the parameters that influence the size and direction of the effect" (Yuker & Hurley, 1987, p. 146, emphasis added), it is disappointing that Yuker and Hurley present a "Contact with Disabled Persons Scale" that simply combines pleasant and unpleasant contact, and equal status and unequal status contact to produce a single quantitative measure of contact.

## Explanations for the Link between Contact and Attitudes

In order to understand the impact of these contact variables on attitudes, it is necessary to review three of the explanations that have been given for the relationship between contact and attitudes.

*Habituation.* The habituation explanation for the improvement of attitudes through contact deals with the emotional aspect of interactions. Research suggests that many nondisabled people experience discomfort when first encountering a person who has a physical disability. This may be due in part to the physiological arousal which occurs when a person is exposed to sensory information that differs from his/her expectations (Mook, 1987). Heinemann, Pellander, Vogelbusch, and Wojtek (1981) found, for example, that college students who participated in a brief experimental interaction with a person who appeared to have a disability, compared to those who encountered a person without an apparent disability, showed significantly more physiological arousal (as measured by skin resistance response). Vander Kolk (1976) suggests that the mere thought of disability may create emotional arousal. Using a voice stress analyzer, he found that nondisabled subjects exhibited anxiety when reading aloud the names of disabilities, a reaction which he suggests might have been caused by imagined threats to the subjects' own body images.

Others suggest that interaction strain may result from interactants' anxiety about saying or doing the wrong thing. Kleck and his colleagues (Kleck, 1966, 1968; Kleck, Ono, & Hastorf, 1966), for example, found that nondisabled student subjects who believed they were interviewing a peer with a disability, compared to those who thought they were interviewing a nondisabled peer, exhibited less motor activity, showed less variability in verbal behavior, expressed more opinions which differed from their previously-reported beliefs, and terminated the interaction sooner. Heinemann et al. (1981) also reported inhibited behavior among nondisabled subjects when interacting with persons who appeared to have disabilities, compared to subjects who were interacting with seemingly nondisabled individuals. They found significantly less eye contact, significantly greater personal distance, and significantly more verbal output (the latter of which they attribute to a desire to avoid awkward silences). It is interesting to note that Comer and Piliavin (1972) found similar motoric and verbal restraint among student subjects with disabilities when they believed that they were interviewing a nondisabled peer, but not when they believed that they were interviewing a student with a disability.

Several researchers (e.g., Fichten, Robillard, Judd, & Amsel, 1989a; Louis Harris and Associates, 1991; Robillard & Fichten, 1983) report that nondisabled subjects openly acknowledged greater discomfort when interacting with persons who have disabilities than when interacting with other nondisabled persons. Fichten et al. (1989a) add that subjects with disabilities expressed similar anxiety when interviewing peers whose disabilities differed from their own. Fichten and her colleagues (Amsel & Fichten, 1988; Fichten et al., 1989a) suggest that this discomfort should be examined in terms of the cognitions which occur during interaction. Amsel and Fichten (1988), for example, found that nondisabled subjects who were anticipating encounters with a peer who had a disability, compared to those anticipating encounters with a nondisabled peer, reported more thoughts overall, and more negative self-referent and other-referent thoughts. (There was no significant difference in positive thoughts.) A survey by Louis Harris and Associates, Inc. (1991) of 1257 nondisabled individuals supports the need for an examination of cognitions. Fifty-eight percent of their subjects reported feeling "awkward or embarrassed" either "often" or "occasionally" when encountering a person with a disability; 47% indicated that they experienced "fear"; and 74% responded that they felt "pity." Harris and Associates point out that their subjects exhibited a high correspondence between feeling "awkward or embarrassed" and "pity." They also note a strong relationship between feelings of awkwardness/embarrassment and educational level, with college graduates significantly more likely than non-high school graduates to report these types of discomfort.

Research also supports a correspondence between previous contact and reduced interaction anxiety. Robillard and Fichten (1983), for example, found interaction comfort to be marginally significantly related to prior contact with individuals with disabilities, and significantly related to prior

*close* contact. Louis Harris and Associates, Inc. (1991) note a very strong relationship between previous contact with persons having specific disabilities and both increased comfort and decreased feelings of awkwardness with people who have those specific disabilities. Amsel and Fichten (1988) found that subjects with previous contact with people who have disabilities, compared to those without such contact, scored higher on a measure of "comfort interacting," verbally reported being more at ease, indicated fewer "other-referent" negative thoughts, and showed a tendency toward fewer "self-referent" negative thoughts. Fichten et al. (1989b) found no significant relationship between a quantitative measure of subjects' contact with persons who have disabilities and their self-reported "ease" in such interactions, but they did find that both variables appeared to have a positive impact on cognitions during interaction. Subjects who reported feeling more at ease when encountering a wheelchair user, compared to those who reported feeling less at ease, indicated stronger self-efficacy beliefs and fewer negative self-focused and other-focused thoughts during interaction. Contact, on the other hand, was found to be related to the presence of positive thoughts and an enhanced ratio of positive self-focused thoughts to negative other-focused thoughts.

Langer, Fiske, Taylor, and Chanowitz (1976) offer another explanation for interaction strain: "Much of the discomfort evident in interactions between handicapped persons and normals exists because one's desire to explore a novel stimulus arouses the fear of violating a social norm against staring" (p. 452). In a test of this hypothesis, they found that nondisabled subjects spent more time staring at a photograph of an individual with a disability than at a photograph of a person who appeared not to have a disability, but only when unobserved (i.e., when perceived sanctions for staring were absent).

Research by Fichten et al. (1989b), though not directly addressing Langer et al.'s (1976) competing motives hypothesis, offers support for part of the equation. Fichten et al. (1989b) found no significant relationship between student subjects' self-reported comfort interacting with a wheelchair user and their "curiosity" thoughts during the encounter. They report, however, a significant positive correlation between curiosity and attitudes toward people with disabilities and a significant negative correlation between curiosity and self-referent positive thoughts. One explanation for these somewhat unexpected results is that, although curiosity indicates a willingness to interact, it may also lead to lowered self-esteem (if it is seen as a violation of social norms). Research by Sagatun (1985) is consistent with this explanation. He showed student subjects videotaped interactions between a person with a disability and a person without a disability, and found a decided preference among subjects for the interactant with the disability when she initiated the conversation, compared to when she did not. Subjects may have interpreted her initiation of the interaction to be a removal of social sanctions inhibiting curiosity.

Regardless of the cause of interaction anxiety--unexpected sensory input, threat to one's body image, fear of saying or doing the wrong thing, or competion between curiosity and inhibition--research suggests that contact may reduce this discomfort. This positive change may be the result of habituation, which Gleitman (1987) defines as "a decline in the tendency to respond to stimuli that have become familiar due to repeated exposure" (p. 69). A study by Langer et al. (1976) strongly suggests the value of habituation in improving the attitudes of nondisabled people toward people with disabilities. Subjects were either allowed or not allowed to observe through a one- way mirror a woman with whom they would be interacting. The woman appeared to have a disability, to be pregnant, or to have no obvious physical condition. Subjects who had not been allowed to observe the woman prior to interaction (i.e., to become habituated to her) sat significantly further from her when she appeared to have a disability or to be pregnant than when her physical condition was not novel, a measure which Kleck, Buck, Goller, London, Pfeiffer, and Vukcevic (1968) found to be significantly related to attitudes toward people with disabilities. On the other hand, subjects in the Langer et al. (1976) study who had been allowed to observe the woman prior

to interaction showed no significant difference in seating distance based on her appearance.

A link between contact and attitudes based on habituation argues strongly for the importance of the three quantitative contact variables: length of the relationship, frequency of interaction, and number of individuals with whom the subject has had contact. Long-term and frequent exposure should lessen physiological arousal in response to a particular individual; exposure to different individuals, all of whom vary from the norm in terms of physical appearance, should lessen physiological arousal in response to others who also differ from the norm. Repeated exposures to persons who have disabilities are likely to make a nondisabled person more accustomed to that sensory stimulus, as suggested by Mook (1987); to comfortably satisfy the nondisabled individual's curiosity, as suggested by Langer et al. (1976); and (assuming that the contacts are either pleasant or neutral) to reduce the nondisabled person's fear of saying or doing the wrong thing, as suggested by Kleck (1966, 1968; Kleck et al, 1966).

***Reduced salience of "deviant" characteristics.*** A second explanation for the relationship between contact and attitudes is based on unconscious linkages between physical appearance and presumed personality traits. According to this interpretation, negative attitudes may be the result of illusory correlations between "deviant" persons and "deviant" behaviors. A study by Langer and Imber (1980) clearly demonstrates this concept. Subjects watched a brief videotape of a man reading a newspaper editorial aloud. Some subjects had been told that he was either "positively deviant" (a millionaire) or "negatively deviant" (an ex-mental patient, a homosexual, a divorcee, or someone who had cancer). Other subjects were simply told to be very attentive to the person whom they would be observing. A control group was given no information about the man and no instructions to be attentive to him. Although all subjects saw the same videotape, subjects who had been given "deviant" information about the man or who had simply been instructed to be attentive to him, compared to control subjects, were significantly more accurate in describing his physical appearance and significantly more likely to describe his behavior as being deviant.

McArthur (1982) suggests that findings such as these are due to illusory correlation. Since physical appearance has salience, there is a tendency to categorize people on the basis of characteristics such as skin color or presence of a physical disability, and a tendency to pay more attention to people who have novel physical appearance. Similarly, there is greater attendance to extreme or negative behaviors, which, in turn, weigh more heavily in impression formation. These two cognitive biases combine to form an illusory correlation: "Subjects perceived an illusory correlation between being a member of the minority group and performing behaviors that were in the minority... [and subjects] tended to overrecall instances of infrequent behaviors by minority group members" (p. 156). Once these stereotypes are formed, according to McArthur, they are reinforced by selective attention to stereotypic behaviors.

A study by Fichten and Amsel (1986) demonstrates the salience of disability as a means of categorization. Subjects were asked to describe one of four hypothetical stimulus persons: a disabled woman, a nondisabled woman, a disabled man, or a nondisabled man. Fichten and Amsel found that, for both socially desirable and socially undesirable traits, disability/nondisability status was more important to categorization than gender. Furthermore, the hypothetical persons with disabilities, compared to those without disabilities, were attributed with more negative traits.

McArthur (1982) suggests that the most effective way to extinguish illusory correlations between "deviant" appearance and "deviant" behavior is to break down the categorization of people by physical appearance through personal contact. Richardson (1971), in an earlier work, arrived at the same conclusion:

The range of cues available to the perceiver in the development of interpersonal relations increases with increasing intimacy, and cues that were salient early in the relationship may become unimportant or be ignored later. Physical handicap is most likely to be a salient cue during the meeting of strangers, when the appearance of a person is evident even before verbal communication begins. The influence of values toward physical handicap on friendship choices is likely, therefore, to be stronger at first meetings than after persons have been together for some time. (p. 254)

Cook and Makas (1979) found support for this concept in their participant observation and interview study on the development of friendships between individuals who have disabilities and those who do not. Many of their interviewees reported that a person's disability or nondisability was much less noticeable after they got to know one another better.

The contact variables can have a dramatic impact on illusory correlations. The three quantitative variables (number of individuals with whom interactions occur, frequency of contact, and length of the relationship) can certainly assist in breaking down the linkage between unique appearance and unique behavior, but only if the interactions are positive ones (i.e., equal status, intimate, and pleasant). If contacts are negative, repeated exposure will actually reinforce a perceived correspondence between unique appearance and "deviant" behavior. Palmerton and Frumkin (1969a), for example, found a significant relationship between frequency of contact and attitude intensity among college counselors; those with extensive contact exhibited both the most positive attitudes and the most negative attitudes toward people with disabilities. Brodwin and Gardner (1978) found a similar relationship among teachers: those who had had greater contact with students with disabilities, compared to those with less contact, expressed both more positive and more negative attitudes.

***Stereotype disconfirmation and individuation of "out-group" members.*** A third explanation for the relationship between contact and attitudes focuses on interaction as a means by which the "out-group" stereotype can be broken down and its members can be seen as individuals rather than as instances of the stereotype. The process involves distinct stages, at each of which, contact plays an important role. In the first stage, from little or no contact to some contact, interaction allows an "out-group" to be perceived more complexly, although still as a unit and still stereotypically. As interaction continues, the transition is made from a depersonalized view of the "out- group" to a more personalized view of the group. At the third stage, the stereotype itself begins to break down because of individuating information. In the fourth and final stage, persons who were once seen as "out-group" members are no longer defined by a stereotype and are perceived, therefore, as potential "in-group" members.

According to Newcomb (1947), individuals seek to increase identification with their own group and to distance themselves from other groups. Heider (1958) suggests that this unconscious behavior can lead to contrast and assimilation biases in cognitive processing in which people fail to acknowledge differences that exist within groups and similarities that exist between groups. Prior to contact, a strong stereotype is not needed to justify distancing oneself from persons in an "out-group"; simple membership in the "out-group" is sufficient to explain the separation. The contrast and assimilation biases suggested by Heider work together to allow an individual to strengthen her/his feelings of cohesiveness with the "in-group" and to distance herself/himself from the "out-group."

These two biases are obvious in a review of the literature by Wills (1978) on the attitudes of "professional helpers" (e.g., social services workers, rehabilitation counselors, special educators, and medical professionals) toward their clients. A majority of the studies found that professional helpers held more negative attitudes than the general public toward people with disabilities. Wills attributes this to the service providers' need to perceive two entirely separate groups, the "helpers" and the "clients," in order to assure the cohesiveness of their own group. He reports that newly-admitted group members tended to conform to the existing "helper" group's negative attitudes toward the "client" group.

Several explanations, all of which support the cognitive need for assimilation and contrast, have been offered for the persistent finding that professionals who interact frequently with people who have disabilities tend to have negative attitudes toward them. Yuker (1988) suggests that "training that emphasizes the central role of the disability and the competence of the professional in contrast to the incompetence of the person with the disability tends to predispose one towards negative attitudes" (p. 268). Research by Elliott et al. (1990) adds another possible factor, the nature of the interaction itself. They found that student subjects who watched a videotaped interview with a man with a spinal cord injury scored significantly lower on a measure of attitudes toward people with disabilities when the man appeared to be depressed than when he appeared not to be depressed. Elliott et al.'s most disturbing finding was that previous contact with other individuals with disabilities had no effect on the ability of the one interview to produce negative attitudes. The unfortunate outcome, according to St. Claire (1986), is that professional-client interactions often occur on an intergroup, rather than an interpersonal level.

Contrast and assimilation can also be seen in research on the attitudes of nonprofessionals. Ravaud, Beaufils, and Paicheler (1987), for example, compared the attitudes of nondisabled adolescents in schools which either had or did not have mainstreamed students. They found greater consensus (i.e., a lower standard deviation) on traits associated with persons who have disabilities among the nondisabled students at the mainstreamed school. They also found that the nondisabled students rated the "standard individual" in their own group as stereotypically as they viewed "out-group" members (thus demonstrating assimilation as well as contrast). Strauch (1970) found a similar pattern among junior high school students. Although students in schools in which peers with mental retardation had been partially integrated did not differ significantly from those in schools without any integration in their expressed attitudes toward "the mentally retarded" or "special class pupils," they did rate "normal people" significantly more positively. Abrams and Hogg (1988) suggest a relationship between stereotyping and self-esteem that may produce assimilation and contrast biases. Their suggestion is supported by Eisenman's (1970) finding of a negative correlation between subjects' self-esteem and their attitudes toward people with disabilities.

Contact with members of an "out-group" allows information about that group to be amassed. A simple accumulation of information, however, does not necessarily lead to the breakdown of a stereotype. To the contrary, initial contact may actually help construct a more complex stereotype. According to Stephan (1985), categorical distinctions increase with limited familiarity (compared to no contact), but extended contact with a members of an "out-group" causes the breakdown of large categories into subcategories. Stephan notes that continued exposure may result in the abandonment of categorization all together. Reed (1980) adds that categorization, including stereotyping of unfamiliar groups, is not necessarily associated with prejudice, and it may actually lower prejudice by providing predictability (and, thus, reduced fear of interaction). This idea is seconded by Abrams et al. (1990): "Stereotypes can also be used to differentiate outgroups from ingroups by making the boundaries clearer, thereby providing a guide for behavior in ambiguous situations" (p. 1087). Reed (1980) found empirical support for this concept in his study of attitudes of Southerners toward Northerners. Subjects who had had little contact with Northerners exhibited high prejudice, but low stereotyping; those who had had moderate amounts of contact indicated less prejudice, but greater agreement with stereotypes; and those who had had considerable contact exhibited low prejudice and low stereotyping.

A study by Langer, Bashner, and Chanowitz (1985) demonstrates the impact of exposure to "out-group" members on the complexity of perceptions of that group. (It should be noted that, even though this study does not include contact, it does suggest the type of visual exposure that may occur during initial encounters.) In the Langer et al. study, children were shown slides of people who either had or did not have a disability and were asked to answer questions related to these slides for 40 minutes a day on four consecutive days. The children were given instructions which encouraged them to think about the slides either less complexly (e.g., if a problem portrayed could be solved) or more complexly (e.g., all the ways in which the problem could be solved). Subjects were then shown slides of children with and without disabilities and were asked to choose partners for various activities. Subjects who had been given the "more complex" instructions (whether the people they had viewed during training had disabilities or not), compared to subjects given the "less complex" instructions, were more likely to choose a blind child as a partner in a game of "Pin the Tail on the Donkey." The Langer et al. study shows the potential impact of increased complexity of perceptions of an "out-group." Although the complexity instructions resulted in a stereotyped view of blind children (i.e., that all blind children would be good partners in a game of "Pin the Tail on the Donkey"), it is worth noting that this more complex stereotype is quite positive since it might encourage the subjects to interact in the future with peers who have disabilities.

The value of increased complexity of stereotypes can also be seen in two studies by Linville and Jones (1980). In one study, white male subjects were asked to sort traits into coherent trait categories while thinking about either a Black man or a white man. This task resulted in significantly more trait categories among subjects conceptualizing the white stimulus persons. In a follow-up study, subjects were asked to evaluate positive or negative law school applications while being attentive to either two or six relevant dimensions. Subjects who were instructed to concentrate on only two dimensions were more extreme in their evaluations of "applicants" (i.e., they rated weak applications more negatively and strong applications more positively) than those who were told to concentrate on six dimensions. Additional support for the value of congitive complexity is found in a study by Katz and Zalk (1978) in which highly prejudiced white children's attitudes toward Blacks were significantly improved by training the children to discriminate among Black stimulus persons.

Continued contact with "out-group" members can lead to gradual changes in the nature of the sterotype. As intimacy with individual "out-group" members increases, the stereotype may become more personalized. This transitional stage of stereotype disconfirmation is demonstrated in two racial/ethnic studies. Deutsch and Collins (1951) found that white women who lived in integrated projects, compared to those who lived in segregated projects, not only attributed fewer negative characteristics to Blacks; they also reported negative characteristics that were more personalized (e.g., "Blacks have an inferiority complex," in contrast to "Blacks are aggressive and dangerous"). Prothro and Melikian (1955) found a similar change in Arab students' perceptions of Americans as a result of contact. Prior to interaction, Americans were described as being "rich," "industrial," "democratic," "materialistic," and "practical" (terms which, according to Prothro and Melikian, represent "national character"). After contact had occurred, these "national" stereotypes were supplemented with other, more personal characteristics (e.g., "jolly," "sociable," and "superficial").

With further interaction, even complex and personalized stereotypes begin to break down. Weinberg (1978), for example, asked college students to describe same- sex persons with a disability and without a disability based on 32 different personality traits. She found that subjects who had had little or no contact with individuals who have disabilities described the two stimulus persons as differing significantly from one another on 14 of the 32 traits; those who had had a moderate amount of contact described them as differing on ten traits; and those who had had considerable contact described them as differing on only five traits.

Deutsch and Collins (1951) suggest that the final breakdown of a stereotype occurs when a person is exposed repeatedly to nonstereotypic behaviors. Rose (1981) adds that stereotype disconfirmation can also include "non-events," when problems feared in interactions do not occur. Yuker (1965)

simply attributes the process to individuation:

> If you have known a person over a period of time, you cannot help but think of him as an individual. You think of him as John or as Dave, not as a cripple, a Negro, a Catholic, or a Jew. You may not like him, but if you don't like him you don't like him as an individual. Or, if you do like him, you like him as an individual. But the attitude is based on him as a person, not as a member of a particular group. (p. 16)

A study by Locksley, Borgida, Brekke, and Hepburn (1980) demonstrates how stereotypes can be broken down through the provision of individuating information, even when that information does not relate to the stereotype. Subjects were asked to estimate the percentage of males and females who are assertive, then asked to assess the assertiveness of individual stimulus persons based on one of three brief descriptions: social category only (whether the person was male or female), low diagnostic information (information not related to the stereotype), or high diagnostic information (information related to the stereotype). In the "social category only" condition, subjects supported the stereotype that males are more assertive than females in their estimates of the relative percentages of men and women in general, and in their assessments of individual stimulus persons. There was no evidence of stereotyping, however, in assessments of stimulus persons in either of the diagnostic information conditions, suggesting that individuating information may reduce or eliminate stereotyping, even when the information is not related to the stereotype. Other researchers have reported similar results for actual contact with target persons: Meltzer (cited in Amir, 1976) on perceptions of Blacks; Cole (1971) on perceptions of blind people; and Chadwick-Jones (1962) on perceptions of Italians.

The final stage of stereotype disconfirmation occurs when persons are no longer seen as part of an "out-group," but, rather, as potential members of the "in-group" to which the observer himself/herself belongs. Heider (1958) suggests that, even though differences between individuals will still be acknowledged, these dissimilarities may be discounted through "mutual assimilation." A study by Genskow and Maglione (1965) demonstrates this final stage in which individuals may be re-categorized as a result of a contact situation. They compared the attitudes of students in a mainstreamed university to those of students in a university without mainstreaming. They found that students at the segregated university were more likely to classify individuals based on the presence or absence of a disability, while those at the integrated university were more likely to categorize individuals based on university affiliation.

It is important to note that the quantitative contact variables alone do not determine an individual's progress through these stages of stereotype disconfirmation. As Bethlehem (1985) points out, exposure to large numbers of Blacks has not necessarily resulted in positive attitudes among white South Africans. Research by Fuchs, Fuchs, Dailey, and Power (1985) supports the importance of the qualitative contact variables. They found no difference either in attitudes toward people with disabilities or in complexity of perceptions of people who have disabilities between professionals who had had experience in assessing test performance of children with disabilities and those who had not. The two groups of professionals described people who have disabilities equally simplistically and equally negatively. As Fuchs et al. suggest, the failure of their study to find a positive relationship between contact and cognitive complexity, and between contact and attitudes may be due to the fact that the contact was professional, rather than personal.

An interesting contrast can be made between the Fuchs et al. (1985) study, which found contact to have had no impact either on cognitive complexity or on attitudes, and the other studies listed above in which contact (or, in some cases, exposure) resulted in greater complexity of perceptions and in more positive attitudes. In the Fuchs et al. study, subjects interacted with children who clearly held status inferior to their own (both as children and as clients). Subjects in the other studies, however, were exposed to people (either through contact or vicariously) who had status

equal to their own. Being in a position of power, the subjects in the Fuchs et al. study, compared to subjects in the other studies, probably had less interaction anxiety and, as a result, less need to be attentive to "out-group" members (i.e., less need to view them complexly). In addition, their superior status would discourage them from seeing "out-group" members as potential candidates for "in-group" membership, thus producing contrast and assimilation biases (as suggested by Heider, 1958).

These explanations for the relationship between contact and attitudes clearly suggest that all of the contact variables can influence the types of attitudes produced. The quantitative variables (number of individuals known, length of contact, and frequency of contact) have an impact on the number of occasions a person has to interact with members of the "out-group" and, consequently, greater opportunity to realize differences within groups and similarities between groups. The qualitative variables (relative status of interactants, degree of intimacy, and pleasantness of contact), however, also contribute to the nature of the attitudes which result from these contacts. Unpleasant interactions with lower status members of the "out-group" that lack intimacy are likely to lead to the reinforcement of stereotypes and to a greater need to distance oneself from the "out-group." On the other hand, if interactions are equal status, intimate, and pleasant (or even neutral), the contact is likely to provide opportunities for the disconfirmation of stereotypes and for the recognition of similarities between oneself and "out-group" members.

A careful review of the literature on attitudes toward people with disabilities leads to the conclusion that interpersonal contact between individuals who have disabilities and those who do not will have an impact on attitudes toward the group as a whole. Each of the explanations offered above provides some insight into the mechanisms by which attitude change can occur, and each of these explanations provides a rationale for careful monitoring of the amount and type of interaction necessary for positive attitude change. "Contact" must be clearly defined and measured, but it must also be carefully assessed in terms of its quantity and quality. If these requirements are successfully met, research is capable of suggesting ways in which contact can help to break down attitudinal barriers separating people with disabilities and those without disabilities, and, consequently, ways in which all people, regardless of their ability/disability status, can participate equally in mainstream society.

********

## REFERENCES

Abrams, D., & Hogg, M.A. (1988). Comments on the motivational status of self-esteem in social identity and intergroup discrimination. *European Journal of Social Psychology*, 18, 317-334.

Abrams, D., Jackson, D., & St. Claire, L. (1990). Social identity and the handicapping function of stereotypes: Children's understanding of mental and physical handicap. *Human Relations, 43*, 1085-1098.

Allport, G.W. (1954). *The nature of prejudice.* Reading, MA: Addison-Wesley.

Altman, B.M. (1981). Studies of attitudes toward the handicapped: The need for a new direction. *Social Problems*, 28, 321-337.

Amir, Y. (1969). Contact hypothesis in ethnic relations. *Psychological Bulletin, 71,* 319-342.

Amir, Y. (1976). The role of intergroup contact in change of prejudice and ethnic relations. In P.A. Katz (Ed.), *Toward the elimination of racism* (pp. 245-308). New York, NY: Pergamon Press, Inc.

Amsel, R., & Fichten, C.S. (1988). Effects of contact on thoughts about interaction with students who have a physical disability. *Journal of Rehabilitation,* 54(1), 61-65.

Anderson, R.J. (1980). The effects of verbal and visual cues on attitudes toward disabled persons (Doctoral dissertation, University of North Carolina, 1980). *Dissertation Abstracts International, 41, 4356A.*

Bethlehem, D.W. (1985). *A social psychology of prejudice.* London: Croom Helm.

Brodwin, M.G., & Gardner, G. (1978). Teacher attitudes toward the physically disabled. *Journal of Teaching & Learning, 3(3),* 40-45.

Chadwick-Jones, J.K. (1962). Intergroup attitudes: A stage in attitude formation. *British Journal of Sociology, 13, 57-63.*

Cole, F.C. (1971). Contact as a determinant of sighted person's attitudes toward the blind. *Dissertation Abstracts International,* 31, 6892A-6893A.

Comer, R.J., & Piliavin, J.A. (1972). The effects of physical deviance upon face-to-face interaction: The other side. *Journal of Personality and Social Psychology, 23,* 33-39.

Cook, S.D., & Makas, E. (1979). *Why, some of my best friends are disabled: A study of the interaction between disabled people and nondisabled rehabilitation professionals.* Unpublished manuscript, The George Washington University, Washington, DC.

Cook, S.W. (1963). Desegregation: A psychological analysis. In W.W. Charters, Jr., & N.L. Gage (Eds.), *Readings in the social psychology of education* (pp. 40-51). Boston: Allyn & Bacon.

Cook, S.W. (1962). The systematic analysis of socially significant events: A strategy for social research. *Journal of Social Issues, 18,* 66-84.

Cook, S.W., & Selltiz, C. (1955). Some factors which influence the attitudinal outcomes of personal contact. *International Social Science Bulletin, 7, 51-58.*

Curtis, C.K. (1985). Education students' attitudes toward disabled persons and mainstreaming. *The Alberta Journal of Educational Research, 31, 288-305.*

Deutsch, M., & Collins, M.E. (1951). *Interracial housing: A psychological evaluation of a social environment.* Minneapolis, MN: University of Minnesota Press.

Donaldson, J. (1980). Changing attitudes toward handicapped persons: A review and analysis of research. *Exceptional Children, 46,* 504-514.

Drake, S.C., & Cayton, H.R. (1945). *Black metropolis: A study of Negro life in a northern city.* New York: Harcourt, Brace and Company.

Eisenman, R. (1970). Birth order, sex, self-esteem, and prejudice against the physically disabled. *The Journal of Psychology, 75, 147-155.*

Elliott, T.R., Frank, R.G., Corcoran, J., Beardon, L., & Byrd, E.K. (1990). Previous personal experience and reactions to depression and physical disability. *Rehabilitation Psychology,* 35, 111-119.

Fichten, C.S., & Amsel, R. (1986). Trait attributions about college students with a physical disability: Circumplex analyses and methodological issues. *Journal of Applied Social Psychology, 16*, 410-427.

Fichten, C.S., Robillard, K., Judd, D., & Amsel, R. (1989a). College students with physical disabilities: Myths and realities. *Rehabilitation Psychology, 34*, 243- 257.

Fichten, C.S., Tagalakis, V., & Amsel, R. (1989b). Effects of cognitive modeling, affect, and contact on attitudes, thoughts, and feelings toward college students with physical disabilities. *Journal of the Multihandicapped Person, 2(2), 119-137.*

Fix, C., & Rohrbacher, J.A. (1977). What is a handicap?: The impact of attitudes. *The Personnel and Guidance Journal, 56, 176-178.*

Fuchs, D., Fuchs, L.S., Dailey, A.M., & Power, M.H. (1985). The effect of examiners' personal familiarity and professional experience on handicapped children's test performance. *Journal of Educational Research, 78*, 141-146.

Furnham, A., & Gibbs, M. (1984). School children's attitudes toward the handicapped. *Journal of Adolescence, 7*, 99-117.

Furnham, A., & Pendred, J. (1983). Attitudes toward the mentally and physically disabled. *British Journal of Medical Psychology, 56*, 179-187.

Gaier, E.L., Linkowski, D.C., & Jaques, M.E. (1968). Contact as a variable in the perception of disability. *The Journal of Social Psychology, 74, 117-126.*

Genskow, J.K., & Maglione, F.D. (1965). Familiarity, dogmatism, and reported student attitudes toward the disabled. *The Journal of Social Psychology, 67, 329-341.*

Gilfoyle, E.M., & Gliner, J.A. (1985-1986). Attitudes toward handicapped children: Impact of an educational program. *Physical & Occupational Therapy in Pediatrics, 5(4), 27-41.*

Gleitman, H. (1987). *Basic Psychology* (2nd Ed.). New York: W.W. Norton and Company.

Heider, F. (1958). *The psychology of interpersonal relations.* New York, NY: John Wiley & Sons, Inc.

Heinemann, W., Pellander, F., Vogelbusch, A., & Wojtek, B. (1981). Meeting a deviant person: Subjective norms and affective reactions. *European Journal of Social Psychology, 11, 1-25.*

Katz, P.A., & Zalk, S.R. (1978). Modification of children's racial attitudes. *Developmental Psychology, 14*, 447-461.

King, S.M., Rosenbaum, P., Armstrong, R.W., & Milner, R. (1989). An epidemiological study of children's attitudes toward disability. *Developmental Medicine and Child Neurology, 31*, 237-245.

Kleck, R. (1966). Emotional arousal in interactions with stigmatized persons. *Psychological Reports, 19*, 1226.

Kleck, R. (1968). Physical stigma and nonverbal cues emitted in face-to-face interaction. *Human Relations, 21*, 19-28.

Kleck, R., Buck, P.L., Goller, W.L., London, R.S., Pfeiffer, J.R., & Vukcevic, D.P. (1968). Effect of stigmatizing conditions on the use of personal space. *Psychological Reports, 23*, 111-118.

Kleck, R., Ono, H., & Hastorf, A.H. (1966). The effects of physical deviance upon face-to-face interaction. *Human Relations, 19*, 425-436.

Langer, E.J., Bashner, R.S., & Chanowitz, B. (1985). Decreasing prejudice by increasing discrimination. *Journal of Personality and Social Psychology, 49*, 113-120.

Langer, E.J., Fiske, S., Taylor, S.E., & Chanowitz, B. (1976). Stigma, staring, and discomfort: A novel-stimulus hypothesis. *Journal of Experimental Social Psychology, 12*, 451-463.

Langer, E.J., & Imber, L. (1980). Role of mindlessness in the perception of deviance. *Journal of Personality and Social Psychology, 39*, 360-367.

Linville, P.W., & Jones, E.E. (1980). Polarized appraisals of out-group members. *Journal of Personality and Social Psychology, 38*, 689-703.

Locksley, A., Borgida, E., Brekke, N., & Hepburn, C. (1980). Sex stereotypes and social judgment. *Journal of Personality and Social Psychology, 39*, 821-831.

Louis Harris and Associates, Inc. (1991). *Public attitudes toward people with disabilities* (Study No. 912028). Washington, DC: National Organization on Disability.

Makas, E. (1989). Disabling stereotypes: The relationship between contact with and attitudes toward people with physical disabilities (Doctoral dissertation, The George Washington University, 1989). *Dissertation Abstracts International, 50(5)*, 2206B.

McArthur, L.Z. (1982). Judging a book by its cover: A cognitive analysis of the relationship between physical appearance and stereotyping. In A.H. Hastorf &

A.M. Isen (Eds.), *Cognitive social psychology* (pp. 149-211). New York, NY: Elsevier/North Holland.

McFarlin, D.B., Song, J., & Sonntag, M. (1991). Integrating the disabled into the work force: A survey of Fortune 500 company attitudes and practices. *Employee Rights and Responsibilities,* 4(2), 107-123.

Mook, D.G. (1987). *Motivation: The organization of action.* New York: W.W. Norton and Company.

Newcomb, T.M. (1947). Autistic hostility and social reality. *Human Relations,* 1, 69-86.

Palmerton, K.E., & Frumkin, R.M. (1969a). Contact with disabled persons and intensity of counselors' attitudes. *Perceptual and Motor Skills, 28, 434.*

Palmerton, K.E., & Frumkin, R.M. (1969b). Type of contact as a factor in attitudes of college counselors toward the physically disabled. *Perceptual and Motor Skills,* 28, 489-490.

Potvin, P., Leduc, A., & Voyer, J.P. (1984). L'utilization de l'information et du contact pour modifier les attitudes des adolescents(es) du secondaire II et IV a l'egard des personnes qui font l'object de discrimination. *Apprentissage et Socialisation,* 7, 181-194.

Prothro, E.T., & Melikian, L.H. (1955). Studies in stereotypes: V. Familiarity and the kernel of truth hypothesis. *Journal of Social Psychology, 41, 3-10.*

Ravaud, J.F., Beaufils, B., & Paicheler, H. (1987). Stereotyping and intergroup perceptions of disabled and nondisabled children: A new perspective. *The Exceptional Child,* 34(2), 93-106.

Reed, J.S. (1980). Getting to know you: The contact hypothesis applied to the sectional beliefs and attitudes of white Southerners. *Social Forces,* 59, 123-135.

Richardson, S.A. (1971). Children's values and friendships: A study of physical disability. *Journal of Health & Social Behavior,* 12, 253-258.

Robillard, K., & Fichten, C.S. (1983). Attributions about sexuality and romantic involvement of physically disabled college students: An empirical study. *Sexuality and Disability,* 6, 197-212.

Rose, T.L. (1981). Cognitive and dyadic processes in intergroup contact. In D.L. Hamilton (Ed.), *Cognitive processes in stereotyping and intergroup behavior* (pp. 259-302). Hillsdale, NJ: Lawrence Erlbaum

Associates.

Rowlett, J.D. (1982). Attitudes of peers toward physically limited students in university resident halls. *Dissertation Abstracts International,* 42, 4740A.

Sagatun, I.J. (1985). The effects of acknowledging a disability and initiating contact on interaction between disabled and non-disabled persons. *The Social Science Journal,* 22(4), 33-43.

St. Claire, L. (1986). Mental retardation: Impairment or handicap? *Disability, Handicap and Society, 1, 233-243.*

Seifert, K.H., & Bergmann, C. (1983). The EKB-Scale--An inventory to measure the attitudes toward physically disabled persons. *International Journal of Rehabilitation Research,* 6(2), 186-187.

Semmel, M.I., & Dickson, S. (1966). Connotative reactions of college students to disability labels. *Exceptional Children,* 32, 443-450.

Shapiro, A., & Margolis, H. (1988). Changing negative peer attitudes toward students with learning disabilities. *Reading, Writing, and Learning Disabilities,* 4, 133-146.

Stephan, W.G. (1985). Intergroup relations. In G. Lindzey & E. Aronson (Eds.), *Handbook of social psychology,* Vol. II (3rd Ed.), (599-658). Reading, MA: Addison-Wesley.

Stewart, C.C. (1988). Modification of student attitudes toward disabled peers. *Adapted Physical Activity Quarterly,* 5(1), 44-48.

Strauch, J.D. (1970). Social contact as a variable in the expressed attitudes of normal adolescents toward EMR pupils. *Exceptional Children,* 36, 495-500.

Thomas, S.A., Foreman, P.E., & Remenyi, A.G. (1985). The effects of previous contact with physical disability upon Australian children's attitudes toward people with physical disabilities. *International Journal of Rehabilitation Research,* 8(1), 69-70.

Vander Kolk, C.J. (1976). Physiological and self-reported reactions to the disabled and deviant.

Weinberg, N. (1978). Modifying social stereotypes of the physically disabled. *Rehabilitation Counseling Bulletin,* 22, 114-124.

Wills, T.A. (1978). Perceptions of clients by professional helpers. *Psychological Bulletin,* 85, 968-1000.

Wilson, E.D., & Alcorn, D. (1969). Disability simulation and development of attitudes toward the exceptional. *Journal of Special Education,* 3, 303-307.

Yuker, H. (1965). Attitudes as determinants of behavior. *Journal of Rehabilitation,* 31, 15-16.

Yuker, H.E. (1988). The effects of contact on attitudes toward disabled persons: Some empirical generalizations. In H.E. Yuker (Ed.). *Attitudes toward persons with disabilities* (pp. 262-274). New York, NY: Springer Publishing Company.

Yuker, H.E. (1983). The lack of a stable order of preference for disabilities: A response to Richardson and Ronald. *Rehabilitation Psychology,* 28, 93-103.

Yuker, H.E., Block, J.R., & Younng, J.H. (1970). *The measurement of attitudes toward disabled persons.* Albertson, NY: Human Resources Center.

Yuker, H.E., & Hurley, M.K. (1987). Contact with and attitudes toward persons with disabilities: The measurement of intergroup contact. *Rehabilitation Psychology,* 32, 145-154.

********

**About the Author: Elaine Makas, Ph.D.** is with the Lewiston-Auburn College of the University of Southern Maine

**Source:** Reprinted with permission from the author who wrote the article specifically for the second edition of *Perspectives on Disability.*

# Living with the Stigma of AIDS
Rose Weitz

## Introduction

In his classic work on the subject (1963:4), Goffman identified three types of stigma:

> First there are abominations of the body~the various physical deformities. Next there are blemishes of individual character..., these being inferred from a known record of, for example,...homosexuality, unemployment, suicidal attempts, and radical political behavior. Finally, there are the tribal stigma of race, nation, and religion, these being stigma that can be transmitted through lineages...

All three types of stigma can affect the lives of persons with AIDS (PWAs as they call themselves). Many PWAs experience stigma because they cannot meet cultural expectations for physical appearance or ability. As the disease progresses, PWAs may become emaciated, exhausted, and, in some cases, covered by disfiguring rashes or cancer lesions. Eventually, they may become unable to walk, talk, see, or care for themselves.

PWAs also may experience stigma because others believe that AIDS is a sign of a "blemished character." Currently, public health officials believe that 89 percent of reported cases of AIDS in the United States have occurred among persons who appear to have contracted AIDS through male homosexual activity or illegal intravenous drug use (AIDS Program, 1989). Because so many PWAs contract AIDS through socially unacceptable activities, even PWAs who have contracted AIDS in other ways frequently find that other people stigmatize them and consider their illness a deserved and divine punishment.

In almost half of all U.S. cases, this stigma is further heightened by notions of inferior or tainted lineage. To date, 41 percent of AIDS cases have occurred among persons already stigmatized because they were born black or Hispanic. Another one percent have occurred among hemophiliacs and one percent

among children who have contracted AIDS in utero. In these cases, others may stigmatize the individual not only for having AIDS but for having inherited somehow tainted or inferior blood.

Goffman's typology of stigma does not acknowledge the additional stigma which accompanies "abominations of the body" that are fatal, contagious, and still considered mysterious by much of the public. In past centuries, life was short and death was an accepted part of life. Now that early death is a rare and terrifying event, dying patients regardless of diagnosis often experience social rejection (Charmaz, 1980:159-61). In addition, because AIDS was idenitified so recently, members of the public may fear that AIDS will prove more readily contagious than physicians now believe. A recent national survey found that, despite the contrary evidence, 22% of adults believe that it is somewhat or very likely that a person can get AIDS from insects. Similarly, 23% feared getting AIDS from "eating in a restaurant where the cook has AIDS virus" (National Center for Health Statistics, 1988). Those fears, reinforced by sources as disparate as fundamentalist ministers and Masters and Johnson (1988), lead many individuals to shun PWAs.

Despite the mass media's extensive coverage of AIDS, few sociologists have yet written about the experience of having AIDS and none have focused on how stigma affects PWAs. However, researchers have investigated how people with other illnesses are affected by and manage stigma. Studies suggest that ill people try to avoid stigma either by revealing their illnesses, so that others will not be shocked or confused by their unusual behaviors, or by concealing their illnesses, so that their differences will not lead others to reject them (Schneider and Conrad, 1983; Hilbert, 1984; Boutte, 1987; Brooks and Matson, 1987). Ill persons also can try to reduce stigma by teaching others the biology of their illnesses and arguing against punitive theological explanations for illness (Gusow and Tracy, 1968).

This article describes how stigma affects PWAs' relationships with families, friends, lovers, colleagues, and health care workers. It explores how PWAs avoid or reduce stigma by concealing their illnesses, learning when and to whom they should reveal their illnesses, changing their social networks, educating others about AIDS, developing nonstigmatizing theories of illness causation, and using bravado to convince others that they are still functioning social beings.

## Methods and Sample

This article draws on interviews I conducted between July, 1986 and March, 1987 with 23 Arizona residents who either had AIDS or AIDS-Related Complex (ARC). For this analysis, I have combined persons with AIDS and persons with ARC because I could not consistently separate the two according to either medical diagnosis or self-diagnosis. For similar reason, the U.S. Centers for Disease Control recently changed its definition of AIDS to subsume most cases previously considered ARC. Although the prognosis for persons with AIDS is grimmer than that for persons with ARC, some persons with AIDS survive longer and with less disability than some persons with ARC. Moreover, some individuals are told by their physicians that they have ARC when they clearly have AIDS and some are told they have AIDS when they appear to have ARC. Some believe that the two diseases are essentially identical while others believe that they are very different. Finally, some people vacillate in their statements about what disease they have and what its prognosis is. Thus, I could not consistently sort cases by either actual or perceived health status.

All respondents discussed in this article were men who described themselves as gay or bisexual (although none mentioned any recent relationships with women). Three of the men had used drugs as well. I also interviewed two heterosexual women who had used intravenous drugs and one man who was seropositive for HIV antibodies but had not yet been diagnosed as having AIDS or ARC.

Because I interviewed only two women and one seropositive but asymptomatic individual, I have only limited understanding of how such individuals' experiences might differ from that of gay or bisexual PWAs. Consequently, I present in this article only data from the interviews with gay and bisexual men.

When my study began, the Arizona Department of Health Services believed that approximately 40 of the 110 known AIDS cases in the state were still living. To contact these and other PWAs, I posted signs in gay bars; announced the study in gay and mainstream newspapers and AIDS political action groups; asked physicians, AIDS support group leaders, and other respondents to inform PWAs of the study; and had non-profit groups which offer emotional or financial support to PWAs send letters describing the study to their clients. Eighteen of the 23 subjects learned of the study through the non-profit groups, two from friends, two from a political action group, and one from a notice in a gay newspaper.

The sample is comparable to the Arizona population in terms of religion and to the state's reported AIDS cases at the time of the study in terms of sex, geographical location (overwhelmingly urban), and mode of transmission (Arizona Dept. of Health Services, February 2, 1987). Because participating in the interviews required mental competence and some physical stamina, the sample undoubtedly underrepresents the most seriously ill PWAs. It also underrepresents persons with Kaposi's sarcoma (1 percent of the sample, but 21 percent of reported cases), even though they tend to be less ill than other PWAs, perhaps because these individuals do not want a stranger to see the disfiguring lesions which Kaposi's sarcoma can cause. In addition, the sample underrepresents nonwhites (0 percent of the sample but 13 percent of reported cases), who typically are less integrated into the AIDS support networks and therefore were less likely to have heard of the study. Finally, the sample overrepresents persons in their thirties (60 percent of the sample, but 42 percent of reported cases) and underrepresents older persons.

The data for this paper were obtained through semistructured interviews. I began with a set list of questions, but during each interview also probed into any unexpected topics that seemed potentially significant. These new topics were then incorporated into subsequent interviews. Thus, all the interviews covered the same basic questions, but the later interviews also included additional ones which emerged as significant in the earlier interviews. Interviews ranged from two to five hours in length, averaging about three hours, and were audio taped and transcribed. Interviews took place at respondents' homes unless they preferred another location (usually my home).

I analyzed the data using themes which emerged from the respondents' statements. With each interview, I began to develop themes which I followed up in subsequent interviews. After completing the interviews, I reread them all to identify additional critical concepts. I then sorted the interview materials according to these concepts to see what patterns emerged. These patterns were used to develop the structure of my analysis in this article.

## THE IMPACT OF STIGMA

Given the extensive media coverage of AIDS, PWAs cannot avoid knowing that many people condemn them and consider AIDS a divine punishment for sin. Several of my subjects described PWAs as the modern world's equivalent of lepers. A few mentioned their fears that they would be quarantined or even killed if the public learned they had AIDS. One expressed the fear that if the "rednecks living across the street...found out a gay person was over here with AIDS, they may decide to get drunk one night and come over and kill the faggot." The sense of stigma was so strong that another said he would rather die than be cured for if he were cured he would have to live the rest of his life with the stigma of having once had AIDS.

The following sections describe how this sense of stigma develops, and how stigma pervades PWAs' relationships with family, friends, lovers, health care workers, and fellow workers. The final section discusses how PWAs cope with this stigma.

**Family.** All PWAs run a risk that their families will reject them, either because of their illness *per se* or because their illness exposes or emphasizes that they are gay or use drugs. One of the men I spoke with was a 27-year old computer operator whose parents lived in a small town in another state. He felt he had a good relationship with his parents, but had never told them of his sexual orientation. When asked how he thought his family would react to news of his diagnosis, he said:

> You just can't predict. They might find it so disgusting that you'll basically lose them. They'll be gone. Or they'll go through the adjustment period and not mind. You really don't know.

Virtually every respondent reported that at least one family member had ceased contact with him after learning of his illness. One source of this rejection is that diagnosis with AIDS can reinforce families' belief that homosexuality is immoral. Families who had always questioned the morality of homosexuality may interpret an individual's illness as divine punishment, regarding it as proof that homosexual behavior should not be tolerated. For example, a 26-year old tailor from a fundamentalist Christian family, whose relatives had not known he was gay, described how AIDS forced him to reveal his sexual orientation and thus "put a wedge" between him and his family. His family considered homosexuality sinful and questioned whether they should help him with his health problems if he would not change his behaviors. He was still in contact with his parents, even though his mother had told him that his homosexuality was an "embarrassment" to her. But he had stopped talking to his sister because he could not abide her constant admonitions "to repent" and "to confess sin."

Even PWAs whose families in the past appeared to accept their lifestyles may find that their families reject them once their diagnosis becomes known. When questioned about this, the PWAs suggested that somehow AIDS made their homosexuality more real and salient to their families. Just as pregnancy forces parents to recognize their daughters are not just living with men but having sex, diagnosis with AIDS apparently forces families to recognize that their sons or brothers are not simply gay in some abstract way, but actually engage or engaged in homosexual activities. As a result, families who have tolerated their relatives' homosexuality despite deep reservations about its morality find that they can no longer do so. A 38-year old business manager reported that when he first told his parents he was gay "their reaction, while it wasn't initially effusive, at least it was grudgingly accepting." Now, however, he felt that his parents had "used this whole AIDS thing against me" by telling him that AIDS was "just desserts for the homosexuality community." Similarly, a 29-year old blue collar worker recounted how his mother, who previously had seemed to tolerate his lifestyle, responded to news of his diagnosis by telling him "I think your lifestyle is vulgar. I have never understood, I've never accepted it...Your lifestyle repulses me." She subsequently refused to let him in her house or help him obtain medical insurance.

Even when families do not overtly reject ill relatives, their behavior may still create a sense of stigma. This can happen when families either hide news of their relatives' illnesses from others altogether or tell others that their relatives have some less stigmatized disease. A 39-year old floral designer, whose Catholic family had all known he was gay before he became ill, reported that his mother refused to tell his brothers and sisters that he had AIDS, and ordered him not to tell them as well. When his siblings finally were told, they in turn would not tell their spouses. Such behavior forces PWAs to recognize that, as one fundamentalist Christian said, "it was an embarrassment to [the family]...that I was gay and...that I have AIDS.' This imposed secrecy places heavy burdens on individuals who subsequently must "live a lie."

Families may reinforce a sense of stigma by adopting extreme and medically unwarranted anti-contagion measures. One family brought their own sheets when visiting their ill son's home. Others refused to allow PWAs to touch any food, share their bathrooms, or come closer than an arm's length away. A 29-year old Mormon salesperson, whose family believed he deserved AIDS as

punishment for his sins, reported that initially his family "wouldn't come in the room unless they had gloves and a mask and they wouldn't touch me...[And] for a time I couldn't go over to somebody's house for dinner. And they still use paper plates [when I eat there]." Even PWAs who feel such precautions are necessary still miss the experience of physical warmth and intimacy. They report feeling stigmatized, isolated, and contaminated.

Although PWAs fear that their families will reject them once their illness becomes known, they also hope that news of their illness will bring their families closer together. A 38-year old store manager who had never had a particularly close relationship with his family described his fantasy "that something like this~an experience where you come this close to death or the reality of death~is when you realize what's really important and not who's right and who's wrong."

For the lucky ones, this fantasy materializes. The oldest man I interviewed, a 57-year old lawyer, had always considered his father a cold and selfish man, and had never been on good terms with him. This situation changed, at least partially, when he became ill. As he described it:

> We've gotten closer....There's the verbal "I love you," there's the letters. One of the nicest things that's ever happened to me...is my father sent me a personal card. In the inside he wrote "God bless you. I love you son"....It meant the world to me.

Another man described how, despite their disapproval of his lifestyle, his fundamentalist Christian family had provided him with housing, money, and emotional support once they learned of his illness. As he described it, in his family, when "little brother needed help...that took priority over all the other bullshit. They were right there."

Diagnosis can also bring families together by ending previous sources of conflict. Whether to preserve their own health, protect others from infection, or because they simply lose interest in sex once diagnosed with a deadly, sexually transmitted disease, PWAs may cease all sexual activity. For health reasons, PWAs may also stop smoking and drinking. As a result, families that previously had disapproved of PWAs' lifestyles may stop considering them "sick" or "sinful," even if the PWAs continue to consider themselves gay. Consequently, some PWAs achieve a new acceptance from relatives who attach less stigma to AIDS than to their former behaviors.

**Friends and Lovers.** At the time of diagnosis, only 7 of the 23 men had lovers (as opposed to sexual partners with whom they had no ongoing relationship). These seven naturally turned to their lovers as well as their families for emotional support. The two whose lovers were also HIV infected did, indeed, receive support from their lovers, as did one man whose lover was HIV negative and two whose lovers do not know their HIV status. The remaining two men, however, were almost immediately abandoned by their lovers.

The PWAs' friends have proven considerably less sympathetic. Typically, PWAs reported that some friends "are very supportive, come around, enjoy coming over here, whatever. But most of them have backed off." A young blue collar worker described how, when his best friend learned of his diagnosis:

> He couldn't get me out of his apartment fast enough....It was to the point (my friends) didn't even want to be in the same room with me....It was just like "don't call us, we'll call you...." They stopped returning calls. When I would see them out (at bars), they would see me coming and they would head out in the other direction.

Because house mates, like other friends, may also reject PWAs once they learn about their illness, PWAs may have to make new housing arrangements shortly after receiving their diagnoses. Some house mates left or asked the PWA to leave as soon as they learned that he had AIDS. In other cases, house mates asked the PWAs to leave once the house mates learned that they too were being shunned by others as possible sources of infection. Because of limited financial resources and social stigma, PWAs who need

new housing may be forced to move in with their families or with other PWAs. Those who move in with their families risk retreating into a childlike dependency, while those who live with other PWAs must cope with their house mates' illnesses as well as their own.

Although rejection by friends and lovers is common, it is not universal. In fact, some men received acceptance and caring from friends and lovers beyond anything they had expected. The 57-year old lawyer quoted above had received many offers of support from friends. He told me, "I never knew I was [so] loved." Similar experiences led the 38-year old business manager described above to conclude "that family are those people who you can really love and trust and care for" and not necessarily one's blood relations.

**Health Care Workers.** That persons who lack medical training should fear or abhor the victims of a new and deadly disease may not seem surprising. Yet even many health care professionals shun PWAs (Katz et al., 1987; Kelly et al., 1987). In Arizona, as in many other places, no nursing home or after-care facility, only a handful of dentists and ambulance services, and relatively few physicians will care for PWAs. Some respondents had experienced discrimination from professionals directly, while more knew of the problem from talking to others.

Through trial and error, most PWAs eventually find primary practitioners who, they believe, provide good and nonjudgmental care. They still face potential stigma, however, whenever they need specialist or hospital care. It may take several phone calls to find a willing specialist. If hospitalization is needed, the problem is less access to care than quality of care. Hospital staff usually cannot refuse to provide care, but they can make their ignorance and prejudice painfully obvious. One man described how hospital nurses made his friends and family "protect themselves" by donning isolation garb, even though his infection could not be transmitted through casual contact. He reported:

> A lot of the nurses were very nervous. It was obvious. Some of them double gloved and some wouldn't come in at all. i mean, they would if you forced them to, but they

weren't going to just drop in and see how you were doing and stuff.

Other PWAs mentioned social workers who refused to enter their hospital rooms and hospital staff who disappeared suddenly once their diagnoses became known. One man first realized that he had AIDS when he suddenly found himself under the care of a new hospital staff team, all of whom appeared gay.

**Work.** By the time individuals receive diagnoses of AIDS, many are physically incapable of working. Others, faced with catastrophic medical bills, must quit their jobs to qualify for state-financed medical assistance.

PWAs who continue working risk additional stigma and discrimination if others learn of their illnesses. Although most courts have rules that PWAs are disabled and thus qualify for protection under anti-discrimination laws (Leonard, 1987), in practice employers can fire PWAs with impunity because few PWAs have the time, money, or stamina to sue successfully (personal communication, Jane Aiken, Arizona Governor's Task Force on AIDS).

Only one man, a mechanic for a large public institution with an established AIDS policy, described his working situation as satisfactory. Every other PWA who revealed his illness was either fired immediately or forced to quit when colleagues or employers made his situation intolerable. An outgoing and amiable young man who had worked as a tailor said that his fellow workers initially responded well, taking only reasonable precautions, such as not sharing drinking glasses.

> Then little things happened....If a pin came from [my department] they would immediately throw it away because [they thought] if they poked themselves, they could get AIDS...[Then they developed] a list of things for me to do at the end of the day like wipe down the scissors and the table and everything that I touched with a weak solution of ten-to-one [bleach]....With all that happening, I kind of lost the desire to work.

He quit his job soon thereafter. Although he appeared to have a strong legal case, he (like all the others in similar situations) decided he did not have the energy, funds, or time to sue.

## Managing the Stigma of AIDS

**Avoiding Stigma.** To maintain as much of their pre-diagnosis lives as possible, PWAs must find ways to avoid or reduce stigma. One basic strategy used by PWAs as well as by people with other stigmatized illnesses (Boutte, 1987; Hilbert, 1984; Schneider and Conrad, 1983) is to hide the nature of their illness.

Hiding can begin at the time of diagnosis. Since AIDS was first identified, Federal law has required physicians to report all cases to the government. A new Arizona law (enacted during the study period) requires physicians to report persons who have ARC or who test positive for HIV, the virus that causes AIDS. Although laws supposedly protect the confidentiality of these reports, physicians and patients fear that the information will leak out. As a result, to protect clients from possible legal, social, and financial repercussions, physicians may circumvent the reporting law. One man, for example, described how his physician diagnosed his illness as ARC rather than AIDS to avoid the stigma which the physician believed would result from diagnosis of AIDS and the necessity to report him to the state. The physician told him:

> "If you diagnoses a person with AIDS, people really do back off from that one. I don't care how knowledgeable people are....We don't want to diagnose people with AIDS if we don't have to diagnose." He [the physician] said, "the first time you go to the hospital with pneumonia or the cancer lesions and stuff like that," he said, "then we got no choice and it has to be reported to the state. But as ARC we don't really have to report ARC cases."

Other physicians avoid reporting by using highly restrictive definitions of AIDS. One physician decided that only his client's pharynx and not his esophagus was infected with candidiasis. This slim distinction allowed the physician to conclude that the client had ARC rather than AIDS and hence did not have to be reported. Physicians can also diagnose each opportunistic infection a client contracts rather than diagnosing AIDS as the underlying cause of those infections.

Fearing that disclosure might result in loss of employment or insurance, PWAs and their physicians also used these tactics to hide diagnoses from insurance companies (and indirectly from employers). A computer operator who was well-read on the biology of AIDS and active in an AIDS political action group described how he and his physician avoided telling his insurance company he had ARC or AIDS.

[We have] been very careful, even so far, never to put the three big letters [ARC] or four big letters [AIDS] on the [insurance] papers. It's always been just candidiasis or anemia or something ridiculous....Anything but. And I prefer to keep it that way, and I think probably even [the physician's] notes reflect that.

For the same reason, and as long as they can afford it, PWAs may only request insurance reimbursement for treatments that will not trigger questions about whether they have AIDS.

In addition to hiding their illness from unknown bureaucrats, PWAs may also hide it from families, friends, and sexual partners as well. Shame about his sexuality had led one 41-year old Catholic man to sever all contact with his ex-wife and young children when he started having gay relationships years ago. After he received his diagnosis, and despite his realization that he was dying, he continued this silence:

I haven't seen my kids for almost 12 years and when AIDS came down, I didn't know how to handle it. How do you tell your kids 2,000 miles away that you're not only homosexual, but you're dying from a killer disease, the "gay plague" as I call it? How do you do that? How do you explain a lifetime in a thirty minute telephone conversation? So I chose not to.

Others chose not to tell their families because they assumed their families would reject them or because the PWAs could not cope with the anguish their news would bring.

Deciding whether to inform sexual partners with whom they were not in continuing relationships was more complex, for it raised the question not only of how to protect oneself from stigma but also how to protect others from infection. This was not an issue for the five men who were in continuing relationships with lovers who knew of their illness. Nor was it an issue for the 14 men who either had sex or had sex only on rare occasions when they were too drunk to make any conscious decisions. Of the remaining four men, two always told their lovers because they felt obliged to inform anyone whom they might infect that they were at risk. The other two disagreed, arguing that they need not disclose their diagnosis as long as they limited themselves to activities unlikely to transmit the virus. Besides, they argued, most gay or bisexual men already had been exposed to the virus. The well-informed computer operator described above stated that he felt no ethical obligation to reveal his diagnosis to sexual partners because "the level of infection in that group is so high that if, in fact, *you* are careful not to exchange body fluids to *them*, then their level of risk out of this encounter is much lower than what they probably did the week before. And they found *that* acceptable." (emphasis in original.)

PWAs use a variety of methods to hide their illnesses from people around them. One man routinely transferred his pills of zidovudine (formerly called azidothymidine or AZT) to an unmarked bottle because he feared others would recognize the drug as one used to treat AIDS. Some selected clothing or used make-up to hide their emaciation or skin problems. Men whose tongues showed the tell-tale whitish spots of candidiasis (an infection that frequently accompanies AIDS closed their mouths partially while smiling or talking.

Most importantly, PWAs learned to gauge how sick they looked. Whenever possible, they tried to look healthy when out in public. A 23-year old salesperson who had always enjoyed going to bars and never enjoyed solitude described how "Every time I go out [to a bar] I try to hide it. I try to act energetic and normal and I always have them put a squeeze of lime in my drinks so it's like a mixed drink.." When their health made it impossible to appear normal, PWAs stayed home. As another man explained, "There are days that I really feel shitty and I look bad and I won't let anybody see me. I won't go around anybody. And then there are days I really force myself to put myself together so I will look decent and I'm not afraid to go out then."

This strategy is no help, however, when PWAs must go out despite visible physical problems. To protect their secret in these circumstances, PWAs may devise plausible alternative explanations for their symptoms. One man explained his weight loss by telling co-workers that he had begun marathon training. Others attributed their physical problems to less stigmatized illnesses, such as leukemia or cancer.

Although hiding one's illness gives PWAs some protection against rejection, it carries a high price. PWAs who hide their illness from employers may lose their jobs when they cannot explain their increased absences and decreased productivity. Those who choose not to tell friends or relatives must endure their illness alone and in silence, without support they might otherwise receive. They must also endure the emotional strain caused by the secretiveness itself. As one man said, "I want to tell. I'm not used to hiding everything from everybody....I'm a basically honest person and I don't like to lie." Finally, PWAs who keep their illnesses secret risk hearing painfully disparaging comments about how AIDS "serves those queers right." On such occasions, PWAs may feel that they cannot respond without risking exposure. A 33-year old salesperson involved with an AIDS political action group said:

> I was at my desk and three secretaries telling AIDS jokes were standing right behind me. It cut and it hurt. I grit my teeth and said nothing....[Occasionally] I try and slide in a little bit of education...but I don't push it to the point where they go, "how come he knows so much?"

To avoid questions about why they don't find AIDS jokes humorous, some PWAs even feel obliged to join in the laughter.

Because both concealing and revealing one's illness can create problems, it is difficult for a PWA to decide what to do. To deal with this dilemma, PWAs learn to predict how various others may react to news of their illness. For example, a PWA can tell a relative that he volunteers for an AIDS education group or that a friend of his has AIDS. The relative's reaction can help the PWA decide whether to tell of his own illness.

PWAs also learn not only whom to tell but when to tell of their illness. A 24-year old blue collar worker who had been abandoned by several close friends said, "I used to tell people up front about my diagnosis, but I don't anymore. I let them get to know me, because I really want them to get to know me before they pass judgment on me." A few PWAs whose families lived out of state had decided not to disclose their illness until they could see their families in person. Others, who expected their diagnosis to precipitate family crises, decided not to tell until death appeared imminent.

In the aftermath of disclosure, PWAs can avoid further stigma by reducing contact with friends and relatives who prove unsupportive. As a result, however, their social lives shrink significantly. The man who put lime in his water at bars said:

> [Before getting AIDS] I was out all the time, I loved to be around people. I hated to be by myself. But now, I find that I don't like to be around people that much except if it's people I know that are not going to reject me because I don't want the rejection. I don't want to be hurt; I'm tired of being hurt.

To replace their former social networks, PWAs can join support groups organized for persons who have this illness. These groups afford them a social life without the risk of rejection or social awkwardness. One man who had experienced painful rejections explained that he socialized mostly with other PWAs "mainly because I guess I'm still afraid of people's reactions" but also "because I think they [other PWAs] can understand more what your feelings are, what is going through your head. It's a lot easier to sit around and have a conversation with someone who is also ill with this disease and you don't have to worry about avoiding certain topics." Similarly, the 39-year old floral designer described above, whose mother had refused to tell his siblings of his illness, experienced further trauma when most of his friends abandoned him. He told me of the pleasure he obtained from a recent potluck social for PWAs:

> I was not alone...I met a lot of really beautiful people, a lot of really nice friends. They took your phone number, they call you, socialize with you, you go to the show with them. You do things with them. If you need any help or whatever, they're there....I went through hiding myself in my house and every time the facial sores started I would be afraid to go out and let people see me. These people don't care. You're not the only one that's had the facial sores and they don't care. You're welcome there....Nobody [at the potluck] was afraid because a person with ARC or AIDS made a dish. We all rather enjoyed the food. It was like all the barriers went down when you were with these other people.

Although socializing with PWAs solves some problems, it creates others. First, PWAs may find that they have nothing but their illness in common. As a result, the relationships they develop are likely to be superficial and unrewarding. Second, as one man explained, these social circles do not permit the PWA "to get away from AIDS and be myself at the same time." Only with other PWAs can they act truly naturally. Yet when they are with other PWAs, they cannot avoid at least thinking about their illness. Third, PWAs who develop new friendships in these circles must then cope with their friends' illnesses and dying as well as their own. thus seeking friendship from other PWAs in the end can increase their own sorrow.

**Reducing Stigma.** Although hiding one's illness and restricting one's social circle help PWAs to avoid stigma, they will not reduce that stigma. Some PWAs therefore consider these strategies inadequate and choose, at least

in some situations, to attack the roots of the stigma.

To reduce the stigma of AIDS, PWAs may "come out of the closet" about their illness~working for community organizations that provide services to PWAs, becoming "resources" for acquaintances who have unanswered questions about AIDS, or even speaking for the media about having AIDS. PWAs who take this course believe it is the only way truly to improve their situation. For example, the man whose mother refused to help him obtain health insurance subsequently became an active speaker about AIDS. He explained, "the only way that I could see getting rid of that stigma is to stick up for myself and become publicly known, to say it's okay to be my friend, it's okay to hug me, it's okay to sit down on a couch with me and watch TV." Other PWAs continue to conceal their diagnosis but nonetheless try to teach people around them that PWAs should not be shunned. One man described a confrontation with a neighbor who accused him of having AIDS and asked him not to use the door in their apartment complex. The PWA denied that he had AIDS, but told the neighbor "ignorance is no excuse. You ought to read up on AIDS, you can't get it that way."

To reduce stigma, PWAs must go beyond educating others about the biology of the disease to challenging the idea that AIDS is a deserved punishment for sin. They do so in two ways. First, PWAs can argue that God is the source of love and not of punishment and that God would not have created gay people only to reject them as sinners. Second, they can argue that all illnesses are biological phenomena, not signs of divine judgment, and that it was simply bad luck that the first Americans affected by AIDS were gay. Several of the men stressed their belief that AIDS had originated among heterosexuals in Africa and thus could not be punishment for homosexuality. As one 28-year old construction worker said, "It didn't start out as a homosexual disease and it's not going to finish that way."

These alternative explanations for AIDS allow PWAs to reject their rejectors as prejudiced or ignorant. The construction worker just quoted went on to describe his reaction to Jerry Falwell's statements that AIDS is God's punishment for sin:

> Somebody like that really ought to be put away. He's doing so much damage, it's pathetic and he doesn't know what he's talking about and that's real sad. And we don't need that~we need understanding.

Other PWAs, however, themselves believe that they deserve AIDS (Weitz, 1989). In these circumstances, they can reduce stigma only by accepting responsibility for their actions, forswearing their former activities, and asking forgiveness from their families, churches, and God.

Finally, PWAs can reduce stigma through bravado~putting on what amounts to a show in order to convince others of the reality that they are functioning and worthwhile human beings. The man who chastised his neighbor for being ignorant about AIDS told how he and other PWAs occasionally go to a bar to "show these people that we can live with AIDS. That we can have a good time. That we can dance, that we can socialize, that we're not people with plagues." Describing a recent visit to his neighborhood bar, he said:

> I just walked in, put my arms around somebody, said "Hi, how're you doing? Everything going OK with you?" and he said, "Well how are you doing?" and I said, "Well, ARC hasn't gotten me down yet, I don't think it will." I said, "I'm going to beat this thing." And I just acted like nothing was wrong.

## CONCLUSIONS

Almost by definition, "to define something as a disease or illness is to deem it undesirable" (Conrad and Schneider, 1980:36). By the same token, to say that someone has a disease or (more strongly) is diseased implies that the person is less whole, functioning, or worthy than "normal" people. Consequently, all chronically ill persons must struggle against stigma.

At present, however, no other physical illness in American society carries stigma as severe as AIDS. For example, while some people believe that herpes or leprosy are divine punishments for sin, far more people believe that AIDS is a divine punishment. Similarly, some health care workers provide only grudging, low quality care to patients whom they consider demanding hypochondriacs, such as people who suffer chronic pain with no clear cause. Few if any health care workers, however, refuse to provide care to such persons. Yet many refuse to provide care to PWAs. The stigma of AIDS reflects the fact that it is contagious, deforming, fatal, imperfectly understood, and associated with already stigmatized groups.

Despite the differences between AIDS and other illnesses, however, PWAs manage stigma in much the same way as other chronically ill people. To avoid stigma, PWAs do not disclose their illness if it is invisible, mask the signs of illness if they are visible, lie about those signs if they cannot be masked, and minimize contact with people who reject them when their illness becomes known. Alternatively, PWAs can reveal their illness and either challenge their detractor's theological and biological assumptions or ask forgiveness for their former deviant conduct. In these ways, PWAs, like people with other illnesses, can limit the impact of illness on their social lives.

********

## Acknowledgments

This research was made possible by a grant from the Arizona Disease Control Research Comission and by a small grant from Arizona State University College of Liberal Arts and Sciences. I also wish to thank Rochelle Kern, Karolynn Siegel and Peter Conrad for their comments on earlier drafts of this paper.

## REFERENCES

AIDS Program (1989). AIDS Weekly Surveillance Report--United States, February 20, 1989. Center for Infectious Diseases, Centers for Disease Control.

Boutte, Marie I. (1987). "The stumbling disease': A case study of stigma among Azorean-Portuguese." *Social Science and Medicine* 2493), 209-217.

**Brooks, Nancy A., and Ronald R. Matson, 1987).** "Managing multiple sclerosis." *Research in the Sociology of Health Care 6, 73-106.*

**Charmaz, Kathy (1980).** *The Social Reality of Death.* Reading, MA: Addison-Wesley.

**Conrad, Peter, and Joseph Schneider (1980).** Deviance and medicalization: From badness to sickness. St. Louis: C. V. Mosby.

**Goffman, Erving (1963).** *Stigma: Notes on the Management of Spoiled Identity.* Englewood Cliffs, NJ: Prentice-Hall.

**Gussow, Zachary, and George S. Tracy (1968).** "Status, ideology, and adaptation to stigmatized illness: A study of leprosy." *Human Organization* 27, 316-325.

**Hilbert, Richard A. (1984).** "The acultural dimensions of chronic pain: Flawed reality construction and the problem of meaning." *Social Problems* 31, 365-78.

**Katz, Irwin, R. Glen Hass, Nina Parisi, JanettAstone, and Denise McEvaddy (1987).** "Lay people's and health care personnel's perceptions of cancer, AIDS, cardiac, and diabetic patients." *Psychological Reports* 60, 615-629.

**Kelly, Jeffrey A., Janet S. St. Lawrence, Steve Smith, Harold V. Hood, and Donna J. Cook (1987).** "Stigmatization of AIDS patients by physicians." *American Journal of Public Health* 77, 789-791.

**Leonard, Arthur S. (1987).** "AIDS in the workplace." pp. 109-125 in Harlon L. Dalton, Scott Burris, and the Yale AIDS Law Project (eds.), *AIDS and the Law: A Guide for the Public.* New Haven: Yale University Press.

**Masters, William H., VirEginia E. Johnson, and Robert . Kolodny (1988).** *Crisis: Heterosexual Behavior in the Age of AIDS,* New York: Grove Press.

**National Center for Health Statistics, D. A. Dawson (1988).** "AIDS knowledge and attitudes for July 1988, Provisional data from the National Health Interview Survey." *Advance Data from Vital and Health Statistics,* No. 161. DHHSS Pub. No. 89-1250, Hyattsville, Md.: Public Health Service.

**Schneider, Joseph, and Peter Conrad (1983).** *Having Epilepsy.* Philadelphia: Temple University Press.

**Weitz, Rose (1989).** "Uncertainty and the lives of persons with AIDS." *Journal of Health and Social Behavior* 30, 270-81.

\*\*\*\*\*\*

**About the Author:** Rose Weitz is a full professor in the Sociology Department at Arizona State University, Tempe, Arizona 85287-210l. She received her Ph.D in 1978 from Yale University, specializing in the sociology of health and illness. She is the author of *Life with AIDS*, Rutgers Univ. Press, 1991, and is a founding member and past chair of the Sociologists' AIDS Network. Currently, she is writing a textbook on the sociology of health and illness for Wadsworth Publishing.

**Source:** Reprinted with permission from *Qualitative Sociology,* Vol. 13, No. 1, Spring 1990, pp. 23-28. Published by Human Sciences Press, New York, New York. 10013-1578.

# On the Situation of African-American Women with Physical Disabilities

William John Hanna
Elizabeth Rogovsky

**Abstract** ~ *This paper explores a category of people with disabilities, African-American women, that is rarely studied by scholars and rarely the subject of education and training within the fields of medicine and rehabilitation. African-American women have a high incidence of physical disability: and among those with disabilities, their socioeconomic situation is less well off than would be predicted on the basis of general patterns of male-female, White-Black, nondisabled-disabled disparity. Drawing upon quantitative surveys as well as qualitative interviews, the authors explore factors which appear likely to contribute to the situation of African-American women with disabilities.*

"The lines between womanhood and blindness are never supposed to meet. And with Blackness on top of that, what must people be seeing!" (Patterson, 1985, p. 243).

"I just felt that people didn't understand me. I had very, very low self-esteem. I felt awful about myself because I was Black and I was deaf. I just felt like I was nobody." (McCaskill-Emerson, 1992).

For decades, popular and scholarly writers as well as medical and rehabilitation specialists have dealt "in general" with people who have disabilities.

These "general" people were usually White males. Women and African-Americans were sometimes not even included in medical trials and rehabilitation impact studies, although the results shaped service practices for all clients. Certainly, scholars and educators must address the issue of culture "to prepare effective rehabilitation counselors for an increasingly pluralistic society" (Dodd, Nelson, Ostward, & Fisher, 1991, p. 46)~~and to increase and improve the utilization of rehabilitation services by underserved segments of the population. The purpose of this paper is to enhance our understanding of African-American women with disabilities so that they will be better served by medical and rehabilitation professionals.

The subject of women with physical disabilities is being addressed with increasing frequency (e.g., Altman, 1984; Deegan & Brooks, 1985; Fine & Asch, 1985, 1988; Hanna & Rogovsky, 1991; Harrison & Wayne, 1986). Women with disabilities may be considered a sub-topic of women and health. Certainly, the study of women's health has significantly expanded within the past few years. For instance, as recently as a decade ago, the Physicians Health Study was launched to ascertain the impact of aspirin on the heart and circulatory system. Not one of the 22,000 subjects was a woman! Women with heart disease are reported to be treated less aggressively than men (Kolata, 1991), and Altman (1985) indicates that women are less likely than men to receive rehabilitation services. Now, however, changes are beginning to take place. There is even an Office of Research on Women's Health at the National Institutes of Health; and it is headed by an African-American woman, Dr. Vivian W. Pinn. And the Commissioner of the Rehabilitation Services Administration, Nell Carney, is a woman with a disability.

Minority group members with mobility, sensory, and other "physical" disabilities are also being given greater attention (e.g., Logan, Freeman, & McRoy, 1990; White, 1990). Research has shown, for instance, that race and ethnicity influence people's attitudes towards the tools of rehabilitation as well as the outcomes of rehabilitation efforts (Dodd, Nelson, Ostward, & Fisher, 1991). The attitudes of rehabilitation workers and other professionals may well be typical in this regard (Smart & Smart, 1992).

The health of African-Americans is comparatively poor. Most generally, the situation may be indicated by life expectancy. Figures from 1990 (Goldstein, 1991) are as follows: White male, 72 years; Black male 65; White female, 79, and Black female, 73. A Commonly cited racial difference is the African-American rate of high blood pressure, which is double that of European-Americans. This differential rate has been attributed to genetic and environmental factors (Leary, 1991). Infant mortality contrasts are equally dramatic. The per-l000 births mortality figures for 1989, recently released, are 17.1 and 8.2 ~ an increased ratio over the previous three decades (Taylor, 1992).

Racial contrasts also appear in disability rates, which are relatively high for African-American men and even higher for African-American women. Women constitute almost two-thirds of those African-Americans with physical disabilities, a relationship that is diminished but still present when controlling for age (Asbury, Maholmes, Rackley, & White, 1989). As but one example, the Public Health Service reports (Squires, 1992) that African-Americans over 40 are four times more likely than European-Americans to become blind from glaucoma.

Differences in health care access and quality, a reflection of personal wealth, may in part be responsible for racial differences in disability rates (Jaynes & Williams, Jr., 1989; Otten, Teutsch, Williamson, & Marks, 1990). "The United States, more than any other developed country, is paying dearly for its social problems once they become medical problems" (Leroy L. Schwartz quoted in Rich, 1991, p. A21). Walker, Asbury, Malhomes, and Rackley (1991) suggest that racial contrasts may be due to poor prenatal, perinatal, and later health care provided and/or sought, poor nutrition, poor education, and higher risk living and working conditions. The rate of preventable deaths is comparatively high among African-Americans (Woodlander et al., 1985).

African-Americans are almost half as likely as European-Americans to have health insurance, and women in the 45-64 age bracket ~ especially African-Americans and Hispanic-Americans (Barringer, 1992) ~ are relatively uninsured compared with their male cohorts. Said one of our respondents, "The help that I need, I can't get. I can't afford it." Insurance and other poverty-related factors such as education may help to explain the National Cancer Institute's figures that fully half of African-American women had not heard of mammography, and many of those who were aware of the diagnostic technique had not used it. Furthermore, public benefits may be less readily available. A congressional investigation revealed that, from initial claims through appeals, African-Americans have a comparatively difficult time obtaining SSDI and SSI benefits (Labaton, 1992).

According to Wolinsky (1992), there are significant differences between the discretionary health services utilization of European-Americans and African-Americans. African-Americans, according to a small-Scale study conducted by Belgrave and Walker (1991), report receiving less physical and occupational therapy than European-Americans. LaViest (in Boodman, 1992) argues that African-Americans are discouraged from using medical services because of the racism they must confront in the health care system. We cannot be sure whether utilization differences are due to supply, resources and other demand factors, or what is most likely, a mixture of the two.

## APPROACH

Our personal observations and experiences added to reports in the scholarly literature lead to the working hypotheses that African-American women with disabilities are especially disadvantaged, and that the disadvantage is linked to their gender, race, and disability. Furthermore, the three stigmatized statuses may be interactive rather than, as usually assumed, additive. One plus one plus one may equal four or more. The disadvantages, causes, and consequences of the interactions should be explored.

A range of sources are used to explore the situation of African-American women with physical disabilities. Especially critical are the Census Bureau's 1984 special survey that included a series of questions about health and disability, and a set of interviews we conducted over the past few years with a non-random sample of Washington metropolitan area women with physical disabilities. Additional insights come from a Louis Harris and Associates' 1986 survey of Americans with disabilities, and our 1988 questionnaire-based studies of undergraduate students' free associations and attributions pertaining to people with disabilities. It should be noted that African-American women with physical disabilities are apparently underrepresented in these studies; intra-racial analysis helps to address this problem.

The quantitative analyses reported here, primarily based upon the Census data, focus on the responses of 40-49 year olds. This choice was made because people in this age category are less impacted on a gender-specific basis by child birth and longevity. That is, women below the age of 40 are in their prime child bearing years; and this impacts employment, income, and other variables. Women aged 50 and above are increasingly likely to be affected by the death of a mate. In the Census data set, there are 2011 respondents in the 40-49 year old bracket; of these, 174 (9%) are European-American and 40 (2%) African-American women with physical disabilities. At this stage of the research, any positive response about a recognized physical disability is used to place the respondent in the disability category. The breadth of disability coverage and possibly some of the severity thresholds may account for the relatively high percent of individuals categorized as disabled. In the 1986 Harris study, the sample included 39 African-American and 270 European-American females with disabilities.

Looking at the Census data, it is surprising to discover that in the 40-49 age bracket, having at least *some* physical disability is much more common among African-American women than is the case with other population groupings. For both African-American and European-American males, the percent with some reported disability is 25%; for European-American females, the figure is 24%. But for African-American women, it is an astounding 42%. Headen and Headen (1986) are apparently correct in observing that "black women are at increased risk (compared with other groups) for illness and disability from a variety of chronic illnesses that require a lifetime of medical care to control both acute and long-term effects" (p. 191).

Initially, the 40-49 year olds in the Census data set were divided into four categories to produce a two-by-two four-cell matrix: nondisabled men, nondisabled women, men with physical disabilities, and women with physical disabilities. A further subdivision produced a four-cell matrix for each of our two focal racial groups, European-Americans and African-Americans. The female/male ratio among the nondisabled category was used to establish a statistical norm of society's gender impact; and for a statistical norm of the impact of physical disability, disabled/nondisabled ratio among men was calculated. This provides a basis for predicting the situation of women with disabilities. For instance, if a particular female-to-male ratio such as percent employed is, say, .7, and the disabled-to-nondisabled male ratio is .6, one would predict the female disabled figure to be .7 x .6 = .42; a lower actual employment figure for women with disabilities suggests that other factors are impacting these women. Finally, the two race-specific four cell matrices are considered to see how the situation of African-American women with disabilities compare with the situation for European-Americans.

## GENDER

The inquiry focuses on gender and then race. The Census data reveal that the overall situation for women with physical disabilities is much worse than would be predicted based on our data-derived norms of sexism and able-ism. Women with disabilities are more likely than expected to be socially isolated, poorly educated, un- or underemployed, and living on a low income. Some of the contrasts are statistically significant, whereas others are not. However, the *direction* of the results is consistent. Indeed, it is the overall pattern which we find impressive~and suggestive of the special situation of women with physical disabilities.

Sociocultural factors appear to be operative. We believe that these factors are primary: Sexism, able-ism, and a set of other factors seemingly associated with the interaction of sexism and able-ism. If gender and disability are often stigmatizing (Goffman, 1963), it may be that the interaction of several stigmas is more than additive in impact. Three related factors appear to be especially critical: nurturing roles, causal attributions, and physical attractiveness.

Women in general, in contrast with men, are typically seen as having nurturing roles in our society, including those of wife-companion, mother, sexual partner, and office worker-pleaser. We note but cannot explore here the potentially oppressive aspects of such roles. Our interviews suggest that women with physical disabilities are viewed differently. In particular, many of the respondents and others often view women with disabilities as incapable of parenting or being a sexual partner. Rather, they are often seen as incapable of nurturing, indeed, as dependent people who must themselves be nurtured.

Within our culture, some differences in people's behavior towards men and women with disabilities may be based on prevailing beliefs about the causes of disabilities. Our exploratory research on this subject, simply summarized, indicates that beliefs about causes may well be relatively positive regarding males but negative for females. The respondents tend to attribute the physical disabilities of males to external "heroic" factors, including war/fighting and work. However, for females, attributions are more likely to focus on "imperfections" of the person such as careless accidents and illnesses. Note that this gender contrast may well be more pronounced within the European-American community due to the culture's negative image of African-American men.

Physical attractiveness is, in American culture, an important determinant of a person's worth~especially for women. Of course, externally defined standards of attractiveness focus on many physical characteristics, from breast shape to skin color. Unfortunately, as Patzer (1985) noted, physical attractiveness influences romance, friendship, and even employment. Disability is linked with attractiveness. Bogle and Shaul (1981) wrote, "The media sex symbol of the day is an impossible standard for any woman to live up

to, but disability places you at an even greater disadvantage" (p. 92). Furthermore, for many people, a visible disability leads to a generalized image (a spread effect) that is relatively negative. This phenomenon even impacts a secondary level of association; males associated with attractive females receive comparatively favorable ratings from peers (Schroedel, 1979).

Some women with physical disabilities are challenged positively by the social and environmental handicaps they face; and many such women are quite successful in meeting the challenges. One of the respondents said, "It is my role to show what a 'disabled woman' can do...Aren't disabled women amazing!' And another, who was injured mountain climbing, sees life as ever more challenging. She has had two children, lectures, swims, and plays competitive tennis. However, the combination of perceived and/or expected deficient nurturing, negative attributions, problematic assessments of physical attractiveness, and other as yet unidentified factors appears too often to lead to a unique socially imposed and individually accepted negative role, that of the low-valued physically disabled woman. Although there are dramatic exceptions, many such women find the challenge of fighting handicaps too overwhelming. Anxiety and depression are common (Taylor & Aspinwall, 1990). These women may well be the ones who are relatively isolated from social contacts and the workplace, poorly educated, lacking in money and other resources, and dependent. They may be taught~and learn~ to be helpless.

## RACE AND GENDER

Does disability produce similar patterns among European-American and African-American women? Certainly, racism is a powerful force within our society; and relationships that might be termed oppressive occur between and even within racial groups. Furthermore, socioeconomic class (African-Americans are on average economically less well off), and environmental conditions (African-Americans tend to live in areas with greater pollution) appear to be powerful influences. Would this study reveal, to borrow a phrase from Barbara Smith (1983), an "interlocking web of oppression" (p. xxviii)?

It is certainly not surprising to find evidence of racism and sexism (Hooks, 1981; Collins, 1990). "Racism," writes Jones (January, 1992), "wounds us in gender-specific ways." But we did not know that African-American women with physical disabilities are much worse off than one might predict on the basis of sex (and sexism), disability (and able-ism), and race (and racism). Clearly, other forces are at work.

Of course, there are many independent and successful African-American females who have physical disabilities (Rousso, 1988). Some of the women with whom we spoke are prime examples. Positive social support and access to quality education and rehabilitation appear to be among the differentiating factors. However, such women tend not to be especially visible within our society at large.

To explore the factor of race, the research again focused on people 40-49 years old in the Census survey. The broad patterns are, of course, that women, people with disabilities, and African-Americans are not well off in contrast with their comparison groups. However, focusing upon women with physical disabilities within each racial group, we find that for virtually every factor studied, African-American women with physical disabilities are absolutely and within-race relatively less well off than their European-American counterparts.

Consider one detailed example, full-time employment. Among European-Americans, the employment figures are nondisabled males, 86%, nondisabled females, 61%, and disabled males, 77%. This provides the basis for predicting a percent for women with disabilities, since a norm for the shortfall due to sexism may be set at 61/86, and for able-ism the norm is 77/86. These shortfall fractions, when multiplied to take into consideration the joint impact of sexism and able-ism, predict 55%, whereas the actual figure is 44%. Thus the full-time employment of European-American women with disabilities is only 44/55 of the expected figure, or 80%. Turning to African-Americans, the percentages for the first three

categories are 75%, 60%, and 57%, and for women with disabilities it is 25%. Thus the calculated expected figure is 46%, and the actual/expected fraction is 25/46, or 54%. Put simply, African-American women with disabilities are worse off than their European-American counterparts, both absolutely (25% to 44%) and relatively (54% to 80%).

## WHAT ELSE IS GOING ON HERE?

Awareness of sexism, racism, and able-ism are essential to an understanding of the situation of African-American women with disabilities. And at the intersections of these three, there appear to be a number of additional sociocultural factors at work.

### Sex Ratio

There may well be a powerful impact upon African-American women with physical disabilities caused by the female-to-male sex ratio. In the mid- 1980s, for instance, Census data indicate that among African-Americans the ratio of unmarried men in the 20-26 age bracket to unmarried women in the 18-24 age bracket was 85 males per 100 females; for European-Americans, the figure was 102 per 100. The undercount of African-American males only slightly reduces the gap (Jaynes & Williams, Jr., 1989). But the sex ratio of so-called "eligibles," i.e., those not stigmatized by being under court supervision (prison, parole, or probation) or likely soon to die (e.g., of AIDS or cancer) is such that there is a dramatic undersupply of work- and mating-eligible African-American males. If unemployment is counted as a further factor reducing the eligibles, the undersupply of males within the African-American community is even more severe. Wilson and Neckerman (1986) report that the ratio of employed young African-American men to women has dropped significantly over the past decade. The situation had led some observers to use the phrase, "the endangered black male" (McAllister, 1989; Lee, 1990). The situation for this study's focal age group, those 40-49, appears to be much worse because of demographic structural changes as well as the importance many men over 40 place on youth as a key element in their assessment of female attractiveness.

Yet another ratio factor is that eligible African-American males are more than twice as likely as their female counterparts to couple with non-African-Americans; and interracial couples have increased three-fold over the past two decades (Statistical Abstract of the United States, 1990). Being seen with a White woman, Jones (June, 1992) observes, "is the pinnacle of personal freedom and power for {an African-American man}." And Lewis (1992) worries, "We transform our women, who should be our closest allies, into the enemy" (p. 5). The enemy status of African-American women in rap music is suggestive in this regard (Wallace, 1990).

Thus there is a large "supply" of eligible African-American women, and males (as well as employers) have many choices among them. "We're without husbands, brothers and sons," comments Black sociologist Gloria Alibaruho (in Wilkerson, 1990, p. A14), reflecting the fact that African-American female-headed households now outnumber those with two parents. Jones (May, 1992) refers to the "sassy-catty-black-woman-alone-again blues."

Marriage and other forms of male-female coupling are said to be based upon a pragmatic partnership (Gwaltney, 1980), and pragmatism also governs the typical employment decision. It appears that these males and employers can be "choosy," rejecting "imperfect" women. Of course, women who have a physical disability are often judged to be imperfect; for instance, a physical impairment or diminished earning potential (Tucker & Taylor, 1989) may be negatively assessed. Powell's (1983) comment is noteworthy: "...Black women are often trapped....We are to be' chosen.' Black men, like white men,...have the power to 'choose' women that is related to our status as reactive, not proactive partners' (p. 287).

### Social Roles

One of our respondents was told, "you're Black, you're a woman, you're supposed to be strong." African-American women appear to have comparatively greater responsibility for nurturing their own and others' children and grandchildren as well as maintaining households. Whether married or not, the women are likely to contribute significantly to household income (Scott, 1991). Such responsibilities have led to the "myth of the super-woman" (Wallace, 1978).

Yet there is another myth, according to some respondents: that African-American women with physical disabilities are not able to nurture or to work. They may well be seen as lacking strength~~to wash clothes, handle office routines, and so forth. A visible physical disability is sometimes generalized; thus they may be seen to lack other attributes such as cleverness and sensuality. Within the African-American community, the perceived gap between the value of nondisabled women and women with physical disabilities may even be greater than in the European-American community. Certainly, there are anecdotal reports of some highly negative attitudes within the African-American community towards women with disabilities. However, one respondent notes, "I have known some Black women who in spite of a disability have been instrumental in holding the family together and have been respected in their role."

### Spatial Mobility

Social roles, economic resources, and exclusionary practices restrict spatial mobility opportunities. It is generally well known that many attractive job opportunities exist outside the disproportionately minority populated inner city; they are mainly in the suburbs as the result of postindustrial deconcentration (Hanna, 1992). Indeed, this trend appears to be rapidly accelerating; whereas the average income of city residents was higher than suburbanites just a few decades ago, it has now dropped to almost half the suburban figure (Ledebur & Barnes, 1992). Many residents of the inner city, African-Americans and others, commute to suburbs for work. A Northwestern University study of low-income African-American mothers in Chicago (Rosenbaum & Popkin, 1990) revealed that the women's job prospects improved significantly by relocating from the inner city to the suburbs. Such a change of prospects surely is not unique to Chicago.

Marriage is also the result of a local market place. As Lichter, LeClere, & McLaughlin (1991) point out, "the mate selection process operates largely at the local area level" and therefore "female marriage rates fluctuate in response to local area economic and demographic conditions" (p. 863). As city employment conditions deteriorate outside postindustrial locations and members of the middle class leave cities, choices for relationships diminish. Here again, the often restricted mobility of the African-American woman with a disability is handicapped.

The spatial mobility of African-American women with physical disabilities appears to be handicapped by the environment in two ways. One is that commuting may be difficult; for instance, they may not have the resources required for specially fitted automobiles. The other is that relocation may jeopardize support from family, church, and others, as well as make meeting social responsibilities difficult.

### Family and Church Support

A key social support factor may be the comparatively greater strength of the African-American extended family (Solomon, 1976) and the church (Lincoln, 1984). These institutions appear to provide significant support for African-American women with disabilities~as indicated by some of our respondents. However, for other women there may be a negative side to such support: dysfunctional dependence. Linda O. Young writes (in Rousso, 1988), "Instead of encouraging you to do and do and do if you have a handicap, you were not really supposed to do anything. That was just their way" (p. 62). A medical specialist told one respondent, "It would be best if you just go home. Let your parents take care of you. It's really hard out here." She chose a college option and will graduate next year.

There may be a difference between a family's emotional and instrumental support. A study by Jenkins and Amos (1983) provides suggestive evidence on differences between college students with and without a disability

within the African-American community. For instance, the items "emotional support by family" and "liked by sisters and brothers" indicate significantly less positive perceptions of others' attitudes as reported by students with a disability (p. 56). However, the instrumental aspects of family relationships do not show this disparity.

### Skin Color

The vocalist Margareth Menezes, in "Elegibo," sings, "My skin is language, and the reading is all yours" (quoted in Dibbell, 1990). Phenotype is a factor in the lives of African-American women (Collins, 1990), and it may impact powerfully those with physical disabilities. Discrimination against African-Americans (and apparently some European-Americans too) is greater for the person with comparatively darker skin and other African physical features (Neal, 1988; Okazawa-Rey, Robinson, & Ward, 1987; Patzer, 1985). In the U.S., phenotype is associated with social class and may well be a screening factor in social class membership.

Research conducted by Keith and Herring (1991) reveal that for African-American women ~ but not men ~ skin color is associated with educational attainment, occupation, and income; and differential attitudes about skin color are held by both European-Americans and African-Americans. According to Hughes and Hertel (1990), this relationship has not significantly changed in recent decades. Although black is beautiful, not everyone realizes that, as director Spike Lee dramatized in his film, -"School Daze." A survey respondent commented, "The lighter, the better, even among Black people."

The situation may be especially critical for African-American women's self-image and the image others have of them. Neal and Wilson (1989) write:

*Even today for many Black Americans, central feelings related to perceived self-worth, intelligence, success, and attractiveness are determined by such factors as the lightness of their skin, the broadness of their nose, and the kinkiness of their hair. Although these concerns affect both men and women, psychologically these effects appear to be stronger for females..."* (p. 324).

If there is greater discrimination against a woman with darker skin color, it may well be that discriminatory actions of professional and other relevant people in a woman's life are likely to increase her chance of experiencing a disabling event and/or of receiving less-than-satisfactory medical and rehabilitation services.

## IMPLICATIONS

Women with physical disabilities must confront multiple handicaps. Put in stronger language, these women are victims of various forms of culturally embedded oppression, including but not limited to sexism, able-ism, and for African-Americans, racism ~ or at the very least, cultural insensitivity. The evidence is persuasive (Smart & Smart, 1992). There is reason to believe that medical, rehabilitation, and other professionals are not independent of their culture. Unfortunately, the changes that may occur as the result of the passage of the Americans with Disabilities Act are not likely to be fully corrective.

Some people suggest that racial matching is needed in rehabilitation and other service delivery dyads. But this solution fails to take into consideration other potentially significant factors, such as class, culture or subculture, and even skin color. Indeed, Kolk (1977) found that African-American counselors working with African-American clients experienced dysfunctional stress. To minimize bias, self-conscious efforts are needed by all service delivery professionals. They should also take into consideration cultural variations in the dyad as well as the clients' unique needs. As an example, the professional's possible attitude about skin color and some client's learned negative self-image in that regard must both be taken into consideration if the probability of successful rehabilitation is to be enhanced. Anderson (1990) suggests that attention be given to "the cultural meanings of such notions as health, illness and disability; family and family roles

and relationships; and language and communication forms" (p.218).

Clearly, equality of rehabilitation services (e.g., in money or time) does not achieve equity, for different needs born of different social experiences and cultural perspectives must be met with a careful and equitable selection of methods. Health scholar Pursley (quoted in Brown, 1992) comments, "I think all physicians and care-givers should look at their own practices and ask whether they are giving care equitably" (p. A10). There is no one best way when dealing with women rather than men and African-American women with disabilities. African-American women in some circles have been looked to increasingly as a source of strength within the community and the family. But as Wallace (1978) argues, it is a myth to think of the African-American female as a "super-woman." She too needs all of the culturally-sensitive support and help that the rehabilitation professional can offer. Policy makers, planners, community leaders, and others can help too: we must all plan and deliver programs that no longer fail African-American women with disabilities.

\*\*\*\*\*\*\*\*

**Note by Authors:** *This paper has been significantly improved by the helpful comments of Cheryl Green of Yale University. Thanks also to this journal's anonymous reviewers, as well as Carolyn McCaskill-Emerson and Barbara D. Hardaway of Gallaudet University, Lauran Newman of the Montgomery County Government of Maryland, and Juanita Jackson, April Morris, Valerie Jean, Sekai Turner, and Caroline Young of the University of Maryland at College Park for sharing their personal views as African-American women. Data tables only summarized in the text due to journal space limitation, are available upon request.*

\*\*\*\*\*\*\*\*

## REFERENCES

**Altman, B. M. (1984).** *Examination of the effects of individual, primary, and secondary resources on the outcomes of impairment.* Unpublished doctoral dissertation, University of Maryland, College Park.
**Anderson, P.P. (1990).** Serving culturally diverse populations of infants and toddlers with disabilities

and their families: Issues for the states. In S. C. Hey, G. Kiger, B. Altman, & J. Scheer (Eds.), *The social exploration of disability* (pp. 217-27). Salem, Oregon: Willamette University and the Society for Disability Studies.

Asbury, C. A., Walker, S., Maholmes, V., Rackley, C., & White, S. (1991). *Disability prevalence and demographic association among race/ethnic minority populations in the United States: Implications for the 21st Century.* Washington, D.C.: Howard University, Research and Training Center for Access to Rehabilitation and Economic Opportunity.

Barringer, F. (1992, May 7). Study says older women face insurance gap. *The Washington Post,* p. A19.

Belgrave, F. Z., & Walker, S. (1991). Differences in rehabilitation service utilization patterns of African Americans and White Americans with disabilities. In S. Walker, F. Z. Belgrave, R. W. Nicholls, & K. A. Turner (Eds.) *Future frontiers in the employment of minority persons with disabilities* (pp. 25-29). Washington D. C.: Howard University, Research and Training Center for Access to Rehabilitation and Economic Opportunity.

Bogle, J. E., & Shaul, S. L. (1981). Body image and the woman with a disability. In D. G. Bullard & S. E. Knight (Eds.), *Sexuality and physical disability: Personal perspectives* (pp. 91-95). St. Louis: C. V. Mosby.

Boodman, S. G. (1992, July 28). The enduring legacy of deprivation. *Washington Post Health,* pp. 16-17, 19-20.

Brown, D. (1992, June 4). Racial disparity in infant mortality persists despite parents' college education, *The Washington Post,* p. A10.

Collins, P. H. (1990). *Black feminist thought: Knowledge, consciousness, and the politics of empowerment.* Boston: Unwin Hyman.

Deegan, M. J., & Brooks, N.A. (Eds.). (1985). *Women and disability: The double handicap.* New Brunswick: Transaction.

Dibbell, J. (1990, August 14). Skin deep. *Village Voice,* p. 82.

Dodd, J. M., Nelson, J. R., Ostward, S. W., & Fischer, J. (1991). Rehabilitation counselor education programs' response to cultural pluralism. *Journal of Applied Rehabilitation Counseling,* 22(1), 46-48.

Fine, M. & Asch, A. (1985). Disabled women: Sexism without the pedestal. In M. J. Deegan & N. A. Brooks (Eds.), *Women and disability: The double handicap* (pp. 6-22). New Brunswick: Transaction.

Fine, M. & Asch, A. (Eds.). (1988). *Woman with disabilities: Essays in psychology, culture, and*

politics. Philadelphia: Temple University Press.

Goffman, E. (1963). *Stigma: Notes on the management of spoiled identity.* Englewood Cliffs, NJ: Prentice Hall.

Goldstein, A. (1991, November 2). Conference looks at inequities in U.S. health care. *The Washington Post,* p. A13.

Gwaltney, J. L. (1980). *Drylongso: A Self Portrait of Black America,* New York: Random House.

Hanna, W. J. (1992, May). *Worrying towards the Twenty-First Century: Looking at the world from my suburban back yard.* Paper presented at the International Conference on Suburban Development and Quality of Life in the USA., Baltimore.

Hanna, W. J., & Rogovsky, B. (1991). Women with disabilities: Two handicaps plus. *Disability, Handicap & Society,* 6(1), 49-63.

Harrison, D. K., & Wayne, B. (1986). Status characteristics in rehabilitation accessibility: Gender influences. *Journal of Applied Rehabilitation Counseling,* 17(4), 14-18.

Headen, A. E., Jr., & Headen, S. W. (1986). General health conditions and medical insurance issues concerning Black women. In M.C. Simms & J. Malveaux (Eds.) *Slipping through the cracks: The status of Black Women* (pp. 183-97). New Brunswick: Transaction.

Hooks, B. (1981). *Ain't I a woman: Black women and feminism.* Boston: South End Press.

Hughes, M., & Hertel, B. R. (1990). The significance of color remains: A study of life chances, mate selection, and ethnic consciousness among Black Americans. *Social Forces,* 68(4), 1105-20.

Jaynes, G. D., & Williams, R. M. Jr. (Eds.) (1989). *Blacks and American society: A common destiny.* Report of the Committee on the Status of Black Americans. Washing, D.C., National Academy Press.

Jenkins, A. E., & Amos, O.C. (1983). Being Black and disabled: A pilot study. *Journal of Rehabilitation,* 49(1), 54-60.

Jones, L. (1992, May 19). Bring the heroines. *The Village Voice,* p.43.

Jones, L. (1992, June 16). Reckless igging, *The Village Voice,* p. 40.

Jones, L. (1992, January 28). Soldier in the style wars. *The Village Voice,* p. 47.

Keith, V. M., & Herring, C. (1991). Skin tone and stratification in the Black community. *American Journal of Sociology,* 97(3), 760-78.

Kolata, G. (1991, July 25). Studies say women fail to receive equal treatment for heart disease. *The New York Times,* pp. Al, B8.

Kilk, C. J. (1977). Counselor stress in relation to disabled and minority clients. *Rehabilitation Counseling Bulletin*, 20(4), 267-74.

Labaton, S. (1992, May 11). Benefits are refused more often to disabled Blacks, study finds. *The New York Times*, pp. A1, 12.

Leary, W. E. (1991, October 22). Black hypertension may reflect other ills. *The New York Times*, p. C3.

Ledebur, L. C., & Barnes, W. R. (1992) Metropolitan disparities and economic growth. *Urban News*, Spring, pp. 1, 4-6.

Lee, F. R. (1990, June 26). Black men: Are they imperiled? *The New York Times*, p. B3.

Lewis, E. (1992). What it means to be a Black man. *Essence*, 23(2), 5.

Lichter, D. T., LeClere, F. B., & McLaughlin, D. K. (1991). Local marriage markets and the marital behavior of Black and White women. *American Journal of Sociology*, 96(4), 843-67.

Lincoln, C. E. (1984), Race, religion, and the continuing American dilemma. *New York: Hill and Wang*.

Logan, S.M.L., Freeman, E. M., & McRoy, R. G. (1990). *Social Work practice with Black Families: A culturally specific perspective*, New York: Longman.

McAlister, B. (1989, December 28). To be young, male and Black. *The Washington Post*, pp. A1, 4, 5.

McCaskill-Emerson, C. (1992). Personal communication.

Neal, A. M. (1988). *The influence of skin color and facial features on perceptions of Black female physical attractiveness.* Unpublished doctoral dissertation, DePaul University, Chicago.

Neal, A. M., & Wilson, M. L. (1989). The role of skin color and features in the Black community: Implications for Black women and therapy. *Clinical Psychology Review*, 2(3), 323-333.

Okazawa-Rey, M., Robinson, T., & Ward, J. V. (1987). Black women and the politics of skin color and hair. *Women and Therapy*, 6(1-2), 89-102.

Otten, M. W., Teutsch, S. M., Williamson, D. F., & Marks, J. S. (1990). The effect of known risk factors on the excess mortality of Black adults in the United States. *Journal of the American Medical Association*, 263(6), 845-850.

Patterson, E. A. (1985). Glimpse into a transformation. In S. E. Browne, D. Connors, & N. Stern (Eds.), *With the power of each breath: A disabled women's anthology* (pp. 240-43). Pittsburgh: Cleis Press.

Patzer, G. L. (1985). *The physical attractiveness phenomena.* New York: Plenum.

Powell, L. C. (1983). Black macho and Black feminism. In B. Smith (Ed.), *Home Girls: A Black feminist anthology* (pp. 283-292). New York: Kitchen Table, Women of Color Press.

Rich, S. (1991, August 23). Tracing medical costs to social problems, *The Washington Post*, p. A21.

Rosenbaum, J. E., & Popkin, S. J. (1990). The Gautreax Program: An experiment in racial and economic integration (Spring Supplement: The Center Report), *Urban Affairs News*, 14(2), 1-4.

Rousso, H. (1988). *Disabled, female and proud! Stories of ten women with disabilities.* Boston: Exceptional Parent Press. Schroedel, J. G. (1979). Attitudes toward persons with disabilities: A compendium of related literature. Albertson, NY: National Center on Employment of the Handicapped.

Scott, K. Y. (1991). *The habit of surviving: Black women's strategies for life.* New Brunswick: Rutgers University Press.

Smart, J. F., & Smart, D. W. (1992). Curriculum changes in multicultural rehabilitation. *Rehabilitation Education*, 6, 105-122.

Solomon, B. B. (1976). *Black empowerment: Social work in oppressed communities.* New York: Columbia University Press.

Squires, Sally. (January 21, 1992). Eye tests to curb blindness. *The Washington Post Health*, p. 9. *Statistical Abstract of the United States.* (ll0th ed.). (1990). Washington, D. C., U.S. Department of Commerce.

Taylor, P. (1992, March 27). U.S. having mixed success in cutting infant mortality. *The Washington Post*, p. A2.

Taylor, S. E., & Aspinwall, L. G. (1990). Psychosocial aspects of chronic illness. In P. T. Costa, Jr. & G. R. VandenBos (Eds.), *Psychological aspects of serious illness: Chronic conditions, fatal diseases, and clinical care* (pp. 3-30). Washington, D. C.: American Psychological Association.

Tucker, M. B., & R. J. Taylor. (1989). Demographic correlates of relationship status among Black Americans. *Journal of Marriage and the Family*, 5l, 655-665.

Walker, S., Asbury, C., Malhomes, V., & Rackley, R. (1991). Prevalence, distribution and impact of disability among ethnic minorities. In Walker, S., Belgrave, F. Z., Nicholls, R. W., & Turner, K. A. (Eds.), *Future frontiers in the employment of minority persons with disabilities: Proceedings of the national conference* (pp. 10-24). Washington, D. C., Howard University Research and Training Center for Access to Rehabilitation and Economic Opportunity.

Wallace, M. (1978). *Black macho and the myth of the superwoman.* New York: Dial.

Wallace, M. (1990, July 29). When Black

feminism faces the music, and the music is rap. *The New York Times,* p. H20.

**White, E. C. (Ed.). (1990).** *The Black women's health book: Speaking for ourselves.* Seattle: Seal.

**Wilkerson, I. (1990, July 17).** Facing grim data on young males, Blacks grope for ways to end blight. *The New York Times, p. A14*

**Wilson, W. J. & Neckerman, K. M. (1986).** Poverty and family structure: The widening gap between evidence and public policy issues. In S. H. Danziger & D. H. Weinberg (Eds.), *Fighting poverty: What works and what doesn't* (pp. 232-59). Cambridge: Harvard University Press.

**Wolinsky, F. D. (1982).** Racial differences in illness behavior. *Journal of Community Health,* 8(2), 87-101.

**Woodlander, S., Himmelstein, D. U., Silber, R., Bader, M., Harnly, T. & Jones, A.A. (1985).** Medical care and mortality: Racial differences in preventable deaths. *International Journal of Health Services,* 15 (1), 1-22.

******

**About the Authors:** William John Hanna is a Professor in the Program of Urban Studies and Planning at the College Park campus of the University of Maryland. in addition to his collaborative work with Rogovsky, his publications include *Urban Dynamics in Black Africa* (2nd ed., 1981), "Decision Making in the Public Sector," *AMA Management Handbook* (1992), and "Time and Administration," *Ways of Knowing.*

Elizabeth Rogovsky is an Assistant Professor in the Department of Social Work at Gallaudet University, Washington, DC.
****
**Source:** Reprinted with permission from the *Journal of Applied Rehabilitation Counseling,* Vol. 23, No. 4, Winter 1992, pp. 39-45. Published by the Journal of Applied Rehabilitation Counseling, New York, New York 10003.

# 3 The Family and Disability

As a social institution, the North American family of the nineties is culturally and socially very different from other decades. There is a revolution of unrest in families, a transformation so sweeping in magnitude and force that as a basic unit of our social organization, confusion and concern reign about its future as the foundation for all other social institutions. Stress for individuals within the family unit is at an unparalleled high as traditional roles and values change rapidly and economic factors increase the pressure on families to live at a higher standard of living than ever before.

During the early decades of the twentieth century it was a societal norm for families to maintain cohesiveness. From 1960 to the present, social pressures on the family have produced increased rates of family dysfunction and breakdown. A disability in one or more family members is one of many stressors that affect the familial institution. From a theoretical perspective, stress related to disability in a family can serve to unify and strengthen the family, or at the other end of the spectrum, it can serve as a factor in family discord. For those on the positive side of the spectrum the family provides all of the advantages necessary to contend with any problems. From the negative side of the spectrum many families do not have the resources to effectively contend with various problems encountered. In this case, forms of family pathology such as alcohol or substance abuse, violence, separation and divorce increase.

The family as a social institution continues to be esteemed as the most important institutional structure. Ideally, the family provides its members with protection, identity, self-esteem, values, and the major focus by which its members view the world. Democratically organized families provide their members with a vital focus and solidarity which gives purpose and structure to life and the achievement of goals. In essence, what the family provides is a set of conceptual guidelines defining for its members a certain 'quality of life'. According to Roberta Renwick,[1] quality of life is not an absolute, but rather is a matter of degree. Quality of life for an individual arises out of his or her unique characteristics and out of the interactions that a person has within various environments. As human beings are biopsychosocial in nature, a holistic approach should be taken in attempting to understand quality of life for individuals or groups. In other words, quality of life is multi-dimensional in nature. When assessing this concept, the same components need to be considered for all people whether they are members of racial, ethnic or religious minorities—~or whether they are with or without disabilities. Disability or any other handicapping condition by itself does not necessarily lead to increased or decreased quality of life. The major perspective is that even though quality of life is assessed using the same components for all people, the quality of life for each person will be different. It is different because individuals place different importance to each component, and because they consider some components to be more important than others in their lives. It is also different because people exercise different amounts of control and levels of satisfaction over different aspects of their lives, and because opportunities differ widely among people.

The modern family is encountering many new influences which were not part of its traditional existence. For instance, with the new tenets of feminism it has been demonstrated to women in all fields that they should no longer be prepared to accept and be affected by traditional patterns of gender exploitation. As well, the family is now utilizing the concepts of advocacy and empowerment in order to gain fair, just, and legitimate treatment for members of families who are affected by disability. Governments at all levels are now counseled to revise social policy in order to allow family members who are disabled to remain in, or provide for, the care and protection of their members with the use of support systems, as well as to be supported as functioning members of mainstream society.

---

[1] Dr. Roberta Renwick defines the "quality of life" concept in, "Quality of Life in Health Promotion and Rehabilitation: Conceptual Approaches, Issues and Applications", a directive to contributing authors in a edited book project, University of Toronto, Toronto, Ontario Canada, January 25, 1993.

*Expanding the Definition of Disability: Implications for Planning, Policy, and Research* written by Susan Reisine and Judith Fifield, examines the relevant concern of gender, employment patterns, family work participation, and disease prevalence as these issues affect individuals with rheumatoid arthritis (RA). The study is particularly revealing as it illustrates the substantial changes in social identity and levels of activity encountered by individuals with this condition. Most importantly, the study illustrates how RA affects family role functioning and the notion that family work does not fall into the paid work category. Hence, the concern is that compensation for this type of work be addressed as an issue in policy planning.

In the second article, *Mothers Who Care: Gender, Disability, and Family Life,* Rannveig Traustadottir explores the role of gender in caring for a child with a disability within the family unit and illustrates how difficult it is for the mothers of children with disabilities to enter the paid labor force and continue to provide the caring and support necessary for the development and nurturing of a child with a disability. Through her research she also examined the caring work that women do within the family and selected women's individual perceptions of "...the meaning of care in the lives of women'".

Parents who have children with disabilities are often affected by divergent perspectives emanating from their relationships with physicians, the clergy, family members and professional counselors. Mary Ellen Zoilko in *Counseling Parents of Children with Disabilities: A Review of the Literature and Implications for Practice,* illustrates the significance of the reactions and strategies which can effectively be utilized by parents and counselors so that family members are able to more effectively support and cope with a child's disability.

Claire Reinelt and Mindy Fried in the article, *A Feminist Perspective on Mothering with a Disability,* illustrate that women with disabilities are asserting their rights to have and raise children in spite of the "shrouded in secrecy" attitude toward the expression of sexuality that society imposes on individuals~particularly women with disabilities. The discovery that women with disabilities are able to accommodate their disabilities and at the same time be successful mothers negates the discrimination which is often encountered. Society is still influenced by a perspective that disabled people lack sexuality and the ability or right to establish a marital relationship and have children. The authors site the fact that the Americans with Disabilities Act (ADA) will have the effect of raising public consciousness so that a favorable political climate will be created for confronting family issues where the expressions of sexuality are concerned and the needs of men and women with disabilities will be "...included in public policies that address child care, family medical leave, sexuality, family planning, and AIDS".

Contending with any type of disability in a family requires a variety of strategies which will maximize the rehabilitative potential of affected individuals as well as provide support for other family members. The article by Adrienne Perry, *et. al., Stress and Family Functioning in Parents of Girls with Rett Syndrome,* illustrates patterns of adaptation and coping as experienced by parents who have daughters with Rett Syndrome~"...a severe developmental disability involving both physical and mental handicaps". While the costs associated with adaptation include limited independence for meeting one's needs and social isolation, the benefits appear to outweigh the difficulties as families experience cohesiveness and a high level of organization and cooperation. The authors suggest that professionals respect the fact that many parents are coping quite well with little or no outside intervention. Positive adaptation by parents of people with disabilities illustrates that disability is now being socially viewed as a legitimate problem that can be successfully overcome within the family structure.

While there are many issues affecting the institution of the family in modern society, it is rewarding to know that disability-related issues are being examined and researched. With further research, education and awareness programs, the family may be strengthened and supported as a secure foundation for future generations. People with disabilities, like other minority groups, will thrive in an atmosphere that allows autonomy and independence which stems from the security and nurturing that a family provides, and which is a valued and supported societal institution.

# Expanding the Definition of Disability: Implications for Planning, Policy, and Research

Susan Reisine

Judith Fifield

The literature on health-related disabilities, particularly those stemming from chronic conditions, is burgeoning. International, federal, state, and research definitions of disability vary widely, however, despite efforts to reach a consensus on the meaning of disability and how to measure it (Reisine and Fifield 1988). Gender presents a particularly troublesome question when defining disability because of the striking differences between men and women in lifetime employment patterns, family work participation, and disease prevalence. The implications of these ambiguities for policy and the well-being of affected individuals are important because politicians and planners may rely on data of limited relevance to persons with disabling health conditions (Greenwood 1984; Alonso and Starr 1987; Kirshner 1990; Scotch 1990; Zola 1990).

In this article we discuss major approaches to the indicators of disability and how well they measure its scope in people with rheumatoid arthritis (RA). We briefly review the best-known definitions and present the available data on arthritis-related disabilities in the United States. Data from an ongoing national study of patients with RA are the basis for constructing rates of disability using common definitions of disability. Finally, we discuss the implications for health care policy of including family work in the definition of disability (Reisine, Goodenow, and Grady 1987).

## Disability and Rheumatoid Arthritis

The issue of disability definitions and the needs of the disabled are particularly relevant to persons with rheumatoid arthritis (RA). RA affects three times more women than men and usually develops during the child-rearing years (Zvaifler 1988, 1990). Because RA is characterized by a pattern of flares and remissions, people with RA may not fit the usual definitions of disability. For example, people with RA often do not qualify for Social Security work disability benefits because their work limitations are episodic rather than long term, as required by the Social Security Administration definition.

Psychometrically sound multidimensional measures have been created for assessing the social, psychological, and physical impact of arthritis (Jette 1980; Guccione and Jette 1990). Among the more commonly used instruments are the Arthritis Impact Measurement Scales (AIMS) (Meenan, Gertman, and Mason 1980; Meenan et al. 1982), the Functional Status Questionnaire (FSQ) (Jette et al. 1986), and the Stanford Health Assessment Questionnaire (SHAQ) Fries, Spitz, and Young 1982.

The literature on RA documents extensive limitations in functional ability. For instance, work disability rates among RA patients average around 50 percent. SHAQ scores, which can range from 0 to 3, tend to average between .8 and 1.1 among people with RA (Fries, Spitz, and Young 1982). When scores on the various subscales of the AIMS are standardized to a score of 0 to 10, they tend to range from a low of 1.0 on the activities of daily living (ADL) scale to 4.8 on the household activity scale to 6.4 on the physical activity scale (Meenan, Gertman, and Mason 1980).

## Work and Family Work Disability

Several investigators examine functional losses in defined social roles among people with RA, including paid work and family roles (Yelin et al. 1987; Allaire, Meenan, and Anderson 1991; Reisine, Goodenow and Grady 1987; Reisine and Fifield 1988; Verbrugge 1990). Most disability research in RA focuses on paid work disability, which is defined as loss of paid employment after the onset of RA. Rates of work disability vary, but cross-sectional studies typically find that about half of the individuals employed before developing RA are no longer working at the time of the study.

One longitudinal study found that more than 50 percent of participants suffered losses in paid employment over a ten-year period (Yelin et al. 1987).

Most arthritis investigators recognize the importance of family functioning, but few examine functional losses in family roles. Studies that do address the issue demonstrate that arthritis does cause disability in family role functioning. Meenan, Gertman, and Mason (1980) reported significant impact on the family economy when the homemaker is affected with RA. Yelin et al. (1987) also found that estimated economic losses in household functioning surpassed those of paid work. Finally, several researchers (Reisine, Goodenow, and Grady 1987; Reisine and Fifield 1988; and Allaire, Meenan, and Anderson 1991) found that women with RA experienced significant levels of disability in both the instrumental and the nurturant dimensions of their work at the home

## Program Definitions of Disability in the United States

Political influences and societal beliefs shape the way in which disability is defined and measured in the United States (Mudrick 1983; Berkowitz 1990; Oliver 1990). Guiding much of U.S. health policy today is a concept of health that defines it as an optimum level of performance in a variety of daily roles and tasks (Sullivan 1971; Parsons 1972; Adams and Hardy 1988). In any society, roles include expectations about proper work for men and women both in the home and in the paid labor market (Deaux and Kite 1987) and the perceived relative value of these roles. In American society, family work is given relatively little monetary value. Sokoloff (1980) suggests that this is because the American market economy relies on cheap labor in the home to maintain these necessary functions for society. American beliefs about health, gender, and the economic value of work in the home all contribute to definitions of disability that assess women's work in the home in only a secondary or limited way. Men's family work is not assessed at all (Pleck 1985).

Social Security programs perhaps wield the greatest political influence in shaping current notions about definitions of disability. Even before the Social Security statutes were expanded to include income replacement programs for the disabled, Social Security legislation of the 1930s was shaped by, and in turn greatly affected, American political thought about women and work and subsequent definitions of disability. Social Security legislation originally was conceived when the country was trying to recover from severe economic problems. Patriarchal political philosophy, reflected in many New Deal entitlement programs, aimed to preserve the nuclear family and the male family wage (Boris and Bardaglio 1983). For example, Mothers' Pensions and Works Progress Administration (WPA) nurseries were restricted to women outside the nuclear family - single mothers or women on relief. Furthermore, the National Industrial Recovery Act of 1933 set women's wages from 14 to 30 per cent lower than men's wages. The Social Security Act of 1935 excluded a number of occupations that were typically women's work, such as hospital and domestic service. This early legislation, which greatly benefited American society, also created a situation that fostered both the financial dependence of women upon men and women's greater responsibility for home and family work and contributed as well to the notion of women's work as being outside the market economy. (Boris and Bardaglio 1983). Even today, women earn, on average, 59 per cent of men's average wages. Many still think that women's natural role is in the work of the home, whereas men need to make a wage to support a family.

Developed as an extension of the Social Security Act of 1935, the Social Security Disability Insurance (SSDI) program became effective in 1956 and provides income replacement for individuals who are unable to do paid work because of disabilities. It covers insured workers who meet both medical and work history criteria. In order to qualify for benefits, a person must be unable to engage in gainful employment, must meet specific medical standards for a given condition, and must have been employed for at least 5 of the 10 years preceding the disability. Unpaid family work is not considered gainful employment. Thus, women are disadvantaged under this program in two ways. Women's work in the home is not considered gainful employment, and the heavy involvement of women in family work means that many do not have a paid work history, making them ineligible for Social Security coverage. Also, women, more than men, tend to be employed in occupations that may not participate in Social Security, such as teaching and domestic services. Despite the restrictions imposed on the SSDI program, 2,786,000 people were receiving income in 1987, with an average monthly benefit of $508 (U.S. Department of Health and Human Services 1991).

Mudricks (1983) analysis of income support programs for disabled women showed that only one-third of married women and one-half of unmarried women are receiving income from this Social Security program. Married women whose work histories are limited by their commitments to working in the home are at an even greater disadvantage than unmarried women. Furthermore, even women who qualify for benefits have a lower percentage of their income replaced than men. In 1971 the median income replacement rate for women was 44 percent of gross earnings (Mudrick 1983). In addition, 12 percent of disabled women were receiving the minimum benefit under SSDI, reflecting long years of low wages. This gap between men and women continues to exist and is growing. Even in 1989, men's monthly average benefit of $646 under SSDI was considerably greater than the monthly benefit of $438 for women. Widows of disabled men fare somewhat better than disabled women. In 1989, the average monthly payment to widows of disabled men was $525.

Although progressive for its time, Social Security definitions of work disability are not consistent with more contemporary notions about women, paid work, and the function of men in the family. Most women are employed outside the home at some point in their lives. Currently, women make up over 50 percent of the paid work force (U.S. Bureau of the Census 1990). Yet, even though 57 percent of women with children under six years of age work outside the home, women still bear major responsibilities for work in the home and experience more erratic work histories. Today, women are more likely to qualify for Social Security payments, but benefits are unlikely to increase because their base salaries upon which benefits are calculated are lower.

Although family work appears to have little direct exchange value when measured by estimated replacement costs (Meenan et al. 1978), functional losses in family work are costly to society, to the family, and to the women who experience losses. The family performs a major social function through its transmission of cultural values, status production, and the stability of the social order (Ferree 1983; Sokoloff 1980). Women who experience losses in family role functioning, particularly the nurturant aspects of family work, report dissatisfaction and a diminished life quality. Yet, despite the importance of family work, it is rarely the central focus of disability reports.

**National Health Surveys**

National health surveys reflect the current view of family work in measuring rates of disability. Functional losses in family work are included as an adjunct to paid work. The best-known health survey in the United States is the national Health Interview Survey (NHIS), which is conducted annually by the National Center for Health Statistics. Compared with other surveys, the NHIS uses a fairly broad definition of disability that includes both paid and family work (Reisine and Fifield 1988; Adams and Hardy 1989). This reflects the policy goals of congressional mandates to estimate disability rates for national needs assessment, program development, and health status evaluation.

Although chronic activity limitations more accurately reflect disability among women in family work, measures of these limitations do not include the nurturant responsibilities of family work (Adams and Hardy 1989). They also underestimate disability among women because household limitations are measured only for unemployed women. That is, if women have some paid employment outside the home, limitations in household responsibilities are not measured.

In 1988, arthritis was the second most common chronic condition in the United States (129.9 per 1,000) (Adams and Hardy 1989). The most recently published reports on limitations of activity associated with selected chronic conditions (Murt, Parsons, and Harlan 1986) show that arthritis is the major cause of activity limitations, accounting for 18.9 percent of all causes of chronic activity limitations. Nearly twice as many women (24 percent) as men (12.4 percent) are limited by arthritis.

In this study, we collected data on several indicators of disability, including information on the number of people actually receiving Social Security disability program payments, paid work disability since onset of disease, and family work disability.

## Methods

Nine hundred ninety-eight patients with a diagnosis of classical or definite RA were recruited from 56 randomly selected private rheumatology practices in the United States (see Fifield, Reisine, and Grady [1991] for details on recruitment). Patients were interviewed by telephone and their doctors submitted medical information from their charts to the study. The interview was a structured questionnaire, consisting of over 100 questions about perceived health status, mood, employment status, work characteristics, family role responsibilities, role functioning, and social support.

## Definitions of Disability

Several definitions of disability are used here:

1. The *Social Security work disability definition* includes all people unemployed at the time of the interview and who report actually receiving Social Security disability benefits.
2. The *NHIS definition* includes persons unable to work because of RA or who report some limitation in housekeeping measured as being affected on at least half of the family role responsibility items discussed below. For women, limitation in housekeeping is counted as a disability only if keeping house is reported as the primary occupation of the respondent (Adams and Hardy 1988).

3. In the *American College of Rheumatology (ACR) definition*, patients were evaluated by their physicians using the college's criteria and were assigned to a functional state category, which is a measure of a physician's assessment of the patient's functional ability. The definitions for each category are as follows:
I. Complete functional capacity with ability to carry on all usual duties without handicaps
II. Functional capacity adequate to conduct normal activities despite handicap or discomfort or limited mobility of one or more joints
III. Functional capacity adequate to perform only a few or none of the duties of usual occupation or of self-care
IV. Largely or wholly incapacitated with patient bedridden or confined to wheelchair, permitting little or no self-care (Steinbrocker, Traeger, and Batterman 1949).
4. **Arthritis Research Definitions:**
   A. Stanford Health Assessment Questionnaire Items (Fries, Spitz, and Young 1982): Each patient completed a modified version of the SHAQ, consisting of 13 items. Questions related to housework activities were not used in order to shorten the questionnaire as much as possible and because of potential correlation in subsequent analyses with other dimensions of disability used in the study. Scores on each item were added and divided by the total number answered, ranging from 0 to 3. Although not directly comparable to the original Stanford Health Assessment Questionnaire, it is a measure of physical disability associated with arthritis.
   B. The *Paid Work Disability* definition includes participants who were employed at the onset of the RA and who are no longer employed because of RA.
   C. In the definition of *Family Work Disability*, family work was conceptualized as having two dimensions, capturing both the nurturant and instrumental aspects of family work (See Reisine, Goodenow, and Grady 1984). An index of disability was created consisting of four and six items, respectively, for each dimension. The measure of disability was whether arthritis affected their ability a lot, some, or not at all. Nurturant items included the ability to listen, take care of sick people, make arrangements for others, and maintain family ties. The instrumental items included ability to cook, clean, shop, care for the car, do yard work, and tend to financial matters.

## RESULTS

*Description of the Sample*

The average participant is 50 years old. The majority of respondents are female, white, and married (Table 1). The educational and income properties of the sample are similar to those of overall U.S. statistics (U.S. Bureau of the Census (1990). In 1987, the median number of school years in the United States was 12.7 and the median money income of families was $30,853 (U.S. Bureau of the Census 1989)

*Prevalence of Disability:* Table 2 presents the prevalence of disability, using different definitions and the percent of those defined as disabled receiving SSDI payments. In our sample, 21 percent of the participants report receiving Social Security disability payments at the time of the interview. Using the NHIS assessment of chronic activity limitation, 34 percent of those in the study have a disability related to arthritis. Notably, only 46 percent of persons defined as disabled by the NHIS are receiving income replacement benefits under Social Security programs, primarily because the NHIS includes family work disability only for unemployed women and Social Security excludes such work.

The ACR functional classification system shows that physicians rated 17 percent of the participants in functional class III. These patients demonstrate serious limitations in functional abilities. Although the functional classification system may not be particularly sensitive, especially given other proven indicators of disability, it overlaps considerably with Social Security definition of disability in this sample. In separate analyses (not shown), 61 percent of persons not employed and in functional class III are receiving Social Security disability income replacement benefits. This overlap probably reflects a reliance on the physician's judgment of physical disability needed to qualify for Social Security income replacement programs.

Using the SHAQ items, the majority of participants have some disability associated with arthritis, as only 9 percent report "no difficulty" with any item. Relatively few people are severely limited, with the vast majority reporting some intermediate level of difficulty, but 27 percent report that they are "unable to do" one or more items on the scale; 3 percent said they are "unable to do" more than half the items (not shown). Although the modified SHAQ scale is a more quantitative indicator of disability, the dilemma of establishing the cut-off score to define disability still remains. There is a positive relation between functional abilities reflected in the modified SHAQ scores and receiving Social Security income replacement benefits. As the modified SHAQ score increases, so does the percentage of people receiving disability benefits; there are also large differences in the modified SHAQ scores between those receiving benefits (mean modified SHAQ=1.6; s.d=.6) and those not receiving benefits (mean modified SHAQ=.59; s.d=.5). This probably reflects the reliance of Social Security program definitions on medical criteria and on measures of limited physical functioning.

The rate of disability varies widely, depending upon how disability is defined. Furthermore, relatively few among the persons who might be defined as disabled are receiving income replacement through Social Security programs.

| Table I Demographic, Family, and Work Characteristics of the Sample (N = 988) | | | |
|---|---|---|---|
| **Variables** | **%** | **Mean** | **s.d.** |
| Age (years) | — | 50 | 10 |
| Female | 77 | — | — |
| White | 87 | — | — |
| Married | 72 | — | — |
| Education (Yrs) | — | 13 | 2.5 |
| No. in family | — | 2.7 | 1.2 |
| Family income ($) | | | |
| < 10,000 | 12 | — | — |
| 20,000-29,000 | 19 | — | — |
| 30,000-49,000 | 28 | — | — |
| 50,000 & above | 22 | — | — |
| Working | 50 | — | — |

| Table 2 Prevalence of Disability Using U.S. Definitions (N = 988) | | Persons receiving Social Security Payments | |
|---|---|---|---|
| Definition | % | % | No. |
| Social Security[a] | 21.0 | --- | --- |
| National Health Interview Survey[b] | 34.1 | 46 | 155 |
| ACR functional class | | | |
| I | 20.0 | 10 | 10 |
| II | 63.0 | 15 | 83 |
| III | 17.0 | 50 | 72 |
| IV | 1.0 | 87 | 7 |
| Modified SHAQ | | | |
| 0 (No difficulty) | 9.1 | 1 | 1 |
| .08 -.99 (some difficulty) | 58.5 | 29 | 60 |
| 1.0-1.9 (much difficulty) | 28.1 | 42 | 118 |
| 2.0-3.0 (cannot do) | 4.3 | 71 | 30 |
| Mean Score (s.d.) | .739 (.6) | | |

[a] This definition includes people who are currently receiving Social Security disability benefits.
[b] The NHIS definition of percent with activity limitation includes those who are not working because of RA and, for women, those who are not working and who report some limitation on at least half of the family role items. *Abbreviations: NHIS, National Health Interview Survey: ACR, American College of Rheumatology; SHAQ, Stanford Health Assessment Questionnaire.*

*Functioning in Work and Family Roles.* Table 3 presents data on ability to function in paid work and family work roles. Thirty-six percent of previously employed persons left work because of arthritis. Only about half of these people (49 percent) are receiving paid benefits under Social Security, illustrating how the Social Security definition of disability under-reports those who are unable to work because of arthritis. There are several possible explanations for why persons unable to work are not receiving replacement income. Some people who apply do not qualify for medical reasons or for work history reasons. However, only about 25 percent of actual applicants are denied benefits. Many people never apply, even though they may qualify. Thus many people who cannot work because of RA are not enumerated in the Social Security data, thereby underestimating paid work disability in this population.

RA also affects family role functioning among these patients. Ninety-one percent of the participants stated that they are affected "a lot or some" on at least one item assessing instrumental activities, and 67 percent are affected on at least one item of the nurturant dimensions of family work. Further, 46 percent are affected on more than half of the instrumental items and 33 percent are affected on more than half of the nurturant items (not shown). Twelve percent are affected "a lot" on more than half of all the items. The instrumental tasks are affected more often than the nurturant dimension, probably because of their physically demanding nature.

Separate analyses of family work disability for persons who are working (not shown) reveal that those who are employed outside the home have fewer functional limitations in family work than those who are disabled at work. Sixty-eight percent of the employed are affected "a lot or some" on cleaning, 63 percent on shopping, 45 percent on maintaining ties, and 28 percent on making arrangements. However, the people who manage to remain employed and who experience functional limitations in family work (particularly in the nurturant dimensions) are never counted in any of American definitions of disability.

Table 3 also presents data showing the relation between family role functioning and Social Security payments. Relatively few of those limited in instrumental and family role functioning are receiving Social Security payments. Again, this may have more to do with having an eligible work history than with medical criteria. Notably, a relatively high percentage of people receiving benefits report difficulties with bills and financial matters.

*Differences Between Men and Women on Functional Disabilities.* Table 4 illustrates differences between men and women in rates of disability. The same percentage of men and women receive benefits from Social Security.

### Table 3
### Prevalence of Disability Using Family and Work Role Functioning Definitions (N = 988)

| Definition | % | Persons receiving Social Security payments[c] % | Number |
|---|---|---|---|
| Paid work role[a] | 36 | 49 | 174 |
| Family work role[b] | | | |
| **Instrumental Activities** | | | |
| Cooking | 65 | 27 | 172 |
| Cleaning | 76 | 24 | 180 |
| Shopping | 71 | 35 | 172 |
| Car Care | 28 | 27 | 73 |
| Yard work | 50 | 21 | 99 |
| Bills/Financial matters | 30 | 36 | 107 |
| Affected on one or more item | 91 | 22 | 196 |
| **Nurturant activities** | | | |
| Maintain ties | 56 | 25 | 138 |
| Care of sick | 41 | 26 | 106 |
| Make Arrangements | 35 | 26 | 89 |
| Listen | 34 | 32 | 108 |
| Affected on one or more item | 67 | 25 | 169 |

[a] This includes only people who were working at the onset of the disease (N = 723). Persons who left their jobs because of RA comprise the "Percent not working." Participants were asked specifically whether RA was the main reason for leaving their jobs.
[b] This includes respondents who reported that they were affected either "a lot" or "some" by their arthritis in their ability to perform each item. "Percent affected on one or more items" includes respondents who said they were affected "a lot" or "some" by their arthritis on at least one item of the scale.
[c] These columns comprise the percent (and number) of people who are affected and who also receive Social Security disability payments.

### Table 4
### Prevalence of Disability Using Social Security, NHIS, ACR, and Modified SHAQ Role Functioning Definitions by Sex (N = 988)

| Definition | % of Females (n=761) | % of Males (n=227) |
|---|---|---|
| Social Security Income | 21.0 | 21.0 |
| NHIS[a] | 36.1 | 27.3 |
| Paid work role- not working b/c of RA | 37.6 | 30.1 |
| **Family work role-% affected some/a lot** | | |
| **Instrumental Activities** | | |
| Cooking | 73.0 | 35.6 |
| Cleaning | 84.7 | 47.8 |
| Shopping | 77.2 | 49.6 |
| Yard Work | 42.9 | 71.4 |
| Car Care | 19.9 | 55.9 |
| Bills/finances | 31.7 | 25.5 |
| % affected on one or more items | 93.3 | 83.7 |
| **Nurturant activities** | | |
| Maintain ties | 60.8 | 37.9 |
| Listen | 35.6 | 29.1 |
| Make arrangements | 38.4 | 24.7 |
| Care of sick | 45.2 | 28.9 |
| % affected on one or more items | 73.2 | 50.0 |
| **ACR functional stage** | | |
| I | 18.3 | 24.5 |
| II | 65.1 | 54.2 |
| III | 15.8 | 20.3 |
| IV | 0.8 | 1.0 |
| **Modified SHAQ items** | | |
| Mean (s.d.) | .786 (.57) | .584 (.57) |

[a] NHIS defines as disabled those who are not working because of RA and, for women, those whose family role functioning is affected "a lot" or "some" on more than half of the items. *Abbreviations: NHIS, National Health Interview Survey; ACR, American College of Rheumatology; SHAQ, Stanford Health Assessment Questionnaire.*

However, relatively more women than men who have lost paid work do not receive Social Security payments. Unemployed women may not be receiving benefits because of work history ineligibilities rather than because of medically defined criteria. These results contrast with a higher overall number of women, compared with men (38 percent of women versus 30 percent of men), who report that they cannot work because of RA (numbers have been rounded).

Using the NHIS definitions, women also have higher rates of disability than men. The NHIS rates of disability in this sample may be somewhat higher than in national samples because this sample was recruited from rheumatology practices, where patients may have more advanced disease. However, the data replicate the data from national surveys by showing a higher rate for women when family role disabilities are included for individuals whose primary occupation is housekeeping.

Women report more physical limitations on the modified SHAQ compared with men. However, significantly more men than women are rated as functional category III-IV by their physicians. Physical limitations cannot explain physicians' judgments about appropriate functional levels for men compared with women, but perhaps these stem from physicians' expectations that men will maintain gainful employment and will assume limited family role responsibilities.

Men and women are affected differently in the home, as they assume very different responsibilities there. Women also are affected to a much greater extent on the nurturant dimension of family work. These differences in responsibilities are a reflection of cultural values as well as the division of labor within the home. The analysis of functional disabilities by sex illustrates the potential for underestimating the extent of this disability when traditional definitions are used.

## Discussion

Our data show that rates of disability vary widely depending upon how disability is defined. A comparison of disability rates, using both Social Security income replacement program and expanded definitions of disability, demonstrates the selectivity of Social Security programs and how the current measures underestimate disability in women. Social Security disability programs exclude a significant number of people who cannot work because of RA, but do not meet work history, medical, or income guidelines. They also exclude persons who experience limitations in life functions other than paid employment. For example, more than half of those who experience chronic activity limitations by NHIS definition used in this study is a fairly liberal estimate of disability. That is, people were defined as having a chronic activity limitation if they were not employed outside the home because of arthritis. Women who stated that housekeeping was their primary occupation had to be affected on at least half of the ten family role items. Using NHIS data., many more people are disabled than receive income replacement benefits. Among persons who state that they are no longer working because of arthritis, the number is even higher. Almost half of the persons employed at the onset of RA stated that subsequently they left their jobs after the onset of the disease because of their health. This statistic is higher than the NHIS measure because it includes women who have left paid work, but who do not have severe functional limitations at home.

We do not think that there should be income replacement programs for full-time homemakers unable to obtain paid work. Rather, attention should be focused on developing programs that meet the needs of persons who experience functional losses in a variety of life domains. We must reassess the scope and focus of the Social Security programs, recognizing and valuing the work of both men and women in the home for the important contribution it makes to the family and the stability of the society. Programs addressing replacement of services in the home, rather than income, should be considered. Further, because women's workforce participation is increasing, we need to examine work patterns over the life cycle in order to assess the possibility of changes in eligibility criteria for SSDI programs in light of family commitments. Finally, surveys of the disabled should include data collected on the perceived needs of persons who experience limitations in functional capacities in order to develop better policies and priorities for meeting these needs.

\*\*\*\*\*\*

**Acknowledgements:** We would like to express our appreciation to Dr. Kathleen Grady and Ms. Norma Lee of the Massachusetts Institute of Behavioral Medicine, Springfield, Massachusetts, for their assistance in collecting the data and for their contributions to the conceptual orientation of this article. This study was supported by the National Institutes of Health, Multipurpose Arthritis Center, Grant # AM 20621

## REFERENCES

**Adams, P.F.,** and A.M.Hardy, 1989.  Current Estimates from the National Health Interview Survey, United States, 1988.  *Vital and Health Statistics, series 10,* no. 173.  Hyattsville, Md.: National Center for Health Statistics.

**Allaire, S.H.,** R.F.Meenan, and J.J.Anderson, 1991. The Impact of Rheumatoid Arthritis on the Household Work Performance of Women. *Arthritis and Rheumatism* 34:669-78.

**Alonso, W.,** and R. Starr. 1987.  *The Politics of Numbers.* New York: Russell Sage Foundation.

**Berkowitz, E.** 1990.  Domestic Politics and International Expertise in the History of American Disability Policy. *ilbank Quarterly* 67:195-227.

**Boris, E.,** and P. Bardaglio.  1983.  The Transformation of Patriarchy: The Historic Role of the State. In *Families, Politics, and Public Policy,* ed. I. Diamond. New York: Longman

**Fifield, J.S.,** Reisine, and I. Grady. 1991.  Work Disability and the Experience of Pain and Depression in Rheumatoid Arthritis. *Social Science and Medicine* 33:579-85.

**Fries, J.F.,** P. Spitz, R.G.Kraines, and H.R. Holman.  1980.  Measurement of Patient Outcome in Arthritis. *Arthritis and Rheumatism* 23:137-45.

**Fries, J.F.,** P.W.Spitz, and D.Y. Young 1982. The Dimensions of Health Outcomes:  The Health Assessment Questionnaire, Disability and Pain Scales. *Journal of Rheumatology 9:*789-93.

**Greenwood, J.** 1984.  Intervention in Work Related Disability:  Need for an Integrated Approach. *Social Science and Medicine 19*: 595-601.

**Guccione, A.A.,** and A.M.Jette, 1988.  Assessing Limitations in Physical Function Among  Patients with Arthritis. *Arthritis Care Research* 1:170-6.

------ **1990.**  Multidimensional Assessment of Functional Limitations in Patients with Arthritis. *Arthritis Care Research* 3:44-53.

**Jette, A.M.**  1980.  Functional Capacity Evaluation:  An Empirical Approach. *Archives of Physical and Medical Rehabilitation* 61:85-90.

**Jette, A.M.,** A. R. Davies. P. D. Clearly, D. R. Calkins, L.V. Rubenstein, A. Fink, J. Kosecoff,

R.T.Young, R.H. Brook, and T.L.Delbanco, 1986. The Functional Status Questionnaire:  Reliability and Validity When Used in Primary Care. *Journal of General Internal Medicine* 1:143-9.

**Kirshner, C.** 1990.  The politics of Disability Statistics:  Who Counts What, and Why. *FDisability Studies Quarterly* 10:1-2

**Liang, M.H.** 1987. The Historical and Conceptual Framework for Functional Assessment in RA. *Journal of Rheumatology* 14:2-5.

**Meenan, R.F.,** P. M. Gertman, and J. H. Mason. 1980. Measuring Health Status in Arthritis:  The Arthritis Impact Measurement Scales. *Arthritis and Rheumatism* 23:146-52.

**Meenan, R.F.,** P. M. Gertman, J.H. Mason, and R. Dunaif, 1982.  The Arthritis Impact Measurement Scales. *Arthritis and Rheumatism* 25: 1048-53

**Meenan, R.F.,** E. H. Yelin, C.J.Henke, D.L.Curtis, and W.V.Epstein. 1978.  The Costs of Rheumatoid Arthritis:  A Patient-Oriented Study of Chronic Disease Costs. *Arthritis and Rheumatism* 21:827-33.

**Mudrick, N.R.** 1983.  Income Support Programs for Disabled Women, *Social Service Review* 57: 125-36.

**Murt, H.A.,** P.E.Parsons, and W.R.Harlan, 1986. *Disability, Utilization and Costs Associated with Musculoskeletal Conditions  United States, 1980.* National Medical Care Utilization and Expenditure Survey, series C, no.5.  DHHS pub. no. 86-20405. Hyattsville, Md: National Center for Health Statistics.

**Oliver, M.** 1990.  *The Politics of Disablement.* New York: St. Martin's Press

**Parsons, T.** 1972. Definitions of Health and Illness in Light of American Values and Social Structure. In *Patients, Physicians, and Illness,* ed. E.G.Jaco, 12-144. New York: Free Press

**Pleck, J.** 1985. *Working Wives/Working Husbands.* Beverly Hills, Calif.: Safe

**Reisine, S. T.**  and J. Fifield, 1988. Defining Disability for Women and the Problem of Unpaid Work. *Psychology of Women Quarterly* 12:401-15.

**Reisine, S.R.,** C.Goodenow, and K.E.Grady. 1987. The Impact of Rheumatoid Arthritis on the Homemaker. *Social Science and Medicine* 25:89-95

**Scotch, R.K.** 1990.  The Politics of Disability Statistics. *Disability Studies Quarterly* 10:14-15.

**Sokoloff, N.** 1980.  *Between Money and Love.* New York: Praeger.

**Steinbrocker, O.**  C.H.Traeger, and R.C.Batteman. 1949. Therapeutic Criteria in Rheumatoid Arthritis. *Journal of the American Medical Association* 140:659-62

**Sullivan, D.F.** 1971. Disability Components for an Index of Health. *Vital and Health Statistics,* series 2, no. 42. DHHS pub. 1000 Washington: National Center for Health Statistics.

**U.S.Bureau of the Census.** 1989. *Statistical Abstract of the United States, 1990,* 109th ed. Washington.

-----**1990.** *Statistical Abstract of the United States 1990,* 110th ed. Washington

**U.S. Department of Health and Human Services,** Social Security Administration. 1991. *Social Security Bulletin, Annual Statistical Supplement, 1990.*

**Verbrugge, L.M.** 1990. The Iceberg of Disability. In *The Legacy of Longevity,* ed. S.M.Stahl. Newbury Park, Calif.: Sage Press.

**Yelin, E.,** D. Lubeck, H. Holman, and W. Epstein. 1987. The Impact of Rheumatoid Arthritis and Osteoarthritis: The Activities of Patients with Rheumatoid Arthritis and Osteoarthritis Compared to Controls. *Journal of Rheumatology* 14: 710-17.

**Zola, I.** Ed. 1990. *Disability Studies Quarterly* 10(3).

**Zvaifler, N.J.** 1988, Rheumatoid Arthritis. In *Primer on the Rheumatic Diseases,* 9th ed., eds. H.R.Schumacher, J.H.Klippel, D.R.Robinson, 83-95. Atlanta: Arthritis Foundation.

-----**1990.** An Introduction to Rheumatoid Arthritis. *Arthritis Care and Research* 2:S17-S23.

\*\*\*\*\*\*\*\*

**About the Authors:** The first author, Susan Reisine, is with the University of Connecticut Health Center, Department of Behavioral Sciences MC 3910, Farmington Avenue, Farmington, CT 06030

**Source:** Reprinted with permission from *The Milbank Quarterly*, Vol. 70, No. 3, 1992, pp. 491-508. Published by The Milbank Memorial Fund, Cambridge University Press, Port Chester, New York 10573.

# Mothers Who Care: Gender, Disability and Family Life
Rannveig Traustadottir

**Abstract~**_Based on a qualitative study of families of children with disabilities, this article examines the role of gender in caring for a child with a disability. Findings reveal caring as a complex phenomenon that has at least three meanings: (a) "caring for," which refers to the caregiving work, (b) "caring about," referring to the love, and (c) "the extended caring role." when mothers of children with disabilities extend their caring to a broader societal concern. The findings, which suggest that the responsibilities for caring are still ascribed on the basis of gender, are discussed in relation to traditional disability family studies and the situation of women in today's society._

**Introduction.** The last decade has seen vigorous research on families of children with disabilities, characterized by an emphasis on the importance of families in the lives of these children (Faraber, 1986; Gallagher & Vietze, 1986: Singer & Irvin, 1989). Much of this literature has attempted to determine the areas where families of children with disabilities need assistance in caring for their children at home and many authors advocate for more family support programs to assist ,families (Covert, 1988; McKaig, Caro, & Smith, 1986; Sherman, 1988; Taylor, Racino, Knowll, & Lutfiyya, 1987). As a result, public policies directed toward families of children with disabilities have been one of the distinguishing features of the 1980's and family support services have emerged as an important component of community-based services (Krauss, 1986).

Although the growing interest in families of children with disabilities should be welcomed, a review of the research literature raises concerns due to the lack of critical examination of the role of gender within these families. The vast majority of the literature that has informed both policies and practices directed toward families of children with disabilities has been based on a view of "the family" as a unit. The family is treated as the smallest unit of analysis, and the differences in activities and experiences of individual family members have for the most part been ignored. These studies are routinely characterized by what Eichler (1988) refers to as "gender insensitivity." That is, they ignore gender as a socially important variable, thereby hiding the differences between mothers and fathers within the family, as well as hiding differences within gender.

The purpose of this study is to explore the role of gender in caring for a child with a disability within the family. Although the concept of "care" is central to the discussion about families of children with disabilities, there have been very few attempts to examine this concept. Most researchers assume a commonsense understanding of caring; everyone "knows" what it is and what it means. They have therefore not seen the need to explore the topic further. The practice of treating the family as the smallest unit of analysis and ignoring gender as an important variable has also served to hide from view the complex and gendered nature of caring. This study examines the activities and meanings that are entailed in caring and how caring for a child with a disability influences the life of the primary caregiver. The study attempts to answer the following questions: How does gender influence the caring for a child with a disability? What is the meaning of care in the life of the primary caregiver? To what extent do mothers of children with disabilities see their experiences of caring as oppressing, and to what extent do they see their experiences as empowering? How do mothers negotiate their caring role within the family with a career outside the home?

My approach to studying family care of children with disabilities is informed by recent Scandinavian and British feminist scholarship (Dalley, 1988; Finch, 1984; Finch & Groves, 1983; Lewis & Meredith, 1988; Ungerson, 1987; Waerness, 1987) and British literature on community care (Bulmer, 1987; Walker, 1982). This article also builds on and is parallel to a growing body of North American feminist scholarship that examines the caring work that women do within the family (Bullock, 1985; DeVault, 1987; Smith, 1987) and the meaning of care in the lives of women (Brabeck, 1989; Tronto, 1989).

## Study Design and Research Methods

The research methods used in this study are qualitative (Bogdan & Biklen, 1982; Hammersley & Atkinson, 1983; Taylor & Bogdan, 1984). Data were collected over a period of 2 years through participant observation in a support group for parents of children with disabilities and in-depth interviews with 14 families of children with disabilities.

**Study Design and Data Analysis.** By their nature, qualitative research studies are flexible and open ended (Bogdan and Biklen, 1982; Lincoln & Guba, 1985). Although qualitative researchers begin their studies with a research focus and a plan of action, the research design evolves in accord with the emerging findings. This study follows what Glaser and Strauss (1967) call the "constant comparative method," a design that involves the combination of data collection with data analysis. This design is commonly used in studies using multi-data sources. In studies with this design, the formal data analysis starts early in the study and is nearly completed by the end of data collection. This approach to qualitative research is most commonly referred to as a "grounded theory approach," a method for discovering theories and concepts from data rather than from a priori assumptions or existing theoretical frameworks (Glaser & Strauss, 1967; Taylor & Bogdan, 1984). This study started with a broad focus on the role of gender in caring for a child with a disability. As data were collected, the research focus was refined as new questions emerged from the data. Starting with the first interview, field notes were

analyzed and coded throughout the data collection process to identify emerging insights, themes, and concepts. This ongoing analysis facilitated the emerging design of the study and structured the data collection. Based on the ongoing analysis, new informants were selected for their potential to provide additional insights or refine or expand already gained insights. This sampling procedure is referred to as "theoretical sampling" (Glaser & Strauss, 1967), an approach most commonly used in qualitative research when data collection and analysis proceed together. Besides selecting informants who would expand already gained insights, I actively searched for negative cases that might not fit evolving insights and concepts. During the final stage of data analysis all data were reread and coded for new insights. The final analysis also involved the comparing of different pieces of data relating to each of the concepts and insights already developed.

Two methods were employed to keep checks on the factual and interpretative accuracy of the analysis. First, during data collection, I kept ongoing checks on my insights by verifying interpretations through follow-up questions to the informants.. In addition, toward the final state of the data collection, I presented the preliminary analysis to a group of parents of children with disabilities, some of whom had participated in the study and some of whom had not been involved. The discussion following the presentation provided valuable additional insights and information. Second, after data collection was completed, a draft of the written analysis was given to three of the mothers who participated in the study. Their verbal and written responses were incorporated into the final write-up of the findings.

**The Sample.** The families identified for in-depth interviews were purposefully selected in such a way that the sample would reflect diversity along a variety of dimensions. The major factors were class, race, educational background, single-parent and two-parent families, families with one and two paychecks, the severity and type of the child's disability, and the age of the child. Four of the 14 families interviewed were upper class, 6 were middle class, and 4 were lower class. Four of the families were African-American and 10 were Caucasian. Three of the families were single-mother families and 11 were two-parent families. The number of children in these families ranged in age from 2 to 16 years and their disabilities had been identified as ranging form "mild" to "severe." Many of these children had been given multiple labels. In most instances the primary label was either "mental retardation" or "emotional disturbance" with an additional handicapping condition such as cerebral palsy, visual impairment, autism, seizure disorder, and so on. Two of the families had placed their children in out-of-home settings; the remaining 12 families had their children living at home at the time of the study. The families were selected for support group, through an agency that runs a family support program, and through personal contacts.

Except for their racial background, the parents who participated in the parent support group were as diverse as the 14 families selected for in-depth interviews. All the parents in the support group were Caucasian. The Support group consisted of about 10 mothers who were regular participants throughout the course of the study, and an additional 13 parents (mostly mothers) who attended meetings irregularly.

**Data Collection.** Each of the 14 families was interviewed once, with the interview lasting from 1 to 2 1/2 hours. All the interviews were open ended, guided by a general interview schedule. The direction of the interview depended on each individual's experiences, and specific questions were asked in the context provided by the individual. Most often, parents were interviewed during a visit to their homes. In five of the families, both the father and the mother were present for the interview; in the remaining interviews, only the mother was present.

Data were also collected through monthly participant observation in a parent support group for a period of 21 months. The purpose of the observations was to gain long-term insight into the processes and experiences of caring. Taylor and Borden (1984) encourage researchers to use more than one type and source of data to gain a deeper and clearer understanding of the topic being studied. Using different sources of data is also referred to as "triangulation," a way of guarding against researcher bias and checking out accounts from different informants. I gained access to the parent support group's first meeting through the person who initiated and organized the group, a mother of a young man with disabilities. My participation in the group was discussed during the group's first meeting, and the parents who were present agreed to allow me to attend meetings.

All the interviews were tape-recorded and then transcribed. Each observation resulted in written field notes with detailed accounts of the event observed. The data collected for analysis consisted of 24 participant observations and 14 interviews. This resulted in close to 700 pages of field notes and transcripts that provided the data that are the basis for the analysis.

In addition to the procedures of data analysis described earlier in this section, my approach to data analysis is informed by the method of doing "sociology for women" developed by Dorothy E. Smith (1987). Smith calls for beginning with women's everyday experiences and then seeking to explain the broader social relations that shape those experiences. This means exploring how individuals' activities are organized by social relations beyond the scope of any one individual's experiences. In an attempt to do this, the article will conclude with a discussion of how the gendered nature of family care of children with disabilities is influenced and organized by social processes that extend outside the everyday lives of the individuals in this study.

## FINDINGS

This study explores how gender relations shape roles, responsibilities, and division of labor within families of children with disabilities. It also takes an in-depth look at the activities and meanings entailed in caring, and how caring for a child with a disability influences the life of the primary caregiver.

## The Meaning of Care

This study treats caring as a problematic topic. Instead of assuming that I knew what caring meant, I tried to rid myself of my own commonsense understanding and listened carefully to what mothers and fathers said about caring. Caring is seen as women's responsibility, and the division of labor assigns far more responsibility for caring to women than to men. All of the mothers I encountered in this study had the main responsibility for caring for the child with the disability. I therefore treated the mothers as "expert witnesses" and listened especially carefully to what they said about caring. This approach revealed caring as a very complex phenomenon that has at least three different meanings.

*Caring for: Work.* The first and the most common way of talking about caring was when the mothers talked about "caring for" or "taking care of" the child. This meaning of care referred to the caring *work*, which can be extremely hard and demanding. Part of this work is the same kind of caring work that all mothers do when they care for their children. But when caring for a child with a disability, the caring work often requires specialized knowledge and techniques that are usually associated with professional work, not housework or traditional "mothering" work.

*Caring about: Love.* The second way of talking about care referred to relationships and emotions. The mothers talked about "caring about," that is *loving* the child. These two meanings of care were often intertwined, and in some cases the mothers did not distinguish clearly between the love and the work. In other instances, it was clear which meaning of care they were referring to. One thing was always clear: The mother was seen as the "natural" caregiver, both in terms of doing the work and giving the love. The fact that the

word *caring* is used to refer to both the work and the love had some unfortunate consequences for the mothers. For example, if the mother thought it was unfair that she should take the main responsibility for *caring for* the child (doing the work) and wanted other people to share the work with her, it could easily be interpreted that she did not *care about* love the child. Not only could other people use this to pressure the mother to do the caring work, it could also create tremendous feelings of guilt within the mother, especially if she did not distinguish between these two different meanings of care. This often created a great deal of pressure on the mother to conform to the traditional role of the selfless, giving mother who devotes her whole life to her child and her family.

*The extended caring role.* The third meaning of care in the lives of mothers of children with disabilities is when the mothers extend their care beyond their own child to broader community or societal concerns. That is, they start caring about what happens to people with disabilities in general and the way that society as a whole treats them. I have chosen to call this third meaning of care "the extended caring role." What may be unique about mothers of children with disabilities is their complex caring role. This caring role seems to work in at least two ways. On one hand, caring can be extremely hard work that limits the mother in pursuing other roles and activities. On the other hand, this role can provide opportunities for more flexibility than the traditional mothering role, and mothers of children with disabilities are sometimes able to extend their caring role to activities that are much more like a professional career than traditional mothering work. One form of this extended caring role is when the mothers go beyond their own children and become advocates for change on behalf of people with disabilities in general. Many mothers of children with disabilities are active, some as leaders, in the "parents' movement," which consists mostly of mothers. These mothers spend much of their time advocating both on behalf of their own child and on behalf of people with disabilities in general and are active in creating social change. They go to meetings, lobby legislators, pressure the school board, argue with government officials, organize parents' groups, and so on. These are activities that are usually not seen as traditional female activities, but when performed by mothers of children with disabilities, they are seen as an extension of the mother's caring role and an expression of the mother's devotion to her child. Thus, at the same time that the caring role of women who have children with disabilities can be very limiting, this role can also provide women with opportunities that are much more like a professional career than traditional mothering work.

## The Experiences of Caring

All the mothers in this study were expected to take primary responsibility for the work required to keep the child within the family. Although all the mothers conformed to these expectations, their attitudes toward caring work differed greatly. Based on their experiences of caring and the meaning they attach to the caring work, the mothers in this study can be divided into four categories.

*Caring as an empowering experience.* The mothers in this category saw it as their "natural" duty to take responsibility for caring for the child. Although caring was a source of satisfaction and pride for all the mothers in this study, this was particularly true for mothers in this category. Caring work was their major source of identity and pride, and they saw themselves as having been empowered by the experience of having a child with a disability. One of the mothers said: "I found in myself a strength I didn't know I had." These mothers were the ones who extended their caring into the extended caring role. They were active within the parents' movement and the disability field, advocating for change on behalf of people with disabilities. This advocacy work gave the mothers a feeling of belonging to a social change movement

fighting for equality and justice. They felt empowered having this mission in life and a vision to fight for. One of the mothers told me: "This work has made me a better person." These mothers distinguished clearly between having a "paid job" and "work." They saw their advocacy as "work," and some of them made a conscious decision not to have a paid job to be able to devote their time to advocacy. They chose to perform this advocacy work on a voluntary basis and saw the advocacy work as more meaningful than a paid job.

There appeared to be a relationship between the mothers who became empowered by their experiences of having a child with a disability and issues of class, race, and education. The mothers in this category were all White, middle-class women with a college education.

*Caring as disrupting.* The second category consists of mothers who also devote their lives to their family and their child. But these mothers did not see themselves as natural caregivers. They took responsibility for caring work because it was the "right thing to do" or because it was the "only thing they could do." Although caring work was a source of satisfaction for them, they also felt disrupted and restricted by it. Miriam Walker[1] is a good example of a mother who saw caring work as having disrupted her life. When Miriam, who is an architect, described to me how having a child with a disability had affected her life, she said:

> I am a case of a totally displaced mother of a child with a disability. I had a career and my own business before I had this child. Now I have neither and am totally displaced from what I was doing before. I have not worked as an architect for 10 years now.

Although Miriam saw herself as being displaced by the experience of having a child with a disability, she devoted her life to caring for her daughter and her two other

---

[1] all of the names of individuals and places that appear in this article are pseudonyms.

nondisabled children. Miriam saw the caring work she did around her daughter as a matter of "life and death," as she phrased it. Miriam's daughter has such severe disabilities that Miriam believes she could never survive in an institution: "When you are faced with issues of life or death of your child, the child's life becomes a priority and you put yourself aside," Miriam said.

There also appeared to be a relationship between the mothers in this category and issues of class, race, and education. With one exception, the mothers in this category were upper-class or middle-class White women who had a college degree or professional training. The one exception was a Black middle-class mother without professional training.

*Caring as one part of life.* This category of mothers reacted to having a child with a disability in a "matter of fact" way; that is, it was just one part of their lives. The fact that their child had a disability did not seem to have a significant meaning for them. "He's my child and I take care of him," one of them explained. She seemed rather surprised by my interest in her son's disability and her caring work. All the mothers in this category were lower-class mothers or mothers who lived in poverty, among them two Black single mothers. Their child's disability was, from their point of view, not their greatest concern. Having enough food and a home were issues of more immediate concern. These mothers devoted a great deal of their time and energy to caring for their child with a disability and cared deeply about that child's well-being. But their economic hardship and their day-to-day struggle for survival, not the child's disability or the caring work, was central to their daily lives.

*Combining caring with a career.* Only one of the mothers in this study combined a professional career with having a child with a disability~Elaine Gensber, who teaches medicine at a large research university. Her experiences will be described in more detail later in the article. Combining a career with having a child with severe disabilities requires an extraordinary amount of work. To do both,

Elaine had to organize her time extremely well and get by with very limited amounts of sleep. To manage everything she had to do, Elaine became an expert manager. As she herself phrased it: "If you are going to survive as a mother [of a child with a disability] in this particular culture and also do your work, you become an expert manager."

### Gender and Responsibilities for Caring

It was the mother who made the final decision to keep the child with the disability within the family. Included in this decision seemed to be the understanding that if the child stayed within the family it would be the mother's role to take responsibility for the caregiving work. This was reflected in the way the mothers described the decision making. Ellen Spencer's 7-year old son, Paul, has mental retardation, a severe seizure disorder, and behavior problems. Paul has always lived with his family, and his mother has not worked outside the home since he was born. Ellen told me about the difficulties in caring for Paul at home and said that, at one point (about a year before I met the family), she felt like she could not handle Paul's behavior any longer and considered

> placing him somewhere. I called the residential school and I had it all set up to place Paul, but I decided I could not send him away. I just could not do it. I want to keep Paul at home; he is a part of this family, and I'm gonna do the best I can.

Ellen did not include her husband when she described who would take the responsibility for the caring work. She described this in terms of "I," not "we."

The parents in this study saw the role of the father as being different from the mother's role. The primary role of the father is to be a supporter. This support role is at least threefold. First, the father is expected to provide financial support; that is, he is supposed to provide the family with adequate income and the economic resources needed to keep the child at home. Second, the father is expected to be supportive of the mother's dedication and devotion to the child and her caring work around the child and the family. The mothers were particularly likely to describe their husbands as "very supportive" if they supported the mother's "extended caring role." As an example of how supportive the father was, a mother often specifically mentioned that the father "baby-sits" when she goes to meetings and other activities relating to her advocacy work. The third part of the father's support role relates to his participation in the caring work within the home and decision making around the child. The mothers are the ones who search for services and investigative programs. If the father takes an active part in discussing the options and making decisions about the child's educational program or other services, the mother sees him as being "very supportive and involved." The same is true if the father takes part in some of the caring work in the home. Both the mothers and the fathers describe this as "helping out."

In families where the father fulfills all, or most, of these support roles, both parents described their marriage as being good, and the couple took pride in their cooperation in raising the child. These couples would typically say: "We work pretty well as a team" If the father did not fulfill these support roles, the mothers expressed their disappointment with the father and his lack of involvement and support. These mothers felt resentful of the fathers and described how their "nagging" about the father's lack of involvement resulted in serious marital problems.

A review of gender roles and responsibilities within families of children with disabilities reveals a division of labor that follows a very traditional pattern where the father's primary responsibilities are related to the world outside the family, and the mother's responsibilities are within the family.

### If It Only Limits the Mother

Caring for a child with a disability can be very demanding, seriously limiting the mother's opportunities to do other things both within and outside of the home. Many of the mothers I encountered arranged their whole lives around the caring work and the child.

Some of the children needed constant attention and could not be left alone for a moment because they could hurt themselves. Others had problems sleeping and kept the mother awake large parts of the night, or the child needed to be tended to and fed during the night.

In addition to the traditional caring work, the mothers also took responsibility for other work required to keep the child within the family. Part of this work was the constant search for appropriate programs and services. Karen Hutton, who has a 12-year old son labeled autistic, described this in the following way:

> My husband, of course, has to work and he leaves most of these things to me. I always discuss the decisions we make about Johnny with him, but basically I do it because I have the time to investigate things and look into programs and what is available and how we could make things available. Unfortunately, how active you are and how forceful you are determines what you get. If you don't fight for your handicapped child you might not get anything. And even if you fight you don't always get what you want, but you have to fight constantly.

In addition to searching and fighting for services for their children, the mothers also coordinate services, benefits, programs, and people - professionals and others - who are involved with their child. One of the mothers who has a daughter with severe physical disabilities explained:

> My daughter is seen by 17 professionals, or at least it was the last time I counted. I'm sure it is way up by now because there are all these computer specialists now. Seventeen professionals! Now who is going to take the responsibility for making sure that all these 17 professionals are seen? That whatever they say is followed up on? That they coordinate and talk to each other, that they

are paid....If you are going to survive as a mother...you become an expert manager.

At the outset I assumed that the severity of the child's disability would be one of the most important factors with regard to the everyday experiences of the families. I therefore made an effort to include a variety of disabilities in the sample. What I learned was that the handicap that the child brought to the family depended only partly on the actual severity of the disability. Instead, the parents tended to evaluate the disability in terms of how much they saw the child as restricting or limiting the family in functioning as a family unit. When the parents described this, it became clear that there were certain critical components of family life which they judged to be most important. These were activities that families do together "as a family" both within and outside of the home. Some of the most important family activities mentioned in this context were the family dinner, being able to go on a vacation, eating out at a restaurant, and so on. If the child hindered the family in doing these activities together, the child was seen as seriously restricting the family.

The lives of the mothers within these families were organized around the child and the caring work frequently limited their possibilities to do other things. When the parents - both the fathers and the mothers - talked about the child as limiting, they rarely brought up how the caring work restricted the mother's life. Thus the majority of the parents did *not* seem to define it as limiting to have a child with a disability if it only limited the mother's life; only if it limited other family members or if it prevented the family from doing things "as a family" was it seen as limiting. Most of the parents seemed to interpret the restrictions placed on the mother as a "normal" part of a traditional mothering role.

## Rejecting the Traditional Mothering Role

The overwhelming majority of the mothers I encountered during this study were full-time housewives and mothers. Only one of the mothers I interviewed, Elaine Gensberg, combined a professional career outside the home with having a child with a disability living at home. Elaine teaches medicine at a large research university. She is one of the three mothers in this study who identified herself as a feminist. Elaine described the pressure on her to quit her career when her daughter was born:

> The agencies; the caregivers; the doctors; the physical, occupational, and speech therapists with whom I came in contact, and with whom I continue to come in contact, assume that I, not my husband, am responsible for this child. That if anything has to be done in order to take care of her, that I am the one who is responsible for that. It was assumed by almost everyone that I would give up my career.

Elaine was the only mother I encountered during the course of this study who clearly rejected the traditional pattern of a nuclear family with a breadwinner husband and a full-time wife and mother. Elaine was very committed to having a family, but this had to be a family in which both she and her husband could combine having children and a career outside the home. Elaine was very aware of how she deviated from other mothers of children with disabilities:

> The Early Childhood Center had a program for children Monday, Wednesday, and Friday for 2 1/2 hours. I would take my daughter there, and I was the only mother who didn't sit around and talk with the other mothers but had to go into another room and do my work for 2 hours. I was usually so exhausted that it would be very difficult to do the work, but I did because it needed to be done. This meant also that I was somewhat alienated from the other mothers, and it was very difficult for them to deal with the fact that I was not only raising this very disabled child but I was also doing "something else."

Elaine's story is informative about the pressure on mother's role. Her story also highlights that if mothers of children with disabilities do not conform to this traditional mothering role they tend to be seen as "deviant" by others, including professionals as well as other mothers of children with disabilities.

There seem to be at least three reasons why Elaine was able to fight the pressure to conform to a traditional mothering role. First, as a feminist, Elaine had an ideology that rejects the idea of a woman as the selfless giving mother who devotes her whole life to the welfare of her family and children. Second, Elaine had the financial resources to hire people to come to her home to take care of her daughter while she was working. And third, because she had a prestigious and highly valued job, Elaine could better afford being seen as "deviant" than most of the other mothers. That is, Elaine had so many highly valued characteristics that it compensated for her deviation form the traditional mother's role. In addition, Elaine's husband is also highly educated and has a professional job, which served to add prestige, status, and financial resources to their family.

We might be tempted to think that Elaine was able to break out of the traditional mothering role because her child had milder disabilities than other children in this study and that Elaine's caring work was therefore less demanding than in the other families. This was not the case. In fact, Elaine's daughter was among the children in this study who had the most severe disabilities. For example, she was one of the children who had to be fed many times each night for the first couple of years, which left Elaine with very limited sleep. We might also be tempted to think that Elaine could continue her career because her husband shared the caring work with her to a greater extent than did other fathers in this study. This was not the case either. Elaine's husband rejected the child in the beginning, and his involvements in the caring work were very limited for the first couple of years. Thus the only way Elaine could manage to keep her child at home and continue her career was to perform extraordinary amounts of work, organize her time extremely well, and get by with very limited amounts of sleep. Elaine could fight the pressure to give up her career, but she still had the main responsibility for the caring of her child.

## DISCUSSION

The findings of this study suggest that families of children with disabilities tend to follow the most traditional pattern of family life with a breadwinning husband and a full-time wife and mother. This traditional family pattern is in contrast to the family pattern most often found in society in general, where over 60% of all women and 59% of all mothers participate in the paid labor force (Russo & Jansen, 1988).

The past few decades have seen a revolutionary increase in women's labor force participation. Women are no longer confined to the domestic realm, but have moved into the public domain. It is commonly assumed that women have permanently moved the boundaries that previously confined them to the home and the family. This study suggests that although the majority of women have managed to enter the public arena of paid work, education, and other activities outside the home, these new and expanded boundaries of women's lives are very fragile. As soon as there is an increased demand for traditional women's work within the home - such as caring for a child with a disability - the boundaries shift and women come under tremendous pressure to leave the public arena and go back into the home. Although a significant number of women have crossed the boundaries of the home and entered the public arena, they seem to have done so without the support of larger structural changes. Women's primary responsibilities are still considered to be within the family, and the bulk of housework, child rearing, and caretaking remains women's work. The changes in women's opportunities and activities outside the home do not reflect lasting structural changes, only a change in some women's behavior. And, as Gerson and Peiss (1985) have pointed out, many women only manage to move the boundaries if they rationalize their activities outside the home as an extension of their roles within the family.

The wage structure is a good example of how the changes in women's opportunities outside the home lack support in the social structure. When the parents in this study made the decision that the father should be the breadwinner and the mother should stay home - because the father could earn a better living - the family was, in fact, being forced into this pattern by the social structure. The family had, in most cases, little choice as to which of the parents should work outside the home but was forced to respond in a certain way because of the wage discrimination against women in the work force - women earn only about 60% of what men earn (Brown & Pechman, 1987). Thus what is often seen as a practical solution to a particular problem is, in fact, an example of how broader social relations shape the everyday lives of individual family members.

The institution of the family, as traditionally structured and presently idealized, has come under wide-ranging criticism from scholars in many fields. The last 2 decades have seen a wealth of literature that has criticized the traditional pattern of family life expressed by the families in this study. This literature has explored traditional gender roles within the family (Dornbusch & Strober, 1988; Thorne & Yalom, 1982), the role of motherhood in the lives of women (Rich, 1986; Trebilcot, 1984; Wearing, 1984), and the work of mothering done by women (Ruddick, 1989; Smith, 1987). This criticism has not yet reached the disability field. Most family studies within the disability field reflect the cultural stereotype of mothers as the natural caregivers and assume that women's primary orientation is as the natural caregivers and assume that women's primary orientation is toward family and motherhood (Traustadottir, 1988). This both reflects and constructs how we see, understand, and interpret the lives of mothers and fathers of children with disabilities. Thus research seems to be one of the social forces that has served to perpetuate and legitimize the traditional family pattern found within families of children with disabilities. The disability field needs to recognize that men and women are not equal participants within the family.

Disability family studies need to look at gender as a critical issue when research questions are formulated, instead of approaching family studies with a gender-blind approach that makes invisible the differences between mothers' and fathers' experiences within families.

********

## REFERENCES

Bogdan, R., & Biklen, S. K. (1982). *Qualitative research for education: Introduction to theory and methods.* Boston: Allyn & Bacon.

Brabeck, M. (Ed.), (1989). *Who cares? Theory, research and educational implications of the ethic of care.* New York: Praeger.

Brown, C., & Pechman, J. a. (Eds.). (1987). *Gender in the workplace.* Washington, DC: Brookings Institution.

Bullock, A. (1985, October). *Community care: Ideology and practice.* Paper presented at the Motherwork Workshop, Simone DeBeauvoir Institute, Concordia University, Montreal, Canada.

Bulmer, M. (1987. *The social basis of community care.* London: Allen & Unwin.

Covert, S. (1988). *A survey of family support needs in New Hampshire.* Durham : University of New Hampshire, Institute on Disability.

Dalley, G. (1988). *Ideologies of caring: Rethinking community and collectivism..* London: MacMillan.

DeVault, M. L. (1987). Doing housework: Feeding and family life. In N. Gerstel & H.E. Gross (Eds.), *Families and work* (pp. 178-191). Philadelphia: Temple University Press.

Dornsbusch, S. M., & Strober, M. H. (Eds.). (1988). *Feminism, children and the new families.* New York: Guilford.

Eichler, M. (1988). *Nonsexist research methods.* Boston: Unwin Hyman.

Farber, B. (1986). Historical contexts of research on families with mentally retarded members. In J. J. Gallagher & P.M. Vietze (Eds.), *Families of handicapped persons: Research, programs, and policy issues* (pp. 3-23). Baltimore, MD: P. H. Brookes.

Finch, J., & Groves, D. (Eds.). (1983). *A labour of love: Women, work and caring.* London: Routledge & Kegan Paul.

Gallagher, J. J. & Vietze, P.M. (Eds.), (1986). *Families of handicapped persons: Research, programs, and policy issues.* Baltimore, MD: P. H. Brookes.

Gerson, J. H., & Peiss, K. (1985). Boundaries, negotiation, consciousness: Reconceptualizing gender relations. *Social Problems, 32(4), 317-331.*

Glaser, B. G., & Strauss, A. L. (1967). *The discovery of grounded theory: Strategies for qualitative research.* New York: Aldine.

Hammersley, M., & Atkinson, P. (1983). *Ethnography: Principles in practice.* London: Tavistock.

Krauss, M. W. (1986). Patterns and trends in public services to families with a mentally retarded member. In J. J. Gallagher & P.M. Vietze (Eds.), *Families of handicapped persons: Research, programs, and policy issues* (pp. 237-248). Baltimore, MD: P.H. Brookes.

Lewis, J., & Meredith, B. (1988). *Daughters who care: Daughters caring for mothers at home.* London: Routledge & Kegan Paul.

Lincoln, Y. S., & Guba, E. G. (1985). *Naturalistic inquiry.* Beverly Hills, CA: Sage.

McKaig, K., Caro, F. G., & Smith, M. (1986). *Beyond the threshold: Families caring for their children who have significant developmental disabilities.* New York: Community Services Society of New York.

Rich, A. (1986). *Of woman born: Motherhood as experience and institution* (10th Anniv. ed.). New York: Norton.

Ruddick, S. (1989). *Maternal thinking: Toward a politics of peace.* Boston, MA: Beacon.

Russo, N. F., & Jansen, M. A. (1988). Women, work and disability: Opportunities and challenges. In M. fine & A. Asch (Eds.). *Women with disabilities: Essays in psychology, culture, and politics* (pp. 229-244). Philadelphia Temple University Press.

Sherman, B. R. (1988). Predictors of the decision to place developmentally disabled family members in residential care. *American Journal on Mental Retardation, 92(4), 3244-351.*

Singer, G.H.S., & Irvin, L. K. (Eds.). (1989). *Support for caregiving families: Enabling positive adaptation to disability.* Baltimore, MD: P. H. Brookes.

Smith, D. E. (1987). *The everyday world as problematic: A feminist sociology.* Boston: Northeastern University Press.

Taylor, S. J., & Bogdan, R. (1984). *Introduction to qualitative research methods: The search for meaning* (2nd ed.). New York: Wiley.

Taylor, S. J., Racino, J. A., Knoll, J. A., & Lutfiyya, Z. (1987)*The nonrestrictive environment: On community integration for people with the most severe disabilities.* Syracuse, NY: Human Policy Press.

Thorne, B., &Yalom, M. (Eds.). (1982). *Rethinking the family: some feminist questions.* New York: Longman.

Traustadottir, R. (1988, August). *Women and family care: On the gendered nature of caring.* Paper presented at the First International Conference on Family Support Related to Disability, Stockholm, Sweden.

Trebilcot, J. (Ed.). (1984). *Mothering: Essays in feminist theory.* Totowa, NJ: Rowman & Allanheld.

Tronto, J. C. (1989). Women and caring: What can feminists learn about morality from caring? In A. M. Jaggar & S. R. Bordo (Eds.), *Gender/body/knowledge: Feminist reconstruction of being and knowing* ((pp. 172-187). London: Rutgers University Press.

Ungerson, C. (1987). *Policy is personal: Sex, gender, and informal care.* London: Tavistock.

Waerness, K. (1987). A feminist perspective on the new ideology of "community care" for the elderly. *Acta Sociologica, 30(2), 133-150.*

Walker, A. (1982). *Community care: The family, the state and social policy.* Oxford: Martin Robertson/Blackwell.

Wearing, B. (1984). *The ideology of motherhood: A study of Sydney suburban mothers.* Sydney:" George Allen & Unwin.

******

**About the Author:** Rannveig Traustadottir, Ph.D. completed her doctoral studies in the U..S. and has moved back to her home country, Iceland. She is currently with the Faculty of Social Sciences, University of Iceland, 101 Reykjavik, Iceland.

**Source:** Reprinted with permission from *Journal of Family Issues,* Vol.12, No. 2, 1991, pp. 211-228. Published by Sage Publications, Inc., California 91320

# Counseling Parents of Children with Disabilities:
# A Review of the Literature and Implications for Practice

Mary Ellen Ziolko

**Abstract** ~ *Parents may respond in a number of different ways to the diagnosis of a disability or serious illness in their child, but there seems to be a fairly reliable pattern of responses in most parents. These responses form a series of stages which end in acceptance of the disabled child. Progress through these stages may be facilitated by a well-trained and caring counselor. Recommendations for a family treatment approach include: awareness of and sensitivity to stages of adjustment to a disability, application of an eclectic counseling model, the use of modeling, the efficacious use of a multidisciplinary team treatment approach, and participation in parent support groups.*

Approximately 30% to 40% of children born this year will suffer from a significant long-term disorder some time during their first eighteen years of life (Whaley & Wong, 1982). Although many families with disabled children manage their lives as effectively as other families, some such families may require counseling or therapy to facilitate the integration of the disabled child into the family (Harris & Fong, 1985). Current studies have demonstrated that there are parental needs at the time of presentation of diagnosis that are not being met and that the parent contact with helping professionals must not end following the diagnostic period (Fischler & Fleshman, 1985; Martin, George, O'Neal, & Daly, 1987; Murdoch, 1984). One reason why intervention with the family of a child with a disability is so important is that the child's adjustment and rehabilitative progress is affected by the family's strengths, weaknesses, and emotional reactions (Power & Dell Orto, 1980). This article addresses family's reactions to learning of disabling conditions in their children and implications for parent counseling.

## Family Reactions to a Child with a Disability

Parents reactions after learning of their child's disability may be better understood by regarding some of the usual thoughts and expectancies most parents have while preparing for parenthood. The typical parent, while looking ahead to the birth of a child, fantasizes about and forms images of the expected infant (Huber, 1979). The image of the way a parent would like the child to be reflects the parents' perceptions of themselves. The parents' expectations may include achievements such as success in a societal role or in a profession or proficiency at some activity. These expectations may be reflected in stereotypes such as the father who buys a baseball and catcher's mitt for his newborn son. When the parents are informed that their child has a disability, the loss of the fantasized child and the discrepancy between these expectations and reality precipitate a crisis reaction typified by feelings of grief and loss (Huber, 1979; Styles, 1986). The grief reaction may be reactivated during later transitions in the life of the child and the family (Konac & Warren, 1984).

Sometimes a child is born with an apparent congenital anomaly and parents are presented with the problem early in the child's life. In these cases, the parents must end the psychological attachment for the child that was idealized during the pregnancy and accept a child who has an imperfection (Whaley & Wong, 1982). The characteristics of an infant born with congenital defects violate the parents' expectations of what their baby should be and are among the most common triggers of disturbed parent-infant relationships (Bassoff, 1982). Often, however, a problem is not discovered until the child is older. Most families are aware that there is something the matter with their child before they receive a diagnosis, but they may "have focused on a rather circumscribed aspect of development" (Robinson & Robinson, 1965, p.416). If the problem is mental retardation, the parents may suspect deafness or worry about behavioral problems or clumsiness, for example. At least one parent will usually admit a serious concern about the child's behavior, but the other will often deny the problem saying that the child will outgrow it (Robinson & Robinson, 1965).

There are frequently practical problems in the management of a child with a disability (Naidoo, 1984). Seven factors to be considered in weighing the family burden are: (a) sleep disturbances the child's disability might cause the parents; (b) physical burdens related to dressing, lifting, feeding, and so on that an illness or disability might create for the parents; (c) complicated diets which require extra time; (d) extra housecleaning which might be necessary; (e) financial stress and strain; (f) adaptations that may be needed in housing and furnishings; and (g) the unpredictability of the disease or disability (Travis, 1986). Parents of infants with disabilities may become over involved in the mechanics of care at the sacrifice of much of the spontaneity and natural enjoyment that is usually a part of parent-infant interaction (O'Sullivan, 1985-86). Parents may unwittingly over-stimulate their infants (O'Sullivan 1985/86 and there is a strong tendency for parents to over-protect the child (Naidoo, 1984). Maladaptive family responses such as overprotection in response to a child's disability may predispose to psychiatric disorder (Rutter, 1977) or to a decrement in IQ (Sharlin & Polansky, 1971).

There are differing reports concerning the divorce rates among families with disabled children, but most studies agree that there is a high level of marital discord between the partners in these families (Whaley & Wong, 1982). Feelings of low self-esteem, helplessness, resentment over excessive demands on time and the burden of financial responsibilities are prevalent in such families and place a great strain upon the marriage. The parent-child relationship provides a context for an infant's acquisition of pertinent developmental skills. Parents of children who are disabled or at-risk need added support to

enhance their interaction skills. To be most effective, interventions should be individualized to address the uniqueness of each family or parent-child dyad (Fitzgerald & Fischer, 1987; Kysela & Marfo, 1983). Four tasks that the parents must master in the situation are griefwork, acknowledgment of their failure to deliver a "normal" child, the resumption and continuation of the parental attachment after hope is given for the infant's survival, and development of an understanding and acceptance of the infant's difference from other children. The father's needs have not received as much attention as those of the mother, but are no less important. Fathers generally have fewer opportunities to help their child directly or to actively participate in the care of the child. As a result, fathers have fewer opportunities to deal with the loss and may have some difficulty appreciating the time and energy involved in the care of the child (Whaley & Wong, 1982). The father may see the circumstances involving the child's problem as a reflection on his masculinity and he may experience guilt feelings. Both parents will need to go through the same tasks in forming an attachment to the child (Opirhory & Peters, 1982).

Many of the needs of the disabled infant are similar to those of any infant, but he or she may need additional tactile, visual, and auditory stimulation. The older child who experiences a serious disability proceeds through three states: withdrawal and depression, preoccupation with self, and a gradual return to reality as the parents become able to adjust to the problem (Whaley & Wong, 1982). The child with a mild or moderate disability may have more difficulty adjusting than a child with a severe disability (Rutter, Graham & Yule, 1970) because he or she is "more able to compete in the ordinary world"..."but not very well" (Rutter, 1976, p.17).

The inability of "any person who is significant to the family" to "accept the abnormal infant as is" may be the factor that interferes with acceptance of the infant most (Opirhory & Peters, 1982, pp. 452-453). Relationships with friends and the extended family may often be helpful to parents in rearing a disabled child, but they may also be sources of stress, particularly if family members cannot accept the diagnosis or if friends ostracize or are critical of the family. Siblings often have feelings of resentment or anger toward the child or the parents. They are often given no explanations or rewards for the disrupted family life and suffer from loss of routine and parental attention. The siblings may fear being affected by the illness that plagues the disabled child. When a disabled child becomes the "youngest" family member by virtue of his or her developmental age, young siblings may feel displaced and experience the burden of responsibilities that would ordinarily be delegated to an older child (Whaley & Wong, 1982).

Many have noted the similarities between the stages parents go through in accepting a child's disability and the attitudes toward death and dying (Opirhory & Peters, 1982; Huber, 1979). Elizabeth Kubler-Ross (1969) described five stages of grieving: denial and isolation, anger, bargaining, depression and acceptance. A similar stage model may be adapted to reflect typical reactions to the diagnosis of a handicap or serious illness in one's child. Stages of family adjustment most often noted in response to a child's disability are: withdrawal or rejection (Whaley & Wong, 1982), denial (Drotar, Baskiewicz, Irvin, Kennell & Klaus, 1975; Pearse, 1977; Willis, Elliott & Say, 1982), fear and frustration (Willis, Elliott & Say, 1982), and adjustment (Power & Dell Orto, 1980).

**Withdrawal or Rejection**

Abnormality in the child is one of the parents' greatest fears during most pregnancies. After these fears are realized, the parents are faced with the task of adapting to the care of a handicapped child while at the same time grieving for the loss of the expected child. Parents are often unable to deal with this task and withdraw from the situation and from the child either physically or emotionally. The parents' perception of the severity of the disability may have an effect on their reactions (Whaley & Wong, 1982). The parents may find themselves unable to visit the child in the nursery, or they may be intellectually concerned with the child's care, but remain emotionally uninvolved focusing on the abnormality rather than on the child.

Symptoms of the withdrawal phase may be exacerbated by complications in parent-infant bonding. Attention has recently been given to the reciprocal nature of the bonding process and to the infant's role in this process (Fraser, 1986; O'Sullivan, 1985/86; Wright, 1986). Not only does the parent stimulate the infant, but the infant stimulates the parent. When a child has a disability that interferes with capacity to give appropriate cues to the parent, parental stimulation and subsequent attachment will be inhibited (Fraser, 1986; O'Sullivan, 1985/86).

**Denial**

Parents are usually stunned and shocked at the diagnosis of a handicapping condition or serious illness in their child. To many, the unfavorable diagnosis is unacceptable, and the denial may take the form of a search for a physician or an agency that will give a diagnosis that coincides with their beliefs (Cruickshank, 1980). For many, precious resources are spent searching for a miraculous cure (Robinson & Robinson, 1976). They may shop from one clinic to another hoping to find a successful treatment. The parent may be even more unwilling to accept the diagnosis if the child shows no outward physical signs of a disability than if the "stimulus properties of the child were congruous ..." (Robinson & Robinson, 1976, p. 59) with the diagnosis. If the child shows a highly visible defect, however, parents may tend to withdraw from social interaction due to anticipatory shame and discomfort over public scrutiny and questioning (Poznanski, 1973).

**Fear and Frustration**

During the process of grieving, the grief may be worse after the initial shock has worn off and denial has begun to dissipate. Parents going through a grieving process may fear losing control because of the depression and other symptoms that are normal aspects of grief. They may need to express their feelings through talking, crying, exercising, or engaging in creative work. Because people grieve at different rates, a parent's spouse may not be very helpful. Reassurance and support from other grieving people may be useful (Frantz, 1984)/

Parents' feelings of guilt and responsibility for the child's illness or disability during this state are exemplified in several cases presented by Willis, Elliott and Say (1982).

> When three-year-old Julie was diagnosed as having a seizure disorder, the mother, searching for her own cause for the seizure disorder, decided she had caused her daughter's medical problem because she bathed her in Phisohex. Parents of a child born with a cleft palate/lip condition have cited God's punishment of them for premarital sex or infidelity as the cause of their child's congenital defect (p.36).

Lack of information is a main reason for some of the anxiety experienced by parents.

## Adjustment

Vernon and Wallrabenstein (1984), in addressing parental reactions to a diagnosis of deafness in a child, posited that parents can begin to constructively cope only after they have acknowledged the irreversibility of the condition and understood and accepted the implications. Acceptance of a child with a disability involves a tolerance for the child's shortcomings and an appreciation of the child's assets (Naidoo, 1984).

The parents, during the stage of adjustment, are able to actively carry out programs to benefit the child. They eventually become adapted to the problem and the family routine may return to normal. The parents' behavior after adaptation may range from over protectiveness to neglect which is the same as the range of behavior in parents of any child. Oveprotection in some cases may be in compensation for feelings of rejection which take the conscious form of fear that the child may die or grow away from the parent. The well-adjusted parent is able to understand realistic limitations that the disability places on the child and to treat the child as nearly normal as possible. Considerable emotional support and information may be needed to help the parents make these adjustments (Kanner, 1972).

Family counseling and parent counseling are potent interventions for families of children with disabilities (Buchan, Clemerson & Davis, 1988; Forest, Holland, Daley & Fallbaum, 1984). Counselors dealing with the parents of a handicapped child must be aware of the profound effect that their intervention may have on the family. They must approach the task with awe and caution.

## IMPLICATIONS FOR PRACTICE

### Awareness of and Sensitivity to Stages of Grief and Adjustment

Awareness of the usual feelings of denial, loss, anger, and withdrawal that accompany the awareness of a disability in one's child will help the professional working with the family to sense when a family's reaction is a maladaptive response which may require more than usual intervention.

As an example, a mother who had over a period of months gradually grown in awareness of the severity of her son's developmental delay was finally presented with a diagnosis of a very disabling form of muscular dystrophy. After leaving the office of the doctor who had made the diagnosis and spent a good deal of time explaining the implications, the mother, carrying her child, stiffened up and turned to me and asked "Does this mean that Johnny is a vegetable?" This search for meaning is described by Power (1988) and is a normal reaction, given this mother's level of understanding and stage of acceptance. She was told that Johnny was the same loving, blue-eyed little boy that he had been before the diagnosis was made. An explanation was given that the purpose of putting a label on Johnny's problem was to qualify the family to receive assistance in obtaining the special equipment which Johnny needed. The implication and long-range outlook were explained in terms she could understand. The mother visibly relaxed and, during the drive home, alternated between mildly tearful periods during which she affectionately held her child and periods during which she asked more questions about what the next several years with her child would probably be like.

The family of Susan, a child with severe multiple disabilities, gradually became aware of Susan's disabilities well before they were noted or diagnosed by the family physician. Susan's mother spent many hours each day holding Susan and rocking her. Susan's mother would not allow anyone else to hold her. She began to show less interest in her husband and in the other children in the family. The father buried himself in his work and withdrew from the family. The siblings also withdrew, spending more and more time in their rooms.

This reaction was seen as maladaptive and intervention was needed to assist the family members in expressing their grief, in helping the mother to allow others to share in the burdens and pleasures of caring for Susan, and in bringing the rest of the family back into the picture.

Huber (1979) made some suggestions to individuals working with parents of disabled children. These suggestions are: (a) feelings of loss should be recognized as normal and even encouraged; (b) it should be recognized that denial or anger may be the best coping mechanism available to parents who are not able to progress to acceptance stage; (c) parents should be allowed to proceed through the stages at their own pace; (d) the parents' feelings should be accepted and may be constructively channeled into activities; (e) parents may need help in seeing that there is some value in being, even when no overt progress is being made; and (f) parents' back and forth movement between the stages should be accepted.

## Six-stage Eclectic Model Applied to Counseling Families of Children with Disabilities

Gilliland, James and Bowman described a six-stage model of eclectic counseling (1989) which is applicable for use in counseling families of children with disabilities. Progression through the stages should be a flexible and fluid process with the focus at the sixth stage cycling back to any earlier stage as needed. The stage progression provides enough structure that the counseling process would be goal-oriented, yet at the same time enough flexibility is allowed to provide for individual differences. As the family progresses through stages of adjustment in response to their child's disability, the counselor can recycle through the stages in the counseling process with attention to the changing needs of the family. In the following paragraphs, the basic model (Gilliland et al., 1989) is described and adapted for use with families of children with disabilities.

The first stage in the counseling process must include the building of a trusting relationship. This may be difficult while the parents are dealing with their overwhelming feelings. The counselor works on gaining their trust by reassuring them and encouraging them to verbalize their feelings, fears and worries. The parents will gradually learn to trust the counselor who exhibits a genuine interest and concern for all aspects of the family and who takes measures to help them feel valued and accepted. The atmosphere should be one that is comforting and permissive and the counselor should attend to the various stages of grieving and remain sensitive to the needs of the family. The use of positive reinforcement for appropriate care of the child or for the development of skills such as verbalization of feelings or concerns is one of the best strategies the counselor may use to establish trust.

Lack of information about the diagnosis, procedures, and treatment is an important reason for anxiety in parents. Parents need more information related to the child's problem, the treatment plan, the prognosis, and on ways they can be involved to help their child (Tuma, 1982). The parents should be encouraged to be together when they are informed of their child's condition and the informing conference should not end with the presentation of this news. The child's strengths, appealing traits, potential for development, and availability of treatment or rehabilitation should also be discussed as well as any positive future expectations for the child (Whaley & Wong, 1982).

The goal of the second stage is the verbalization of the emotional and factual aspects of the client's problem. The process is continued until counselor and client can both understand and agree on problem definition (Gilliland et al., 1989). Tasks that might be addressed during stage two are presentation of test results, monitoring family response to information that is provided, observation of family interactions, and assessing strengths and burdens with attention to the full hierarchy of human needs.

The family members' individual strengths and reactions to the child should be assessed in order to determine the family's needs. Asking the parent how he or she would explain the child's condition to a stranger is one good way to elicit information. Some of the important areas outlined by Whaley and Wong (1982) for assessment in order to determine the family's strengths are: available support systems, particularly relationships between family members; perception of the event, including the influences of knowledge of the problem, past experiences, religious beliefs, imagined cause, and perceived effects; and coping mechanisms.

Different illnesses and disabilities might create different burdens on the family and weighing and assessing the burden is another step in uncovering the needs of the family. Maslow's (1970) entire hierarchy of needs should be considered when examining family strengths and weaknesses. A counselor cannot expect a family to follow up on recommendations for therapeutic treatment for their child if, for example, they are not able to provide food or heat for themselves and the rest of their immediate family. The counselor should be familiar with local resources that are available to assist families with needs for food, clothing, shelter, and financial assistance.

Family interactions should be analyzed and attended to. Some of the mother's behaviors that are observed and reinforced are:

*making positive statements about her infant, touching the infant ... attempting to establish eye contact, talking to the infant, smiling frequently to her baby ... relating the infant's characteristics to other family members ... (Opirhory & Peters, 1982, pp.451-454). Or when the child is hospitalized, number and frequency of calls and visits, specific questions asked about the baby's condition, involvement in care when appropriate, reluctance to leave, and willingness to wait until the baby is*

*sleeping before leaving (Opirhory & Peters, 1982, p. 453).*

Father-infant interaction is also assessed and includes:

*the quality and frequency of touching the child, speaking to the child, playing with the child, frequency of calls and visits, seeking information about the infant, responses to the infant's activity and participation in the child's care ...(Opirhory & Peters, 1982 (p.453)*

The third, fourth, and fifth stages involve: identification and evaluation of alternatives and commitment to a plan of action. Any reasonable alternatives available to help the child or the family adapt to the disability should be expressed and examined. The types of alternatives explored will depend upon the particular needs of the child and the family. It is important for the counselor to be aware of and maintain contacts with referral sources available in the community for such needs as medical treatment, occupational therapy, speech therapy, physical therapy, educational services, follow-up counseling, and special equipment. Parents should be encouraged to seek or create their own "novel solutions to special problems" (Darling, 1988, p.141).

The alternatives identified in stage III should be critically evaluated. The counselor assists by helping the client to decide which alternatives are appropriate and by teaching, modeling, or mentoring when needed. The client makes a specific commitment to a series of workable action steps with the support of the counselor.

In the sixth stage, the client summarizes progress made and client and counselor evaluate the level of goal attainment then cycle back through with attention to family's stage of adjustment and other changes in strengths, needs, and pertinent available resources.

## Modeling

"One of the fundamental means by which new modes of behavior are acquired and existing patterns are modified entails modeling and vicarious processes" (Bandura, 1969, p.118). Not only is it helpful to observe and reinforce positive statements about the child and touching, holding, and caring for the child; it is very beneficial in many instances to model some of these behaviors for the parents. Many parents have noted, particularly in the case of children who react to being handled with abnormal flexion or extension, that very few people outside the nuclear family have ever held the child. Some have even commented that some professionals have seen and made recommendations for the child in the course of an office visit without ever touching the child. These parents reportedly felt that the people who dealt with their child in such a manner were afraid that they might be affected by the disability. Holding the child in a caring and confident manner and making comments about positive aspects of the child's appearance or personality appears to have the effect of strengthening the trusting relationship between the parents and the counselor and facilitating the parents' progress toward acceptance of their child.

## Consultative Intervention in the Multidisciplinary Treatment Setting

The treatment of a disabling condition in a child often involves the contributions of a multidisciplinary team of specialists. Through sharing knowledge from a variety of disciplines, coordinated services may be provided. Poor communication, dangers inherent in specialization, and problems of respect and trust among treatment providers may, however, impede effective service delivery (Jacques, 1970). It is important for team members to be able to effectively communicate with other professionals as well as with the child and family (Mesibou & Johnson, 1982).

Each member of the multidisciplinary treatment team, in addition to providing specific input into the diagnostic procedure or treatment plan, might serve as resource person to the other team members providing training and information that would enable each professional to do his or her job more effectively. For example, a physical therapist working in a setting where treatment is provided to children with neuromotor disorders could give a lecture/demonstration on positioning and handling. A speech therapist might give a presentation on speech development so that the other workers would be better able to tell when speech is developing normally in the child with a disability. The participation of team members in a cooperative, consultative role would tremendously enhance the benefits inherent in the multidisciplinary team approach while reducing the potential drawbacks.

## Parent Support Groups

Increasing numbers of parents are joining special interest groups associated with particular childhood disorders. There are many self-help organizations in existence which promote and emphasize the educational component, promote services for children as well as utilize strategies to bring parents with similar problems together for support (Halper & Kissel, 1976). Parents of disabled children often derive a sense of mutual support from participation in a group and are generally relieved to learn that others in their situation experience similar emotions and responses.

## DISCUSSION

The diagnosis of a disabling condition in a child may have a traumatic effect on the entire family and may predispose both child and family to concomitant problems of adjustment. A broad, integrated program of services that considers the needs of the family should be available.

It has been widely recognized that parents, after learning of a child's disability or serious illness, experience a pattern of feelings and responding similar to that exhibited by other parents in that situation. Using the knowledge of the stages and typical reactions, the well-trained counselor can often provide valuable support to the family during this crisis situation. The support and information provided by a counselor and by parent support groups or advocacy groups can facilitate the adjustment process and help to ease the family's progress through an extremely stressful situation.

*****

## REFERENCES

Baker, B.L. & Brightman, R.P. (1984), Training parents of retarded children: Program-specific outcomes. *Journal of Behavior Therapy and Experimental Psychiatry, 15 (3), 255-260.*

Bandura, A. (1969) *Principles of behavior modification.* NY: Holt, Rinehart and Winston, Inc.

Bassoff, E. S. (1982). Identifying, preventing and treating disturbances between parents and their infants. *Personnel and Guidance Journal, 61, (4), 228-232.*

Brookman, B.A. (1988). Parent to parent: A model for parent support and information. *Topics in Early Childhood Special Education, 8 (2), 88-93.*

Buchan, L., Clemerson, J. & David, H. (1988). Working with families of children with special needs: The parent adviser scheme. *Child Care, Health and Development, 14 (2), 81-91.*

Cruickshank, W.M. (Ed.) (1980) *Psychology of exceptional children and youth.* Englewood Cliffs, N.J.: Prentice-Hall, Inc.

Darling, R.B. (1988). Parental entrepreneurship: A consumerist response to professional dominance. *Journal of Social Issues, 44 (1), 141-158.*

Fischler, R.S. & Fleshman, C. (1985). Comprehensive health services for developmentally disabled Navajo children. *Journal of Developmental and Behavioral Pediatrics, 6 (12), 9-14.*

Fitzgerald, M.T. A family involvement model for hearing-impaired infants. *Topics in Language Disorders, 7 (3), 1-18.*

Forrest, P., Holland, C., Daly, R. & Fellbaum, G. (1984). When parents become therapists: Their attitudes toward parenting three years later. *Canadian Journal of Community Mental Health, 3(1), 49-54.*

Frantz, T.T. (1984). Helping parents whose child has died. *Family Therapy Collections, 8, 11-26.*

Fraser, B.C. (1986). Child impairment and parent/infant communication. *Child Care, Health and Development, 12(3), 141-150.*

Gilliland, B.E., James, R.K. & Bowman, J.T. (1989. *Theories and strategies in counseling and psychotherapy.* New Jersey: Prentice-Hall Inc.

Halpen, W.I. & Kissel, S. (1976). *Human resources for troubled children.* NY: John Wiley & Sons.

Harris, S.L. & Fong, P.L. (1985) Developmental disabilities: The family and the school. *School Psychology Review, 14(2), 162-165.*

Hornby, G. & Murray, R. (1983). Group programmes for parents of children with various

handicaps. *Child Care, Health and Development, 9(4),185-198.*

Hornby, G., Murray, R. & Jones, R. (1987). Establishing a parent to parent service. *Child Care, Health and Development, 13(4), 277-286.*

Huber, C.H. (1979). Parents of the handicapped child: Facilitating acceptance through group counseling. *Personnel and Guidance Journal, 57(5), 267-269.*

Jacques, M. E. (1970). *Rehabilitation counseling: Scope and services.* Boston: Houghton Mifflin.

Kanner, L. (1972) *Child psychiatry.* Springfield, IL: Charles C. Thomas.

Konanc, J.T. Warren, N.J. (1984). Graduation: Transitional crisis for mildly developmentally disabled adolescents and their families. *Family Relations: Journal of Applied Family and Child Studies, 33(1), 135-142.*

Kubler-Ross, E., b. *On death and dying.* NY: Macmillan Publishing Co., Inc.

Kysela, G.M. & Marfo, K. (1983). Mother-child interactions and early intervention programmes for handicapped infants and young children. *Educational Psychology, 3(3-4), 201-212.*

Maslow, A.H. (1970) *Motivation and personality (2nd ed.).* NY: Harper & Row.

Mesibov, G.B. & Johnson, M.R. (1982).b Intervention techniques in pediatric psychology. In Tuma, J.M. (Ed.) *Handbook for the practice of pediatric psychology.* NY: John Wiley & Sons.

Murdoch, J.C. (1984). Immediate post-natal management of the mothers of Down's syndrome and spina bifida children in Scotland 1971-1981. *Journal of Mental Deficiency Research 28(1), 67-72.*

Naidoo, R. M. (1984). Counseling parents with handicapped children. *British Journal of Projective Psychology and Personality Study, 29(1), 67-72.*

Opirhory, G. & Peters, G.A. (1982). Counseling intervention strategies for families with the less than perfect newborn. *Personnel and Guidance Journal, 60, (8), 451-454.*

O'Sullivan, S.B. (1985-86). Infant-caregiver interaction and the social development of handicapped infants. *Physical and Occupational Therapy in Pediatrics, 5(4), 1-12.*

Pilon, B. H. & Smith, K.A. (1985). A parent group for the Hispanic parents of children with severe cerebral palsy. *Children's Health Care, 14(2), 96-102.*

Pomerantz, B. R. (1984). Collaborative interviewing: A family-centered approach to pediatric care. *Health and Social Work, 9(1), 66-73.*

Power, P.W. & Dell Orto, A.E. (1980) *Role of the family in the rehabilitation of the physically disabled.* Baltimore: University Park Press.

Poznanski, E.O. (1973). Emotional issues in raising handicapped children. *Rehabilitation Literature, 34, 322-326.*

Robinson, N.M. & Robinson, H.B. (1976). *The mentally retarded child.* St. Louis, MO: McGraw-Hill Brook Co.

Rutter, M. (1977). Brain damage syndromes in childhood: Concepts and findings. *Journal of Child Psychology and Psychiatry, 18, 1-21.*

Rutter, M., Graham, P. & Yule, W. (1970). A neuropsychiatric study in childhood. *Clinics in Developmental Medicine, Nos. 35/36,* SIMP/Heinemann: London

Sharlin, S.A. & Ponansky, N.A. (1971). The process of infantalization. *American Journal of Orthopsychiatry, 42, 92-102.*

Styles, B. (1986). The unseen handicap. *Emotional First Aid: A Journal of Crisis Intervention, 3(2),* 19-22.

Vernon, M. & Wallrabenstein, J.M. (1984). The diagnosis of deafness in a child. *Journal of Communication Disorders, 17(1),* 1-8.

Whaley, L.F. & Wong, D.L. (1982). *Essentials of pediatric nursing.* St. Louis, MO: The C.V.Mosby Co.

Willis, D.J., Elliott, C.H. & Jay, S.M. (1982). Psychological effects of physical illness and its concomitants. In Tuma, J.M. (Ed.) *Handbook for the practice of pediatric psychology.* NY: John Wiley & Sons.

Wright, B.M. (1986). An approach to infant-parent psychotherapy. *Infant Mental Health Journal, 7(4),* 247-263.

********

**About the Author:** Mary Ellen Ziolko completed her Ph.D. in Counseling Psychology from Mephis State University in 1991 and is currently working as a psychologist in private practice in Blytheville, Arkansas. She has worked for eight years in early intervention with families of developmentally disabled preschoolers, and has also taught college classes in developmental and adolescent psychology. She may be reached at Blytheville Psychological Group, 1104 Medical Drive, Blytheville, Arkansas 72315.

**Source:** Reprinted with permission from *Journal of Rehabilitation,* Vol. 57, No. 2, April/May/June 1991, pp. 29-34. Published by The National Rehabilitation Association, Alexandria, Virginia.

# "I am this child's mother": A Feminist Perspective on Mothering with a Disability

Claire Reinelt
Mindy Fried

**Introduction** ~ The choice to have a child, while taken for granted by many women, is for women with disabilities an act of resistance to the dominant social norms regarding who should be a mother. When a disabled woman decides to have a child, she is affirming her right to be sexually active, involved in intimate relationships, and have and raise a child. This paper will explore the experiences of mothering with a disability. We focus on the choice to become a mother, the impact of having a disability on children and on the division of labor between partners in the home.[1]

Sexuality and family life are among those areas of human experience that are most shrouded in secrecy. Our society severely limits the available public space for discussing and exploring sexualities that affirm in healthy ways our sexual identities. This lack of openness has ramifications for all people, but it can be particularly severe for women with disabilities. There is so much silence about the sexuality of women with disabilities that many girls grow up thinking of themselves as asexual beings. [2] When they do become sexually active they often lack basic knowledge about how to protect themselves from disease and pregnancy.

Unlike sexuality, motherhood is often revered in public discourse. Actual mothers, however, find little public support for the work they do. Mothers with disabilities are likely to find even less. All mothers are adversely affected by the lack of public investment in affordable quality child care. Mobility-impaired mothers face the additional task of finding day care that is accessible. Another critical need for mothers with disabilities is availability of adaptive equipment. Very little public or private investment has been made in designing and manufacturing accessible cribs, changing tables and carriers for parents with disabilities.[3] There also is a need to rethink the guidelines for personal care attendants. Right now, mothers are not allowed to have their attendants assist in any way with caring for children. These services support the right to work at a job outside the home, not the right to have and raise a child. In addition to unmet physical needs, mothers with disabilities are constantly having to defend their ability to be good mothers. While all mothers experience criticism about how they mother, mothers with disabilities continually have to endure surprise and disbelief from people who cannot even imagine that they could be mothers at all.

Like sexuality, family life has been privatized. There is a deep reluctance on the part of many policy makers, judges and others in positions of power to interfere in private family matters. If we look a little deeper we realize that the reluctance to interfere refers mainly to able-bodied, heterosexual, nuclear families with adequate financial means. There is plenty of interference for single mothers on welfare, mothers with disabilities, lesbian mothers and others who are considered unfit or undesirable parents. Very little, if any, of this interference comes in the form of financial or social support.

During the 1960s and 70s, personal and private issues were moved onto the public agenda by feminist and lesbian and gay activists. Reproductive rights, violence against women, the right to claim one's sexuality without being discriminated against have all been given public attention. The rights and needs of disabled women have not been visible in these movements. There is a pervasive able-body-ism that excludes women with disabilities from comfortably participating. According to Fine and Asch, non-disabled feminists are reluctant to engage with disabled women because they perceive them as dependent, passive, and needy. They are seeking instead to advance more powerful, competent, and appealing female icons. [4]

This same attitude has also contributed to the ambivalence that feminists have historically felt towards the institution of motherhood. Mothers have been perceived as dependent, passive, and needy, while career women have been perceived as independent and powerful. Only recently have White, able-bodied, middle-class feminists begun reclaiming motherhood - defining it as a meaningful personal choice, not a female obligation.

Women with disabilities have also begun to claim motherhood. Their struggle, while linked in some ways to the struggle of able-bodied women, must be understood in a different historical context. Women with disabilities have never been expected to be mothers. Excluded from the experience, they have had to fight for the right to become mothers. The empowerment of disabled women has occurred to a large extent through participation in the disability rights and independent living movements, and to a somewhat lesser extent in the women's movement. Despite the importance of these movements, family issues are still not a priority on the political agenda of the disabled community. The same political forces that have kept family issues off the wider public agenda have been at work in the disability rights and independent living movements. Family issues have been privatized and relegated to women.

Recently, disabled women have been raising these and other women's issues at movement conferences. They still feel, however, that their issues are being ghettoized. [5] Moving the issues raised by women to the center of the political agenda has not yet occurred. Even in the area of access to employment, housing and transportation which have been at the top of the disability movement's agenda, very little attention has been given to exploring whether women's access issues are different from men's. For mothers, access to daycare centers, schools, public playgrounds and low-income family housing are all fundamental access issues that do not even make it on to movement questionnaires that are assessing accessibility.[6]

Disabled feminists are developing a political agenda. In the area of reproductive rights they have raised concerns about the information and support women are given when they learn they are carrying a fetus that will be born with a disability. They are discussing issues of violence against disabled women, aging issues, self-image issues, sexuality, discrimination within the disability rights movement and within the women's movement. There are an increasing number of books, articles, and conference workshops that are devoted specifically to disabled women's issues.[7]

Some of these writings and workshops have addressed mothering issues, but there is still a lot about the experience of being a mother with a disability that has not been explored. With this paper we hope to add to the available information on mothering with a disability. We address the choices women make to become mothers and what it means to them, how women perceive their disability having an impact on their children, and its impact on relationships with partners.

## Research Participants

The material in this paper is based on nine interviews. Six of the women we interviewed were connected in some way to a support group for parents with disabilities; three were not. We draw no conclusions in this paper about the impact of women's participating in the support group but we believe that such groups provide valuable opportunities for women to reduce their isolation and find others who share similar experiences, all of which is conducive to a sense of well-being and improved parenting skills.

There was some diversity among the women we interviewed although not as much as we would have liked. Eight of the women were White, one was Black. One woman was upper-class, because of her family's finances, the others were working and middle-class. All of the women were heterosexual. Six of the women were married, two were single, and one was divorced. One woman had seven children, the rest had one each at the time of this interview. Two of the women have since had a second child.

Women had a variety of disabilities, although the majority were mobility-impaired. Two of the women had Multiple Sclerosis and were in wheelchairs; two others were in wheelchairs from spinal cord injuries, two others had post-polio syndrome; one woman had a severe speech impairment and another woman had been blind since birth.

The following chart provides a summary of information about the nine women we interviewed to make it easier for the reader to follow along in the paper.

| Particip ant | Nature of Disabili t | Child's Name/A ge | Support Group | Partner / Spouse |
|---|---|---|---|---|
| Maggie | polio | Jennifer (5) | facilitator | Tom (who is blind) |
| Alison | MS | seven children Susan (10), interviewe | no | Harry |
| Abby | Blind | Seth (3) | yes | John |
| Lisa | MS | Amy (4) | yes | Sam |
| Beth | polio | Sasha (13) | no | ------ |
| Debra | Speech impairmen t | Michael (6) | yes | ------ |
| Ann | paraplegia | Nancy/Eve (twins (4)) | no | Stan |
| Rose | Quadri- plegia | Laura (8) | yes | Rick |
| Karen | arthritic wrists | Joe (12) | yes | divorced |

## Choosing Motherhood

In many ways, women with disabilities are no different than other women; many of them desire to have and raise a child. What is different is that women with disabilities are not expected to have children, in fact they are often actively discouraged from even considering the possibility. Abby, who has been blind since birth, says,

When I was a child, there was a definite subliminal message that I was not supposed to have children. I was the youngest child in the family and I had very little experience caring for children. The blindness was definitely part of the reason I took so long to have a child...Whenever I

was around young children, my mother would get tense and give me more instruction.

Maggie talks about having to come to terms with relationships and intimacy before being able to have a child with her husband Tim. Tim is visually limited and Maggie has post-polio syndrome. She says,

Both of us had major relationship things to work through in our 20s and 30s. We're just going to have a child late, and that's better than not doing it at all.... I'm 44 and he's 37. From the age of 20 he thought he would never have a child because he didn't want to pass on his disability. He changed his mind real quick when it was clear that I was open to having a child if he wanted one. He hadn't realized how much he was saying that because he knew that none of the women he went out with would want to have a blind child. For both of us the timing of this child has been very influenced by disability. This is a first marriage for both of us and that is clearly disability totally. I had real similar things about men wanting to go out with me but I thought they would never want to marry me. So it took us a long time.

Most disabled women report that their parents encouraged them to have careers, but not to form intimate relationships. While parents often demand equity for their disabled children in educational and vocational arenas, they are much more ambivalent about their children's sexual lives.[8]

When disabled women become pregnant they may initially face disapproval from their family. Abby says,

My family was shocked that I was going to have a child. I'm a renegade in my family. They often say, "You can do anything", and then they are indirect about their disapproval of my actions. That's how they were at first, but once they saw that [Seth] is doing well, I think they are more accepting.

Disabled women also encounter disapproval from the medical profession.

Rose, who has quadriplegia, tried to see a doctor at a local hospital when she suspected she was pregnant.

> I felt bad that [the doctors] weren't taking my concerns seriously about the post-polio syndrome and how it might affect me later [in pregnancy]. So I sent letters out to people that knew and asked them if they knew any post-polio syndrome mothers who went through delivery and what happened. I didn't know if my respiratory system would be overstressed. [The doctors] finally did send me in to see how to use a respirator if I needed that. I didn't feel like I was getting the attention I wanted.

Lack of both sensitivity and knowledge continues to create problems for women even when they are at the hospital giving birth to their children. Abby tells about trying to claim her baby before leaving the hospital. As she was preparing to leave after five days in the hospital, a nurse came by to have the release forms signed verifying that Seth was indeed her child.

> Initially, the hospital personnel refused to allow me to sign the form and to identify Seth as my child. I took the paper and said, "I am going to sign this paper," and they said, "oh no wait until your husband gets the car, he can sign the paper." And I said, "I am this child's mother, you have had him twice in the nursery in the entire five days he's been alive, this is my child. I gave birth to him, I will sign the paper."

As you can see from these stories, disabled women spend a lot of time advocating for themselves and claiming what is rightfully theirs. Many disabled women are well-prepared for these encounters through years of experience facing discrimination, yet it is clear that no woman should be subjected to this kind of treatment.

*A postscript to Abby's story:* She recently had her second baby at the same hospital. This time her experience was completely different. The nurses were comfortable and friendly with her and she felt supported by them. The nurses hadn't changed. Abby claims *she* had. Her own confidence and knowledge about her ability to be a mother transformed how the nurses related to her. What this story points out is the importance of women like Abby sharing their knowledge and experience with disabled women who are pregnant for the first time, so that they will not have to go through what she did the first time around.

### Raising Children

The experience of raising a child varied tremendously for the women we interviewed. Some had more support than others, some were more comfortable with their disability than others, and some had better parenting skills. All of the women had to devise ways to parent their children that recognized and respected their disability. Beth learned to change her daughter's diaper using her mouth. Women with wheelchairs designed carriers so their babies could ride with them. Abby attached a beeper to her son Seth when they went out so she could keep track of him. Ann was very firm with her twins about holding on to her wheelchair whenever they were out in public. Maggie builds in rest times during her day that her daughter has learned to accept. Mothers with physical disabilities teach us that good mothering can take many different forms.

What is the impact of the mother's disability on the child? This is a question that able-bodied professionals seem particularly interested in. We listened to mothers talk about their children and found a number of similarities in their descriptions of their children. They described them as independent, self-sufficient, empathetic, sensitive, and helpful. Many mothers thought their disability had had little negative affect on their children or had in fact been positive. While they also discussed the hardships and the pain, all but one of the women we interviewed were very happy to be mothers.

Alison's youngest daughter has been able to get up in the morning and get her glass of milk since she was three. Alison says of her children:

> I can talk them through a lot of things. If you take the time and the trouble to give

step by step instructions you'll find that even a small kid can really be quite helpful. You give them praise afterward and they are quite happy.

Alison does not see her disability as a burden for her children, but rather as an opportunity to build their self-esteem and confidence.

In addition to being independent and self-sufficient, some children enjoy the feeling of being helpful. Susan, Alison's ten-year old, says:

> I don't know what it would be like to have a mother who could walk. I don't think that would be right for me because I am so used to having a mother that I can help out - I mean really, really help out; most kids don't feel that. You just feel more confident with yourself when you are helping someone in your family.

Alison nurtures this feeling in her children while at the same time being sensitive not to overburden them with responsibilities or expect more than they can give for their age.

There is a fine line to walk between asking too much of a child and helping them to be self-sufficient and self-confident. Beth acknowledges that Sasha got tired of helping her so much.

> She carried bags when she was so little, my mother used to say, "You're going to go to jail, you're having that little girl do so much for you."

Beth realized that she needed to get a Personal Care Attendant both for herself and for the relationship with Sasha.

Many of the children express a unique sense of empathy and sensitivity to others who are disabled. Susan, Alison's daughter, says:

> I think I understand when other people have different diseases when I know that my mom has a disease too. I know that they are real people and they are not weird. Others may stare and think "Oh my god, what are those creatures." I think I am more understanding because I know my mom has MS, she has a disease. I know she's alive, she's living, and she's happy,

and she has children and everything and I really think that I look at different people, like who have AIDS or handicaps, and I know I'm more secure with them than most other people would be.

Sensitivity manifests itself in other ways as well. When Beth's daughter, Sasha, encounters someone with a disability who looks like they might need help, she always asks them, "Would you like me to help you?" She does not just jump in and start helping them without asking.

One of the most frustrating things for the women we spoke with was feeling or being treated as though they were incompetent. Lisa feels that it has been hard to establish her competence with Amy because there is so much she can't do with her. One day, however, Amy came into the room while Lisa was tutoring (she used to be a teacher). "Amy said, 'Mom, you're a teacher.' And that was one of the first times she was really looking up to me."

Parental competence is often undermined in public interactions. Abby speaks about how frustrated she gets when she is asking for directions and the adult turns and tells Seth the directions.

> When we're in public...there have been times that I ask for directions and the person will tell Seth. With Seth this is more upsetting. I'm trying to field his questions, his needs, trying to get us out of being lost. I also don't want him to think I'm incompetent.

Rather than hold in her reaction, Abby uses this opportunity to teach Seth about discrimination as well as share her own feelings about the way she has been treated.

> I'll say to Seth that these people are silly, or these people are stupid, or some people don't understand, or that makes mommy angry.

As children grow older they may become very protective of their mothers. So you can see that while some of the women at times feel inadequate and some of the children at times feel overburdened, having a mother with a disability or being a mother with a disability has many positive aspects as well.

## Caregiving and the Division of Labor Between Partners

Traditionally, women are expected to assume the family caregiving role. What happens when the woman is disabled? How does this affect the division of labor between partners?

Two of the women we interviewed have husbands who are full-time caregivers. Rose's husband cares for both Rose and their daughter Laura. Rose says that her husband would like to work but there is a financial disincentive for him to do so because she receives medical benefits totaling $30,000 a year. Without Medicaid, she and her husband would have a difficult time paying for her medical needs. Consequently, they have to make sure that they keep their income below the benefit threshold. Rose comments:

> It's not a good system they have set up. I don't understand why the husband and wife can't both work. If we were divorced, we could get a lot more benefits than if we were married. It's crazy.

Rose thinks that the divorce rate is so high among couples with disabilities because of the financial disincentive of the marriage relationship.

It is often difficult for husbands to assume a caregiving role because of society's attitude toward male caregiving. Rose says:

> What I don't like is the attitudes of society towards my husband, that the man should be the financial earner the old-fashioned way, and the wife stays home. Who could ask for anything more rewarding than taking care of wife and child, rather than going out and rushing around. People don't realize the work involved; it's more than a full-time job. People look at him like he's a bum. I hate that. If you had to pay him for all the work he does it would be $60,000.

Whether it is men or women who perform caregiving work, this work is undervalued. Male caregivers face the additional disapproval of not providing financially for their families.

Alison's husband is also a full-time caregiver. They arrived at their arrangement not out of financial necessity, but through deliberate planning and choice. During the early stages of Alison's MS she and her husband began to plan for the day when she would no longer be able to care for the children. He switched jobs and worked overtime in order to make more money. They invested the money in the stock market until they had a nest egg that allowed him to retire. When Alison's last child was born, she was at the end of being able to consider having and raising a child.

> I had her and gave her to my husband and said she's yours. He changed every diaper. We divide the family into two families actually. My family is the first four when he was working and I was raising the kids and managing alright. The last three are his family where he has been more or less the mother and I've been the father, sort of watching and supporting but he's doing the work. So we've kind of switched our roles half way through. So if you want to have a lot of kids with MS you probably will run into that time when you have to switch your roles around, but if you are good and flexible you can do it.

Not all women have switched roles with their husbands. Ann feels that it is primarily the mother's responsibility to stay home with the kids and for the father to work to support them. Ann is able to do much of the caregiving work herself, particularly now that her daughters are older. In addition, she has a Personal Care Attendant (PCA) who can help her with caregiving responsibilities. Despite Ann's commitment to staying home with her children, she does work part-time. Working is a source of self-fulfillment for her as well as a financial contribution to the family. Ann's embrace of traditional gender roles affirms for her the normalcy of their family situation. In Ann's case her husband knew that he was marrying a disabled woman so there were no issues for them such as those that arise if a woman becomes disabled during the marriage.

Unlike Ann, Lisa acquired her disability after she and Sam were married. Part of the stress in their relationship comes from coping with the disease because it was not a 'given' in their relationship.

> It's a bitch of a disease.  It's so unrelenting.  You just get on top of it.  You feel like you're riding the wave and then you're under again.  It's really, really hard. And I feel sympathy for [Sam], which I think is part of what therapy has done for me.  I used to feel really angry at him and I started to realize that I had it first and now I feel like he has the disease.  As long as he's connected to me, he has this disease too.

Recognizing that the whole family is affected by her MS is a positive step for Lisa and has helped her feel more sympathy for Sam. Nevertheless, her increasing disability takes its toll on the relationship.

Sam wants to be a traditional husband: he wants to come home from work, put his feet up and have his wife prepare and serve him dinner.  Lisa says that he does more caregiving than the average husband, but he clearly resents having to do it.  In their case, negotiating who does how much housework and child care (an issue that every couple deals with) is complicated by the fact that she has MS.  She is very conscious of how tired she is getting and works hard to stay within her limits.  While she needs to do this for herself, Sam isn't always understanding.  Lisa does not have a PCA.

The availability of a PCA can be very important to a relationship.  Beth, a single parent, believes that her relationship with her child's father might have been different if she had had a PCA.

> He used to do everything for me.  We never used to argue about it or anything, but it could have been something that he wasn't hot about.  It could have played a big role in our breaking up.

PCA's are a critical resource for disabled people.  Their availability can free the couple to pursue a relationship that is not imbalanced by the imposition of daily care.

**Conclusion**

The disabled women we talked to are asserting their right to have and raise children. They are discovering how to parent in ways that accommodate their disability and meet the needs of their children.  They are learning how to confront the professional attitudes of doctors and social workers who continue to perceive disability as a problem, rather than part of who someone is.

Parenting is never easy work and in some ways it is extra hard for people with disabilities, but most of the women we spoke with were very happy to be parents.  One of the biggest challenges continues to be confronting the skepticism and disapproval of others who believe that disabled women cannot be good mothers.  To combat this we need more education on parenting with a disability for professionals, the general public and for disabled people themselves.  The disability rights and independent living movements need to place sexuality and family issues squarely on the movement's agenda.

With the passage of ADA, the next decade offers a unique opportunity to move disability issues into the public consciousness. It would be a serious oversight for both women and men if sexuality and family issues were excluded from public discussion and action. Likewise, given the more favorable political climate for confronting family issues that has come with the election of President Clinton, we need to make sure that the needs of men and women with disabilities are included in public policies that address child care, family and medical leave, sexuality, family planning, and AIDS.

**NOTES**

[1]  There are other important issues for mothers with disabilities that we address in a longer version of this paper.  They include issues of governmental and workplace support for parents with disabilities, combining work and family lives, and policy recommendations that support the caregiving work that parents with disabilities do.

[2]  **Barbara Faye Waxman and Anne Finger**. The Politics of Sex and Disability, *Disability Studies Quarterly*, Vol. 9, No. 3, Summer 1989.

[3]  Megan Kirshbaum at **Through the Looking Glass** in Berkeley, California recently received a

three-year grant to develop and design adaptive equipment for disabled parents and their babies.

[4] Adrienne Asch and Michelle Fine. Introduction Beyond Pedestals, in *Women with Disabilities: Essays in Psychology, Culture, and Politics.* Philadelphia: Temple University Press, 1988, p.4.

[5] This issue was raised by Corbett O'Toole at a workshop on *Women and Disabilities* held during the 1991 Independent living Movement Conference in Oakland, California.

[6] At the 1991 Independent Living Movement Conference, the World Institute on Disability handed out a lengthy Accessibility Survey that did not include any questions designed to determine accessibility for parents with disabilities.

[7] For an extensive annotated bibliography and review of the issues facing women with disabilities, see Rannveig Traustadottir, *Women with Disabilities: Issues, Resources, Connections,* The Center on Human Policy, Syracuse University, 200 Huntington Hall, 2nd Floor, Syracuse, NY 13244-2340.

[8] Marilyn Rousso, "Daughters with Disabilities: Defective women or Minority Women?," in Michelle Fine and Adrienne Asch, (Eds), *Women with Disabilities: Essays in Psychology, Culture, and Politics,* Philadelphia: Temple University Press, 1988.

## REFERENCES

**Books:**

**Browne, Susan and Debra Connors and Nanci Stern,** *With the Power of Each Breath,* Pittsburg: Cleis Press, 1985. (Includes a section on being a mother.)

**Campion, Mukti Jain.** *The Baby Challenge: A Handbook on Pregnancy for Women with a Physical Disability,* London: Routledge, Chapman, and Hall, 1990.

**Campling, Jo, (Ed.,)** *Images of Ourselves: Women with disabilities talking,* London: Routledge and Kegan Paul, 1981. (Many of the women included in this collection are mothers.)

**Deegan, M.J. and N.A. Brooks, (Eds),** *Women and Disability: The Double Handicap,* Transaction Books: New Brunswick, NJ, 1985. (Includes a chapter on mothering).

**Finger, Anne.** *Past Due: A Story of Disability, Pregnancy, and Birth.* Seattle, WA: The Seal Press, 1990.

**Matthews, Gwyneth Ferguson,** *Voices From the Shadows: Women with Disabilities Speak Out,* Toronto: The Women's Press, 1983. (Includes a chapter on 'Bringing up Baby').

**Morris, Jenny, (Ed.)** *Able Lives: Women's Experience of Paralysis,* London: The Women's Press, 1989. (Includes a chapter on being a mother).

**Pies, Cheri,** *Considering Parenthood: A Workbook for Lesbians.* San Francisco: Spinsters Ink, 1985. (Includes a section for disabled lesbians considering parenthood.)

**Rogers, Judith.** *Mothers-to-be: A Guide to Pregnancy and Birth for Women with Disabilities,* Demos Publications, 1992.

**Journal:**

*Disability, Pregnancy and Parenthood International,* **Mukti Jain Campion, (Ed.).** The journal is published in England. For subscription information in the United States write to DPPI, Auburn Press, 9954 South Walnut Terrace #201, Palos Hills, Illinois, 60465. The first issue was published in January 1993.

**Non-Profit Organization:**

*Through the Looking Glass,* 801 Peralta Avenue, Berkeley, California, 94707. Megan Kirshbaum, Executive Director. (Through the Looking Glass is currently involved in developing adaptive equipment and techniques for physically disabled parents and their babies.)

**About the Authors:** **Claire Reinelt** is a Ph.D. candidate in Sociology at Brandeis University, Waltham, MA. She is completing a dissertation on mothers with disabilities. She has been active for many years in feminist and family policy organizations. Her other research interests include social movements, non-profit organizations, and the state.

**Mindy Fried** is a Ph.D. candidate in Sociology at Brandeis University, Waltham, MA. Her dissertation is on attitudes towards, and use of parental leave policies. She has been active in child and family policy work for many years and was a fundraising and organizational consultant to the Project on Women and Disability in Massachusetts.

**Source:** Reprinted with permission from the authors. From a paper presented at the Society for Disability Studies Meetings, Oakland California, June 1991.

# Stress and Family Functioning in Parents of Girls with Rett Syndrome

Adrienne Perry,
Natalie Sarlo-McGarvey,
David C. Factor

**Abstract ~** *Mothers and fathers of 29 girls with Rett syndrome provided data about their levels of parenting stress, marital adjustment, and family functioning. Their scores were compared to normative and clinical samples. The parents of girls with Rett syndrome reported more stress, lower marital satisfaction, and certain adaptations in family functioning compared to norms. However, most parents scored in the normal range on most measures and their scores were not related to SES. There was little relationship between specific characteristics of the daughter with Rett syndrome, such as her age and level of functioning, and her parents' scores on these measures. There were few significant differences between mothers' and fathers' scores. Results are discussed in terms of patterns of family adaptation and coping. Clinical implications are also discussed.*

Rett Syndrome is a severe developmental disability (DD) involving both physical and mental handicaps. It affects only girls, and appears after an apparently unremarkable prenatal, perinatal, and early infancy period. Symptoms, typically first noticed between 6 and 24 months, include the loss of purposeful hand use (replaced by characteristic hand wringing or other mannerisms); the loss of previously acquired speech (if any); severe psychomotor retardation; and an ataxic and apraxic gait. There may also be respiratory dysfunctions, EEG abnormalities, seizures, scoliosis of the spine, and other physical symptoms (Hagberg, Aicardi, Dias, & Ramos, 1983; Perry, (1991) Rett Syndrome Diagnostic Criteria Work Group, 1988).

There has, to our knowledge, been no empirical research on families who have a daughter with Rett syndrome. One might expect these parents to be particularly highly stressed because the children are so severely incapacitated and require considerable caretaking throughout their life; because the disorder is progressive and there is little hope for significant treatment gains; and because the child seems healthy initially, allowing parents to form expectations about her future, which are then dashed.

There does exist, however, a great deal of clinical and empirical literature on families of children with other disorders, including autism and mental retardation. Parents of DD children can be said to experience greater stress, depression, and health problems than parents of normal controls (Donovan, 1988; Friedrich & Friedrich, 1981; Holroyd, 1974; Wilton & Renault, 1986, Wolf, Noh, Fisman, & Speechley, 1989).

A DD child is often thought to have a negative effect on his or her parents' marriage, but some parents report positive effects as well (Blackard & Barsh, 1982; Carr, 1988; DeMyer, 1979; Friedrich & Friedrich, 1981; Gath & Gumley, 1984). For example, some report that having the DD child has brought them closer together. The literature indicates that a strong marital relationship is one of the most important factors which can mediate parental distress (Bristol, 1984; Bristol & Schopler, 1984; Friedrich, Wilturner, & Cohen, 1985; Perry, 1990).

It is widely believed that mothers are more adversely affected by having a DD child than are fathers, and it is generally acknowledged that the burden of caretaking falls disproportionately on mothers (Bristol, Gallagher, & Schopler, 1988; DeMyer, 1979; Gallagher, Scharfman, & Bristol, 1984; Konstantareas & Homatidis, 1987; Milgram & Atzil, 1988). Some literature has begun to focus on fathers' experience of having a DD child, suggesting that it is qualitatively different from that of mothers, but not more or less difficult (Bristol & Gallagher, 1986;

Gallagher, Cross & Scharfman, 1981; McConachie, 1982; Meyer, 1986; Vadasy, Fewell, Meyer, & Greenberg, 1985).

Undoubtedly, the whole family is affected by the DD child, with different issues emerging at different stages in the family life cycle which can have positive or negative consequences for the family (Turnbull, Summers, & Brotherson, 1986; Wikler, Wasow, & Hatfield, 1983). One aspect of family life which is frequently reported to be particularly adversely affected is the family's recreational and recuperative function (Bristol, 1984; Bristol & Schopler, 1983; Cutler & Kozloff, 1987; DeMyer & Goldberg, 1983).

Individuals, couples and families cope with the situation of having a DD child in many different ways and, ultimately, the majority cope well (Bristol, 1984; DeLuca & Salerno, 1984; Kornblatt & Heinrich, 1985). This is accomplished by employing a variety of coping resources, including factors in their larger social context (e.g., social support from friends) as well as factors within themselves (e.g. personality and beliefs.) Religious faith, in particular, has been reported to be an important coping resource in families of DD children (Bristol, 1984; Fewell, 1986; Friedrich, Cohen, & Wilturner, 1988).

It is often assumed that specific child characteristics are directly correlated with the parents' level of stress. These include age, sex, diagnosis, IQ. level of self-help skills, and so forth. Clearly, these characteristics do make an important contribution to parents' stress level (Bristol, 1987; DeMyer, 1979; Factor, Perry & Freeman, 1990; Friedrich et al., 1985; Marcus, 1984; Morgan, 1988; Perry, 1990), but it is not a simple linear function and many other factors must be taken into account (Perry, 1990).

The purpose of the current study is to present the first empirical investigation of parental stress, marital satisfaction, and family functioning in parents of girls with Rett syndrome. We set out to answer three questions. First, what is the level of stress experienced by these parents compared to norms? Second, what is the relationship between specific child characteristics (such as chronological age, severity of disorder, and age at onset) and the family variables? Third,

what are the similarities and/or differences between mothers' and fathers' experiences of stress and family functioning?

# METHOD

## Subjects and Procedure

Subjects for the study were recruited in two ways. First, letters describing the study were sent by the Canadian Rett Syndrome Association to 53 Ontario families who had a daughter with Rett syndrome. To preserve the confidentiality of the Association's mailing list, parents who wished to participate were asked to contact the investigators. Thirteen of the 53 families (25%) responded. Because of this method of subject recruitment, it was not possible for the investigators to contact families directly to follow up and/or determine reasons for nonparticipation. Second, 16 families were approached directly at a Rett syndrome conference in Western Canada, and 14 of these (88%) agreed to participate. A further two families contacted one of the investigators who was giving a presentation at another Rett Syndrome conference.

There were three components to the study. First, parents were interviewed in order to gather demographic and diagnostic information and to obtain an estimate of the girl's current level of adaptive functioning using the Vineland Adaptive Behavior Scales (Sparrow, Balla, & Cicchetti, 1984). Second, parents were asked to complete a package of questionnaires (see Measures) and return them. There was a 93% return rate and, in the case of two-parent families questionnaires were completed separately for mothers and fathers in all cases. Third, whenever access to the daughter with Rett Syndrome was possible, she was assessed using the Cattell Infant Intelligence Scale (Cattell, 1940).

The final sample consisted of 29 families (including 6 single mother families), though not every family completed each component of the study. Twenty-six families completed both interview and questionnaires; two families were interviewed but did not return the questionnaires despite repeated follow-up; and one family completed the questionnaires but could not be interviewed because of distance. All were biological parents with the exception of three stepparents one grandmother who was the primary caregiver for the child. In addition, 15 of the girls with Rett Syndrome were assessed (all families seen in their homes as well as two whose daughters attended the conference).

Families were predominantly white Canadians, two were European immigrants, and one was from the United States. The sample was close to normally distributed in terms of socioeconomic status (SES), calculated according to the Blishen system (Blishen & Carroll, 1978; Blishen and McRoberts, 1976) (see Table I).

**Table 1.   Socioeconomic Status of Families according to Blishen and McRoberts (1976)[a]**

| SES Class[b] | n | % |
|---|---|---|
| 1 | 3 | 10.4 |
| 2 | 5 | 17.2 |
| 3 | 9 | 31.0 |
| 4 | 7 | 24.1 |
| 5 | 3 | 10.4 |
| 6 | 2 | 6.9 |

[a]Family SES defined as either the higher of the two parents' individual SES categories in the case of two-parent families, or mother's SES in single-mother families.
[b]Class 1 is the highest SES, Class 6 the lowest

The girls with Rett syndrome ranged in age from 2 years 11 months to 19 years 6 months with a mean of 9 years 5 months (see Table II).  The actual diagnosis of Rett Syndrome (Hagberg et al., 1983; Rett Syndrome Diagnostic Criteria Work Group, 1988) was made independently of the present study, primarily by pediatric neurologists (79% of the children), including 4 cases (14%) diagnosed by Dr. Rett himself.  The remaining 21% were diagnosed by geneticists and other

**Table II. Age Distribution of Subjects (N=28)**

| Age Range-yrs/months | n | % |
|---|---|---|
| 0-00 to 4-11 | 5 | 17.9 |
| 5-00 to 9-11 | 12 | 42.9 |
| 10-00 to 14-11 | 8 | 28.5 |
| 15-00 to 19-11 | 3 | 10.7 |

medical specialists.   The cognitive and adaptive behavior level of the girls was assessed for the present study and, as shown in Table III, all girls were found to be profoundly developmentally disabled.  These results are described more fully in a separate report (Perry, Sarlo-McGarvey, & Haddad, 1991).

**Table III.  Characteristics of Rett Syndrome Sample**

| | M(mos) | SD | n |
|---|---|---|---|
| Chronological age | 113.3 | 56.2 | 28 |
| Age of onset | 12.1 | 7.4 | 28 |
| Cattell mental age | 3.0 | 2.0 | 15 |
| **Vineland Adaptive Behavior Scales** | **Range** | | |
| Communication | 11.0 | 5-28 | 28 |
| Daily Living Skills | 14.0 | 4-34 | 28 |
| Socialization | 10.0 | 14-36 | 28 |

## MEASURES

*Parenting Stress Index (PSI).*   The PSI (Abidin, 1986 is a 101-item scale intended to identify parent-child subsystems under stress.   The total Child Domain score and seven Parent Domain subscales (Depression, Attachment, Restriction of Role, Sense of Competence, Social Isolation, Relationship with Spouse, and Health) were used.  The PSI has good psychometric properties and norms for various samples.

*Dyadic Adjustment Scale (DAS).*  The DAS (Spanier, 1976) is composed primarily of Likert type items designed to assess the quality of relationship in married (or cohabiting) couples.   It has four factors:   Dyadic Consensus, Dyadic Satisfaction, Affectional Expression, Dyadic Cohesion, and a total score called Dyadic Adjustment.  The DAS is very well known, has excellent reliability, and clearly differentiates married from divorcing couples.

*Family Environment Scale (FES).* The FES (Moos and Moos, 1981) is a 90 item true-false instrument designed to tap various aspects of family functioning.   It has 10 rationally derived subscales:   Cohesion, Expressiveness, Conflict, Independence, Achievement Orientation, Intellectual/Cultural Orientation, Active/Recreational Orientation,

Moral/Religious Emphasis, Organization, and Control. Internal consistency and test-retest reliability are good to high. norms are available for "normal" and "distressed" families, and the scale has been used with various clinical populations.

## RESULTS

Means and standard deviations for the stress and family functioning variables are shown in Table IV along with values for the normative samples. These results indicate that parents of girls with Rett syndrome differ from norm groups in a number of ways. however, many of these differences are modest and, on all measures, the majority of individual parents scored in the normal range.

On the PSI, scores for the Child Domain were, not surprisingly, substantially higher than norms, indicating that the girls with Rett syndrome were perceived as much more stressful than children in the normative sample. The Parent Domain scores were also significantly higher, indicating greater parenting stress in the present sample. There were four significant differences on the seven individual subscales. Parents of girls with Rett syndrome experienced greater stress in their feelings of Attachment to their daughters, greater Social Isolation, more stress in their Relationship with Spouse, and more parental Health problems than did parents in the normative sample. Between 23 and 31% of parents scored in the "clinical range" on these subscales.

The analyses of the DAS scores (excluding the six single mothers) are also shown in Table IV. According to the overall Dyadic Adjustment score and three of the subscales, the parents in this sample were less satisfied with their marital relationships than were the "happily married" normative group. Of the four DAS subscales, the biggest difference was found on the Consensus score, indicating that the couples in the current sample experience more disagreement about a variety of issues (family, friends, money, religion, sex, etc.). On the Satisfaction and Affectional Expression subscales there were small but significant differences, indicating less happiness in the current sample compared to norms. Interestingly, on the Cohesion

subscale, the sign of the $t$ statistic is opposite, indicating that the present sample reports their marriages to be closer, more supportive, and more cohesive. It should be noted that these couples were, on the whole, much more similar to the norms for the happily married group than to those for couples who were divorcing.

As shown in Table IV, 5 of the 10 FES subscales showed significant differences compared to the norms. Parents in the current study reported significantly less open Conflict than norms for "happy families" and considerably less than norms for "distressed families". There was also less Independence for family members to do things on their own and a much lower Active/Recreational Orientation. On these two scales, the present sample scored very similarly to the distressed norm group. However, the parents of girls with Rett syndrome had a higher Moral/Religious Emphasis. They also reported greater family system Organization compared to norms, and scored much higher in this respect than the distressed families. In addition, families in the present sample reported somewhat more Cohesion ($p = .06$) than norms, again scoring considerably higher than distressed families.

All stress, family functioning, and marital satisfaction variables were analyzed according to SES. None of the 24 correlations between individual parents' SES and their test scores was significant, indicating that there was no linear relationship between SES and family variables. One-way ANOVAs for the six SES categories were also calculated for each variable. There were 3 of 24 significant $F$ values, but in 2 of these 3 cases, Scheffe post tests indicated no significant group differences. The remaining significant ANOVA was for the FES Conflict subscale, but the Scheffe post test indicated a significant difference between Groups 2 and 3 only. This result can probably be attributed to chance. It was clear from careful examination of the six SES means scores for each variable that there was no consistent ordering of family variables by SES.

**Table IV.  Comparison of Means and Standard Deviations for Stress and Family Functioning Measures for Current Sample and Norm Sample.**

| Measure & Subscale | Current sample / Norm Sample | | | | |
| --- | --- | --- | --- | --- | --- |
| | M | SD | M | SD | t |
| **PSI (n=48)** | | | | | |
| Child domain | 131.6 | 16.6 | 98.4 | 19.2 | 11.85 |
| Parent domain | 132.8 | 21.5 | 122.7 | 24.6 | 2.79[b] |
| Depression | 20.0 | 5.2 | 20.4 | 5.6 | |
| Attachment | 13.6 | 3.2 | 12.6 | 3.1 | 2.20[a] |
| Restriction of Role | 20.1 | 5.4 | 19.0 | 5.2 | |
| Competence | 30.6 | 5.8 | 29.2 | 6.3 | |
| Isolation | 15.1 | 3.8 | 12.8 | 3.8 | 4.16[c] |
| Relationship with Spouse | 19.7 | 4.7 | 16.8 | 5.1 | 3.93[c] |
| Health | 13.2 | 3.2 | 11.9 | 3.3 | 2.79[b] |
| **DAS (n=42)** | | | | | |
| Consensus | 46.4 | 7.3 | 57.9 | 8.5 | -8.86[c] |
| Satisfaction | 37.5 | 6.1 | 40.5 | 7.2 | -2.74[b] |
| Affectional expression | 8.2 | 2.1 | 9.0 | 2.3 | -2.15[a] |
| Cohesion | 14.7 | 3.8 | 13.4 | 4.2 | 1.99[a] |
| Dyadic adjustment | 106.9 | 15.7 | 114.8 | 17.8 | -2.89[b] |
| **FES (n=47)** | | | | | |
| Cohesion | 52.8 | 14.4 | 50.0 | 10.0 | |
| Expressiveness | 48.1 | 15.0 | 50.0 | 10.0 | |
| Conflict | 46.9 | 12.5 | 50.0 | 10.0 | |
| Independence | 45.7 | 13.4 | 50.0 | 10.0 | |
| Achievement orientation | 49.4 | 8.7 | 50.0 | 10.0 | |
| Intellectual\ cultural orientation | 48.1 | 11.9 | 50.0 | 10.0 | |
| Active/recreational orientation | 45.1 | 13.2 | 50.0 | 10.0 | -3.38[b] |
| Moral/religious emphasis | 55.2 | 11.2 | 50.0 | 10.0 | 3.59[c] |
| Organization | 54,2 | 11,3 | 50.0 | 10.0 | 2.88[b] |
| Control | 51.8 | 12.1 | 50.0 | 10.0 | |

*a) p < .05  b) p < .01 c) p < .001*

To address the study's second question, correlations [3] were computed between the principal child characteristics as shown in Table III and the stress and family variables.   Looking first at the child's chronological age, 7 of the 24 correlations with family variables were significant, though only moderate in size (-.31 to -.48).  These were 3 of 10 FES subscales (Cohesion, Expressiveness, and Intellectual/Cultural Orientation) and 3 of 4 DAS subscales (Consensus, Satisfaction, and Cohesion) as well as total Dyadic Adjustment.  (None of the PSI subscales was correlated with child's age.)  All seven significant correlations were negative, indicating that parents of older girls reported greater marital or family problems.

Age of onset of Rett syndrome was also correlated with the family variables. Eight of 24 correlations were significant though, again, only of moderate size (-.29 to -.39).  These were the PSI Child Domain, 3 of 10 FES subscales (Expressiveness, Conflict, and Independence), 3 of 4 DAS subscales (Satisfaction, Affectional Expression, and Cohesion) as well as total Dyadic Adjustment. All correlations were in the direction of greater marital and family problems as age of onset increased.  Generally speaking, there were few significant correlations between the child's cognitive and adaptive behavior scores and the family variables.

The third question for investigation concerned mother-father differences.  For the 21 couples, paired t tests were calculated for all stress and family variables.  These values, shown in Table V, indicate that husbands and wives perceived their family situation quite similarly, for the most part.  Of 24 t tests computed, only 3 detected significant differences, although several others approached significance.  The three were all from the FES and suggest that mothers perceived their families more positively than fathers.  Mothers reported significantly greater Cohesion, greater Expressiveness, and greater Independence than did their husbands.

[3] Correlations are available by writing to the first author.

# DISCUSSION

Looking at the profile of subscale similarities and differences compared to norms, it seems as though these families, as a group, have developed a pattern of adaptation to their situation that is sensible and essentially healthy. The family is close and cohesive, there is little open conflict, there is a high degree of organization, and religious beliefs are an important coping mechanism. However, there are costs associated with this pattern of adaptation, both to family members as individuals and to the marital relationship. For individuals, there is limited independence for meeting one's own needs (especially as felt by fathers), a lack of opportunity to engage in recreational activities, a degree of social isolation, and consequences in terms of parents' health. In the marriage, although there is a sense of closeness, there is some disagreement about important issues. However, there is little openly expressed conflict (especially as perceived by fathers), suggesting that discussion of issues is not a prevalent coping strategy in these families. It is likely that a great deal of the couple's energy is channeled into parenting rather than into their relationship.

It must be stressed that this "pattern of adaptation" is based on group means and does not necessarily apply to all families or all individuals. It is also speculative on our part to suggest that it has developed in response to the presence of the daughter with Rett syndrome, since we do not know how these families functioned prior to having the child with Rett syndrome. However, the finding that questionnaire scores were independent of SES is consistent with the notion that there is a characteristic pattern of adaptation in families with a severely DD child. Furthermore, a virtually identical pattern of subscale differences and similarities was found in a previous study of parents of children with autism (Perry, 1990).

In general, there was very little relationship in the present study between specific child-functioning indices and family variables. From a statistical point of view this is not surprising, since there was very little variability in the intellectual level and adaptive behavior of the girls with Rett syndrome.

The finding that some of the marital and family variables tended to be related to the daughter's age is likely to be a reflection of several factors. The constant caretaking demands (changing, feeding, etc.) over a long period take an increasing toll on the resources and energy of parents. Also, the parents are themselves growing older, and there may be a decline in marital satisfaction as part of normal family life-cycle changes.

The correlations of family stress variables with age of onset are somewhat difficult to interpret. One hypothesis is that, after the child is born and appears to be developing normally, parents build up a set of expectations about the child's future. The longer parents have to do this (i.e., the later the age of onset), the more difficult it is to relinquish these dreams and aspirations when it becomes clear that the child will never attain them.

There were a very few significant mother-father differences in this study. Although mothers' scores were slightly higher on a number of stress-related variables, the only three statistically significant sex differences in the study did not support the popular clinical assumption of greater maternal distress.

Most parents in this sample scored in the normal range and, as a group, the sample was more similar to normal than distressed norms except for a few specific family functions. Clearly, it cannot be assumed that all parents of girls with Rett syndrome are devastated. However, since this was a volunteer sample of parents who, it may be claimed, are particularly well adjusted, the results may not be generalizable to all parents of girls with Rett syndrome. However, the unrepresentativeness issue is a common and inevitable concern in research of this type.

These findings need to be considered within the complex reality of the social situation of the families. Parents of DD children are, without doubt, exposed to additional stressors compared to other parents. However, the potential negative consequences resulting from these additional stressors are mediated by the quality of the marital relationship prior to the child's diagnosis, the level of support from their social network, and the individual parents' personality, beliefs, and coping abilities. Future research should attempt to deal with this complexity as far as possible, both in terms of concepts and variables measured and in selection of suitable data analysis procedures.

There are a number of clinical implications that emerge from this study. Clearly, one major avenue of intervention involves strengthening the marriage. This could include teaching communication skills, which would enable the couple to more effectively express their feelings and deal with disagreements. A second major area is to help parents achieve a balance between meeting the needs of the family and their own individual needs. Each parent should have the opportunity to have some outside interest or activity as a source of self-esteem, social support, and general mental health. Provision of respite care is one of the most effective ways that professionals can help individuals and couples meet these other needs. Given the importance of religious beliefs as a coping strategy for many of these people, it is possible that religious communities and organizations could be a significant source of social support and validation. Most importantly, professionals should respect the fact that many parents are coping quite well with little or no outside intervention.

\*\*\*\*\*\*\*\*

**Table V.  Mother-Father Comparison Within Couples**

| Measure & Subscale | Mothers | | Fathers | | Prd |
|---|---|---|---|---|---|
| | M | SD | M | SD | *t* |
| **PSI (*n*=21)** | | | | | |
| Child domain | 134.4 | 18.5 | 129.3 | 15.7 | --- |
| Parent domain | 134.1 | 26.7 | 128.2 | 15.1 | --- |
| Depression | 20.9 | 5.6 | 18.8 | 4.9 | --- |
| Attachment | 13.0 | 3.4 | 14.3 | 3.4 | --- |
| Restriction of Role | 21.1 | 5.4 | 18.6 | 4.9 | --- |
| Competence | 30.8 | 7.6 | 29.4 | 3.7 | --- |
| Isolation | 14.9 | 4.5 | 15.1 | 3.0 | --- |
| Relationship with spouse | 20.1 | 5.2 | 18.5 | 3.9 | --- |
| Health | 13.4 | 3.6 | 13.1 | 3.2 | --- |
| **DAS(*n*=19)** | | | | | |
| Consensus | 47.8 | 6.8 | 45.2 | 7.1 | --- |
| Satisfaction | 38.0 | 5.0 | 37.5 | 5.4 | --- |
| Affectional expression | 8.4 | 2.3 | 8.2 | 2.0 | --- |
| Cohesion | 14.6 | 3,6 | 14.5 | 4.0 | --- |
| Dyadic adjustment | 108.7 | 13.1 | 105.9 | 16.0 | --- |
| **FES (*n*=20)** | | | | | |
| Cohesion | 58.1 | 11.9 | 51.2 | 14.3 | -3.21[b] |
| Expressivenes | 55.5 | 12.8 | 42.7 | 14.9 | -5.15[c] |
| Conflict | 46.0 | 11.6 | 48.5 | 14.2 | --- |
| Independence | 48.2 | 11.5 | 42.3 | 14.3 | -2.19[a] |
| Achievement orientation | 49.3 | 8.8 | 49.6 | 7.9 | --- |
| Intellectual/cultural orientation | 49.6 | 13.0 | 45.8 | 10.8 | --- |
| Active/recreational orientation | 48.6 | 11.7 | 43.3 | 12.3 | --- |
| Moral/religious emphasis | 56.5 | 11.0 | 54.9 | 11.8 | --- |
| Organization | 55.2 | 11.2 | 50.3 | 10.7 | --- |
| Control | 48.6 | 13.0 | 53.7 | 11.0 | --- |
| *a) p< .05  b) p< .01  c) p< .001* | | | | | |

## REFERENCES

**Abidin, R.R.** (1986). *Parenting Stress Index-Manual* (2nd ed.) Charlottesville, VA: Pediatric Psychology Press.

**Blackard, M.K.** & Barsh, E. T. (1982) Parents' and Professionals' perceptions of the handicapped child's impact on the family. *Journal of the Association for Persons with Severe Handicaps, 7,* 62-70.

**Blishen, B.R.** & Carroll W.J. (1978). Sex differences in a socioeconomic index for occupations in Canada. *Canadian Review of Sociology and Anthropology. 15,* 352-371.

**Blishen, B. R.** & McRoberts, H.A. (1976). A revised socioeconomic index for occupations in Canada. *Canadian Review of Sociology and Anthropology, 13,* 71-79.

**Bristol, M. M.** (1984). Family resources and successful adaptation to autistic children. In E. Schopler & G.B.Mesibov (eds.) *The effect of autism on the family* (pp.289-310). New York: Plenum Press.

**Bristol, M.M.** (1987). Mothers of children with autism or communication disorders: Successful adaptation and the Double ABCX model. *Journal of Autism and Developmental Disorders, 17,* 469-486.

**Bristol, M.M.** & Gallagher, J.J. (1986. Research on fathers of young handicapped children: Evolution, review, and some future directions. In J.J.Gallagher & P.M.Vietze (eds.) *Families of handicapped persons: Research, programs, and policy issues* (pp.81-100). Baltimore, MD: Brookes

**Bristol, M.M.,** Gallagher, J.J. & Schopler, E. (1988). Mothers and fathers of young developmentally disabled and nondisabled boys: Adaptation and spousal support. *Developmental Psychology, 24,* 441-451.

**Bristol, M.M.** & Schopler, E. (1983). Coping and stress in families of autistic adolescents. In E. Schopler & G.B.Mesibov (Eds.), *Autism in adolescents and adults* (pp.251-278). New York: Plennum Press.

**Bristol, M.M.** & Schopler, E. (1984). A developmental perspective on stress and coping in families of autistic children. In J. Blacher (Ed.), *Severely handicapped young children and their families: Research in review* (pp.91-141) Orlando, FL: Academic Press.

**Carr, J.** (1988). Six weeks to twenty-one years old: A longitudinal study of children with Down's syndrome and their families. *journal of Child Psychology and Psychiatry,29,* 407-431.

**Cattell, P.** (1940). *Infant Intelligence Scale.* New York: Psychological Corp.

**Cutler, B. C.** & Kozloff, M.S. (1987) Living with autism: Effects on families and family needs. In D.J.Cohen & A.M.Donnellan (Eds.) *Handbook of autism and developmental disorders* (pp. 513-527). New York: Wiley.

**DeLuca, K.D.** & Salerno, S.C. (1984) *Helping professionals connect with families with handicapped children.* Springfield, IL: Charles C. Thomas

**DeMyer, M.K.** (1979) *Parents and children in autism.* New York: Wiley.

**DeMyer, M.K.** & Goldberg, P. (1983). Family needs of the autistic adolescent. In E. Schopler & G.B.Mesibov (Eds.) *Autism in adolescents and adults* (pp.225-250). New York: Plenum Press.

**Donovan, A.M.** (1988). Family stress and ways of coping with adolescents who have handicaps: Maternal perceptions. *American Journal on Mental Retardation, 92,* 502-509.

**Factor, D.C.,** Perry, A., & Freeman, N.L. (1990) Stress, social support, and respite care use in families of autistic children. *Journal of Autism and Developmental Disorders, 20,* 139-146.

**Fewell, R.R.** (1986. Support from religious organizations and personal beliefs. In R.R.Fewell & P.F.Vadasy (Eds.) *Families of handicapped children: Needs and supports across the life span* (pp.297-316). Austin, TX: PRO:ED.

**Friedrich, W.N., Cohen, D.S.** & Wilturner, L.T. (1988). Specific beliefs as moderator variables in maternal coping with mental retardation. *Children's Health Care, 17,* 40-44.

**Friedrich, W.N.** , Friedrich, W.L. (1981). Psychosocial assets of parents of handicapped and non-handicapped children. *American Journal of Mental Deficiency, 85,* 551-553.

**Friedrich, W.N.,** Wilturner, L.T. & Cohen, D.S. (1985). Coping resources and parenting mentally retarded children. *American Journal of Mental Deficiency, 90,* 130-139.

**Gallagher, J.J.,** Cross, A., & Scharfman, W. (1981). Parental adaptation to a young handicapped child: The father's role. *Journal of the Division for Early Childhood, 3,* 3-14.

**Gallagher, J.J.,** Scharfman, W., & Bristol, M.M. (1984). The division of responsibilities in families with preschool handicapped and nonhandicapped children. *Journal of the Division of Early Childhood, 8,* 3-11.

**Gath, A.,** & Gumley, D. (1984). Down's syndrome and the family in mid-childhood: A follow-up of children first seen in infancy. *Developmental Medicine and Child Neurology, 26,* 500-508.

Hagberg, B. Aicardi, J., Dias, K., & Ramos, O. (1983). A progressive syndrome of autism, dementia, ataxia, and loss of purposeful hand use in girls. Rett's syndrome: Report of 35 cases. *Annals of Neurology, 14,* 471-479.

Holroyd, J. (1974). The Questionnaire on Resources and Stress: An instrument to measure family response to a handicapped family member. *Journal of Community Psychology, 2,* 92-94.

Konstantareas, M.M. & Homatidis, S. (1987, May). *Stress and differential parental involvement in families of autistic children.* Paper presented at the Don't Blame Mother conference, Toronto.

Kornblatt, E.S. & Heinrich, J. (1985). Needs and coping abilities in families of children with developmental disabilities. *Mental Retardation, 23,* 13-19.

Marcus, L.M. (1984). Coping with burnout. In E. Schopler & G.B.Mesibov (Eds.) *The effects of autism on the family* (pp.311-326). New York: Plenum Press.

McConachie, H. (1982). Fathers of mentally handicapped children. In N. Beail & J. McGuire (Eds.), *Fathers: Psychological perspectives* (pp.144-173). London: Junction Books.

Meyer, D.J. (1986) Fathers of handicapped children. In R.R.Fewell & P.F.Vadasy (Eds.) *Families of handicapped children: Needs and supports across the life span* (pp.35-73). Austin, TX: PRO-ED.

Milgram, N.A., & Atzil, M. (1988) Parenting stress in raising autistic children. *Journal of Autism and Developmental Disorders, 18,* 415-424.

Moos, R.J. & Moos, B.S. (1981). *Family Environment Scale.* Palo Alto, CA: Consulting Psychologists' Press.

Morgan, S.B. (1988). The autistic child and family functioning: A developmental-family systems perspective. *Journal of Autism and Developmental Disorders, 18,* 263-280.

Perry, A. (1990). *An empirical test of a new theoretical model of stress in families of children with autism.* Unpublished doctoral dissertation, York University, Toronto, Canada.

Perry, A. , (1991) Rett syndrome: A comprehensive review of the literature. *American Journal on Mental Retardation, 96,* 275-290.

Perry, A. , Sarlo-McGarvey, N., & Haddad, C. (1991). Cognitive and adaptive functioning of 28 girls with Rett syndrome. *Journal of Autism and Developmental Disorders, 21,* 551-556.

Rett Syndrome Diagnostic Criteria Work Group. (1988). Diagnostic criteria for Rett syndrome. *Annals of Neurology, 23,* 425-428.

Spanier, G.B. (1976). New scales for assessing the quality of marriage and similar dyads. *Journal of Marriage and the Family, 38,* 15-28.

Sparrow, S.S., Balla, D.A. & Cicchetti, D.V. (1984). *Vineland Adaptive Behavior Scales.* Circle Pines, MN: American Guidance Service.

Turnbull, A.P., Summers, J.A. & Brotherson, M.J. (1986. Family life cycle: Theoretical and empirical implications and future directions for families with mentally retarded members. In J.J.Gallagher & P.M.Vietze (Eds.) *Families of handicapped persons: Research, programs and policy issues* (pp.45-65). Baltimore, MD: Brookes.

Vadasy, P.F., Fewell, R.R., Meyer, D.J. & Greenberg, M.T. (1985). Supporting fathers of handicapped young children: Preliminary findings of program effects. *Analysis and Intervention in Developmental Disabilities, 5,* 151-163.

Wikler, L.M., Wasow, M., & Hatfield, E., (1983). Seeking strengths in families of developmentally disabled children. *Social Work, 28,* 313-315.

Wilton, K. & Renaut, J. (1986. Stress levels in families with intellectually handicapped pre-school children and families with non-handicapped preschool children. *Journal of Mental Deficiency Research, 30,* 163-169.

Wolf, L.C., Noh, S., Fisman, S.N. & Speechley, M. (1989). Psychological effects of parenting stress on parents of autistic children. *Journal of Autism and Developmental Disorders, 19,* 157-166.

********

**Acknowledgements:** The authors gratefully acknowledge the Canadian Rett Syndrome Association and Jo Nanson for assistance in recruiting subjects, and all the parents who participated. We also thank Carol Haddad for her help with data collection and assessing the girls. Portions of this paper were presented at the Ontario Association of Developmental Disabilities annual conference, Ottawa, Ontario, March 1991. We appreciate the administrative support of Thistletown Regional Centre and the Thistletown Foundation. However, the views expressed in the article are those of the authors and do not necessarily represent the views of Thistletown Regional Centre or the Ontario Ministry of Community and Social Services. We sincerely thank Dugal Campbell of the Ontario Mental Health Foundation for his flexibility and kind support. The program was sponsored by the Ministry of Community and Social Services, Ontario; administered by the Research and Program Evaluation Unit in cooperation with the Ontario Mental Health Foundation; and funded from the "Interprovincial" Lottery Research Program.

**About the Author:** The first author, Adrienne Perry, is Coordinator of Research, TRE-ADD, Thistletown Regional Centre, 51 Panorama Court, Rexdale, Ontario, Canada M9V 4L8

**Source:** Reprinted with permission from *The Journal of Autism and Developmental Disorders*, Vol. 22, No. 2, 1992, pp. 235-247. Published by Plenum Publishing Corporation, New York, New York 10013-1578.

# 4 Sexuality and Disability

Society has emerged from the Victorian era where sexuality was considered a taboo topic. However, since the turn of the century years of sexual repression have given way to a sexual revolution. Issues relating to sexuality have emerged from the closet. We have became a nation consumed by matters of sex and sexuality spawned by the 1960's decade which proliferated the notion of full sexual expression. However, until recently there had been a tradition which granted sexuality to only those people considered to be 'normal'. Sexuality was considered immoral and deviant for various other groups of people and establishing sexual relations with people of the same sex, different cultures, different religions, different classes, and people with disabilities was considered to be socially and morally wrong.

In some societies laws were passed to restrict or even prohibit sexual relations between various groups of people. Perhaps the foremost illustration of this orientation emerged in South Africa with the formal establishment of apartheid which served to sever relationships, especially in the sexual realm, between those defined as whites, blacks, and coloreds. Similar laws emerged in some paternalistic societies which denied people with disabilities normal healthy sexual outlets and restricted for them the possibility of marriage and raising a family. As David Baker maintains in his article in Chapter Six, "There exist a number of laws which have such a stifling effect on disabled people. For example, until recently, it was a criminal offence to have sexual relations with a "feeble-minded" person. This prohibition made anyone, including a mentally handicapped person who was engaging in healthy, consensual sexual relations with another mentally handicapped person, liable to prosecution. The purpose of the law was clearly to prevent mentally handicapped people from engaging in sexual activity of any type, and only secondarily to protect the person from exploitation."

Clearly laws of this nature were a thinly disguised attempt to deter people with disabilities from dating, engaging in sexual activity, getting married, or raising a family. Most segments of society have been influenced by a positive orientation towards current social change which directs the active involvement and participation of all minorities in all activities in society, including the right to participate in and enjoy aspects of sexuality.

In some jurisdictions, people with disabilities who were capable of being involved sexually were sterilized because their parents or the state believed that they were incapable of successfully bearing or raising children. People with Down syndrome, cerebral palsy, paraplegia and quadriplegia, and a host of other disabilities, have now become successful parents. Society's perspective has indeed changed and this is certainly reflected in Harlan Hahn's article, *Can Disability be Beautiful?* Visual images which are presented to the general public, as well as the ongoing development by people with disabilities themselves of alternative standards of physical attractiveness play a major role in alleviating this form of prejudice, stereotyping and law-making about the right to sexuality for people with disabilities. Sandra Keller and Denton Buchanan's article, *Sexuality and Disability: An Overview,* introduce the psychological and physical aspects of a number of disabilities "...with an emphasis on practical solutions to common problems..." within the domain of the disabled and their expressions of sexuality.

As we emerge from a sexually repressed society to a society where matters of sexuality are easily discussed, many serious concerns regarding sexual exploitation have come to the fore. Sexual abuse within the family and outside of the family has emerged as a critical topic of investigation. The investigation has reflected the strength of a sociological axiom - that those who have the least power are the most vulnerable. Hence, wives, children, dating teenagers and people with disabilities have been most vulnerable to sexual abuse. In addition to all other groups of people who are sexually abused, those with disabilities who are victimized by sexual abuse also encounter problems imposed by the power of caregivers . Exposing caregivers as abusers can bring about the possibility of destroying one's family, or having the threat of necessary care withheld.    The victim is put in a perilous position  and lack of self esteem,  which may accrue from the vulnerability of the disabled status, leads to a state of 'learned helplessness'.

The article by Deborah Tharinger, et al, *Sexual Abuse and Exploitation of Children and Adults with Mental Retardation and Other Handicaps,* illustrates the vulnerability and problems imposed as a result of sexual abuse as it affects people with disabilities in general and the mentally retarded in particular.  There is a recognition that this type of exploitation is widespread and the challenge for professionals is to protect persons who are disabled from further abuse while at the same time provide therapeutic interventions which will assist the individual to regain self-esteem, some control over his or her life, and continue with emotional and social development.

Fred Kaeser in *Can People with Severe Mental Retardation Consent to Mutual Sex?* explores  the concerns that have emerged with regard to the establishment and maintenance of sexual relations between people within and outside of institutional settings.  Kaeser makes excellent points for redefining consent within the population.  As well, he outlines and provides helpful and appropriate modalities for the management of sexuality through an interdisciplinary approach.

Although the next article, *Ethical Aspects of Sexuality of Persons with Mental Retardation,* by author K. R.  Held,  centers on the ethical aspects of sexuality and mental retardation, and may seem to be more appropriate for the chapter on ethical issues and disability, it provides an additional  complementary focus for Kaeser's article.  Held maintains that by applying  principles fundamental to modern ethics  the key  issue "..is the acceptance of the human rights of personal inviolability, self-determination, in marrying and founding a family, and voluntary procreation of mentally disabled persons in respect to prevailing parent-family and parent-citizen models".    Held further rationalizes that  issues involving compulsory sterilization of the mentally retarded must be carefully and thoroughly  debated  as this practice seems only justified when there is increased risk of sexual exploitation to the individual.  Obviously this is a very difficult situation where the rights of the people involved and the obligations and cost to society must be considered.  It is encouraging to note that with increased debate and public awareness, society is in the process of creating support systems to all groups of disadvantaged people.

Corbett O'Toole and Jennifer Bregante present their article, *Lesbians with Disabilities: Multicultural Realities* - another important aspect of disability and sexuality.  These authors contend that lesbians with disabilities face not only one area of discrimination - that is sexism - but discrimination of homophobia, ableism and racism.  However, there is a positive and dramatic trend being established toward self-advocacy and self-determination in each community which affects the lives of lesbians with disabilities as the voices of these women are challenging the  stereotypical attitudes toward race, gender, disability and sexual orientation.

Sandra Cole's still timely article, *Facing the Challenges of Sexual Abuse in Persons with Disabilities* heightens our awareness of the vulnerability of the person with a disability.  It is often more difficult for people with disabilities to tolerate this type of violence because of their compromised social esteem, their dependence on caregivers, their emotionality, and their tenuous sense of self identity.  Cole illustrates that sexual abuse includes visual, physical or verbal aggression.   As she illustrates, sexual abuse is a crime almost always suffered in silence "...shrouded in such fear that the offenders are able to continue for years or perhaps a lifetime without being apprehended".  Cole explores the characteristics, the myths, the emotional impact, and the ways in which sexual abuse can be recognized and prevented.  It is imperative for all those who are victims of sexual abuse to be treated with sensitivity in any interventions undertaken to achieve justice for these victims and permit their recovery.

And finally, Dick Sobsey and Sheila Mansell examine some of the existing prevention programs and provide alternate sexual abuse prevention strategies for people with disabilities in their article, *The Prevention of Sexual Abuse of People with Developmental Disabilities.* As they articulate, "Effective programs must consider the potential victims of abuse, potential offenders, and the settings in which abuse often takes place.

In contemporary society sexuality has become a foremost concern of people. The authors in this chapter illustrate the prime concerns which must be addressed for the protection of people with disabilities, for the development of healthy attitudes toward sexuality by and toward people with disabilities, and for the functions of professionals who are involved in maintaining and promoting a healthy adaptation of people with disabilities to the concerns often posed by matters relating to sexuality.

# Can Disability Be Beautiful?
Harlan Hahn

**Introduction:** In a decade that has often turned its back on the political aspirations of Black , Hispanic, feminist, gay, aging, and other disadvantaged groups, there is an increasingly urgent need to develop a means by which the disability rights movement can mobilize a potential 27 to 36 million [1] disabled citizens to join the ranks of a powerful progressive coalition. This process could enable persons with disabilities to gain a new kind of political identity and nondisabled groups to develop an innovative basis for forging electoral alliances. Both goals represent admittedly difficult tasks, but I believe they can be achieved through an enhanced awareness of the significance of discrimination based on perceptible physical differences.

The foundation for these developments has already been established by research that recognizes disabled Americans as a minority group and by a sociopolitical definition of disability that identifies their problems primarily as the product of a disabling environment rather than of personal deficiencies. [2] In the present human-made milieu which was not designed to accommodate the interests or needs of this minority, people with disabilities have experienced one of the highest rates of unemployment, poverty and welfare dependency in the country. They have usually been sent to separate or segregated schools and they have been prevented from interacting, or integrating, with their nondisabled peers in transportation, housing, and public accommodations by barriers and policies as rigid as the most restrictive practice of apartheid. By contrast, in an environment adapted to the needs of everyone, which appears to be both technologically and economically possible, disabled and nondisabled persons could become functionally equal; the only remaining distinction between them would be the presence of irreducible physical differences that result from labeling or visible characteristics. [3]

The most salient features of many disabled persons are bodily traits similar to skin color, gender, and other attributes that have been used as a basis for differentiating people for centuries and without which discrimination probably could not occur. In fact, in a recent survey, 45 percent of disabled Americans said that they considered themselves "a minority group in the same sense as ... Blacks and Hispanics." [4] Unlike other minorities, however, disabled men and women have not yet been able to refute implicit or direct accusations of biological inferiority that have often been invoked to rationalize the oppression of groups whose appearance differs from the standards of the dominant majority. Since most disabled children and adults have been raised by nondisabled parents or guardians, they also lack a sense of generational continuity that might otherwise allow the legacy of their experience to become an important solace in an uncaring and inhospitable world. Perhaps even more significantly, people with disabilities have been forced to bear a stigma that virtually defines them as "not quite human." [5]

The sources of aversive and unfavorable attitudes toward disabled women and men seen to be deeply rooted in the psychic and social structure of the nondisabled majority. Recently, however, I have suggested that such views may reflect "existential " anxiety (the projected threat of the loss of physical capabilities or "aesthetic" anxiety (the fear of others whose traits are perceived as disturbing or unpleasant).[6] Both worries can result in discriminatory behavior.

Employers who refuse to hire a disabled applicant for a job because they are reminded of their own physical vulnerability are not less guilty of prejudice than those who would consider the presence of a disabled employee unsightly or upsetting to customers. Yet, government leaders and courts may be more likely to outlaw discrimination based on the simple fear of others who are regarded as alien or strange than to prohibit prejudicial acts founded on apprehensions concerning clinically demonstrable physiological defects. Hence there is a pressing need to focus increased attention on the "aesthetic" dimension of perceptions of disabled individuals.

Ironically, however, many persons with disabilities have been reluctant to acknowledge the existence of discrimination based on aesthetic criteria. Although a recent note in the *Harvard Law Review* indicates that the prejudicial treatment of people with so-called unattractive attributes might already be illegal under Section 504 of the Rehabilitation Act of 1973, [7] this aspect of the stigma imposed on disabled citizens probably has been the major obstacle to the development of a political identity that would allow them to emerge as a strong and cohesive voting bloc. Disabled Americans thus are forced to confront an awkward dilemma. Certainly, no one wants to be considered unattractive. Epithets that characterize another person as ugly or unappealing may be the most vicious insults that can be hurled at a human being. And yet the failure to examine candidly the extent to which unfavorable assessments of people with disabilities are determined by feelings that might not be encompassed by "existential" anxiety could impede the efforts of the disability rights movement to achieve equal rights.

Prior researchers have tended to ignore the aesthetics of disability; if they mentioned the subject at all, they have cast disability almost exclusively in negative terms. Fisher, for example, states:

Despite all efforts invested by our society in an attempt to rally sympathy for the crippled, they still elicit serious discomfort. It is well documented that the disfigured person makes others feel anxious and becomes an object to be warded off. He is viewed as simultaneously inferior and threatening. He becomes associated with the special class of monster images that haunts each culture.[8]

Kern even seems to imply that the exclusion of disabled men and women from the ranks of the aesthetically pleasing may be desirable:

As long as physical beauty determines sexual choices, human relations will be guided by fortuitous, pleasing compositions of bone, muscle, and skin. Elites of the beautiful will continue to live privileged lives, and character and "inner" beauty will continue to take second place in the contests for sexual partners. It is tempting to condemn this rewarding of physical beauty by pointing to the riches and fame we shower on fashion models and athletes while the aged and the deformed are hidden away in poverty and neglect. But perhaps our condemnations are in bad faith and even a bit silly... It is after all, the physical expression of sexual desire that produces offspring. Though erotic stimuli vary from one age to another, they are always based on physical attraction, and as long as that is the case, we will remain dominated by the mysterious and enduring power of the body to generate sexual tension and release sexual pleasure. [9]

The subject of disability probably represents one of those issues in which politics and sexuality are juxtaposed in unexpected ways. In view of the overwhelming failure of prior investigations to discover any positive features of the aesthetics of disability, it is not surprising that many persons with disabilities have tended to deny this aspect of their oppression. Most relevant studies have imposed unacknowledged taboo or censorship on the discussion of this topic, and even the burgeoning literature on sexuality and disability has not provided a means of transcending the supposedly unattractive qualities of obvious physical differences. In fact, the effort to persuade disabled citizens to adopt a social and political identity based on a recognition of this type of discrimination might even be construed as a request that they sacrifice their personal lives for the sake of their public agenda.

Clearly, what is needed is an equivalent to the "Black is Beautiful" phenomenon of the 1960s that would allow disabled persons to redefine their identity in a positive manner. Even though the phrase "disability is beautiful" hardly flows trippingly from the tongue, history discloses abundant proof that images of beauty have changed continually and that physical differences or disabilities sometimes have changed continually and that physical differences or disabilities sometimes have been considered attractive and appealing. By examining this evidence, disabled men and women might gain both an enhanced appreciation of their history and a new basis for developing a political identity. And, in this process, nondisabled observers also may acquire valuable insights about varying concepts of physical appearance as well as a firm foundation for working cooperatively with the disability rights movement.

## THE HISTORY OF A SUBVERSIVE SENSUALISM

In many respects, the history of perceptions of disability has appeared to reflect two contrasting tendencies. On the one hand, disability sometimes has been associated with what might be termed a "subversive sensualism" reflecting a curiosity and fascination that is frequently infused with erotic impulses. On the other hand, views of physical differences or disabilities also have been shaped by a supposedly more civilized tradition of charity and help that has seemed to transform disabled adults into sexless beings. In order to unravel these conflicting and often overlapping trends, I intend to develop a brief and somewhat revisionist interpretation of the limited but significant historical evidence available concerning people with disabilities from antiquity to the modern era.

Perhaps the oldest known disabled individual was the Neanderthal "Nandy", whose bones excavated in the Shanidar cave in Iraq not only disclose congenital deformity but also "show that even in death his person was an object of some esteem, if not respect, born out of close association with a hostile outside."[10] Several thousand years seemed to elapse before definitive information about the social role of people with disabilities reappears, although it does seem significant that many artifacts from ancient fertility cults resemble men and women who, in modern eyes, might be regarded as grotesque, distorted, or deformed rather that as aesthetically pleasing. [11]

Folk tales transmitted by oral traditions include a disproportionately large cast of disabled characters who appear to denote a persistent fascination - perhaps of both attraction and repulsion - with physical differences and disabilities. [12] In the fairy tales collected by the Grimm brothers, for example, there are several figures such as the stepsisters of Cinderella who disable themselves in order to enhance their attractiveness. [13]

Perhaps the first evidence that disabilities could be perceived as valued characteristics, paradoxically, may be found in competitive bidding for impaired Roman slaves who, like their counterparts in Aztec civilizations and in later medieval courts, were often entertainers at intemperate and uninhibited banquets or festivals. [14] In fact, the appearance of disability often has been especially conspicuous at festive celebrations associated with a relaxation of personal restraints and a heightened sense of eroticism.

Early records concerning the role of disabled people in many societies indicate that, although they have generally been oppressed and exploited, the physical differences represented by disabilities have also been perceived as socially and sexually desirable. In many cultures, humans continue to disable themselves through techniques ranging from sacrification and mutilation to tattooing, resculpting, and painting in order to achieve commonly accepted standards of physical beauty. [15]

There are also indications that, in some societies, persons with distinctive physical differences have been especially prized as sexual partners. Among the Hopis, for example, the sexual activity of a tiny proportion of the population has perpetuated an unexpectedly high rate of albinism. [16] Ironically, persons of short stature, who appeared to be favorites of many royal courts of Europe until the seventeenth century, [17] have encountered rejection in modern times that had perhaps been partially responsible for placing an unusual reliance on their own organizational resources to facilitate processes of family formation. [18]

From the decline of the Roman Empire to the end of the Middle Ages, the careers of many disabled adults who survived as comedians or entertainers appeared to follow different paths. Some, including several famous individuals of short stature and other seemingly retarded adults, managed to attach themselves to Royal courts, as jesters or "fools,' a role in which they were granted more satirical freedom and other privileges than were available to most members of the entourage. [19] The highly eroticized nature of their status is underscored by the fact that, in the thirteenth century, many of them apparently were naked when they performed. [20]

In addition, groups "of wandering minstrels who were blind, deaf, and lame traveled from manor to manor, carrying information and providing entertainment in exchange for food and shelter." [21] Less is known about these bands, but they seemed to play not only an important role in the life of medieval society but also in festivities such as the Feast of Fools, an occasion for gaiety, mirth and heightened feelings of sexuality. Hence, physical disabilities during the Middle Ages, both in feudal courts and among the general populace, appeared to be related to revelry, debauchery, and laughter rather than to inferiority, ugliness, and tragedy.

All of these activities were strongly condemned by the medieval church that sought to control the social and sexual conduct of its members. And yet, for hundreds of years, neither religious nor secular authorities seemed capable of suppressing the popular excitement that was associated, at least symbolically, with physical difference or disability.

The explanation of this phenomenon can only be sought in speculation based on the fragmentary information available about public emotions and behavior in the pre-modern era. In a legacy extending from ancient rites and Roman civilization into the Middle Ages, perhaps persistent human curiosity and fascination about physical differences connected with fertility, along with the dialectical reversals that permeate uninhibited conduct, have been stimulated as

often by physical traits that modern observers would consider unattractive as by attributes that would be perceived as aesthetically beautiful by contemporary viewers.

This propensity has been most clearly described by Bakhtin in his interpretation of the work by Rabelais: "The acute awareness of victory over fear is an essential element of medieval laughter ... All that was terrifying becomes grotesque ... The people play with terror and laugh at it; the awesome becomes a 'comic monster.'" Perhaps Bakhtin's most penetrating comment, however, was: "Various deformities such as protruding bellies, enormous noses, or humps are symptoms of pregnancy or of procreative power. [22] This sentence implies the interesting and significant possibility that both the process of pre-modern thinking and its symbolic content might betray an undercurrent of dialectical or dialogical images.

Such perceptions also are infused with political implications that manifest themselves most clearly on festive occasions. "Carnival masks, costumes, and grotesque distortions of the body served to destabilize fixed identities and role differentiations." [23] The prominence of physical differences or disabilities at festivals, therefore, posed a threat that the established order of bodily images might be overthrown by unleashing repressed instincts that could exceed the repressive capacities of civil or religious leaders. While some visible impairments have been interpreted as implying that their bearers were unlovable and aesthetically unlovely, [24] the physical symptoms of other disabilities such as tuberculosis continued to evoke erotic connotations throughout the nineteenth century. [25] The sexual feelings triggered by atypical physiques have exerted consistent and disturbing effects on the social and political perceptions of the nondisabled majority.

The revolutionary potential of eroticized images of physical differences or disabilities, however, was overwhelmed and diffused by economic forces. In the Middle Ages, men and women with disabilities were the heirs to two contrasting and ambiguous legacies. In one tradition emanating from the early treatment of disabled persons as parasites, mascots, or scapegoats who might bring good fortune to those who responded to their plight with compassion and generosity, some people with disabilities were beggars who wandered through the countryside until they became the first group to receive outdoor relief under the English Poor Law of 1601 and subsequent legislation. [26] Others became entertainers, minstrels, and court jesters. The relative status of disabled citizens in medieval society is indicated by the fact that many individuals during this era intentionally disabled themselves in order to join either group. [27]

Even though the intensely curious and intriguing nature of physical disabilities continued to find expression at exhibitions in carnivals throughout the nineteenth century, [28] historical trends depicting human differences both as an inverted antidote to the prospect of increasing debility and as sensually provocative traits finally succumbed to legacies that have portrayed disabled women and men as the aesthetically neutered objects of benevolence and assistance.

## THE MORAL ORDER OF THE BODY

The human body is a powerful symbol conveying messages that have massive social, economic, and political implications. In order to perpetuate their hegemony, ruling elites have attempted to impose what might be termed a moral order of the body, providing images that subjects are encouraged to emulate. By manipulating prescribed forms of appearance, they also have been able to maintain control of a significant aspect of human behavior. Since physical disabilities during the Middle Ages commonly had been linked with relatively unrestrained social and sexual conduct, officials sought to establish a standard that would stress similarities rather than differences among human beings.

Instead of exalting the visible differences that had long been associated with uninhibited sensuality, the medieval church and secular leaders turned to another disability as a source for images of a new moral order of the human body. As evidence of their intense commitment to denial of the flesh, mortals-- especially women--with anorexia nervosa were widely promoted as a physical model that the laity ought to imitate. [29] This look was

later endorsed by Protestant leaders such as John Wesley who invoked nutritional as well as moral arguments in urging parishioners to strive for the slender and svelte figure that has, ironically, become the idealized symbol of modern hedonism. [30] These comparatively restricted bodily contours, of course, not only have excluded persons with a wide range of so-called deformities or disfigurements such as visible scars, scoliosis, amputated limbs, and readily identifiable orthopedic or sensory impairments, but they also have eliminated others perceived as too short, too fat, or too old from the category of those who might be considered aesthetically attractive.

Perhaps the most influential modern agent promoting images of the moral order of the body inherited from the Middle Ages has been the mass media, which emerged after the Industrial Revolution as a potent ally of capitalists seeking to promote mass consumption as a natural corollary of mass production. In fact, advertisers probably have been less successful in selling their products to consumers than they have been in persuading the public to seek to mimic virtually unattainable standards of physical appearance that, of course, have reinforced the social and economic unacceptability of individuals with disabilities or other so-called deviant characteristics. [31]

Visual depictions of disability have continued to serve as a focal point of film and television dramas, but these traits are employed as a vehicle to portray malevolence or maladjustment. [32] The reinterpretation of disability from a sensually stimulating attribute to a socially and aesthetically devalued characteristic has advanced to a point where even venerable fairy tales such as Cinderella have been transformed from a story about women who mutilate themselves in order to win male approval to a legend that teaches the rewards of hard work and incomparable beauty. And, Snow White could never have retained her purity or her reputation by living with seven adult males if they had not been described as harmless "dwarfs."

Another explanation for the increasing devaluation of physical differences and disabilities probably can be traced to the growing proclivity of modern civilization to study and discuss human sexuality to a far greater extent than any prior epoch. [33] Contemporary men and women have a vast wealth of statistical data with which to compare their private fantasies and desires. Hence, although sexual feeling might conceivably be elicited more by atypical physiques than by convention or ordinary appearances, they are also more likely to be suppressed by men and women who fear that such emotions are unusual or "abnormal." In order to preserve a belief in the "normality" of their behavior, many may be willing to sacrifice their own satisfaction and fulfillment. The use of this research as a benchmark for assessing personal conduct therefore, probably has contributed to the perceived unattractiveness of physically disabled persons who are not ordinarily included in such studies.

Perhaps the most significant facet of the pervasive effect of mass media on aesthetic perceptions is exemplified by the fact that, for the first time in history men and women are inundated with physical images of others who can only be found outside the confines of their immediate vicinity. Modern individuals have been taught to compare the appearance of those they encounter in their everyday lives with the idealized models they see in the media instead of appreciating the heterogeneity that surrounds them.

The ubiquitous views of a restricted range of physical characteristics disseminated by the media seem to encourage observers to focus on the similarities between these pictures and their personal acquaintances rather than on the enduring fascination of human differences. As a result, most men and women who attempt to approximate these images not only have been doomed to disappointment, but they also have deprived themselves of the rich experience to be gained from recognizing the value of physical diversity -- a world in which, fortunately, everyone does not look alike. And, of course, conventional viewpoints seem automatically to eliminate most people with obvious disabilities from the ranks of the aesthetically desirable. While treatment as "sexual objects" had been a major grievance of the women's movement, many disabled adults have been perceived in modern society as "asexual objects."

## TOWARD A NEW UNDERSTANDING OF DISABILITY

There is an alternative means of resolving the complex issues of disability, sexuality, stigma, and political identity. Basically, physical attractiveness can be defined as a multi-dimensional, dialectical phenomenon encompassing traits that the culture defines as unattractive as well as characteristics that are popularly perceived as attractive or appealing. The multi-dimensional component involves perceptions focused less on the total composition of the body than on a diverse range of physical details that the viewer finds exciting or pleasurable. The fascination of personal attraction is based less on the gestalt, or unified whole, of the body than on its separate and discrete parts. The phenomenon is also dialectical because it encompasses a shifting kaleidoscopic series of intriguing images rather than static or unidirectional observations contributing to a definitive impression.

This unfolding of sensual emotions is molded by cultural expectations, but, contrary to modern beliefs, attraction is not stirred exclusively by attributes that society designates as aesthetically pleasing. Nor, of course, can such feelings be aroused solely by opposite characteristics. Instead, true attractiveness emanates from the tension produced by these contrasting elements. It is, after all, the unique convergence of these features that comprises individuality and that stamps one person as the special object of admiration and affection. Rather than stressing the similarity between idealized media images and the physiological traits of a specific woman or man, this approach to physical appearance focuses on the intrinsic appeal of the differences that are embodied in a particular individual. By reclaiming an aesthetic tradition that originated in one of the earliest eras of human history and by overturning the moral order of the human body imposed by authorities such as the organized church and the mass media, it is possible to assert proudly that "disability is beautiful."

The capacity to affirm this statement with dignity and pride has profound social, political, and aesthetic implications for nondisabled as well as disabled people.

Ironically, perhaps the major advantages of a renewed appreciation of the value and appeal of visible differences might eventually be conferred on the nondisabled community. For decades, nondisabled viewers have been bombarded with almost unattainable media images of physical "perfection " that most of them could never possibly approximate. Magazine, billboard, and television advertisements are basically designed to trigger anxiety in the minds of viewers about their own appearance, and a multi-billion dollar industry has been created to assuage these worries by peddling an awesome range of products that promise to improve attractiveness. But the ultimate futility of these efforts has even been recognized by sex symbols such as Brigitte Bardot who said:

I do not want to die, so I have to accept old age, right? It is horrible; you rot; you fall to pieces; you stink. It scares me more than anything else. There's a beach not far away, but I never go during the day. I'm 48 and not so pretty. I wouldn't inflict this sight on anyone anymore. [34]

By developing awareness of the beauty to be discovered in the physical differences that distinguish human beings rather than the similarities between them and idolized media images, everyone could be liberated from the conformity perpetuated by these depictions and acquire a heightened aesthetic appreciation of anatomical variations. Perhaps even more importantly, by accepting alternative standards for assessing the aesthetic pleasure of bodily attributes, the nondisabled might uncover a reciprocal advantage that could sustain an enduring coalition with the disabled minority.

Eventually, every person must confront the inescapable reality that most are not likely to resemble the models of youth and beauty promulgated by the mass media and that their chances of receiving the rewards bestowed on the physically desirable are almost certain to diminish as they grow older. Hence, both nondisabled and disabled individuals have a vested interest in expanding the restrictive confines of physical models that, though they seem deeply implanted through media socialization, are not necessarily irreversible. As the history of physical differences demonstrates, humans have always exercised the right to make choices about the anatomical features they consider desirable or interesting, and, at times, these options have included rather than excluded women and men with disabilities.

Perhaps the most significant effects of the realization that attraction can be elicited by a visible disability, however, are apt to be experienced by disabled people themselves. Saddled with a stigma that appears to render them unlovable as well as unacceptable, the personal lives of many disabled people have been plagued by reduced odds, options, and opportunities, the increased risk of rejection, "settling" for less desirable partners, isolation, and perhaps worst of all, a denial of their identity as people with disabilities.

Private concerns previously have seemed to exert disastrous consequences on the public status of the disabled minority. Since many have been understandably reluctant to confront candidly the dire impact that disability might have on personal lives, we have been equally reticent about embracing an identity that may otherwise have permitted us to organize a potentially large segment of the electorate. As a result of this unusual conjunction of private and public considerations, disabled persons have been trapped by the discriminatory effects of the stigma that we have also identified as our greatest enemy.

Just as other disadvantaged groups have sometimes uncovered solutions to their problems by re-examining their own history, research on people with disabilities seemingly provides a solid foundation for the development of a positive sense of personal and political identity. For thousands of years, in a legacy that appeared to emerge from ancient fertility rites and that persisted until religious and economic interests managed to impose another order of the human body, the appearance of physical differences seemed to be associated with festiveness, sensuality, and entertainment rather than with loss, repugnance, or personal tragedy. These trends seem to form a sufficient basis for the redefinition of the identity of persons with disabilities.

I believe that this revitalization of personal and political identity can be most effectively achieved by three means. First, disabled people could play a significant role as the critics of a culture that places inordinate stress on a rather conformist vision of external attractiveness and on a vain search for "the body beautiful." In a society that often seems to have gone berserk in a futile quest to achieve unattainable physical standards, women and men with disabilities may need to offer an alternative model of attraction that would permit both disabled and nondisabled persons to discover enhanced aesthetic satisfaction in the appearance of the ordinary men and women whom they encounter in everyday life.

Second, disabled individuals might appropriately stress the innate appeal of physical differences that contribute richness and diversity to human perceptions. In a fundamental sense, disability demonstrates the superficiality of physical standards in modern society. In a world that can be adapted to accommodate the needs of everyone, the presence of people with disabilities may also signify the dangers of an otherwise drab environment in which everyone begins to appear increasingly alike.

Finally, all persons may need to realize that the occurrence of disability is not necessarily a tragic fate. In many respects, it is also an opportunity to play a significant role in a major process of social change. In the immediate aftermath of a disability, an individual is compelled to answer two of the most difficult metaphysical questions that can be posed to any human being: why? and why me? In the past, they have been given little assistance in their efforts to grapple with such imponderables. Increasingly, however, disabled Americans are beginning to recognize that they have a unique chance to become involved in an historic struggle to extend and expand the definition of human rights. And there are perhaps few other activities that can

provide greater meaning and purpose in life. In this sense therefore, disability can also become an important source of empowerment and a major potential for promoting the increased acceptance of human differences in modern civilization.

In addition, efforts to reduce prejudice based on aesthetic considerations can be facilitated by changes in public policy. One scientist has even proposed that sharply increased taxes should be imposed on products solely designed to improve personal attractiveness. [35] Educational institutions, from elementary and secondary schools to universities, also might focus increased attention on teaching about the salience of physical appearance and alternative means of perceiving individual attraction. For a generation that has been exposed to supposedly ideal physical models via television and films, at least some instruction might be appropriately offered to allow students to evaluate the impact of these forms on their own perceptions of other people.

A method then must be found to affect policies that govern the presentation of visual images to the general public. Perhaps the major initiative in this field might be taken in the private sector by television and film producers, who might rediscover the interest and fascination of human characteristics that represent a departure from - rather that a conformity with - idealized notions of physical appearance.

Eventually, policymakers also need to become aware that visual displays of physical features convey messages that are just as political as the content of verbal declarations. In the past, such communications have had an effect on the disabled minority and other groups that have been subjected to discrimination on aesthetic grounds. By regaining appreciation of the historical legacies that have shaped earlier perceptions of human differences and by promoting the development of alternative standards of physical attractiveness, however, disabled people themselves can play a major role in combating this form of prejudice.

********

# NOTES

[1]     Estimates of the number of disabled persons in the United States vary considerably, depending on the definitions and methods used to identify them. The 27 million figure is reported in *The ICD Survey of Disabled Americans: Bringing Disabled Americans into the Mainstream* (New York: Louis Harris and Associates, 1986), p.iii. thirty six million is described as " the most widely quoted estimate" by Frank Bowe, *Handicapping America: Barriers to Disabled People* (New York: Harper & Row, 1978), p. 17.

[2]     See, for example, Harlan Hahn, "Civil Rights for Disabled Americans: The Foundation of a Political Agenda," in Alan Gartner and Tom Joe (eds.), *Images of the Disabled, Disabling Images* (New York: Preager, 1987), pp 181-203.

[3]     See Harlan Hahn, "Disability and the Urban Environment:    A Perspective on Los Angeles," *Society and Space* 1986), pp. 273-288.

[4]     *The CD Survey of Disabled Americans*, p. 114.

[5]     Erving Goffman, *Stigma: Notes on the Management of Spoiled Identity* (Englewood Cliffs, N.J.: Prentice Hall, 1963), p.5.

[6]     Harlan Hahn, "The Politics of Human Differences:    Disability and Discrimination," Journal of Social Issues (forthcoming).

[7]     "Facial    Discrimination:    Extending Handicapped Law to Employment Discrimination on the Basis of Physical Appearance," *Harvard Law Review* (June, 1987), pp. 2035-2052

[8]     Seymour Fisher, *Body Consciousness: You Are What You Feel* (Englewood Cliffs, N.J.: Prentice Hall, 1973), p. 73.

[9]     Stephen Kern, *Anatomy and Destiny: A Cultural History of the Human Body* (Indianapolis: Bobbs-Merrill, 1978), p. 256.

[10]     Ralph S. Solecki, *Shanidar, the First Flower People* (New York: Alfred A. Knopf, 1971), p. 196; Erik Trinkaus, The Shanidar Neanderthals (New York: Academic Press, 1983), pp. 401-413.

[11]     Janet and Colin Bord, *Earth Rites: Fertility Practices in Pre-Industrial Britain* (London: Granada, 1982), pp. 69-80; Reay Tannahill, *Sex in History* (New York: Stein and Day, 1980), pp. 33-35.

[12]     Shari    Thurer,    "Disability    and Monstrosity: A Look as Literary Distortions of Handicapping    Conditions," *Rehabilitation Literature* (January/February, 1980), pp. 12-15.

[13]     Alan Dundes (ed.), *Cinderella: A folklore Casebook* (New York: Garland, 1982).

[14]     Dr. Doran, *The History of Court Fools* (New York: Haskell-House, 1966, originally published in 1855), pp. 32-40, 79-80, 41-61.

[15]     Robert Brain, *The Decorated Body* (New York: Harper & Row, 1979); Bernard Rudofsky, *The Unfashionable Body* (Garden City, N.Y.: Doubleday, 1971).

[16]     Charles M. Woolf and Frank C. Dukepoo, "Hopi Indians Inbreeding, and Albinism," *Science* (April, 4, 1969), pp. 30-37.

[17]     Leslie Fiedler, *Freaks: Myths and Images of the Secret Self* (New York: Simon and Schuster, 1978), especially pp. 47-63.

[18]     Joan Albon, *Little People in America: Social Dimensions of Dwarfism* (New York: Praeger, 1984).

[19]     Enid Welsford, *The Fool: His Social and Literary History* (New York: Farrar and Reinehar, n.d.), pp. 113-127.

[20]     Sandra Billington, *A Social History of the Fool* (New York: St. Martin's Press, 1984), pp. 4-5.

[21]     Debra Connors, "Disability, Sexism, and the Social Order," in Susan E. Browne, Debra Connors, and Nanci Stern (eds.). *With the Power of Each Breath: A Disabled Women's Anthology* (Pittsburgh: Cleis Press, 1985), p. 95.

[22]     Mikhail Bakhti, trans. by Helen Iswolsky, *Rabelais and His World* (Cambridge: MIT Press, 1969), p. 91.

[23]     Robert Anchor, "Bahktin's Truths of Laughter," *Cilo* (Spring, 1985), p. 240.

[24]     See Douglas Biklen and Lee Bailey (eds.), *Rudely Stamp'd: Imaginal Disability and Prejudice ( Washington, D.C.: University Press of America, 1981).*

[25]     Susan Sontag, *Illness as Metaphor* (new York: Farrar, Straus , and Giroux, 1978).

[26]     Deborah A. Stone, *The Disabled State* (Philadelphia: Temple University Press, 1984), pp. 51-55.

[27]     C. Esco Obermann, *A History of Vocational    Rehabilitation    in    America* (Minneapolis: T.S. Denison, 1965), pp. 58-59; Victor Finkelstein *Attitudes and Disabled People* (New York: World Rehabilitation Fund, 1980), pp. 8-9.

[28]     Robert Bogdan "The Exhibition of Humans with Differences for Amusement and Profit," *Policy Studies Journal* (March, 1987), pp. 537-550.

[29]     Rudolph M. Bell, *Holy Anorexia* (Chicago: The University of Chicago Press, 1985); Caroline Walker Bynum, *Holy Feast and Holy Fast: The Religious Significance of Food to Medieval    Women* (Berkeley: University of California Press, 1987).

[30]     Brian S. Turner, *The Body and Society: Exploration in Social Theory* (Oxford, England: Basil Blackwell, 1984).

[31]     Harlan Hahn, "Advertising the Acceptably Employable Image: Disability and Capitalism," *Policies Studies Journal* (March, 1987), pp. 551-570.

[32]     Paul K. Longmore, "Screening Stereotypes: Images of Disabled People, " *Social Policy* (Summer, 1985), pp. 31-37.

[33]     Michael Focault, trans. by Robert Hurley, *The History of Sexuality* (New York: Pantheon, 1978).

[34]     quoted in Alexandra Dundas Todd, "Women and the Disabled in Contemporary Society *Social Policy* (Spring, 1984), pp. 44-45.

[35]     Don B. Giddon, "Through the Looking Glasses of Physicians, Dentists and Patients," *Perspectives in Biology and Medicine* (1983), pp. 451-458.

****

**About the Author:**  Harlan Hahn, at the writing of this article, is a professor of political science at the University of Southern California

**Source:**  Reprinted with permission from *Social Policy,* Winter 1988, pp. 26.32.  Published by the Social Policy Corporation, New York, New York 10036.  Copyright 1988.

# Sexuality and Disability: An Overview

Sandra Keller, Ph.D.
Denton C. Buchannan, Ph.D.

**Introduction:** Sexuality is psychological and physiological. From a psychological perspective, sexuality is an expression of intimacy, affection and love. When one acquires a disability, the subsequent worries and outright emotional disruption and anxiety cloud the ability to express and perceive such tender emotions. Injury or disease often produces a lowered self-confidence, self-esteem and self-worth. The ability to see oneself as attractive, masculine or feminine is threatened. It is difficult to either express or feel love and affection when one loses respect for one's own body.

Similarly, able-bodied partners can experience difficulty in the expression of intimacy. A decrease in sexual performance can become an early symptom of the stresses and strains within the partnership as both adjust to the disability. The non-disabled partner may fear making the disorder worse through sex, for example by increasing blood pressure and thus risking another heart attack or stroke. Some fear contagion or genetically impaired offspring as a result of the disease. Muscular dystrophy and multiple sclerosis are occasionally thought of in these terms. Unfortunately, these false beliefs and needless concerns are often unspoken yet produce an atmosphere that perpetuates sexual problems.

From a physiological standpoint, experimental research with animals has given us some understanding of brain function in relation to sexuality. Animals appear to be primarily dependent upon hormonal influences. Specifically, the release of hormones initiates sexual behavior in almost all species that have been studied. Males, for example, are stimulated by a pheromone or odor emitted from the female during estrus. Similarly, an inhibitory system in the brain serves to decrease sexual drive. In contrast, the cortex appears to play only a minimal role in animals. For example, female rats can mate, become pregnant and deliver pups with the majority of the cortex removed, while male

rats which require more neuromotor involvement, can complete sexual behavior with as much as 60% of the cortex removed.

However, the pattern for humans does not appear to be the same as for animals. Human female sexual behavior is not dependent upon the estrus cycle, and sexual arousal in the male can occur independent of any changes in sex hormones. In man, sexual arousal and behavior are functions of personality and emotion, which depend on the cerebral cortex.

This article will introduce many aspects of sexuality and disability. Psychological and physical aspects of a number of disabilities are discussed with an emphasis on practical solutions to common problems, and the illumination of current research and perspectives within the domain of sexuality.

## Multiple Sclerosis

Multiple Sclerosis (MS) has a significant effect on an individual's sexuality since it is a disorder of the nervous system that most commonly strikes most young adults at an age when sexual performance and attractiveness are paramount. As its name implies, MS can occur in multiple areas of the body and consequently has varying affects on different individuals. In general, however, MS affects sensory motor neurons, causing impairments in the individual's ability to perceive or enjoy sexual stimulation and the muscular ability to sustain sexual behavior. The most common physical symptoms in men are fatigue, weakness, and a loss of the ability to attain and sustain erections. Women report reduced numbers of orgasms, numbness, decreased vaginal lubrication resulting in pain or discomfort during sex, and muscle spasms that interfere with sexual performance. One survey of MS individuals reported that 91% of men and 72% of women experienced changes in their sexual performance ranging from a mild loss of sensation to severe impairment. For example, between 20% and 40% of MS males report total failure to attain an erection.

It is important to realize that despite the physical symptoms, people with MS have a normal interest in sex.  Their symptoms therefore cause frustration and embarrassment. It is common to develop significant feelings of inadequacy and lack of confidence because of their difficulty in expressing attitudes of affection and intimacy.

Although MS is a progressive disease, it is common for symptoms to wax and wane, being absent for long periods of time then reappearing without any apparent cause. Therefore, both patient and partner must continually readjust. This creates uncertainty about one's ability to perform sexually each time an attempt is made and can produce a total avoidance of sex to escape embarrassment of failed performance. Jealousy and suspicion that the spouse is seeking affection elsewhere can be an offshoot of this lack of confidence.

Pregnancy is another concern.  MS strikes at an age when couples are planning children.  Males worry about their ability to father a child.  Females are concerned about the impact of pregnancy upon the course of the disease.

Women with MS usually continue to menstruate and ovulate, and therefore have a normal chance of becoming pregnant. However, pregnancy may make the symptoms worse.  These difficulties appear to be transient, related to the hormonal changes that occur during the 9-month gestation period. A larger problem appears to be the early post-partum period when the hormonal fluctuations are at their peak.

Questions of heredity and of contagion often arise in the topic of sexuality and MS.  MS is not contagious and sexual contact produces no risk.  Similarly, breast feeding causes no risk for the infant.  There is however, an increased risk of contracting MS in the offspring of MS parents.  A child has approximately one percent chance of getting MS if one parent has the disease.  The complicated interaction between genetics and environment is not totally understood.

Many recommendations can be made to increase the MS patient's enjoyment of sex. Open communication between partners is essential.  Emptying the bladder before lovemaking removes the fear of loss of bladder control.  Women can use sterile water-soluble lubricant jellies, such as KY Jelly. Recognizing that fatigue is a major obstacle, couples can often overcome this problem by experimenting with different positions and different times of the day to increase strength. There are several surgical procedures that have been tried, such as implants to the penis to provide an erection.

For the reader interested in the topic of sexuality and MS, a comprehensive booklet is available through the Multiple Sclerosis Society: *Sexuality and Multiple Sclerosis* by Michael Barrett.

## Spinal Cord Injury

The spinal cord injured (SCI) male may experience erections in response to external stimulation to the body below the level of the cord lesion (reflex erection), or as a result of internal stimulation such as bladder distention (spontaneous erection).  Research has shown that while a small percentage of men report the sensation of ejaculation, the seminal fluid backs up into the bladder rather than being expelled (retrograde ejaculation).  Thus, the male's reproductive capacity is greatly reduced or eradicated.

In contrast, the female's reproductive capacity is unimpaired.  Although the menstrual cycle may be temporarily interrupted, it is restored in almost all women within a year.  Pregnancy is as possible as it was prior to injury.  Not only are women capable of carrying a fetus to term without serious medical problems, but most are capable of vaginal deliveries.  In fact, caesarean sections are no more common among SCI women than they are among able-bodied women.

Because of the loss of sensation to the genital region, the utilization of fantasy can enhance sexual experience.  A large number of spinal cord injured people, both male and female report that they can achieve fantasized orgasms that seem similar to those experienced by neurologically unimpaired individuals. By concentrating on sensations being received from enervated areas of their body and transposing that stimulation to the genitals, some SCI men and women report multiple orgasms during a single sexual encounter. Thus, portions of the body that retain feeling may become more highly eroticized than they were before injury.

Many of the problems of SCI are similar to those of MS. Spinal injured people have normal libidos while experiencing changes in sensation and muscle strength. The major difference is that the disorder is sudden rather than gradual, thereby requiring an immediate adjustment by both spouse and patient. Although it is not uncommon for marital difficulties to develop from feelings of frustration and inadequacy, once adjustment is achieved the SCI patient does not have to cope with progressive deterioration.

Several group programs and literature exist for counseling and education. Training in social skills for young SCI people is as essential as sexuality counseling. With the sudden switch to a wheelchair, confidence in social relationship is often lost, and routine activities such as dating can become frightening.

## Brain Dysfunction

There are many social myths concerning the sexuality of individuals with brain dysfunction. A stereotype of sexual deviance resulting from brain damage exists, yet there has been little research done on brain damage and sexual behavior.

We do know that sexual behavior results from an interaction between two major areas of cerebral cortex: the frontal and temporal lobes, and the underlying limbic system. Damage to the top of the frontal lobes (which is beneath the forehead) causes a general loss of initiative and of the ordering of sexual behavior. Damage to the orbital frontal cortex (underneath the brain above the eye orbits), in contrast, appears to cause loss of inhibition, or moral or ethical restraint. This can result in sexual misconduct and inappropriate behavior.

When the temporal lobes of the brain (located above the ears) are damaged, either an increase in appropriate sexual behavior or a reduction in sexual interest and performance can result. Although precise areas within the temporal lobes affecting sexual behavior are not as well understood as the frontal lobes, the primary area appears to be the anterior temporal lobe.

It is important to recognize that these two large areas of the brain, the frontal lobes and the temporal lobes, are most prone to damage in closed head injury. Thus, it is not only possible, but likely, to experience changes in sexual functioning following a blow to the head. However, it is much more difficult to predict the nature of the change.

Several studies have looked at the impact of a cerebral vascular accident or stroke upon sexual functioning. Bray deFrank and Wolfe studied the sexual interest, function, and attitude of thirty-five patients before and after a stroke. They found that there was a significant reduction in sexual ability following the stroke. Only 46% of the men could maintain an erection and only 29% could experience an ejaculation. Similarly, only 9% of the women could achieve an orgasm and only 27% continued to menstruate after the stroke.

Allsup-Jackson conducted a telephone survey in 1981 of fifty stroke patients between the ages of 45 and 60. She found that 60% of the men had a reduction in sexual contact and 70% of females reported a decrease in sexual behavior following the stroke. Of these, 20% reported that sexual contact had stopped completely.

There are a number of reasons for reduced sexual behavior after stroke. Hemiplegia and the resulting neglect of one side of the body and visual field cause patients to have less sensory enjoyment and to notice fewer sexual cues from their partner. Muscle weakness and awkwardness impair sexual performance. Speech difficulties also impair sexual communication. However, the major cause for the lack of performance when interest remains the same is emotional in nature.

In temporal lobe epilepsy, more than any other disorder, there exists a folklore and stigma of bizarre sexual behavior. However, several recent studies have clearly shown that the most common sexual change in temporal lobe epilepsy is a reduction in sexual interest and behavior (hypo sexuality).

It is important to distinguish between behavior that occurs during a seizure and behavior that occurs at other times. Seizures can produce sexually deviant behavior that cannot be controlled by the person at the moment. Such behavior may include automatic acts such as undressing, verbal utterances, and even public masturbation. These events are rare and do not represent the most common experience of epileptics. Quite the opposite, temporal lobe epileptics generally have a lower than normal interest in sex.

### Coronary Dysfunction Disease

Patients who have suffered a myocardial infarction (MI) have been shown to reduce the frequency of sexual activity. One study reported a 58% decrease in sexual activity in post-infarct patients. This finding has been confirmed more recently with reports of the wives of MI patients.

Another study demonstrated that the frequency of orgasm declined as well. Furthermore, this decrease in sexual activity or even outright abstinence from sexual intercourse has been found as late as forty-seven months after MI. When interviewed, the most common cause reported by males is impotence and decrease in sexual desire. Ten percent of post-infarct males reported performance impotence. The incidence of additional sexual difficulties had been reported as premature ejaculation in 37% of the patients, retarded ejaculation in 54%, and 60% manifested erectile difficulties at least half of the time.

Although the majority of the studies have evaluated the various aspects of the sexual life of males, study of the female coronary patient appears to have been neglected. Abromov compared the sexual activity of 100 female patients with acute MI to that of a control group of 100 female general medical patients. Sexual frigidity and dissatisfaction were among 65% of the coronary patients as compared with 34% of the controls. The coronary patients were also found to have a significantly earlier menopausal age that the patients hospitalized for other diseases.

Little attention has been paid to the concerns of the spouse. Spouses have been found to contribute to the difficulties by being overprotective, overly solicitous, afraid to make demands or induce emotional upset. Ambiguous instructions from physicians often add to their confusion and accentuate their concern.

Extensive work by Hellerstein and colleagues has determined that there are few, if any, physiological reasons for the cardiac patient to suffer sexual dysfunction. A "sexercise" tolerance test, using electrocardiograph tape-recordings during sexual activity, showed that the energy expended during sexual intercourse is significantly lower than the energy expended in most everyday tasks. Furthermore, they found that the mean maximal heart rate achieved during orgasm was 117.4 beats per minute, while the mean maximal heart rate during the performance of usual occupational activity was 120.1 beats per minute.

The prescription of a physical conditioning program may increase the cardiac patient's cardiovascular and respiratory fitness. Indeed patients in one study indicated that both the frequency and quality of sexual activity improved significantly as a result of a physical fitness program. Moreover, 67% of the patients reported much fewer, or complete absence of cardiac symptoms during sexual activity. However, a conditioning program must be highly individualized, and personal limiting factors such as angina, dyspnea, and body weight must be considered before advising a patient to resume physical activity - sexual or otherwise. Another means of gradually returning a post-coronary patient to sexual activity is to recommend masturbation, not only to allay fears, but also to allow time for experimentation of one's limits and to gain confidence.

### Chronic Obstructive Lung Disease

Chronic obstructive lung disease (COLD) refers to a group of chronic respiratory disorders including asthma, emphysema, and chronic bronchitis. It has been reported that COLD can precipitate diverse sexual difficulties such as impotence and frigidity, loss of spontaneity in sexual contact, premature ejaculation, sexual inhibitions, and reduced libido. However, the extent to which these difficulties occur has not been settled. One study of 100 male respiratory patients found that only 17 were impotent. Details from the case histories led the authors to speculate that these dysfunctions were due to life long patterns of behavior not due to the disease. In contrast, two studies contended that COLD was detrimental to sexual physical expression in as many as 74% of the patients.

Individuals suffering from lung disease are chronically short of breath and it is not uncommon for some to develop anxiety about participating in physical activity of any kind. Given the increased depth and rate of respiration during sexual excitement, it is easily understood why many patients are afraid that they may suffocate during sexual activity. The patient and partner should be educated and reassured by the research findings which show that effort required for intercourse does not jeopardize blood pressure, heart rate or respiratory rate.

Chronic coughing and phlegm production may be a source of embarrassment and patients may suffer from a poor self-image because of physical alterations such as a caved in or barrel-shaped chest. Regular physiotherapy could increase not only exercise tolerance, but could also add to the patient's self-confidence. The able-bodied partner could also be advised to assume a more active role in lovemaking.

## Assessment

Sexuality counseling is a vital component in the rehabilitation of disabled people. Since some patients feel uncomfortable discussing the topic of sex, and indeed will never initiate such a discussion, it is often incumbent upon the therapist to introduce the subject, preferably as a matter of routine. The person's religious and sexual attitudes must be considered. A sexual history should include prior sexual activity and address such variables as frequency of coitus, level of sexual desire, capacity for arousal and orgasmic experience. A program can then be designed that will take all of this information into account. Whether sexual counseling is delivered individually or in a group, it should be supportive and reassuring, striving to facilitate communication between patient and partner.

A number of assessment inventories have been devised to help the clinician in determining a treatment program. In fact, since Masters and Johnson published *Human Sexual Inadequacy* in 1970, mental health professionals have exhibited a widespread interest in the treatment of sexual dysfunction. Research on the clinical treatment of sexual dysfunction has been greatly impeded by the lack of objective, valid, and reliable testing methods. There are a number of simple behavioral checklists which are used to assess the range of sexual behaviors a person engages in heterosexual - homosexual orientation, and masculinity -femininity. However, there are relatively few assessment devices that focus on actual sexual functioning and satisfaction.

The Sexual Interaction Inventory is a paper and pencil self-report inventory that assesses the nature of a couple's sexual relationship in terms of sexual functioning and sexual satisfaction. It is valuable both as a measure of the effectiveness of treatment and as a diagnostic tool. As a descriptive system for sexual dysfunctions, it examines the desire, arousal, and orgasm phases of the sexual response. The Sex History Form, to be used before the initial intake interview, helps the clinician become aware of the areas of sexual functioning requiring a closer assessment.

The Sex Knowledge and Attitude Test (SKAT) is a self-administered multiple choice test which measures sexual attitudes, knowledge and degree of experience in a variety of sexual activities. The attitude section of this test comprises a heterosexual relations scale that deals with an individual's general attitude toward pre- and extra marital heterosexual behavior; a sexual myths scale is concerned with the individual's acceptance or rejection of commonly held sexual misconceptions about sex education, homosexuality, etc.; an abortion scale; and a masturbation scale. The knowledge section of the SKAT yields a score based on the respondent's general store of factual information concerning the physiological and social aspects of sexual functioning.

The Minnesota Sexual Attitude Scales require respondents to give their emotional reaction to the notion of different persons (e.g. mid-adolescents, unmarried adults. married adults) engaging in certain categories of sexual activities. On the Sexual Attitude and Behavior Survey, respondents indicate under what circumstances they would find different sexual behavior or thoughts to be permissible.

## Intervention Strategies

There are many articles and studies on intervention techniques to improve sexuality in physically disabled people. Space does not permit a review of these reports. However, there are two conceptual frameworks that can be of assistance to rehabilitation professionals and clients alike. These are the Plissit Model outlined by Jack Annon and the Developmental Skill Based Approach described by Shrey, Kiefer and Anthony.

The Plissit Model is a conceptual scheme for behavioral treatment of sexual problems in general and not specifically for the disabled. The title "Plissit" is an acronym derived from the four stages: permission (P), limited information (LI), specific suggestions (SS), intensive therapy (IT). Each stage is a more advanced approach than the one preceding it.

Permission implies that many patients merely need to have the reassurance that their behavior, coping strategies, fantasies, and ideas are normal and acceptable. Such permission often removes sexual anxieties and barriers to sexual expression.

Limited information is seen as providing clients with specific factual information directly relevant to their particular sexual concerns. This imparting of information needs to be directed at a specific sexual concern and at dispelling sexual myths.

It is not intended as a broad-based session on all human sexual behavior.

Clinical experience has shown that the majority of sexual obstacles are met during the first two stages, of relieving anxieties and providing limited information.

The third level of treatment. specific suggestions, involves direct attempts to help the client change his behavior in order to overcome specific sexual problems. For the problem to be clearly understood by both the patient and the therapist, a clear sexual history is needed. The necessary treatment approach becomes obvious with a clear understanding of the problem.

In the fourth stage, intensive therapy, the patient is referred to a specialist in sexual problems and treatment approaches to develop a specific program.

The second model to be discussed here, the Development Skill-Based Approach, which falls within the specific suggestion and intensive therapy stages of the Plissit Model. This approach provides the clinician with a three phase strategy in interviewing clients and developing treatment plans for change.

The first phase is called *exploration.* Through discussions, both therapist and client gain insight into the sexual needs and capabilities of the client. Physical impairments and capabilities as they relate to sexuality are discussed. Information concerning physical capacity is also obtained from the patient's partner, physicians, and other health care professionals, with care being taken to observe the rule of confidentiality. Similarly, psychological assets and disadvantages are explored. Areas of concern may include feelings of unattractiveness, lack of motivation, or fears regarding sexuality, interpersonal and social skills, and satisfaction with current sexual behavior. The client's sexual values are also discussed. Religious beliefs concerning birth control and sexual freedom, cultural beliefs, and the client's attitudes toward sexual activities such as masturbation and body positions are important sources of information.

The second phase is called *understanding.* It helps the client to acquire the knowledge and skills necessary for sexual adjustment. During this phase, the client develops methods to overcome sexual barriers and sets priorities on the various concerns he or she may have. The therapist and client determine the steps needed to establish a behavior change program. This may involve community resources, physical aids, etc.

The third phase in this model is the *action* phase in which a step by step plan to overcome sexual adjustment problems is developed by the client and the therapist. Each step identifies specific behavioral goals and completion dates.

This overview is not meant to be a definitive study of all aspects of sexuality and disability. It is simply intended to be an introduction to the experience and current research which has contributed to our knowledge of this long neglected, yet vital subject.

### How to Find Help

If you have concerns or problems with sexual functioning, you can improve your chances of finding a qualified therapist by seeking sex therapy at centers that are affiliated with universities, medical schools or hospitals, or by contacting reputable professional associations for referral.

In Canada, referrals can be obtained by contacting **Sex Education Council of Canada** (SIECCAN) at 423 Castlefield Avenue, Toronto, ON. M5N 1L4, or by calling Michael Barrett, SIECCAN Chairperson, (416) 978-3488. For Ontario only, contact BESTCO, The Board of Examiners and Counselling in Ontario, c/o OAMFT, 271 Russell Hill Road, Toronto, ON. M4V 2T5, (416) 968-7779.

In the United States, AASECT publishes listings of qualified therapists including certified Canadians. Contact:

### American Association of Sex Educators, Counsellors and Therapists

5010 Wisconsin Avenue N.W.
Suite 304
Washington, D.C. 20016 (Cost $2.00)

The telephone directory yellow pages may list Sex Therapists under Marriage and Family Therapy. Be certain to check out

qualifications; request names of physicians or health clinics who refer patients to this therapist; ask the therapist for information about their education and training in Sex Therapy; avoid therapists who make unrealistic promises to guarantees of cure; request treatment costs, whether medical insurance coverage is available, and the particular therapy approach used by the therapist.

In many centers, well-trained and qualified sex therapists are few in number or non-existent. Careful shopping and perhaps a willingness to travel to a city where there is a clinic or a number of qualified therapists will result in a greater chance of success and prove both a financial and emotional saving.

### Professional Training in Sex Therapy

Training and certification in Sex Therapy are difficult to obtain in Canada. Since there is no English University sexology degree program available, completion of a Master's Degree or Doctorate Degree in a discipline such as psychology, sociology, social work or medicine is usually a prelude to subsequent specialization in sex counseling and therapy. It is necessary to search out programs, courses, workshops, and clinical supervision in sex therapy. This may mean going to the United States.

Two professional organizations, the Society for Sex Therapy and Research, New York (SSTAR) and the American Association of Sex Educators, Counsellors and Therapists, Washington D.C. (ASSECT) publish national directories. ASSECT has a sex therapist certification process and also sponsors courses and programs which are credited towards certification. SIECCAN (address above) also provides information on professional education programs.

~ Marg Jacobs
Professor of Human
Sexuality - Algonquin
College

There is a Master of Science (M.Sc.) degree in family studies offering the opportunity to specialize in the field of human sexuality. For more information, contact the Chairman, Department of Family Studies,

University of Guelph, Guelph, ON.  N1G 2W1 (519) 824-4120 Ext. 3968.

Humber College in Toronto offers a multi-disciplinary advanced certification program in human sexuality to professionals already working in institutional and community settings.  For more information on Human Sexuality: Counselling and Teaching Program contact:    Paul Pieper, Coordinator, Community Health Education Programs, Health Sciences Division, Humber College, 205 Humber College Blvd., Rexdale, ON. M9W 5L6. (416) 675-3111, Ext. 587.

********

**About the Authors:**  At the time of writing, Sandra Keller, Ph.D. and Denton C. Buchanan, Ph.D. were with the Royal Ottawa Regional Rehabilitation Centre in Ottawa, Ontario, Canada

**Source:**  Reprinted with permission from *Rehabilitation Digest*, Vol. 15, No. 1, Spring 1984, pp. 3-7.  Published by CRDC, Toronto, Ontario, Canada  M2N 5W9.

# Sexual Abuse and Exploitation of Children and Adults with Mental Retardation and Other Handicaps

Deborah Tharinger,
Connie Burrows Horton,
Susan Millea

*Abstract ~ There is growing recognition that children, adolescents, and adults who are mentally retarded are particularly vulnerable due to their often life-long dependence on caregivers, relatively powerless position in society, emotional and social insecurities, and lack of education regarding sexuality and sexual abuse. In addition the mental health functions and emotional development of individuals who are mentally retarded are not well understood, and many professionals remain uneducated about their mental health needs. To work effectively with this population, mental health professionals and educators must be alert to what is known about the sexual abuse and exploitation of persons with mental retardation. Furthermore, they need to become educated about the rights of these persons to special legal protection from abuse and neglect and to appropriate and effective mental health interventions. The challenge for mental health professionals and educators is to protect persons who are mentally retarded from sexual abuse and exploitation, to provide appropriate psychotherapeutic interventions when abuse occurs, to respect their right to developmentally appropriate knowledge about sexuality and sexual abuse, and to allow the fulfillment of their sexuality.*

**Key Words-** Mental retardation, Children, Adults, Sexual abuse.

Since the passage of the Child Abuse Prevention and Treatment Act of 1974 (Public Law 93-247), which included sexual abuse and exploitation on its definition of child abuse (National Center on Child Abuse and Neglect, 1978), sexual abuse has received widespread media coverage that has resulted in heightened professional and societal awareness of the problem. Concern for the legal protection of persons with intellectual disabilities from sexual abuse and exploitation has been noted as far back as 1899. The Queensland Criminal Code Act states:

> *Any person who...knowing a woman or girl to be an idiot or imbecile, has or attempts to have unlawful carnal knowledge of her is guilty of a misdemeanor and liable to imprisonment with hard labor for five years... (Muller, 1984).*

Although the language is derogatory and offensive in today's parlance, the identified need for protection of a special group of people is clear. Also evident is that the sexual and reproductive rights of females who are mentally retarded were being controlled by the same statute. This situation identifies the difficult task at hand today: protecting persons with mental retardation from sexual abuse and exploitation while enabling them developmentally appropriate knowledge about and the fulfillment of their sexuality. Similarly, legal debates about children's rights to protection also involve the question of whether children can make informed decisions about sexual or other matters. The main argument is whether parental responsibility consists of an obligation to protect or whether it also includes a measure of enablement, that is of helping children to become independent and capable of making informed, autonomous decisions (Ennew, 1984). A balance must be struck between the extent of protective and enablement measures and must take into account the developmental stages and capacities of the individual, whether an adult or a child.

The reality that children and adults with intellectual disabilities are sexually abused or exploited by family members, caretakers, acquaintances, or strangers indeed is disturbing and perhaps even more difficult to accept than the fact that non-handicapped individuals are abused. Pervasive myths exist, suggesting that people with disabilities are not vulnerable to sexual abuse because they are objects of pity, are asexual, or are undesirable (Anderson, 1982; O'Day, 1983). In reality, persons with handicaps often are targets of violence, perversion and assault. There is growing recognition that individuals with disabilities, including children, adolescents and adults who are mentally retarded, are particularly vulnerable to sexual abuse (American Psychiatric Association, 1987; Finkelhor, 1984; Gordon, 1971; Krents, Schulman, & Brenner, 1987; Mayer, 1988; Morgan, 1987; O'Day, 1983; Sullivan & Scanlan, 1988; Zirpoli, 1986).

An estimated 1% of the population living in the United States is mentally retarded, indicating that there are a little over two million individuals with mental retardation. Within the retarded population, approximately 85% function in the range of mild retardation (IQs between 55 and 70), 10% function in the moderate range (IQs between 40 and 55), 3-4% function in the severe range (IQs between 25 and 40), and 1-2% function in the profound range (IQ below 25) (American Psychiatric Association, 1987). In making a determination of mental retardation, level of adaptive functioning also is taken into account. That is, an individual's social skills, communication skills, daily living skills, personal independence, and self-sufficiency are evaluated along with intelligence. Among the population of mild to moderate retarded, sexual development and sexual interest has been shown to occur at approximately the same age as for the normal population (Haavik & Menninger, 1981; Szymanski & Jansen, 1980). However, these individuals have little opportunity to understand their sexuality and to explore their curiosity, and as a result, they may become easy targets of sexual abuse and exploitation.

Although there has been recognition that persons who are intellectually disabled are at high risk for sexual abuse, there is little professional literature documenting their abuse and exploitation. There are few case study reports, scant empirical research findings, few specially designed prevention education materials, and an absence of guidelines for treatment programs. The mental health functioning and emotional development of persons who are mentally retarded have been addressed only recently, and thus many professionals still remain uneducated about the mental health needs of the population of individuals who are mentally retarded (Matson & Barrett, 1982.; Menolascino & McCann, 1983; Stark, Menolascino, Albarelli & Gray, 1988; Tanguay & Szymanski, 1980). To work effectively with children and adults with intellectual disabilities who are victims of sexual abuse, educators, social workers, physiologists, psychiatrists, and other mental health professionals must be alert to knowledge about their abuse and exploitation. Professionals also need to become educated about the rights of persons who are mentally retarded to obtain appropriate and effective mental health interventions to receive sexuality education and to actualize their sexuality.

## Socio-Legal Considerations

Two issues are pertinent to a discussion of the special protections from abuse and neglect afforded to the intellectually disabled and of their personal sexual rights: their classification as a special group of people and the ability of the mentally retarded to give legal consent to a relationship. The process of class legislation accords to certain persons or classes of persons, as defined by established criteria (in this case predicted upon appropriate determination of mental retardation), the grant of privileges or imposition of burdens to individuals by virtue of their membership within the class (Black, 1968).

While class legislation may be intended to safeguard the rights of persons who are mentally retarded, in effect, certain rights may be, in some circumstances, grossly restricted. This has been true historically with regard to sexuality issues. Consequently, during the past 15 years the constitutional issues of equal protection and due process for persons with mental retardation have been addressed with regards to their rights to engage in sexual relationships, marriage, and family life, and the prevention of sterilization without consent. Given this historical contest, the legal dilemma of providing protection from sexual abuse and exploitation becomes more understandable. What is asked of the legal system for this class of people is both protection of their legal right to engage in sexual relationships by virtue of their intellectual disability and limited capacity to protect themselves.

The situation is further complicated in that the label "mental retardation" constitutes an ambiguous and potentially discriminatory class of disabled people. Both the profoundly impaired person with severely limited verbal and motor ability and the mildly impaired person capable of competitive employment and independent living are contained within this class. More than simply an intellectual deficit, mental retardation encompasses a complex set of adaptive behaviors, some of which may be a function of the retardation while others may be totally unrelated. This complexity is particularly evident in the area of socio-sexual behavior. Yet the constitutional right to equality of treatment is dependent upon the reliable treatment of each person within this class, regardless of their idiosyncrasies. This legal concept of reliability refers to those factors which assure the consistency of the legal process to be provided to persons who are mentally retarded ( Woody, 1974). This concept of legal reliability in conjunction with the provision for the sexual rights and necessary protections from abuse requires that behaviors be clearly defined for an ambiguous population, a task that many of the social sciences have grappled with for years.

As a special class, persons who are mentally retarded are entitled to special legal protection from abuse and neglect, comparable to that for children and for the elderly. Laws providing protection and requiring the reporting of abuse, as well as investigative procedures for incidents of suspected sexual abuse, of adults with mental retardation vary by state. Many states now have legislation comparable to Minnesota's "Reporting of Vulnerable Adults Act". This act requires the reporting by professionals of suspected cases of neglect or physical or sexual abuse of vulnerable adults including persons 18 or older who are residents of nursing homes, day care centers, or residential facilities serving the mentally ill, mentally retarded, or chemically dependent, as well as those unable to report abuse or neglect due to impairment (O'Day, 1983). The protected status of mentally retarded persons may be affected by their age and independent status. In Texas, children and adults who are mentally retarded are protected from abuse within the statewide service system, where any allegation of sexual maltreatment is investigated as a Class 1 abuse (Highest priority). Within Texas there is a mandatory reporting law for abuse or neglect, including sexual abuse of persons who are mentally disabled, if an alleged abuse has occurred at the hand of a caretaker. However, there is little special protection for intellectually disabled adults living independently within the community. For example, if a child younger than 17 is manually molested in the genital area external to the clothes, this would be defined as "indecency by contact", a felony offense. If the same incident occurred in the community to an adult who is mentally retarded, it would be considered a random crime, a "simple assault", which is a misdemeanor offense.

The concept of legal consent is fundamental to protection. It is generally defined to encompass three elements: (1) having the capacity or aptitude to acquire knowledge and become informed; (2) being informed, this is, the ability to understand the advantages and disadvantages associated with the decision to be made, and the ability to choose a course of action after considering the information; and (3) voluntariness, which is the lack of coercion or force through the entire decision-making process (Ames, Hepner, Keaser, & Penler, 1988). According to the report, in the "overwhelming majority of cases" the ability of an individual who is mentally retarded to consent to sexual relations has been evaluated with indicators that were "woefully inadequate" (Ames et al., 1988).

## Incidence and Prevalence of Sexual Abuse in the Population of Persons with Mental Retardation

Not surprisingly, accurate statistics describing the prevalence of sexual abuse and exploitation with mentally retarded persons and handicapped populations do not exist. Generally, professionals in the field believe the incidence of assault in handicapped populations is higher than it is in non-handicapped populations (Anderson, 1982). Since individuals with mental retardation or handicaps face barriers in reporting sexual assault crimes not faced by others, the problem of under reporting is likely more pervasive among this population (O'Day, 1983). Some estimates suggest that only 1 in 30 cases of sexual abuse/assault of persons with disabilities is reported, compared to 1 in 5 cases with the nondisabled (James, 1988). A study of hospital charts and parental interviews of 87 adolescent females with mental retardation reported that 25% of the girls had been sexually abused (Chamberlain, Rauh, Passer, McGrath, & Burkett, 1984). For the purposes of the study, sexual abuse was defined as "attempted or successful coerced intercourse", suggesting that the finding of an incidence of 25% is an underestimate of the total number of girls who were sexually abused. Of the victims, 34% were mildly retarded, 26% were moderately retarded, and 9% were severely retarded.

## The Increased Vulnerability to Sexual Abuse of Children and Adults who are Mentally Retarded

A first and major area that places persons with mental retardation at risk is often lifelong dependency on caregivers (O'Day, 1983). In some cases, such arrangements are necessary due to the severity of their handicaps. In other situations, individuals who are retarded are capable of functioning quite independently, but habits of dependency have been established and are difficult for both the caregivers and the individuals to change. In either situation, a vulnerability is created. Varley (1984) explained that this "long term dependency causes them to unquestioningly follow the direction of supposedly nurturing adults". Compliance with caregivers often is overemphasized at the expense of lessons in assertiveness or independence (Anderson, 1982). This over dependence and unquestioning compliance makes persons with mental retardation especially vulnerable to

sexual abuse, as it places them in situations of unusual trust and enhances the possibility of coercion.

In addition, sexual abuse takes place in the very institutions designed to protect individuals with mental retardation, which speaks to their social powerlessness.. Protection and advocacy agencies were mandated by Congress partially to help prevent and/or investigate cases of abuse and neglect. The vast majority of these agencies appear to have a very limited budget and staff size and are basically unable to manage this charge (Zuckerman, Abrams, & Nuehring, 1986). There are no accurate statistics about the incidence of institution-based abuse partially because it is seldom reported and in some cases may be covered up. Szymanski and Jansen (1980) also note that caregivers in residential facilities may unconsciously sexually exploit residents who are intellectually disabled while unconsciously rationalizing their activity. Furthermore, often the handicaps that cause children and adults who are mentally retarded to require institutionalization also make them extra vulnerable. Individuals with profound mental retardation are the most likely to be institutionalized. Their limited verbal skills create a situation where coercion may not be necessary (Anderson, 1982). If the client who is abused has no verbal ability whatsoever, the chances of his or her being able to prevent or report an attempted sexual abuse incident is severely limited. Persons who are mentally retarded and also physically handicapped may not have the strength to fight or the ability to run to escape. In addition, offenders in institutional settings and in the community may be aware of the vulnerabilities of individuals who are mentally retarded and, thus, find them attractive targets for sexual abuse (O'Day, 1983).

The need of people who are intellectually disabled to be valued and accepted also can place them at risk (Matson & Sevin, 1988). For many individuals with mild retardation the desire is to fit in and to have friends in the "normal" population. This quest for acceptance makes them especially vulnerable to coercion since many will do almost anything that they believe or are told will help them to fit in with the normal crowd. Their emotional and social insecurities again raise their vulnerability.

Children and adults who are mentally retarded frequently are not taught about sex or sexuality. Some parents have strong views that their children with retardation should not be taught about sexual issues (Piper, 1976). Others are anxious or unsure about appropriate techniques for sexual education of their retarded children (Alcorn, 1974; Hammar, Wright, & Jenson, 1967). Barriers to the provision of sexuality education in institutionalized settings exist as well. This deficit may be partially attributed to the attitudes of staff members. Mitchell, Doctor, and Butler (1978) found that nearly one-third of the staff members of residential facilities believed that no sexual behavior, including simple physical contact, is acceptable for persons who are retarded. Furthermore, persons who are mentally retarded are often thought of as asexual beings who will not understand or need sexuality information and therefore should not be educated. In reality the situation is quite different. The sexual drive and development of individuals with mild and moderate retardation are no different than for the non-handicapped (Gordon, 1071; Hall, Morris, & Barker, 1973). They are confronted with a similar variety of sexual stimuli, and as adolescents and adults are, in fact, sexually active (Chamberlain, et al., 1984). Still for many parents and professionals the myth continues, and sexuality issues are not taught to many in this population.

Just as people with mental retardation often fail to receive information about sexuality in general, there is a void in their exposure to information about sexual abuse prevention education programs. Even when they are mainstreamed and do see such a presentation in the normal classroom, it is generally not at a level they can comprehend. There is very limited information on sexual abuse adapted to the needs of the mentally retarded population (O'Day, 1983). This lack of education compounds the vulnerability of the person who is mentally retarded.

Thus, children and adults with mental retardation appear to be extra vulnerable to abuse and exploitation. As described above, they often are dependent on caregivers their whole life, are relatively powerless in society, are easily coerced, are emotionally and socially insecure and needy, and usually are not educated about sexuality and sexual abuse among this population.

## The Nature of the Sexual Abuse and Exploitation of Persons with Mental Retardation

A general description of sexual abuse of individuals who are mentally retarded is difficult as there is much variety in the extent of the abuse, the relationship with the offender, the perception of the experience, the response to disclosure, and the effects. However, there are a few research articles that provide clues about the nature of sexual abuse among this special population. In a sample of 87 adolescent females who are retarded (Chamberlain. et al., 1984), 22 were found to have been sexually abused (Defined as attempted or successful coerced intercourse). Of the whole sample, 9 of the women (10%) were victims of incest. In seven of the incest cases, the offender was the father, stepfather or foster father. The incest generally continued for long periods of time, typically 2-6 years, with other family members often aware of the ongoing sexual abuse. Two incest cases were brother-sister incidents which appeared to have been isolated episodes. Of the other adolescent victims, nine were victims of rape. Two had been sexually assaulted at school; one by a teacher. The authors point out that their data suggest that, contrary to parent's belief that their retarded daughters are at the greatest risk of being sexually assaulted by strangers or other retarded persons, assailants are most likely to be family members or people well known to the victim.

Three case reports of adolescent mentally retarded female victims of sexual abuse are described briefly by Varley (1984). In one case, the 16 year old victim reported that she had been recently sexually assaulted by a friend of the family and also had been a long-standing victim of incest. In the second case, a 14 year old had been sexually assaulted by a boy at school. In the third case, the victim was 17 years old. and the offender was a neighborhood boy.  Thus while there is clearly a need for additional information regarding the nature of sexual abuse of this population, we know that the abuse is at times extensive and ongoing and is often perpetuated by people known to the victim.

## Initial and Long-term Effects of Sexual Abuse in the Population of Persons with Mental Retardation

Little is known about the initial and long-term effects of sexual abuse on the emotional, psychological, or social development of mentally retarded victims; only one article was located that addressed these effects (Varley, 1984). The paucity of research may be due to the difficulty of assessing the impact of and  the ongoing effects of sexual abuse on individuals who are mentally retarded.  Little attention has been paid to the emotional, psychological, and personality development of this population. Furthermore, even less is known about the relationship between personality factors and emotional disturbance (Lewis & MacLean, 1982).    Although  persons  with  mental retardation are susceptible to the same range of behavioral and emotional disorders as non-intellectually impaired individuals, few mental health  professionals  have  focused  their research  or  practice  on  the  emotional development of persons with mental retardation as a group (Matson & Sevin, 1988).

The incidence of mental disorders in the population of individuals who are mentally retarded has been difficult to determine based on existing studies because of differing interpretations  of  the  diagnosis  of retardations, biased selection of samples studied, and the lack of uniform use of psychiatric  diagnostic  classification. However, the limited research that has been conducted indicated that there is a high incidence of psychiatric disorders in the population of persons with mental retardation (Szymanski, 1980). Almost without exception, epidemiological studies have supported that there is a greater prevalence of psychiatric disorder among the mentally retarded than in the general population (Lewis & MacLean, 1982).  For example, the Isle of Wight studies reported five

to six times the rate of emotional disturbance in children with mental retardation compared to a randomly selected control group (Rutter, Tizard, & Whitmore, 1980).

Thus there is reason to believe that reactions to sexual abuse in the population of persons who are mentally retarded will be more severe than in the non-handicapped population.    As  stated  recently,  "Their response to sexual assault may be qualitatively different from that of non retarded victims" (Varley, 1984). In three case studies described by  Varley  (1984),  the  mildly  retarded adolescent victims' reactions to being sexually abused were so severe that they developed schizophreniform psychoses. The occurrence of the abuse was not discovered or disclosed until the psychoses had cleared.

## Professional Response to Sexual Abuse and Exploitation of the Mentally Retarded

Of  importance  is  the  need  for professionals to acknowledge and dispel the myths that persons with mental retardation are not vulnerable to sexual abuse or are not affected by its occurrence. The myths constitute a basis for denying the existence of sexual abuse in this handicapped population.  This denial may take the form of minimizing  the seriousness of the problem, showing a reluctance to accept the prevalence of the problem, expressing disbelief in the credibility of a mentally retarded person's disclosure  of  symptoms,  failing  to  report suspected abuse, failing to recommend or provide appropriate and effective interventions, or failing to provide prevention education.

**Identification and Reporting:** There are two major ways for education and mental health professionals to identify cases of sexual abuse in this population.  The first is to provide a trusting  atmosphere  and  knowledge  and communication skills so that individuals with mental retardation who have been sexually abused will feel comfortable and able to discuss the abuse.  This can be a difficult task because there are many reasons for mentally retarded victims not to disclose.  These include difficulties communicating , not knowing who to tell, feeling guilty and responsible, being coerced, fearing that they won't be believed, and the willingness to put up with the abuse in order to be liked, to feel normal, or to receive rewards. In addition, the sexual abuse may be on top of psychological abuse and neglect or extensive psychopathology. For a sexually abused child or adult who is mentally retarded, the ability of the interviewer to establish rapport, to gain trust, to diffuse anxiety, and to communicate at a mental age level about sexual and emotional issues is critical. It also is essential for professionals to remember that the disclosing individual often will be pressured by family members or perhaps institutional staff to recant his or her accusations. The person to whom the individual disclosed also may feel pressure to disbelieve or suppress disclosure. Awareness of these possibilities may equip the professional to advocate the rights of the victim.

The second method to identify cases of sexual abuse is to be aware of physical, behavioral, psychological, and family signs and symptoms that are indicators of sexual abuse. A child or adult who is mentally retarded may not directly disclose sexual abuse but may show behavioral or emotional signs in school, at home, in the neighborhood, in a community home, or in an institution. Behavioral, emotional, and family signs of sexual abuse are not as conclusive as physical evidence or the individual directly disclosing the abuse. In confirming the reasonableness of indicators of sexual abuse, a cluster or pattern of indicators is sought rather than a single sign. The role of professionals is to be aware of clusters of signs that may be related to sexual abuse and to pursue the possibility if indicators are present. At the present time, the professional needs to consider the signs and symptoms that are available in the literature concerning sexually abused, non-handicapped children (Vevier & Tharinger, 1986). With further work identifying sexual abuse in disabled populations, unique signs and symptoms may be identified.

Following disclosure of sexual abuse by the individual or the evaluation that physical, emotional, behavioral, and family indicators constitute suspicion of sexual abuse, the professional is legally required to make a report to the designated statutory authorities. The designated authority is typically the local law enforcement agency and/or an agency designated by the courts to be responsible for the protection of children (e.g. child welfare). Educators and mental health professionals must know the requirements and procedures for reporting suspected cases in their state. Following the report, investigations will be made to ascertain the status of current protection in place for the individual and to gather evidence that may be used to prosecute the alleged offender. Although some often maintain that victims who are mentally retarded cannot provide reliable information or act as credible witnesses on their own behalf and thus investigations are futile, recent work indicates that, by following developmentally sensitive procedures, victims who are mentally retarded can provide evidence leading to the prosecution of offenders (Kaufhold & VanderLaan, 1988).

## Therapeutic Interventions with Sexually Abused Mentally Retarded Persons

With the exception of some helpful but general guidelines provided by Szymanski and Jansen (1980), no published material was found addressing therapeutic interventions for individuals with mental retardation who have been sexually abused. This was not surprising as this population clearly is underserved in regard to all their mental health needs (Hoshman, 1985; Matson, 1984). For instance, many community mental health systems are set up with separate divisions of mental health and mental retardation as if to imply that one cannot or does not need the services of both divisions (Matson, 1984). Few therapists specialize or are trained in treating this population (Balbernie, 1985; Lewis & MacLean, 1982;). Little research has been conducted regarding the efficacy of therapeutic modalities in the treatment of persons who are retarded. In fact, mental retardation is generally an automatic rule out criterion when selecting patients for psychotherapy research studies (Matson, 1984). Thus, effective therapeutic interventions for facilitating recovery from sexual abuse in the life of an individual who is retarded have not been researched. However, some clues may be provided by reviewing the growing positive response toward providing psychotherapy for individuals with mental retardation and the available literature concerning interventions with nonhandicapped individuals sexually abused as children.

Psychotherapy with persons who are retarded and nonretarded is essentially similar, but therapeutic goals and techniques need to be adapted to the retarded person's unique life circumstances and developmental levels. In addition, the therapeutic needs of the sexually abused or exploited person who is mentally retarded basically do not differ from those of nonretarded persons (Szymanski & Rosefsky, 1980). Sexually victimized children and adults who are mentally retarded are in need of psychotherapeutic interventions that facilitate their working through their emotional reactions. The choice of treatment for the mentally retarded victim of sexual abuse or exploitation depends on the same factors as for a nonretarded person: the person's age, cognitive and social developmental levels, gender, diagnosis, family and living situation, as well as the availability of services. Interventions may be used to provide support during the crisis that surrounds the reporting of sexual abuse to prevent some of the sequelae that have been associated with sexual abuse, to work on the reactions that present, and to examine long-standing problems. The goals of therapy often are to promote the individual's self-esteem, help him or her regain some control over his or her life, and reinstate emotional and social development.

In general, the most common mental health interventions provided persons who are mentally retarded include psychotropic medications and behavior modification (Matson, 1984; Matson & Sevin, 1988). While these interventions may be useful adjuncts, they do not deal adequately with the emotional and psychological trauma of sexual abuse victimization. Unfortunately, individual, group, and family psychotherapy with persons who are retarded often have been overlooked due to assumptions that persons who are mentally retarded lack the verbal abilities, introspective nature, and insight needed to benefit from this form of treatment. Although

this is likely the case for individuals with severe and profound retardation, it is not accurate in regard to individuals who are mildly and moderately retarded (Matson & Sevin, 1988). However, because of these assumptions, persons who are mentally retarded seldom are exposed to psychotherapy, asked to share their personal experiences, or given the credit for the validity of their experiences (Hoshman, 1985). Important to remember is that the goal of psychotherapy with the retarded is not to cure the retardation but to ameliorate the mental disturbance that may be preventing the retarded from actualizing their potential (Szymanski, 1980). Psychotherapy has been described as being effective with this population in individual (Balbernie, 1985; Bernstein, 1985; Hurley & Hurley, 1986, 1987; Lubetsky, 1987) and in group situations (Fletcher, 1984; Hoshman, 1985; Monfils, 1985; Szymanski & Rosefsky, 1980). Clients have been found to share themes of the desire for independence, lack of self worth, loneliness, personal loss, and other introspective topics, indicating an ability to benefit from inclusion in psychotherapy.

Treatment models for nonhandicapped child victims of sexual abuse and for adults who were abused as children vary in their theoretical orientation and duration (Boatman, Borkan, & Schetky, 1981; Giarretto, 1982; Hall, Kassees, & Hoffman, 1986; James & Nasjleti, 1983; Mayer, 1983). However, they typically include addressing the issues listed above and involve individual, group, and for treatment of child and adolescent victims, family therapy. There is reason to believe that sexually victimized individuals with mild and moderate retardation can benefit from these approaches. Individual therapy can be used as a sole treatment modality or in conjunction with family or group therapy. With accompanying family therapy, individual therapy may be the treatment of choice for the child for whom play is the natural medium of exchange. Children who are preoccupied with sexual trauma may work it through in play and at the same time may gain some verbal mastery and understanding of their feelings and family situation (Knittle & Tuana, 1980). Individual therapy also may be the treatment of choice for the beginning stages of recovery, regardless of age. The client-therapist relationship offers the child or adult victim the chance to have an intimate relationship with a healthy adult, which is neither overwhelming nor self-serving, and one that may foster a sense of trust that the client has not previously experienced.

Group therapy has the potential of offering peer support to preadolescent and adolescent victims and adults who were abused as children. The shared experiences promote group cohesiveness and help members overcome some of their fears of isolation and deviancy. Advantages of group therapy include reduction of anxiety due to universal issues faced by all group members and the presence of peers which reduces isolation and increases opportunities for trying new behaviors through role modeling (Lamb, 1986). In addition, clients may perceive the group as a supportive club, and resistance to attending may be lower. Directed self-help groups, which use professional group facilitators, e.g., Parents Anonymous and Parents United (Giarretto, 1982), are prevalent and perceived positively. Family group treatment is useful when an operational family structure exists in a victim's environment. This could involve therapy of the family in which the sexual abuse occurred, substitute families, such as foster homes, or group-home family networks.

## SUMMARY AND CONCLUSIONS

There is growing recognition that children, adolescents, and adults who are mentally retarded are particularly vulnerable to sexual abuse and exploitation. They are vulnerable because they are often dependent on caregivers their whole life, are relatively powerless in society, are easily coerced, are emotionally and socially insecure and needy, and usually are not educated about sexuality and sexual abuse. The challenge for professionals is to protect persons who are mentally retarded from sexual abuse and exploitation, to provide appropriate psychotherapeutic interventions when abuse occurs, to respect their right to developmentally appropriate knowledge about sexuality and sexual abuse, and to allow for the fulfillment of their sexuality. Professionals involved in education, research, and clinical efforts need to join together to meet this challenge.

********

## REFERENCES

Alcorn, D. A. (1974). Parental views on the sexual development and education of the trainable mentally retarded. *The Journal of Special Education, 8*, 119-130.

American Psychiatric Association. (1987). *Diagnostic and statistical manual of the American Psychiatric Association* (Rev. 3rd ed.). Washington, DC: Author.

Ames, T. H., Hepner, P. J., Kaeser, F., & Penler, B. (1988). *Guidelines for sexuality education and programming for the next decade.* Presented at the International Conference on Developmental Disabilities: Employment, Integration, and Community Competence. New York, NY.

Anderson, C. (1982). *Teaching people with mental retardation about sexual abuse prevention.* Santa Cruz, CA: Network Publications.

Balbernie, R. (1985). Psychotherapy with a mentally handicapped boy. *Journal of Child Psychotherapy, 11*, 65-76.

Bernstein, N. R. (1985). Psychotherapy of the retarded adolescent. *Adolescent Psychiatry, 12*, 406-413.

Black, H. (1968). *Black's Law Dictionary* (Rev. 4th ed.). St. Paul, MN: West.

Boatman, B., Borkan, E., & Schetky, D. H. (1981). Treatment of child victims of incest. *The American Journal of Family Therapy, 9*, 43-51.

Chamberlain, A., Rauh, J., Passer, A., McGrath, M., & Burket, R. (1984). Issues in fertility control for mentally retarded female adolescents: I. Sexual activity, sexual abuse, and contraception. *Pediatrics, 73*, 445-450.

Ennew, J. 91984). *The sexual exploitation of children.* Cambridge: Polity Press.

Finkelhor, D. (1984). *Child sexual abuse: New theory and research.* New York: Free Press.

Fletcher, R. (1984). Group therapy with mentally retarded persons with emotional disorders. *Psychiatric Aspects of Mental Retardation Reviews, 3*, 21-24.

Giarretto, H. 91982). *Integrated treatment of child sexual abuse: A treatment and training manual.* Palo Alto, CA: Science and Behavior Books.

Gordon, S. G. 91971). Missing in special education: Sex. *The Journal of Special Education,* 5, 351-354.

Haavik, S., & Menninger, K. 91981). *Sexuality, law, and the developmentally disabled person: Legal and clinical aspects of marriage, parenthood, and sterilization.* Baltimore: Paul H. Brookes.

Hall, J. E., Morris, H. L., & Barker, H. R. (1973). Sexual knowledge and attitudes of mentally retarded adolescents. *American Journal of Mental Deficiency, 77,* 706-709.

Hammer, S L., Wright, L. S., & Jensen, D. L. (1967). Sex education for the retarded adolescent: A survey of parental attitudes and methods of management in fifty adolescent retardates. *Clinical Pediatrics, 6,* 621-627.

Hoshman, L. T. (1985). Phenomenologically based groups for developmentally disabled adults. *Journal of Counseling and Development, 64,* 147-148.

Hurley, A. D., & Hurley, F. J. (1986). Counseling and psychotherapy with mentally retarded clients: I. The initial interview. *Psychiatric Aspects of Mental Retardation reviews,* 5, 22-26.

Hurley, A. D., & Hurley, F. J. (1987). Psychotherapy and counseling: II Establishing a therapeutic relationship. *Psychiatric Aspects of Mental Retardation Reviews, 6,* 15-20.

James, B., & Nasjleti, M. (1983). *Treating sexually abused children and their families.* Palo Alto, CA: Consulting Psychologists Press.

James, S. K. (1988). *Sexual abuse of the handicapped.* Paper presented at Deaf/Blind/ Multiple Handicapped Conference, Austin, TX.

Kaufhold, M., & VanderLaan, R. (1988). *Evaluating developmentally disabled victims of sexual abuse.* Paper presented at the National Symposium on Child Abuse, San Diego, CA.

Knittle, B. J., & Tuana, S. J. (1980). Group therapy as primary treatment for adolescent victims of intrafamilial sexual abuse. *Clinical Social Work Journal, 8,* 236-242.

Krents, E., Schulman, V., & Brenner, S. (1987). Child abuse and the disabled child: Perspectives for parents. *The Volta Review, 89,* 78-95.

Lamb, S. 91986). Treating sexually abused children: Issues of blame and responsibility. *American Journal of Orthopsychiatry, 56,* 303-307.

Lewis, M., & MacLean, W. (1982). Issues in treating emotional disorders. In J. L. Matson & R. P. Barrett (eds.), *Psychopathology in the mentally retarded* (pp. 1-36). New York: Grune & Stratton.

Lubetsky, M. J. 91987). The psychiatrist's role in the assessment and treatment of the mentally retarded child. *Child Psychiatry and Human Development, 16,* 261-273.

Matson, J. L. (1984). Psychotherapy with persons who are mentally retarded. *Mental Retardation, 22,* 170-175.

Matson, J. L., & Barrett, R. P. (1982). *Psychopathology in the mentally retarded.* New York: Grune & Stratton.

Matson, J. L., & Sevin, J. A. (1988). *Psychopathology in persons with mental retardation.* Oxford, MS: Behavior Intervention Specialists.

Mayer, A. (1983). *Incest: A treatment manual for therapy with victims, spouses and offenders.* Holmes Beach, FL: Learning Publications.

Mayer, P. (1988). *Sexual abuse of children with disabilities: A vulnerable population in need of protection.* Paper presented at the National Symposium on Child Abuse, San Diego, CA.

Menolascino, F. J., & McCann, B. M. (1983). *Mental health and mental retardation: Bridging the gap.* Baltimore: University Park press.

Mitchell, L., doctor, R. M., & Butler, D. C. (1978). Attitudes of caretakers toward the sexual behavior of mentally retarded persons. *American Journal of Mental Deficiency, 83,* 289-296.

Monfils, M. J. (1985). Theme-centered group work with the mentally retarded. *Social Casework, 66,* 177-184.

Morgan, S. R. (1987). *Abuse and neglect of handicapped children.* Boston, MA: Little, Brown.

Muller, N. D. (1984). The law: A point of view--sexuality, intellectual handicap and Queensland legislation. Questions for service providers, policy makers and families. *Australia and New Zealand Journal of Developmental Disabilities, 10,* 179-181.

National Center on Child Abuse and Neglect (NCCAN). (1982). *Profile of child sexual abuse.* Rockville, MA: Clearinghouse on Child Abuse and Neglect Information.

O'Day, B. (1983). *Preventing sexual abuse of persons with disabilities: A curriculum for hearing impaired, physically disabled, blind, and mentally retarded students.* Santa Cruz, CA: Network Publications.

Piper, P. (1976). *The aspirations and dilemmas involving sex education for the mentally retarded.* ERIC document ED172506.

Rutter, M., Tizard, J., & Whitmore, K. (1980). *Education, health, and behavior.* New York: Wiley.

Stark, J. A., Menolascino, F. J., Albarelli, m. H., & Gray, V. C. (1988). *Mental retardation and mental health: Classification, diagnosis, treatment services.* New York: Springer-Verlag.

Sullivan, P. M., & Scanlan, J. M. (1988). *Abuse issues with handicapped children.* Paper presented at the National Symposium on child Abuse, San Diego. CA.

Szymanski, L. S. (1980). Individual psychotherapy with retarded persons. In L. S. Szymanski & P. E. Tanguay (Eds.), *Emotional disorders of mentally retarded persons: Assessment, treatment, and consultation* (pp. 195-214). Baltimore: University Park Press.

Szymanski, L. S., & Jansen, P. E. (1980). Assessment of sexuality and sexual vulnerability of retarded persons. In L. S. Szymanski & P. E. Tanguay (Eds.), *Emotional disorders of mentally retarded persons: Assessment, treatment, and consultation* (pp. 173-194). Baltimore: University Park Press.

Tanguay, P. E., & Szymanski, L. S. (1980). Training of mental health professionals in mental retardation. In L. S. Szymanski & P. E. Tanguay (Eds.), *Emotional disorders of mentally retarded persons: Assessment, treatment, and consultation* (pp. 19-28). Baltimore: University Park Press.

Varley, C. K. (1984). Schizophreniform psychoses in mentally retarded girls following sexual assault. *American Journal of Psychiatry, 141,* 593-595.

Vevier, E., & Tharinger, D. (1986). Child sexual abuse: A review and intervention framework for the school psychologist. *Journal of School Psychology, 24,* 293-311.

Woody, R. (1974). *Legal aspects of mental retardation: A search for reliability.* Springfield, IL: Charles Thomas.

Zirpoli, T. J. (1986). Child abuse and children with handicaps. *Remedial and Special Education, 7,* 39-48.

Zuckerman, M., Abrams, H., & Nuehring, E. (1986, Aug.). Protection and advocacy agencies: National survey of efforts to prevent residential abuse and neglect. *Mental Retardation,* pp. 197-201.

\*\*\*\*\*\*

**About the Author:** Reprint requests my be sent to Deborah Tharinger, Ph.D., Associate Professor, EDB 504, The University of Texas, Austin, Texas 78712.

**Source:** Reprinted with permission from *Child Abuse and Neglect,* Vol. 14, 1990, pp. 301-312. Published by Pergamon Press Ltd., Oxford, England.

# Can People with Severe Mental Retardation Consent to Mutual Sex?

Fred Kaeser

**Abstract~** *One of the most pressing issues confronting service providers who work with people with severe mental retardation is how to negotiate mutual sex behaviors which occur among this population. Uncertainty surrounding whether individuals have the capacity to consent, fear of legal repercussion, and staff not understanding what their responsibilities and roles should be, each contribute to the difficulty which the service provider experiences. This article examines in detail all aspects of consent and ways for determining consent as well as the responsibilities an interdisciplinary team has for managing mutual sex behaviors.*

**Introduction~** It is 11:00 in the evening and the newly hired home health aide at residence "A" is walking by Tom and Robert's bedroom. As he does he hears what appears to be grunting and groaning sounds coming from within the bedroom. As his responsibility is to insure client safety, the health aide peers around the door to take a look inside to make sure all is okay. After a few seconds of adjusting his sight to the dimly lit room he sees what he has been secretly told by other aides happens from time to time between Tom and Robert after they've both gone to bed. They have sex. What he thought was the other employee's way of kidding with a new hiree was in fact accurate and real. Tom and Robert were having anal intercourse!

Not that two men having anal intercourse is unusual. However, these two men are severely retarded with I.Q.'s somewhere in the low 30's. What is he supposed to do, how is he to handle this, who does he refer this to, or should he? These and many more questions flood his thinking. "What a way to begin a new job," he says to himself.

Historically people with mental retardation have been denied access to sexual expression and freedom (1,2,3,4). For a variety of reasons the prevailing view was to

roadblock and prevent these people from experiencing what others in the general population took for granted: the right to have a sexual relationship with another person. On the coattails of this ideology rode a host of other wrongdoings fueled by a plethora of myths and misconceptions about the mentally retarded. They were prevented from marrying and procreating (3) were thought to be oversexed and dangerous to others (5), and detrimental to the gene pool were they ever to have children (6).

Fortunately, during the last fifteen years these myths and others like them have been sufficiently debunked and restrictive laws and practices have fallen by the wayside. According to this author's observations, the number of residential service providing agencies which sanction mutual sexual expression among their clients (sexual expression with another) have steadily increased over the last ten years. However, this perceived increase tends to reflect only those individuals who would be considered to be mildly mentally retarded. There is still a great amount of reluctance on the part of service providing agencies to allow mutual sexual involvement among persons with a greater degree of mental retardation.

### Mutual Sexual Expression and People with Severe Mental Retardation

Unfortunately, the literature generally treats the mutual sexual needs of people with severe mental retardation with little regard. Not only does it say very little about the subject, when it does, it suggests that the more retarded an individual is the more limited her or his interest in and involvement with sexual matters (3,7,8,9). While this statement is accurate for the most part it does, nevertheless, tend to distract one's attention from the fact that there are indeed individuals within this functional category who are very much involved in mutual sex behaviors. Only one study to date has concerned itself solely with the sexual behavior of people with severe mental retardation. During one calendar month fifteen of thirty one individuals were observed in sex play (touching of genitals and breasts) and seven were involved in sexual intercourse (10).

Could it be that the actual incidence of mutual sex behavior among people with severe mental retardation is greater than is suspected? Indeed this author has conducted workshops and presentations on the topic of sexuality for scores of service providing agencies in six different states and has yet to encounter one which does not have its fair share of mutual sex involvement cases. He has also worked with a considerable number of individuals with mental retardation who have been sexually involved with others. In any event, regardless of the true incidence of mutual sex involvement the question of what to do about these behaviors still remains.

## The Issue of Consent

While many reasons have been cited for denying sexual opportunity for people with mental retardation, perhaps there is one which looms the greatest: consent. Consent means knowing, intelligent, and voluntary agreement to engage in a given activity (11). Indicia of competency identified in court cases (cases involving a male who was clearly competent who had had sexual relations with a woman whose competency was being questioned) which have been used to demonstrate an individual's capacity to consent to sexual matters have included the person's ability to read, write, and tell time, and to know the right and wrong  of the sexual act (12); an understanding of the sexual act, its nature and possible consequences (People v. Blunt, 1965); and an ability to appreciate how coitus would be considered within the framework of societal environment and the different taboos people are exposed to (13).

Clearly, indicia  of competency such as these were established to protect people with mental retardation from sexual coercion (14). Interestingly, however, such a standard of competency can ultimately work to the disadvantage of such people.  It would be

difficult at best for many people with mental retardation, much less those with severe retardation, to demonstrate the capacity to consent to mutual sex relations under the terms of the present standard. While it is true that mental incompetence does not necessarily mean incompetence in all areas of one's life (15), one would be extremely hard pressed to find many people with moderate, severe, or profound mental retardation who could appreciate how coitus would be considered within the framework of societal environment and the different taboos people are exposed to.

A state's compelling interest in protecting its citizens from harm is warranted. Yet, the laws which are designed to protect this special group of people from harm are the same laws which work to exclude them from ever engaging in mutual sex behaviors.

## The Need to Protect Vs.  The Right to Express

According to Paul Freidman (16), "Under too lax a standard of competency, persons will be allowed to act in ways which are contrary to their best interests.  Under too strict a standard, the opportunity for self determination may be undermined and personal integrity denigrated by the paternalism of the state." Balancing the need to protect people with mental retardation from harm with their inherent right to express their sexuality is a very difficult challenge for the service provider. Unfortunately, it appears as though this balance has continually fallen on the protection from harm side.  It should be apparent to anyone who had a reasonable understanding of mental retardation that too strict a standard of competency regarding mutual sex behavior has been established. All the sex education and training in the world will not afford a significant number of these people to become informed decision makers.

Expressions of sexuality can certainly be life enhancing.  By coming to terms with the fact that all people with mental retardation are sexual and should be allowed opportunity to express themselves sexually should only serve to enhance their chances for overall adjustment (17, 3).  Certainly most all of us can testify to the  pernicious effects we encounter when we are unable to enjoy the sexual company of another for extended periods of time or when we are confronted with some negative experience in our sexual lives.

The need to protect people with mental retardation from harm cannot be so great as to categorically preclude one's chances for personal choice and right to privacy. Individuals with mental retardation are permitted to be involved in activities which pose risk particularly when that risk can be minimized with the help and assistance of others (18). This standard should include, where and when possible, sexual activity as well. Reflecting back to the opening scenario posed herein, to automatically deny these two men the opportunity to be managed in a reasonably safe manner would be, in this author's opinion, an unconstitutional deprivation.

There are very few guarantees in life. Any time two people with mental retardation are involved in sex there are always risks to consider. Then again, many activities of daily living pose inherent risks. The answer in most cases is not to discontinue the activity. Rather, attempts should be made to modify the environment and/or facilitate the individual as the activity is engaged in. The service provider must determine whether the benefits of an activity outweigh the risks and if they do, how best to structure that activity.

The risks associated with sexual expressions can be very real. We know all too well that any people within the general population have compromised their health status through sexual activity. Yet, given their ability to consent and understand the costs and benefits to their behavior they were permitted to behave in ways which were harmful (e.g. AIDS/HIV, sexually transmitted diseases, unintended pregnancy, etc.). People within the general population however, have made far more mistakes in their sexual lives than the mentally retarded ever have or ever will. One of the wonderful benefits this society has to offer its citizens is the right to fail, to make mistakes, and try again. The overprotecting nature of service providers, however, make them extremely hesitant to allow people with mental retardation the right to do the same.

With specific regard to sexual abuse, assault, and rape, each of which are acts of coercion, and/or force, people in the general population utilize their knowledge, decision making abilities, and their experience to insure that the risk of any one of these happening to them is at its lowest. This same process should be utilized by the interdisciplinary team of a service providing agency which should have the responsibility for developing management plans for negotiating client sexual behaviors.

Any attempt to redefine consent would include not only a determination of what the individual would want could she/he advocate and speak for her/himself but also what is in the individual's best interests. If we return to the opening scenario involving Tom and Robert what would be some of the more important issues which an interdisciplinary team would need to address in the investigatory process?

Trying to ascertain what Tom and Robert's wants are and what is in their best interests is not a very difficult endeavor. Those of us who have worked for any length of time with people who are severely mentally retarded are able to understand fairly well what their likes and dislikes are and whether or not they want or do not want certain things. When they are engaged in particular activity we look to see how they respond, Do they appear happy and content? Does their body language signal you that they want to remain involved in the activity? Or, do they appear duressed? Do they try to escape from the activity? Do they seem to be experiencing any discomfort? Have they engaged in the activity willfully? Do they make repeated attempts to engage in the activity on their own? If they are capable of verbally expressing themselves do they tell you they enjoy the activity or not? If they are unable to but could what do you think they would say? These are all very important questions necessary when determining whether individuals with severe mental retardation enjoy what they do and whether they want to do it. There are also the same questions the interdisciplinary team members would ask regarding activities which are sexual.

Should the team's decision indicate that the individuals in question both desire and like their sexual involvement this would still not be sufficient grounds to grant them permission. Additional questions and concerns related to the couple's health and safety would need to be addressed. The team would need to be reasonably assured that both individuals can remove themselves from an unwanted activity. If not, will they be able to express their displeasure in an adequate fashion in order to alert team members? Is either of the individuals in question overly aggressive in his general behavior patterns creating a danger for those who have contact with him? If so, is the risk for potential harm to another so great as to preclude his sexual involvement even if it appears to be what he wants and desires? Can a management plan for this client behavior be effectively implemented by employees? After due care and deliberation in this matter does the interdisciplinary team believe that they have acted in the client's best interests? If their decision was to allow for their mutual sex needs do they feel that they have created a plan which ensures a reasonable degree of client health and safety?

### Aspects of a Management Plan

The primary goal of any management plan which addresses mutual sex behavior should be to ensure, to the maximum degree possible, the health and safety of the individuals while still allowing for the occurrence of the behavior. To do so requires a well thought out plan of action and the ability to carry it out.

The interdisciplinary team needs to decide the degree to which education and training of any related concept can be made. Can the individuals be taught to request their sexual desires? If nonverbal, perhaps they can be taught signs which may be used to initiate the sexual courtship. If intercourse is part of the couples interaction, can at least one of them be taught to use a condom even if the success rate for its correct use is minimal at best? Perhaps they can be taught how to clean and wash themselves on completion. These are but a few of the tasks which the interdisciplinary team might consider as potential topics to be taught.

It has been this author's experience that the extent to which people with severe or

profound mental retardation can integrate and learn educational concepts such as those mentioned above will vary from individual to individual. As an example, the author has been successful in teaching two men with profound retardation to learn to ask each other if they'd like to have sex by gesturing a sign to each other. This was accomplished by constant practice and positive reinforcement. The author and an assigned direct care staff would have the two gentlemen practice each evening the courtship repertoire. This involved assisting one man, Edgar, in presenting the sign for intercourse to his partner John. Coupled with the verbal prompt "Does John want to have sex?," one of the staff would shake John's head to reply "Yes". "Yes, John wants to have sex", was repeated to the author which was followed by having both men escorted to their bedroom. Upon entering the bedroom the author would say, "When John shakes his head 'yes' you may have sex," and the author would then point to the bed. Immediately after this the two men were brought back out of the bedroom and the procedure repeated, only this time with the shake of the head "no." The author would say , "No, John doesn't want to have sex. Edgar you can go to the bedroom and masturbate instead," and the author would offer Edgar the sign for masturbation. The author would then take Edgar to his bedroom and using the penis model would stroke the penis and say, "See Edgar, you can masturbate. No sex with John, you can masturbate."

The above procedure was practiced five to ten times daily for approximately two months at which time Edgar had completely learned his new courtship behavior. After seven years Edgar still signs to John when he desires to have sex with him.

The author was unsuccessful however when he tried to teach a severely retarded woman named Maryann that she should not engage in indiscriminate sex with just any man in her fifty- bed residence.. He attempted to explain to her that her activity should be confined to those men who she liked and who treated her well. This was a woman who could have sex with any man who presented her with any type of trinket; a comb a hairpin a barrette, etc. He also tried to roleplay with her the various sexual situations she would encounter. He had hoped that he would be successful in teaching her to discriminate the appropriate and inappropriate times for intercourse. Unfortunately, he was unable to do so.

Whenever an individual demonstrates an inability to grasp particular concepts which are needed in order to act in a more independent manner, which was the case with Maryann, it becomes the responsibility of the interdisciplinary team to decide to what degree staff may act for her.   The interdisciplinary team convened to discuss Maryann's case and to decide what path intervention would take.   While they determined that Maryann gave every indication that she enjoyed her sexual involvement with men they also decided that the potential risks associated with being involved with so many different men were great enough to warrant placing certain restrictions upon her.  During their discussions and associated fact finding it was revealed that Maryann demonstrated a genuine fondness for the company of one man in particular.  Rather than eliminate her mutual sex activity altogether they would explore what possibilities existed with regard to limiting her sexual interactions to her favorite companion.

It was at this point that the interdisciplinary team's decision making powers become fully operational.  They had decided that Maryann consented to her mutual sex behavior.  She was both willing and desirous and would, if she was capable of doing so, advocate that she would like to continue.  A behavior management plan was developed by the behavioral therapist in conjunction with a consulting human sexuality expert (the author) for the purpose of ensuring to the extent possible, that Maryann would be able to have sexual relations with her favored companion only.  The author also wrote a program which attempted to teach the man (Ricky) how to use a condom (Maryann was already receiving oral contraceptives for several years).  It was further decided that attempts would be made by direct care staff to teach Maryann and her partner to wash their genitals after each encounter.  An associated program was developed by the behavioral

therapist, the author, the case manager, and one of the attending direct care staff.

Each time Maryann attempted to engage herself with any of the men at the residence ( e.g. another man entering her room or her his) staff were instructed to intervene and say, "No, Maryann you may not have sex with him." and she would then be redirected to another activity.  Only when Ricky approached her would she be allowed sexual opportunity.  Staff would say to her, "It is all right Maryann, it is Ricky," at which point Ricky would be issued a condom.  Staff were asked to monitor each of these encounters in a minimally restrictive manner by listening intermittently by the door to ensure that Maryann was not being harmed.   Upon finishing their lovemaking staff would have both Maryann and Ricky proceed to the bathroom to wash their genitals.

Ultimately, the staff were able to manage this entire situation quite well.  Maryann only had relations with Ricky although she attempted to engage with others.  They learned to wash themselves after each get-together but Ricky's success in using condom was poor at best.  While the lack of effective condom usage was troublesome the potential risks for contracting a sexually transmitted disease or HIV were not perceived to be great enough to cease their interaction. The fact that both Maryann and Ricky had been sheltered institutionally for years as were the other clients at the facility the chance that HIV infection existed was viewed as minimal. While the fears surrounding the spread of HIV is an obvious concern for all service providers, particularly residential service providers, the chances for client infection need to be weighed against the perceived benefits of the sexual interaction before a decision is made whether "condom-less" sex can be allowed, While one is usually never certain of the HIV status of people with mental retardation, a reasonable determination of at-risk levels can be made by examining the sexual histories of the individuals in question.   It is this author's opinion that the vast majority of people with severe profound  mental retardation would be HIV free given the relatively limited population from which potential sexual partners might be chosen.

The above two examples demonstrate the roles and responsibilities of the interdisciplinary team with regard to managing client sexual expression. The team is responsible for determining whether the individuals desire their sex behavior, whether it is in their best interests, which related concepts they can be taught and the necessary intervention to manage the situation. Whether the team's decision is to allow or to disallow sexual interaction, it is their responsibility for designing appropriate strategies for negotiating the behavior. Whether the individuals in question can be taught specific concepts to enable them to act more independently or whether they require team members to act for them, the behavior(s) become manageable.

The team decides which member(s) investigate the situation, which ones are to develop a management plan, and which ones carry out the plan. The entire team monitors and ultimately evaluates the plan.

## Conclusion

There are so many difficult decisions confronting the service provider who works with people with severe mental retardation. Decisions regarding client sexual behaviors are often times the ones most difficult to make. Certainly, to make a decision to accommodate for the sexual expression of a person who is severely retarded, especially when that expression involves another person, only serves to enhance the degree of difficulty. However, if one reflects back on the history of people with mental retardation it is astonishing just how much positive change has occurred so quickly. Twenty-five years ago just the thought of people with severe retardation being allowed to live anywhere other than in an institution was unfathomable. Now, many live in group homes and apartments right on "Main Street". If service providers are as committed as we say we are to assist this special group of people to live as complete a life as possible then we must acknowledge that this includes a life of sexual expression and opportunity as well - even if this does present an element of risk.

Statutory regulations would suggest that anytime two people with severe mental retardation are engaged in mutual sex expression it is a crime. However, what are service providers to do about the many individuals who do not understand this and only know that they enjoy their mutual sex expressions? They spend countless hours monitoring them, separating them and doing their best keeping one from the other, Clearly, a new standard of competency regarding sexual relations between two people with severe mental retardation needs to be established. One that takes into consideration that two such people might actually enjoy and desire sexual contact with each other. Additionally, service providers need to be allowed decision making capabilities for sanctioning such behaviors. Just as they are allowed to make decisions for all other aspects of a person's life, they should be granted the opportunity to make sexual decisions as well.

********

## REFERENCES

1. **Deisher, R.W.** Sexual Behavior of Retarded in Institutions. in *Human Sexuality and the Mentally Retarded.* De La Cruz, F.F. and La Veck, G.D. (Eds.). New York: Brunner/Mazel, 1973, pg. 145-152
2. **Hall, J.** Sexuality and the Mentally Retarded. In *Human Sexuality: A Health Practitioner's Text.* Green, R. (ed.). Baltimore: Williams and Wilkens, 1975.
3. **Haavik, S.F. and Menninger, K.A.** *Sexuality, Law and the Developmentally Disabled Person: Legal Clinical Aspects of Marriage, Parenthood and Sterilization.* Baltimore: Paul H. Brooks, 1981.
4. **Ames, T.R.H.** Some Considerations for effective Sex Education and Counseling with the Developmentally Disabled, Chapter in *From the '60's into the '80's: An Educational Assessment of Articles and Services for the Developmentally Disabled.* Levy, J.M., Levy, P.H., Leibmen, N., Dern, T.A., Rae, R., Ames, T.R. (Eds.). New York: YAI Press, 1982.
5. **Burt, R.A.** Legal Restrictions on Sexual and Familial Relations in Mental Retardates--Old Laws, New Guises. In *Human Sexuality and the Mentally Retarded* De La Cruz, F.F. and La Veck, G.D. (Eds.). New York: Brunner/Mazel, 1973, pg. 206-214.
5. **Reed, S.C. and Anderson, V.E.** Effects of Changing Sexuality on the Gene Pool. n *Human Sexuality and the Mentally Retarded* De La Cruz,

F.F. and La Veck, G.D. (Eds.). New York: Brunner/Mazel, 1973, pg. 111-125.

7. **Meyorowitz, J.H.** Sex and the Mentally Retarded *Medical Aspects of Human Sexuality,* November 1971. pg. 95-118.

8. **Gebhard, P.H.** Sexual Behavior of the Mentally Retarded. In *Human Sexuality and the Mentally Retarded* De La Cruz, F.F. and La Veck, G.D. (Eds.). New York: Brunner/Mazel, 1973, pg. 29-50.

9. **Griffiths, D.M. and Hingsburger, D.** *Changing Inappropriate Sexual Behavior: A Community Based Approach for Persons with Disabilities.* Baltimore: P.H. Brooks, 1989.

10. **West, R.R.** The Sexual Behavior of the Institutionalized Severely Retarded. *Australian Journal of Mental Retardation.* Vol. 5, No. 11, 1979, pg. 11-13.

11. **Stavis, P.** Counselor's Corner: More on the Law, Sex, and Mental Disabilities. *Quality of Care,* Sept-Oct., 1987, pg. 2-3.

12. **Commonwealth vs. Saltzberger,** 62PA., 1951.

13. **People vs. Easley.** 42N.Y. 2nd 50, 1977.

14. **Abramson, P.R. and Weisberg, S.R.** *Sexual Expression of Mentally Retarded People: Educational and Legal Implications,* American Journal on Mental Retardation, Vol. 93, No. 3, 1988, pg. 328-334.

15. **Stavis, P. and Tarantino, L.** Counselor's Corner: Sexual Activity in the Mentally Disabled Population: Some Standards of the Criminal and Civil Law. *Quality of Care,* Oct-Nov., 1986, pg. 2-3

16. **Freidman, P.** Legal Regulation of Applied Behavior Analysis in Mental Institutions and Prisons, 17 *Arizona Law Review,* 40, 77, 1975.

17. **Mulhern, T.J.** Survey of Reported Sexual Behavior and Policies Characterizing Residential Facilities for Retarded Citizens. *American Journal Of Mental Deficiency,* Vol. 79, No. 6, 1972, pg. 670-673.

18. **Part 633 of Title 14 N.Y.C.R.R. Client Protection,** State of New York, Office of Mental Retardation and Developmental Disabilities, 1987.

\*\*\*\*\*\*

**About the Author:** Fred Kaeser is currently the Director of Health Education and Services for Community School District Two, New York City, New York. He provides extensive consultation to service providers throughout the United States on all issues pertaining to sexuality and people with mental retardation. Specifically, his specialities relate to masturbation training for orgasmically dysfunctional men and women with severe and profound mental retardation and the issue of how to negotiate the mutual sex expression of people living in residential care facilities.

**Source:** Reprinted with permission from the author and from *Sexuality and Disability,* Vol. 10, No. 1, 1992, pp. 33-42. Published by Human Sciences Press, Inc. New York, New York. 10013-1578.

# Ethical Aspects of Sexuality of Persons with Mental Retardation

K. R. Held, M.D.

**Abstract~** *Current trends towards "normalization" of the disabled provide opportunities especially for mentally retarded adolescents to enjoy satisfying sexual experience. However, the right of mentally disabled persons to their own sexuality has become an emotionally discussed topic among professionals and lay people because of concerns about unwanted pregnancies, venereal diseases and sexual exploitation. The key ethical issue is the acceptance of the human rights of personal inviolability, self-determination in marrying and founding a family and voluntary procreation of mentally disabled persons in respect to prevailing parent-family and parent-citizen models. It is argued that in discussing ethical aspects of the sexuality of mentally disabled persons standards of consistency should be upheld by applying principles fundamental to modern ethics.*

Because of firmly entrenched moral visions, the sexual concerns of mentally disabled persons have been largely ignored by most societies in the past. Changes in societal attitudes throughout the last 20 years have resulted in recognition of the various emotional needs of mentally disabled people (1). The current trend towards "normalization" has provided new opportunities especially for mentally retarded adolescents to enjoy satisfying sexual experiences (2). However at the same time parents and guardians have realized that this gain in personal freedom could imply an increased risk of sexual exploitation, venereal diseases, and unwanted pregnancies (2,3,4,). As a consequence, the right of mentally disabled persons to their own sexuality has become an emotionally discussed topic among professionals and lay people. It seems obvious that the loss of traditional morality in pluralistic societies requires the finding of ethical principles independent of individual moral visions to solve various problems associated with the sexuality of mentally disabled persons.

The complexity of the ethical and social issues connected with the sexuality of mentally disabled persons is usually not adequately acknowledged in present discussions. As a result the arguments put forward often seem to be one-dimensional, i.e. the various positions and conflicting interests of persons and groups involved are not sufficiently recognized. Since the present discussion centers around a question of rights, attention will be focused in this paper on the rights of the individual person, the family members, and the society at large.

It has often been argued that the sexual development of mentally disabled persons is not only a matter of the individual, but of great concern to parents and others as well. This argument cannot be denied. However, it must not be used to suppress normal sexual development. Though self-evident to most, arguments regarding the right of mentally disabled persons to their own sexuality will be sketched and briefly defended in this paper. In this context some biological facts should be mentioned which are generally acknowledged but not sufficiently recognized in public discussions.

Each human is unique and not interchangeable. It is therefore normal to be different.

Each individual has according to his or her uniqueness different mental abilities and talents.

In the realm of mental ability no one is exclusively disabled (5).

Sexuality is a fundamental need of man. It is an integral part of being human and part of one's personality.

Thus the individual experience of sexuality is influenced by one's intellectual abilities. There is, however, no intellectual threshold known as an incontestable condition for having one's own sexuality.

The right of the mentally disabled persons to their own sexuality results directly from the principles of universalizability and equality. It is, therefore, not a matter of generosity of the mentally competent to grant mentally disabled persons this right. In essence this means that all forms of sexuality are to be accepted which are compatible with human dignity. In the context of a defense of the right to one's own sexuality, regardless of the degree of mental ability a person possesses, the following topics have surfaced regarding the individual person.

There are numerous statements to the effect that mentally disabled persons have to accept restrictions regarding their sexual freedom because of an increased risk of becoming victims of sexual exploitation. Naturally, the mentally disabled person is in need of help and guidance in the development of his sexuality. It is a defensible position to argue that the principle of fairness implies that he or she is protected in his or her sexual development against exploitation and deceit as much as in all other executions of his or her daily routine. The need of protection of the disabled in this particular respect poses a challenge to society. It must not be used as an argument for the oppression of the sexuality of mentally disabled persons.

The view that a restriction of the right to one's own sexuality in mentally disabled persons is justifiable because the risk of sexually transmitted disease is deeply rooted in our society. This is quite certainly an indefensible position. Again, we are confronted with the undeniable fact that the disabled person is in need of protection and guidance. But it makes good sense to argue, that AIDS and all other sexually transmitted diseases are primarily medical and social challenges to the society and not a specific problem of mentally disabled persons. A restriction of sexual freedom could only be argued in a situation where there is sufficient evidence to assume that a severe health problem is inevitable and where this risk cannot be avoided by social help. In fact, the aspect of sexually transmitted diseases is analogous to the aspect of sexual exploitation. It should thus be used as an argument for social help. A help which promotes rather than restricts or even oppresses the individual's sexual development.

The contention concerning the inability of mentally disabled persons to have a meaningful sexual relationship has often been brought forward in discussions as an argument for restricting free sexual development. This notion is scientifically ill-founded. One would have to ask for the degree of intelligence necessary to qualify for having a meaningful sexual relationship and for a definition of the specific characteristics of "meaningful". Anyhow, there is no good reason for setting higher standards in respect to harmony and stability for sexual relationships of mentally disabled persons as compared to other relationships. (5)

Sexuality, and in particular, heterosexual relationships, imply the aspect of procreation. Unquestionably having a child affects more than just the interests of the respective parents (6). The discussion about sexual development and sexual freedom of mentally disabled persons centers accordingly around the question of family planning, specifically around the aspect of prevention of unwanted pregnancies by sterilization (7). The critical question thus being, should legal constraints regarding procreation be imposed on mentally disabled individuals who may not function as satisfactory parents.

In mentally disabled persons, sterilization as a method of family planning would not pose a specific ethical problem if they were able to give voluntary informed consent. In medicine any treatment performed without free and informed consent has generally been judged unethical. Accordingly, in several industrial countries sterilization is considered lawful only if informed consent is given (8). It makes good sense to suspect that voluntary informed consent cannot be given by a person in whom sterilization seems warranted because of the inability to function as a satisfactory parent even with a reasonable level of support. In essence, the concept of voluntary sterilization of a mentally disabled individual is inconsistent in itself. Thus, the pursuit of sterilization conflicts with the fundamental human rights of self-determination and inviolability. Applying the principle of equal consideration of interests, suspending these rights could only be defended by showing that the right of voluntary procreation of mentally disabled persons affects vital interests of other persons. In discussing the conflict of interests in this context attention will be focused on:

- the rights of a child to be,
- the rights of parents and family members
  of mentally disabled persons
- the rights of society

A frequently used argument in the discussion about compulsory sterilization of mentally disabled persons is based on the notion that the right of a child exists to be born free of a genetic defect or any other serious health problem (6). It is doubtful that this is a defensible position. In every pregnancy a significant risk of a congenital defect exists. This is to say that genetic risks are an integral part of a human being; in addition mental disability is often not genetic in nature. Consequently, the recurrence risk is low in most cases. The argument may be valid though in cases of mental deficiency with a dominant or a specific chromosomal etiology. However, the argument seems weak since in democratic societies sterilization is not imposed on individuals found to be at high risk of transmitting a serious genetic disease to potential progeny if they are of normal intelligence. Consequently the criticism exists that this situation violates the principle of equality.

The contention that a child has a right to satisfactorily functioning parents is understandably shared by many. From the point of view of the child's welfare it is certainly a most desirable condition, but it is a right which can be argued for on ethical grounds only with difficulty. But even if one accepts this concept it seems most questionable whether this right overrides the fundamental human rights of the parents to self-determination and voluntary procreation. In respect to the high divorce rate of mentally competent couples in industrialized countries imposing sterilization on mentally disabled persons because of the lack of ability to function satisfactorily as parents would violate

again the principle of equality. In any case, before a sterilization is carried out one would have to evaluate whether the needs of the child could not be satisfied by giving social help and guidance to the parents. This is not to say that one should not strive for an education permitting mentally disabled individuals a realistic perception of their abilities in respect to parenthood and the extent of responsibility it implies (5).

Sterilization may be justified if there is sound evidence that a severely mentally disabled person would be incapable of coping with the emotional and physical stress of pregnancy and of functioning as a satisfactory parent. In this situation sterilization is not only the best method of contraception as far as social and medical aspects are concerned, it is also ethically justified. The principle of equality requires that sterilization should be available as a method of contraception to mentally disabled persons of all ability levels to the same extent as to the general population (8). There is no sound reason to assume, that mentally competent persons would not accept sterilization as a method of choice for contraception if they were permanently incapable of coping with the emotional or physical stress of pregnancy.

Unquestionably, most parents of mentally disabled persons find it difficult to arrange a family's life so as to integrate the disabled individual. Their striving to maximize the potential of the affected child often reaches the limits of their abilities (7). The notion of not only having to carry the burden of an affected child but of having to take the risk of an unwanted pregnancy is viewed as being extremely unfair by most parents. This concern must not be underestimated. It is, however, necessary to point out that this concern is often unjustified. Some of the affected are infertile due to genetic or other reasons. Others tend not to have frequent sexual encounters due to their severe mental disability. The common practice of compulsory sterilization seems only justified in situations where fertility has been proven and due to an unfavorable social environment an increased risk of sexual exploitation has to be assumed. A pregnancy occurring under such circumstances could cause a burden to the individual involved and her parents or guardians which outweighs the restrictions of the person's human rights. As a special problem in this context, it should be noted that severely retarded girls do not have the highest risk of a sexual assault. Investigations have shown that mildly disabled girls have the greatest risk in this respect and that the risk of severely retarded girls is less than for the girl of average intelligence (2). The dilemma being that the individual with the highest risk might very well function satisfactorily as a parent with the necessary social help. One should take into consideration that the individual cannot be evaluated with certainty in adolescence. This is reason enough to advocate early sterilization only with great caution. Fertility control of mentally disabled adults is a special situation. Many, perhaps most, can cope with the challenge of sexuality without contraceptive measures (2). In any case it seems necessary to evaluate each situation individually and to find a balance between safety and effectiveness which takes the needs of the affected individual and the concern of the parents into consideration (3). This is not to say that the parents have a fundamental right to influence the development of sexuality, the choice of partners, and the family planning of their mentally disabled children. The principle of equal consideration of interests requires however, that in weighing the interests of the persons involved the need of the parents carry an equal weight to the need of their retarded children.

It should be noted that the societies of most industrial countries display a considerable interest in the number and "quality" of the children born. This is demonstrated by publicly supported family and health programs, but most of all by the regulations of sterilization and abortion (6). The suspicion is not unfounded that this interest of the society is aimed at the reduction of the number of persons requiring social welfare. This contention can only be justified if the concerns of the society are given a higher priority than the interests of the individual citizen. However, history has shown up to the present time that whenever the concerns of the society are placed above the

rights of the individuals, this results in the long run in a suspension of human rights.

The arguments put forward in this connection refer to cost and potential health risks of future generations. It is argued that the society has an obligation to prevent pregnancies of mentally disabled persons if they are not able to function as satisfactory parents. In this situation the society would have to take charge of parental duties causing high costs. It is overlooked that the protection of individual rights by the society always causes considerable costs, for example, external and internal security, health care, etc. In this context it is indefensible to exclude social care.

The second argument consists of the contention that the society had an obligation to prevent pregnancies of mentally disabled persons because of the existing risk that the child would be mentally disabled as well. It has already been mentioned that this contention is based on the incorrect notion of a genetic cause of mental deficiencies with a high recurrence risk in the majority of cases. There is no sound reason to assume that unrestricted procreation of mentally disabled persons leads to a significant deterioration of the genetic composition of a population since the genetic composition of further generations is influenced by many factors. Even in cases with a high recurrence risk the right of society to impose sterilization is questionable. The principle of equality would require sterilization of mentally competent persons with a high risk of transmitting a genetic disease as well. This can be enforced only in a totalitarian society. Realizing that this had led to the perception of many liberals that unrestricted procreation of mentally disabled persons is a smaller problem than the enforcement of eugenic concepts by compulsory sterilization. Some see a way out of this conflict by advocating prenatal diagnosis. They consider prenatal diagnosis as ethically unproblematic because the method is increasingly accepted by the general public. Naturally, it should be available as well to mentally disabled persons. This position is indefensible. The requirements for carrying out a prenatal diagnosis are not fulfilled. In addition to a lack of voluntary informed consent there is a lack of plausible motivation

(Why should a woman with Down Syndrome not want a child with Down Syndrome?). For the reason given compulsory prenatal diagnosis is legally indefensible in many countries.

For the sake of clarity other forms of contraception besides sterilization have not been discussed. The use of oral contraceptive agents, injectable progesterons, or IUDs may be better indicated in some situations than a sterilization (2,4). It should be kept in mind that applying these methods of contraception requires the same condition as sterilization, i.e. voluntary informed consent. Every form of compulsory contraception raises the suspicion of a social eugenic objective and is therefore exceedingly questionable.

Discussing the obvious conflicts between individual rights and the interests of parents and society within the context of sexuality of mentally disabled persons standards of consistency should thus not be abandoned. The dilemma can appropriately be dealt with by applying principles of reasoning fundamental to modern ethics.

**\*\*\*\*\*\*\*\***

## REFERENCES

1. Ames, T-R. H.: Guidelines from Providing Sexuality-Related Services to Severely and Profoundly Retarded Individuals: The Challenge for the Nineteen-Nineties. Sexuality and Disability, Vol. 9, 2:113-122, 1991.
2. Chamberlain, A., Rauh, J., Passer, A., McGrath, M., Burket, R.: Issues in Fertility Control for Mentally Retarded Female Adolescents: I. Sexual Activity, Sexual Abuse, and Contraception. Pediatrics Vol. 73 4:445-450, 1984.
3. Passer, A., Rauh, J., Chamberlain, A., McGrath, M., Burket, R.: Issues in Fertility Control for Mentally Retarded Female Adolescents: II. Parental Attitudes Toward Sterilization. Pediatrics Vol. 73, 4:451-454, 1984.
4. Kreutner, A.K.: Sexuality, Fertility and the Problems of Menstruation in Mentally Retarded Adolescents. Ped Clin North America, Vol. 28, 2:475-480, 1982.
5. Bundesvereinigung Lebenshilfe fur geistig Behinderte: Grundsatz programm der Lebenshilfe. 1-16, 1990.
6. Twiss, S.B.: Ethical Issues in Genetic Screening. Models of Genetic Responsibility. In: Ethical, Social and Legal Dimensions of Screening for Human Genetic Disease. D. Bergsman (Ed.). Birth Defects: Original Article Series Vol. X, No. 6, 225-261, 1974.
7. Karp, L.E.: Sterilization of the Retarded. Am J Med Gen 9:1-3, 1981.
8. Macer, D.R.J. (Ed.): Sterilization of the Mentally Incompetent. In: Shaping Genes. Ethics, Law and Science of Using Genetic Technology in Medicine and Agriculture. Eubois Ethics Institute, 228-230, 1990.

**\*\*\*\*\*\***

**About the Author:** K. R. Held, M.D. at the time of writing is with the Institute of Human Genetics, University Hospital Eppendorf, Martinistrasse 52, 2000 Hamburg 20, Fed. Rep. Germany.

**Source:** Reprinted with permission from *Sexuality and Disability*, Vol. 10, No. 4, 1992, pp. 237-243. Published by Human Sciences Press, Inc. New York, New York. 10013-1578.

# Disabled Lesbians: Multicultural Realities

Corbett Joan O'Toole
Jennifer Luna Bregante

**Introduction:** "According to Kirk and Madsen, 'Many if not most, straights would undoubtedly find it hard to believe... that there are nearly as many gays as blacks in America today, half again as many Hispanics, and more than three times as many Jews. The practice of homosexuality may be a more commonplace activity than, say, bowling (6 percent), jogging (7 percent), golfing (5 percent), hunting (6 percent), reading drug store romance novels ( 9 percent), or ballroom dancing (2 percent)' " (Simon, 1991).

Ten percent of America is gay, lesbian or bisexual. Eleven percent of America is disabled. Ten percent of all gay people, even before the onset of AIDS were disabled.

All disabled lesbians exist in a multicultural context, yet as Fine and Asch (1988) point out, "To date almost all research on disabled men and women seems to assume the irrelevance of gender, race, ethnicity, sexual orientation, or social class. Having a disability presumably eclipses these dimensions of social experience" (p.3).

The four primary communities that affect all disabled lesbians are: disability, women, lesbian, and racial. These communities do not easily interact with each other (O'Toole & Martinez, 1991).

All disabled lesbians live multicultural lives. They usually have a primary and secondary affiliation. The ways that these intersect depend on the life experience of each disabled lesbian. While they have the advantages of four sets of communities, they also face four distinct sets of discrimination: homophobia, sexism, ableism*, and racism.

Karen Thompson met with resistance from the disabled community when she asked for help for her newly disabled lover*, Sharon Kowalski: "[I had] trouble getting disability groups to be willing to put their names behind the issue because they saw it as a gay rights issue. One of the leaders in the disability rights community told me, "We think Sharon's rights are being violated, but we can't afford to get involved in a gay rights issue" (K. Thompson, 1992).

At a meeting of Disabled People's International, the invisibility of Disabled women was addressed. "A man from Asia asked the "women to keep reminding us of your rights. I have a mindset that I have developed not to think of them" (Dreidger, 1989, p.88).

While all these communities have increased their visibility in mainstream culture, the effects are not always positive. Schwanberg (1990) found that the increased attention on homosexuals resulted in increasingly negative articles in professional journals. Fine and Asch (1988) documented that two decades of work by disabled women in the women's movement did not facilitate either increased access or acceptance.

This article examines the impact on lesbians with disabilities of being an invisible minority. For many disabled lesbians there is a homelessness of the heart. They belong to so many separate communities, but they rarely find acceptance in any. As the voices of the women in this article tell us, being a disabled lesbian is not the problem, it is the ignorance and negative attitudes of others.

The lack of awareness of disabled lesbians as multicultural prompted one disabled lesbian writer to title her article, "What's It Like to be Blind? (And please keep all that other stuff quiet. We can only deal with one minority at a time.)" (Myers, 1989).

### Searching for Images

Investigating the problems of disabled lesbians is difficult. There is limited information about disabled lesbians, Researchers tend to see both disability and homosexuality as monocultural constructs with neither disabled people (Davis, 1991) nor lesbians (O'Toole & Bregante, 1992b) having positive societal value.

Accurate information about lesbians has been difficult to obtain; information that is available had been extrapolated from studies of homosexual men, which rarely addresses the critical issues of lesbians (Saunders et al, 1988).

When lesbians are not being subsumed under articles about gayness which focus on gay men, they are seen relative to heterosexual women and found lacking (Magee & Miller, 1992).

The multicultural barriers of heterocentrism, homophobia, ignorance and guilt prevent us from getting accurate information about lesbians and gay men. Heterocentrism causes people to regard only the work of heterosexuals as significant. Homophobia makes society label anything homosexual or lesbian as abnormal and contagious ( Gaard, 1992).

The policies and practices of libraries have created barriers through heterosexist prejudices, ignoring the information needs of gay and lesbian patrons, censorship, inadequate indexing of lesbian and gay materials, and inappropriate subject headings (Gough & Greenblatt, 1992). When lesbian and gay literature is published, it is written primarily by white gays and lesbians (Brownworth, 1992).

Women with disabilities have been excluded from research (Wight-Felske, 1991). When they are included, they are assumed to be monocultural. The majority of literature on disabled women assumes them to be Caucasian and physically disabled. Beginning in the early 1980's a number of books were written by disabled women. Yet, with a few rare examples, the voices of disabled lesbians were minimal if at all present. Only if the editors were lesbians were they most likely to be recorded. (O'Toole & Bregante, 1992b).

An extensive literature search consistently offered only one story of a disabled lesbian - that of Sharon Kowalski and her lover Karen Thompson. Otherwise, the lives and accomplishments of disabled lesbians are completely invisible.

In the introduction to their breakthrough book, *With the Power of Each Breath* (1985), the authors discuss their experience: "When we decided to do a workshop on disability together, we found that we learned far more about ourselves by talking

with each other than we ever had by reading literature, whether traditional or feminist" (Browne, Connors & Stern, 1985, p.9).

REGARD, a Canadian self-advocacy organization for disabled lesbians and gay men, articulates the need for their organization to exist: "REGARD (campaigning organization of disabled Lesbians and Gays) was established as a result of two processes: rampant heterosexism in the disability movement where the lives of disabled Lesbians and Gays were invisible - therefore, no accountability or representation; ignorance of issues resulting in bad practices including offensive terminology and negative images. To admit sexual expression of disabled people by itself challenges myths. Thus to embrace the sexuality of disabled lesbians and gays is too threatening for many disability organizations.

Simultaneously, the multiple oppression of disabled lesbians and gays was resulting in isolation and distress. Individuals' lives were being compartmentalized. At the same time valuable experience gained in other liberation struggles was being lost to the disability movement" (Gillespie-Sells, 1992, p.111).

In an early and important work *"Sexism Without the Pedestal"* (1981), Adrienne Asch, a disabled scholar, and Michelle Fine, a nondisabled scholar, found that disabled women have access to fewer socially sanctioned roles than either nondisabled women or disabled men.

The rolelessness is in itself a handicapping condition that impedes career and personal options. Adult disabled female role models could help to counter this problem, but all too often these women are also invisible (Fine & Asch 1981), Disabled women's entire post- disability lives are shaped by this lack of a socially valued role (Fine and Asch, 1981).

Without roles to adopt, or reject, and without role models to emulate or deviate from, disabled girls grow up feeling not just different, but inferior. While we recognize that role models alone would not solve the problem, their absence may introduce feelings of worthlessness which complicate disability (Fine & Asch, 1981).

As long as we deny any socially viable roles to disabled women, there can be no room for the sexually active disabled woman. Disabled women who live normal lives are seen as exceptions (Off our backs, 1981). As Fine and Asch (1988) point out:

> Exempted from the 'male' productive role and the 'female' nurturing one, having the glory of neither, disabled women are arguably doubly oppressed - or, perhaps, 'freer' to be untraditional. Should they pursue what had been thought nontraditional, however, the decision to work, to be a single mother, to be involved in a lesbian relationship, or to enter politics may be regarded as a default rather than a preference (p.13).

The experience of rolelessness is not unique to disabled women but seems to be shared by other multicultural women. Here a Chicana lesbian speaks about her struggle:

> " ¿[A] quién fregados tengo que imitar? Entonves no hay patrón, No existe un rol a jugar, y tienes que crear un nuevo rol. Y esa es la razón por que digo yo ahora ya sé cual es me meta" (Castillo, 1991, p.36).

> [trans] *Who the heck do I have to imitate? So there is no model. There doesn't exist a role to play, and you have to create a new role. And that is why I now say I know what my goal is.*

Birth families* are often unable to assist a disabled lesbian with her struggle for a role. Families know that the lesbian is giving up all the privileges of heterosexuality, often including acceptance by her family (C. Thompson, 1992). While relationships with some family members may remain positive, token support does not equal acceptance.

One study sought out mothers who were publicly supportive of their lesbian daughters. Even they continued to struggle with unresolved feelings toward homosexuality; had feelings of loss and concern over discrimination; had a self-consciousness about themselves as being the mother of a lesbian daughter ; and, they often wished their daughters were heterosexual (Pearlman, 1990).

Even with these obstacles, the adverse consequences of parental disapproval were overshadowed by benefits derived from the decision to affirm one's lesbian identity and to acknowledge a couple relationship by "coming out" to parents (Murphy, 1989).

## The Price of Invisibility

Disabled lesbians, as other lesbians, have the responsibility and pressure to break the silence about sexual preference. Yet disabled lesbians have much to lose by being open with homophobic people because many people hold negative attitudes (O'Toole & Bregante, 1992b).

Faced with social isolation, prejudice, and discrimination disabled lesbians are frequently encouraged to minimize the effects of their disability and to hide their lesbianism in order to be accepted by nondisabled heterosexual people. Any attempt to hide their needs or desires can have long term consequences.

Pretending to be nondisabled or heterosexual, "passing"*, has a number of negative affects. It keeps the passing person both isolated and invisible. When disabled women pass, it encourages them to deny the need for accommodation, encourages public denial of reality ("I'm not disabled"), reinforces the hierarchy of disability (disabled people who can pass are "better" than those who cannot), and most importantly, takes away any disabled role model (Women and Disability Awareness Project, 1989; Klobas, 1989).

> *"The compensations were endless, long sleeves in the heat of the summer to conceal my arm brace, high necklines to hide my shoulder straps, nothing too sheer, nothing too thin - nothing that would draw attention to me... I was on the street hoping to pass, and once safely at home the final act of frustration, anger and pain culminated in my ripping "my helper" [artificial arm] from my body and flinging it against the wall"* (Rome, 1989, p.37).

The next few quotes are from the 1989 issue of *Sinister Wisdom* that focused on disabled lesbians. Here they discuss the reasons for, and impact of passing.

> *"this stripping away of the lies of the past gives me clarity about the present. One*

*piece of clarity is a realization of how much I pretend to forget. I pretend to forget how deeply disabled people are hated. I pretend to forget how this is true even within my chosen home, the lesbian and feminist communities. My survival at every level depends on maintaining good relationships with able-bodied people\*. Pretending can make this easier" (Lambert, 1989, p.72).*

*"Much of the silence of the disabled springs from the near impossibility of being treated with dignity once able-bodied others know of the indignities imposed upon us by or because of our disabilities" (Cardea, 1989, p.127).*

*"now here, i stand because i'm a lesbian - none even knows i'm disabled. it feels much easier" (Zana, 1989, p.21).*

*"For the past five years, Susan Koppleman had been nudging me to deal with my identity as a disabled women, And for the past five years, I have refused. I was too embarrassed, too afraid of the stigma, too afraid of its threat to my professional identity. Too afraid that naming it would give it control over my life.*

*"I have spent the past fifteen years as a radical feminist, a Marxist, a lesbian, a fighter, But this is an issue that I have been terrified to take on. To speak about disability renders you vulnerable to the charge of hypochondria and malingering. Or maybe - even worse- of being needy..." (Koolich, 1989, p.91).*

Disabled lesbians are frequent targets of violence. Being in three risk groups seems to increase the likelihood of being assaulted. Disabled women seem most at risk from people in their immediate environment (O'Toole & Bregante, 1992a; O'Toole, 1990).

Yet violence against disabled lesbians is largely ignored. Barbara Waxman (1992), a disabled woman, analyzes it this way: "The main reason for the consistent denial of hatred as a motivation for violence against disabled people is that we are not perceived as

constituting a viable, separate group in society" (p.7).

Violent assaults on all women, straight\* and gay, rose 49% in the 1980's. Lesbians lack access to capital and are prone to male violence just like other women (Adler & Brenner, 1992). Lesbian victims of assault find little sympathy or skill in the medical support community (Brownworth, 1991). Although graffiti vandalism was the most common expression of racial and religious bigotry, assault was the most common type of sexual orientation crime (Hatcher, 1991). Gay activists say that gays and lesbians are now more socially acceptable as targets of violence (Gallagher, 1991). This violence attacks lesbians everywhere, even on university campuses (D'Augelli, 1989).

Violence against disabled lesbians can occur in many places, even medical settings. Disabled lesbians can receive the negative attention of health care workers because they are often considered unpopular. They may be perceived as having low moral worth, or being incurable (Kus, 1990). As one lesbian nurse documents, lesbian hospital patients are discussed in hushed tones during shift changes (Stephany, 1988).

Consequences of unpopularity with nurses can be significant: withholding pain medications, ignoring call lights, staff being cool and detached, staff turning other staff against patient (Kus, 1990).

**Disabled Lesbian Families**

Choosing to make a family is complicated for disabled lesbians. They are dealing with double stereotypes that do not see them as possible partners or parents.

Richard Simon (1991) wrote about his new contact with gay and lesbian families when his publication, the *Family Therapy Networker,* devoted an issue to gay men and lesbians:

> Over the past couple of months, I've come face to face with family constellations that didn't match anything in my own experience - gay men bringing up adopted children together, lesbians living as spouses while pretending to their children they are

'just friends,' gay widows afraid to tell anyone that they're mourning. Certainly, I was generally aware of the range of family arrangements gays and lesbians create for themselves, but as I learned more about them, I was startled by my own naiveté and how alien they seemed to me. My reaction is not unusual (Simon, 1991).

The story of Sharon Kowalski and Karen Thompson illustrates the incredible odds that they faced after Sharon became disabled (Thompson & Andrezejewski, 1988). Sharon Kowalski and Karen Thompson lived together as lovers for four years, owned a home, and considered each other as permanent partners.   At this time they were both nondisabled.   They were not identified ("out*") as lesbians to their families, nor did they have any paperwork, medical or legal, identifying them as partners.

Sharon was hit by a drunk driver. She was permanently and severely disabled, requiring extensive hospitalization.  Her birth family presumed themselves to be Sharon's only family.  Karen was systematically denied any role in Sharon's recovery.  She has spent nearly a decade in the courts and in the press to get recognition of their relationship.

As the case of Sharon Kowalski graphically demonstrated, partners of disabled lesbians have no automatic rights.   The disabled lesbian's right to choose her family can be made dependent on her type of disability combined with the attitudes of a judge.

Unfortunately, Karen Thompson's experience is familiar to disabled lesbians (O'Toole & Bregante, 1992b; Fine & Asch, 1988; Anstett. Kiernan, & Brown, 1987). Karen came to realize that the stigma of disability, and the myth of asexuality, encompasses her and her partner (Thompson & Andrezejewski, 1988).

Few nondisabled partners are rewarded for dating a disabled woman. Nondisabled families often question the nondisabled partner's choice of a disabled partner, particularly if the relationship is permanent (Bullard & Knight, 1981).

The nondisabled partner is usually viewed as a nonsexual caregiver and expected to compensate for physical barriers.

Nondisabled friends will often expect the nondisabled lover to interpret for the deaf woman, or to carry the woman who uses a wheelchair.      Creating a give-and-take balance of help within the relationship is critical for both the disabled and the nondisabled partner (Califia, 1988).  Disabled partners who do need assistance often find that seeking necessary help outside the relationship allows both partners more choice (Boston Women's Health Book Collective, 1984).

Yet the experience of disabled lesbians are difficult to find documented.  Fine and Asch (1988) commented on the invisibility of lesbian relationships in disabled women's literature in general and *With the Power of each Breath* (Browne, Connors & Stern, 1985) in particular:

> Although many of the women represented are lesbians, none discusses an ongoing intimate relationship or provides a glimpse of the trials and pleasures of meeting a lover and maintaining a valued partnership (Fine & Asch 1988, p.14).

Although reproduction is the defined social role for females, most disabled females are actively discouraged from motherhood (Fine & Asch, 1988).  Disabled women are more often than nondisabled women advised not to have children, or to be threatened by, or be victims of, involuntary sterilization (Fine & Asch, 1981).  Many disabled women have the right to become mothers (O'Toole & Bregante, 1992a).  Disabled mothers confront many obstacles.  It is not uncommon for disabled mothers to have to "prove" their ability to raise their own birth children.  Nondisabled people frequently assume that any woman with a visible disability adopted her children (O'Toole & Bregante, 1992a).  Disabled lesbians must deal with the belief that both as lesbians (DiLapi, 1989) and as disabled women (Holmes, 1991) they are considered "inappropriate mothers".

Even when the woman is heterosexual, married, and has substantial income, she faces problems.  Bree Walker is a television newscaster in Los Angeles.  She is also a woman with a genetic disability.  When she became pregnant with her second child, a popular radio talk show, without consultation with Ms. Walker, dedicated an entire show to whether she should be allowed to have children (Holmes, 1991).

Lesbians, whether disabled or not, are actively struggling to have their relationships societally validated. Some cities and some corporations allow lesbians to register their relationships. As Karen Thompson points out, "If we had had a legally sanctioned relationship, this never would have had to happen" (K. Thompson, 1992). Yet there is significant resistance in some quarters to this idea. One Methodist bishop said that gay and lesbian marriage ceremonies bring pain and confusion and should not be performed (UMC Bishop, 1992).

Researchers find that lesbian couples have solid and happy relationships. In one study couples with children scored significantly higher on relationship satisfaction and sexual relationship (Koepke et al, 1992). Yet there is a need to articulate a lesbian family cycle (Slater & Mencher, 1991). Another study found these helpful coping strategies used by lesbian parents to deal with the stress of living in a heterosexual and homophobic environment: emphasize social support, lesbian identity, and developing oneself. Least helpful coping strategies were: disclosure of lesbian identity to unsupportive people or social institutions (Levy, 1992). As one disabled person says, "In the end it is only relationships which matter or which give our lives meaning." (Hevey, 1992c).

Connie Panzarino, a disabled lesbian, articulated the problems facing disabled lesbians this way:

> Disabilities are categorized as taboo and untouchable, and sexuality is part of this untouchability. Either society isolates disabled people - like lepers - or worships us as psychic and intuitive. Either way, we are not allowed to be sexual beings and are not allowed to have offspring (off our backs, 1981).

The missing discourse on women's sexual desire is an important barrier to disabled lesbians (Browne, Connors & Stern, 1985). When access barriers combine with attitudinal barriers, it is difficult for disabled women to meet potential sexual partners. Women who internalize the myth that disability equals an asexual life will not even venture out to find a partner (Thornton, 1981). Disabled women generally engage in sexual behaviors later than their nondisabled peers (Rousso, 1988).

Hiding her sexuality can have a high price for a disabled lesbian - damaged self-esteem, distancing from family and peers, and self-conscious attempts to avoid disclosure (Remafedi & Blum, 1986).

> We've learned - in the teeth of all the romantic novels and television sitcoms and glossy advertising to the contrary - that the bodies we inhabit and the lives those bodies carry on need not be perfect to have value (Mairs, 1992, p.26).

Merely removing the myth that disabled lesbians are asexual is not enough, Many other myths move in to 'explain' disabled people's sexual behavior: all women's sex is heterosexual (Rubin, 1981; Loulan, 1987; Anstett, Kiernan & Brown, 1987); only independently functioning disabled people can handle sexual relations (Hyler, 1985); disabled women cannot be mothers (Pastina, 1981); if a mother becomes disabled, her children are not getting a real mom (Ferris, 1981); in relationships, the nondisabled person runs the relationship (Lenz & Chaves, 1981); disabled women are too fragile for vigorous sexual activity (Daniels, 1981).

Many sexuality health services for disabled women focus on two narrow needs: birth control and sex education. Some disabled women argue that this reflects nondisabled people's discomfort with disabled women's emerging independence (O'Toole & Bregante, 1992a).

The attempts to control reproduction, sometimes to the point of sterilization, and the emphasis to teach disabled women to say no to sexuality reflect this. This narrow focus demonstrates the tremendous resistance to the idea that all disabled women are not heterosexual (O'Toole & Bregante, 199b). Discussing sexuality related issues is important for disabled lesbians since it is their sexual preference that removes them from the heterosexual mainstream.

Joseph Capell, a parent of a disabled child and an advocate for sexuality, notes that although he is a frequent consultant to other doctors, no one has ever identified a disabled adolescent's lack of sexuality information or curiosity as a problem (Capell & Capell, 1981).

As the disabled women's theater group Wry Crips, advises "Tips for crips* #15 is: "Baffle the world, have a sex life" (Pols, 1991).

## Closing

Disabled lesbians are emerging into the mainstream culture. They are defining their own roles and forcing their primary communities to expand the definition of who is included (O'Toole & Martinez, 1991). Studies by disabled women identified these areas of concern: employment, poverty, health, violence against women with disabilities, mothering, self-image, and reproductive technologies (Mamvura, 1992; Wight-Felske, 1991). Other areas of concern included sexuality, participation in the women's movement, and inclusion in research and policy development. (Marks & Rousso, 1991; Trausadottir, 1990; Boyle, 1988).

Bapst (1991) examined the ways that teachers can integrate gay and lesbian concerns: including explicitly lesbian/gay literature in assigned course work; rejecting texts and eliminating assignments which exclude lesbians and gays; using oral examples of lesbian/gay issues, role models, and individuals; creating specific lesbian/gay elective classes; 'coming out'* as lesbians, gay men and supporters of gay equality.

Wight-Felske (1991) offers specific recommendations for research guidelines regarding values (e.g. generation of research questions by women with disabilities through advocacy organizations); methodology (e.g. disabled women should be involved as consultants when research tools are being developed); dissemination (e.g. disabled women need publishing grants and sponsorship to attend and organize conferences).

At the South Korean Women's Seminar of Disabled People's International in 1986 a man asked Dr. Fatima Shah, a disabled women's organizer: " 'What do you women want? To be equal to able-bodied women? To disabled men? Or to able-bodied men' "? To which Dr. Fatima Shah asked, " What do you want?" He said, 'I want to be equal to anybody.' She replied,'"We want the same". (Dreidger, 1989, p.89).

The following are a few examples of work done in the lesbian and disability community that is changing the ways in which disabled lesbians are seen:

The Ladder was the first widely circulated lesbian publication in the United States. With the increased militancy of the homophile movement, lesbians were less tolerant of negative images of lesbians (Esterberg, 1990).

The Lesbian History Archives in Brooklyn New York, is the oldest and largest lesbian archive worldwide. Founded in 1972 by Joan Nestle and Deborah Edel, it houses documents and artifacts expressive of lesbian culture and achievements from various countries (Strock, 1992).

Exciting research has taken place within the lesbian community that has more to do with what is relevant to lesbian life-styles and less to do with proving that homosexuality is a viable life-style (Sang, 1989).

The Networking Project for Disabled Women and Girls in New York City is increasing disabled adolescent girls' social, sexual, educational, and vocational aspirations and options through role models of successful disabled women in the community (Rousso, 1986).

Each community that affects the lives of disabled lesbians has undergone a dramatic shift towards self-advocacy and self-definition in the 20th century. Whether it be race, gender, disability or sexual orientation, the challenges confronting the members of these communities are being articulated and defined.

We end with the voices of disabled

women who are members of many different communities:

*Politically my fluctuating impairment and I are comfortable. The disability, those years of not owning my body, still cause anger but now it's becoming constructive. It is society that is wrong, not me (Hevey, 1992a).*

*She doesn't think the purpose of disabled people, in life or on film, is to be symbols of fortitude or suffering for others. 'I think the negative or taboo things are more interesting,' she says (Pollack, 1991, p.21).*

Cheryl Marie Wade, a disabled woman poet, says: *"Many of us couldn't fit into the mainstream view of the world if we wanted to - and some of us wouldn't want to if we could" (Younkin, 1989, p.31).*

*Disability, though not the main focus of my life,* says [Pamela] Walker, *flavors everything about me" (Younkin, 1989, p.30).*

*"I am very proud to say I was born colored and crippled. I am black and disabled" (Gainer, 1992, p.31)*

*People who assume I live for the day when a cure is found, when I (or future generations) can live disability-free, simply don't understand my reality...There's an issue of pride involved. Disability is part of my whole identity, one I'm not eager to change (Hershey, 1992, p.16).*

*"Eventually you stop trying to fool yourself and you even respect what you are" (Hevey, 1992b).*

*"The pious compassion shown to disabled people cannot be demonstrated to lesbians and gays. Conversely, the violent hostility shown gays and lesbians is hidden due to our disability. In a word, we are too different.*

*"However, we are proud of our non-stereotypical multi-identities, and this power will force our communities to expand their own horizons of the 'acceptable'. All disabled people are viewed as asexual, but we challenge that oppression twice. Our social challenge is that our sameness and our difference are included.*

*"We are in the struggle and we are OUT about it" (Hevey, 1992d).*

## NOTES

\* The language used in both the disabled and lesbian communities contains words unfamiliar to many people. Here is a brief glossary of terms:

**Able-bodied** - refers to people who are nondisabled.

**Ableism** - oppression of disabled people by non-disabled people; similar to racism and sexism.

**Birth family** - used to designate which family is being referred to; a lesbian's adult family is called her 'chosen family'.

**Coming out -** the process and actions that accompany the lesbian or gay man acknowledging their sexual orientation; often shortened to 'out'.

**Crip** - shortened form of 'cripple', a term used with pride by some disabled people; it is always considered derogatory when used by a nondisabled person.

**Lover** - a common lesbian designation for one's sexual partner, often used in the same context as the heterosexual terms 'spouse' 'wife' 'husband'.

**Passing** - the act of not identifying membership in a minority community.

**Straight** - heterosexual.

## REFERENCES

**Adler, S. & Brenner, J.** (1992). Gender and Space: Lesbian and Gay men in the city. *International Journal of Urban and Regional Research*, 16(1), pp. 24-35.

**Anderson, L.** (1985). The Lois Anderson story. In S.E. Browne, D. Connors, & N. Stern (Eds.). *With the Power of Each Breath: A Disabled woman's anthology.* San Francisco: Cleis Press.

**Anstett, R., Kiernan, M., & Brown, R.** (1987) The Gay-Lesbian Patient and the Family Physician. *Journal of Family Practice*, 25(4), 1987, pp.339-344.

**Bapst, D.** (1991). *The Lesbian and Gay Student.* Paper presented at the Annual meeting of the Conference on College composition and Communication (42nd, Boston, Ma, March 21-23, 1991).

**Boston Women's Health Book Collective.** (1984). *The new our bodies ourselves.* New York: Simon and Schuster.

**Boyle, G. et al** (1986).  Women with Disabilities: A National Forum. *Entourage,* 3 (4), pp. 9-13.

**Browne, S.E., Connors, D. & Stern, N.** (1985). *With the power of each breath: A disabled women's anthology.* San Francisco: Cleis Press.

**Brownworth, V.**  (1991, November 5).  An unreported crisis. *The Advocate,* pp.50-53.

**Bullard, D.F., & Knight, S.E.** (1981). *Sexuality and physical disability: Personal perspectives.* New York: Mosby.

**Califia, P.**  (1988). *Sapphistry:  The Book of lesbian sexuality.* Tallahassee, Fl: NAIAD Press.

**Capell, B., & Capell, J.** (1981).  Being Parents of children who are disabled. In D.G. Bullard & S.E. Knight (eds.), *Sexuality and physical disability: Personal Perspectives,* New York: Mosby.

**Cardea, C.** (1989-1990, Winter)  Snapshots of a decade and more. *Sinister Wisdom,* pp.119-127.

**Castillo, A.** (1991) La Macha: Toward a Beautiful Whole Self.  In Carla Trujillo (Ed.), *Chicana Lesbian: The girls our mothers warned us about.* Berkeley:  Third Woman Press.

**Daniels, S.M.** (1981).  Critical issues in sexuality and disability. In *Sexuality and physical disability: Personal perspectives.* New York: Mosby.

**D'Augelli, A.R.** (1992).  Lesbian and gay men's experiences of discrimination and harassment in a university community. *American Journal of Community Psychology,* 17(3), pp.317-323.

**Davis, L.** (1991) *Feminism, Disability & Education -- For What?*  Paper presented to the Women's Studies and Education Conference (North Ryde, Australia, October 26, 1991).

**DiLapi, E.M.** (1989).  Lesbian mothers and the motherhood hierarchy. *Journal of Homosexuality,* 18(1-2), pp.101-132.

**Dreidger, D.** (1989). *The Last Civil Rights Movement:  Disabled People's International.* London: Hurst & Company.

**Esterberg, K.G.** (1990).  from Illness to action: conception of homosexuality in 'The Ladder', 1956-65, *The Journal Of Sex Research,* 27(1), pp. 65-81.

**Ferris, L.,** (1981). Being a Disabled mother. In *Sexuality and physical disability: Personal perspectives.* New York: Mosby.

**Fine, M. & Asch, A.** (1981). Sexism without the pedestal. *Journal of Sociology and Social Welfare,* 8(2), p.233-48.

**Fine, M & Asch, A.** (1988) *Women with disabilities:  Essays in psychology, culture, and politics.* Philadelphia: Temple University Press.

**Gaard, G.** (1992). Opening up the canon: The importance of teaching lesbian and gay literatures. *Feminist Teacher,* 6(2), pp.30-34.

**Gainer, K.**  (1992, September/October). I was born colored and crippled. Now I am black and disabled. *MOUTH, The National Magazine of People with Brains.* p.31.

**Gallagher, J.** (1991, November 5).  August: a month of hate, an epidemic of violence. *The Advocate,* pp.42-51.

**Gillespie-Sells, K.** (1992). *Equality of Opportunity for disabled Lesbians and Gays.* In Independence 92:  International Congress and Exposition on Disability - Book of Abstracts, Vancouver, British Columbia, p.111.

**Gough, C. & Greenblatt, E.** (1992).  Services to gay and lesbian patrons:  Examining the myths. *Library Journal,* 117(1), pp.59-63.

**Hatcher, B.N.** (1991). *Hate Crime in Los Angeles County 1990: A report to the Los Angeles County Board of Supervisors.*  Los Angeles County Commission on Human Relations.

**Hershey, L.** (1992, September/October).  Laura Hershey on Cure. *Disability Rag,* p.16.

**Hevey, D.** (1992a). *Liberty, Equality, Disability - Images of a Movement:* One of six.  In The creatures time forgot:  photography and disability imagery. London: Routledge.

**Hevey, D.** (1992b). *Liberty, Equality, Disability - Images of a Movement:* Three of Six.  In The creatures time forgot:  photography and disability imagery. London: Routledge.

**Hevey, D.** (1992c). *Liberty, Equality, Disability - Images of a Movement:* Four of Six.  In The creatures time forgot:  photography and disability imagery. London: Routledge.

**Hevey, D.** (1992d). *Liberty, Equality, Disability - Images of a Movement:* Five of Six.  In The creatures time forgot:  photography and disability imagery. London: Routledge.

**Holmes, S.A.** (1991, August 23).  TV anchor's disability stirs debate. *New York Times,* p.A16(N), p.B18(L).

**Hyler, D.** (1985).  To Choose a child, In S.E. Browne, D. Connors, & N. Stern (Eds.). *With the power of each breath:  A disabled woman's anthology.* San Francisco: Cleis Press.

**Klobas, L.** (1989).  Television distorts lives of disabled. *New Directions for Women,* 18(5), p.5.

**Koepke, L, et al.** (1992).  Relationship quality in a sample of Lesbian couples with children and child-free lesbian couples. *Family Relations,* 41(2), pp.224-229.

**Koolish, L.** (1989-1990, Winter).  from We are the canaries: Women, disability and coalition-building. *Sinister Wisdom,* pp.91-93.

**Kus, R.J.** (1990).  Nurses and unpopular patients. *American Journal of Nursing,* June, pp.63-66.

**Lambert, S.** (1989-1990, Winter).  from Disability and violence. *Sinister Wisdom,* p. 72.

Lenz, R. & Chaves, B. (1981). Becoming active partners. In D.G. Bullard & S.E. Knight (Eds.), *Sexuality and Physical Disability: Personal perspectives.* New York: Mosby.

Levy, E.F. (1992). Strengthening the coping resources of lesbian families. *Families in Society: The Journal of Contemporary Human Services,* 73(1), pp.23-32.

Loulan, J. (1987). *Lesbian Passion.* San Francisco: Spinsters Ink.

Magee, M. & Miller, D.C. (1992). "She forswore her womanhood": Psychoanalytic views of female homosexuality. *Clinical Social Work Journal,* 20(1), pp.67-88.

Mairs, N. (1992, Summer/Fall). Good enough gifts. *Kaleidoscope,* p.26.

Mamvura, L. (1992). *Disabled women organizing themselves.* Paper presented as Independence 92: International Congress and Exposition on Disability, Vancouver, B.C., Canada.

Marks, L. & Rousso, H. (1991). *Barrier free: Serving young women with disabilities.* YWCA of New York City, NY.

Murphy, B.C. (1989). Lesbian couples and their parents: The effects of perceived parental attitudes on the couple. *Journal of Counseling and Development,* 68(1),pp.46-51.

Myers, T. (1989-1990, Winter). from What's it like to be Blind? *Sinister Wisdom,* pp.77-78.

*off our backs* (1981). *Women with disabilities.* 11(5). Entire issue.

O'Toole, C.J., (1990). Violence and sexual assault plague many disabled women. *New Directions for Women,* 19(1), p.17.

O'Toole, C.J. & Bregante, J.L. (1992a. Disabled women: The myth of the asexual female. In S. Klein (Ed.), *Sex equity and sexuality in education.* Albany, NY: SUNY Press.

O'Toole, C.J. & Bregante, J.L. (1992b). Lesbians with disabilities. *Journal of Sexuality and Disability,* 10(3).

O'Toole, C.J. & Martinez. K. (1991). Disabled women of color. *New Directions for Women,* 20(1).

Pastina, L. (1981). Impact of a genetic disability, In D.G. Bullard & S.E. Knight (Eds.), *Sexuality and physical disability: Personal perspectives.* New York: Mosby.

Pearlman, S.F. (1990) *Heterosexual Mother/Lesbian Daughters: Parallels and similarities.* Paper presented at the Annual Convention of the American Psychological Association. (98th, Boston, MA., August 10-14, 1990).

Pollack, E. (1991, Summer/Fall). The scars we all hide: A profile of Sharon Greytak. *Kaleidoscope,* 00.21-22.

Pols, M. (1991, September). Moving over the edge. San Francisco Guardian.

Remafedi, G. & Blum, R. (1986). Working with gay and lesbian adolescents. *Pediatric Annals,* 15(11), pp.773-783.

Rome, J. (1989-1990, Winter). Untitled. *Sinister Wisdom,* pp.35-40.

Roush, S.E. (1986). Health Professionals as contributors to attitudes toward persons with disabilities: a special communication. *Physical Therapy,* (66)10, pp.1551-1554.

Rousso, H. (1986). Positive Female Images at Last! *Exceptional Parent,* 16(2), pp.10-12.

Rousso, H. (1988). Daughters wit Disabilities: Defective Women or Minority Women. In M. Fine & A. Asch, *Women with disabilities: Essays in psychology, culture and politics.* Philadelphia: Temple University Press.

Rubin, N. (1981). Clinical issues with disabled lesbians: An interview with Ricki Boden. *Catalyst 12,* pp.40-43.

Saunders, J.M., et al. (1988). *A lesbian profile: A Survey of 1000 lesbians.* Report prepared for the National Lesbian Rights Conference (San Diego, CA, October 1988).

Sang, B.E. (1989). New Directions in Lesbian Research, Theory and Education. *Journal of Counseling and Development,* 68(1), pp.92-96.

Saxton, M. & Howe, F. (Eds.). (1987). *With wings: An anthology of literature by and about women with disabilities.* New York: Feminist Press.

Schwanberg, S.L. (1990). Attitudes towards homosexuality in American health care literature 1983-1987. *Journal of Homosexuality,* 19(3), pp. 117--136.

Simon, R. (1991). From the Editor. *The Family Therapy Networker,* January/February 1991, p.2.

*Sinister Wisdom.* (1989-90, Winter). On Disability. Entire issue.

Slater, S. & Mancher, J. (1991). The lesbian family cycle: A contextual approach. *American Journal of Orthopsychiatry,* 61(3), pp.372-283.

Stephany, T.M. (1988). Lesbian Nurse. *Nursing Outlook,* November/December, pp.295.

Strock, C. (1992, July-August). Three-dimensional history. *Ms. Magazine,* p.59.

Thompson, C.A. (1992). Lesbian grief and loss issues in the coming out process. *Women & Therapy,* 12(1-2). pp.175-186.

**Thompson, K.** (1992, March/April).    Karen Thompson talks about the case that never should have had to happen. *Disability Rag.*

**Thompson, K., & Andrezejewski, J.** (1988) *Why can't Sharon Kowalski come home?* San Francisco: Spinsters/Aunt Lute.

**Thornton, V.** (1981).   Growing up with cerebral palsy.   In D.G. Bullard & S.E. Knight (Eds.), *Sexuality and physical Disability:    Personal Perspective.* New York: Mosby.

**Traustadottir, R.** (1990). *Women with disabilities: Issues, resources, connections.*    Syracuse Univ., NY:  Center on Human Policy.

**UMC bishop rejects gay union liturgies.**  (1992, Oct, 21). *The Christian Century,* 109(30), pp.928-931.

**Waxman, B.F.** (1992, May/June).    Hatred: The Unacknowledged dimension in violence against disabled people. *Disability Rag*, pp.6-10.

**Wight-Felske, A.** (1991)   *Research by/for/with Women with disabilities,* G. Allen Roeher Institute, Toronto, ON.

**Women with Disability Awareness Project.** (1989). *Building community: A manual exploring issues of women and disability.*    New York: Education Equity Concepts.

**Younkin, L.** (1989, May/June).   Crips on Parade. *Disability Rag,* pp.30-33.

**zana.**    (1989-1990, Winter).    going shopping. *Sinister Wisdom,* pp. 18-22.

\*\*\*\*\*\*

**Source:**   Reprinted with permission from the authors who wrote this version of *Lesbians with Disabilities* specifically for the second edition of *Perspectives on Disability.*

# Facing the Challenges of Sexual Abuse in Persons with Disabilities
## Sandra S. Cole, AASECT, CSE, CSC

**Definition~** Child abuse has been defined in the literature to include any act of commission or omission that endangers or impairs a child's physical or emotional health and development. It may be evidenced by an injury or series of injuries appearing to be non-accidental in nature and which cannot reasonably be explained. The most frequently recognized forms of child abuse are physical abuse (including neglect or lack of adequate supervision), emotional abuse or deprivation and sexual abuse.[1]

All children, unfortunately, are candidates to experience sexual abuse. This includes children who were born with or have acquired a disability. They may be living in foster homes or institutions or with their families.

Sexual abuse can consist of visual or verbal aggression which can be perceived as unwanted sexual activity. This is particularly true about the victim who is less than the age of consent. Sexual assault or abuse includes any form of unwanted sexual touching, nonconsensual sexual intercourse, other ongoing sexual exploitation, or perhaps isolated incidences of physical harassment which is experienced as sexual intent.

The Illusion Theater in Minneapolis, Minnesota [2] defines sexual abuse as occurring when a person is "manipulated, tricked or forced into touch or sexual contact". A helpful definition of sexual abuse to use with children is: forced or tricked touch or sex. This touch can begin anywhere on your body and may mean the person touches your breasts, buttocks, the vagina or penis. Sexual abuse can also involve oral, anal or vaginal penetration. Rape is sexual abuse with penetration. For children, a way to discuss penetration is to say that one part of a person's body (finger, tongue or penis) goes into a part of another person's body (vagina, anus, mouth). Penetration may occur with an object or a body part.

There is also sexual abuse without touch as when someone forces or tricks another person to look at their genitals or forces or tricks an individual into exposing his or her own genitals. Another type of sexual abuse without touch is an obscene phone call, as when a person calls and talks about sex (ways he/she wants to touch a person's body or be touched him/herself)."

Sexual abuse of children involves someone too young to give informed consent but who has been involved in a sexual act. The exploitation of an individual who lacks adequate information to recognize such a situation or who is unable to understand or communicate is also labeled sexual abuse (i.e. the mentally or physically disabled children).

Sexual abuse or assault is a violation of the whole person and is not restricted to "just a sexual act". It results in indignation and an overwhelming sense of violation and invasion which can affect the victim in a physical, psychological and social way. Frequently the aftermath of the assault or abuse is more severe that the actual event. This is particularly true of disabled individuals who cannot (or do not) access support systems and services that may be available.

It is a crime committed by adults who have forgotten or not adequately learned that it is their responsibility to protect children or to respect the privacy and integrity of another person. These adults instead force or coerce their victims into sexual encounters, the specifics and ramifications of which are beyond their comprehension. For many reasons, these victims cannot resist what they perceive as the authority of the offender.

The effects of these crimes may be short term, but in many cases there is virtually irreparable psychological harm done to the victim. Sexual exploitation, molestation and incest are devastating types of abuse. Some explanation will clarify here that victims include children but also frequently include women, adolescents, the disabled (physically or intellectually) and the female sexual partners of aggressive dominant men, especially if fear of abandonment because of children is involved. The societal taboos surrounding this type of abuse have kept it from widespread exposure. Until recently, it has received very little publicity, helping to keep it a hidden form of abuse. The media is now daily recording such events and demanding our attention.

The nature of sexual abuse also makes it difficult to observe and therefore more threatening to report. The guidelines given for its detection are by no means comprehensive. Several publications are now available in the literature to assist and guide the public and professional in recognizing the signs and symptoms of sexual abuse. These symptoms may exist singly or in various combinations of behavior and attitude as well as physical manifestations.

Illusion Theater [2] reminds us that it is important to remember that this form of abuse can make a child or individual both a victim and a prisoner. Those who seek help are often accused of lying. This results in embarrassment, fear, shame and confusion. Society particularly does not want to accept the fact that disabled persons have become victims of abuse, assault or rape. The assumption that this is unthinkable creates even more difficulty for persons with disabilities to receive specific services which could help protect them. Many people perceive the disabled asexual or not eligible to receive the attention of others in a sexual way. These resistant attitudes are pervasive and also exist in agencies, facilities, courts, homes and police stations. Families don't want to hear/believe these things. This disbelief can result in unnecessary questioning and pressure on the victim, adding yet another burden of victimization. [3]

## A Perspective

As children, we are taught to obey adults and persons in authority. In addition, victims of sexual abuse are often pressured into secrecy about sexual activity by the abuser, leaving the victim feeling helpless and guilty about the behavior. Victims often perceive that they have no place to run for help and no acceptable way out. Frequently they have been coerced, manipulated, bribed or threatened. Frequently they are filled with feelings of self-blame, fear and, for the physically disabled, increased concerns about being repulsive to others.

Children, adults with disabilities, intellectually impaired individuals, and those in institutions, can experience feelings of social powerlessness which make them particularly vulnerable to exploitation and they may not be able to exert their will against the will of the offender. In some cases the victim does not fully understand what is happening because of intellectual limitations, a lack of experience, or a lack of knowledge. It is also recognized that the powerlessness of children, the disabled, or otherwise limited individuals is socially legitimized and even supported. Isolation from society is a major contributor to this feeling of powerlessness. Inability to be viewed as adult or credible because of societal myths about their inabilities and rights further contributes to potential exploitation.

It is dehumanizing to be objectified because of a disability. It is further dehumanizing to be omitted or disbelieved as ever being a candidate for molestation, exploitation or assault. In some cases abuse is not viewed as a serious crime because it occurred to someone who is considered "different" or lacking in power and dignity. The perceived damage won't affect society as a whole or in general; therefore, it won't get the full attention of society.

In the last few years, there has been an increase in the media reporting of sexual abuse [4]. Statistics have been presented which speculate that a child is molested every two minutes in the United States. The majority are between the ages of eight and thirteen. Some estimated that for every victim revealed, nine are hidden from the authorities. Because of recent events, we are now forced to recognize that thousands of youngsters fall prey to deviant day care workers, teachers, coaches, and others entrusted with their care. Recent television programs have devoted extensive attention to this topic. The parallel here is that the disabled or institutionalized who are dependent on others fall prey to their care providers in the same way as do children to their assailants. At present, society does not really recognize these parallels.

## Characteristics

Finklehor [5] in his recent studies indicates that a quarter of all abuse occurs before the age of seven. Others suggest that over a third of all those who suffer sexual abuse are victimized before the age of nine. These statistics vary depending on different sources, and it is difficult to know the exact numbers which occur because each study has its own limitations. But it is important to recognize the fact that probably most assaults and molestation events are not reported or reflected in the statistics at all. A general estimation is that 20% of cases are reported, the rest are silenced. One of the most uncomfortable facts is that perhaps as much as 50% of sexual abuse occurs within the family [4] (again statistics vary depending on the study).

Sexual abuse is a crime almost always suffered in silence, shrouded in such fear that the offenders are able to continue for years or perhaps a lifetime without being apprehended. It is recognized that the average molester may have abused as many as an appalling total of 70 victims. Many speculations estimate that a typical offender within the family may have committed as many as 80 acts of incest with female children. It is recognized that child molesters reveal far more sexual assaults than the number for which they were originally charged. Sex offenders can be sentenced ranging from dismissal and forgiveness to forty years in prison.

Facts about family sexual abuse can be disturbing and confusing. Families differ in values surrounding touch and behavior. A distinction must be made between *normal* family practices of affection, touching interaction and that which is defined as incest. Touching, communication patterns, behavior and play patterns may change from culture to culture and family to family. Families will react in different ways to hugging, cuddling and snuggling of children, to levels of nudity permitted in the family and permissible topics of conversation. Families of disabled children frequently are on either extreme - avoidance of touch (affectional deprivation) or excessive touch (overcompensating, especially with touch). This can confuse both child and adult and appropriate boundaries are crossed or blurred.

The Illusion Theatre has created a "touch continuum"[2] the difference between good touch and bad touch and what you do when the touch is confusing. "Most touch is good: That means it feels good, warm, fun or playful. Good touches may include a kiss, hug or handshake. Some types of touch are bad: that means the touch hurts our feelings or our bodies. Bad touches may include a slap, kick or punch. Bad touch also includes sexual abuse - where the touch is tricked or forced sexual contact. Some types of touch are confusing: that means we are mixed up about whether the touch is good or bad, but we do know that something doesn't make sense or feel right. The good or fun touches, including tickling, wrestling, or 'touch games' can become confusing if it doesn't feel like a game anymore or we begin to feel uncomfortable, mixed up or hurt by the touch. Sometimes people are not used to touch, or don't like to be touched. We need to respect people's right not to be touched if they don't want to be. We also need to understand that severe deprivation of touch has some of the same effects on children as abusive touch and leaves them very vulnerable to being manipulated by what seems to be "affectionate contact". We need to consider the importance of teaching these principles, particularly to persons with disabilities and their families.

## Special Considerations

Exploitive situations become more complicated when individuals have a developmental or physical disability. In some cases involving sexual abuse, when the offender is identified as a family member or perhaps a caregiver, the victim may be unaware of being victimized and may lack the information to recognize exploitation or may be confused about what the activity really means or what the intent of the offender is [6]. In fact, frequently the victim is told that this activity is "special", and in return for compliance and secrecy will be given rewards. Of paramount importance in these situations is recognizing frequently the individual who is dependent on relatives and care providers for personal care (i.e. hygiene, dressing, grooming) can become very confused and unable to distinguish appropriate affectionate behavior and touch from exploitive touch which is expressly designed for the sexual gratification of the offender -- *not* the victim.

This inability to differentiate basic assistance with personal care activities of daily living (ADL) from sexual exploitation renders them ultimately vulnerable. In a recent NIMH study by the Institute for the study of Sexual Assault (ISSA)[7] which was designed to identify patterns of sexual abuse of patients in psychiatric settings, it was discovered that orderly psychiatric aides, technicians, and nurses (predominantly male staff) were the most frequent offenders. Their victims were patients, mostly female, who were most dependent and needing constant physical contact. "Testing" of the patient which involved gradual escalation of physical contact wherein the victim was assessed for cooperation resulted in staff perpetrator assaults, which included the full range of sexual acts: intercourse, oral copulation, masturbation and/or sexual battery. The study also reports that although staff assailants often did not directly force patients, they simply took advantage of them because many were completely helpless, in restraints, medicated or, in some cases, physically limited.

The physical affects of sexual abuse may range from almost nonexistent to venereal diseases or pregnancy. Violent attacks often result in bruises and lacerations. Although relatively few instances of sexual molestation are rape or committed with intended violence, it is very easy for the larger, more powerful person to cause serious injury to the child or to the physically limited individual whether or not they resist or try to defend themselves.

## Emotional Impact of Abuse

It is well recognized that the two factors of shame and guilt (either one or the other or both in tandem) are the prime psychological injuries. Both of these devastating repercussions are the result of the internalization of the offense. Victimized individuals frequently view themselves as the cause and as responsible and perhaps ultimately "bad".

Shame is the emotion most experienced out of feelings of defeat and weakness in such situations. There is a sensed loss of self-control with accompanying loss of self-esteem. Victims may be pressured, forced or tricked and still feel themselves to be accessories to the sexual activity even though they do not truly consent and/or perhaps do not fully understand. The adult can completely dominate and manipulate the victim. Following these experiences is a loss of self esteem. The main dilemma of shame is that it becomes a part of the individual's personality. When this happens, shame manifests itself in the feeling that the individual has no worth to self or society. Thus, another "disability" is added to the existing physical or intellectual disability of victims.

One of the more common fears of victims is that of being abandoned. Children and dependent or limited individuals particularly can feel at risk if they are unsafe in their environment. When adults do not believe them, or if disclosure threatens their safety, they are further victimized. In some cases this can lead to the belief that they are deserving of this punishment and they begin to experience not only a loss of self-esteem but a general discounting from family members or society.

The victim can also feel the devastating psychological effects of guilt. The individual may have enjoyed the attention and "love" given to some degree and may believe they have created the situation or been responsible for the problem. Children and others who are vulnerable are told they will be doing a misdeed if they do not agree to the pressure of the offender, and they're put into the difficult situation of having to agree or go against that which they have been taught is authority and must be obeyed, In most cases the offender lets the victim know that there is something wrong about the act itself by the mere fact that the child is sworn to secrecy. In essence, the victim can feel caught in a double bind. This process is also commonly recognized in the workplace and is called "sexual harassment". There is now legislation to protect the victim from the molestation and exploitation, including verbal harassment. Those who are not in the workplace deserve the same protection.

Feelings of guilt are further created by offenders in incest situations when they tell the child/victim that to reveal the sexual abuse would be to destroy the family. This sense of culpability can be reinforced by the management of the abuse cases when the child, not the parent, is removed from the home. This guilt becomes part of the person as much as does shame and is incorporated into the individual's development. When these incidences remain unidentified and are not appropriately dealt with, the psychological impact of the sexual trauma is carried exclusively and alone.

### Recognition and Prevention

There is a direct correlation between the results of training professionals to understand and identify sexual abuse and the number of cases reported. However, low statistics of reported cases do not necessarily mean that the situations do not exist. It is generally recognized in our society that the topic of sexual abuse, exploitation and molestation is a difficult one to discuss, and many people are not comfortable and/or will not believe it occurs. In spite of all this reluctance, it does. David Finklehor reports in his book *Sexually Victimized Children* [8] that one in every five female children and one in every ten male children will be sexually abused before the age of 18. There is indication that over 80% of the sexual abuse of children is by someone the child knows, not a stranger. However, in a study conducted by the Seattle Rape Relief and Sexual Assault Center [9] over a seven year period, it was revealed that 99% of all developmentally disabled reported victims were sexually abused by relatives and caregivers (residential staff, bus drivers, recreation workers, volunteers, work supervisors and others serving in care-giver capacities). Only one percent were strangers to the victim. These are dramatic statistics and serve to alert all of us working in the area of rehabilitation health

care. As a first step toward prevention, we must begin to realize that sexual abuse is common. The most recent statistics and general unpublished reports reflect that the number and incidence is higher than has previously been documented in the literature. Some therapists and mental health workers with sex offenders report or discuss among themselves the possibility that perhaps as many as one in three girls experiences molestation by the time she is fourteen and that perhaps as much as 50% of victimization occurs within the family.

Prevention of sexual abuse starts with recognition and acknowledgment that it is happening. Many victims of sexual abuse suffer long term and permanent effects not only of shame, guilt, fear and lowered self-esteem, but also health disorders, learning problems, delinquent behavior and chemical abuse [2]. Efforts aimed at prevention must necessarily involve an intention to stop the assaults before they occur. It is essential to identify and change societal beliefs and norms which permit sexual abuse and exploitation to continue. The power structure in our society sets up males as more powerful than females, able-bodied persons as more powerful than the physically disabled, white persons as more powerful that those of color, the wealthy as more powerful than the poor, and adults as more powerful than children. The child or disabled individual is particularly a candidate to be victimized since there is an imbalance of age, size, power, self-control or knowledge.

Children have the right to grow in a safe environment. Because they are vulnerable, they look to adults for protection. As previously mentioned, victims of sexual abuse are often tricked, not forced, by the offender who is likely to be someone the child knows and trusts. It is easy to understand that the child may not believe or even perceive that this person could/would possibly ever hurt him/her. The same rationale can be applied to adult individuals with intellectual or physical disabilities, those who are institutionalized, the elderly.

Prevention efforts must include programs for individuals which inform them of their right to trust their feelings, to say "no", to tell someone, to live in a safe environment, to not permit any touch or behavior which frightens, confuses or hurts them.

The media in the recent five years has made great strides toward publicizing this problem which is reaching a national health hazard proportion. General information, highly publicized public service announcements, docu-dramas, talk shows, special news reports help increase public awareness and reporting. In an effort to teach individuals some prevention techniques, the books, media, theater companies, and instructions include basic guidelines:

- say "no" if touch or situation is uncomfortable
- tell someone if help is needed
- do not keep secrets if it feels uncomfortable
- ask questions if confused or frightened by touch behavior
- right to privacy and to not permit anyone else to touch their body in any way without permission
- right to be taught appropriate touch behavior
- right to learn alternative ways of expressing affection without intimate or inappropriate touch

## Indications of Sexual Abuse

Suspicion of sexual abuse is indicted if:

- clothing appears stained or bloody
- there are reports of injury or neglect by the parents
- the child (victim) has a diagnosis of venereal disease of eyes, mouth, anus, genitalia
- the child (victim) reports pain or itching, bruises or bleeding in the genital area
- over adaptive behaviors that meet the parent's needs rather than the child's (victim's)
- there is extreme fearfulness, withdrawal or fantasy
- the child (victim) exhibits behavioral extremes (passive, very compliant to rageful and extremely aggressive), stealing, hoarding, habit disorders or

neurotic traits, hyperactivity, running away, lagging in development
- there is severe emotional conflict at home
- the child (victim) shows fear of intervention
- there is past history of abuse by the parent or parents
- there is an unwanted pregnancy
- there is inappropriate dress
- there is seductive behavior
- sleep disturbances are being manifested
- there are mood swings, feelings of humiliation, anger, nightmares, eating pattern disturbances, fear of sex, development of phobias about the attack

Specialists who work in the field of sexual abuse consistently state that when an individual does take the risk to identify the abuser and report information related to sexual exploitation or activities, it is crucial that he or she is believed. It may be the only time that they risk revealing the taboo and may be the only cry for help that will be given.

There is relatively little written on the topic of sexual abuse and individuals with physical disabilities. However, with the statistics which are available, combined with the knowledge of the personal and societal pressures generally experienced by an individual with a disability, it is not difficult to understand that physically disabled persons are potentially at higher risk than the general population. The mere fact that they are in many ways more dependent on the care-providers to assist them in activities of daily living creates multiple opportunities for them to be vulnerable in ways that the able-bodied are not. Not only do they lack privacy, but also they may lack the ability to be spontaneous in protecting themselves. Many individuals are without speech or language abilities and limited in or without mobility. Some may be so totally dependent on others for health care needs for daily living survival that to consider resisting anything from a care-provider or family member may seem too frightening for their own existence. They may also not know in whom to confide for assistance were they to try to identify abusive behavior. They may already have experienced a disenfranchisement from society and would not be willing to risk a further separation. It is understandable that handicappers may predict that their stories may not be believed because their credibility would be pitted against that of an able-bodied person. It is commonly recognized that many sex offenders are viewed as pillars of the community - respected and trusted. Offenders themselves often state that they are aware of the vulnerability of their victims and deliberately plan this abuse since the likelihood of its being reported is minimal.

The emotional reactions and adjustments of someone who has been denied his or her personal integrity by being assaulted are the same as those of someone who has been denied personal integrity by being institutionalized. Because of the denial of freedom, personal decision-making, privacy, economics, independence, and decreased feelings of personal strength, many persons who have been institutionalized share outward characteristics which indicate a history of abuse. [10]. This makes recognition somewhat difficult at times.

An obvious preventive measure is to encourage and assist parents and families in being comfortable with discussing sex and sexuality and in having the skills and information necessary to provide sex education and prevention techniques. Often parents have difficulty doing so. They may not have received any particular education in sexual health and may find themselves limited and perhaps confused in their own knowledge and skills. This leads many families to avoid the issue and to cloak it in further silence. Individuals who live in institutions may experience the same kind of silence from the institutional staff for the same reasons.

Sexual abuse is not restricted to any social or economic class and, contrary to some popular beliefs, parents with higher levels of education or income are not providing better sex education and abuse-protection techniques than parents who have less education and a lower income. A family containing a physically disabled member, particularly a child, is often seen closing around that individual in a self-containing way in an effort to protect itself from the community and society. Not only might a family be naturally more protective of a child with a disability, but also it might isolate itself in a cautious way from society and its insensitivities. Although it is subtle, it creates yet another barrier for the sexually abused disabled child who might otherwise reach out. Frequently, the only community the disabled child knows is that of the family and the care providers upon whom she or he is dependent.

Although evidence indicates that most children don't reveal their victimization and, even when they do, that many families try to shroud the incident in silence lest they call attention to themselves and sexually inappropriate behavior or make a false accusation, increasing numbers of treatment programs are needed to respond to victims. All children, particularly the disabled, must be taught personal safety lessons, preventing sexual abuse, and protecting the right and dignity of their well-being. Books have been written for children helping them to identify "good" and "bad" touch. Audio-visual materials are being created regularly, materials are being written for families to use together and efforts are being taken to train professionals to recognize and identify the events surrounding sexual exploitation. However, in an effort to adequately prepare children to recognize sexually exploitive situations, they must understand that a normal looking person, or even someone they know, could molest them. Most importantly, they must be given the message that they can tell anything to the parent or a trusted adult and that they will be believed and loved. If we can teach children to say "no" and to yell for safety, even if a family member, the local school coach or teacher, attendant, scout leader, transporter, or the next door neighbor is the abuser, we will participate in enabling safety for the vulnerable individual.

Reporting is also directly proportional to the number of education programs operating in the community; and although children often know the difference between touch which is given in love and exploitive touch, they are generally reluctant to acknowledge this unless asked directly by a trusted individual in what they perceive to be a safe setting, free from harm.

Linda Sanford, in her brochure for parents entitled "Come Tell Me Right Away", emphasizes that we must tell the children that we believe them, that the offender did something wrong, and that it is not the child's fault. We must report to the authorities (professionals are obligated by law to report suspected sexual exploitation within twenty-four hours). She instructs that we not confront the offender in the child's presence and that we be sure that the child has a physical examination to reassure him/her that his/her body has not been harmed or changed. Most importantly, she stresses that we allow the child to talk about the incident at his or her own pace, that counseling is helpful and that covering up the incident will not make it go away. The same criteria is applicable for other vulnerable persons.

## Myths

Some of the more common myths about sexual exploitation, particularly as it relates to disability, are that nice girls don't get raped, that society feels compassion toward disabled individuals and therefore would not think to do such a thing, that people who are handicapped are not really sexual or attractive and are therefore not eligible to be sexually assaulted, that rapists/abusers are strangers to their victims; that someone who can't speak or doesn't have full mental capabilities wouldn't really understand what happened to them anyway and also probably can't be believed. Other myths are that the mentally retarded or physically disabled lie about assault or are promiscuous and "ask for what they get". Many disabled individuals may participate in sexual acting out behavior which is then labeled as offensive or inappropriate by care-providers. Usually in these circumstances no effort is made to modify the negative behavior. These same individuals are also candidates to be treated in a trivial manner and kept socially isolated, reinforcing their sexual ignorance and ultimate vulnerability [12].

## Recovery

The most difficult step in recovery from sexual exploitation is actually identifying the sexual abuse. Most therapists acknowledge that "telling the secret" is threatening and traumatizing in and of itself and creates feelings of isolation and further vulnerability. When an individual's life has been violated by a parent or adult who has forced himself or herself as a lover, it results in a loss not unlike that which is experienced with an acquired or traumatic disability. It can be extremely disruptive and create enormous vulnerability. It is common for victims to say "He robbed me of my childhood... of my dignity", and "I am broken".

Incest continues to be perceived as the most damaging form of sexual abuse because of the ambivalence created between hating and loving the offender-family member. Frequently the offender may have been the more nurturing of the family members, and the victim experiences further isolation and loss by severing this tie.

A recognized common response to sexual abuse of families and of accused offenders is denial, followed by anger toward the victim. This can result in further shame, increased vulnerability and at times panic, retreat, and even rescinding the accusation. When support groups, networks, counseling and therapy can be provided, the therapeutic process can result in reduced suffering and positive, though difficult recovery. The emotional scarring can be pervasive and can affect a person's feelings of safety and well being for the rest of his/her life.

At times of crisis intervention, it is important to determine what the victim needs: to assess his/her immediate health needs to be assured that he or she is not at fault and to validate the feelings of fear, anxiety and revulsion being felt. We must stand by and assist the victim with problem solving skills for further situations and we must let the individual know that he/she has a right to be safe. These simple guidelines are essential to the healing process.

## Responses

Reluctance to talk about assault and exploitation, particularly of children and those with disabilities, is common. The reasons tend to be consistent throughout our society. Parents are afraid of unnecessarily frightening the child by giving them information about abuse. They are often reluctant to talk about sex education mainly for feelings of inadequacy and discomfort of their own.

It is generally regarded as inadequate to discuss abuse in isolation from sex education. Without the context and perspective of sexual health, it is difficult and very frightening for an individual to understand abuse.

Common community resistance often appears in the form of denial that the issue is really a problem in "our neighborhood". Communities are reluctant to inform the individuals about sexual information for fear that they will try out all of the sexual activities, act inappropriately, make up false reports or be terrorized. Although most parents support sex education and preventive education for their children, they are most critical of *who* provides it. Interestingly, Finklehor [13] reports that only "29% of the parents give their children information about sexual abuse despite their awareness of the prevalence of child sexual abuse". Generally, communities struggle over who should teach prevention programs and how much information they should contain or cost. Some community groups suggest task forces or child protection teams should do the training, others say the schools, others the police, clergy, rape centers, parents, etc. It is generally acknowledged that specific, professional training needs to be provided to those who teach these topics.

Another concern of communities is limited financial resources. Particularly in times when some conservative elements in the community are against sex education communities are concerned that talking about anything sexual (healthy or otherwise) is inappropriate and will not be supported financially. There are no easy answers to the dilemma of persuading communities to invest in educational programs, but clearly the intervention techniques are necessary if we are to continue to provide all individuals, able-bodied and disabled, with the right to sexual health.

It is also timely and appropriate to routinely provide sex education, including the area of sexual exploitation, to professionals working in the health care and rehabilitation milieu. It is time for us to aggressively address these unacceptable situations and establish clear directions which mandate respect, dignity and integrity.

********

## REFERENCES

1. Children's Village U.S.A. Child Abuse and You, National Headquarters  Woodland Hills. California.
2. Anderson, Cordelia:  No Easy Answers, Secondary Curriculum on Sexual Abuse, *Illusion Theatre,* Minneapolis, MN.  Available from Network Publications, Santa Cruz, CA, 1983.
3. Aiello, Denise, Capkin, Le, Catania, Holly: Strategies and Techniques for Serving the Disabled Assault Victim:  A Pilot training Program for Providers and Consumers, *Sexuality and Disability*, Volume 6, Number 3/4, Fall/Winter 1983.
4. Life Magazine:  Special Report on Childhood Sexual Assault, December, 1984.
5. Finklehor, D.: Child Sexual Abuse: Theory and Research, New York Free Press, NY, 1984.
6. Ryerson, Ellen:  Sexual Abuse and Self-Protection Education for Developmentally Disabled Youth:  A Priority Need, *SIECUS, Where the Action is,*  Developmental Disabilities Project, Seattle Rape Relief, 1825 South Jackson, Suite 102, Seattle WA 98144.
7. Musick, Judith: Patterns of Institutional Sexual Assault, *Response to Violence in the Family and Sexual Assault,* Volume 7, No. 3, May/June 1984.
8. Finklehor, D.: Sexually Victimized Children, New York Free Press, NY, 1979.
9. Developmental Disabilities Project, Seattle Rape Relief, 1825 South Jackson, Suite 102, Seattle WA 98144.
10. Assault Prevention Training Project: Women Against Rape, P.O. Box 82024, Columbus, Ohio 43202.
11. Sanford, Linda Tschirhart:  Come Tell Me Right Away, Ed-U-Press Inc., P.O Box 583, Fayetteville, NY 13066, 1982.
12. O'Day, Bonnie:  Minnesota Program for Victims of Sexual Assault:  Preventing Sexual Abuse of Persons with Disabilities:  A Curriculum for Hearing Impaired, Physically Disabled, Blind and Mentally Retarded Students, Network Publications, Santa Cruz, CA. 1983.
13. Finklehor, D.:  Public Knowledge and Attitudes about Child Sexual Abuse:  A Boston Survey, Paper presented to the National Conference on Child Sexual Abuse, Washington, D.C., 1982.

**About the Author:**    At the time of writing this article, Sandra S. Cole was a Clinical Professor, Health Educatior at the University of Michigan Medical School, Ann Arbor, Michigan. 48109.

**Source:** Reprinted with permission from *Sexuality and Disability,* Vol. 7, No. 3-4, 1986, pp. 71-86. Published by Human Sciences Press, New York, New York. 10013-1578.

# The Prevention of Sexual Abuse of People with Developmental Disabilities

Dick Sobsey

Sheila Mansell

**Abstract** ~ *Considerable research demonstrates that both children and adults with disabilities experience a much greater risk of sexual abuse and sexual assault (Sobsey, Grey, Wells, Pyper & Reimer-Heck, 1991). However, the available information concerning prevention and treatment of sexual assault and sexual abuse for the disabled is scarce. This paper examines some of the existing prevention programs and proposes alternate sexual abuse prevention strategies for disabled persons.*

*Some of the strategies discussed in this paper developed out of work completed by the University of Alberta Sexual Abuse and Disability Project[1] . This project began in 1987 and has completed a comprehensive review of the literature (Sobsey, Gray, Wells, Pyper & Reimer-Heck, 1991) and an analysis of more than 150 victims' reports (Sobsey, in press; Sobsey & Doe, in press). The current work of the project is designed to validate prevention components extracted from the two previous phases. Many of these prevention strategies are discussed in this chapter.*

## Education and Training

Training can be an important component in a risk reduction program. Training potential victims to avoid or resist abuse has been the standard approach to sexual abuse prevention for some time. Nevertheless, it is unrealistic to expect that any program which places sole responsibility for abuse prevention on potential victims will adequately protect or serve the needs of the disabled.

[1] Portions of the project that provided the basis for this chapter were funded by National Health Research and Development Program, Health and Welfare Canada under projects 6609-1465 CSA and 6609-1597 FV. Findings and opinions expxressed are those of the author and not necessarily those of the funding agency.

Researchers suggest that prevention training programs also may produce several unwanted effects. Detrimental effects may result from prevention programs which focus responsibility for sexual abuse and/or assault prevention on potential victims but fail to assign ultimate responsibility for sexual victimization to offenders (Trudell & Whatley, 1988; Gilgun & Gordon, 1985). For example, if potential victims fail to prevent sexually abusive or assaultive situations, by implication they may be held responsible for the occurrence. Ironically, prevention training programs that intend to help potential victims protect themselves may ultimately contribute to victim blaming.

Although many children and adults with disabilities possess adequate information and the will to avoid victimization, they still may be powerless to prevent abuse. Despite the problems associated with training programs, there are several types of training which appear to be useful in addressing the needs of the disabled.

**Appropriate Sex Education:** Everyone, whether disabled or not, needs appropriate education and training in sexuality. The culturally pervasive myths surrounding disability continue to influence both societal perceptions and treatment of the disabled (Warnemuende, 1986). These myths may also contribute to offenders' rationalizations for sexually abusing disabled persons. For example, one myth portrays people with disabilities as non-sexual. This erroneous belief not only denies the sexuality of disabled persons, it also may be used to justify denying access to sex education to people with disabilities. Denying the disabled access to sex education may produce several related consequences. It may increase the vulnerability of people with disabilities to possible pregnancy and venereal diseases, but also to potential abuse by those who will exploit their lack of knowledge about sexuality. For example, in our own research of sexual abuse victims with disabilities, we found cases in which sexual abuse was rationalized by offenders as a form of sex education. This rationale for abuse is not unique to cases involving victims with disabilities; however, Marshall and Barrett report that many incest offenders and child molesters use the same type of rationalization (1990). Those who fail to receive an appropriate and healthy sex education may be condemned to an inappropriate and brutal sex education at the hands of those who will exploit and abuse them. Appropriate sex education for the disabled clearly is an important resource in sexual abuse prevention.

Sex education programs for people with disabilities should be individually tailored to the person's age, environment, and communication skills. In sex education programs, although it is necessary to impart explicit information about sexual behavior, choices, and risks, it is also important to reach beyond the biological and address the social and emotional aspects of sexuality.

A critical component in sexuality education is sexual abuse prevention. Several different skills may be involved such as learning to recognize and avoid dangerous situations and becoming aware of personal feelings of discomfort (Watson, 1984; Ryerson, 1981). Learning how to seek advice and help when it is needed are also important skills. For example, students need to learn how to let others know that something doesn't feel good, and that letting others know immediately, before the situation becomes more serious, may prevent escalation to abuse. Sex education, however, is not the only educational intervention that can help prevent sexual abuse of the disabled.

**Other Educational Needs:** Assertiveness training, choice-making, and personal rights education are essential educational content areas for people with disabilities. Unfortunately, special education programs have often focused on generalized compliance as a goal for students. An unfortunate consequence of this approach is that our best students have been effectively trained to be

victims of psychological, sexual and physical abuse (Sobsey, 1988). Education should emphasize an awareness of the range of lifestyles available and help students develop the abilities to choose among these. The development and enhanced access to appropriate social and sexual relationships can reduce vulnerability to more abusive relationships (Shaman, 1986). Therefore, the programs that attempt to isolate or de-sexualize people with disabilities are likely to increase the likelihood of abuse (Musick, 1984).

An important self-protection strategy for many individuals with disabilities is learning enhanced communication skills. Individuals who cannot communicate their feelings are more vulnerable to abuse. Research suggests that offenders seek victims who they consider to be vulnerable and unable to seek help or report the abuse (Lang & Frenzel, 1988). Communication skill deficits may contribute to an offender's perception of victim vulnerability and to the selection of potential victims. Increased vulnerability of deaf children is clearly demonstrated by research that indicates that deaf children experience a greater incidence and risk for sexual abuse than hearing children (Sullivan, Vernon & Scanlan, 1978). Conversely, improved communication skills probably decrease the perception of vulnerability and the risk of sexual abuse.

**Staff Training:** Disabled children and adults can clearly benefit from some of the previously described educational interventions. However, staff members who are providing educational, vocational, residential, and other related services could also benefit from training (Sundram, 1984). It is important for staff to have an early introduction to a clear policy regarding abuse and sexual behavior. Staff should be trained to recognize and respond appropriately to early signs of abuse, and to their own feelings of aggression or sexual attraction that may arise. Research suggests that many service providers occasionally experience feelings of sexual attraction to one or more clients (Pope, Keith-Spiegel & Tabachnick, 1986). Most service providers, however, maintain appropriate standards of professional conduct. Frequently, the individuals who inappropriately act out their aggressive or sexual feelings have failed to anticipate the possibility of these feelings and have never developed strategies for appropriately dealing with them (Pope et al., 1986). Establishing both clear standards of conduct and boundaries between appropriate and inappropriate behavior, along with access to formal or informal counselling, may help staff cope more appropriately with their feelings.

Staff need to know not only the procedures for reporting abuse but also to be trained to detect the signs of sexual abuse. These preventions components may seem to be "after-the-fact" and perhaps too late to have any preventive effect. However, there are several indicators that these can be powerful prevention strategies. The presence of effective prevention and reporting systems can have powerful deterrent effects on offenders. Potentially abusive staff members who believe that others are not only unlikely to detect but also unlikely to report them, are likely to become active abusers. Alternately, when they believe that they are likely to be detected and reported, their potential abuse is often effectively inhibited. Furthermore, most abusers have many victims. Child molesters, for instance, have on average 70 victims before they are first apprehended (Barbaree & Marshall, 1988.) Consequently, both undetected and unreported cases of sexual abuse allow more people to be victimized. Therefore, while it may be too late to prevent the victimization of past victims, potential future victims may be protected. Also our research suggests that most victims are not sexually abused on only a single occasion (Sobsey & Doe, in press). The abuser typically repeats the offense with the same victim many times over periods of months or years unless the abuse is reported. Therefore, detection and reporting may protect victims from repeated and prolonged abuse.

## Administrative Reform

Our research suggests that sexual abuse often takes place in the "disability" service delivery system and abusers are often paid caregivers (Sobsey, in press). The implications of this finding suggest that system reform is an essential part of prevention. There are several administrative reforms that could be implemented in this system to have powerful effects in sexual abuse prevention for the disabled.

**Staff Screening:** In a number of cases that have come to our attention, known sex offenders have taken jobs providing personal care to people with disabilities in institutions, group homes, and private residences. Although the number of previously convicted and currently charged applicants is small, the number of victims that each will be likely to have if allowed into the system is large (likely 100 or more). Therefore careful and thorough reference and police checks are essential to the screening process (Musick, 1984). The interview process provides an employer with an important opportunity to determine the suitability of a prospective employee. Using open-ended situational questions may help an employer determine a prospective employee's attitudes towards the disabled and reactions to personal feelings of aggression, stress or arousal in providing personal care to the disabled. Employers in the service delivery system need to be both sensitive to the problems produced by sexual abuse of people with disabilities and conscientious about screening staff in order to prevent it.

In the past, many abusers have been allowed to resign from an agency rather than facing charges for their offenses. Unfortunately, many of these individuals move on to another service delivery setting and continue to abuse the individuals in their care. It is imperative that whenever possible charges be laid and convictions obtained to prevent the possibility of abusers moving from agency to agency. When employees leave an agency because of concerns over the nature of their interaction with service consumers, it is essential that this fact be included in any reference information provided to prospective future employers.

**Agency Responsibility:** Service providers must accept greater responsibility for the clients they serve. For example, when they fail to provide a reasonably safe environment, they must acknowledge their responsibility for the resulting harm done to the people in their care. Failure to adequately screen staff is one example of agency irresponsibility, but there are several others. Many institutional settings cluster potentially sexually aggressive and vulnerable people together with little attention to the prevention of violence. Institutionalization of dangerous individuals may improve safety in the community, but without adequate safeguards to protect vulnerable people living in institutions, such residents will be at great risk for victimization. Certainly, violence among residents is rarely condoned and typically some attempt is made to maintain order, but institutions have failed to recognize their legal obligation to maintain a level of personal safety similar to that of the general community.

Several recent court decisions suggest that this irresponsibility will no longer be tolerated. In at least three American cases, courts found that mental institutions did not protect residents adequately against sexual assault from other residents (Sobsey, 1988). One American institution for people with developmental disabilities had federal funding withdrawn for the same reason (*School for the disabled loses* ..., 1989). Canadian courts have also recognized this principle. For example, a recent case found a nursing home to be responsible for a physical assault by a resident (Stewart v. Extendacare, 1986). Staff were held responsible because they knew that the developmentally disabled resident was assaultive and failed to take appropriate action to prevent the assault.

Institutions cannot entirely eliminate risk for residents, but they do have a responsibility to provide a level of safety that is not substantially worse than the level currently available in the community. Institutional staff have a responsibility to take reasonable precautions to reduce the risk of abuse for residents.

Responsibility also needs to be established for contract staff. For example, many schools and other programs contract for transportation services to convey students with disabilities to specialized programs. Our research has found many cases of these transportation providers sexually assaulting disabled students (Sobsey & Doe, in press). Once schools and other service providers have knowledge of this risk, they have a responsibility to control it.

**Integration and Reduction of Isolation:** It is difficult to precisely compare the relative risks for sexual abuse in institutional and community environments. The available research suggests that the risk of being sexually abused within an institutional setting is two to four times as high as for being sexually abused in the community (Rindfleisch & Bean, 1988; Rindfleisch & Rabb, 1984; Shaughnessy, 1984). Therefore, serving more people with disabilities within the community and fewer in institutions may be a powerful prevention strategy.

For individuals who continue to be served in institutional settings, however, reducing the isolation of this service delivery system may have similar preventive effects (Crossmaker, 1986; Musick, 1984). The privacy of individuals living within institutions is both a legitimate and significant concern. Ironically, many of the practices defended in the name of protecting the privacy of the individual have resulted in the isolation of these individuals, thereby increasing their risk for abuse.

**Behavioral Control:** Two other service reforms need careful consideration. The extensive use of psychotropic drugs for behavior control of people with developmental disabilities may also increase their vulnerability to abuse. In some cases the same people who recommend, prescribe, or administer these mind altering drugs are also the offenders who sexually abuse their drugged victims. The drug may be used deliberately to reduce the resistance of victims or to interfere with the victim's ability to make a complaint. Breggin (1983) has described widespread use of these drugs to control political dissenters, prisoners, and the elderly, in addition to people with intellectual and behavioral disabilities. Animal and human studies reported in these studies document the effects of tranquilizers in suppressing escape and avoidance responses, interfering with the abilities required for self-protection. In some cases, these drugs may be used with good intention but with equally damaging effects. For example, drugs may be prescribed and administered by treatment team members who are unaware of the cause of the behavior to control non-compliant or other "inappropriate" behavior. They may be unaware that the behavior that they are "treating" developed in response to abuse or that they are suppressing the victim's only available means of defense. Similarly, intensive and aversive behavior management programs are sometimes used to control non-compliant, aggressive, sexually inappropriate or other problem behavior of people with disabilities. Unfortunately, these programs are often employed with little attention to the discovery of the cause of the inappropriate behavior. In many cases, the cause of such behavior turns out to be abuse of the individual. Suppressing this behavior through behavioral control may take away the victim's last defence against abuse and silence their only way of letting people know that they are being abused. Abusers may even use such programs as a coercive tool to ensure silence from sexual abuse victims. It is essential that attempts be made to identify the real cause of "behavior problems" before caregivers attempt to eliminate them through the intrusive use of drugs or punishment procedures (Sobsey, 1990).

Various forms of restraint that are sometimes used to control people with atypical behavior also leave them vulnerable to abuse and assault. In our review of cases, we have also come across cases in which "therapeutic restraint" left victims vulnerable to abuse and assault. Whether restraint is accomplished physically, chemically, or through behavioral coercion, its use creates the extreme inequality of power that often leads to abuse. Packard (1875), in her classic description of her own experience as a patient in a 19th century insane asylum, suggests that the "most heinous wrong of our present system consists of the fact that inmates of insane asylums are denied the primeval right of self defense" (cited in Crossmaker & Merry, 1990). Little has changed this fundamental fact in the last century. Only the new, more sophisticated methods of chemical and behavioral restraint

have been added to supplement physical restraint. The use of any of these procedures is rarely if ever justified. If they are ever to be used, there must be more stringent controls in place to prevent abuse.

## Detection, Reporting, Prosecution and Treatment

The processes of detection, reporting, prosecution and treatment of sexual abuse may seem to be activities that occur only after prevention has failed and therefore of little value in preventing sexual abuse. However, these activities are essential components of prevention programs. Poor detection, reporting, and prosecution results in repeated offenses against the same victims and also to the additional victimization of others. The perception that these crimes go unreported and unpunished encourages potential offenders to act out their drives (Sundram, 1984). Treatment for victims and offenders is also important. Offenders who go untreated are likely to commit future offenses. There is also evidence that many adult sex offenders were victims of sexual abuse as children (Fagan & Wexler, 1988; Langevin, Wright & Hardy, 1989; Finkelhor, 1984). Thus, by effective treatment of victims of child sexual abuse, we may not only help the victim but also decrease the chance that some victims will later become offenders.

**Detection:** Detection of sexual abuse of people with disabilities has often been hampered by several different factors. Society's de-sexualized image of people with disabilities often results in our failure to recognize the possibility of sexual abuse of children and adults with disabilities (Shaman, 1986). A greater public understanding of the frequency of this crime is necessary in order for people to recognize and react to its symptoms. Just as people with disabilities are often stereotyped, caregivers are often viewed as patient, dedicated, quasi-religious figures who are beyond reproach. Consequently, we may have difficulty believing that the same man who was honored by his international religious and fraternal organizations for his dedication in adopting handicapped children from the third world countries, is now charged with sexually abusing these children. It would be equally wrong, however, to stereotype all caregivers as merciless exploiters. Like individuals found in all segments in society, caregivers are variable and complex individuals. We cannot afford to dismiss suspicious events or behavior simply because we believe some individuals are beyond reproach.

Special emphasis should be placed on teaching children and adults to recognize and respond to early signs of abuse. Caregiver-abusers often attempt to disguise their abuse as part of treatment and this ploy may be quite convincing especially at early stages. Symptom-masking is another obstacle to successful detection. Many of the symptoms of sexual abuse may be easily attributed to the victim's disability and thus overlooked (Sobsey, in press). For example, if a physician finds that an adolescent girl is not sleeping well, having difficulties in school, seems fearful of people, and resists physical examination, he should begin to wonder about the possibility that she is being abused. If that child, has a diagnosis of mental or emotional disability, he may be likely to attribute the symptoms to her disability and thus be less likely to detect abuse.

**Reporting Abuse:** Much of the sexual abuse of people with disabilities currently goes unreported for several reasons. Many service consumers are often intimidated by the abuser or afraid of disruption of essential services. Some service consumers are unable to communicate about their abuse because of their disability or because their isolated living situation prevents them from having free communication with someone they can trust. Many service providers fail to report abuse for fear of direct retaliation by the abuser or administrative retaliation from authorities who are embarrassed by the reports of abuse within the service delivery system for which they have responsibility.

Complainant protection legislation is essential to combat these obstacles and has been adopted in some states and provinces. Provisions of this legislation may vary, but may include some combination of important elements. First, there is usually a legally mandated requirement to report suspected abuse. Second, there is often protection from legal action taken by the alleged abuser if the charges are not supported. This protection against being sued by the alleged abuser is normally absolute except in the case where it can be proven that the report was made without grounds but rather with malice and intent to injure the accused. Service consumers may be protected against service interruption or withdrawal, subsequent to making a report.

Similarly, service providers who report may be legally protected against administrative retribution. It is very important to have provisions that ensure that all reports go to authorities independent of the service delivery system that is involved, and that administrative investigation cannot be used as a substitute for law enforcement investigation appropriate to the reported crime. In some states and provinces, independent advocates have been appointed to facilitate such reports since an employee of an institution or service system under investigation cannot be expected to act impartially.

**Investigation and Prosecution:** Good investigation and prosecution procedures are essential to prevention, because failure to convict perpetrators of these crimes allows abusers to continue their abuse and encourages others to believe that they can also become abusers without the fear of punishment for these offenses. Currently, many victims with disabilities are so severely disadvantaged in the criminal justice system that their rights to personal security and equal protection of the law under sections 8 and 15 of the Charter of Rights and Freedoms are almost certainly violated. Legislation will be necessary to restore the balance of rights for disabled victims with those accused of abusing them.

Changes in evidentiary rules are required. Currently, many disabled victims are not allowed to testify in court because they are considered to be incompetent. Others are not allowed to utilize their most effective method of communication to testify. Every citizen who becomes a victim of a crime should have a right to present the best evidence they can in a manner that is most suited to their abilities.

Clarification of issues related to consent are also required in many countries. For example, in Canada, if an offender "honestly believes" that a victim is consenting, no crime has been committed. The law, however, is unclear regarding what constitutes reasonably honest belief in consent. The inability of an individual to fight off an attacker or to clearly communicate should be grounds for a finding of consent to sexual assault.

Complainant protection or "whistleblower" legislation is an essential component in deterring abuse. People with disabilities should not be in jeopardy of service interruption or more restrictive placement as a result of reporting abuse. Service providers should not be in jeopardy of administrative harassment or other consequences that have occurred in response to their reports of abuse.

## Treatment Programs

Many community programs that treat victims of sexual abuse or assault remain inaccessible to people with disabilities or offer programs that are inappropriate to their individual needs. Nevertheless, many treatment centres across Canada have acknowledged this gap in their services and are making excellent progress toward attaining appropriate and accessible services for all. Physical accessibility. alternative telephone devices, provision of translating services, and non-print alternatives for reading materials are among the basic accommodations required. More work needs to be done to identify appropriate treatment alternatives for people with cognitive and communicative impairments that make traditional insight therapy difficult (Sullivan, Scanlan, Knutson, Brookhauser & Schulte, in press).

## Attitudes about Disability

The myths surrounding sexual assault and sexual abuse combined with the cultural images of people with disabilities may act as powerful influences in the perpetuation of sexual abuse (Shaman, 1986). Most sexual offenders develop myths about their victims that they employ to both justify their own inappropriate behavior and reduce their behavioral inhibitions. For example, rapists often blame their victims describing them as "asking for it". We need to carefully examine the cultural myths surrounding people with disabilities to determine not only how these attitudes may contribute to abuse and also how changing attitudes may function as a sexual abuse prevention strategy. Five such attitudes are discussed here as examples, but there are several others.

**The "Dehumanization" Myth:** Sadly, people with disabilities are still portrayed and viewed as less than full members of our society. Labels such as "vegetative state" suggest an image of the person with a disability as not quite human. Such images allow offenders to fuel their existing justifications with the belief that their offenses are less problematic because the victim is not really a fellow human being. Since the offender sees himself as more human and therefore more valuable, he sees nothing wrong with exploiting the less valued individual to meet his own needs.

**The "Damaged Merchandise" Myth"** Closely associated with the dehumanization concept is the view of the disabled person as damaged merchandise. This is perhaps most clearly articulated by those who advocate for euthanasia of severely handicapped children. They argue that the "potential quality of life" for such a person is so poor that the child is better off dead than alive. Indeed, this myth allows society to kill handicapped children and provides the rationalization which asserts that it is ultimately in their "best interest!" In fact, we have little reason to believe that the euthanasia advocates' presentation of so-called indicators of quality of life have any relationships to the individual's own perception of the quality of his or her own life.

The damaged merchandise myth asserts that because the life of the disabled person is worthless, they have nothing to lose in death. The sexual abuser may employ similar reasoning which allows him to regard his victim's life as worthless. Therefore, it provides an offender with a rationalization not only for the choice of victim, but also may alleviate any guilt or inhibition about exploiting a disabled person.

**The "Feeling No Pain" Myth:** People with disabilities, especially emotional disorders and mental handicaps, are often described as immune to pain and suffering. In fact, there is no basis for this belief since these people are subject to experiencing the same range of feelings as any person. This myth allows offenders to believe that because some victims may not fully understand what is happening to them, they suffer less. Therefore, they rationalize their crime by saying that the victim really wasn't hurt by it. Research shows that people with all kinds of disabilities suffer just as much emotional trauma, physical injury, and social consequences of abuse as any other victim (Stuart & Stuart, 1981; Sullivan,Vernon & Scanlan, 1987).

**The "Disabled Menace" Myth:** People with disabilities have sometimes been portrayed and viewed as deviant menaces to society who are both dangerous and unpredictable. For the offender, this view often contributes to rationalizations which blame the victim for the abuse. For example, caregivers who sexually abuse their clients may believe that the event occurred as a result of the sexual aggression of the victim. The reality is often the opposite. Sexually inappropriate behavior is often seen in victims of sexual abuse or sexual assault, but it often occurs as a result of their abuse, and should never be used as an excuse for the cause.

**The "Helplessness" Myth:** Even the portrayal of people with disabilities as vulnerable or helpless may contribute to their abuse. The perception of vulnerability is known to affect the selection of victims by sex offenders. This raises ethical concerns about exposing the frequency of sexual victimization of people with disabilities, since this exposure of vulnerability may encourage future victimization. However, attempting to hide the problem may produce worse problems because it protects abusers. The real answer to combating the myth of helplessness is through the evolving empowerment of people with disabilities and developing positive, more

realistic images appropriate to this empowerment. A more encompassing goal for the empowerment of people with disabilities involves promoting positive societal attitudes towards disability.

**Changing Attitudes:** Clearly, society's attitudes about people with disabilities continues to contribute to their disempowered position and vulnerability to sexual abuse. Changing societal attitudes towards persons with disabilities may be an important, encompassing and long term empowerment and sexual abuse prevention strategy. A more relevant objective for sexual abuse prevention for persons with disabilities, however, is directly addressing the attitudes of professionals who work with persons with disabilities (Sundram, 1984)

There are a few strategies such as educational programs, contact with the disabled and disability simulation which appear to be successful in promoting positive attitudes towards persons with disabilities (Westwood, Vargo & Vargo, 1981). However, the results from studies attempting to alter attitudes toward persons with disabilities tend to be both conflicting, inconclusive and subject to methodological differences and problems, (Westwood et al., 1981). Despite these methodological problems, however, there may be important applications for use of these strategies in professional training programs. Ibrahim & Herr (1982) studies educational and role playing attitude change strategies in undergraduate students in helping professions, and discovered that role playing appeared to be more successful in altering attitudes towards the disabled. Professional training programs promoting positive attitudes toward people with disabilities, combined with increased employer screening, may act together to help reduce the risk of sexual abuse for persons with disabilities.

**Summary**

People with disabilities experience increased risk for sexual assault and sexual abuse, however, much of their excessive risk can be eliminated through appropriate abuse prevention strategies. Effective programs must consider the potential victims of abuse, potential offenders, and the settings in which abuse often takes place. The problems of sexual abuse and sexual assault in our society are not unique to people with disabilities. The most effective forms of prevention must consider all members of society regardless of disability status, however, the most relevant issues for people with disabilities have been presented as the focus of this article.

\*\*\*\*\*\*

## REFERENCES

**Barbaree, H.E.** & Marshall, W.L. (1988) *Treatment of the adult male child molester: Methodological issues in evaluating treatment outcome* Kingston, ON: Queen's University.

**Breggin, P.R.,** (1983) *Psychiatric drugs: Hazards to the mind.* New York: Springer Publishing Company.

**Crossmaker, M.** (1986) *Empowerment: A systems approach to preventing assaults against people with mental retardation and/or developmental disabilities.* Columbus, OH: The National Assault Prevention Center.

**Crossmaker, M.,** & Merry, D. (Eds.) (1990) *Stigma: Stereotypes and scapegoats.* Columbus, OH: Ohio Legal Rights Service.

**Fagan, J.** & Wexler, S. (1988). Explanations of sexual assault among violent delinquents. *Journal of Adolescent Research, 3* (3-4), 363-385.

**Finkelhor, D.** (1984) *Child sexual abuse.* New York: The Free Press.

**Gilgun, J.** & Gordon, S. (1985). Sex education and the prevention of child sexual abuse. *Journal of Sex Education and Therapy, 1* (1) 46-52.

**Ibrahim, F.,** Herr, E. (1982). Modification of attitudes toward disability: Differential effect of two educational modes. *Rehabilitation Counselling Bulletin, 26* (1), 29-36.

**Lang, R.A.** & Frenzel, R.R. (1988). How sex offenders lure children. *Annals of Sex Research, 1* (2), 303-317.

**Langevin, R.,** Wright, P., & Handy. L. (1989) Characteristics of sex offenders who were sexually victimized as children. *Annals of Sex Research 2* (3), 227-253.

**Marshall, W.L.** (1990). *Criminal neglect: Why sex offenders go free.* Toronto: Doubleday Canada Limited.

**Musick, J.L.** (1984) Patterns of Institutional sexual assault. *Response to Violence in the Family and Sexual Assault, 7*(3), 1-2, 10-11.

**Packard, E.P.** (1875). *Modern prosecution or insane asylums unveiled.* Hartford, CT: Arno Press.

**Pope, K.S.,** Keith-Spiegel, P., & Tabachnick, B.G. (1986). Sexual attraction to clients: The human therapist and the (sometimes) inhuman training system. *American Psychologist, 41,* 147-158.

**Rindfleisch, N.** & Bean, G.J. (1988) Willingness to report abuse and neglect in residential facilities. *Child Abuse and Neglect, 8,* 33-40.

**Ryerson, E.** (1981). Sexual abuse of disabled persons and prevention alternatives. In D. G.Bullard & S.E.Knight (Eds.) *Sexuality and physical disability: Persona; perspectives* (pp.235-242). St. Louis: C.V.Mosby.

**School for the disabled loses federal support.** **(1989)** *Washington Coalition of Sexual Assault Programs Newsletter* (March, 1989), pp. 1-2.

**Shaman, E.J.** (1986). Prevention for children with disabilities. In M. Nelson & K. Clark (eds.), *The educator's guide to preventing child sexual abuse* (pp.122-125). Santa Cruz, CA: Network Publications

**Shaughnessy, M.F.** (2984). Institutional child abuse. *Children and Youth Services Review, 6,* 311-318.

**Sobsey, D.** (1990). Modifying the behavior of behavior modifiers: Arguments for counter control against aversive procedures. In A. Repp, & N. Singh (Eds.) *Perspectives on the use of non-aversive behavior and aversive interventions for persons with developmental disabilities.* (pp.421-433). Sycamore, IL: Sycamore Publishing.

**Sobsey, D.** (in press). Sexual abuse of individuals with intellectual disability. In A. Craft (Ed.) *Practice issues in sexuality and intellectual disability.* London: Routledge.

**Sobsey, D.** (1988). Sexual victimization of people with disabilities: Professional and social responsibilities. *Alberta Psychology, 17*(6) 8-9.

**Sobsey, D.** & Doe, T. (in press). Patterns of sexual abuse and assault. *Sexuality and Disability.*

**Sobsey, D.,** Gray, S., Wells, D., Pyper, D., & Reimer-Heck, B. (1991). *Disability , sexuality, & abuse: An annotated bibliography.* Baltimore: Paul H. Brookes.

**Stewart v Extendacare Ltd.** (1986 (4.W.W.R. (Sask.Q.B.)

**Stuart, C.K.,** & Stuart, V.W. (1981). Sexual Assault: Disabled perspective. *Sexuality and Disability, 4* (4), 246-253.

**Sundram, C.J.** (1984). Obstacles to reducing patient abuse in public institutions. *Hospital and Community Psychiatry, 35 (3),* 238-243.

Sullivan, P.M., Scanlan, J.M., Knutson, J.E., Brookhauser, P.E. & Schulte, L.E. (in press). The effects of psychotherapy on behavior problems of sexually abused deaf children. *Journal of Child Abuse and Neglect.*

Trudell, W., & Whatley, M. (1988). School sexual abuse prevention: Unintended consequences and dilemmas. *Child Abuse & Neglect, 12,* 103-113.

Warnemuende, R. (1986). Misconceptions and attitudes about disability and the need for awareness. *Journal of Applied Rehabilitation Counselling,* 17, (1), 50-51.

Watson, J.D. (1984). Talking about the best kept secret: Sexual abuse and children with disabilities. *Exceptional Parent, 14*(6), 15, 16, 18-20.

Westwood, M., Vargo, J., & Vargo, F. (1981). Methods for promoting attitude change toward and among physically disabled persons. *Journal of Applied Rehabilitation Counseling,* 12 (4), 220-225.

\*\*\*\*\*\*\*\*

About the Authors:  Dick Sobsey and Sheila Mansell are with the University of Alberta, Edmonton Alberta, Canada.  Requests for reprints should be addressed to Dick Sobsey, Department of Educational Psychology, 6-102 Education North, University of Alberta, Edmonton, Alberta, Canada, T6G 2G5

Source:  Reprinted with permission from *Developmental Disabilities Bulletin*, Vol. 18, No. 2, pp. 51-66, 1990.  Published by the Faculty of Education, University of Alberta, Edmonton, Alberta, Canada.

# 5 Medical and Psychological Concerns and Disability

Medical and paramedical personnel because of their status positions perform crucial functions in the diagnosis and treatment of disability. Nurses, rehabilitation professionals, medical doctors, psychologists and social workers are front line authorities because they convey to people with disabilities the realities and difficulties posed by disabled statuses. As front line people, they are able to convey the outcomes of habilitative and rehabilitative strategies, but this is often difficult as people with a wide range of disabilites illustrate different levels of motivational potential. Some people are able to overcome the severest handicaps while others find it difficult, and sometimes impossible, to overcome the realities posed by lesser disabling conditions. Multidisciplinary and eclectic approaches to improving the quality of life for people with all disabling conditions must be considered if rehabilitation is to be successful.

Physicians identify the disease and disability, legitimate temporary release from social obligations and certify for the patient the impact of the disease. In many instances, the role of the physician becomes somewhat ambiguous for the patient because the patient often expects a utopian scientific diagnosis which will always produce a cure. As is known, many disabling conditions or potentially disabling conditions are difficult to diagnose because people are often reluctant, or are unable to convey all the symptoms, or because many symptoms convey the probable existence of many diseases or disabling conditions. For understandable reasons, people are often traumatized when disabling conditions are diagnosed. Some people will attempt to maximize their rehabilitative potential by precisely following medical directives and in the process they also attempt to maximize their quality of life. For other patients faced with similar diagnosis, the illness and the disabling condition becomes the central organizing aspect of their identities and they relinquish any and all role participation. Physicians and other medical personnel relaying such diagnoses may become targets of aggression when patients find it difficult to adjust to permanent disabling conditions. In addition, some people go to extremes to validate or deny the diagnosis by seeking several opinions and options for cures.

In the field of psychiatric disability, it is understandably difficult for the physician to certify an individual as 'different' because of the social stigma and implications that mental illness has in contemporary society. Individuals faced with this type of psychiatric diagnosis will attempt to construct a social identity and manner of behavior that is acceptable to others. Difficulties arise when different methods of counseling and drug therapies produce vastly different results on individuals who are diagnosed with the same problem. The result? Not only the scientific, but the social definition of illness and/or disability presents wide and differing ramifications for the helping professional, for the person who has been diagnosed, and for all those with whom the person with the condition interrelates.

However, professionals in all fields of disability-related concerns are often able to convey the most positive prognosis to people who encounter the consequences of severe disability. Technological innovations evolving from computer technology and modern therapeutic techniques have served to increase the rehabilitative potential of many individuals and have allowed people to maintain or increase their independence and autonomy. In some societies the resources necessary to maximize rehabilitative potential are readily available. In other societies, because of fiscal reality factors, people with disabilities find it difficult and sometimes impossible to avail themselves of the therapeutic techniques available. However, many individuals with disabilities overcome the severest of conditions as a consequence of self motivation, while others are able to affiliate with peers and organizations representing their particular disability. Peer group affiliation then becomes instrumental in achieving maximum rehabilitation potential. These organizations provide personal support, resources and facilities in order to take advantage of the most efficient rehabilitative strategies which in turn motivates members to achieve maximum habilitative and rehabilitative potential. In addition, governments at all levels are now establishing and mandating policies which serve to mainstream people with disabilities into their respective societies. This strategy is a progressive thrust as in the past people with disabilities were often institutionalized, were limited in accessing rehabilitation techniques, and were prevented from full integration into their respective societies.

To be sure, barriers continue to exist. For instance, there have been cutbacks in many services for people with disabilities due to the emphasis on fiscal responsibility and government debt reduction. It would still seem that the groups in society with the least power, and who are the most vulnerable, are usually the first victims of such "economy drives". However, because of the determination, the empowerment, the awareness of new techniques and technology and the positive directions for integration and acceptance that have been achieved by and for the disabled community, many barriers have been overcome and the rights of people with disabilities are "now in place".

There are still many disability issues and concerns to confront, research, and develop habilitative strategies for. Professionals working with people with disabilities often find themselves in ambivalent ethical and moral positions when confronted with the dilemma of whether to prescribe technologies and innovations which can control if not eliminate the prospect of disability. Chapter Seven will address some of the ethical questions, philosophical debates and legal ramifications that affect people with disabilities. However, professionals who are the front line workers must deal on a daily basis with the realities of particular disabilities as they affect their patients and clients. Innovative research is now allowing surgery to be performed on fetal tissue during pregnancy. Where such interventions can lessen the possibility of disabled status for a newborn, they should be encouraged. However, there are some medical technologies which need more critical examination from ethical and moral perspectives. President Clinton, in March 1993, allowed continued research in fetal tissue. The ethical factors that arise from this research concern the fact that some individuals may choose to become pregnant in order to provide fetal tissue that may alleviate conditions such as Parkinson's disease. Are these reasons for becoming pregnant valid? Another area of great concern to people with Down Syndrome is the use of the procedure of amniocentesis. Results of this procedure have been used as a decision-making tool to abort fetuses. There are many individuals affected by Down syndrome and other conditions which may be detected before birth who have been carried to term and have subsequently become productive, self-sustaining, accepted and integrated human beings. Who can morally and ethically make decisions for a fetus?

Therefore, the roles of medical and paramedical personnel who work with people with disabilities are vital, challenging, and instrumental to the well being of these individuals, their families, and their communities. The goals of these professionals should be to act in the best interests of their clients. This is often personally and professionally difficult due to the issues raised above and to those issues addressed in the following articles.

The extensive and varied field of rehabilitation is endeavoring to establish a 20th century philosophical tenet that considers an empowerment approach to rehabilitation. In William G. Emener's article, *Empowerment in Rehabilitation: An Empowerment Philosophy for Rehabilitation in the 20th Century,* four critical areas of rehabilitation service delivery are considered: systems (agencies, facilities and companies); professionals (counselors, surpervisors, managers and administrators); families; and clients. As he states, "The true value of rehabilitation services, even in an era of accountability, is not vested in the number of 'closures' but in its impact on the quality of life and on the happiness in life of each individual client served."

Researchers must develop better communication skills with their informants when research with people with severe retardation takes place. Sari Knopp Biklen and Charles Moseley discuss the modifications needed in qualitative research methodology for interviewing people with severe retardation. They offer excellent guidelines and suggestions for new approaches to this type of research in their article *"Are you Retarded?" "No, I'm Catholic": Qualitative Methods in the Study of People with Severe Handicaps.*

The nursing professionals and others who work closely with adolescents who have acquired a disability will benefit from the article, *Developmental Competence in Adolescents with an Acquired Disability* by Kathleen J. Sawin, and June Marshall. The challenge to promote self-esteem and feelings of competence in this vulnerable group is an important aspect in this area of concern. As the authors suggest, nurses who work with adolescents and their families "have regular opportunities to affect developmental outcomes" and the research indicates that "interventions aimed at increasing adolescents' skills in decision making are crucial to the achievement of competence."

Eli Isakov, an eminent rehabilitationist with the Loewenstein Hospital Rehabilitation Center in Tel-Aviv, Israel, wrote the article *Giving Hope to Severely Disabled People*. The newest computer technology being used for people with severe spinal cord injury is described in technical detail and provides hope for future advances and new developments for persons with paraplegia.

Elaine Westerlund explores the challenges of counseling people with deafness *and* incest histories in the article, *Thinking About Incest, Deafness, and Counseling*. No matter how horrible the experiences have been, the author is moved by "the incredible capacity of children to persevere, and even triumph, in the face of injustice and cruelty."

As well, Patricia M. Sullivan and John M. Scanlan discuss the development of new therapeutic intervention techniques with sexually abused children with disabilities in the article, *Psychotherapy with Handicapped Sexually Abused Children*. Included in the article are thirteen goals for psychotherapeutic treatment plans and nine therapeutic techniques used in working with this group of children. The authors acknowledge that professionals in this field are "pilgrims in the evolution of psychotherapy for handicapped sexual abuse victims" and that "therapists need to be both scientists and healers" if they are to help children who have endured this abuse to lead productive lives.

As twentieth century demographics demonstrate, we are all living longer than ever before. Consequently, we must deal with the issues of disability and aging. Nancy Crewe, *Ageing and Severe Physical Disability: Patterns of Change and Implications for Services,* explores the challenges that are presented to service providers as people with severe disabilities such as spinal cord injury or polio live to an advanced age. As she states, "As professionals, we are challenged to recognize, respect, and capitalize on the expertise of these survivors" and that there is much to be learned by the professionals by "see[ing] things from the survivor's point of view." In addition, authors Cheryl Cott and Seanne Wilkins explore the differing experiences of aging of "those who are disabled and become old" and "those who are old and become disabled". The need for professionals who work with this population to examine the many concerns that deal with aging and disability is apparent and commands that adequate knowledge and expertise be in place for the near future.

Mental illness is a very critical area of disability that is currently being recognized as deserving of attention from health care professionals and social planners alike in the article, *Depression as a Mental Illness*. Ellen Frank and David Kupfer examine the area of clinical depression as a disabling illness and provide suggestions for mental health practitioners, consumers, and family members when dealing with this often misunderstood, but often crippling condition. Treatment programs are discussed in terms of phases, interventions, maintenance, and failures. A great deal of stigma still exists for the person who has experienced any form of mental illness. Unfortunately, many people do not recognize that mental illness is not selective: that it is, in fact, a condition which can strike anyone.

David Coulter presents an interesting discussion on the prevention of mental retardation through a "paradigm shift in how mental retardation is conceptualized and in how services are provided." New approaches to prevention will include greater attention to environmental variables which will impact the service delivery community and which will "realize a comprehensive, coordinated, and integrated strategy that reflects the ecology of prevention and will improve the lives of people at risk for mental retardation."

With so many areas to examine in the prevention, cure, or rehabilitation of the disabled community, the challenges are never-ending. However, it is rewarding and exciting to discover that many of these challenges are being met and that education and research in all areas of disability is forward moving, positive and enlightening--not only to people with disabilities, but to society in general. As work in the field continues and expands, we can look forward to a new philosophy of meaningful integration, acceptance, and empowerment in the twenty-first century for people with disabilities.

# Empowerment in Rehabilitation: An Empowerment Philosophy for Rehabilitation in the 20thCentury

## William G. Emener

**Abstract** ~ *Following discussion of pertinent, a priori philosophical tenets of the field of rehabilitation, relevant assumptions underlying an empowerment approach to rehabilitation service delivery are presented and discussed. External and internal considerations and illustrations of empowerment are offered within four critical areas of rehabilitation service delivery: (a) rehabilitation systems (e.g., agencies, facilities and companies); (b) rehabilitation professionals (e.g., rehabilitation counselors, supervisors, managers and administrators); (c) families (of individuals with disabilities); and (d) rehabilitation clients. Conclusions and recommendations are designed to facilitate a self-empowerment approach to rehabilitation service delivery.*

The field of rehabilitation, its systems, agencies, facilities, companies, and especially its rehabilitation professionals, individually and collectively share major responsibilities in responding to the needs of the estimated 34 million individuals with disabilities in the United States. For purposes of addressing the primary phenomena of this paper, *rehabilitation* is defined as "a process of helping handicapped individuals move from positions of dependency in their community toward positions of independency in a community of their choice" (Emener, Patrick & Hollingsworth, 1984, p. 6). Furthermore, the following considerations of "empowerment" presume some of rehabilitation's basic, a priori, philosophical assumptions such as those articulated by Dowd and Emener (1978).

*First, the profession has consistently held the belief that each individual is of great worth and dignity. Second, rehabilitation professionals have maintained that every person should have equal opportunity to maximize his or her potential and is deserving of societal help in attempting to do so. Third, the rehabilitation profession assumes that* people by and large strive to grow and change in positive directions, reflecting both traditional American optimism and the belief in human perfectibility characteristic of the Age of Enlightenment. *Fourth, the rehabilitation profession assumes that individuals should be free to make their own decisions about the management of their lives* (p.35).

Thus, pertinent empowerment issues such as locus of control (Lefcourt, 1976), especially in terms of the roles and functions of rehabilitation professionals (Emener & Cottone, 1989), are critically contingent upon rehabilitation's a priori philosophical tenets. For example, Condeluci (1989) poignantly offered that "the concept of community integration and the empowerment model have their roots in social vaporization, right to choose and risk, individualization and consumer control" (p.16). There are, however, other critical aspects of rehabilitation theory and philosophy which also are germane to considerations of empowerment.

There are numerous divergent positions regarding the interface between what people "need" versus what people "want". For example, the author of this paper frequently has felt that what some people need is to learn that they cannot always have what they want. What does "independence" mean for an individual with a severe disability - especially if considerations are given to the vicissitudes of economic independence, functional independence, social independence and psychological independence. Similar considerations also are pertinent to the concept of "freedom". Perhaps independence is sine qua non to freedom. Nonetheless, if rehabilitation professionals are dedicated to issues of individual independence and freedom on behalf of individuals with disabilities, then it indeed would appear fitting to assure that "empowerment" is a critical construct and guiding operational value within rehabilitation's systems, agencies, facilities, companies and professional service delivery personnel.

## EMPOWERMENT

The process of empowering an individual or a system, means "to give power or authority to; to authorize; as, the president is empowered to veto legislation" (*Webster, 1978, p.595*). Thus the rehabilitation professional committed to an empowerment approach to rehabilitation service delivery should facilitate and maximize opportunities for individuals with disabilities to have control and authority over their own lives. This approach involves modifications and controls both internal and external to the individual. For example, as an individual with a severe disability it is important for me to be internally empowered - I should be helped to empower myself so that I see myself as being powerful, and in a position of authority, over my own life. To a great extent, empowerment is a mind-set. Likewise, from an external point of view, the laws, rules and regulations governing aspects of my life also should be designed to accommodate my self-empowerment (Hahn, 1982, 1985). If I want to fly to another city, for example, the aviation laws should assure that I can board an airplane. Importantly, this model promotes rehabilitation professionals' activities that attend to me as an individual as well as to the environment in which I live and work. This model also surfaces the importance of modeling.

If it is critical for individuals with disabilities to be empowered, then it would be fittingly consistent for rehabilitation systems, agencies, facilities, companies, and rehabilitation professionals to likewise be empowered. It should behoove rehabilitation professionals to practice in their own lives those life-style considerations which they attempt to promote within, and on behalf of, their clients.

### Empowerment: Internal and External Considerations

There are four areas of rehabilitation service delivery within which empowerment is critical:  (a) rehabilitation systems (e.g., agencies, facilities and companies); (b) rehabilitation professionals (e.g., rehabilitation counselors, supervisors, managers and administrators); (c) families (of individuals with disabilities); and (d) rehabilitation clients. Important internal and

Figure l. Four Critical Factors (Systems, Professionals, Families, and Clients) and to Areas of Empowerment (External and Internal) Critical to Rehabilitation Service Delivery

### AREAS OF LOCUS OF CONTROL

| KEY FACTORS | |
|---|---|
| SYSTEMS:<br><br>Laws<br>Negotiations<br>External Systems Management<br>Image Control and Marketing<br>Efficiency and Effectiveness | Organizational Philosophy<br>Policies and Procedures<br>Competent Staff<br>Leadership Style |
| PROFESSIONALS:<br><br>Competency<br>Efficiency and Effectiveness<br>Professional Sanctions<br>Negotiations<br>Image Control and Marketing | Competency<br>Knowledge and Skills<br>Professional Self-Concept<br>Collegiality<br>Networking |
| FAMILIES:<br><br>Economic Security<br>Family Management Functions<br>Effectiveness | Communications<br>Individual Competency<br>Individual Input |
| CLIENTS:<br><br>Economic Security<br>Effective Living<br>Life-style Management | Individual Competency<br>Healthy Self-Concept<br>Meaningful relationships<br>Networking |

external considerations of empowerment pertinent to these four areas of rehabilitation service delivery are displayed in Figure 1.

The following discussion highlights and offers illustrative examples of critical internal and external empowerment considerations within each of these four areas.

## Systems

*External.* It is important to remember that as the world and society continues to change, the field of rehabilitation and the rehabilitation systems within it must continuously and proactively change (Emener, Luck & Smits, 1981; Emener & Stephens, 1982; Hahn, 1986). It is critical for proposed and enacted public laws and policies to empower systems so that they can have the power and control they need to establish and implement negotiations with other systems in ways that facilitate effective and efficient services to individuals with disabilities. Moreover, rehabilitation systems should manage their relationships with other systems, control and market others' perceptions of them, and thus be one of many human service systems within society that collectively and synergistically attend to the needs of all citizens including those with disabilities. When discussing the importance of independence on behalf of rehabilitation facilities, Van Doren, Smith and Beigel (1986) aptly state, "properly used, marketing helps to sharpen the social service direction so that everybody wins" (p.14). And when social service systems are empowered by, and on behalf of, society, everybody wins.

*Internal.* McDaniel and Jacobs (1981) stated that "an organizational philosophy is a system of beliefs or value statements that serve as a basis for decision making" (p.193). The organizational philosophy of a rehabilitation system, including its policies and procedures, should be written and operationalized so that the system empowers itself for purposes of self-direction, self-improvement and self-governance (consult Sussman, 1982). For example, it is quite understandable that rehabilitation professionals frequently become frustrated when the systems in which they work do not accommodate their need for freedom and autonomous functioning. And it is also interesting to note that in situations like this rehabilitation professionals are often very tempted to blame people for systems problem.

Thus, it is not only important for rehabilitation systems to be empowered as systems, but to be designed, managed and therefore postured to facilitate empowerment on behalf of the professionals working within them as well. Moreover, it is critical for rehabilitation systems to recruit, retain and manage competent professional staff. Lorenz, Larson and Schumacher (1981) suggested that "personnel management in rehabilitation in the future will be a complex, decentralized task, and will require technically competent personnel specialists with well-developed leadership skills at the helm" (p.367). Leadership in these domains is critical (Bordieri, Reagle & Coker, 1988; Emener & Stephens, 1982; Galvin & Roessler, 1986; Latta, 1987). As Frayne (1989) recently and accurately stated "As employees' demands for flexibility, autonomy and challenge increase, managers are struggling to find an approach that accommodates both the employees' need for freedom and the organization's need for control. Self-management may be one solution" (p.46), and "Perhaps the time has come to implement an approach to management that includes training people to manage themselves more effectively"(p.50).

## Professionals

*External.* Rehabilitation professionals, in order to be assured of having external empowerment (viz., to enjoy the luxuries of having social, professional, legislative and regulatory empowerment), must be competent (Emener & Cottone, 1989; Emener, Patrick & Hollingsworth, 1984). Demonstrating high level skills and efficient and effective service delivery are tantamount to receiving professional sanctioning, negotiating desired opportunities with other systems and professionals, and establishing and maintaining a desired public image. The author of this manuscript often has suggested that when the Rehabilitation Act of 1973 legislatively mandated the utilization of an Individualized Written Rehabilitation Plan IWRP) with all clients served through the state-federal vocational rehabilitation program, the professional autonomy of the rehabilitation counselor was infringed upon. In effect, this *un*empowering aspect of the law told rehabilitation counselors how to serve their clients (consult Emener & Andrews, 1977). "Who do I serve?" "How do I serve?", and "When do I terminate services?" are three questions which are critical to the professionalism of the rehabilitation counselor. It is also suggested that Congress's perceived need to enact this aspect of the legislation, was a societal indictment of the quality of the clinical case management component of rehabilitation service delivery. It is somewhat ironic that this legislated mandate (viz., the required utilization of the (IWRP), which was designed to empower rehabilitation clients, when implemented systematically, had a disempowering effect on rehabilitation counselors. Nevertheless, it is critical for professionals to assure that they are not externally impeded from having self-management and self-regulatory controls, and that they have the external empowerment necessary to advance and enhance their professionalism.

*Internal.*  It is very important for rehabilitation professionals to be internally empowered (Pinkard & Gross, 1984). For example, Majumder, MacDonald and Greever (1977) reported that rehabilitation counselors who have a more internal orientation tend to have more positive attitudes toward the economically poor, higher levels of job satisfaction, better morale, higher performance ratings, and more positive attitudes toward supervision. In addition to having high level skills and abilities, rehabilitation professionals should also embrace a philosophy of helping commensurate with the philosophy of client-empowerment. Ruffin (1984), for example, offered that "the goals of therapy should not be to help the individual find meaning. Rather, it should be to help individuals accept the responsibility to face meaninglessness, and through their creativity to bring order out of chaos" (p.42). The professional's professional self-concept and professional identity are also critical (Kyril, 1988). For example, as a rehabilitation counselor in the state of Florida, I could ask myself: "Am I an employee of the State of Florida who happens to be a rehabilitation counselor, or am I a professional rehabilitation counselor who happens to be working for the State of Florida?" Responses

to questions such as these can provide rehabilitation professionals with helpful insights into their concepts of themselves as professionals, their sense of collegiality, corresponding networking critical to their career and professional endeavors, and the extent to which they, as professionals, are self-empowered.

### Families

*External.*  The critical role(s) of the family in a disabled individual's rehabilitation, have been clearly documented (e.g., Cook & Ferritor, 1985; Cottone, Handelsman & Walters, 1986; Dew, Phillips & Reiss, 1989; Marlatt, 1988; Power & Dell Orto, 1986). For example, in order for families of individuals with disabilities to maximize their potentials for externally oriented empowerment, it is suggested that rehabilitation counselors work with families and assist them in establishing and maintaining economic security. Roessler (1987) suggested that "vocational rehabilitation counselors must be informed about national economic projections, shifts in their local economies, vocational preparation opportunities, and entry requirements of new employment areas" (p.90). Comparisons of rehabilitation counselors' roles and functions indicate an increase in attending to, and working with, the families of individuals with disabilities (Emener & Rubin, 1980; Pubin, Matkin, Ashley, Beardsley, May, Onstott & Puckett, 1984). It would appear very appropriate and helpful for rehabilitation counselors to occasionally ask themselves, "Is it possible that one of my client's family members could be more helpful to my client that I could be? And if this is the case, how can I facilitate the family member's providing such helpful assistance?" The importance of assisting families in managing themselves and maximizing their functional effectiveness cannot be underscored enough (Herbert, 1989). From an external empowerment perspective, it is imperative for the family to be empowered to attend to itself and its family members.

*Internal.*  Families should be encouraged and assisted to empower themselves to prevent and ameliorate difficulties and issues pertinent to individual family members as well as to the family as a whole. For example, the author of this manuscript once was working with a teenager who had recently had a severe and permanent loss of vision as a result of an automobile accident. When talking with his family during a home visit, the young man's nine-year-old sister began crying and asked, "Will Jerry still be able to go swimming with all of us next summer?" It would be understandably tempting for a rehabilitation counselor to say something in a situation like this one; however, it was more important that Jerry turned to his sister and said, "Yes, I will, and you can help me." A family's potentials for internal empowerment are critically related to the individual family members' abilities in communication with each other (Clifford, 1987). Herbert (1989), for example, recently stated that "while rehabilitation counselors are not trained as family therapists, counselors should be able to assess family dysfunction as it relates to rehabilitation adjustment issues and be able to make referrals to qualified personnel" (p.49). The individual competence and assistance of family members should be reinforced and input on behalf of family members should be encouraged. Minimally, "practitioners must become involved intimately enough with the family to know about transitions and to determine the impact on the disabled member's needs" (*Rehab Brief., 1984*, p.4.). With family participation, "the vocational rehabilitation counselor can develop a plan that will help the family achieve a healthy balance between meeting the requirements of the disability and the needs of the family, which in turn increases the likelihood of a successful vocational rehabilitation outcome for the client" (Dew, et al., 1989, p.43). When a rehabilitation counselor thinks, for example, "What can I do with my client if her family is going to continue to sabotage what I am accomplishing with her?", it is suggested that the question be reframed to, "What can I do to help her family to be more helpful to my client?".

**Clients**

*External.* External empowerment considerations must include economic security (Roessler, 1987) and social networking phenomena critical to being able to govern one's own life. In the journey of life, happiness is not a station we arrive at; rather, it is a manner of traveling - it is a by-product of effective living. In the teaching of independent living skills to individuals with disabilities, it is important to include attending to their life-style management and self-management skills (Iceman & Dunlap, 1984). In his evaluation study of the teaching of self-management skills to individuals with disabilities, Farley (1987) reported that "Rehabilitation clients who completed the social skills class independent of the self-management training made significantly less gain from class assessment to the 3-month follow-up as compared to rehabilitation clients who completed the social skills class plus self-management training" (p.50). In effect, it is important to teach individuals with disabilities how to manage their external environments so that their potentials for self-empowerment are not impeded or negatively affected.

*Internal.* It is critical that individuals with disabilities empower themselves (Bruyere, 1985; Condeluci, 1989). It is important for them to conceptualize and operationalize self-empowerment from an internal perspective. Lefcourt (1976), in summarizing research on locus of control phenomena, stated that "it is fairly safe to conclude that the perception of control has some profound effects upon the manner in which organisms come to grips with adversity". (p.144). Having a healthy self-concept, meaningful interpersonal relationships, and supportive social networks, combined with a high level of self-esteem and self-management (Kazdin, 1974), indeed places an individual in a good position to empower himself or herself to be in charge of his or her life. Rehabilitation professionals must remember that they frequently are in excellent positions to initiate and reinforce internalized empowerment on behalf of their clients. For example, when an individual with a disability says to a rehabilitation counselor, "I would appreciate your telling my boss that I need that ramp complete as soon as possible," one alternative empowering response may be, "Yes, I could do that, but I would prefer that since you have been taking more and more responsibility for your life and you have the ability to express your needs and wants to other people, that we discuss how you would tell him yourself."

## Empowerment is a Mind Set

As stated earlier, empowerment is a mind set. Congress and executive boards can legislate and mandate rehabilitation agencies, companies and facilities so that they are technically empowered, but unless they consider themselves as being empowered, they are not empowered. Agencies and facilities can tell the professionals working within them that they are empowered, but unless they think of themselves as being empowered, they are not empowered. Families and clients can be told that they are empowered, but unless they feel empowered, they are not empowered. When rehabilitation agencies, companies and facilities and the rehabilitation professionals working within them consider themselves, think of themselves and feel empowered, then they truly are in positions of facilitating and modeling self-empowerment within and on behalf of individuals with disabilities and their families.

## Recommendations and Concluding Comments

An interesting "Catch 22" can emerge when considering issues pertinent to internal empowerment and external empowerment. For example, it could be argued that internal empowerment is a prerequisite for facilitating external empowerment; likewise, it could be argued that external empowerment is a prerequisite for internal empowerment. Rather than to debate an understandable "the chicken or the egg" question, it would appear more realistic and functional to suggest that systems, professionals, families and individual clients must attend to both their external empowerment and their internal empowerment issues simultaneously and continually. The benefits of such, indeed, are worth the effort. For example, William Holahan (1988) shared his transitional learning and movement toward self-empowerment as he progressed from being an intern to being a senior staff member in a counseling center:

In the end, I have also become more self-nurturant, and this is the finest result of my quest to understand the transition experience. Because I function with considerable autonomy, I can no longer rely solely on nurturance from others. I have begun to be self-encouraging and self-reinforcing, skills that I am sure I shall need as I continue to develop and assume professional positions with less supervision and more autonomy (p.120).

Myrya Kyril (1988) reported a similar experience and concluded that "I had come into my own" and had a renewed appreciation for the "phenomenological experience of its meaning in the larger context of my professional development" (p.121).

Living and modeling an internally empowered lifestyle is critical to rehabilitation service delivery. Bruyere (1985), for example, suggested that "as counselors, we should explore with clients meaning in life for them, so we are better able to set with clients both vocational and larger life goals consistent with this meaning. To do so better assures the ultimate value of rehabilitation services in the life of a given client" (p.40). The true value of rehabilitation services, even in an era of accountability, is not vested in the number of "closures" but in its impact on the quality of life and on the happiness in life of each individual client served.

Rehabilitation systems, professionals, clients' families and clients themselves need to be encouraged and assisted in the process of enhancing and managing their externally oriented empowerment considerations. Likewise, they need to attend to the internal, self-empowerment aspects of their lives. While addressing the disability of cerebral palsy, Condeluci (1989) recently offered a poignant observation and recommendation relevant to the broader field of rehabilitation: "...we must bridge the gap from the medical model to an empowerment model. We are learning that when people with cerebral palsy are given the opportunity to be in control of their situation, good things happen. People want to belong and be a part of their community. An empowerment approach can make this happen" (p.16). If autonomy, freedom and independence are the by-products of effective living and the heart of happiness in life, then empowerment is the backbone of rehabilitation service delivery. It is imperative for rehabilitation professionals to maximize every opportunity they have to facilitate each client's self-empowerment. Individuals with disabilities can grow toward independence when they can experientially discover their key to freedom, which was so beautifully expressed by Dr. Shirley Kashoff:

*I used to think that Freedom*
*Was what someone gave to me*
*Until I found that I was bound*
*By nameless heavy chains*
*I could not see.*

*I used to think that Freedom*
*Was what someone gave to me*
*Until I learned that what I'd earned*
*Was simply my permission*
*To use that very freedom*
*That no one but myself*
*Could give me.*

*Those locks and bonds and prisons*
*Are the things we've learned to hate*
*Yet those most despised constructions*
*Are identically the ones*
*We have masterfully come to create*

*I spent my lifetime waiting*
*For someone to set me free*
*I could not grow*
*I didn't know*
*That in my hands I held*
*The key.*

---(Shostrom, 1972, pp. 163-164)

And in the broader scheme of rehabilitation in America, this is what it is all about!

\*\*\*\*\*\*\*\*

**Acknowledgments:** For their suggestions, recommendations and critical review of an earlier draft of this manuscript, sincerest appreciation is extended to five members of an advanced graduate Field Research Seminar in the Department of Rehabilitation Counseling at the University of South Florida: Margaret A. Darrow, David E. Layman, Marilyn N. McClain, A. Miranda Ray, and Wendy L. Struchen.

This manuscript is based on a symposium proceedings paper, "Empowerment: The Backbone of Rehabilitation Service Delivery", presented by the author at the National Rehabilitation Counseling Association's Seventh Annual Professional Development Symposium, in Boston, Massachusetts, on February 10, 1990. Appreciation is extended to Dr. Tennyson J. Wright, Coordinator of the Symposium and Editor of the Symposium's *Proceedings*, for his review of this manuscript and for granting permission to submit it to the *Journal* for consideration for publication.

For their valuable assistance in modifying and expanding this manuscript from the Symposium *Proceedings* paper, a hearty "Thank you" is respectfully forwarded to Dr. Bobbie J. Atkins, Professor of Rehabilitation Counseling at San Diego State University and to Margaret A. Darrow, a doctoral student in the Department of Special Education at the University of South Florida.

\*\*\*\*\*\*

## REFERENCES

**Bordieri, J.E.,** Reagle, D.Y., Coker, C.C. (1988). Job Satisfaction and leadership style of rehabilitation facility personnel. *Rehabilitation Counseling Bulletin, 32* (2, 149-160.

**Bruyere, S.M.** (1985). An existentialist approach to rehabilitation counseling. *Journal of Applied Rehabilitation Counseling, 16* (4), 36-40.

**Clifford, T.** (1987). Assertiveness training for parents. J*ournal of Counseling and Development, 65* (10), 552-554.

**Condeluci, A.** (1989). Empowering people with cerebral palsy. *Journal of Rehabilitation, 55* (2), 15-16.

**Cook, D.,** & Ferritor, D. (1985). The family: A potential resource in the provision of rehabilitation services. *Journal of Applied Rehabilitation Counseling, 16* (2), 52-53.

**Cottone, R.R.,** Handelsman, M.M. & Walters, N. (1986). Understanding the influence of family systems on the rehabilitation process. *Journal of Applied Rehabilitation Counseling, 17* (2), 37-40.

**Dew, D.W.,** Phillips, B., & Reiss, D. (1989. Assessment and early planning with the family in vocational rehabilitation. *Journal of Rehabilitation, 55* (1), 41-44.

**Dowd, E. T. ,** & Emener, W.G. (1978). Lifeboat counseling: The issues of survival decisions. *Journal of Rehabilitation, 9* (2), 34-36.

**Emener, W. G.** & Andrews, W., (1977). The individualized written rehabilitation program: Perceptions from the field. *Journal of Applied Rehabilitation Counseling, 7* (4), 215-222.

**Emener, W. G.** & Cottone, R.R. (1989). *Pro*fessionalization, *de*professionalization and *re*professionalization of rehabilitation counseling according to criteria of professions. *Journal of Counseling and Development, 67* (10), 576-581.

**Emener, W. G.,** Luck, R.S., & S. J. Smits, (Eds.) (1981). *Rehabilitation administration and supervision.* Baltimore, MD: University Park Press.

**Emener, W. G.** & Rubin, S.E. (1980). Rehabilitation counselor roles and functions and sources of role strain. *Journal of Applied Rehabilitation Counseling, 11 (2)*, 57-69

**Emener, W.G.,** & Stephens, J. (1982). Improving quality of working life in a changing rehabilitation environment. *Journal of Rehabilitation Administration, 6,* 114-124.

**Farley, R.C.** (1987). Self-management training and the maintenance of selected career enhancing social skills: A pilot study. *Journal of Rehabilitation, 53,* (2), 48-51.

**Frayne, C.A.** (1989). Improving employee performance through self-management training. *Business Quarterly, 54* (1), 46-50.

**Galvin, D.,** & Roessler, R.T. (1986). Employee support services: A sound investment. *Personnel, 63,* 54-58.

**Hahn, H.** (1982). Disability and rehabilitation policy: Is paternalistic neglect really benign. *Public Administration Review, 73,* 385-389.

**Hahn, H.** (1985). Changing perceptions of disability and the future of rehabilitation. In L.G.Perlman and G.F.Austin (Eds.), *Social influences in rehabilitation planning: A blueprint for the 21st century* (pp.53-64), Alexandria, VA:National Rehabilitation Association.

**Hahn, H.** (1986). Public support for rehabilitation programs: The analysis of U.S. disability policy. *Disability, Handicap and Society, 1 (2),* 121-137.

**Hebert, J.T.** (1989). Assessing the need for family therapy: A primer for rehabilitation counselors. *Journal of Rehabilitation, 55* (1), 45-51.

**Holahan, W.** (1988).From intern to senior staff: Movement toward self-nurturance. *Journal of Counseling and Development ,67* (2), 120d.

**Iceman, D.J.,** & Dunlap, W.R. (1984). Independent living skills training: A survey of current practices. *Journal of Rehabilitation, 50* (4), 53-56.

**Krazdin, A.E.,** (1974). Self-monitoring and behavior change. In M.J.Mahoney & C.E. Thoreson (Eds.), *Self-control: Power to the person* (pp.221-246). Monterey, CA: Brooks/Cole.

**Kyril, M.B.** (1988). Toward the emergence of professional identity. *Journal of Counseling and Development, 67* (2), 121.

**Latta, J.** (1987). Excellence in rehabilitation: The leadership connection. *Journal of Rehabilitation Administration, 11,* 52-59.

**Lefcourt, H.M.** (1976). *Locus of control: Current trends in theory and research.* Hillsdale, NJ.: Erlbaum.

**Lorenz, J.R.,** Larson, L., & Schumacher, B. (1981). Prologue to the future. In W.G.Emener, R.S.Luck, & S.J.Smits (Eds.) *Rehabilitation administration and supervision* (pp.355-370). Baltimore, MD: University Park Press.

**Majunder, R.K.,** MacDonald, A.P., & Greever, K.B. (1977). A study of rehabilitation counselors: Locus of control and attitudes toward the poor. *Journal of Counseling Psychology, 24,* 137-141.

**Marlatt, J.** (1988). The role of the family in rehabilitation. *Journal of Rehabilitation, 54* (1), 7-8, 77.

**McDaniel, R.H.** & Jacobs, M.F. (1981). Administration of rehabilitation services in a rehabilitation facility. In W.G.Emener, R.S.Luck & S.J.Smits (Eds.), *Rehabilitation administration and supervision* (187-204). Baltimore, MD: University Park Press.

**Pinkard, C.M.** & Gross, P. (1984). Modification of locus of control among rehabilitation counseling graduate students. *Rehabilitation Counseling Bulletin, 28* (1), 39-45.

**Power, P.W.,** & Dell Orto, A.E., (1986). Families, illness and disability: The roles of the rehabilitation counselor. *Journal of Applied Rehabilitation Counseling, 17* (2), 41-44.

*Rehab Brief.* (1984). Disability and families: A family system approach. Washington, DC: National Institute of Handicapped Research.

**Roessler, R.T.** (1987). Work, disability, and the future: Promoting employment for people with disabilities. *Journal of Counseling and Development, 66* (4), 188-190.

**Rubin, S.E.,** Matkin, R.E., Ashley, J., Beardsley, M.M., May, V.R., Onstott, & Puckett. F.D. (1984). Roles and functions of certified rehabilitation counselors. *Rehabilitation Counseling Bulletin, 27,* 199-224.

**Ruffin, J.E.** (1984). The anxiety of meaninglessness. *Journal of Counseling and Development, 63* (1), 40-42.

**Shostrom, E.** (1972). *Freedom to be.* New York: Bantam Books.

**Sussman, M.** (1982). VR perspectives for policy analysis and change. In J. Rubin & V. LaPorte (Eds.), *Alternatives in rehabilitating the* *handicapped* (pp.151-188). New York: Human Sciences Press.

**Van Doren, D.C.** , Smith, L.W. & Beigel, D. (1986). Helping the rehabilitation facility live a more independent life through marketing. *Journal of Rehabilitation, 52* (4), 11-15.

**Webster's** *new twentieth century dictionary of the English language: Unabridged. (Second Edition). (1978). William Collins-World Publishing Company.*

********

**About the Author:  William G. Emener** is with the Department of Rehabilitation Counseling, University of South Florida, Tampa, Florida 33620-8100

**Source:**  Reprinted with permission from *Journal of Rehabilitation,* Vol. 57, No. 2, pp. 29-34, 1991. Published by National Rehabilitation Association, Reston Virginia.

# "Are you Retarded?" "No, I'm Catholic": Qualitative Methods in the Study of People with Severe Handicaps

Sari Knopp Biklen
Charles R. Moseley

**Abstract** ~ *Qualitative research methods generally depend heavily on good communication between researcher and informant. When qualitative methodologists study informants with severe retardation whose use of language may be limited, what do they do?*

*If the researchers plan to study the world of the informant, then traditional participant observation guidelines are useful. But when the researcher wants to interview the informant, some modifications need to be made. The authors suggest several guidelines to follow:*

**Descriptors:** interviewing, participant observation, qualitative research.

As outsiders, people who have not been diagnosed as severely mentally retarded may assume that the presence of this disability is the most salient feature of a person's identity. People with severe retardation may not view themselves in that way, preferring to identify with members of particular religious groups, as certain kinds of workers, employees of particular companies, or as fans of particular sports teams. Asked directly, in other words, individual people with severe retardation have preferences about how to present themselves to others. As outsiders, researchers cannot take for granted the views or positions of insiders unless we study these perspectives directly.

Qualitative research methods study perspectives. They can document the patterns of people's lives and reveal how research subjects construct meaning around these patterns. Prominent qualitative methods such as participant observation, in-depth interviewing, and life history also allow researchers to study the construction of meanings. In particular, qualitative methods are used most frequently to examine this process of making meaning, or the perspectives of various categories of people

such as teachers (Grant, 1988; McPherson, 1972; Spencer, 1986,) students (Cusik, 1973; Everhart, 1983), parents involved in busing (Cottle, 1976), medical students (Becker, Geer, Hughes, & Strauss, 1961; Bosk, 1979), marijuana users (Becker, 1963), corporate workers (Kanter, 1977) and people with mental retardation who live in the community (Bogdan & Taylor, 1982; Edgerton, 1967).

A rich tradition of discussing methodological considerations has developed in education and in other fields. In this article we examine the contributions of qualitative methods to the study of a particular category of people, those with severe disabilities. What specific issues arise for the researcher studying people with severe handicaps? Are there certain types of research questions that seem particularly suited to the use of qualitative methodologies? In addition, do qualitative methods have to be adapted in any way for the study of people with severe disabilities? Here we offer some guidelines for the application of qualitative research methods to such a study. We will first briefly share our interpretation of the qualitative approach and will then focus upon some strategies for adapting the qualitative approach in the field as we have learned about them through fieldwork.

## The Qualitative Approach

By qualitative research methods we mean strategies such as participant observation (McCall & Simmons, 1969; Spradley, 1980), ethnography, the study of a group's culture through first-person immersion in that culture and hence the presentation of one culture through the lens of another (Geertz, 1973; Hammersley & Atkinson, 1983; Metz, 1983; Wolcott, 1975), interviewing and life histories, which bring the researcher into the places where people actually live their lives (Bogdan & Biklen, 1982). The phenomenological basis of the qualitative approach means that the researcher studies how informants make meaning out of their situations. Hence, the informants' own interpretations of their lives assume a prominent place. The qualitative researcher describes what the research subjects (informants) do and the meaning they make of it (Biklen & Bogdan, 1986). To do this, researchers typically case themselves in the role of students to let informants teach them about their lives.

Basic to the qualitative approach is the belief that people act on the basis of interpretations that they make about the world; the role of the researcher is to discover the nature of these interpretations and how they are contextually situated (see, for example, Berger & Luckmann, 1967; Blumer, 1969). The purpose of the research is not to prove a particular hypothesis or test for the effect of a set of variables, but rather to come to understand the experience from the perspective of the individual involved. Language, whether in oral or written form, is central to most qualitative research because of the emphasis on symbolic understanding and communication. Qualitative data take the form of narrative rather than numbers.

The emphasis placed on language by qualitative traditions such as in-depth interviewing raises questions about how these methods might have to be adapted to study people with severe disabilities. But qualitative methodologists have studied talkative and nontalkative people and groups and have found ways to communicate with them. When anthropologists traveled to distant lands to study indigenous peoples, it often took a long time to learn a language with which to communicate. Hence, qualitative methods are labor-intensive, because they demand that the researcher spend substantial time in the environment to be studied in order to gain informants' trust and to understand the individuals' lives.

## Background

Qualitative researchers have studied people with both physical and mental disabilities (see, for example, Biklen & Bogdan, 1978; Bogdan & Taylor, 1976, 1982; Brightman, 1984; Edgerton, 1967, 1984; Edgerton & Bercovici, 1976; Edgerton, Bollinger, & Herr, 1984; Ferguson, 1987; Foster, 1987; Goode, 1979, 1984)[1] They have also examined social issues generated by civil rights concerns for people with disabilities including integration in public schools (Biklen, 1985; Sutton, 1988), deinstitutionalization (Rothman & Rothman, 1984), and group homes (Biklen & Bogdan, 1978). Scholars also have discussed the uses of qualitative methods for investigating general research problems in special education (Stainback & Stainback, 1984), and observing people with mental retardation in particular (Edgerton & Langness, 1978).

Researchers tend to take two approaches to the study of people with severe disabilities. These approaches can be illustrated by examining two studies. When Bogdan and Taylor (1976, 1982) interviewed two people who had been labeled mentally retarded, they described the meaning that these individuals made out of their lives and particularly out of the label of retardation. In this case, they were able to rely on words as the language of interchange.

Biklen and Bogdan (1978) studied what happened when people with severe retardation were taken out of an institution where they had exhibited violent and aggressive behavior and were placed in a group home. These informants were nonverbal, and rather than studying their perspectives directly, the researchers studied their worlds, relying on the verbal interpretations of others closely connected to them and on their own observations.

These studies differ in two important ways. The interview study totally depends on language, while the participant observation research does not depend so heavily on the informant's own description of his or her situation. The first, however, studies two people labeled mentally retarded as they

[1] Here we use the term "severe intellectual disabilities" to refer to those "who function intellectually within approximately the lowest 1% of a naturally distributed general population" (Albright, Brown, VanDeventer, & Jorgensen, in press). We also use the term "severe disabilities" to mean those persons who have disabilities and need many support services.

personally construct their worlds. The second depends on the view of significant others in the lives of the informant and less on the particular views of the informants themselves.

Studies that depend primarily on in-depth interviewing of people with severe disabilities approach the world from the perspective of the informant. This kind of research requires articulate research subjects.[2] Studies that depend on participant observation of people with disabilities and the settings where they live as well as on in-depth interviews with people connected to these individuals such as staff in a group home, friends, and caseworkers, do not demand articulate informants. This kind of study examines the world of the informant. Both approaches reveal the qualitative emphasis on gaining an empathic understanding of subjects.

This kind of understanding is central to the qualitative approach. Hence, researchers try to study groups where developing empathy is not impossible. But it is not always an easy task. Perhaps the closest observers of children with severe disabilities, at least those who live at home, are their parents. Even parents, however, have reported difficulties in discovering the perspectives of their children. Helen Featherstone (1980), for example, in describing her son, wrote that "it is almost impossible for us to imagine his world" (p.6). Josh Greenfield (1970) concurred when he described his family's efforts to reach his son, who is labeled autistic: "(we are) constantly trying to pierce his perimeters (p.169). If parents have a hard time learning the perspectives of their children, how can the qualitative researcher manage?

In this article we present some of the problems qualitative researchers have faced and some strategies they have developed to handle these difficulties. Although we discuss interviewing and observation separately, we emphasize that in both cases the researcher wants to learn the perspectives of the informants. These methods are not separate. Moseley (1987), for example, depended heavily on observations even as he interviewed

all of his subjects. As you will see, some circumstances require expansion of the qualitative approach, while others reaffirm its typical practice.

## Deciding What and Where to Study

Design and analysis are closely related (Bogdan & Biklen, 1982; Goetz & LeCompte, 1984). The questions researchers ask, therefore, shape the findings they can report. Hence, disability rights researchers, for example, do not study the question; Does school integration work? Rather, they study; What is the nature of model school integration programs? (Biklen, 1985). Two sorts of questions have led researchers to further the analysis of successful integration of people with severe disabilities into society: questions which look at model programs and questions which examine promising practices. Taylor (1983) studied model school integration programs. he solicited nominations of model school programs from "state and local administrators, parent leaders, and university personnel known for their expertise in the area of the severely handicapped and their commitment to the principle of integration" (p.43). Researchers made telephone calls to check on specific information about the programs before observers conducted 2-day site visits. The research was "oriented toward identifying and documenting integration strategies and practices rather than verifying educational approaches or evaluating programs" (p.43). Research teams also have used similar strategies in the study of promising practices for serving people with disabilities in the community (Biklen, 1987, 1988; Bogdan, 1986, 1987; Ferguson, 1986,; Searl & Wickham-Searl, 1985; Taylor, 1985, 1987a).

Different kinds of relationships, particularly friendships, are another promising area where qualitative researchers are studying people with severe disabilities (Biklen, 1986; Biklen, Corrigan, & Quick, in press; Bogdan, 1987, Bogdan & Taylor, 1987; Evans, 1983). When you study a particular category of people, you study not only those who are members of the group, but individuals with whom labeled people

---

[2] Qualitative researchers have a broad definition of articulate verbal behavior. Fine (1987) has written about issues involved in interviewing children.

regularly interact such as neighbors, friends, and professionals.

It is important when studying any people who have been labeled to remember that individuals feel differently. Qualitative methods are biased toward this view. However, the researcher can distinguish between factions or affiliated peoples. The qualitative researcher who studies special education faculty, for example, can distinguish between those whose perspective reflects disability rights issues and those whose perspective is rooted in a charity ideology.

## Interviewing

Researchers who interview people with severe disabilities find that observation is an important part of the process, especially during initial sessions before the informants get to know the researchers and rapport is developed. Interviewers feel challenged to provide enough structure so that the subjects know what is being asked of them, yet not so much that subjects' answers are proscribed (Spradley, 1979). Like all informants at the early stages of a study, subjects with severe mental retardation may be included to please the interviewer and may frame their answers according to what they think the interviewer wants to hear rather than giving their "own" responses. Although many research subjects respond in a like manner, those who have been closely supervised by the human service system may be very accustomed to responding in a way they think most acceptable to staff (Goode, 1984; Taylor, 1987b).

Interviewers may encounter six general kinds of difficulties. These include misunderstandings of what was said (on the part of both researcher and respondent); problems with open-ended questions; the interview environment; the "same-answer" problem; pleasing the interviewer; and the use of significant others.

**Misunderstandings** ~ Qualitative researchers learn qualitative methods in university classes, where language is generally assumed to be a developed skill available to both parties involved in an interview. Although we may discuss social class differences between interviewer and interviewee and how these

differences might affect the interview, we are less likely to think of problems encountered with informants who have severe mental retardation. Qualitative researchers often develop a mental picture of an interview situation which demands that the researcher use "small talk" to develop rapport with the interviewee. This approach, based on an assumption of mutual understanding and familiarity with typical patterns of communication, may result in continuation of discussions when neither party understands fully what is being discussed. Interviewers' difficulties tend to center on their inability to understand the actual language of the informant, while the interviewee may have a difficult time with the concepts of the interviewer.

In one study of work (Moseley, in press), the interviewer (1) struggled to communicate with Pete, the research subject (P):

1. How are supervisors different than counselors?
P. Oh, I like it.
1. How are they different?
P. Pretty good.
1. Are they the same?
P. Oh yea.
1. They do the same jobs? (P. Yup) Or, do they do different jobs? (P. Yea). What does the supervisor do?
P. Well, they have to clean up the stuff.

The interviewer was finally able to determine how the jobs differed by asking Pete to describe his first supervisor's job and then that of his counselor. Pete was not able to bring the supervisor and counselor together to compare them. One strategy used to overcome these cognitive difficulties, then, is to ask about people, things, and activities separately, rather than asking the respondent to provide a comparison or analysis.

Sometimes respondents may not understand what you are talking about (or vice versa). Interviewers in a project to study long-term relationships between people with disabilities and their advocates, for example, often struggled to learn how respondents described their own histories. The interviewers discovered that informants often confused time sequences and settings (Biklen, 1986) and found it possible to obtain more detailed histories through interviews with advocates.

Some misunderstandings require repetition and honesty to overcome. During one conversation, D. Biklen (1987) repeated his preference several times while developing rapport with Pat, a group home resident.

Pat: Doug, would you like a nice cold coke? Doug, a coke on ice?

Doug: Thanks, but you know, I'd rather have water if you have it.

Pat: Coke, Doug? Want a nice cold coke, Doug? A coke on ice?

Doug: (smiles) No thanks, but I'd love a cold glass of water.

Pat: Water it is, Doug (p.16)

Biklen's honesty heightened their communication and revealed Pat's ability as a flexible and gracious hostess.

Taping interviews with subjects who are severely mentally retarded may help researchers to better understand the informant's pronunciation. Moseley (in press) found it easier to understand language when he listened to the tapes than when he was in the actual interview situation. Taping the interviews also enabled him to replay sections when desired.

**Open-Ended Questions** ~ Most qualitative researchers are trained to ask open-ended questions in order to allow respondents to frame answers from their own perspectives. When interviewing persons with severe mental retardation, however, such questions may become more confusing than clarifying. When the interviewer in the study of work (Moseley, in press) asked questions such as "Tell me about your work" or "What do you think about what you are doing?", he received answers such as "It's okay," "Alright," or sometimes no response at all other than a smile or a stare. We suggest avoiding open-ended questions. Break requests for information into parts and ask separate questions about each. One researcher, for example, broke down the original question

"What did you do before you worked here?" to "When did you start working here?" "Were you going to school or were you in a workshop, or just at home?" (Moseley, in press). This process may elicit richer responses and answers to other questions as well. You can obtain a response to queries involving more complex concepts if you can determine the right form to use.

In order to get past difficult spots and find this form, you can ask the informant questions which can be answered by "yes" or "no" or by giving a short answer. In this way the researcher can develop an understanding of the problem through a series of successive approximations. It is helpful to view this process as temporary rather than routine, however, because there are problems with it as well. Moseley (in press) found that respondents sometimes did not see a relationship among a series of short answer questions, and he felt the lack of continuity. Another danger with short answer questions is that they represent the concerns of the interviewer rather than the interviewee. Moseley, however, did do extensive observations at informants' work sites before interviewing them and asked questions based upon those observations. We suggest using a structured interview approach along with observations.

**The Interview Environment** ~ Effective interviews need to occur in situations where the informant feels comfortable. Qualitative researchers talk about building "rapport" and interviewing people in settings where they feel most natural. This is no less true when interviewing a person labeled severely mentally retarded. Because institutions usually make people more anxious and because people with disabilities may have been negatively evaluated in institutional settings (cf., Goode, 1984), a home-like environment may be more comfortable. In one interview by Moseley, an individual living in a group home expressed great anxiety when she thought she would be interviewed in the group home office and requested that her bedroom be used. In such cases you can ask the informant to tell you about objects in the room, a topic which often elicits more data about the individual's experiences.

**The "Same Answer" Problem** ~ What do respondents mean when they use the same phrase over and over again in response to different questions?   Moseley (1987), for example, found that one respondent frequently repeated "What I like to do is do all my work and get the job done, and that is what I like best."   Perhaps the informant added this statement to many of his answers to reassure the interviewer that he was a good worker, or perhaps just to have something to say. Another informant would respond "Oh I like it" to virtually any question that he did not understand.  Other respondents might not talk at all, but would simply smile and nod.  As an interviewer you can use these repetitions as signals that respondents may not know the answer to your question (but will not say so), that you may not be asking questions that they find important, or that they may not understand the question.

Phrases may also be repeated because the respondent is preoccupied by a particular concern or problem which is unsolved.   In response to virtually any open-ended question, for example, one woman said something like "Oh, I don't want to work at the recycling company, I want to go out.  Do you think they will let me?  I don't think they will."  She repeated this basic statement again and again. In this situation, Moseley (1987) acted more like a counselor than a researcher.   When informants repeatedly mentioned a worry or concern in response to any question, he attempted to reflect the problem back to the individual and would ask "Well, what are you going to do about it?" or "What do you think you could have done in that situation?" Asking questions that encouraged respondents to think of other options seemed to help them concentrate on what they could do and moved the conversation along.

**Pleasing the Interviewer** ~ All interviewers worry about the extent to which the interviewee says that the researcher wants to hear.  When interviewing persons with severe retardation, this typical methodological problem may be heightened, as discussed earlier, by the informant's institutional experiences.  This problem can be especially apparent when the informant is not sure who the researcher is and may mistake him or her for an institutional staff member. Institutionalized people may become so accustomed to telling staff members what they want to hear in order to gain control over their lives that they will not be able to express readily what is on their minds.   Moseley frequently was asked if he were a staff member, and when he replied that he was not, they did not know where to "place" him, so he added that he was from the university, or that he did not work for anyone and was just there to observe.   For some informants this alternative role identity worked to loosen the connection with institution staff.

**Significant Others** ~ One strategy to handle language difficulties and communication problems is to use important people in the lives of informants.  There are both advantages and disadvantages to this approach.   One advantage is clear.   The friend, parent, or advocate frequently has spent considerable time with the subject and has a better understanding of the individual's language and methods of communication.  In addition, these friends or family members often know specific dates or events that the respondents do not know or remember.    In the study of relationships fostered by the Georgia Advocacy Office, for example, there were many instances in which the advocate expanded on answers that the protegé gave or clarified situations where the protegé combined two incidents into one (Biklen, 1986).  In this case, because the relationships were being studied, the oral historians interviewed both parties as part of the method.

This approach has clear drawbacks as well, the most serious being that the friend, advocate, or parent may act, not just as a translator, but as a filter as well.  In fact, it is impossible not to get the perspective of the other person.  To some people, like the George advocates, it is important that the story of the person with disabilities be told and a studied attempt is made to tell a story from the point of view of their friend.  It depends on what stake this significant other has in the story.

In his study of the meaning of work to people with severe mental retardation, Moseley (1987) had such a difficult time understanding one young woman that he needed her mother to help him figure out what the person was saying. Although the mother's translation was helpful, her interpretations were less so; she filtered the informant's perspective through her opinions of what should or should not be discussed, or how the daughter felt. For example, when the interviewer asked the daughter if she thought her employer was giving her enough hours (she was working part time), the mother answered, "No, they are not, are they, sweetie?" Fortunately the daughter seemed to feel no compunction about saying what she felt, frequently stating her own opinions. The mother would help translate if necessary (although as time went on, the better Moseley understood the daughter), but she also interacted with her daughter, offering opinions on her behavior such as "Oh Alice, you know you shouldn't do that either." The daughter would then giggle or say something like, "Mom, I do it myself." An added benefit of relying on the parent was that the interviewer learned something about how the mother and daughter each felt about a particular issue and something of the dynamics of their relationship.

Biklen, who studied relationships between students labeled typical and handicapped in integrated fourth grade classrooms, interviewed the teachers who became co-researchers. The teachers kept a log of student interactions with each other so that researchers could examine how interactions changed over time (Biklen et al., in press).

Nothing is trivial to qualitative researchers, and we can use situations that are not ideal to make the situation itself data. The researchers' need for the help of the informant's mother, for example, produced field notes on the mother-daughter relationship. The context in which researchers collect data must be included as part of field notes.

## Observing

Researchers should seek opportunities to get unfiltered responses; hence, observations play a key role in studying persons with severe disabilities.

Qualitative researchers use participant observation to study subjects in the context of their worlds. Although language is important to the participant observer, it is possible to study a situation from the perspective of the individual with mental retardation who may also be nonverbal. The goal is to discover the meaning that subjects make of their world. In this section we use examples from the field to illustrate three issues to take into account: observe over a period of time in varied settings, get to know the person, and use significant others.

**Observe Over a Period of Time in Varied Settings~** Participant observation is labor-intensive research. The effort sustains insights. Goode (1948) observed a man with severe mental retardation in the institutional setting where he was tested and in the group home where he lived. The institutional staff asserted that the man had no language, although his friends in the group home insisted and the researcher observed that he spoke and communicated just fine. The informant did not experience the setting of the test as comfortable enough to risk talking, so he never did.

Some people are more difficult to know than others. Although this is not always language-related, language does give the researcher data. For the nonverbal person, however, the researcher must find other windows on the soul. Observing Chris, an institutionalized girl who was blind, deaf, and severely mentally retarded, over time, Goode (1979) discovered the ways she attempted to manipulate her environment. Goode realized that Chris did not perceive the world with the same senses that he did. Concluding that he and Chris occupied two different perceptual worlds, he wanted an experimental basis for discovering hers. He spent time watching her rock back and forth engaging in rhythmic banging of a spoon or rattle, and observed that she always held her head in a particular position. He surmised that she had slight hearing in one ear and impaired sight in one eye. In order to understand her world, he bandaged one of his own eyes completely and the other slightly, and he closed one of his ears off completely and the other slightly. Then he used the strategy of imitating her as she sought pleasure. He let her be the teacher and discovered that her rocking motion allowed light and sound to form rhythmic patterns that were stimulating and pleasurable.

There are stages in Goode's work. First, he recognized that he and his subject lived in two separate worlds. Second, he realized he needed to experience her world in order to understand it. Third, he tried the strategy of letting her lead him.

Goode was interested in how Chris' given world looked to her. Though he has argued elsewhere about the socially produced identities of institutionalized people (Goode, 1984), here he did not study the structural effects of institutionalization on her behavior. Although rocking may have provided pleasure, given her situation, another setting may have encouraged entirely different behavior.

Others have used contrived disabilities as a consciousness-raising tool, but it is important to recognize the risks Goode took with this innovative approach. If the researcher is in an academic setting, such risk-taking may appear unattractive. It is important to remember, however, that many issues must continually be negotiated in the research process. We still negotiate with graduate students, for example, over how many subjects should be interviewed for their dissertation research. Strategies for studying nonverbal subjects can be negotiated as well.

**Get to Know the Person** ~ One way to get to know subjects in their natural environment is by spending time with them. You get to know their preferences, their habits, and their modes of interacting. Getting to know the informant well allows you to see the person empathically. Reactions to characteristics, mannerisms, or appearance may change over time. Daniels (1983), for example, found that her original alienation from army psychiatrists or upper-class volunteer women dissipated after she spent time with them. She gained sympathy with their perspectives.

The importance of getting to know a person with severe mental retardation well is grounded in the idea that early impressions are simply that - early impressions. There is someone to get to know. Goode (1984) argues

that people try to interpret what it means to be retarded without knowing well the person with retardation. This tendency reflects Becker's "hierarchy of credibility" (1967), the idea that the more important or powerful the person, the more claim or legitimacy the person has to define the situation. Although it may be intellectually difficult to get to know the informant who is retarded, it is an obstacle to overcome. Moseley (in press) worries that as adults we have very few ways of conversing with persons who are not as smart as we are. Most of the ways we have developed of communicating cast them in the role of child, as incompetent, or even worse, as insignificant.

Experimentation and risk-taking become important, because we need to develop ways to talk and interact with individuals who have intellectual deficits that do not place them in a lesser position. Goode took risks in his attempt to enter Chris's perceptual world.

**Use Significant Others** ~ Significant others are as important in observing as they are in interviewing. Although there are dangers in depending on advocates, friends, or parents to interpret meaning, there are benefits as well. Ideally, the researcher would want to compare official records about an informant's life with the person's perspective. If this is impossible to achieve, the researcher can depend on others who know the person well enough to help. Biklen and Bogdan (1978) led a team of researchers to study community placement of 10 men labeled severely retarded who were judged to be the most violent residents in an institution. They relied on significant others to learn about the well-being of the men. The director of the men's former institution unit told the researchers that his observations of the intact furniture in the group residence suggested to him that one former inmate, Johnny, had improved his behavior in his home. Otherwise, he said, the furniture would have bite marks on it. Leading the team into a bedroom, he argued that a dresser filled with clothes showed that the resident was using the toilet and not ripping his clothes, two problems staff had faced in the institution. In this case the research team depended on people who knew the house residents well to interpret the meaning of activities and events. Had they not had the assistance of people who were familiar with the residents, they would have walked into the house and seen the furnishings as ordinary. They would not have looked for bite marks on furniture, ravaged carpets, or empty bureau drawers had they not been comparing the men's present lives to their former lives in the institution.

The difficulty of depending on significant others, of course, is whether or not to trust the person's views. This is a generic problem for qualitative researchers, but the difficulties in using language as a satisfactory means of communication make the researcher more conscious of this issue. The best way to judge the adequacy of important others is by the quality of the data they give. Rich data, full of examples, given about a variety of situations over time will provide enough details for the researcher to make a decision.

## CONCLUSION

We have tried to show that basic guidelines of qualitative research hold up fairly well in the study of people with severe disabilities, primarily because the guidelines are, in themselves, flexible. We have suggested that sometimes certain rules (e.g., the importance of staying in the field over time) are vital. On other occasions (e.g., Goode's [1979] investigation of a young girl's alternative perceptual view of the world), bending the parameters of academic research guidelines may yield richer data.

The researcher's major concern is language. The dependence of the qualitative researcher on language, and the image of the ideal informant (particularly in American field work) as an articulate person (e.g., Doc, in Whyte, 1955), may call for some creative tactics in the face of the informant who cannot verbally inform. It is important for the qualitative researcher who wants to learn about the worlds of subjects with severe mental retardation to supplement information received through verbal discussion with observations in the places where they live and work.

Qualitative researchers enter natural environments to find out what meanings people make of their situations, as well as to

examine the conditions of people's lives (hence, the camera has been an important tool, cf. Blatt, Ozolins, & McNally, 1979; English, 1988), but we need a framework in which to place these meanings and to help explain conflicting perspectives. It is for this reason that the design of the research project is so important. If the design of the study, takes the improvement of living, educational, and working conditions for people with severe disabilities as the starting point, then the analysis of the data will be based upon this orientation.

**Acknowledgements:** The authors would like to thank Luanna Meyer, Cindy Sutton and *JASH* reviewers for their comments on earlier drafts of this article.

******

## REFERENCES

**Albright, K., Brown, L., VanDeventer, P., & Jorgensen, J.** (in press) Characteristics of educational programs for students with severe intellectual disabilities. In D. Biklen, D. Ferguson, & A. Ford (Eds.,) *Schooling and Disability.* Chicago: National Society for the Study of Education.

**Becker, H.** (1963). *Outsiders: Studies in the sociology of deviance.* New York: The Free Press.

**Becker, H.** (1967). Whose side are we on? *Social Problems 14,* 239-247.

**Becker, H.S., Geer, B., Hughes, E.C. & Strauss, A.** (1961)/ *Boys in white: Student culture in medical school.* Chicago: University of Chicago Press.

**Berger, P., & Luckmann, T.** (1967). *The social construction of reality.* Garden City, NY: Doubleday.

**Biklen, D.** (1985). *Achieving the complete school.* New York: Teachers College Press.

**Biklen, D.** (1987) *Small homes: A case study of Westport Associates.* Syracuse University, Center on Human Policy.

**Biklen, D.** (1988, June) *Lessons from families.* Paper presented at the annual meeting of the American Association on Mental Retardation, Washing, DC.

**Biklen, D. & Bogdan, R.** (Eds.,) (1978). *Unconditional care.* Syracuse: Syracuse University, Center on Human Policy.

**Biklen, D., Corrigan, C. & Quick, D.** (in press) Beyond obligation: Students' relations with each other in integrated classes. In D. Lipsky & A. Gartner (eds.,) *Beyond separate education.* Baltimore: Paul H. Brookes.

**Biklen, S.** (Ed.) (1986). *Just friends: Oral histories of citizen-advocate relationships.* Atlanta: Georgia Advocacy Office.

**Biklen, S. & Bogdan, R.** (1986). On your own with naturalistic evaluation. In D.D.Williams (Ed.), *Naturalistic evaluation* (pp.93-110). New Directions for Program Evaluation, no.30, San Francisco: Jossey Bass.

**Blatt, B., Ozolins, A., & McNally, J.** (1979). *The family papers.* New York: Longman.

**Blumer, H.** (1969). *Symbolic interactionism: Perspective and method.* Englewood Cliffs, NJ: Prentice-Hall.

**Bogdan, R.** (1986). *The No Name Program: Three severely multiply disabled people who live at the Petrone's in Burlington, Vermont.* Syracuse University, Center on Human Policy.

**Bogdan, R.** (1987). *We care for our own":* Georgia citizen advocacy in Savannah and Macon.* Syracuse: Syracuse University, Center on Human Policy.

**Bogdan, R. , & Biklen, S.** (1982). *Qualitative research for education.* Boston: Allyn and Bacon.

**Bogdan, R. & Taylor, S.** (1976). The judged, not the judges: An insider's view of mental retardation. *American Psychologist. 31,* 47-52.

**Bogdan, R. & Taylor, S.** (1982). *Inside out.* Toronto: University of Toronto Press.

**Bogdan, R. & Taylor, S.** (1987, Fall). Toward a sociology of acceptance: The other side of the study of deviance. *Social Policy, 18,* 34-39.

**Bosk, C.** (1979). *Forgive and remember.* Chicago: University of Chicago Press.

**Brightman, A.** (Ed.), (1984). *Ordinary moments. The disabled experience.* Baltimore: University Park Press.

**Cottle, T.** (1976). *Busing.* Boston: Beacon Press.

**Cusick, T.** (1973). *Inside High School.* New York: Holt, Rinehart & Winston.

**Daniels, A.K.** (1983, Fall). Self deception and self-discovering in fieldwork. *Qualitative Sociology, 6,* 195-214.

**Edgerton, R.** 1967). *The cloak of competence.* Berkeley: University of California Press.

**Edgerton, R.** (Ed,.). (1984). *Lives in process: Midly retarded adults in a large city.* Washington, DC: American Association on Mental Deficiency.

**Edgerton, R. & Bercovici, S.** (1976). The cloak of competence: Years later. *American Journal of Mental Deficiency, 80,* 485-497.

**Edgerton, R. Bolinger, M. & Herr, B.** (1984). The cloak of competence: After two decades. *American Journal of Mental Deficiency, 88* (4), 345-351.

**Edgerton, R., & Langness, L.** (1978). Observing mentally retarded persons in community settings: An anthropological perspective. In G. Sackett (Ed.), *Observing behavior, Volume 1, Theory and applications in mental retardation* (pp.335-348). Baltimore: University Park Press.

**English, F.W.** (1988, May). The utility of the camera in qualitative inquiry. *Educational Researcher, 17* (4), 8-16.

**Evans, D.P.** (1983). *The lives of mentally retarded people.* Boulder, CO: Westview Press.

**Everhart, R.** (1983). *Reading, writing and resistance.* Boston: Routledge and Kegan Paul.

**Featherstone, H.** (1980). *A difference in the family.* New York: Basic Books.

**Ferguson, D.** (1986). *Site visit report, Boise group homes, Boise, Idaho.* Syracuse: Syracuse University, Center of Human Policy.

**Ferguson, D.** (1987). *Curriculum decision making for students with severe handicaps: Policy and practice.* New York: Teachers College Press.

**Fine, G.** (1987). *With the boys.* Chicago: University of Chicago Pr ess.

**Foster, S.** (1987). *The politics of caring.* London: Falmer Press.

**Geertz, C.** (1973). Thick description: Toward an interpretive theory of culture. In C. Geertz (Ed.), *The interpretation of cultures* (pp. 3-30) New York: Basic Books.

**Goetz, J. & LeCompte, M.** (1984). *Ethnography and qualitative design in educational research.* Orlando, FL: Academic Press.

**Goode, D.** (1979). The world of the congenitally deaf-blind: Towards the grounds for achieving human understanding. In H. Schwartz & J. Ja cobs, *Qualitative sociology* (pp. 381-396). New York: Free Press.

**Goode, D.** (1984), Socially produced identities, intimacy and the problem of competence among the retarded. In L. Barton & S. Tomlinson (Eds.), *Special education and social interests* (pp. 228-248). New York: Nichols.

**Grant, G.** (1988). *The world we created at Hamilton High.* Cambridge, MA: Harvard University Press.

**Greenfeld, J.** (1970) *A child called Noah.* New York: Holt, Rinehart & Winston

**Hammersley, M. & Atkinson, P.** (1983). *Ethnography, Principles in practice. d* London: Tavistock.

**Kanter, R.** (1977) *Men and women of the corporation.* New York: Basic Books.

McCall, G. & Simmons, J. (Eds.), (1969). *Issues in partipant observation.* Reading, MA: Addison-Wesley.

McPherson, G. (1972). *Small town teacher.* Cambridge, MA: Harvard University Press.

Metz, M. (1983). What can be learned from educational ethnography? *Urban education, 17* (4), 391-418.

Moseley, C. (1987, October) *Job satisfaction of workers in supported employment.* Paper presented at the annual meeting of The Association for Persons with Severe Handicaps, Chicago, IL.

Moseley, C. (in press). *What work means: People with severe disabilities in the workplace.* Unpublished doctoral dissertation, Syracuse University, Syracuse.

Rothman, D. & Rothman, S. (1984). *The Willowbrook wars.* New York: Harper & Row.

Searl, S. & Wickham-Searl, P. (1985). *Site visit report, Working Organization for Retarded Children, Flushing, New York.* Syracuse: Syracuse University, Center on Human Policy.

Spencer, D. (1986) *Contemporary women teachers.* New York: Longman.

Spradley, J. (1979). *The ethnographic interview.* New York: Holt, Rinehart & Winston.

Spradley, J. (1980). *Participant observation.* New York: Holt, Rinehart & Winston

Stainback, S., & Stainback, W. (1984). Methodological considerations in qualitative research. *Journal of The Association for Persons with Severe Handicaps, 9,* 296-303.

Sutton, C. (1988). *The newcomers: Students with severe disabilities.* Unpublished doctoral dissertation, Syracuse University, Syracuse.

Taylor, S. (1983) From segregation to integration: Strategies for integrating severely handicapped students in normal school and community settings. *Journal of The Association for the Severely Handicapped, 7,* 42-49.

Taylor, S. (1985). *Site visit report, State of Michigan.* Syracuse, NY: Syracuse University, Center on Human Policy.

Taylor, S. (1987a). *Community living in three Wisconsin counties.* Syracuse: Syracuse University, Center on Human Policy.

Taylor, S. (1987b). Observing abuse: Professional ethics and personal morality in field research. *Qualitative Sociology, 10,* 288-302.

Wolcott, H. (1975). Criteria for an ethnographic approach to research in schools. *Human Organization, 34* (2), 111-127.

Whyte, W.F. (1955). *Street corner society.* Chicago: University of Chicago Press.

**About the Authors: Sari Knopp Biklen** may be reached through the Cultural Foundations of Education and Curriculum, 259 Huntington Hall, Syracuse University, Syracuse, NY 13244.

**Charles R. Moseley** may also be reached at Syracuse University. He is also affiliated with the Vermont Division of Mental Retardation.

**Source:** Reprinted with permission from the authors and *JASH,* Vol. 13, No. 3, pp. 155-162, 1988. Published by The Association for Persons with Severe Handicaps, Seattle, Washington. 98133-8612

\*\*\*\*\*\*

# Developmental Competence in Adolescents with an Acquired Disability

Kathleen J. Sawin, DNS RN C
June Marshall, MS RN

**Abstract** ~ *Several authors have proposed that disability may present adolescents with unique barriers to achieving the competencies necessary for transition into young adulthood. The purposes of the pilot study detailed in this article were to establish the reliability of proposed instruments and to identify factors associated with competence in adolescents with spinal cord injury. Both overall self-worth and domain-specific competencies were explored. Decision making, friendship patterns, specific and general future expectations, and parental over-protectiveness were associated with overall self-worth in a convenience sample of 32 adolescents with spinal cord injury. Several variables were associated with the eight domain-specific competencies.*

Achieving developmental competencies such as positive self-esteem, a sense of self, and the ability to interact with others is crucial for all adolescents. Several authors (Cadman, Boyle, & Szatmari, 1987; McAnarney, 1985; Melamed, Siegel, & Ridley-Johnson, 1988; Resnick, 1986; Yoos, 1987) have proposed that disability may present unique barriers to achieving these competencies. If this proves accurate, the adolescent with a disability may be more at risk from the lack of developmental competencies than from the physical disability itself. The purpose of the pilot study described here was to identify factors associated with the perception of individual and interpersonal competence in adolescents with an acquired spinal cord injury. The model generated in this study will be used in subsequent examinations of larger populations with multiple disabilities or chronic illnesses.

## BACKGROUND:

### *Developmental competence:*

Developmental theorists have proposed that adolescents must achieve competence in three arenas: individual, interpersonal, and social (Greenberger & Sorenson, 1974; Kinopka, 1973). Individual competence includes developing overall self-esteem; becoming comfortable with one's body; and developing school, job, and athletic competence. Interpersonal competence encompasses the ability to develop peer, romantic, and family relationships. Social competence implies the ability to participate as a citizen and function as a responsible member of society. This study addressed the perceptions of individual and interpersonal competence.

### *Factors related to individual and interpersonal competence:*

Determination of the achievement of individual competence is complicated by the varied way that developmental issues are conceptualized and operationalized. For example, self-esteem is measured differently by different researchers (Long & Hamilin, 1988; Resnick & Hutton, 1987; Rosenberg, 1965). Resnick and Hutton (1987) discussed resilience factors; McAnarney (1985) focused on social maturation, and others have proposed developmental tasks (Greenberger & Sorenson, 1974).

Self-esteem, or the evaluative assessment one makes regarding satisfaction with role(s) and quality of performance, is critical to development. There have been conflicting reports about the effect of disabilities on self-esteem. Cadman and colleagues (1987) studied a large random sample of Canadian children and found adjustment and self-esteem related to physical disability but not chronic illness. Kellerman, Zelter, and Ellenberg (1980), using the Rosenberg (1965) measure of self-esteem, found that females, both with and without disabilities, had lower self-esteem than males. Further, McAnarney (1985), evaluating controlled studies in the literature, concluded that, as a group, chronically ill adolescents do not have lower self-esteem but that specific subgroups, homogeneous in their illness, might. Studies of children and adolescents with cystic fibrosis (McAnarney, 1985), diabetes (Saucier, 1984), and renal transplants (Korsch, Negrete, & Gardner, 1973) have shown no relationship between disability and self-esteem. However, adolescents with spina bifida (Hayden, Davenport, & Campbell, 1979; McAndrew, 1979) and sickle-cell disease (Kumar, Powers, Allen, & Haywood, 1976) were found to have lower self-esteem.

Achieving comfort with one's body and sexuality are reported in the literature as particularly significant for adolescents with disabilities (Bogle & Shaul, 1981; McKown, 1984; Sawin, 1986). Women with disabilities are reported to be especially at risk for being perceived by society as asexual, unattractive, and incompetent in relationships (Sawin, 1986). Only a limited number of studies have addressed these issues specifically in adolescents with disabilities.

Autonomy or independence is viewed by professionals in the field as impaired in adolescents with disabilities, but differences in the definition of autonomy make generalizations difficult. In a study of 110 adolescents with cerebral palsy, those with any household responsibilities beyond self-care were found to have greater self-esteem and more positive body image even when severity of illness was statistically controlled (Resnick & Hutton, 1987). In addition, in this same study, having friends other than a best friend and spending time with friends were related positively to individual competence. In a study of groups of adolescents with cystic fibrosis, asthma, and small stature with a comparison group of healthy adolescents (N = 70), Sinnema (1986) identified eight dimensions of responsibility. He found differences only in the dimensions of dating, body hygiene, and social conflicts. The differences, however, varied by age and type of disability. Responsibility for household chores was not explored.

The patterns of interpersonal relationships with family and peers are not well delineated for adolescents with disabilities. Although disability is assumed to have a negative impact on both peer and family interactions (Yoos, 1987), few studies have addressed this issue. An exception is Resnick and Hutton's (1987) study. These authors adapted a parental overprotectiveness tool, confirmed its factor structure, reported acceptable reliabilities (a = .72), and, by using multiple regression, found it to be a significant predictor of adolescent self-image, even controlling for severity of illness, chores done in the home, and types of friendships. The authors, however, made no attempt to control for intellectual level.

McAnarney (1985) found little support for the importance of dysfunctional family communication or school problems in the literature on adolescents with disabilities. When family relationship differences were reported, however, they were associated with physical disabilities rather than chronic illness. Both Resnick and Hutton (1987) and McAnarney (1985) reported relationships between decreased quantity and quality of peer interactions and negative self-perceptions.

*Other factors:*
Characteristics of the disability itself, such as severity of disability (Perrin, Ramsey, & Sandler, 1987; Pless, 1984), functional ability of adolescents with disabilities (Perrin et al., 1987; McAnarney, 1985), and age (McAnarney, 1985) have been shown to be related to developmental or psychosocial outcomes for adolescents. The relationship between these characteristics and the adolescent's interpersonal relationships is not clear, however.

*Framework for the study:*
The literature delineates both self-esteem, or overall sense of competence, and domain-specific competencies as important in adolescent development (Harter, 1988). The relationships of predictive factors to both overall competence and domain-specific competence are important to understanding the adolescent's achievement or nonachievement of developmental tasks. Identifying factors

## TABLE 1. DEFINITION OF STUDY VARIABLES

| Conceptual Definition | Operational Definition |
|---|---|
| **Proposed Factors Affecting Competence** | |
| Coping | A-COPE subscales (Patterson & McCubbin, 1987):<br>    **Venting feelings**<br>    **Seeking diversion**<br>    **Seeking spiritual support**<br>    **Engaging in demanding activity**<br>    **Being humorous**<br>    **Avoiding activities**<br>    **Investing in others** |
| Autonomy | A-COPE subscale:<br>    **Developing self-reliance**<br>Decision-making scale* |
| Division of household responsibility<br>Expectations of self/future | Chores subscale*<br>Specific future scale*<br>Hope scale (general future scale) |
| Family interactions | A-COPE subscale: Solving family problems<br>Parental Overprotectiveness Tool<br>Family activities pattern*<br>FACES III (Olson et al., 1985)<br>Family AGPAR (Smikstein, Ashworth, & Montano, 1982) |
| Friendship Patterns | Peer activities pattern* |

### Outcome Measures of Individual Competence

| | |
|---|---|
| Self Esteem/overall self-worth | Harter's Tool subscale: Self-worth |
| Body image | Physical appearance |
| Intelligence | Scholastic competence |
| Job | Job competence |
| Sports | Athletic competence |
| Behavior | Behavioral conduct |

### Outcome Measures of Interpersonal Competence

| | |
|---|---|
| Social | Harter's Tool subscale: Social acceptance |
| Establishing peer friendships | Close friendships |
| Romantic relationships | Romantic Appeal |

### Other Variables

| | |
|---|---|
| Severity of disability | Severity index (adapted from Perrin, Ramsey, & Sandler, 1987) |
| Age | Age in years |

## * Scales developed for this study

Sources Consulted: Olson, D. H., McCubbin, H.I., Barnes, H., Larsen, A., Muxes, M., & Wilson, M. (1985). *Family inventories.* St. Paul, MN: Family Social Science Department of the University of Minnesota.
Patterson, J.M., & McCubbin, J.I. (1987). A-COPE: Adolescent Coping Orientation for Problem Experiences. In H.I. McCubbin & A.I. Thompson (Eds.), *Family assessment inventories for research and practice* (pp. 225-243). Madison, WI: University of Wisconsin-Madison.
Perrin, .C., Ramsey, B.K., & Sandler, H.M. (1987). Competent kids: Children and adolescents with a chronic illness. *Child Care, Health and Development,* 13, 13-32.
Smikstein, G., Ashworth, C., & Montano, D. (1982). Validity and reliability of the family APGAR as a test of family function. *Journal of Family Practice,* 15, 303-311.

associated with positive or negative developmental outcomes is the first step in designing interventions to facilitate the achievement of these tasks in adolescents at risk due to chronic illness or disability. The factors proposed to affect individual and interpersonal competence in this study are summarized in Table 1.**Methodology**

Data were collected from 32 individuals who sustained spinal cord injury (SCI) and were part of a larger study of adolescents with physical disability or chronic illness (N = 85). The convenience sample for this study of individuals with SCI was obtained from three sources: a children's hospital, a rehabilitation hospital, and the State of Virginia Spinal Cord Injury Registry. All the subjects were enrolled in an educational setting and functioning at grade level. Their ages ranged from 12 to 22 years (mean = 18.06), with 22 males and 8 females. The average subject had been disabled for 3.6 years (range = 9 to 120 months), had experienced 1.44 medical complications, had missed 9 days of school/work, had an average grade of C, and had been hospitalized for 0.92 days in the past year. The researchers conducted semistructured interviews in the patients' homes using a variety of standardized tools. Five scales were developed for the larger study. Scale items were developed from three sources: clinical experience, a review of the literature, and qualitative interviews with 15 adolescents. The first of these scales focused on adolescents' perceptions of their future -- that is, the specific expectations they hold for themselves. This 15-item scale measured the individual's confidence that he or she would achieve future goals (e.g., go to a college or technical school, have a romantic relationship, raise a family, live independently). The Adolescent Psychosocial Functional Assessment Tool (APFAT) encompassed the four scales developed for this study to measure adolescents' function (in other words, what they did and how often they did it) on four dimensions--decision-making patterns they followed, chores and/or responsibilities they had, activities they engaged in with their peers, and activities they engaged in with their families.

The APFAT decision-making scale was a 21-item Likert-type scale measuring adolescents' perceptions of how decisions are made in their families. Adolescents indicated whether decisions such as setting curfews or determining how much allowance they got were made totally by the parent, made by the parent with input from the adolescent, made jointly (50/50), made by the adolescent with input from the parent, or made totally by the adolescent. The chores scale is a Likert-type scale of chore/job frequency. Both the peer activities and the family activities scales contained items proposed by adolescents in the qualitative interviews. Adolescents were asked to indicate the frequency of the listed activities (e.g., once a week, a couple of times a month, once a month, once in 6 months, never) with peers and family.

Content validity was established by a panel of three experts in pediatric nursing and rehabilitation. To explore the construct validity of the five scales, factor analysis was employed using the total sample of the larger study (N=85). As the number of items in the proposed scales was less than the number of the subjects in the larger study, it was impossible to analyze the instrument as a whole. Each of the proposed scales (decision making, friendship patterns, family patterns, chores/job) as well as the future-expectations scale items was entered into the factor analysis independently. Factor analysis supported the existence of unidimensional scales for chores, job, family activities, and specific future expectations. Two problem solving and two peer-activity scales were identified. The first problem-solving scale encompassed the decisions adolescents described as personal--decisions about the clothes they wore or the friends they chose. The second problem-solving scale addressed decisions the adolescents described as more like rules--decisions about curfew, how late the teen stayed up, rules about dating, and restrictions on activity. The two peer activities scales differed in the size of the network and nature of the activities, with the first reflecting everyday activities done with a limited number of friends ("hanging out" at home, listening to music, going to a movie) and the latter encompassing special activities done in larger groups (going to school events, going to parties). The scales developed for the larger study of adolescents with chronic illness or disability (N=85) were used to report the results for adolescents with SCI.

Established tools were used to measure other factors proposed to affect competence. Adolescent coping was measured by the Adolescent Coping Orientation for Problem Experiences (A-COPE) (Patterson & McCubbin, 1987). This 54-item scale with 12 factors was developed and confirmed with three middle-class samples and subsequently was used to predict smoking and drug use in adolescents (Patterson & McCubbin, 1987). Family functioning was measured by both the Family APGAR (Smikstein, Ashworth, & Montano, 1982) and Olson's FACES III (Olson et al., 1985); the first is a 5-item summary screening tool and the second is a well-established 20-item tool addressing family cohesion and adaptability.

## Figure 1. Sample Items from the Harter Tool

(Note: The subjects chose one of the two statements separated by the "BUT" and then indicated whether that statement was somewhat true or very true for them.)

### Overall competence/Self-Worth

Some teenagers often are disappointed with themselves BUT Other teenagers are pretty pleased with themselves.

Some teenagers don't like the way they are leading their lives BUT Other teenagers are often happy with their lives.

### Domain-Specific Competencies

| Close friendship | Athletic competence | Romantic appeal |
|---|---|---|
| Some teenagers are able to make really close friends BUT Other teenagers find it hard to make really close friends. Some teenagers don't have a friend who is close enough to share really personal thoughts BUT Other teenagers do have a close friend with whom they can share personal thoughts and feelings. | Some teenagers think they could do well at just about any new athletic activity BUT Other teenagers are afraid they might not do well at a new athletic activity. Some teenagers feel that they are better than others their age at sports BUT Other teenagers don't feel they do as well in sports. | Some teenagers feel that if they are romantically interested in someone, they will be liked in return BUT Other teenagers worry that when they like someone romantically they won't be liked in return. Some teenagers feel that people their age will be attracted to them romantically BUT Other teenagers worry about whether people their age will be attracted to them. |
| **Behavioral conduct** | **Job competence** | **Scholastic competence** |
| Some teenagers feel really good about the way they act BUT Other teenagers don't feel very good about the way they often act. Some teenagers do things they know they shouldn't do BUT Other teenagers hardly ever do things they know they shouldn't do. | Some teenagers feel they are old enough to get and keep a paying job BUT Other teenagers do not feel that they are old enough yet to handle a job really well. Some teenagers feel they could do better at work they do for pay BUT Other teenagers feel that they really are doing well at work they do for pay. | Some teenagers feel that they are just as smart as others their age BUT Other teenagers are not so sure and wonder if they are as smart. Some teenagers do very well at their class work BUT Other teenagers don't do very well at their class work. |
| **Physical appearance** | | **Social Acceptance** |
| Some teenagers are not happy with the way they look BUT Other teenagers are happy with the way they look. Some teenagers wish their bodies were different BUT Other teenagers like their bodies the way they are. | | Some teenagers find it hard to make friends BUT Other teenagers find it pretty easy. Some teenagers feel that they are socially accepted BUT Other teenagers wish that more people their age accepted them. |

* Reprinted with permission from Harter, S. (1988). *Manual for the self-perception profile for adolescents.* Denver: University of Denver.

Generalized future expectation was measured by the Hope Scale (Snyder et al., 1991), a 12-item scale with factor analysis revealing two subscales of hope and optimism. Protectiveness was measured by an adaptation of Resnick's (1986) Parental Protectiveness Scale.

The severity-of-disability index was developed by Perrin et al. (1987) and included age of onset, duration of illness, frequency of hospitalizations, and proportion of days absent from school.

Developmental outcomes were measured by Harter's (1988) Perceptual Profile, which generates an overall perception of individual competence or self-esteem and perceptions about eight specific domains of competence (close relationship, behavioral, physical, athletic, job, romantic, scholastic, and social). Each scale has five items; subjects choose one of the bipolar statements and then indicate whether the statement is "really true for me" or "sort of true for me" (see Figure 1). Cronbach's alpha was used to determine the reliabilities of previously established scales and of those developed for this study. Any scale with a reliability of less than .60 was deleted. (This included several of the A-COPE scales and one of the parental overprotectiveness scales.)

**Table 2. Means and Reliabilities for All Competence Scales**

| Variable | Mean | SD | Minimum | Maximum | Reliability |
|---|---|---|---|---|---|
| Overall competence/self-worth | 17.2 | 3.00 | 9 | 20 | .81 |
| Close Friendship | 17.63 | 3.24 | 5 | 20 | .84 |
| Behavioral conduct | 15.47 | 3.27 | 9 | 20 | .79 |
| Physical appearance | 15.34 | 3.61 | 9 | 20 | .82 |
| Athletic competence | 14.52 | 4.44 | 5 | 20 | .87 |
| Job competence | 16.86 | 2.61 | 10 | 20 | .72 |
| Romantic appeal | 15.77 | 3.39 | 5 | 20 | .78 |
| Scholastic competence | 12.56 | 2.72 | 7 | 20 | .71 |
| Social Acceptance | 18.09 | 2.10 | 12 | 20 | .63 |

**Results and discussion**

This sample's competence scores generally were high (see Table 2). Overall self-worth or self-esteem scores ranged from 9 to 20 with an average of 17.12. Most adolescents felt the positive statements were "really true for me." Domain-specific competencies in which students held the most positive perceptions were social competence, forming close relationships, and job competence. Adolescents felt moderately competent (i.e., the majority responded that positive statements were "sort of true for me") in the areas of physical, behavioral, and romantic competence. They perceived themselves as only minimally competent in scholarship. In addition, the participants saw themselves as moderately involved in decisions, with the adolescent usually deciding about clothes and friends. The average subject made decisions jointly with parents on rules in the household. These subjects occasionally did chores, did everyday things frequently and special things sometimes with their friends, and sometimes engaged in family activities with their families. They were generally satisfied with their families, saw their families as frequently cohesive and sometimes adaptable, and were positive about accomplishing specific and general future expectations.

Pearson correlations indicated that age, severity of disability (onset, number of days hospitalized, and numbers of missed days of work/school), grade point average, family activities, and sex were not related to overall developmental competence (self-worth), nor were they related to any of the domain-specific competencies in the sample of adolescents with SCI. Fourteen variables were associated with overall self-worth/self-esteem (see Table 3). All eight of Harter's specific competencies (with correlations ranging from .41 to .71), two decision-making subscales, friendship activities, both the general and specific future expectations scales, and the parental protectiveness subscale were related to the adolescent's perception of overall competence.

Factors associated with individual competencies varied somewhat, depending on the specific competence (see Table 4). Friendship activities were related to all five of the domain-specific individual competencies (physical, job, scholastic, athletic, behavioral). Family functioning was related only to the behavioral competence. Family cohesion and adaptability were higher in adolescents perceiving themselves as "behaving as I should." Future expectations were related to three of the individual competence scales: behavioral, scholastic, and job. Subjects who held higher specific expectations for themselves (to go to school, to raise a family, to be happy, to be independent) were more likely to have higher perceptions of job and scholarly competence. Subjects who had higher general expectations and assessments of themselves ("energetically pursue goals" or "can generally figure out solutions to a problem") also had higher perceptions of job, scholastic, and behavioral competence. Adolescents who used avoidance as a coping strategy had poorer perceptions of their intelligence and job competence. High adolescent involvement in decision making, controlling for age, was related to positive perceptions of behavioral and physical competencies.

Several factors consistently were associated with aspects of interpersonal competence (see Table 5). Both future expectation scales were related to all of the interpersonal scales. Friendship activities

were related to establishing friendships (social competence and establishing close relationships). Adolescents who saw themselves as able to establish close friendships and comfortable in social settings had more positive perceptions of the future and spent more time with their friends. Higher levels of decision making were related to greater perceived competence in establishing relationships and to romantic competence, while use of the coping strategy of "investing in friends" was related to romantic and social competence. Frequency of domestic responsibility (chores) was related only to romantic competence.

**Table 3. Factors Associated with Overall Self-Worth (Including Other Competence Scales**

| Variable | Pearson Correlation Coefficient |
|---|---|
| **Domain-Specific Competencies** | |
| Close friendship | .41 |
| Behvioral Conduct | .62 |
| Physical appearance | .65 |
| Athletic competence | .43 |
| Job competence | .71 |
| Romantic appeal | .46 |
| Scholastic competence | .45 |
| Social Acceptance | .45 |
| **Other Factors from Proposed Framework** | |
| Decision Making (2) | .61 |
| Friendship patterns | .57 |
| Decision making (1) | .41 |
| Future expectations (specific) | .41 |
| Future expectations (general) | .53 |
| Parental overprotectiveness | .40 |

In summary, the data from this study indicate that adolescents who (a) have high expectations for themselves, (b) have an overall optimistic or hopeful attitude about the future, (c) spend more time with their friends, (d) are involved in decision making, and (e) do not perceive their parents as overprotective and perceive themselves more positively in general and in specific domains of competence. This study supports the view that adolescents with disabilities generally have a positive perception of self (McAnarney, 1985; Resnick, 1986). The scores on domain-specific competencies, however, give insight into specific problems and the factors associated with them. For example, these data support Resnick's view of parental overprotectiveness as a limiting factor in the development of overall competence. Frequency of friendship activities, as in several other studies (Resnick, 1986), was associated with positive developmental outcomes. The activity itself did not seem to be as important as just doing something with friends. Unlike Resnick's study, in which responsibility for chores in addition to self-care were related to self-concept, this study found that adolescents generally had some domestic responsibilities. The frequency of these responsibilities was not related to overall self-esteem or to any specific competence except romantic competence.

## Table 4. Factors Associated with Domain-Specific Individual Competencies

### Physical Appearance

| Variable | Correlation |
|---|---|
| Decision Making (1) | .41 |
| Friendship activities | .42 |

### Job Competence

| Variable | Correlation |
|---|---|
| Friendship activities | .45 |
| Future expectations (specific) | .54 |
| Future expectations (general) | .46 |
| Coping scale: Avoiding | .45 |

### Scholastic competence

| Variable | Correlation |
|---|---|
| Coping scale: Avoiding | .37 |
| Friendship activities | .37 |
| Future expectations (specific) | .39 |
| Future expectations (general) | .50 |

### Athletic competence

| Variable | Correlation |
|---|---|
| Friendship activities | .48 |

### Behavioral conduct

| Variable | Correlation |
|---|---|
| Family cohesion (FACES III) | .44 |
| Family adaptability (FACES III) | .39 |
| Decision making (2) | .56 |
| Friendship activities | .43 |
| Future expectations (general) | .37 |

## Implications for nursing practice

Nurses working with adolescents and their families have regular opportunities to affect developmental outcomes. The findings from this study, combined with those in the existing literature, indicate that interventions aimed at increasing adolescents' skills in decision making are crucial to the achievement of competence. Didactic content that addresses the stages of decision making, encourages role-playing situations to help patients practice decision-making skills, and informs parents of the benefits of incremental and guided decision making for adolescents should be developed.

-----------

## Table 5. Factors Associated with Domain-Specific Interpersonal Competencies

### Social Acceptance

| Variable | Correlation |
|---|---|
| Friendship activities | .45 |
| Future expectations (general) | .54 |
| Future expectations (specific) | .46 |
| Coping: Investing in friendships | .37 |

### Romantic Appeal

| Variable | Correlation |
|---|---|
| Coping: Investing in others | .58 |
| Use of demanding activities | .42 |
| Future expectations (general) | .59 |
| Future expectations (specific) | .65 |
| Chores | .44 |
| Decision Making (2) | .42 |

## Close Relationships

| Variable | Correlation |
|---|---|
| Future expectations (general) | .68 |
| Future expectations (specific) | .40 |
| Friendship activities | .36 |
| Decision making (2) | .37 |
| Decision making (1) | .45 |

Building adolescents' assertiveness skills can facilitate their acquisition of decision-making skills. This approach is consistent with the literature (Spivack & Shure, 1989) that proposes that children and adolescents with significant life stresses need to build their overall mental health skills (communicating, problem solving, labeling of feelings, owning problems) before focusing on the problem at hand. For example, a study exploring a model of three levels of intervention for children and adolescents in families experiencing divorce (support, support plus skill building, support plus skill building plus family involvement) showed increasing benefits at each level (Stolberg & Mahler, 1990). Support for the adolescent is not sufficient; skill building is essential. When the interventions involve parents in the support and skill-building process, the outcomes are optimized.

In this study, only a few coping strategies were associated with competence outcomes. It is possible that it is not the coping strategy itself (or the mix of strategies) that is the predictive factor, but instead the effectiveness of the coping strategy in establishing the desired outcome. It would be useful to assess the coping strategies of adolescents perceiving themselves to be deficient in domain-specific competencies. If there are factors blocking the adolescent's ability to use friends as a coping strategy, these barriers could be addressed by the nurse. Older adolescents with disabilities who are not pursuing chores and/or jobs might be using avoidance as a way of coping: they might benefit from a discussion of both the negative consequences of abusing that coping style and the positive aspects of having responsibilities in one's life.

Peer activities had the most consistent impact on overall and domain-specific competence. Specific interventions must be developed to integrate young people with disabilities into activities both at school and in the community. Nurses need to direct interventions at schools, parks and recreation programs, and the community at large. By adolescence, each individual with a disability or chronic illness should have experienced activities that build skills in independent living, such as spending the night with friends or a week at camp.

Interventions designed to influence developmental outcomes should involve the family and focus on developmentally appropriate strategies. It is difficult for parents to change their style when children become adolescents. Yet, the same parental behaviors that are appropriate to ensure the safety of a preschooler often limit the development of an adolescent's autonomy. Panels of young adults and adolescents with disabilities, other parents, and professionals could be helpful in addressing some of the concerns of parents who continue to be overly protective of their teens. Peer counseling often can prove effective in intervening with the adolescents themselves. Perhaps the most powerful teaching tool is seeing success in action. Thus, a matching system could be developed in which parents who have navigated this developmental stage successfully with their at-risk adolescents could be paired with those needing guidance. The expectations for future achievement held by parents are correlated with their adolescent's expectations and may be even more strongly correlated with outcomes than their adolescent's own expectations (Overbaugh & Sawin, 1992). Programs that provide mentorship by exposing adolescents to successful young adults with disabilities or chronic illness also can affect expectations positively.

## Conclusions

This study was limited by the size of the sample and its homogeneous nature (i.e., one medical diagnosis, one geographic setting) and by the fact that sample selection was clinic-based and the sample was one of convenience. For the purposes of pilot testing of instruments and a general interview schedule, however, the sample was adequate. The study has generated a model delineating the complex relationships of study variables to specific and overall developmental competencies. Further research to test this model is needed with a larger sample of adolescents, as adolescents with other disabilities and/or chronic illnesses might differ significantly in the variables under study. If these preliminary results are supported by further research, nurses will be able to design interventions to target decision-making activities, peer activities, and future expectations in adolescents with disabilities. Further research then must focus on the evaluation of these interventions.

********

## REFERENCES

Bogle, J. E., & Shaul, S. L. (1981). Body image and the woman with a disability. In D. G. Bullard & S. E. Knight (Eds.), *Sexuality and physical disability* (pp. 131-157). St. Louis: The C. V. Mosby Company.

Cadman, D., Boyle, M., & Szatmari, P. (1987). Chronic illness, disability and mental and social well-being: Findings of the Ontario child health study. *Pediatrics, 79*, 805-813.

Greenberger, E., & Sorenson, A. (1974). Toward a concept of psychosocial maturity. *Journal of Youth and Adolescence, 3*, 42-49.

Harter, S. (1988). *Manual for the self-perception profile for adolescents.* Denver: University of Denver.

Hayden, R. W., Davenport, S. L. H., & Campbell, M. M. (1979). Adolescents with myelodysplasia; Impact of physical disability on emotional maturation. *Pediatrics, 64*, 53-59.

Kellerman, J., Zelter, A., & Ellenberg, M. (1980). Psychological effects of illness in adolescence: Anxiety, self-esteem and perception of control. *Journal of Pediatrics, 97*, 126-131.

Konopka, G. (1973). Requirements for healthy development of adolescent youth. *Adolescence, 8*, 292-316.

Korsch, B. M., Negrete, V. F., & Gardner, J. E. (1973). Kidney transplant in children. Psychosocial follow-up study on child and family. *Journal of Pediatric, 83*, 379-408.

Kumar, S., Powers, D., Allen, J., & Haywood, L. J. (1976). Anxiety, self-concept, and personal and social adjustments in children with sickle cell anemia. *Journal of Pediatrics, 88*, 859-863.

Long, K. A., & Hamlin, C. M. (1988). Use of the Piers-Harris self-concept scale with Indian children: Cultural considerations. *Nursing Research, 37*, 42-46.

McAnarney, E. R. 91985). Social maturation: A challenge for handicapped and chronically ill adolescents. *Journal of Adolescent Health Care, 6*, 90-101.

McAndrew, I. (1979). Adolescent and young people with spina bifida. *Developmental Medical Child Neurology, 21*, 619-621.

McKown, J. M. (1984). Disabled teenagers: Sexual identification and sexual counseling. *Sexuality and Disability, 7*, 17-26.

Melamed, B., Siegel, L., & Ridley-Johnson, R. (1988). Coping behaviors in children facing medical stress. In T. Field, P. McCabe, & N. Schneiderman (Eds.), *Stress and coping* (pp. 109-137). Hillside, NJ: Lawrence Ehlbaum.

Olson, D. H., McCubbin, H. J., Barnes, H., Larsen, A., Muxen, M., & Wilson, M. (1985), *Family inventories.* St. Paul, MN: Family Social Science Department of the University of Minnesota.

Overbaugh, K., & Sawin, K. J. (1992). Future life expectations and self-esteem of the survivor of childhood cancer. *Journal of Pediatric Oncology Nursing, 9*(1), 8-15.

Patterson, J. M., & McCubbin, J. I. (1987). A-COPE: Adolescent Coping Orientation for Problem Experiences. In H. I. McCubbin & A. I. Thompson (Eds.), *Family assessment inventories for research and practice* (pp. 225-243). Madison, WI: University of Wisconsin-Madison.

Perrin, E. C., Ramsey, B. K., & Sandler, H. M. (1987). Competent kids: children and adolescents with a chronic illness. *Child Care, Health and Development, 13*, 13-32.

Pless, I. B. (1984). Clinical assessment: Physical and psychological functioning. *Symposium on Chronic Disease in Children, 31*, 33-45.

Resnick, M. D. (1986). Sociological & social psychological factors influencing self-image among physically disabled adolescents. *International Journal of Adolescent Medicine and Health, 2*(3), 2-12.

Resnick, M. D., & Hutton, L. (1987). Resilience among disabled adolescents. *Psychiatric Annals, 12*, 796-800.

Rosenberg, M. (1965). *Society and the adolescent self-image.* Princeton, NJ: Princeton University Press.

Saucier, C. P. (1984). Self concept and self-care management in school age children with diabetes. *Pediatric Nursing, 10,* 135-138.

Sawin, K. J. 1986). Physical disability. In J. Griffith-Kenney (Ed.), *Contemporary women's health* (pp. 236-256). Menlo Park, CA: Addison-Wesley Publishing Company, Inc.

Sinnema, G. (1986). the development of independence in chronically ill adolescents. *International Journal of Adolescent Medicine and Health, 2*(1), 1-15.

Snyder, C. R., Harris, C., Anderson, J. R., Holleran, S. A., Irving, L. M., Sigmon, S. T., Yoshinobu, L., Gibb, J., Langelle, C., & Harney, P. (1991). The will and the ways: Development and validation of an individual-differences measure of hope. *Journal of Personality and Social Psychology, 60, 570-585.*

Spivack, G., & Shure, M. B. (1989). Interpersonal cognitive problem solving (ECPS): A competence-building primary prevention program. *Prevention in Human Services, 6,* 151-178.

Stolberg, A. L., & Mahler, J. (1990). Protecting children from the consequences of divorce: An empirically derived approach. In R. Lorion (Ed.), *Prevention in human services* (pp. 161-176). New York: Haworth.

Yoos, L. (1987). Chronic childhood illnesses: developmental issues. *Pediatric Nursing, 13,* 25-28.

******

About the Author: Kathleen J. Sawin, DNS, CPNP, is an Assistant Professor with the Medical College of Virginia, Virginia Commonwealth University, Department of Maternal Child Nursing, Box 567, Richmond, Virginia 23298-0567

Source: Reprinted from *Rehabilitation Nursing Research,* Vol. 1, Issue 1, with permission of the Association of Rehabilitation Nurses, 5700 Old Orchard Road, First Floor, Skokie, IL 60077-1057. Copyright © 1992 Association of Rehabilitation Nurses.

# Giving Hope to Severely Disabled People
## Eli Isakov, MD

**Introduction~**Progress in science and technology during the last two decades led to the development of new devices and treatment methods, giving new hopes and opening possibilities to better rehabilitation of paralyzed patients.

Spinal cord trauma or disease may lead to an incomplete or complete active functional inability to stand up and to walk. As a result, spinal cord injured (SCI) patients are destined to wheelchairs for the rest of their lives. Paraplegics and quadriplegics, more than any other group of invalids, are forced into a very long period of hospitalization for rehabilitation purposes. One of the main goals in the rehabilitation of SCI patients is to restore standing and ambulation abilities in order to make them more independent in daily life.

Spinal cord injured subjects are encouraged to become and to keep as physically fit as possible. Paralysed athletes are more successful than non-athletes in avoiding the major medical complications to which they are at risk. Standing upright and walking are important to the well-being of paraplegic patients and is believed to improve the physiological processes in the body,( i.e. blood pressure, blood circulation to the lower limbs and functioning of the gastrointestinal and urinary tract systems) [1] Weight bearing on the legs has a positive effect on the long bones of the lower limbs and controls osteoporosis to a great extent [2]. Low physical endurance capacity was found to coexist with an increased number of medical complications and more dependency during daily life activities. Therefore, physical endurance training such as being involved in standing and ambulation is recommended as a prophylactic measure against medical complications [3].

Researchers have been trying to challenge the SCI invalidity by investigating rehabilitation engineering. In order to achieve goals such as standing up and walking, efforts have been invested in three different directions. First, improvement of conventional long leg braces. Second, through the application of electrical stimulation for functional activation of the lower limb muscles via implantable and surface electrodes. Third, by combining braces and FES into an "hybrid orthosis".

## Mechanical and Physiological Gait Factors

Evaluations of the physical effort of individuals with different locomotor disabilities during ambulation is of major interest [4]. In doing so, it is relevant and convenient to use the gait of normal and healthy individuals for reference. The evaluated parameters include walking speed and energy consumption expressed in terms of oxygen consumption per unit of body weight, per unit of distance traveled [5]. Alternatively, energy consumption is also defined as the oxygen consumption per unit of body weight, per unit of time. However, the first definition is found preferable as it is more closely related to efficiency of walking.

Concerning the walking speed of normal individuals, Finley and Cody [6] observed the gait of 1006 pedestrians during ambulation along sidewalks in urban areas, under natural conditions. The average walking speed was reported to be 82 m/min in men and 74 m/min in women. In another study, Coccoran and Brengelmann [7] found that the mean walking speed in unrestrained gait was 83 m/min. They also reported the oxygen consumption of 0.167 ml/kg/m.

According to Saunders et al. [8], minimization of the metabolic energy cost during ambulation is dependent on biomechanical determinants, aimed at limiting and smoothing out the displacement path at the center of gravity of the body. Lack of one or more of these determinants, as in the case of a locomotor disability, results in reduced mechanical efficiency of gait and, hence, increased energy consumption. An extreme example is the gait of paraplegic patients in which the lower limbs participate minimally, or do not participate at all, in weight-bearing and walking unless supported by long braces mounted on the patient. The main effort required is thus accomplished by the upper extremities and trunk muscles above the level of the lesion. This kind of gait is very costly and inefficient in terms of metabolic energy expenditure.

In paraplegia, mobility is possible only with the help of crutches, long-leg-braces or wheelchairs. Fisher and Gullickson [9] have shown the existence of a relationship between metabolic energy cost during ambulation and the level of injury. For instance, in paraplegics with a high thoracic lesion and walking with crutches, the metabolic energy cost was 0,.675 ml/kg/m, compared to 0.508 ml/kg/m in lower level lesion paraplegics. This difference is attributed to increased difficulties in controlling the pelvis in patients with a higher spinal level lesion.

In comparison to crutches, ambulation of paraplegics by wheelchair was found to be much less energy consuming. Smith et al. [10] studied paraplegics moving at the speed of 50 m/min. The resulting oxygen consumption was 0.203 ml/kg/m. Similar results were also reported by Waters et al. (1978), who found that the comfortable speed during pushing of a wheelchair was 85 m/min. The resulting oxygen consumption was 0.191 ml/kg/m.

## 1) Mechanical Orthosis

Until recently, the only way of helping SCI patients to reach standing and walking abilities was by fitting them with conventional long leg braces. However, the usage of such mechanical orthosis supports is very limited (11,12,13). The main reason for not using these orthoses is the difficulty experienced by the patients in attaching them to their spastic limbs, which sometimes requires help from another person. These braces are also heavy and cumbersome and many patients stop using them soon after discharge from hospital (12,13,14). It should also be remembered that walking with these aids requires high energy expenditure from the patients [9]. Furthermore, only incomplete low level paraplegics may benefit and then to

a limited extent only from such braces. All others find the wheelchair more practical as it requires a smaller energy demand for daily mobilization [5].

This development of substitutes for the existing mechanical aids is thus of great interest. The pneumatic orthosis [15,16] presents a new concept in the field of orthotics. It consists of a lightweight nylon garment with integral pneumatic tubes which, when inflated, form almost rigid exoskeleton.

Various swivel walkers have been described [14,17,18]. The principle of the swivel walker consists on using side-to-side oscillation together with a forward center of gravity to promote ambulation. The swivel walker consists essentially of a light, stiff frame, hinged at the knees and hips and mounted on a swiveling foot mechanism. The advantages of these walkers include stability, easy mobility, and the ability of the wearer to ambulate with free hands. Disadvantages include slow velocity of locomotion, comparative metabolic inefficiency, awkwardness of getting into and from the standing position, and inability to be used on uneven surfaces.

Important contributions in the field of orthosis were accomplished through the development of the hip guidance orthosis (HGO) [19] and the reciprocating gait orthosis (RGO) [20]. These custom-made braces enable SCI patients to reach functional standing and efficient ambulation [21]. Isakov et al. [22] observed that as far as locomotion is concerned, the general principles of these orthoses are similar. The body is braced from the mid-trunk to the feet, with knees and ankles immobilised. The hips are allowed to flex and extend, but are prevented from moving into adduction when the leg is lifted off the ground. Walking is achieved by pulling the trunk forward, using crutches or rollator, then tipping the pelvis so that the trailing leg is lifted clear of the ground, thus allowing it to move forward and take a step. The hip joints on the HGO are free to flex and extend between stops, whereas on the RGO there are twin cables linking the two hip joints of the brace which permit a range of motion of approximately 15 degrees extension and 45 degrees flexion. During ambulation, when the patient shifts his weight on to the forward stance leg and pushes his upper trunk backwards, the Bowden cable system of the RGO is being activated providing a push-pull type of mechanism. An extension in the brace hip joint of the stance leg brings the cable into a state of tension. This mechanical energy is being transferred to the opposite brace hip joint and as a result it pulls forward into flexion the swinging contra lateral limb. The existence of a solid ankle-foot orthosis positioned in approximately 7 degrees of plantar flexion assists in raising the body center of gravity during heel-off through toe-off phases. As a result, no lateral trunk shift is required for the ground clear-off of the swing leg.

## 2) Functional Electrical Stimulation

Functional electrical stimulation (FES) as a therapeutic technique for physical treatment and rehabilitation is constantly expanding. Liberson [23] pioneered work concerned with functional electrotherapy to motor deficit rehabilitation in patients with a central nervous system lesion. In his study on stimulation of the peroneal nerve in hemiplegics he defined functional electrotherapy as a form of replacement therapy, required in cases where the impulses coming from the central nervous system are lacking. At the very time of stimulation the resulting muscle contraction has a functional purpose in locomotion, prehension, or in other muscle activity. Spastic paraplegics suffer from upper motor neuron lesions with normal spinal arc reflex. In these patients, the paralysed muscles can be activated by electrical stimulation. At tetanic stimulation and with proper frequency and intensity, these muscles can be strengthened [24]. Investigation of the cumulative influence of electrical stimulation on muscle strength has shown that atrophied muscles can be brought to a strength equal to that of normal stimulated muscles. In the two patients studied by Kralj et al. [25] a significant increase in muscle force and reduction in fatiguing was reported. It may be of interest to note the effect of electrical stimulation on muscle strength in healthy young adults as studied by Romero et al. [26], who found an increased isometric strength of the quadriceps muscles after a treatment period of 5 weeks.

Authors have suggested that FES offers further advantages such as the prevention of muscle contractures, and the reduction in spasticity [27]. Isakov et al. [28] investigated the reaction to effort related to the activation of the lower limb muscles by FES while the patient sat inactive in a wheelchair. Data of heart rate and oxygen consumption were taken in rest and following 30 minute of FES application. Results indicated that FES caused an increase in the heart rate by over 20 percent and oxygen consumption increase was of the order of 100 percent.

Electrical stimulation of the neuromuscular structures provides active forces for the patient to stand up, maintain the standing position and perform primitive walking. Standing up of a paraplegic patient by a two-channel electrical stimulator was analyzed by Bajd et al. [29] and compared with standing up of a healthy subject. Kralj et al. [25] reported on an orthotic device using FES that enables the patient to stand supported by his own bones and muscle forces, substituting the less effective long-leg-brace calipers that require complicated daily mounting procedures.

Isakov et al. [30,31] demonstrated that reciprocal gait of paraplegic patients with complete lesion of the spinal cord can be generated by an electrical stimulator and surface electrodes. In the double stance phase of gait the knee extensor muscles of both knees are stimulated and in the single phase, the knee is kept extended only on the supporting side. Swing of the contralateral lower extremity is achieved by cutaneously stimulating the afferent nerves and thus triggering the flexor reflex mechanisms. The optimal location of electrodes for electrical stimulation is summarized by Benton et al. [32].

While the vast majority of researchers make use of surface electrodes, there exists a tendency to introduce implanted electrodes which directly activate the muscle or nerve [33]. The main advantage of implanted FES is presented by the low stimulation currents or voltages required for muscle activation. In this way, smaller energy sources are needed, providing more specific excitation possibilities and considerably reduced size of stimulators.

Apart from surface and implanted FES, there also exists the third modality of delivering electrical stimuli to the paralysed muscles [34]. This technique is presented by the use of percutaneous intramuscular electrodes where the main advantage is the possibility of activation of many different muscles. However, lifetime of the wire electrodes is limited, cosmetic appearance is poor and there are difficulties in toileting.

The Loewenstein Biomechanics Laboratory group has been conducting an intensive research program into FES for the last 9 years, and has evaluated the influence of FES on different physiological systems and the biomechanical aspects of standing and walking by means of FES [28, 30, 31]. At present, the Loewenstein Rehabilitation Center offers a FES rehabilitation program, directed to SCI patients, which relies on a self-developed FES system [35].

**Patient Prerequisites** ~ The following are the criteria for patient selection:

1)  spastic paralysis of the lower limbs due to complete or incomplete upper motor neuron lesion.
2)  anesthesia of the lower limbs
3)  full range of motion in the joints of the lower limbs
4)  adequate balance
5)  no pressure sores
6)  satisfactory psychological condition
7)  general good state of health, motivation, and good cooperation.

•  Patients should be clinically examined to exclude cardiovascular, pulmonary or renal problems. Routine blood and urine laboratory tests should be performed.

The contraindications for FES application are the following:

•  Osteoporosis, heterotopic ossifications, confractures, peripheral nerve lesions, obesity, and severe spasticity.

**Training Program** ~ The training program is divided into three main stages: The first stage is dedicated to these steps:
a)  The motor points of the quadriceps and gluteus muscles and the triggering points on the legs which serve to provoke the flexion response should be determined. The exact location of the electrodes is established in every patient at the motor points, where the response to the stimulus is maximal. There is no difficulty to re-establish the same location of the electrodes for every patient.

The quadriceps are stimulated, 5 cm above the patella and 8 cm distally to the inguinal area. The flexion reflex is activated by stimulation of the shank, by placing the electrodes on the antero-lateral expect of the leg, just below the head of the fibula. The result is simultaneous flexion of the hip and knee, together with dorsiflexion of the foot. It is especially important to avoid stimulation too near the head of the fibula, as this gives plantar instead of dorsi-flexion of the foot because of the simultaneous activation of the tibialis posterior nerve. Placement of the proximal electrode is 4 cm below and 4 cm medial to the head of the fibula; placement of the distal electrode is 10 cm below and 3 cm medial to the head of the fibula.
b)  The patient's muscles are strengthened. Isotonic contractions of the quadriceps and activation of the flexion reflex are achieved by using the FES when the patient is in the sitting position on the wheelchair. Training is performed with all the electrodes connected, except those of the gluteus muscles. The sequence of automated stimuli given during the strengthening procedure is similar to the sequence used at a later stage to generate gait.

Stimulation of the quadriceps raises the lower leg against gravity up to full extension of the knee. Upon release of the quadriceps, the flexion reflex is stimulated. After approximately 2 weeks of training 500 g sand bags are attached to the ankle to increase the resistance during the strengthening process. Adequate padding behind the legs is prepared to prevent their bumping against the wheelchair.

Stimulation of the gluteus maximum muscles is found necessary in patients with high dorsal lesion, due to the very limited control of their pelvic girdle. Stimulating these muscles in the sitting position is technically difficult because hip extension may result in slipping down from the wheelchair. Strengthening of the gluteus maximus muscles during the training period is therefore abandoned and is done in the standing phase instead.

In the second stage, the patients are trained to stand up and maintain the standing position. This is achieved by applying continuous FES to the quadriceps muscles and in some patients to the gluteus maximus as well. The upright time is adjusted to the ability of each patient and is limited, when bending of the knees is first noticed. As first supports, parallel bars are used. However, when the patient is able to maintain equilibrium with a walker or with Canadian crutches, these are used instead.

The third stage is devoted to ambulation training while the patient is being supported on a walking aid, the type of which is determined to fit the patient's needs and abilities. It is possible to proceed into this stage only whenever the patient is able to stand steadily between the parallel bars for at least 5 minutes.

**System Description ~** The Loewenstein FES rehabilitation system [35] includes a small and light-weight portable stimulator and an adaptable instrumented walker. The system was designed to serve paraplegic patients as a primary tool for muscle restrengthening and for the restoration of standing and reciprocal walking. The system components, stimulator and walker, are simple to use and are controlled entirely by the user.

**Stimulator ~** The stimulator has six individually controllable current source channels. The pulse trains in each channel consist of asymmetrical rectangular biphasic pulses. The stimulus current characteristics ranges are 0-400mA for intensity, 10-50Hz for frequency and 100-300 microseconds for pulse width. All these parameters are individually adjustable for each channel. The power source is 12 V/500mAh from 10 rechargeable nickel cadmium batteries. The run time is 1.5 hours, with a load of 200 mA in four channels. The

stimulator's overall dimensions are 154 x 85 x 60 mm, and the total weight including batteries is 850 g.

The stimulator can be operated in either a local or a remote mode. The local mode is basically a preprogrammed mode. The stimulus parameters are 24 Hz for frequency and 250 microseconds for pulse width. The current intensity is the only parameter which can be altered during the course of stimulation, as required for the continuous re-adjustment in the process of muscle fatigue. This mode is used for the actual running of the three main programs. The remote control mode is hosted by the IBM PC or compatible computer and allows re-adjustment of all the stimulus parameters (i.e.current intensity, pulse width and pulse frequency) and saves these values in the computer. Communication between the stimulator and host computer is through a serial port, isolated by optocouplers within the stimulator, and a specially adapted card installed in the computer. This interface is designed so that the stimulator continues to function even if the host computer is accidentally switched off.

The stimulator and its control keys are shown in Figures 1 and 2. The key functions are as follows: Front Panel - (1) Program button: this allows the user to select one of the three main operating programs - exercise, stand, or walk. (2) Run button: this controls the 'standby' position. (3) Plus and minus buttons: these serve to increase and decrease current intensity for each channel individually. (4) Channel selection buttons: these are six separate buttons, three for the right and three for the left limb (e.g. RQ, RG, RP = right quadriceps, gluteus and peroneal muscles respectively). (5) Display: an eight character alpha-numeric LCD display provides the user with visual control over each stage of the treatment and with data on the state of the stimulator. Whenever the stimulator is switched on, 'SELF TEST' followed by 'GOOD' messages appear on the display. One can also read the name of the program in use, the chosen channel and the adjusted intensity of each of the six channels. Six miniature red lights for each channel button and one green light permit visual feedback of the instantaneous operating state of the stimulator. A blinking character on the LCD display warns the patient if the battery is running down, meaning that the stimulator should be shut down within five minutes.

Back panel - (1) Switch on/off button: for safety reasons, each time the stimulator is switched on, the initial current levels supplied in all six channels are of 1 mA only. (2) Port socket: for communication of external commands, which can be used when exercising and walking. They allow the patient or trainer to control the timing duration and intensity of the activating stimuli. (3) Electrodes/charger socket: for connection of the channels or charger wires. (4) Walker socket: for connection of the walker control wires.

**Walker** ~ A reciprocating-type walker was equipped with two control units to allow the patient to obtain the self-standing and walking functions. The control units were attached to each of the walker handles, positioned on the medial aspect of the handle, enabling the patient to control each with his thumb (Fig.3). Each set included (1) a joystick, with a double function. The first function is channel selection: inclining the joystick laterally activates the quadriceps muscles channel, while medial inclination activates the peroneal muscles channel. The second function is adjustment of current intensity: forward inclination results in increment and backward inclination in decrement of the current intensity to the preselected channel. (2) A swing activator button. When being pushed down it activates the peroneal channel and assists in swinging the leg forward. (3) A solitary run button, attached either to the left or right handle set. It substitutes the stimulator 'RUN' button, functioning as a program 'standby' position. When pressed, it activates the 'STAND' program. The walker control units are connected to the stimulator and can be also attached to the handles of a pair of Canadian crutches or tripods.

**Clinical Function** ~ Before using the stimulator, the surface electrodes should be properly attached to the lower limbs. These water-soaked, flexible carbon-fibre electrodes are easily attached to the skin using adhesive micropore-type or Velcro straps. The three main muscle groups to be activated in each limb are the glutei, quadriceps and tibialis anterior and peroneals. The first two groups are the main antigravitatory extensors, important in obtaining the functions of self-raising from sitting and maintaining supported standing. The third group is the dorsi flexors of the ankle joint. The surface electrodes attached over the anteriolateral leg muscles have a double function: (1) to generate ankle dosiflexion, enabling an easy ground clear-off (2) to provoke the withdrawal or flexion reflex of the entire lower limb, allowing the limb to swing forward while taking a step.

When the stimulator is switched on, the messages 'SELF-TEST' and 'GOOD" appear after one another on the display. Thereafter, the appropriate program can be selected by pressing the 'PROG' button on the front panel, after which the stimulator is set to the 'standby' position. The stimulator programs provide the following functions.

**Muscle Strengthening Program** ~ Three basic exercises have so far been incorporated. (1) Serial activation of the two legs: activation of each leg consists of stimulation of the quadriceps for knee extension followed by stimulation of the ankle dorsi flexors and elicitation of the withdrawal reflex of the same limb. (2) Alternate activation of the two legs: stimulation of the quadriceps of one leg is followed by the activation of the ankle dorsi flexors of the opposite leg. (3) Synchronous activation of both legs: the quadriceps and the dorsi flexors of the opposite limb are activated simultaneously.

Whenever a program has been chosen and the stimulator is in the 'standby' position, the patient can start the muscle test procedure. First the channel is selected by pressing one of the six related buttons and the required initial current intensity is then adjusted by pressing the 'plus' button. The current is increased until the required muscle response is obtained. When the desired current intensity has been established, the 'RUN' button is pressed and the preselected program is transferred from the 'standby' position to the active mode.

**The Standing Program ~** This uses a combination of the stimulator and the instrumented walker. In this program, continuous and simultaneous electrical impulses activate the four channels to the antigravitatory muscles. Prior to program activation, the current intensity to the muscles is adjusted while the stimulator is still in the 'standby' position . The patient then inclines himself forward in his wheelchair to shift his upper trunk over his feet whilst holding the walker handles. At this moment he presses the solitary run button attached to one of walker handle sets and the 'STAND' program is activated. The electrical stimulation of the involved muscles causes a strong enough contraction to raise the patient from the wheelchair to the upright position. For smooth transition, the current is supplied by an ascending ramp. While standing, the patient can readjust the current intensity to the quadriceps by operating the walker handle joysticks. To sit down smoothly, the patient can gradually decrease the current intensity and lower himself into a chair. In case of accidental stimulator shut-down, the current stops via a descending ramp, to prevent a sudden fall.

**The Walking Program ~** This is divided into two stages. The first stage is similar to the 'STAND' program. The second stage consists of the reciprocal gait activation. Generation of a step forward is accomplished by pressing the swing activator button of the walker handle set. As long as this button is kept pressed, the current to the quadriceps and glutei in the ipsilateral side is interrupted, whilst the peroneal muscles channel is activated. The shank electrodes on the same limb stimulate the dorsi flexors and elicitate the withdrawal reflex. At the moment when the entire limb is raised to start the swing phase, the patient releases this button and the quadriceps and glutei are reactivated, while the peroneal channel is interrupted. The contracting quadriceps extend the knee and the patient can shift his trunk forward over the supporting leg to enter the double stance phase. During the swinging maneuver, the antigravitatory muscles in the opposite leg are isometrically

activated to support the paraplegic's body weight.

During ambulation, quadriceps muscle fatigue may result in the collapse of the relative knee while the limb is in stance. Therefore, whenever the user realizes that his knee tends to bend, he should immediately increase the current to the corresponding muscle by using the joystick on the walker handle. At the end of ambulation, the patient can sit down using the same procedure described in the standing program.

### 3) The Hybrid System

The concept of combining orthotics together with FES was first described in 1972 [36]. This combines the benefits of passive long leg braces intended for the standing and walking of paraplegic patients with the possibilities given by FES. The main advantage of hybrid systems is higher patient safety. Within a hybrid orthosis, the mechanical component serves to support the subject's body weight, while electrical stimulation is used to provide propulsion. Investigators have evaluated the advantages of different hybrid systems. Functions such as standing up and sitting down as well as ambulation become more efficient and require less energy consumption when combining FES with HGO [37] or with RGO [38, 39].

Isakov et al. [22] described the clinical and technical principles of a hybrid system composed of RGO and FES. the efficacy of this system was evaluated while performing the tasks of stand-up and sit-down as well as ambulation. The results obtained with the hybrid system were compared with those obtained with the RGO only. Although influences of the hybrid system on speed of gait were small, the reduction in effort demand was found to be impressive. Values of physiological cost index [40] during walking with RGO and with the hybrid system decreased from 2.55 bts/min to 1.54 bts/min respectively. Stand-up and sit-down have been found to be much easier using the hybrid system, indicating that this system enables a higher number of repetitions in 2 minutes and a smaller demand in effort as there is a much smaller increase in heart rate. Subjective reports from the patient indicate that the hybrid system allows a better control on steps, it is comfortable and less tiring when using it.

## Conclusions

In recent years a considerable amount of time, effort and money has been directed towards permitting paralysed people to walk again using reciprocal gait. There are three approaches currently under development; mechanical orthoses, functional electrical stimulation, and hybrid devices which combine the first two alternatives.

Continuing research and corresponding advances in medical technology mean that the future may hold many exciting new developments, with corresponding benefits to the paraplegic person.

****** 

## REFERENCES

[1] Petrofsky JS, Heaton HH, Phillips CA. Outdoor bicycle for exercise in paraplegics and quadriplegics. J. *Biomed Eng 5:292-298, 1983.*

[2] Phillips, CA, Petrofsky JS, Hendershot DM, Stafford D. Functional electrical exercise. A comprehensive approach for physical conditioning of the spinal cord injured patient. *Orthopedics 7:1112-1119, 1984.*

[3]Hjeltnes, N, Lannem, A., Functional neuromuscular stimulation in 4 patients with complete paraplegia. *Paraplegia 28:235-243, 1990.*

[4] Isakov E., Susak Z., Energy expenditure and cardiac response in above-knee amputees while using open and locked knee joints. *Scand J Rehabil Med (sup) 12:108-111, 1985.*

[5] Waters, RL, HislopHJ, Perry J, Antonelli, D., Energetics: Application of the study and management of locomotor disabilities. *Orthop Clin N Am 9:351-377, 1978.*

[6] Finley FR.., Cody KA. Locomotive characteristics of urban pedestrians. *Arch Phys Med Rehabil 51: 423-426, 1970.*

[7] Corcoran PJ, Brengelman, GL. Oxygen uptake in normal and handicapped subjects, in relation to speed of walking beside velocity-controlled cart. *Arch Phys Med Rehabil 51:78-87, 1970.*

[8] Saunders, JB, Inman, VT, Eberhart, HD. The major determinants in normal and pathological gait. *J Bone Joint Surg 35(A): 543-549, 1953.*

[9] Fisher, SV, Gullickson G. Energy cost of ambulation in health and disability: a literature review. *Arch Phys Med Rehabil 59:124-133, 1978.*

[10] Smith, PA, Glaser, RM, Petrofsky, JS, Underwood PD, Smith GB, Richard JJ. Arm crank vs handrim wheelchair propulsion: Metabolic and cardiopulmonary responses. *Arch Phys Med Rehabil 64:249-254, 1983.*

[11] Coghlan JK, Robinson, CE, Newmarch, B, Jackson G. Lower extremity bracing in paraplegia: A follow-up study. *Paraplegia 19:379-385, 1981.*

[12] Hong, C, Luis, S, Chung, S. Follow-up study on the use of leg braces issued to spinal cord injury patients. *Paraplegia 28:172-177, 1990.*

[14] Henshaw, JT. "Walking" appliances for paraplegics and tetraplegics. *Paraplegia 17:163-168, 1979-80.*

[15] Lehmann, JF, Stonebridge, JB, Lateur, B.J. Pneumatic and standard double upright orthoses: Comparison of their biomechanical function in three patients with spinal cord injuries. *Arch Phys Med Rehabil 58:72-79, 1977.*

[16] Ragnarsson, KT, Sell, GF, McGarrity, M, Ofir, R. Pneumatic orthosis for paraplegic patients: Functional evaluation and prescription considerations. *Arch Phys Med Rehabil 56:479-483, 1975.*

[17] O'Daniel, WE, Hahn, HR. Follow-up usage of the Scott-Craig orthosis in paraplegia. *Paraplegia 19 :373-378, 1981.*

[18] Seymor, RJ, Knapp, CF, Anderson TR, Kearney, JT. Paraplegia use of the Orlau swivel walker: Case Report. *Arch Phys Med Rehabil 63:490-494, 1982.*

[19] Rose, GK. The principles and practice of hip guidance articulations. *Prosthet Orthot Int 3:37-43, 1979.*

[20] Douglas, R, Larson, PF, D'Ambrosia, R, McCall, R. The LSU reciprocation gait orthosis *Orthopedics 6:834-838, 1983.*

[21] Jefferson, RJ, Whittle, MW. Performance of three walking orthoses for the paralysed: A case study using gait analysis. *Prosthet Orthot Int 14:103-110, 1990.*

[22] Isakov, E, Douglas, R, Berns, P. Ambulation using the reciprocating gait orthosis and functional electrical stimulation. *Papaplegia 30: 239-245, 1992.*

[23] Liberson, WT, Holmquest, HJ, Scot, D, Dew, M. Functional electrotherapy. Stimulation of the peroneal nerve synchronized with the swing phase of the gait of hemiplegic patients. *Arch Phys Med Rehabil 42:101-105, 1961.*

[24] Kralj, A, Bajd, T, Tur, R, Krajnik, T, Benko, H. Gait restoration in paraplegic patients: A feasibility demonstration using multichannel

surface electrode FES. *J Rehab Res Dev 20:3-20, 1983.*

[25] Kralj, A, Majd, T, Turk. Electrical stimulation providing functional use of paraplegic patient muscles. *Med Prog Technol 7:3-9, 1980.*

[26] Romero, JA, Sanford, TL, Schroeder, RV, Fahey, Td. The effect of electrical stimulation of normal quadriceps on strength and girth. *Med Sci Sports Exer 14: 194-197, 1982.*

[27] Lagasse, PP, Roy, MA. Functional electrical stimulation and the eduction of co-contraction in spastic biceps brachi.*Clin Rehabil 3:111-116, 1989.*

[28] Isakov, E., Mizrahi, J Najenson, T. Biomechanical and Physiological evaluation of FES-activated paraplegic patients. *J Rehabil Res & Dev 23(3): 9-19, 1986.*

[29] BajdT, Kralj, A, Turk R. Standing-up of a healthy subject and a paraplegic subject. *J Biomech 15:1-10, 1982.*

[30] Isakov E, Mizrahi, J, Graupe D, Becker, E, Najenson, T. Energy cost and physiological reactions to effort during activation of paraplegics by functional electrical stimulation. l*Scand J Rehabil Med 12 (supp):102-107, 1985.*

[31] Mizrahi J, Isakov , E, Susak Z, Becker, D. Mechanical and physiological gait factors of above knee amputees and of paraplegics activiated by functional electrical stimulation. *Ergonomics in Rehabilitation.* Eds. A. Mital and W. Karwowski. Taylor & Francis Ltd., London. pp. 211-230, 1988.

[32] Benton, LA, Baker, LL, Bowman, BR, Waters, RL. Functional electrical stimulation - a practical clinical guide (2nd ed.) Downey, CA, *Rancho Los Amigos Rehabilitation Engineering Center,* Downey Hospital, 1981.

[33] Strojnik, P, Acimovic, R, Vavken, E, Simic V, Stanic U. Treatment of drop foot using an implantable peroneal underknee stimulator. *Scand J Rehab Med 19:37-43, 1987*

[34] Marsolais EG, Kobetic R. Implantation techniques and experience with percutaneous intramuscular electrodes in the lower extremities. *J Rehabil Res Dev 23:1-12, 1986.*

[35] Isakov, E, Mizrahi, J. FES system for self-activation: an electrical stimulator and instrumented walker. *Clin Rehabil 7:67-72, 1993.*

[36] Tomovic, R, Vukobratovic, M., Vodovnic, L. Hybrid actuators for orthotic systems - hybrid assistive system. *Proceeding of International Symposium on External Control of Human Extremities.* Dubrovnik, Yugoslavia. pp. 73, 1972

[37] McClelland M Andrew BJ, Patrick JH, Freeman, PA, El Masri, WS. Augmentation of the Oswestry parawalker orthosis by means of surface electrical stimulation: gait analysis of three patients. *Paraplegia 25:32-38, 1987.*

[38] Phillips, CA, Hendershot, DM. Functional electrical stimulation and reciprocating gait orthosis for ambulation exercise in a tetraplegic patient: A case study. *Paraplegia 29: 268-276, 1991.*

[39] Hirokawa, S, Grim, M, Le T, Solomonow, M, Baratt, RV, Shoji H, D'ambrosia, RD. Energy consumption in paraplegic ambulation using the reciprocating gait orthosis and electric stimulation of the thigh muscles. *Arch Phys Med Rehabil 71:687-694, 1990.*

[40] Butler, P, Engelbrecht, M, Major, RE, Tait, JH, Stallard, J, Patrick, JH. Physiological cost index of walking for normal children and its use as an indicator of physical handicap. *Dev Med Child Neyrol 26:607-612, 1984.*

******

**About the Author: Dr. Eli Isakov** is a specialist in Physical Medicine and Rehabilitation (PMR) at the Loewenstein Hospital Rehabilitation Center, Tel-Aviv University Medical School, 278 Ahuza Stree, P.O. Box 3, Raanana 43100, Israel. Presently, he divides his time between clinical, academic and research activities as a vice-departmental head of the Orthopaedic Rehabilitation Department and a lecturer at the School of Medicine at Tel-Aviv University. He is also engaged in lecturing and research projects in overseas academic institutes in Europe, the United States and South Africa.

**Source:** Reprinted with permission from the author who wrote this article specifically for the second edition of *Perspectives on Disability.*

# Thinking About Incest, Deafness, and Counseling
Elaine Westerlund, Ed. D.

**Introduction** ~ Childhood incest is now recognized as a trauma that *at least* one hearing woman in six has experienced (Belmonte & Boyer, 1983; Russell, 1983, 1986; Wyatt, 1985). There is little reason to assume that deaf[*] women are any less often victimized as children, and there may, in fact, be reasons to believe that deaf women may be more vulnerable as children.

For incest to occur and continue, the sexual offender must choose a victim who will likely remain silent. Or he must choose a victim who will not be believed in the event that she tells. The vast majority of deaf children (over 90%) come from hearing families (Woodward, 1982). During the years that today's adult women grew up, almost 90% of families with deaf children did not use sign language (Mindel & Vernon, 1971). The young deaf child has frequently been prohibited from using sign language both at home and in the school on the mistaken assumption that this would prevent the child from ever developing appropriate speech (i.e. from ever becoming "normal"). For similar reasons, contact with Deaf adults and the Deaf community has also often been systematically avoided. Thus, in many instances, particularly in the past, the young deaf child has essentially been barred from reporting sexual abuse. Also, if a deaf child <u>did</u> try to disclose incest (in spite of such language difficulties and the restrictions these difficulties impose on relationships), the incest offender could, with relative ease, claim "misunderstanding" or "miscommunication."

It would seem reasonable then to speculate that incest offenders may have viewed (and may continue to view) deaf children as "disabled" children and as "safe" targets. If so, the percentage of deaf women in the United States today who have experienced incest could well be higher than the estimated 16-33% of hearing women with such histories (Belmonte & Boyer, 1983; Russell, 1983, 1986; Wyatt, 1985).

What is obvious, with or without comparative statistics, is that the experience of incest could be that much more complex for deaf women. Whatever issues are associated with the incest, deafness surely adds its own dimension and power, as the following discussions on denial, stigma, self-blame, self-esteem, confusion, body perception, powerlessness, and loss will illustrate.

**Denial** ~ Incestuous families are families adept at denial, families unable to acknowledge and confront problems. A frequent complaint heard from women with incest histories is, "No one ever paid attention to the fact that there were a lot of problems in our home. Everybody just pretended that nothing was happening and that we were an ordinary, happy family. No one ever listened to me about anything else, so why would I bother to tell them about the incest?"

For deaf women, many of whom may have grown up in hearing families that denied their deafness, that refused to communicate in sign language, and that may have even insisted that they conceal their deafness as much as possible, such issues could clearly be magnified.

**Stigma** ~ Women with incest histories commonly experience an extreme sense of alienation and isolation, of being different in such a way as to feel outside the realm of humanity.

Deaf women, all of whom experience devaluing attitudes toward deafness outside the home, and many of whom are exposed to such attitudes inside the home, are made painfully aware of their "differentness". This could obviously compound feelings of shame, abnormality, and nonbelonging that incestuous experiences generally produce.

---

[*] In this paper, the use of the lower-case "deaf" refers to audiological deafness, and the use of the capitalized "Deaf" refers to cultural (i.e., sociological) deafness, as originally proposed by James Woodward (1972).

**Self-Blame** ~ As children there is little choice but to blame oneself for whatever might be wrong in the family. It is far too threatening for a child to believe that the people life depends upon are "bad" or, worse yet, "crazy". And it is far too risky for a child to express her rage at the adults in her life. In incestuous families, children often receive messages that if they were just better children everything would be all right. Such children internalize these messages and, when incest occurs, they assume responsibility for that, too. They believe the incest is the result of something they did or failed to do; they believe it's because of who they are or who they're not.

For deaf women, many of whom have received messages as children that they fell short of parental expectations or weren't working hard enough at becoming "normal" (through speech and speech-reading), self-blame and guilt could be exacerbated.

**Self-Esteem** ~ Since the self must be viewed as "bad" and anger turned inward when incest occurs, feelings of self-hatred and worthlessness are commonly experienced by women with incest histories.

Deaf women may additionally develop a sense of inferiority as children in response to others' attitudes toward them or rejection of them for their deafness. As adults, assuming they identify as culturally Deaf, negative self-image may be strengthened by societal (and often continued family) devaluation of their language and culture.

**Confusion** ~ Incest is a highly confusing event or, more often, series of events, in the life of <u>any</u> child. For the deaf child, the confusion experienced with incest may be that much greater.

The problems with language development that accompany deafness severely restrict the information the child receives about the world (through the customarily available channels). This imposes limitations on the child's ability to comprehend what is happening and how she feels. A deaf child may have greater difficulty for this reason labeling her experience abusive or exploitive. Since deaf people continue to be denied access to information, a deaf woman's adult understanding of the incest violation and its meaning to her life might, likewise, be delimited.

**Body Perception** ~ Ambivalence or negativity related to the body are common among women with incest histories. Many women report feeling "broken", "damaged," or "not whole" as a result of the incest.

Deafness may well complicate and intensify these feelings since deaf children are taught by hearing children (and hearing adults, including parents sometimes) to view themselves as physically deficient, incomplete, or defective.

**Powerlessness** ~ Women with incest histories are often routinely controlled and humiliated within their families. They may come to view themselves as helpless and ineffectual in the world, and may continue to be victimized in adulthood.

Deaf women may additionally develop a false sense of inadequacy or a perception of themselves as dependent due to widespread negative attitudes toward deafness and the greater power wielded (and not infrequently abused) by the hearing majority.

**Loss** ~ Every woman with an incest history must mourn the loss of childhood and the loss of the ideal family as part of the healing process. For deaf women with incest histories, these losses may clearly be multiplied.

In addition to the ways in which deafness might influence the issues for a woman with an incest history, there are ways in which deafness might influence the therapy relationship should a woman seek counseling.

**Confidentiality** ~ Confidentiality is a primary concern for any woman with an incest history. However, for a woman who is deaf, confidentiality can become a major problem.

The Deaf community is somewhat comparable to a small town in which everyone knows one another. Deaf women may meet acquaintances coming from or going to therapy. In fact, given the limited number of clinicians who work with deaf people, this is likely to occur. Or deaf women may be observed at locations where it is known that certain events (such as incest groups) take place on particular evenings. Such information may then leak to other Deaf people and become a source of speculation or gossip among members of the Deaf community.

If a woman's therapist is Deaf, or is involved to any degree in the Deaf community, social contact is very likely to occur (whatever the therapist-client boundaries) because of the nature of the Deaf community. In these instances, privacy for the therapist as well as confidentiality for the client may become problematic.

Another factor to consider is that breaches of confidentiality have frequently been part of the experience of deaf women growing up. In school settings for deaf children, where a sense of "family" sometimes exists, administrators or teachers may be given access to information from counseling sessions. In hearing schools, confidentiality may be breached simply because hearing teachers and administrators find it easier to talk to hearing parents than to a deaf child. Such occurrences may contribute later on to concerns on the part of deaf women that confidentiality will not be respected by the therapist.

**Trust ~** Trust is an equally important concern for any woman with an incest history, given the betrayal that occurs with incest. For deaf women, additional layers of mistrust may have developed due to their experiences with hearing people.

Historically, deaf people have been viewed from a clinical-pathological perspective. For years deaf people were vulnerable to misdiagnosis and confinement in institutions for the mentally retarded and mentally ill because mental health professionals didn't understand deafness, couldn't communicate, and were culturally insensitive. In school settings, which have traditionally been controlled by hearing people, deaf women may have experienced a variety of betrayals. They may also have been taught in such settings to view counseling as discipline for "bad girls".

Deaf women with incest histories may approach therapy (which generally occurs

with a hearing professional whose loyalties are questionable) with double suspicion and a justifiable fear of humiliation.

**Power and Control ~** In the therapy session, power and control automatically rest with the therapist. This is something that women with incest histories may be acutely aware of and something that therapists should be sensitive to.

For deaf women with incest histories, the experience of therapy directed by a hearing clinician may well be overwhelming. Adding a hearing interpreter may obviously compound the issues.

The hearing therapist should recognize, particularly with miscommunication, that she/he may be identified with the hearing parent. This means that the transference may be to an incest offender who had total control over the client (and, perhaps the family) or to, at best, a nonoffending parent who didn't have sufficient power within the family to protect the client as a child. Power and control issues (and the complexity of transference phenomena that may arise in relation to both the hearing therapist and the hearing interpreter) would clearly be minimized in situations where the hearing therapist is fluent in ASL (American Sign Language) and chooses not to work with an interpreter, or where the therapist is also deaf.

**Avoidance ~** Many women with incest histories report having had the experience of meeting with a clinician (even over time) who was unable to directly discuss the incest. The therapist's avoidance, often rationalized as the client's inability to "handle it," generally conveys several messages to the client. These are: (1) maybe it's not really so. (2) It's true, but how much difference could it make? (3) It's true, but it's too unpleasant to confront. (4) We don't talk about such subjects here.

Likewise, avoiding direct discussion related to the origin and history of a client's deafness (assuming an alliance has developed) conveys similar messages. These messages may be very reminiscent of the messages the client received from her family regarding her deafness. This, again, could create negative transference situations. Denial and mini-mization, assumption (from a "nonmember" mind set), and inadvertent insensitivity are common to both work in the field of incest and work in the field of deafness.

**Protection** ~ Work with women with incest histories may provoke (among other things) powerful rescue fantasies in the therapist. If these are not well managed by the clinician, boundaries and identities may become blurred and confused. The therapist who attempts to compensate for all past parental failings experienced by the incest client may invite client regression, discourage the growth of autonomy, and interfere with the development of a healthier self-image.

If the incest client is deaf, she may be perceived by the rescuing therapist as that much more in need of care. The therapist may become inappropriately involved in the life concerns of the deaf client (employment, housing, etc.) under the assumption that this will be welcomed. In fact, the deaf incest client may experience such caring as humiliating or intrusive experiences. There is a difference between acknowledging the real needs of a deaf client (such as assistance with a telephone call) and undermining the client's sense of independence and competence.

The therapist would do well to keep in mind, with both deaf and hearing women, that incest is likely to produce a strong need for independence (symbolic of safety) and a deep longing, despite the fear, for dependency (symbolic of the lost childhood). Even appropriately offered help or protection may be difficult for the incest client (who has clearly experienced a lack of parental protection or help) to accept. For the deaf incest client, this difficulty may be complicated by the fact that she may also have experienced a lack of parental protection or help in relation to cultural and linguistic oppression.

The complexity of issues for the deaf woman with an incest history may not be fully recognized until well into therapy. The compounding of effects from the two experiences may present what appear to be insurmountable challenges at times. And yet,

as with incest, the experience of deafness often produces remarkable strengths and internal resources to draw upon. When I think of deaf women with incest histories, I think of the incredible capacity of children to persevere, and even triumph, in the face of injustice and cruelty.

****** 

## REFERENCES

**Belmonte, F., & Boyer, J.** (1983). NCAN statement on incest. *NCAN News, 13,* 2.
**Mindel, E., & Vernon, M.** (1971). *They Grow in Silence.* Silver Spring, MD: National Association of the Deaf.
**Russell, D.** (1983). The incidence and prevalence of intrafamilial and extrafamilial sexual abuse in female children. *Child Abuse and Neglect: The International Journal, 7,* 133-146.
**Russell, D.** (1986) *The secret trauma: Incest in the lives of girls and women.* New York: Basic Books.
**Woodward, J.** (1972) Implications for sociolinguistics research among the deaf. *Sign Language Studies, 1,* 1-7.
**Woodward, J.** (1982) How you gonna get to heaven if you can't talk with Jesus: On depathologizing deafness. Silver Spring, MD: *T.J.Publishers, Inc.*
**Wyatt, G.** (1985). The sexual abuse of Afro-American and white women in childhood. *Child Abuse and Neglect: The International Journal, 9,* 507-519.

******* 

**About the Author: Elaine Westerlund, ED.D.** is a psychologist in Cambridge, MA. Request for reprints may be sent to Incest Resources, Inc. Cambridge Women's Center, 46 Pleasant Street, Cambridge, MA. 02139.

# Psychotherapy with Handicapped Sexually Abused Children

Patricia M. Sullivan
John M. Scanlan

**Introduction** ~ In response to the vulnerability of handicapped children to maltreatment, the Boys Town National Research Hospital established the Center for Abused Handicapped Children in 1984. Thus far, the Center has provided therapeutic services to over 600 handicapped children from 28 U.S. states and three provinces in Canada. This patient base provided an opportunity to develop therapeutic intervention techniques and study their effects on behavioral problems typically manifested in sexually abused handicapped victims.

The field of psychotherapy with sexually abused children is less than 10 years old. Accordingly, everyone in the field has less than a decade's worth of experience. Most sexual abuse therapists are self-trained practitioners who have learned their skills on the job. Psychotherapy typically takes place behind closed doors, and much of the undertaking is necessarily subjective. Due to these factors, confusion is the general state of affairs for all psychotherapeutic intervention, that is, we do not know the process that takes place between the therapist and the child or what makes one therapist or therapeutic method more effective than another.

This chapter describes the psychotherapy treatment program at the Center for Abused Handicapped Children and discusses therapy treatment plans, including typical goals and therapy methods and techniques. This treatment program is considered within the context of psychotherapy research with nonhandicapped children, including both individual and group therapy. The psychological dynamics and behavioral sequelae of sexual abuse which necessitate psychotherapeutic intervention is discussed, and the manifestations of Post-Traumatic Stress Disorder and its diagnostic applicability to sexually abused handicapped children are examined. Finally, a summary of the results of an efficacy study on the therapeutic program at the Center is presented.

## Therapy with Nonhandicapped Samples

Systematic research on intervention with sexually abused youngsters or perpetrators of sexual abuse is not available (Knutson, 1988). In clinical practice, virtually all forms of child or adolescent psychotherapy have been provided for victims. Treatment strategies are typically a function of implicit theories of abuse, and treatment seems to differ according to whether youngsters are seen as victims or perpetrators in the episode.

The most ambitious treatment article in the literature on sexual abuse of children was completed in 1982 in California. Giarretto (1982) studied psychotherapeutic services provided to over 4000 youngsters and their families and worked exclusively with incest victims. Although systematic process and outcome data were not provided, Giarretto reports that 90% of the children were reunited with their families, and the recidivism rate was less than 1%. He recommends a sequence of therapy that begins with individual counseling for all participants (i.e. mother, father, child,) followed by mother-daughter counseling, marital counseling, father-daughter counseling, family counseling, and then group counseling.

## Individual vs. Group Therapy

In the literature dealing with psychotherapy of sexual abuse victims, individual therapy is viewed, for a variety of reasons, as the main form of treatment as well as the initial phase of the therapeutic process (Haugaard & Reppucci, 1988). It is the least threatening form of treatment, especially during the early stages of therapy, the most easily tailored to the specific needs of the child, and the form of treatment for preparing the child for other forms of treatment. If the child later begins group or family therapy, concurrent individual treatment can help the child explore issues that arise during these sessions or to work through issues that the child does not yet feel able to reveal in the other settings.

Group therapy also has some advantages and disadvantages. It is often cited as the preferred method of treatment for the victim and the abuser (Forseth & Brown, 1981), and it can take place at the same time as, or subsequent to, individual treatment and can be concurrent with family treatment. Group treatment can provide victims with experiences not in individual or family treatment, and thus, it can be a valuable complement to other forms of therapy. Indeed, in a practical vain, group treatment may be more cost effective than individual therapy; however, there are some negative aspects of group treatment. The main disadvantage is that it may "suggest" symptoms or concerns to some group members. The concern is that some group members will develop symptoms or beliefs because other members have them. Group treatment does offer members a chance to interact with other abuse victims, reducing each member's sense of being the only one to have suffered abuse and offering members the opportunity to understand how others have reacted to and/or handled their abuse. When employed in residential settings, the possibility exists that group members will taunt other members outside the group meetings and that confidentiality of the therapy session may not be maintained. Scapegoating weaker group members can occur both in and out of group therapy sessions.

Therapy at the Center for Abused Handicapped Children has been primarily individual in nature. This treatment strategy is used because the majority of children served do not have the sophisticated verbal or language skills necessary to handle the intense verbal interactions that typically occur in group therapy. In addition, the Center has treated many hearing impaired children who characteristically have problems following the content of group psychotherapy sessions even when an interpreter is present. It may be that group psychotherapy is the treatment of choice with highly verbal nonhandicapped

adolescents; however, research is needed to demonstrate the therapeutic process and outcome differences between individual and group therapy with handicapped participants.

## Psychological Sequelae of Sexual Abuse

A growing body of research among nonhandicapped victims of sexual abuse indicates that the effects of abuse are long-term (Eth & Pynoos, 1985; Browne & Finkelhor, 1986), and if left untreated, sexual abuse results in disastrous consequences for the victim's overall adjustment to life. (Van Der Kolk, 1987). One of these disastrous consequences is Post-Traumatic Stress Disorder, and the Center for Abused Handicapped Children was among the first mental health centers to apply the diagnosis of Post-Traumatic Stress Disorder to child victims of sexual abuse. This has subsequently become the diagnosis of choice for victims of child abuse (Eth & Pynoos, 1985). The ramifications of this disorder on the overall functioning of its victims are just becoming known in the psychological and psychiatric literature. Two primary findings are that the victims are disordered because of the initial stressor, and the effects of the trauma are long-term in nature, with manifestations in various aspects of the victim's life. This can occur regardless of the number of times the child was sexually victimized. For example, youngsters who are victimized only one time can exhibit pronounced psychological difficulties. In a comprehensive review of the literature on the impact of child sexual-abuse, Browne and Finkelhor (1986) found that long-term effects include depression, self-destructive behavior, anxiety, feelings of stigma and isolation, poor self-esteem, impaired ability to trust, substance abuse, and sexual maladjustment.

The manifestations of Post-Traumatic Stress Disorder include (American Psychiatric Association, 1980) the existence of a recognizable stressor, re-experiencing the trauma by recurrent and intrusive recollections of the event, recurrent dreams of the event, sudden action or feeling as if the traumatic event were recurring because of an association with an environmental or ideational stimulus, numbing of responsiveness and a reduced involvement with the external world (including markedly diminished interest in activities, feelings of detachment and/or estrangement from others, and constructed affect), hyper alertness or exaggerated startle responses, sleep disturbance, guilt about survival when others have not, or about behavior required for survival, memory impairment or trouble concentrating, avoidance of activities that arouse recollection of the traumatic event, and intensification of symptoms by exposure to events that symbolize or resemble the initial traumatic event. Symptoms may begin immediately or soon after the trauma; however, it is not unusual for the symptoms to emerge after a latency period of months or years following the trauma. The impairment may be either mild or affect nearly every aspect of life. Phobic avoidance of situations or activities resembling or symbolizing the original trauma may result in academic, occupational, or recreational impairment. The condition may also interfere with interpersonal relationships such as marriage or family life. Emotional liability, depression, and guilt may result in self-defeating behavior or suicidal reactions. Substance abuse disorders may also develop. The Center for Abused Handicapped Children has seen many of these diagnostic characteristics in the children it has served. Also, periods of exacerbation and remission of symptoms among the children have been noted.

Victims of sexual abuse, handicapped or not, require psychotherapeutic intervention to address the psychological injury inflicted by the abuse. Both psychological difficulties and behavioral problems often result from abuse and must be addressed within any given treatment program. Four traumagenic dynamics have been hypothesized to explain the effects of child sexual abuse (Finkelhor & Browne, 1985). The first, traumatic sexualization, is the process by which the child's sexuality is shaped in a developmentally inappropriate and interpersonally dysfunctional fashion. Betrayal, the second dynamic, occurs when the child discovers that someone on whom he or she was vitally dependent has caused them

harm. The third dynamic describes how victims are rendered powerless by the sexual abuse. The child's body space is repeatedly violated, and the resulting sense of powerlessness is reinforced when his or her attempts to halt the abuse are futile. The final dynamic, stigmatization, refers to the negative connotations and feelings (i.e. guilt, shame, badness) that are often communicated to the child within the context of the abuse and which often become incorporated into the child's self-image. Finkelhor and Browne (1985) suggest that these dynamics alter the child's cognitive and emotional orientation to the world, resulting in a distorted self-concept, diminished affective capacities, and a distrustful world view. This model of traumagenic dynamics has applications for use in the assessment of trauma among sexual abuse victims as well as in the establishment of treatment goals.

## Center for Abused Handicapped Children-Therapy Program

In establishing a therapeutic program for victims of sexual abuse at the Center for Abused Handicapped Children, we reviewed the available literature on therapeutic intervention with non-handicapped children. We then applied our knowledge of handicapped children and developed a therapy program which delineated specific treatment goals and therapeutic methods to be employed to achieve these goals.

An individual treatment plan is developed for each child receiving psychotherapy at the Center for Abused Handicapped Children. We provide parents or appropriate personnel with a copy of the child's treatment plan as well as formalized psychotherapy progress reports which are given approximately every six months. The psychotherapy treatment plan includes a relevant case history and background information section, specific counseling goals and objectives, treatment methods that are used with the child to meet the goals outlined in the report, and a prognostic statement about how long the child will need to remain in counseling. The psychotherapy progress report summarizes the child's progress to date in meeting the goals and objectives outlined in the treatment plan, treatment methods that were used in meeting the counseling goals, and specific recommendations regarding the child's counseling.

The following are typical goals included in the psychotherapy treatment plans (Sullivan & Scanlan, 1987).

*1. To alleviate guilt engendered by the sexual abuse and to assist the child in regaining the ability to trust peers and adults.* Much time is spent with every child involved in therapy in order to emphasize to them that the maltreatment they endured was not their fault. This goal also entails providing the child with appropriate methods for preventing and/or avoiding future sexual abusive situations. This helps to restore the child's ability to trust peers and adults.

*2. To help treat the depression that is often manifested by children who have been sexually abused.* A primary secondary behavioral characteristic of sexually abused children is depression. The symptoms include sleep disturbance, difficulties in concentrating, loss of appetite or excessive eating, ruminations, and sometimes suicidal thoughts, gestures, and attempts. If the child manifests symptoms of depression, these are addressed within the treatment.

*3. To help the child learn to express anger relating to the sexual abuse in appropriate and productive ways.* Victims of sexual abuse generally express anger regarding this victimization at some time in their therapy; therefore, the therapy needs to teach the child how to express this anger in appropriate and productive ways rather than harboring it for years and leaving it unexpressed. Sometimes this anger is expressed toward men or women in general (depending upon the sex of the perpetrator), and it can

potentially interfere with healthy interpersonal relationships.

*4. To teach basic information about normal human sexuality and interpersonal relationships.* A major component of a therapy treatment plan is to provide, through didactic and directive counseling techniques, basic sex education concepts and knowledge about establishing and maintaining appropriate interpersonal relationships with peers, family members, teachers, and adults. This didactic technique is undertaken at a level appropriate to the chronological age of the child. It is an integral part of the therapy program because, often, parents and caregivers consider handicapped individuals to be asexual, and accordingly, they neglect this aspect of the handicapped child's development.

*5. To teach the child sexual preference and homosexual issues, when appropriate.* Many adolescents who experience sexual abuse by adults or older peers of the same sex exhibit sexual identity problems regarding their sexual preference. Didactic counseling techniques are useful for teaching these adolescents the meanings of the terms heterosexuality, homosexuality, and bisexuality. We have found that handicapped adolescents often have many misconceptions about the various sexual preferences.

*6. To teach sexual abuse issues, when appropriate.* The major objective of this goal is to teach the children, at a level appropriate to their developmental status, information about the meanings of sexual abuse and incest. This goal assists the children in understanding what happened to them and helps alleviate the guilt and "damaged goods' syndrome that is often associated with sexual victimization.

*7. To teach the child self-protection techniques.* This goal entails teaching the children how to recognize and exhibit their own personal strengths and powers, how to identify potentially dangerous situations and respond assertively, how to exhibit assertive body language and the mechanics of saying "no", and how to demonstrate effective communication skills when seeking help. Children are taught specifics about sexual abuse laws and about the appropriate people to report sexual abuse to, including parents, school officials, police officials, and social service workers. Emphasis is placed on self-protection strategies that can be used when someone who is well known to the child attempts to abuse them. This is emphasized because 98% of the children served at the Center were abused by known perpetrators.

8. *The development of an affective vocabulary to label emotions and feelings.* Before emotions can be appropriately expressed, the child must know the language. We have found that most handicapped children have a limited affective vocabulary and often have an emotional label repertoire limited to happy, sad, mad, and bored; therefore, each child's treatment program includes the teaching of various language concepts for emotions. The children are encouraged to express their emotions and are given language labels for them. Part of the process for encouraging the expression of emotions is the "feelings box" technique, a technique where the children are encouraged to express emotions and collect a label signifying these emotions in their "feeling box." Degrees of emotions are also taught by giving the child a "feeling line," a quantitative visual aid where the children can assign the degree of intensity to a given emotion.

9. *The attainment of emotional independence.* This goal entails assisting the child in learning how to recognize and express his/her emotions,

accept the consequences of the expression of these emotions, and thereby to develop independence from external individuals for permission and validation for the expression of emotions. This goal is attained by teaching the children to understand their own personal strengths and powers and how to employ a decision-making model in order to analyze a situation, determine the appropriate emotional responses to this situation, and make an appropriate choice about the emotion to display.

10. *Assistance in the establishment of a meaningful and stable identity.* This goal entails engendering a positive self-concept and feeling of self-worth in the child. Characteristically, children who have been victims of sexual abuse have low self-concepts. Part of each therapy session is spent in enhancing their self-concepts.

11. *Development of a personal value system.* This goal entails teaching the children appropriate and inappropriate social behavior as well as the ability to make value judgments about their own behavior and the behavior of others. Some children who are victims of sexual abuse also victimize other children. When therapy begins, these youngsters typically have little or no understanding about sexual abuse and why it is inappropriate. These youngsters, who became offenders as a result of being victimized themselves, need to understand the difference between an abusive and a non abusive situation. Directive, didactic, non directive, and insight-counseling techniques are used with the children in order to meet this goal.

12. *The development of a capacity for lasting relationships and for both tender and genital love.* This goal entails teaching the children, at a level appropriate to their developmental status, how to make friends, maintain friendships, establish dating

relationships, terminate dating relationships, choose whether or not to engage in sexual activity with another individual, and choose a marriage partner. It is generally used with adolescent children, but some of these concepts are taught at a rudimentary level to younger children.

*13. Treatment of secondary behavioral characteristics.* Many children who have been the victims of sexual abuse exhibit secondary behavioral or emotional characteristics as a direct result of the abuse. Indeed, these secondary behavioral or emotional characteristics are often the original reason for referral to mental health service providers. The existence of these secondary behaviors have been well documented in the literature and include depression, suicidal ideation, suicidal gestures, aggressive acting-out behavior, poor peer relationships, school phobia, regressive behaviors, enuresis and/or encopresis, promiscuous acting-out behaviors, inability to empathize, negative attention-seeking behaviors, and chemical dependency. If present, these difficulties are also addressed in a given child's treatment plan through behavior modification programs co-ordinated between the therapist, school, and home.

The following therapeutic techniques are used with the children at the Center for Abused Handicapped Children (Sullivan & Scanlan, 1987). These techniques are eclectic in nature and consistent with that current trend in psychotherapy in general (Zeig, 1987):

1. *Nondirective Counseling.* This counseling technique encourages an atmosphere of unconditional positive regard (Rogers, 1951) toward the child, thereby encouraging the child to express his/her thoughts and feelings in the psychotherapy session. This technique also encourages the child to develop insights into his/her difficulties

and to make decisions based upon those insights. Insight techniques are generally limited to those handicapped youths who have sufficient affective vocabularies and language-reasoning skills to benefit from them; however, attempts are made to correct these deficits.

2. *Directive Counseling.* This counseling approach provides the child with options about how to make decisions and choices in life. It is directive in nature and is required for those children and youths who do not have good decision-making skills. In addition, we have found that therapists need to be a bit more directive in their therapy with handicapped children and youths than therapeutic orthodoxy generally prescribes. Although some children will not discuss the sexual abuse unless asked about it, the therapist takes steps to ensure that he or she does not direct all aspects of the therapy session.

3. *Play Therapy.* This is a nondirective psychotherapeutic technique that encourages the child to express his/her thoughts and feelings during play (Axle, 1947). It is most beneficial with handicapped children who possess speech and language difficulties, visual impairments, hearing impairments, and intellectual impairments. We consider art therapy to be an adjunct to play therapy, and we have also found this to be most heuristic in allowing children with communication disorders to express their feelings. It is also useful for teaching children affective vocabulary concepts, for example, the children draw their feelings and then the therapist labels these emotions.

4. *Didactic Counseling.* This counseling technique teaches the child specific things that relate to his/her individual therapy goals, for example, concepts regarding human sexuality, interpersonal relationships, and

affective vocabulary. We have found that therapy with handicapped children has many didactic components, and these are particularly apparent in the instruction of self-protection skills.

5. *Reality Therapy* (Glasser, 1965). This technique is an *in vivo* approach to therapy, a technique where the child is directly confronted with the consequences of his/her behavior. This assists the child in making reality-based decisions for action, controlling impulses, anticipating consequences for behavior, and learning to accept the consequences of behavior. It is particularly useful with handicapped adolescent perpetrators.

6. *Transactional Analysis* (Berne, 1964, 1972). This is a therapeutic approach in which the child is taught basic interaction patterns in his/her life, including transactions between parents, adults, children, and all possible permutations of these interactions. This approach is useful for teaching the child about the various interaction patterns that he/she might possibly encounter in life.

7. *Behavior Therapy*. The entire gamut of behavior therapy techniques are used to address the specific behavioral management difficulties exhibited by a given child. Both classical and operant behavior modification techniques are applied. Shaping, chaining, and fading techniques are particularly heuristic with multihandicapped and intellectually impaired children. Systematic desensitization and counter conditioning procedures (Wolpe, 1982) may also be implemented. Social learning theory principles (Brandura, 1977) are heavily employed, and Gentle Teaching, a nonaversive behavioral teaching and modification system designed primarily for the intellectually impaired (McGee, Menolascin, Hobbs, & Menousek, 1987) is used with all handicapped children.

8. *Psychodrama and Role-playing*. We have found these techniques to be most useful with handicapped adolescents, particularly visually-impaired, hearing-impaired, language-disordered, and learning-disabled youngsters. This technique is used in both individual and group psychotherapy sessions where the youths are asked to act out meaningful situations in the presence of peers. This helps the youngster understand him/herself and to act spontaneously, which facilitates self-understanding. These techniques are particularly useful in teaching self-protection skills. We have also used these techniques with adolescent perpetrators and had the youngsters portray roles of both victims and victimizer. This is useful in building empathy skills in perpetrators.

9. *Generalization Training*. The therapists provide follow-up and generalization of concepts which are presented and discussed within the therapy setting in *in vivo* situations. Handicapped children characteristically have difficulties generalizing concepts taught in a specific situation, such as the therapy setting, to appropriate settings outside the therapy setting. Generalization training in specific situations helps to overcome this difficulty.

**Efficacy Study**

Among hearing impaired children, there are some data which indicate that those who do not receive therapy exhibit more behavioral problems than those who do receive it (Sullivan, Scanlan, Brookhouse, Schulte, & Andrew, in press). The following describes a study that examined the efficacy of the therapeutic methods used at the Center for Abused Handicapped Children.

The subjects in this study were 51 boys and 21 girls, aged 12 to 16, who attended a residential school for the deaf. During individual police interviews, all of the children in this study indicated that they had been sexually victimized more than once by dormitory staff, family members, and/or older students. The Child Behavior Checklist (CBC) was used to record the behavioral problems and competencies of the subjects (Achenbach & Edelbrock, 1983) prior to and after receiving therapeutic intervention. A non treatment control group was possible because approximately half of the parents of the 72 children refused the offer of free psychotherapy services for their child. Subject assignment to treatment and non treatment groups was accomplished by parental response to the offer of psychotherapy. Parents of 21 of the boys and 14 of the girls accepted the offer of psychotherapy.

The CBC was completed by house parents at the residential school before treatment began, and these ratings served as pretests in the study. One year after the implementation of psychotherapy, the CBC were again completed by house parents on all children who participated in the study. These ratings were used as post-tests in the study. The psychotherapy treatment goal and methods were identical for all children and have been thoroughly described in this chapter.

Results indicate that there were no differences between the treatment and non treatment groups for both girls and boys on the CBC prior to the institution of therapy. Both the treatment and non treatment groups had significantly elevated scores on the CBC. One year after the onset of therapy, the girls in the treatment groups had significantly lower scores than the non treatment group. Therapy with the girls was found to be particularly effective in alleviating symptoms of depression, aggression, and cruelty. For boys, the treatment groups had significantly lower scores on the aggression, hyperactivity, delinquency, immaturity, hostile withdrawal, and uncommunicative scales.

## Conclusion

It was only a century ago that Freud's pioneering work in the psychological aspects of medicine led to the birth of psychotherapy. One of the characteristics that separates humans from other animal species is that we use others to help ourselves overcome feelings of distress and despair. In the evolution of humanity, we only recently have come to value intelligence over physical prowess (Zeig, 1987). It is only within the last twenty-five years that we have become concerned about the maltreatment of our children. Ironically, the first mention of child abuse in the medical literature (Tardieu, 1860) appeared before Freud's time and was virtually ignored for eighty years (Knight, 1986). The field of handicapped abuse is a mere five years old; consequently, we are all pilgrims in the evolution of psychotherapy for handicapped sexual abuse victims. Therapists need to be both scientists and healers. As scientists, we need to engage in and encourage research on the efficacy of the treatment methods and techniques we employ with children. As healers, we need to assist the children in processing the abuse they endured and help them to lead productive lives.

\*\*\*\*\*\*

## REFERENCES

**Achenbach, T.M.**. & Edelbrock, C. (1983). *Manual for the child behavior checklist and revised child behavior profile.* Burlington, VT: Department of Psychiatry, University of Vermont.

**Axline, V.** (1947). *Play Therapy.* Boston: Houghton-Mifflin

**American Psychiatric Association,** (1980). *Diagnostic and statistical manual of mental disorders (3rd ed.)* Washington, DC: American Psychiatric Association.

**Bandura, A.** (1977) *Social learning theory.* Englewood Cliffs, NJ: Prentice-Hall, Inc.

**Berne, E.** (1964). *Games people play.* New York: Grove Press.

**Berne, E.** (1972). *What do you say after you say hello?* New York: Grove Press.

**Browne, A.,** & Finkelhor, D. (1986). Impact of child sexual abuse: A review of the research. *Psychological Bulletin, 99 (1),* 66-77.

Eth, S., & Pynoos, R.S. (1985). *Post traumatic stress disorder in children.* Washington, DC: American Psychiatric Press.

Finkelhor, D., & Browne, A. (1985). The traumatic impact of child sexual abuse: A conceptualization. *American Journal of Orthopsychiatry, 55 (4),* 530-541.

Forseth, L.B., & Browne, A. (1981). A survey of intra familial sexual abuse treatment centers: Implications for intervention. *Child Abuse and Neglect, 5,* 177-186.

Giarretto, H. (1982). A comprehensive child sexual abuse treatment program. *Child Abuse and Neglect, 6,* 263-278.

Glasser, W. (1965). *Reality therapy.* New York: Harper & Row.

Haugaard, J.J. & Reppucci, N.D. (1988). *The sexual abuse of children.* San Francisco: Jossey-Bass.

Knight, B. (1986). The history of child abuse. *Forensic Science International, 30,* 135-141.

Knutson, J.F. (1986). Physical and sexual abuse of children. In D.K. Routh (Ed.), *Handbook of pediatric psychology* (pp.32-70). New York: Guilford Press.

McGee, J.J., Menolascino, F.J., Hobbs, D.C. & Menousek, P.E. (1987). *Gentle teaching: A non-aversive approach to helping persons with mental retardation.* New York: Human Sciences Press, Inc.

Rogers, C.R. (1951). *Client-centered therapy.* Boston: Houghton-Miffin.

Sullivan, P.M., & Scanlan, J.J. (1987). Therapeutic Issues. In J. Garbarino, P.E. Brookhouse, & D.J.Authier (Eds.) *Special children - special risks: The maltreatment of children with disabilities (*pp.127-159). New York: Aldine de Gruyter.

Sullivan, P.M., Scanlan, J.M., Brookhouser, P.E., Schulte, L. & Andrew, J. (in press). *The effects of psychotherapy on behavior problems of sexually abused deaf children: A comparative study.*

Tardieu, A., (1860) Etude medico-legal sur les services et mauvais traitements exerces sur des enfants. *Annales d'Hygeine Publique et Medecine Legale, 13,* 361-398.

Van Der Kolk, B.A., (1987). *Psychological trauma.* Washington, DC: American Psychiatric Press.

Wolpe, J. (1982). *The practice of behavior therapy (3rd ed.)* New York: Pergamon Press.

Zeig, J.K. (1987). *The evaluation of psychotherapy.* New York: Brunner-Mazel.

**About the Author:** Requests for Reprints should be addressed to Patricia M. Sullivan, Boys Town National Research Hospital, 555 North 30th Street, Omaha, NE 68131, USA.

**Source:** Reprinted with permission from *Developmental Disabilities Bulletin,* Vol. 18, No. 2, pp. 21-24, 1990. Published by the Faculty of Education, University of Alberta, Edmonton, Alberta, Canada T6G 2G5

\*\*\*\*\*\*\*\*

# Ageing and Severe Physical Disability:
# Patterns of Change and Implications for Services

Nancy M. Crewe

**Abstract** ~ *For the first time in history, numbers of people with severe physical disabilities such as spinal cord injury or polio are surviving to old age. Ageing-related changes combined with pre-existing impairments present new challenges for these individuals and for service providers. Implications for professionals include the need to foster more collaborative relationships between themselves and recipients, to emphasize services that enable independence, to coordinate new services, and to address issues of wellness, not only disability.*

**Key words** ~ Ageing, Polio, Spinal cord injury, Geriatric medicine, Health care services

**Introduction** ~ The fields of ageing and rehabilitation have many shared concerns and much can be learned about one field by studying the other, yet historically their literature and areas of service have been quite separate. This situation has been changing, however, and interest in the combined topic of disability and ageing is growing. One reason for this interest is the shift in the population demographics. During most of history, only about one person in 10 lived to the age of 65; now almost eight of 10 do.[1] The fastest growing segment of the population is people over the age of 85.

Although many elderly people are in good health, normal changes in all bodily systems accompany ageing. Many kinds of disability (for example, visual and hearing impairments) are correlated in incidence with age. Thus, larger numbers of people are living long enough to experience life with disabilities. Rehabilitation medicine always has served some older people, such as those with strokes, but the field's attention primarily has been focused on people with disabilities that typically begin at younger ages - for example, spinal cord injury, polio, developmental disabilities, and traumatic brain injury. The American Congress of Rehabilitation Medicine acknowledged the changing balance, however, in the theme of its 1986 annual convention, "Rehabilitation reality in an ageing America: new wrinkles in geriatric rehabilitation".

Another reason for the current interest in disability and ageing is that advances in medicine and rehabilitation have resulted in remarkable increases in the life expectancy of people with varied kinds of earlier-onset disabilities. For the first time in history, large numbers of people are living for 30, 40, and more years after contracting polio or sustaining spinal cord injuries. They are pioneers in essentially uncharted territory, without previous generations of role models and facing medical questions that sometimes can be answered only with educated guesses.

**Ageing with spinal cord injury** ~ Menter [2] summarized the evolution of the treatment and prognosis for people with spinal cord injuries over the past 50 years. Prior to 1940, people did not survive except very briefly following spinal cord injury. Soldiers who sustained such injuries during the Second World War were expected to die, so minimal efforts were made to provide medical care. Rehabilitation medicine was in its infancy, and what would later become principles of rehabilitative care were just being discovered.

Nevertheless, in the 1940s a small number of individuals, most with injuries in the lower back, surprised their physicians and everyone else by refusing to die. No antibiotics were available to prevent recurrent urinary tract infections, and no one expected that the patients would ever be able to leave the hospitals. The treatment goal was just extended existence. By the 1950s a limited number of antibiotics became available, offering the possibility that some paraplegics, even those with higher injuries, would be able to survive at home. Further advances occurred in the 1960s, resulting in the survival of increasing numbers of individuals with low cervical injuries, and the first realistic possibilities of life beyond sedentary existence, actually including some community involvement, began to emerge.

By the 1970s, with advances in emergency medical services and the development of specialized spinal cord injury centers, individuals with higher levels of quadriplegia were being saved. Even some who required ventilators for breathing were able to exist outside hospitals and long-term care institutions. The independent living movement was thriving, and there arose increasing concern about the quality of life available to people with spinal cord injury. Expectations for community involvement continued to grow, and for some there were even pressures toward over achievement.

Spinal cord treatment has continued to change during the present decade. Medical centers are seeing increasing numbers of people with incomplete injuries, [3] meaning that the cord is not completely severed so some degree of usable function or sensation remains. This is mostly because of better evacuation techniques following accidents. In the past, untold numbers of originally incomplete injuries probably were made complete as people were pulled from damaged vehicles and transported to hospitals by whatever makeshift means could be devised. Now trained emergency medical technicians and helicopter units are available to bring people to expert care in record time. With larger numbers of incomplete injuries, the rehabilitation focus goes beyond preventing catastrophic complications and includes concerns with the broader issues of wellness. Concurrently, in this decade, issues of adjusting to ageing *and* disability are receiving more attention.

Given the substantial changes in medical care over the decades, the question of how spinal cord injury affects the ageing process cannot be answered simply. Researchers now are able to interview and to study individuals in their 50s and 60s who have lived for years with the condition, so new data are becoming available. Trieschmann [4] summarized the published research and her own investigation on the incidence of health problems among this group and identified the following as being of special concern: renal disorders, bladder cancer, and cardiovascular conditions, especially hypertension and related cardiac problems. But one cannot assume that these conditions always will be the primary consequences of spinal cord injury. Many of the people in her sample lived through endless bouts of urinary tract infections before antibiotics and improved methods of catheterization were available.

The pattern of expectations and concomitant stressors also has shifted over the years. Some of the complications seen in people who were injured during the 1940s and 1950s may have been due to inactivity, whereas individuals who were injured after the 1950s may show the effects of excessive wear and tear on joints and muscles. As another example, the incidence of respiratory problems may increase significantly among later cohorts that include more people with cervical injuries.

Therefore, cross-sectional studies will not be sufficient to explain the effects of ageing on people with spinal cord injury. Even longitudinal studies will not tell the complete story. Comprehensive data will be needed that take into account multiple factors including the era in which the disability began, the age of the person at that time, and the age and duration of injury at the time of follow-up.

The evidence indicates that a very significant number of people with spinal cord injury do begin to experience a variety of problems that are new, if not in kind, at least in degree, as they age. Fatigue is probably the single most common complaint, followed by a variety of physical concerns such as bones that break easily and skin that breaks down more readily than in past years. Trieschmann [4] concluded that these developments seemed to be more related to duration of disability than to chronological age. As a consequence, some individuals who were injured as teens began to experience the problems in their 30s and 40s, long before their peers who did not have disabilities.

**Ageing with polio** ~ Interest in the ageing process also has grown tremendously among the survivors of polio during the past decade. Some notable similarities and differences exist between spinal cord injury and polio. Whereas spinal cord injury is most often caused by trauma (although tumors or other disease processes account for some cases), polio is caused by a virus. Although references to such a disease go back much further, polio was identified as a distinct entity in Europe in the eighteenth century. [5] It has tended to strike in epidemics, with major ones occurring in the United States in the 1940s and 1950s. With the development of the Salk vaccine in 1955 and the Sabin oral vaccine in 1960, polio has been almost eradicated from the United States. The field of rehabilitation medicine was growing, particularly by the time of the later epidemics, and its practitioners willingly applied their efforts and their emerging philosophy to the treatment of polio. Radical new ideas about therapy were offered by Sister Elizabeth Kenney, an Australian nurse, and many people benefited with greater return of function that otherwise would have been possible.

Polio, like spinal cord injury, traditionally has been considered a stable rather than a progressive disability. Following onset, a period of intensive treatment brought people back to the best level of functioning of which they were capable. Those who required respirators often became permanent residents of hospitals or extended-care facilities. Others returned home and adapted as well as they could, with or without the aid of others, in their new circumstances.

For many people, even though some functional limitations remained, their personal battle against polio seemingly had been won. They went to school, got jobs, married, and reared families, often making it a point of pride to refuse any special consideration or allowances. During the past decade, however, 30 to 40 years after the last major epidemics, a significant number (some estimate approximately 25%) have begun to experience a range of unwelcome changes in functioning. [5] These changes included unaccustomed fatigue, breathing problems, weakness in previously unaffected muscles, and pain. Many of those first affected had difficulty getting their physicians to understand and to accept the functional changes they were experiencing.

Eventually, the pattern was recognized so widely that it was given the label 'post-polio syndrome' and has been the subject of conferences and articles. Various theories have been advanced about the cause, one of the most common being that there has been premature ageing caused by over-work in the motor neurons that survived the polio virus. [4] Other theories have been advanced, including the possibility of the reactivation of the long-dormant virus.

Agreement on the cause of the problems that people have experienced has not been reached, and controversy exists about what affected individuals should do to minimize them. Some experts advise staying in shape with a carefully designed exercise programme. Yet overwork, particularly of muscles that have long been compensating for the weakness of other muscles that were denervated by the virus, may be even more harmful than disuse. So the 'use it or lose it' maxim is in direct conflict with the perspective that says one's energy resources literally are finite and that what is invested in one activity will never be available for future activities. Apart from the debate about long-term consequences, the undeniable fact of decreased energy and strength requires these individuals to reprioritize their activities and cut back, often drastically, on their commitments.

Carolyn Vash, a rehabilitation psychologist who had polio years ago, wrote about her own experience. [5] She began to have a variety of problems, including the addition of about 10 pounds in middle age to her previously 90-pound frame. Unable to eliminate them with diet alone, she increased her physical activity and then experienced losses in neck and shoulder functioning. Her physician warned her that she could be causing irreparable microtears in her muscles, so she quickly went back to her normal activity level and only partially recovered her strength. She also began to question the impact of her multiple work and travel commitments on her health.

The shifting pattern of expectations from one's self or society that has been noted across the decades for people who have spinal cord injury has also affected those with polio and no doubt, those with other disabling conditions as well. Perhaps the physical changes are, as Vash suggested, a direct result of the increasing demands for work, for competition, and for other contributions that make for an active and integrated life. Perhaps the diminished functioning is simply the result of the evolution of the disabling conditions that would have occurred anyway.

**Societal changes and disability ~** The shifting expectations of people with disabilities have not been accidental or isolated. They are part of major societal changes, and they have served to change the relationship between these individuals, the health care system, and rehabilitation professions. In the 1940s and 1950s, the rehabilitation philosophy and vision were revolutionary. Regardless of their impairments, people with disabilities were no longer to be left in back wards and attics, watching the days pass without risk, significance, or achievement. Each one would be evaluated and provided with services that would bring the individual to the highest level of functioning. Encouragement, education, and assistive devices would provide maximal functioning in the activities of daily living. Counseling, job training, and employment would enable each to make productive contributions to the society.

This revolutionary philosophy for rehabilitation has not disappeared, and it is not even hopelessly outdated. It no longer, however, represents a full picture of the relationship between individuals with disabilities and rehabilitation practitioners. The service paradigm began shifting somewhere in the early 1970s.[6] People with disabilities were no longer eternal patients who looked to the experts to provide them with services that would make them whole or as whole as possible. They began to recognize that many of their problems were not the result of their own deficiencies, but rather reflected the barriers that had been erected by an unthinking and sometimes hostile society. In the process, many people became politicized, realizing they would have to fight to meet needs that had been unmet for years. They began to perceive themselves as consumers of services and to insist on retaining control of their own decisions and directions.

**Implications for service providers ~** Such changes in self-perception inevitably will make a difference in the way these ageing individuals with long-standing disabilities relate to health care professionals. Compared with the person who experiences the onset of a new disability in later years, most of these individuals will be in a significantly different position. It became very important to these individuals that health and service providers respect and enhance their strengths rather than force them into molds that may better fit other situations. Their special characteristics include psychological adaptation to disability and change, development of expertise with respect to their own conditions, and accumulation of knowledge about systems and services.

Rehabilitation psychologists have long tried to identify the process of adjustment to disability, just as gerontologists have theorized about what constitutes successful adaptation to the ageing process. Some well-known theories maintain that individuals go through a series of stages, beginning with shock and denial, progressing through acknowledgment and depression, and finally arriving at the re-establishment of equilibrium and the development of new values and satisfaction. No doubt these theories have been taken too literally by many health care providers in the past, some of whom have fairly demanded that people display an 'appropriate' amount of depression in order that they might 'legitimately' achieve adjustment.

Such excesses aside, and allowing for the fact that not only the pace but also the pathway will be somewhat different for each person, adaptation is a process that unfolds slowly through the experience of living. Longitudinal research on people with spinal cord injury [7] confirms that duration of disability is positively correlated with measures of productivity and life satisfaction. At least for the 15-year period for which Krause and I currently have data, the longer people live with a disabling condition, the better their adjustment seems to be.

A second major difference between people with long-standing and with recent disabilities is that the former, over the years, have developed tremendous expertise with respect to their condition and their own bodies.

Very often the person with spinal cord injury can recognize the onset of yet another urinary tract infection, whereas a relatively inexperienced physician feels the need to run time-consuming tests before providing medication. This is not to say that the individual has all the answers or does not need expert care. The changes that accompany ageing can be new, confusing, and frightening, but the person with the familiar disability has substantial context into which to place new knowledge.

Third, the person who is accustomed to a disability often has had substantial experience with health care providers and with service systems, for better or for worse. This experience enables them to know better where to turn and how to manipulate the systems in order to obtain needed resources. Based on these differences, several implications for services to people who are ageing with disabilities may be identified.

**Consultant/Consumer Relationship** ~ For those individuals who desire it, a consultant/consumer relationship may be far more productive than the traditional professional/patient pattern. A man in his mid-50s told of his first meeting with the woman who became his personal physician. The doctor began by saying, 'I already know most of what the textbooks say about muscular dystrophy. Now I'd like to have you tell me about what it is like for you.' And with that she sat back to listen and take notes for several minutes. The man said that was the most positive experience he had ever had with a health care professional.

Most people with long histories of patienthood have had the experience of being given authoritative information that later proved incorrect, predictions that never materialized, and advice that turned out to be detrimental. As a result, they are less inclined to tolerate arbitrary directives, unnecessary delays, and arrogant manners. With the equality implied in a consumer/consultant relationship, the individual with a disability is less likely to be a passive recipient. In addition, the individual is in a much better position to bring past experience and knowledge to bear on current problems, and by

cooperating, the individual and the health care professional are much more likely to arrive at adequate workable solutions.

**Services to promote self-sufficiency** ~ Services should enhance independence, not just in terms of keeping individuals with disabilities out of institutions but also in terms of enhancing their control over their life situations. In this regard, the distinction between a rehabilitation perspective and that of a more traditional social services perspective is essential. Rehabilitation is essentially an educational process -teaching individuals to find new ways of accomplishing their daily activities when their usual ways are blocked by the onset of disability. For example, if a person has a cervical spinal cord injury and loses upper extremities function, the ability to cook may be lost. The preferred rehabilitation approach would be to teach the use of adaptive techniques and devices to regain that functional ability. Only if that fails would we look to a service such as meals on wheels that provides the prepared food to the person. Similarly, for the individual who has become unable to get around the community because of a severe visual impairment, the first goal would be to provide orientation and mobility training that would enable the regaining of that ability. In the event that that did not prove feasible, then the alternatives of providing special transportation or a helper would be considered.

Services are provided to promote self-sufficiency to the greatest degree possible. Even this principle must not be carried beyond reason, however, to a point of heroic sacrifice for the sake of independence at any cost. The measuring stick must always be that of the greater good for the individual being served. The philosophy of rehabilitation maintains that maximal independence usually will serve that goal, so it is given high priority.

When a person's needs are such that assistance is required to meet the demands of living, the rehabilitation perspective still remains primary. The central issue remains one of control over decisions. The individual with a disability must be recognized as the employer of the person who is retained to provide attendant care of homemaker services, not perceived as a patient who must follow the instructions of the service provider. With this point of view, who physically is performing the task is of little importance. Who is responsible for deciding what gets done and how is of prime importance.

**Health care systems and wellness** ~ The implications of health care systems and wellness probably apply equally to individuals who are ageing with a long-standing disability and those with a recent condition. Health care systems are complex, even for someone who has been dealing with them for years. For the person who is ageing with a disability, new programmes that would be helpful to meet new needs may have been developed. Given the amount of fragmentation in the service systems and the traditional chasm that has existed between service providers in ageing and those in rehabilitation, good opportunities are almost sure to be missed unless a knowledgeable person is available to help coordinate access to new programmes and resources.

We need to attend not just to the specific medical problems that accompany disability but also to the full range of health and wellness concerns that apply to everyone. Nutrition is a particularly important consideration for people who use wheelchairs through much of their lives. Reduced physical activity may lead to weight gain, and added pounds can produce even more serious consequences that would result for other people.

The lack of weight-bearing by long bones in the lower extremities also may contribute to the development of osteoporosis and to the danger of easy fractures. Good nutrition is an important part of maintaining overall health and avoiding complications, but some of the secondary effects of disability may make achieving good nutrition difficult. Frequent shopping for fresh fruits, vegetables, and meats may be difficult for someone with mobility and transportation limitations. Fixed income may present even greater restrictions.

The need for physical conditioning may present a comparable dilemma. Cardiovascular fitness requires activity, but how does this fit with the problems of increased weakness and fatigue that many individuals with long-standing disabilities experience? Time is another consideration: all of the ordinary activities of daily living take longer, so even if there were energy and time left over for fitness after work, maintenance activities may be limited or nonexistent. These issues of health and wellness are just beginning to receive some recognition in the rehabilitation community, and much more needs to be done.

## Conclusion

This article has identified some of the changes that seem to be occurring frequently in the lives of the first substantial generation of people to reach advanced age who have lived 30 to 40 years with some severe physical disabilities. Changes were reviewed that have occurred concurrently in society and in the lives of these individuals that together provide them with a unique perspective on health care services and professionals. Normal, and perhaps accelerated or amplified physical changes of ageing, have affected individuals with disabilities and have precipitated new needs for services. As professionals, we are challenged to recognize, respect, and capitalize on the expertise of these survivors. A great botanist once said, "My green thumb came only as a result of the mistakes I made while learning to see things from the plant's point of view." Surely, the greatest contributions also will come as a result of trying to see things from the survivor's point of view.

\*\*\*\*\*\*

## REFERENCES

[1] Zola, I.K. Aging and disability: toward a unifying agenda. *Educational Gerontology 1988*; **14**: 365-387

[2] Menter. R.R. *Aging: normal vs spinal cord injury, specific issues.* Paper presented at the regional meeting of the American Congress of Rehabilitation Medicine, Minneapolis, MN, April 1989.

[3] Young, J., Burns, P., Bowen, A., McCutchen, R. *Spinal cord injury statistics.* Phoenix, AZ: Good Samaritan Medical Center, 1982.

[4] Trieschmann, R.B. *Aging with a disability.* New York: Demos, 1987.

[5]     National  Institute  on  Disability  and Rehabilitation  Research.     The  late  effects  of poliomyelitis. *Rehab Brief 1986;* **9 (9).**

[6]   DeJong, G.   Defining and implementing the independent living concept.  In:  Crewe, N.M., Zola I.K.  and  associates  (eds.)  *Independent  living  for physically disabled people.*  San Francisco: Jossey-Bass, 1983;  pp. 4-27.

[7]   Crew,  N.M.,  Krause,  J.S.   *An eleven-year follow-up  of  adjustment  to  spinal  cord  injury.* Manuscript submitted for publication.

******

**About the Author:**  Nancy M. Crewe is with the School  of  Lifelong  Education,  Michigan  State University,  332  Erickson  Hall,  East  Lansing,  MI 48824.

**Source:**  Reprinted from *Educational Gerontology,* 1990; 16:525-534. with permission in *International Disability Studies,* Vol. 13, No. 4, 1991, pp. 158-161.   Copyright © 1990, 1991 Taylor & Francis Group, London WCIN 2ET, UK.

# Aging, Chronic Illness and Disability

Seanne Wilkins

Cheryl Cott

**Abstract** ~ *Although increasing age is associated with increasing disability, most older people are not disabled. However, there are two groups of elderly people who do experience disability in later life: those who are old and become disabled, and those who are disabled and become old. The differing experiences of being old and being disabled for these two groups are explored.*

## Introduction:

Increasing numbers of individuals are living to more advanced ages[1]. Living longer may result in worsening health and increase the risk of becoming disabled (Verbrugge, 1991). However, our understanding of the experience of being old and disabled is limited. While there are extensive literatures on aging and on disability, for the most part, the disability literature deals with disability acquired in early or middle adulthood and does not address the experience of being old and disabled.

Aging is often regarded as a biological process that is universal, unavoidable and associated with deterioration. In contrast, McPherson (1990) defines aging as a complex, dynamic social process involving physical, psychological and social changes and adaptation over the life course. Individuals and age cohorts experience different rates and types of aging. Genetic, physical, psychological, environmental and social factors are directly and indirectly involved.

Similarly, disability is a complex process that also involves physical, psychological and social processes. Disability is defined as "any restriction or lack ...of ability to perform an activity in the manner or within the range considered normal for a human being" (World Health Organization, 1980). Often disability is measured on surveys by questions about activities of daily living (ADL), such as eating, bathing and dressing; and instrumental activities of daily living (IADL), such as shopping, preparing meals and light housekeeping. Performance of these basic obligatory activities is used to assess whether the individual can survive and maintain a household in the community. Difficulty doing these activities is taken to mean varying degrees of disability (Verbrugge, 1990). The limitation of this operationalization of disability is that it does not take into consideration many life activities that might be important or meaningful for the older individual (Verbrugge, 1991). Verbrugge (1991) provides a more comprehensive definition: "Disability refers to how chronic conditions affect people's ability to act in typical and personally desired ways in their society. The essential notion ... is how much difficulty people have doing valued activities .... [which] can be obligatory, committed, or discretionary" (p. 225). Obligatory activities include personal and household care, committed activities include paid employment and child care and discretionary activities include hobbies and social activities.

Although aging is often associated with chronic illness and disability, most older people are not disabled. There are changes that are associated with increasing age that have implications for an older person's functional level. However, for the most part these are adapted to and do not result in disability. Only a small number of older people are disabled. For those who are disabled, there are two distinct groups, those who are old and become disabled and those who are disabled and become old. The former refers to older people who, often as the result of chronic illness, develop varying degrees of disability in later life. The latter group refers to the increasing number of individuals who are living longer with a disability acquired in early life. The experience of being disabled and old will be different for these two groups because of their differential access to various resources (e.g., physical, social, psychological and financial) throughout their lives, which in turn, have implications for the interaction of age and disability and the different perceptions of aging and disability held by these individuals.

This chapter will address the particular issues and concerns relevant to the experience of aging and disability for the following three different groups of older individuals: 1)those with usual age changes that affect functional capacity but which are usually adapted to and do not result in disability; 2) those who are aging and become disabled as a result of chronic illness; and 3) those who have a disability acquired earlier in life and who are now aging.

## Usual Aging

Despite an increase in disability with age, the older population generally remains functionally well until very advanced ages (Health and Welfare Canada, 1982). Canadian survey data indicate that over 60% of elderly people report that their health is good or excellent (McPherson, 1990) and approximately 80% report that they are capable of living independently and caring for themselves, despite a high incidence of chronic health problems (Health and Welfare Canada, 1982). In the U.S. approximately 69% report their health as good to excellent (Verbrugge, 1989).

Older people may report good health even in the presence of chronic illness because they may expect illness with aging and therefore alter their definition of health. Because elderly people see many of their illnesses as natural consequences of aging, they may isolate or discount them in judging their overall health status. Thus, an elderly person may say, "Considering my age, I'm in excellent health" (Keller, Leventhal, Prohaska and Leventhal, 1989b, p. 254).

There are biological, psychological and social changes that occur with age and

have an impact on the older person's ability to function but do not necessarily result in disability. Changes in sensory functioning, particularly changes in vision and hearing, affect an older person's ability to interact with his or her environment. Visual changes include a decline in visual acuity, restriction of the visual field, increased susceptibility to glare, deficient gaze stability, decline in colour vision, and decreased perception (Andreasen, 1980; Spooner, Sakala and Baloh, 1980). These visual changes may result in the need for increased illumination, difficulty performing tasks that require visual acuity, and difficulty reading, particularly small print. As well, these visual changes have implications for the older person's ability to interact with his or her physical environment to guide locomotion and avoid obstacles and falls (Owen, 1985).

Hearing changes include a loss of ability to hear higher frequency sounds in music and speech (presbycusis), difficulty distinguishing conversations in the presence of background noise and difficulty with verbal recall. Hearing losses in particular have implications for social interaction. Diminished hearing can affect the older person's ability to follow conversations and result in a decreased quality of social interaction, and in extreme cases the misperception that the older person is confused, particularly if he or she does not hear instructions or statements correctly. However, in most cases these sensory impairments are not severe, come on gradually and can be compensated for through rehabilitation (Corso, 1981).

Changes in physiological capacities such as changes in cardiovascular, musculoskeletal and neuromuscular functioning affect an older individual's ability to be physically active. Cardiovascular changes include a decrease in maximum achievable heart rate and stroke volume resulting in a decrease in maximum cardiac output and aerobic capacity (Fitzgerald, 1985). Age changes in the muscular system lead to a decrease in strength, speed and endurance (Vandervoort, Hayes and Belanger, 1986).

These changes result in quicker onset of fatigue during physical activity. Age-related changes in postural control have implications for the older person's gait and balance, leading to an increased susceptibility to falls (Holliday, Cott and Torresin, 1992).

Although these biological changes have been associated with aging, even for these so-called usual age changes there are serious questions about their inevitability. Some researchers suggest that about 50% of aging decline can be delayed or offset by participation in regular exercise programs (McPherson, 1990; O'Brien and Vertinsky, 1991). However, involvement in physical activity declines with age, particularly amongst women and individuals with lower levels of formal education. These declines in physical activity often do not reflect declines in physiological capacity for exercise. Most cross-sectional studies of activity patterns throughout the life cycle indicate that, although physical activity declines with age, factors such as social status, education, income, martial status and gender also affect activity patterns within age cohorts (McPherson and Kozlik, 1987).

While a number of alternative explanations for this pattern of declining involvement by age have been proposed, a definitive explanation is lacking. Nevertheless, it appears that the salient factors involve some combination of inadequate early life socialization and, during the adult years, a lack of opportunity, a lack of commitment for a variety of reasons, a lack of role models, and, because of ageism, the presence of cultural norms that devalue physical activity in adult lifestyles. (McPherson, 1990, p.168)

Changes in psychological functioning with age include decrements in neuropsychological functioning, memory and certain types of intelligence (Craik and Jennings, 1991; Salthouse, 1982). Changes in memory result in slower and less efficient memory processes. However, these are neither inevitable nor irreversible. Older people generally are better able to remember distant events more readily than recent events. Intelligence that is affected by physiological and neurological capacity (fluid intelligence) reaches a peak during adolescence and then declines with age whereas intelligence that is based on learning and experience (crystallized intelligence) increases with age (Horn, 1982). Usually age changes do not affect older persons' ability to learn or to solve problems, although they tend to perform better in situations where they can set their own rate and speed of performance.

Although these biological and psychological age changes may increase the susceptibility of elderly individuals to certain chronic disabling conditions, they are usually not sufficient to create significant disability in and of themselves. Instead, these age changes lead to different degrees of physical, perceptual or cognitive losses that require varying degrees of adaptation. This adaptation depends on the individual's previous lifestyle and life experiences, personality structure and coping style, support from significant others, socioeconomic status, race, gender, and marital status (McPherson, 1990).

There are social changes with aging that have implications for older persons' health and functional levels. These changes include role transitions, the two most notable of which are retirement and widowhood. Although myths exist as to the relationship of health and retirement, research indicates that poor health is a cause rather than a consequence of retirement, and retirement may produce health benefits (Ekerdt, Baden, Bosse & Dibbs, 1983; Ekerdt & Bosse, 1982; Palmore, Burchett, Fillenbaum, George & Wallman, 1985; Shapiro & Roos, 1982;).

In contrast, widowhood is the single most disruptive life course transition affecting both morbidity and mortality (Martin Matthews, 1987, 1991). There is evidence of increased mortality due mainly to heart disease among the recently bereaved (Marshall and Rosenthal, 1993). As well, problems with deteriorating health and with insomnia, irritability and weight-loss may occur, particularly in the first few years after a spouse's death (George, 1980; Lopata, 1979).

Retirement and widowhood have implications for the older person's income, an important consideration for health. Although gains in income maintenance for older persons have occurred, great variability in income levels still exist. Maintaining an adequate income is still difficult for many older individuals. The majority of older North Americans are poor or "near poor" (National Advisory Council on Aging, 1991; Smeeding, 1990). Particularly at risk of poverty are elderly women, who as widows, often have limited access to pension income due to lack of spousal survivor benefits and who have irregular or nonexistent work histories. In addition, they must then live longer on these limited incomes (Clark, 1990; Gee & Kimball, 1987; Marshall & Rosenthal, 1993). Poverty influences older persons' health and functional levels by affecting their housing, dietary intake and nutrition, and access to resources such as transportation and formal services requiring payment.

Other social changes with age that have implications for health and function include changes in family structure and social support. Contrary to popular myths, most older people are active participants in family networks, although there are variations depending upon gender, marital status, social class, and geographic proximity (Bengtson, Rosenthal & Burton, 1990). Most older persons have children, grandchildren and siblings and most older men have a spouse (Connidis, 1989). With advancing age, the size and composition of family networks change. They become smaller and increasingly composed of women, many of whom have mobility and functional losses (Connidis, 1989).

Caregiving and social support flow between the older person and other family members. This flow of care is not unidirectional, although the nature and extent of caregiving and support may differ between the different family members. Older married couples often have an interdependence that provides mutual support in dealing with physical problems of aging and may actually act as a deterrent to institutionalization (Johnson, 1983; Stoller and Earl, 1983). Aging parents are often involved in giving and receiving emotional support, plus giving assistance in the form of home services, monetary assistance, assistance in times of crisis and child care services (Rosenthal, 1987). However, as the older individual becomes increasingly frail they may be less able to be a full partner in the caregiving relationship and the balance of support may shift to the older person receiving more support than they are able to give.

Although elderly people are aware of these age changes, their overall impressions of aging are positive (Connidis, 1987). In a study of healthy community-dwelling adults aged 50 to 80, Keller and associates (1989a) found that while aging was associated with physical health difficulties and losses, both interpersonal and job related, it was most often described as a natural and gradual process without remarkable features; as a period of life evaluation, philosophical reflection or increased wisdom and maturity; and as a period of increased freedom, new interests and fewer demands. The contrast between negative age changes and positive impressions of aging might be explained by the wide range of coping strategies these people used in response to aging-related changes (Keller et al., 1989a).

In summary, although increased age is associated with increased disability, most older people are not disabled. They may have biological, psychological and social age changes that have an impact on their functional levels, but these are usually adapted to and do not create significant disability in and of themselves. However, these usual age changes can develop more significance if they co-exist with disability. Functional limitations might be increased and the ability to adapt to disability compromised.

## Aging, Chronic Illness and Later Life Disability

Illness in old age includes diseases from which most people die (heart disease, stroke and cancer), acute illnesses (acute trauma, pneumonia) and chronic illnesses (arthritis, diabetes, depression). Although not usually disabling, some acute conditions, particularly hip fractures, can result in considerable morbidity and disability for older persons. Some chronic illnesses may result in disability and the severity of disability differs for different conditions. Commonly reported generalized symptoms such as pain, fatigue, malaise and weakness have considerable impact on an older person's well-being and functioning (Verbrugge, 1991). Diabetes, depression and high blood pressure are common chronic illnesses which result in little or no disability for the older person. Other conditions such as arthritis, dementia and stroke, can be severely disabling (Ford et al., 1988). The prevalence of nonfatal chronic conditions increases with age, thereby increasing the risk of disability (Verbrugge, 1991).

There are certain characteristics of the chronic illness that influence the degree of disability experienced by the older individual. The suddenness of the onset of the disease and the predictability of its course affect the older person's ability to adapt and incorporate changes into his or her everyday life (Strauss et al., 1984). Illnesses that come on gradually and have a predictable course allow the older person more time to adapt and adjust to the disability and incorporate it into their everyday routines (Becker, 1993).

The degree of disability is also influenced by a number of considerations in addition to the nature of the chronic illness. The presence of more than one chronic condition at the same time, in the same individual (co-morbidity) is common amongst older people and can exacerbate disability (Guccione, 1993; Verbrugge, 1991). Usual age changes can affect adjustment to disability so that the older person may take longer to adapt to changes caused by the disability than a younger person might (Becker, 1993). Variations in levels of frailty amongst older individuals due to usual age changes, genetic characteristics, previous lifestyle characteristics and risks accumulated over the life course create variation in their relative risks of disability (Verbrugge, 1991).

Furthermore, the relationship between chronic conditions and disability is not fixed but can be influenced by the physical environment, social resources, economic resources, psychological states and medications (Kaplan, 1991). People who are old and become disabled will have differential access to many of these resources which in turn will have implications for the degree of disability they experience.

Although 85% of elderly persons have one or more chronic conditions, for only 46% does this result in some form of disability, most of which relate to mobility (Chappell, 1990a; Dunn, 1990). Most of these elderly people live in households, a small percentage with severe disabilities live in institutions. The majority of disabled elderly people do not require any assistance with daily tasks except heavy household chores but there are some who require help with some or all of their ADL and this increases with age. Elderly women experience higher levels of disability than elderly men and disabled women are at greater risk of institutionalization.

Being old and becoming disabled has considerable implications for the older person both personally and socially. Personally, the experience of being old and becoming disabled is an important consideration. Increasing levels of disability can lead to losses of independence, social roles, and income and can result in social isolation or institutionalization. Socially, these changes affect not only older individuals but also their families and social networks, particularly when there are issues around the provision of support needed to perform everyday activities.

Although the social gerontology literature includes research on older people's perceptions of aging[2] and the sociology of chronic illness literature addresses the meaning of disability[3], little research has been conducted to consider the meaning of *aging, chronic illness and disability* for elderly people. From the limited research available, it appears that the experience of developing a chronic illness and disability in later life is not as negative as for those who acquire a disability in younger years. "Aged men and women often assumed that they would lead narrowed, even restricted, lives .... they believed that reasonable people should expect to feel worse as they age .... [they] defined the 'appropriateness' of illness in relation to the life course" (Charmaz, 1991, p. 61). Older people may already have experienced some functional declines as a result of usual age changes and so may already have developed some coping strategies. As well, age has freed them from some roles and responsibilities, changing time and energy resources available to manage chronic illness (Belgrave, 1990). Because of the prevalence of chronic illness among elderly people, older people who acquire later life disabilities do not consider themselves to be particularly different from their age peers. Having such ailments does not set them apart, and because these conditions are experienced in common with their cohort there is an opportunity for support. The presence of these chronic conditions becomes problematic when the ability to continue valued activities is affected by the extent to which the body and its care dominates everyday life (Belgrave, 1990).

Chronic illness and disability are seen as normative by elderly people themselves (Charmaz, 1991; Belgrave, 1990). They may not seek attention for health problems but rather accept chronic illness as inevitable. These views are often shared by health care providers and families of elderly people, thereby limiting access to rehabilitation. Moreover, rehabilitation has traditionally been concerned with restoring function and independence. Since a loss of function and independence with aging is regarded as "normal", rehabilitation may not be considered appropriate for the older individual with a later life disability (Becker & Kaufman, 1988).

Another key issue for older people who acquire a disability in later life is that they may require support in order to perform usual everyday activities. Although the majority of non- institutionalized older individuals are self-sufficient, for those who do require more care, it is usually provided by a spouse. Women are more likely than their husbands to assume caregiving roles because women marry men older than themselves and have a greater life expectancy (Chappell, 1990a; Marshall,

1987). Children provide care when a spouse is not available. Daughters and sons usually assume different roles; daughters provide hands-on and emotional care while sons provide financial aid and advice, home repairs and decision-making (Rosenthal, 1987). In the absence of a daughter, daughters-in-law accept responsibility for personal care (Stoller and Earl, 1983). However, changes in the availability of these middle-aged female caregivers due to increased labour force participation of women has made it more difficult for women since they must combine caregiving and employment roles (McPherson, 1990). If neither a spouse nor children are available, another relative such as a sibling, niece or nephew who has strong family ties with the elderly person may be involved. Only after all these avenues of informal support have been exhausted do elderly people rely on friends and neighbours (Cantor, 1979; O'Bryant, 1985; Stoller & Earl, 1983).

Depending on the level of care required by the elderly individual with a disability, heavy demands can be made on caregivers (Chappell, 1990b). The most common problems identified by spousal caregivers are missing the way the spouse used to be, worrying about what would happen if the caregiver became ill, feeling depressed and finding it physically difficult to perform care-related tasks (Barusch, 1988).

Children as caregivers of elderly parents present different experiences. A great deal has been written about the "sandwich generation" or "women in the middle" (Brody, 1981, 1990). This refers to daughters who are providing care for elderly parents while there are still young children at home requiring attention. Recent increases in labour force participation by women may mean that these women are also working full-time. While not overly prevalent (Rosenthal, Matthews & Marshall, 1989), the phenomenon of having dual responsibilities creates some problems. The CARNET Work and Family Survey (1993) found employees with dual caregiving responsibilities (ie. children and an older relative) had the highest levels of stress, work-family conflict, and absenteeism compared to persons with only one type of or no care responsibilities.

Caregiving may become a burden. This may occur when the elderly person being cared for experiences a significant degree of physical or cognitive impairment. If the elderly person is to  remain in the community, the caregiver may be required to give additional heavy care, an increased time commitment and emotional support. It is beyond the scope of this chapter to fully explore the issue of caregiving to older adults. There is a vast literature on caregiver stress and burden (for an overview, see Chappell, 1990b). What is important to a discussion of aging and disability are the two different but linked aspects of caregiving. On the one hand, for the already disabled elder the issue is the availability of caregivers when other family members are themselves aging and on the other hand, for the caregiver the issue is the implications of providing elder care for one's own health.  A 92 year old woman may be receiving care from her 70 year old daughter who may have her own chronic illness and disability to manage in addition to providing care for her mother. This situation may result in institutionalization of the elderly mother and increased risk of poor health for the daughter.

As the elderly person with a later life disability requires increasingly extensive care, spouses or children may not be able to continue to provide the level of informal care required, thus, institutionalization or formal care may be the only alternative. It has been estimated that for disabled elders in the community, 80% of care is provided by informal sources and 20% provided by formal services (Branch & Jette, 1983; Chappell, Strain and Blandford, 1986). Once formal services are necessary, the options available to older persons and their families are limited by the way that health and social services are delivered.

The development of health care systems in North America has resulted in medical care focusing on acute, short-term illnesses primarily treated in the hospital setting. Reviews of this issue are found in Chappell (1987, 1990b) and Kane and Kane (1990). Since most elderly people have chronic illnesses, this medical care system does not provide the care needed by most elderly people. Community-based programs that are more appropriate for maintenance of elderly people in their communities are usually an add-on to medical services and thus, receive limited funding (Chappell, 1987).

While Kane and Kane (1990) indicate that in the U.S. 5% of those 65 and over are in nursing homes, Canadian census data for 1986 indicated that 8% of those 65 years and older receive care in an institutional setting (McPherson, 1990). Those elderly individuals most likely to be institutionalized are: 85 years of age and over; female; without a spouse; no longer physically or mentally competent to continue living independently in the community; and either have no families or their families are unable to care for them.  Also at risk are those who live in areas where community-based support services are unavailable or inaccessible, and those who have small social networks and low income (Statistics Canada, 1988; Young & Olson, 1992).

While some elderly people will continue to require institutionalization, many prefer and would be able to stay in their own homes if alternative support services were available in their communities. These support services may include home care programs, hospital-based day treatment programs, foster care programs, respite care services, employee assistance programs and adult day care programs. For a comprehensive review of models of community-based long term care, see Marshall (1989).

In summary, although most older people are not disabled, there is a small percentage of the elderly who develop disability in later life.  However, decreasing functional abilities are considered normative by many older people, their families and health care providers.  As a result, it does not appear that being old and becoming disabled has the same meaning for these individuals as does developing a disability in younger years.  A more important consideration for the older disabled person is the availability of the support they may need to perform everyday activities and the resulting risk of institutionalization.

## Aging with a Lifelong Disability

Life expectancy has been increased for those with chronic disabilities because of improved medical practice related to secondary infections and to improved drug and surgical interventions for diseases such as diabetes, spinal cord injuries, poliomyelitis and multiple sclerosis (Gerhardt, 1990; Rice & LaPlante, 1988). For example, with traumatic spinal cord injuries, the most striking changes are related to a large decrease in deaths due to renal disease. Researchers have postulated that this is as a result of improved renal care related to the use of antibiotics, renal dialysis, medical and surgical procedures and educational counselling (Geisler, Jousse, Wynne-Jones & Breithaupt, 1983).

The implications of being disabled and becoming old have only begun to be recognized. As a result there is little written about the impact of aging on those with a lifelong disability. Exceptions include the work of Becker (1980), Zola (1988, 1990), The Developmental Consulting Program (1988), Rosenthal, McColl and McNair (1992) and the Kauferts (1984).

Canadian data estimate that 13.2% of the population experience some form of disability with the rates increasing with age from 5.2% for individuals from birth to 14 years old to 45.5% for people 65 and older (Dunn, 1990). Estimates of the number of people with disabilities in the U.S. vary depending on the purpose and source of the data (Zola, 1988). In reviewing data from different sources, Zola (1988) noted that estimates of persons with disabilities range from 8-17% of the population. Pfeiffer (1986) argued that these were underestimated and that 30 to 45% of the current population either have a disability or are regarded as having one.

The Canadian Health and Disability Survey, 1983-84, (Department of the Secretary of State of Canada, 1986) indicated that more women than men reported having a disability and mobility limitations were mentioned more frequently, followed by restriction in body movements and by hearing and sight limitations. Having a disability has implications for education, labour force participation and income. Adults reporting a disability tended to have received less formal education than non-disabled people and among younger people, those reporting a disability had a lower school attendance rate than non-disabled youth. Among those working (15-64 years), only 48% of disabled people were in the labour force in contrast to 75% of non- disabled people. Generally, those with a disability had a lower income than the Canadian population. Fifty-four percent of disabled respondents earned less than $10,000 with some reporting no income. Disabled women tended to have lower incomes. Eighty percent of those reporting no income were disabled women as opposed to 43% of disabled men.

These inequities have implications for the disabled persons as they age. Trieschmann (1988) argues that disability exacts a "penalty" on individuals in terms of the psychological, physical and economic costs of living. Lifelong disability combined with aging causes this penalty to increase exponentially.

There are two key issues related to aging with a lifelong disability: the experience of being disabled and becoming old; and, access to care.

An increased life expectancy is not without problems for disabled people. Living longer means that people with disabilities will be at risk for all of the chronic illnesses associated with aging (The Developmental Consulting Program, 1988). The physical, psychological and social changes associated with usual aging may interact with the existing disability to produce additional or more severe decline in function. Functional changes may occur earlier than expected. Weaknesses or deficits associated with the lifelong disability may be aggravated as the usual biological and psychological changes with age occur. As well, the ability of the aging disabled individual to adapt to some of these age changes may be affected by the presence of already existing functional limitations. Furthermore, chronic stresses experienced by disabled people as they compensate for their disability may produce further pathology (The Developmental Consulting Program, 1988).

Rosenthal and her associates (1992) reported that, in their sample of 40 men, 45 years and older (mean age 58.6 years; average years since injury 33) with spinal cord injuries, physical changes occurred at an earlier age and the consequences were more severe than for non-disabled older adults. The increased possibility of becoming dependent on others was imminent and real for these men. Rather than gradual adjustments to functional changes as would occur with usual aging, these men reported loss of energy, strength, stamina, mobility and flexibility that quickly and directly impinged on their abilities to carry out basic activities of daily living.

Another important aspect of chronic conditions related to aging is that, although these conditions are permanent, they are not necessarily static and thus may require continuing adaptation over time (Zola, 1990). Zola describes current concern with post- polio syndrome. Until recently, poliomyelitis was considered a stable chronic condition. After the original onset followed by rehabilitation, most people reached a plateau relative to physical functioning and expected to continue functioning at that level. But for at least 25% of people with polio, new problems have arisen 20 to 40 years after the original onset. These problems include fatigue, weakness in muscles previously affected and unaffected, muscle and joint pain, breathing difficulties, intolerance to cold (Zola, 1988), decreased endurance for usual activities and changes in lifestyle (Holman, 1986). Kaufert and Kaufert (1984), in their discussion of the long term impact of poliomyelitis in a Canadian sample, describe medicine's responses to these changes: some physicians argued that long term pathological processes specific to polio caused the symptoms, others proposed that the cumulative stress of impaired functioning over an extended period of time was the cause while others suggested that these changes were the product of normal aging. Regardless of the causes of these symptoms, the course of the disability again becomes uncertain for those

individuals experiencing the changes - the future course of their disability is no longer stable but may change requiring further adaptation or focus on coping strategies (Kaufert & Kaufert, 1984).

In a comprehensive report for the Ontario Federation for the Cerebral Palsied, the Development Consulting Program at Queen's University (1988) considered the implications of aging for people who had lived since childhood with a severe physical disability (i.e., those acquiring a disability prior to age 21 who were now over age 45) and living in the community. Cerebral palsy, congenital anomalies (spina bifida, meningomyelocele), poliomyelitis, arthritis, muscular dystrophy and injuries including but not limited to amputations, spinal cord injuries and head injuries were reviewed. In addition to prevalence, physical changes and complications associated with aging and disability, they identified the social and psychological factors affecting the aging disabled population. They suggested that, while the onset of problems related to aging may begin earlier in people with lifelong disabilities, many of the psychosocial effects due to aging would be similar to those encountered by the general elderly population. An extensive literature review and responses from 20 key informants resulted in identifying particular psychological and social factors (i.e., coping and adaptation, feelings of control, anxiety and fear, depression, energy and motivation, meaningful activity, isolation and social contact, self-esteem, and life satisfaction). They found that the psychosocial needs of an individual aging with a lifelong disability varied according to personality factors and particular environments; whether the disability was progressive or static; and the degree to which the individual perceived and coped with stresses and barriers in the environment.

In some cases the effect of living adult life with a disability can facilitate the development of skills which assist in dealing with issues related to aging (The Development Consulting Program, 1988). Becker (1980), in a study of aging and being old in the deaf community, found that the ways that deaf individuals learned to cope with deafness early in life enhanced their ability to cope with aging, particularly in terms of self- image. She argued that having a disability and being old are both devalued statuses in North American society. However, the individual who experiences loss of status early in life has a greater chance of learning to cope with it than does the individual who loses status later in life. In other cases having a disability serves to drain the individual of energy and motivation to cope with new challenges (The Development Consulting Program, 1988). Most of the men with spinal cord injuries in Rosenthal and associates' (1992) study felt that the changes they experienced with aging were qualitatively different than those of the general population - they experienced the same changes in a more intense way or their problems were compounded with other difficulties peculiar to the disability. Problems associated with a need for more assistance because of declining physical function may be compounded by the lack of financial and other resources. There was also the potential for increased isolation and possibly institutionalization.

Considering the context within which disabled people experience aging, employment and income issues provide examples of problems that may arise. More than half of those with disabilities are not in the labour force and those that are may have a lower income due to less educational preparation and less stamina to work full-time. With increased disability with aging, additional expenses may be incurred by the need for modifications to their living environment, special equipment, and personal care or other services. The individual may reduce his or her employment to part-time or take early or partial retirement because of increased disability. If full-time employment has not been possible over his or her lifetime, pensions may be unavailable. The increased expenses along with a change in income create an added burden to living with a disability (The Development Consulting Program, 1988).

Kaufert and Kaufert (1984) found that as those with poliomyelitis aged, the direction their actual lives had taken was described in terms of how it fit with the "normal" or "expected" pattern. The age of onset of polio was important in understanding the physiological and social consequences of long term disability. Those acquiring polio as adults had already established careers and thus, had to deal with disruptions of these. In contrast, those who were children when they contracted polio experienced issues around access to education, marriage and parenthood, and employment. The uncertainties of aging related not only to the physiological changes with poliomyelitis but also related to whether individuals would "be able to maintain the social fabric of their life unchanged" (p.614). This was particulary salient for those dependent on others for support and help. For some the concern was not for their own aging but for the aging of those providing support.

As with elders with later life disability, issues of caregiving are of concern for the aging adult with a lifelong disability. Declines in function with aging will result in an increase in the amount of assistance needed to maintain disabled individuals in their communities. In situations where spouses have assumed the care of their severely disabled partners for a number of years, they may have assumed responsibility for providing physical care as well as taking on more responsibility for traditionally gender specific roles such as household tasks, house maintenance and repair. Some may be the sole support of the family or hold jobs outside the home to supplement the family income. Some may also be involved in the care of aging parents. Individuals in their 50s and 60s may also have developed their own health problems. The burden of care created by these competing demands are potential sources of stress that may result in a neglect of family responsibilities and marital conflict (The Development Consulting Program, 1988).

Parents who have assumed the care of a disabled child may be faced with similar problems to the spouses described above. As their disabled adult child ages into his or her 50s or 60s and requires more care, they too at 75 years or older may acquire later life disabilities necessitating finding alternative formal services to provide the care needed.

Institutionalization of their aging child may become necessary as aging parents become unable to provide the necessary care either because of their own aging or death.

The Development Consulting Program (1988) reported, as did the Kauferts (1984), the concern of disabled people regarding the additional work and restrictions imposed on their caregiving parents, spouses, relatives and friends. Physical and mental fatigue felt by caregivers may result in them giving up their jobs, restricting social contacts and activities, reducing leisure activities and incurring additional expenses (The Development Consulting Program, 1988).

In summary, individuals who acquire disability in earlier life are also increasingly living to older ages. Very little is known about this phenomenon although it does appear that being disabled and becoming old is a much different experience to being old and becoming disabled.

## Conclusion

Although increasing age is associated with increasing disability, most older people are not disabled. Usual aging involves biological, psychological and social changes that may have implications for an older person's ability to function, but usually these changes are adapted to and do not result in disability. Only a small percentage of elderly people experience disability in later life. Some are old and become disabled in later life. Others are disabled before becoming old. It is not clear how the experiences of being old and of being disabled interact. The presence of the two together may compound the experience of either being old or being disabled. Usual age changes may affect the experience of disability and the presence of a disability may influence the experience of aging. It appears that the experience of being old and disabled differs depending on the age of onset of the disability, the nature of the disability itself, its suddenness of onset, and the predictability of its course. These factors change both the experience of being old and the experience of being disabled by creating differential access to various resources, particularly in young and middle adulthood, that influence one's ability to cope with the aging process and/or the ability to cope with being disabled.

*****

**Acknowledgements:** Seanne Wilkins gratefully acknowledges the support of the Royal Canadian Legion and the Canadian Occupational Therapy Foundation for the PhD studies on which this chapter is based. Cheryl Cott gratefully acknowledges the support of the Ontario Ministry of Health through a Health Research Personnel Development Fellowship.
We would like to thank Carolyn Rosenthal and Victor Marshall for their comments on an earlier draft of this chapter.

## NOTES

[1.] While the proportion of old people in the population increased from 5.2% in 1901 to 10.9% in 1991, it is projected to be 23.9% by 2031 (Marshall & Rosenthal, 1993; Messinger & Powell, 1987). One of the reasons for this change is that life expectancy has increased over time. Based on mortality conditions in 1931, a newborn male could expect to live about 60 years; a newborn female, 62 years. In 1986 the life expectancy at birth in Canada had increased to 73.0 for males and 79.7 for females (Chappell, 1990a; Denton, Feaver & Spencer, 1987). This increase in life expectancy is attributed to better sanitation, improved living conditions and medical technology that have decreased the likelihood of someone dying of contagious or parasitic diseases at a young age (Olshansky, Rudberg, Carnes, Cassel & Brody, 1991).

[2.] See for example, Breytspraak, 1984; George, 1980, 1990; Kaufman, 1986; Matthews, 1979; Ryff, 1986.

[3.] See for example, Bury, 1982; Charmaz, 1991; Corbin & Strauss, 1988; Locker, 1983; Williams, 1984.

## REFERENCES

Andreasen, M.E.K. (1980). Colour vision defects in the elderly. *Gerontological Nursing,* 6, 383-384.

Barusch, A.S. (1988). Problems and coping strategies of elderly spouse caregivers. *The Gerontologist,* 28, 677-685.

Becker, G. (1980). *Growing old in silence.* Berkeley, CA: University of California Press.

Becker, G. (1993). Continuity after stroke: Implications of life- course disruption in old age. *The Gerontologist,* 33, 148- 158.

Becker, G. & Kaufman, S. (1988). Old age, rehabilitation and research: A review of the issues. *The Gerontologist,* 28, 459-468.

Belgrave, L. (1990). The relevance of chronic illness in the everyday lives of elderly women. *Journal of Aging and Health,* 2, 475-500.

Bengtson, V., Rosenthal, C. & Burton, L. (1990). Families and aging: Diversity and heterogeneity. In R.H. Binstock and L.K. George (Eds.), *Handbook of aging and the social sciences* (3rd ed.) (pp. 263-287). San Diego, CA: Academic Press.

Branch, L.G. & Jette, A.M. (1983). Elders use of informal long term care assistance. *The Gerontologist,* 23, 51-56.

Breytspraak, L. (1984). *The development of self in later life.* Boston, MA: Little, Brown.

Brody, E.M. (1981). "Women in the middle" and family help to older people. *The Gerontologist,* 21, 471-480.

Brody, E.M. (1990). *Women in the middle: Their parent-care years.* NY: Springer.

Bury, M. (1982). Chronic illness as biographical disruption. *Sociology of Health and Illness,* 4, 167-182.

Cantor, M. (1979). Neighbours and friends: An overlooked resource in the informal support system. *Research in Aging,* 1, 434- 463.

CARNET: The Canadian Aging Network. (1993). *Work and family: The survey findings.* Geriatric Research Centre, University of Guelph, Guelph, ON: Author.

Chappell, N. (1987). Canadian income and health-care policy: Implications for the elderly. In V.W. Marshall (Ed.), *Aging in Canada: Social perspectives* (2nd ed.) (pp. 489-504). Markham, ON: Fitzhenry and Whiteside.

Chappell, N. (1990a). *The aging of the Canadian population* (S2- 184/6-1990). Ottawa, ON: supply and Services Canada.

Chappell, N. (1990b). Aging and social care. In R.H. Binstock and L.K. George (Eds.), *Handbook of aging and the social sciences* (3rd ed.) (pp. 383-396). San Diego, CA: Academic Press.

Chappell, N., Strain, L. & Blandford, A. (1986).

*Aging and health care: A social perspective.* Toronto, ON: Holt, Rinehart & Winston.

Charmaz, K. (1991). *Good days, bad days: The self in chronic illness and time.* New Brunswick, NJ: Rutgers University Press.

Clark, R.L. (1990). Income maintenance policies in the United States. In R.H. Binstock and L.K. George (Eds.), *Handbook of aging and the social sciences* (3rd ed.) (pp. 383-396). San Diego, CA: Academic Press.

Connidis, I. (1987). Life in older age: The view from the top. In V.W. Marshall (Ed.), *Aging in Canada: Social perspectives* (2nd ed.) (pp. 451-472). Markham, ON: Fitzhenry and Whiteside.

Connidis, I.A. (1989). *Family ties and aging.* Toronto, ON: Butterworths.

Corbin, J. & Strauss, A. (1988). *Unending work and care: Managing chronic illness at home.* San Francisco, CA: Jossey-Bass.

Corso, J. (1981). *Aging sensory systems and perception.* Englewood Cliffs, NJ: Prentice-Hall.

Craik, F.I.M. and Jennings, J.M. (1991). Human memory. In F.I.M. Craik & T.A. Salthouse (Eds.), *The handbook of aging and cognition* (pp. 51-109). Newark, New Jersey: Lawrence Erlbaum Associates.

Denton, F., Feaver, C. & Spencer, B. (1987). The Canadian population and labour force: Retrospect and prospect. In V. Marshall (Ed.), *Aging in Canada: Social perspectives* (2nd ed.) (pp. 11-38). Markham, ON: Fitzhenry & Whiteside.

Department of the Secretary of State of Canada. (1986). *Profile of disabled persons in Canada* (S2-173/1986). Ottawa, ON: Supply and Services Canada.

Developmental Consulting Program, The. (1988). *Aging with a lifelong physical disability.* Toronto, ON: The Ontario Federation of the Cerebral Palsied.

Dunn, P.A. (1990). *Barriers confronting seniors with disabilities in Canada: Special topic series from the health and activity limitation survey* (82-615, Vol 1). Ottawa, ON: Statistics Canada.

Ekerdt, D.J., Baden, L., Bosse, R., & Dibbs, E. (1983). The effects of retirement on physical health. *American Journal of Public Health,* 73, 779-783.

Ekerdt, D.J. & Bosse, R. (1982). Changes in self-reported health with retirement. *International Journal of Aging,* 15, 213- 223.

Fitzgerald, P.L. (1985). Exercise for the elderly. *Medical Clinics of North America,* 69, 189-196.

Ford, A., Folmar, S., Salmon, R., Medalie, J., Roy, A. & Galazka, S. (1988). Health and function in the old and very old. *Journal of the American Geriatrics Society,* 36, 187-197.

Gee, E. & Kimball, M. (1987). *Women and aging.*

Toronto, ON: Butterworths.

**Geisler, W., Jousse, A., Wynne-Jones, M. & Breithaupt, D. (1983).** Survival in traumatic spinal cord injury. *Paraplegia*, 21, 364-373.

**George, L. (1980).** *Role transitions in later life.* Monterey, CA: Brooks/Cole.

**George, L. (1990).** Social structure, social processes, and social-psychological states. In R. Binstock & L. George (Eds.), *Handbook of aging and the social sciences* (3rd ed., pp. 186-204). San Diego, CA: Academic Press.

**Gerhardt, U. (1990).** Patient careers in end stage renal disease. *Social Science and Medicine*, 30, 1211-1224.

**Guccione, A. (1993).** Implications of an aging population for rehabilitation: Demography, mortality and morbidity in the elderly. In A. Guccione (Ed.), *Geriatric physical therapy* (pp. 4-18). St. Louis, MO: Mosby.

**Health and Welfare Canada. (1982).** *Canadian governmental report on aging.* Ottawa, ON: Minister of Supply and Services.

**Holliday, P.J., Cott, C.A. & Torresin, W.D. (1992).** Preventing accidental falls by the elderly. In J. Rothman and R. Levine (Eds.), *Prevention practice: Strategies for physical and occupational therapy* (pp. 234-256). Philadelphia, PA: W.B. Saunders.

**Holman, K.G. (1986).** Post-polio syndrome. *Post-Graduate Medicine*, 79, 44-53.

**Horn, J.L. (1982).** The theory of fluid and crystallized intelligence in relation to concepts of cognitive psychology and aging in adulthood. In F.I.M. Craik & S. Trehub (Eds.), *Aging and cognitive processes* (pp. 237-278). New York: Plenum.

**Johnson, C.L. (1983).** Dyadic family relations and social support. *The Gerontologist*, 23, 377-383.

**Kane, R.L. & Kane, R.A. (1990).** Health care for older people: Organizational and policy issues. In R.H. Binstock and L.K. George (Eds.), *Handbook of aging and the social sciences* (3rd ed.) (pp. 415-437). San Diego, CA: Academic Press.

**Kaplan, G. (1991).** Epidemiologic observations on the compression of morbidity. *Journal of Aging and Health*, 3(2), 155-171.

**Kaufert, P. & Kaufert, J. (1984).** Methodological and conceptual issues in measuring the long term impact of disability: The experience of poliomyelitis patients in Manitoba. *Social Science and Medicine*, 19, 609-618.

**Kaufman, S. (1986).** *The ageless self: Sources of meaning in later life.* NY: Meridian.

**Keller, M., Leventhal, E. & Larson, B. (1989a).** Aging: The lived experience. *International Journal of Aging and Human Development*, 29, 67-82.

**Keller, M., Leventhal, H., Prohaska, T. & Leventhal, E. (1989b).** Beliefs about aging and illness in a community sample. *Research in Nursing and Health*, 12, 247-255.

**Locker, D. (1983).** *Disability and disadvantage: The consequences of chronic illness.* London, UK: Tavistock.

**Lopata, H. (1979).** *Women as widows: Support systems.* NY: Elsevier.

**Martin Matthews, A. (1987).** Widowhood as an expectable life event. In V. Marshall (Ed.), *Aging in Canada: Social perspectives* (2nd ed., pp. 343-366). Markham, ON: Fitzhenry & Whiteside.

**Martin Matthews, A. (1991).** *Widowhood in later life.* Toronto, ON: Butterworths.

**Matthews, S. (1979).** *The social world of old women: Management of self-identity.* Beverly Hills, CA: Sage.

**Marshall, V.W. (1987).** The health of very old people as a concern for their children. In V.W. Marshall (Ed.), *Aging in Canada: Social perspectives* (2nd ed., pp. 473-485). Markham, ON: Fitzhenry and Whiteside.

**Marshall, V.M. & Rosenthal, C.J. (in press, 1993).** Aging and later life. In R. Hagedorn (Ed.), *Sociology* (5th ed.). Toronto, ON: Holt, Rinehart.

**Marshall, V.W. with S. Rappolt & S. Wilkins. (1989).** *Models of community-based long term care: An analytic review.* Ottawa, ON: Health & Welfare Canada.

**McPherson, B.D. (1990).** *Aging as a social process* (2nd ed.). Toronto, ON: Butterworths.

**McPherson, B.D. and Kozlik, C.A. (1987).** Age patterns in leisure participation: The Canadian case. In V.W. Marshall (Ed.), *Aging in Canada: Social perspectives* (2nd ed.) (pp. 211-227). Markham, ON: Fitzhenry and Whiteside.

**Messinger, H. & Powell, B. (1987).** The implications of Canada's aging society on social expenditures. In V. Marshall (Ed.), *Aging in Canada: Social perspectives* (2nd ed., pp. 569-585). Markham, ON: Fitzhenry & Whiteside.

**National Advisory Council on Aging. (1991).** *The economic situation of Canada's seniors.* A fact book (H71-3/14- 1991E). Ottawa, ON: Supply and Services Canada.

**O'Brien, S.J. and Vertinsky, P.A. (1991).** Unfit survivors: Exercise as a resource for aging women. *The Gerontologist*, 31(3), 347-357.

**O'Bryant, S.L. (1985).** Neighbours' support of

older widows who lived alone in their own homes. *The Gerontologist*, 25, 305- 310.

Olshansky, S. J., Rudberg, M., Carnes, B., Cassel, C. & Brody, J. (1991). Trading off longer life for worsening health: The expansion of morbidity hypothesis. *Journal of Aging and Health*, 3, 194-216.

Owen, D.H. (1985). Maintaining posture and avoiding tripping. Optical information for selecting and controlling orientation and locomotion. *Clinics in Geriatric Medicine*, 1, 581-599.

Palmore, E., Burchett, B.M., Fillenbaum, G. G., George, L.K., & Wallman, L.M. (1985). *Retirement: Causes and consequences*. NY: Springer.

Pfeiffer, D. (1986, April). *The number of disabled persons in the U.S. and its policy implications.* Paper presented to the Society for the Study of Chronic Illness, Impairment, and Disability, Reno, NV.

Rice, D. & LaPlante, M. (1988). Chronic illness, disability, and increasing longevity. In S. Sullivan & M. Lewin (Eds.), *The economics and ethics of long-term care and disability* (pp. 9-55). Washington, DC: American Enterprise Institute for Public Policy Research.

Rosenthal, C. (1987). Aging and intergenerational relations in Canada. In V. Marshall (Ed.), *Aging in Canada: Social perspectives* (2nd ed., pp. 311-342). Markham, ON: Fitzhenry & Whiteside.

Rosenthal, C., Matthews, S. & Marshall, V. (1989). Is parent care normative? The experience of a sample of middle-aged women. *Research on Aging*, 11, 244-260.

Rosenthal, C, McColl, M.A. & McNair, T. (1992, November). *Aging with a disability: Perceptions of aging among men with spinal cord injury.* Paper presented at the annual meetings of the Gerontological Society of America, Washington, DC.

Ryff, C. (1986). The subjective construction of self and society: An agenda for life-span research. In V. Marshall (Ed.), *Later life: The social psychology of aging* (pp. 33-74). Beverly Hills, CA: Sage.

Salthouse, T.A. (1982). *Adult cognition: An experimental psychology of human aging.* New York: Springer-Verlag.

Shapiro, E. & Roos, N.P. (1982). Retired and employed elderly pensioners: Their utilization of health care services. *The Gerontologist*, 22, 187-193.

Smeeding, T.M. (1990). Economic Status of the Elderly. In R.H. Binstock and L.K. George (Eds.), *Handbook of aging and the social sciences* (3rd ed.) (pp. 362-381). San Diego, CA: Academic Press.

Spooner, J.W., Sakala, S.M. & Baloh, R.W. (1980). Effect of aging on eye tracking. *Archives of Neurology,* 37, 575-576.

Statistics Canada. (1988). *Canada's seniors* (98-121). Ottawa, ON: Supply & Services Canada.

Stoller, E.P. & Earl, L.L. (1983). Help with activities of everyday life: Sources of support for the non- institutionalized elderly. *The Gerontologist*, 23, 64-70.

Strauss, A.L., Corbin, J. Fagerhaugh, S., Glaser, B.G., Maines, D., Suczek, LB., & Wiener, C. (1984). *Chronic illness and the quality of life,* St. Louis: C.V. Mosby.

Triecsmann, R.B. (1988). *Spinal cord injuries: Psychological, social, and vocational rehabilitation* (2nd ed.). NY: Demos.

Vandervoort, A., Hayes, K.C., and Belanger, A.Y. (1986). Strength and endurance of skeletal muscle in the elderly. *Physiotherapy Canada*, 42, 99-107.

Verbrugge, L. (1989). Gender, aging, and health. In K. Markides (Ed.), *Aging and health: Perspectives on gender, race, ethnicity, and class* (pp. 23-78). Newbury Park, CA: Sage.

Verbrugge, L. (1990). The iceberg of disability. In S. Stahl (Ed.), *The legacy of longevity: Health and health care in later life* (pp. 55-75). Newbury Park, CA: Sage.

Verbrugge, L. (1991). Survival curves, prevalence rates, and dark matters therein. *Journal of Aging and Health*, 3(2), 217-236.

Williams, G. (1984). The genesis of chronic illness: Narrative re-construction. *Sociology of Health and Illness*, 6, 175- 200.

World Health Organization. (1980). *International classification of impairments, disabilities, and handicaps.* Geneva, Switzerland: Author.

Young, R. & Olson, E. (1991). Introduction. In R. Young & E. Olson (Eds.), *Health, illness, and disability in later life: Practice issues and interventions* (pp. 1-7). Newbury Park, CA: Sage.

Zola, I. (1988). Policies and programs concerning aging and disability: Toward a unifying agenda. In S. Sullivan & M. Lewin (Eds.), *The economics and ethics of long-term care and disability* (pp. 90-130). Washington, DC: American Enterprise Institute for Public Policy Research.

Zola, I. (1990). Aging, disability and the home-care revolution. *Archives of Physical Medicine and Rehabilitation*, 71, 93-96.

******

About the Authors: Seanne Wilkins, M.Sc., Ph.D. (in progress) is an occupational therapist and a Doctoral Candidate in the Graduate Department of Community Health (Behavioural

Science) and the Centre for Studies of Aging, University of Toronto.

**Cheryl Cott, M.Sc., Ph.D. (in progress)**, is a Lecturer in the Division of Physical Therapy and a Research Project Coordinator in the Centre for Studies of Aging at the University of Toronto. She is currently a Doctoral Student in the Graduate Department of Community Health (Behavioural Science), University of Toronto.

*Correspondence may be addressed to* either author, c/o Centre for Studies of Aging, University of Toronto, 455 Spadina Avenue, Suite 305, Toronto, Ontario, M5S 2G8.

**Source:**  Reprinted with permission from the authors, Seanne Wilkins and Cheryl Cott who wrote this article specifically for the second edition of *Perspectives on Disability*.

# Depression as Mental Illness
Ellen Frank
David J. Kupfer

**Abstract** ~ *Depression is a very disabling illness. This article describes what depression is, how it disables individuals, why it gets so little medical attention, problems in the treatment of depression, phases in the treatment of depression, types of treatment interventions, the impact of psychotherapy on depression, indications for hospitalization and common reasons why treatment fails. The authors provide many practical suggestions for mental health practitioners, consumers, and family members.*

## Depression: What is it?

The term "depression" is probably the most unfortunate term ever used to describe a major mental illness. It fails to distinguish this serious and disabling condition from the everyday experience of normal, healthy individuals. Everyone has transient periods of low, bad, or blue mood that last a few hours or a few days. Clinical Depression or Major Depression, the mental illness, is a syndrome that includes sad or irritable mood lasting at least 2 weeks a month *and* pronounced changes in sleep, appetite, energy, ability to concentrate and remember, interest in usual activities, and capacity to experience pleasure. Frequently, when all of these symptoms coexist at a severe level for a long time, individuals become so discouraged and hopeless that death seems preferable to life. This leads to passive suicidal wishes, suicidal plans, and even attempted and completed suicide.

Sleep and appetite can either increase or decrease from an individual's usual levels. The more typical picture of depression is that of an individual who has difficulty falling asleep, wakes throughout the night, and awakens an hour to several hours earlier than desired in the morning. However, approximately 20% of individuals experiencing depression sleep more than the usual amount. In all cases, the person experiencing depression awakes without feeling rested.

Most people in a clinical depression experience a decrease in appetite and weight loss that is occasionally considerable. About 15% will experience an increased desire to eat and will gain weight, but most of these people will still report that the food they are eating does not actually appeal to them.

The inability to concentrate and make decisions experienced by individuals with depression can be the most frightening aspect of the disorder. In the midst of a severe depression, individuals may find that they cannot follow the thread of a simple newspaper article or the story line of a half-hour situation comedy on television. Major decision making is impossible. Even minor decisions, such as which shirt to wear or which brand of green beans to buy, can seem overwhelming to an individual experiencing depression. This often leads depressed individuals to feel as though they are literally losing their minds. Equally distressing is the loss of energy and profound fatigue experienced by both those who sleep more and those who sleep less during their episodes.

## How Disabling is Depression?

Depression is often thought of as the "common cold" of mental illnesses because it affects so many people. The most recent epidemiologic data suggests that about one in five to one in seven women will experience a depression sometime during her lifetime, as will approximately one in 15 men. Approximately half of those who experience a single episode of depression will never have another. The other 50% may have episodes that occur as frequently as once or even twice a year. If untreated, they may be quite long-- anywhere from 6 months to over a year.

A recent study by the Rand Corporation demonstrated that depression is as disabling, in terms of time spent away from work and loss of work productivity, as hypertension and diabetes. However, although people never question the heart patient's need for special treatment and time to recuperate, they generally assume that individuals with depression should be able to pick themselves up by their own bootstraps. In fact, people with depression are no more capable of treating their own disorder than are cardiac patients or diabetics.

## Why Depression Gets So Little Attention

The vast majority of depressions go untreated and undiagnosed. Why does such a disabling condition receive so little medical attention? Perhaps the most important reason is that depression is often not recognized at all, or it is not recognized as a mental illness. Even if it is viewed as a mental illness, many people avoid seeking treatment because of the stigma associated with depression. Depression may be stigmatizing because its symptoms often appear to the outsider to be mere laziness or overreaction to life events.

The lack of an obvious cause can hinder recognition and treatment of depression: those around the individual may well ask, "What could you possibly have to be depressed about?" Because the behavior of the person with depression typically does not fall outside the normal (i.e., they are rarely bizarre in their behavior, almost never experience hallucinations, and only rarely experience delusions), a depression must become extremely severe--reaching the point at which the individual no longer cares for him or herself--before hospitalization is considered. Unlike mania or other extreme conditions, the behavior of the depressed individual, while quite worrisome to family members and friends, rarely disrupts the lives of others. The depression does not *appear to* be a threatening illness. Yet the statistics on suicide among people with depression contradict this impression. Depression is actually a quiet killer. Perhaps 50% of the people who succeed in committing suicide are thought to have been depressed.

## Problems in the Treatment of Depression

As stated above, depression is typically not noticeable in the way that other kinds of illnesses, such as schizophrenia or alcoholism, may be in normal social situations. Often the depressed individual suffers in silence. Further complicating the picture is the tendency of depressive illness to masquerade as physical ailments. Often the most persistent complaints are headache, stomach ache, backache, and other pain symptoms. The person often focuses on these symptoms, partly because they are more socially acceptable than the profound feeling of sadness, inability to concentrate, or total loss of pleasure in usual activities. Indeed, the physical symptoms may help the person with depression to explain why nothing is fun anymore.

Another barrier to recognizing depression can be the individual's own assumptions about what is normal. This is particularly true for those who have seasonal variations in mood that may have persisted since their late teens or early twenties. They often come to accept their lack of motivation and energy as a normal part of winter. Likewise, they may accept as normal the fact that they can count on spring and summer to be times of accomplishment and high energy. They adapt their lives to fit their seasonal variation in mood, but never seek treatment for it. Another problem may be the coexistence or comorbiditiy of another psychiatric or medical condition. In most cases, treatment of depression is necessary, regardless of the accompanying disorder. However, one must be aware of diagnostic and treatment complications in treating two disorders simultaneously.

## Phases in the Treatment of Depression

*How Many Phases in the Treatment of Depression?*

For people experiencing their first episode of major depression, there are two phases of treatment: acute treatment and continuation treatment. For those individuals who have experienced previous episodes of depression, treatment should be thought of in three phases:    acute, continuation, and preventive maintenance therapy.    This is especially true if the person has had two or more previous episodes spaced relatively close together.

*Acute Treatment*

The goal of acute treatment is to eliminate the symptoms of depression.  We believe that, even when the treatment is primarily by medication, the clinician needs to deliver the treatment in a psychotherapeutic environment.    Indeed, probably the most effective therapeutic intervention relies on both      psychopharmacologic      and psychotherapeutic approaches.   Combined treatment in all phases of the disorder may provide the best model in which to develop an alliance between the person receiving treatment and the clinician, as well as with the family, if appropriate.   A successful acute treatment brings the person back to an essentially symptom-free state and to a level of functioning comparable to before he or she became ill.    Unlike the common cold, depression is not an illness that can be cured in a matter of days.  At the very *minimum*, a good response to antidepressant medication or psychotherapy focused on the treatment of depression will take 4 weeks.  It may take as long as 12 to 16 weeks, and , in some cases, even longer.  During that time, individuals in treatment who are unfamiliar with depressive illness should receive as much information as possible about the illness and its treatment. This should include both general information and retrospective inquiry, with the treating clinician, into the development of the episode. It is very important for the individual to try and establish in his or her own mind the sequence of symptom development, because this sequence is likely to be repeated in the future.

*Continuation Treatment*

Probably the greatest mistake made in the treatment of depression (other than the failure to give an adequate dose of medication) is the failure to continue a successful treatment long enough.    This is true both for pharmacotherapy and psychotherapy, in which therapists may feel it important to stick to a short-term treatment contract.    The risk of relapse is exceptionally high in the first 4 to 6 months after symptomatic recovery, and even someone experiencing a first episode of depression should continue in treatment for 4 to 6 months after the complete resolution of symptoms and return to normal functioning.  If the treatment is a psychotherapeutic one, the frequency of visits can usually be safely decreased during this period.   On the other hand, the dose of medication should definitely not be altered during continuation treatment.

*Maintenance Treatment*

In the area of unipolar (as opposed to bipolar or manic depressive) illness, the concept of maintenance treatment is a relatively new one.   While it has long been agreed that people with bipolar illness require maintenance treatment with lithium carbonate or some other medication, the concept of preventive maintenance in recurrent unipolar disorder has been relatively slow in developing.   The few research studies that have addressed this question, however, clearly point to the advantage of continued pharmacotherapy, psychotherapy, or both in preventing new episodes or lengthening the time period between episodes.  Any individual who has had even a single previous episode of depression should be considered for preventive maintenance treatment.    Certainly, those individuals with two or more previous episodes that have occurred close together should have a maintenance treatment plan. Depending on the particular person and his or her life circumstances, this could include maintenance pharmacotherapy, maintenance psychotherapy, or a combination of the two.

*Intervention with People who Do Not Respond to Treatment*

About   70%   of   people   with nonpsychotic depression will respond to the first treatment  tried; about 30% will not.  For those who have not achieved good progress toward recovery after 6 to 8 weeks of consistent therapy, there are several strategies that can be tried.  The first is to add lithium carbonate   to   the   tricyclic   antidepressant regimen.   A second strategy, which can sometimes be helpful especially for women who have slightly subnormal or low-end-of-normal thyroid function, is the addition of T3 or cytomel. A third strategy is to switch from a tricyclic antidepressant to a monoamine oxidase inhibitor. If none of these more traditional strategies is effective, one of the "new" antidepressants, such as fluoxetine (Prozac) or sertraline (Zoloft), can be tried.

*Intervention with Psychotic Depression*

People experiencing psychotic depressions usually receive treatment in the hospital, rather than as outpatients. Although such individuals often respond to high doses of tricyclic antidepressants, in most cases additional therapy is necessary. Probably the most common treatment strategy with people experiencing psychotic depression is to combine a tricyclic antidepressant with a phenothiazine. These drugs are sometimes referred to as the "major tranquilizers" and include thorazine, stelazine, and mellaril. Haldol, which is not actually a phenothiazine, is also considered one of the major tranquilizers, and may also be combined with a tricyclic antidepressant.

Another extremely effective approach is the use of electroconvulsive therapy (ECT or EST), followed by a tricyclic antidepressant. ECT appears to be extremely effective in bringing people with psychotic depression out of the episode. Without continuation treatment with a tricyclic, however, relapse is extremely common. Thus, as with the individual who responds to tricyclics initially, the individual who responds to ECT should have a 4- to 6-month continuation treatment on tricyclic antidepressants.

**Indications for Hospitalization**

While most people with unipolar depression can be treated on an outpatient basis, there are several circumstances under which hospitalization is indicated. An individual who has a complicating medical illness should, in most instances, be treated in the hospital, not so much because of the severity of the depression, but because of the need to watch for any changes in the medical illness as treatment for the depression is introduced. Furthermore, if the individual is already on several medications for the medical

illness, this may complicate the drug treatment of depression; a hospital setting provides considerably more safety for treatment. While comorbidity may refer to the presence of other psychiatric or other medical disorders, we are referring here to the comorbidity due to medical disorders.

Hospitalization should always be considered in the face of suicidal behavior or suicidal thinking that the individual seems unable to control. In some such instance, family members can be counted on to help the individual through the initial stages of treatment. However, very careful consideration must be given before placing this responsibility on family members. This should only be considered when there are very strong reasons for keeping the person out of the hospital and there is a high level of confidence in the family member's ability to restrain the person.

Typically, delusions or hallucinations are also indications for hospitalization, since these are associated with the most severe episodes of depression. Treatment of delusional depression is more complicated than that of the nonpsychotic variety, and can be accomplished more efficiently in a hospital setting.

Extreme agitation or anxiety can also signal a need for hospitalization. When individuals are so agitated that their behavior is frightening to others, the endurance of family members and friends often wears quickly. Like a person experiencing delusion, someone who is extremely agitated can be treated more efficiently in the hospital, thus giving quicker relief to these very distressing symptoms.

Finally, hospitalization should be considered when there is no close support person nearby. Such a situation often exists with elderly persons whose families no longer reside in the same city with them, or when young singles have moved from home to take a job but are not yet well integrated into the community.

*How Long Should Hospitalization Last?*

Hospitalization should last long enough to bring about a resolution of symptoms sufficient to allow the person to return to his or her normal roles. That is, within a few days of returning home, the person should be able to resume the majority of normal work or homemaking functions. Unfortunately, many people today find that their insurance coverage does not last long enough to permit this level of symptom resolution.  In these instances, a clear plan should be developed for outpatient management until such symptom resolution can be brought about.

**Why Treatment Fails**

A major problem in the treatment of depression is the failure to treat with sufficient intensity.  While the D/ART programs and other attempts to educate health professionals about depression have resulted in increasing recognition of the disorder and in the better choice of appropriate treatments by the treating clinician, one of the most common reasons for failure to resolve an episode of depression is that treatment was not offered with sufficient intensity.  As more and more is understood about how the antidepressant medications work, increasing recognition is being given to the substantial variability in how different individuals process these medications in their systems.

It was once thought that a rough estimate of the correct amount of medication could be made by taking into account one's size and weight (presumably, smaller, lighter individuals required less medication) and age (presumably, elderly individuals required less medication than younger ones).  We now recognize that, while it is true that elderly individuals, on average, will require less of the same medication than younger individuals, some elderly people need as high a dose as does a younger person.  It appears that other factors, such as whether the individual smokes (nicotine interferes with the absorption of medication), whether the individual is on other medications (certain drugs can enhance the amount of antidepressant that is available in the system), and how rapidly the individual's liver breaks down the medication, is much more important in determining the correct dose of medication than is size or weight.

Unfortunately, many doctors stop treatment as soon as an individual comes close to the upper end of the "average" dose for a given antidepressant medication, without testing to see that the person has achieved the blood level (amount of medication in the blood for active treatment of the disorder). The doctor thus may not realize that a particular person is nowhere near the blood level expected for the dose being given. Such a person may require 50 or even 100% more than the average dose in order to achieve good therapeutic effect.  For example, in the case of imipramine, a standard antidepressant, the average person can be expected to respond to a dose somewhere between 175 and 225 mg/day.  However, some individuals may require as little as 75 mg; others may require 400 or 450 mg to achieve the same blood level that the average person achieves at 200 mg. The larger number of side effects experienced by the person who requires only 75 mg will usually be a signal to the doctor to *reduce* the dose. It is much more unusual for someone's failure to respond to 175 or 200 mg to be interpreted as a signal that the dose needs to be increased, perhaps as much as 100%. Such a person is often seen as a treatment failure, or given an alternate medication, when simply increasing the dose of the first medication would have resulted in a good treatment response.

*Failure to Treat Long Enough*
Another problem in the pharmacologic or drug treatment of depression is the failure to treat long enough.  This is really a two-part failure: a failure to treat with a single substance long enough to determine whether it is really effective, and a failure to treat long enough once a response has been obtained.  The first failure seems to come from a lack of recognition of how long it sometimes takes for the antidepressant drugs to work effectively. for some individuals, the descent into an episode of depression is a precipitous one; for others, it is a long, drawn-out process. Likewise, some people seem to respond quite quickly to medication, while others take much longer to respond adequately. As long as there is steady progress toward recovery, even if it is painfully slow, sticking with a single drug for as long as 12 weeks is advisable.  Many clinicians will give up on a particular drug if full recovery has not been achieved in 6 to 8

weeks. We argue that, as long as steady progress is being made, the best course of action is often to stick with the original compound.

Failure to treat long enough also occurs when people do achieve a good response. Once a recovery is obtained, there is pressure from the individual, family members, and sometimes even the treating physician to discontinue treatment as soon as possible. Several recent studies of the treatment of depressive illness, however, indicate that the early discontinuation of treatment is probably the single largest cause of relapse. Thus, after a good response has been achieved, treatment should be continued without change for a minimum of 4 to 6 months. This continuation of treatment is necessary even if the person does not experience any symptoms.

*Failure to Recognize Recurrent Depression*

For a long time, recurrent unipolar depression was thought of as being quite different from manic depressive disease, which was conceptualized as a lifelong illness. We now recognize that an individual who has two episodes of depression in close succession ought not to be thought of as having two discrete episodes of illness, but as having what is very probably a lifelong illness. This then brings up the consideration of maintenance treatment. When medication has been used to bring about remission of the acute episode, we would argue that individuals with recurrent unipolar illness should be offered ongoing pharmacotherapy at the acute treatment dose (the dose needed to achieve a good treatment response for the acute episode) for at least the length of 2.5 treatment cycles. Thus, if the person has had yearly episodes, maintenance treatment should be continued for at least 2.5 years. If the person only has episodes every 2 years, maintenance treatment should be continued for a period of at least 5 years in order to maximize the probability that he or she will remain illness-free. At the end of that time, the individual and the clinician can discuss the pros and cons of stopping medication. If stopping medication is decided upon, it should be done very gradually, over an extended period of time.

**About the Authors:** **Ellen Frank, Ph.D.,** is Associate Professor of Psychiatry and Psychology in the Department of Psychiatry at the University of Pittsburgh School of Medicine, and the Director of the Western Psychiatric Institute and Clinic's Depression Prevention Program. Under grants from the National Institute of Mental Health (NIMH), Dr. Frank is currently conducting a series of long-term treatment studies with individuals suffering from recurrent depression, and another in the area of manic-depressive illness.

**David J. Kupfer, M.D.,** is professor and Chairman, Department of Psychiatry, University of Pittsburgh School of Medicine. Dr. Kupfer is also Chairman of the MacArthur Foundation's Mental Health Research Network I: Psychobiology of Depression and Other Affective Disorders. He is an internationally recognized expert in the areas of sleep and affective disorders research.

**Source:** Reprinted with permission from *Support,* the newsletter for the Depressive and Manic-Depressive Association of Nebraska (DMDA), Vol. 4, No. 2, February 1993, pp. 1,5,7,8. Copyright © Innovations and Research in Clinical Services, Community Support and Rehabilitation, Boston, MA. 12215.

# An Ecology of Prevention for the Future

David L. Coulter, MD

**Abstract** ~ *The field of mental retardation is being changed by a paradigm shift in how mental retardation is conceptualized and in how services are provided. This new way of thinking is reflected in the 1992 AAMR definition of what mental retardation is (Luckasson, et. al., 1992). Prevention efforts must also reflect this new way of thinking, which focuses on the interaction between individuals and their environment. In this paper, the stage was set for adoption of a new vision of prevention that incorporates an ecological approach to understanding the causation of mental retardation. The articles in this symposium were reviewed and their relevance to this new vision discussed. A comprehensive, coordinated, and integrated prevention program is needed that includes new strategies addressing a variety of personal, social, and environmental risk factors and the interactions among them.*

## What Are We Trying to Prevent?

Research, teaching, and service delivery in the field of mental retardation are being challenged by what has been termed a *paradigm shift* in how the basic ideas of the field are conceptualized (Bradley & Knoll, 1990). This shift is nothing less than a dramatic change in the dominant theoretical perspective (paradigm) that organizes the way in which the majority of workers in the field think about what they are doing. Earlier perspectives were dominated first by an institutional model and, more recently, by a developmental-behavioral model. Both models identified the "problem" as being located within the individual, so services to "correct the problem" were directed at the individual. The purpose was to treat, train, or change the individual with mental retardation. Highly sophisticated schemas for producing change were developed, including the use of pharmacologic, aversive, and nonaversive behavioral interventions. As change ("growth") was produced, the individual was permitted to move along a predetermined continuum from more restrictive to less restrictive settings. This model faltered in recent years as workers in the field realized that the continuum had failed to deliver on its promises. Individuals with mental retardation were now living in smaller programs, but they were still surrounded by professionals, isolated from the community, and learning "skills" that had little relevance to personal choices or full community participation. The shift away from this failing model has been energized by the emergence of a new way of thinking about what mental retardation really is.

In recent decades, society has given increasing recognition to the importance of understanding the relation between organisms and their environment. The original, biological concept of ecology (Odom, 1959) was adapted for the study of human development (Bronfenbrenner, 1979) to describe the complex interactions between individuals and their social environment. For many years, a small group of workers studied these relations and developed the idea that disability was the result of the interaction between the individual and the environment. This idea achieved "mainstream" recognition with the Institute of Medicine's (1991) report, *Disability in America*, in which *functional limitation* was defined as the effect of specific impairments on the performance or performance capability of the individual. *Disability* was the expression of such a functional limitation in a social context (Institute of Medicine, 1991). The importance of this idea was recognized by the American Association on Mental Retardation (AAMR) in its new conceptualization of mental retardation. The AAMR now views mental retardation as a description of an individual's present functioning, which reflects the impact of intellectual and adaptive limitations on coping with the demands of the environment in which the individual lives, learns, works, and socializes (Luckasson et al., 1992). This new concept of mental retardation is consistent with and reflects the paradigm shift that will guide our thinking in the 1990s and beyond.

The fundamental components of the new paradigm include a commitment to the community and family, an emphasis on human relationships, person-centered programming, and a recognition of real choice and control by people with disabilities (Bradley & Knoll, 1990). The focus is on the individual's personal choices for living in the community and on how person-centered supports can be utilized to enhance social inclusion and functioning within this environment. The new AAMR definition of mental retardation reflects this paradigm when it states that application of the definition assumes that the existence of limitations in adaptive skills occurs within the context of community environments typical of the individual's age peers and is indexed to the person's individualized needs for supports (Luckasson et al., 1992).

Mental retardation no longer represents a diagnosis of a medical or psychological disorder. In this new way of thinking, mental retardation represents a description of how a person with intellectual and adaptive limitations functions within a community environment. If this is what mental retardation is, then this is what we are being challenged to prevent. This requires a critical change in how we think about prevention. Prevention efforts can no longer be constrained by an outdated medically based or "disease" model of what mental retardation is. Mental retardation is about people and how they function in a community environment. Thus, prevention efforts in the 1990s and beyond will have to focus more on how people can be helped to improve their functioning within this environment.

**An Ecological Approach**

This new way of thinking about what mental retardation is also requires a new way of thinking about how it can be prevented. Consistent with the new paradigm, we are challenged to direct prevention efforts increasingly toward the interaction between the individual and the community environment (Luckasson et al., 1992). This interaction determines how the person actually functions within that environment. Knowledge about this interaction is needed to understand the

nature of mental retardation and how it can be prevented. The most appropriate way to describe this body of knowledge is to utilize an ecological approach. *Ecology* is defined as the study of the relation of organisms or groups of organisms to their environment or the science of the interrelations between living organisms and their environment (Odom, 1959; Webster's, 1979). Our challenge, then, is to develop an ecological approach to the prevention of mental retardation. We must use the knowledge gained from the science of ecology in order to understand how people with mental retardation function within community environments. This knowledge must then be incorporated into new strategies for prevention.

We should not underestimate the magnitude of the challenge involved in rethinking prevention and in adopting an ecological approach. Many will say, "Why bother?" Why change the focus of 3 decades of prevention efforts, which have largely concentrated on preventing the occurrence (or improving the outcome) of some of the most important diseases that are associated with mental retardation? Certainly, many of these efforts have been very successful, such as the virtual elimination of mental retardation due to untreated phenylketonuria. One reason to change is that 3 decades of prevention efforts have not significantly reduced the overall incidence or prevalence of mental retardation (Coulter, 1991). Crocker (1992b) correctly pointed out in this symposium that simple counting or charting of changes in the overall incidence and prevalence of mental retardation is not a sufficient way to evaluate prevention. He offered several reasons for rejecting this measure as an evaluation tool, but his reasons actually represent the failure of current evaluation efforts to incorporate an ecological approach. When he referred to prevention gestures affecting only one part of a complex equation, he was really saying that mental retardation often results from complex interactions between multiple causative factors. In the Institute of Medicine (1991) report, the observation was made that multiple risk factors often converge to pre-dispose an individual to the disabling process and that these risk factors may interact at different stages of the disabling process. In the new AAMR manual of definition, classification, and systems of supports in mental retardation (Luckasson et al., 1992), four categories of causative or risk factors were recognized: biomedical, social, behavioral, and educational. Understanding the interactions among these various factors, some of which describe the individual and some of which describe the environment in which the person functions, requires an ecological approach. Thus, Crocker was really saying that accurate evaluation of the overall impact of prevention efforts requires an ecological approach to understanding the complex equation that operates to determine the functional outcome.

Crocker (1992b) also argued that evaluating prevention efforts by simple charting changes in the incidence and prevalence of mental retardation may overlook significant improvement or reduction in the level of disability experienced by people who continue to qualify for a diagnosis of mental retardation. Accurate evaluation of this outcome of prevention efforts requires measurement of how the person actually functions in the environment in which the person lives. An ecological approach that measures the interaction between the person and the environment in terms of how the person functions would provide the means to assess this outcome of prevention efforts. Once again, current approaches to evaluating the impact of prevention programs may have failed to demonstrate an effect on the overall incidence and prevalence of mental retardation, in part because they have not incorporated an ecological understanding of what mental retardation is and how it occurs.

## Why Change? An Illustration

The principal reasons to change to an ecological approach to prevention are as follows: (a) It will help us to understand better what it is we are trying to prevent; (b) it will lead to new and potentially more effective strategies that are focused on improving the interactions between individuals and their environment; and (c) it will help us to measure better the impact of these prevention efforts.

To understand how such an ecological approach to prevention might work,

consider the following real-life example (the name has been changed). This example illustrates how multiple risk factors interacted at different stages to result in this child's disabilities and how an ecological approach to prevention might have prevented her disabilities.

Julie was born prematurely at 32 weeks gestation. Her mother was infected with HIV and used cocaine throughout the pregnancy. Julie had respiratory distress after birth and was on a ventilator for several weeks. On the third day of life she had a severe intracranial hemorrhage with bleeding into the right cerebral hemisphere and into both cerebral ventricles. She subsequently developed progressive hydrocephalus, which stabilized with medical therapy, and she never required a shunt. She was discharged to her mother's care. Her mother had received drug counseling and was no longer using cocaine, but she was not very compliant with medical care for her HIV infection. During the next few months of life, it was discovered that Julie was not infected with HIV. A CT scan showed that the hydrocephalus had resolved, but there was persistent damage in the right frontal lobe. This brain damage was felt to be the cause of Julie's cerebral palsy and left hemiparesis. She developed seizures when she was about a year old and asthma shortly after that. Although she was referred for early intervention services, she never received these services consistently because of a long waiting list, disorganization in her mother's life and in the family home, and Julie's own frequent hospitalizations for seizures or asthma. A comprehensive evaluation when she was 3 years old found that Julie's cognitive skills were at approximately the level of an 18-month-old. The evaluation team noted that Julie had a "sunny" disposition and was a happy, loving child who could make everyone around her smile and want to play with her.

The causes of Julie's mental retardation include biomedical factors (prematurity, intracranial hemorrhage, hydrocephalus), social factors (her mother's illness and the disorganization of the family home), behavioral factors (her mother's drug use), and educational factors (lack of early intervention services). The interactions among these factors are readily apparent. Her mother's drug use probably caused her to deliver Julie prematurely and may have affected Julie's prenatal brain development. Furthermore, her mother's illness and the chronic disorganization of the family home contributed to Julie's lack of educational intervention. An ecological approach to causation in Julie's case would focus on understanding these interactions and how they contributed to her mental retardation.

How might an ecological approach to prevention have worked in Julie's case? What prevention strategies would have been necessary to prevent her mental retardation and cerebral palsy? The key point is that a prevention strategy that focused on only *one* of the causative factors present in her case would probably not have been effective. If we only delivered a drug treatment program to help her mother stay away from cocaine, we might have prevented Julie's premature birth, but we would not have prevented the social disorganization of the family home or the inadequate provision of educational intervention services. If we only gave better neonatal care, we might have prevented the intracranial hemorrhage, but we also would not have prevented the social disorganization or lack of intervention. If we only removed Julie from the family home, placed her in a good foster home, and enrolled her in an adequate early intervention program, we would not have prevented her premature birth and the intracranial hemorrhage. An ecological approach to prevention in Julie's case would require a comprehensive, coordinated, and integrated set of strategies that included (a) a drug treatment program for her mother (including ongoing care to prevent relapse), (b) complete prenatal care for Julie's mother, (c) adequate medical care for both Julie and her mother, (d) provision of appropriate and continuing social supports to the family, (e) and Julie's prompt enrollment in a comprehensive educational intervention program. Furthermore, an ecological approach would require a service coordinator who would monitor all of these programs and ensure their integration and effectiveness.

This illustration summarizes the reasons for adopting an ecological approach to prevention. We need a new vision of prevention that incorporates an ecological understanding of the interaction among all of the personal, social, and environmental factors that cause mental retardation in order to help individuals like Julie function optimally in their own personal environment of home, school, and community.

## The Symposium on Prevention

Allen Crocker asked me to review the articles included in this special issue and reflect on how well they capture the spirit of what the prevention of mental retardation means for the 1990s. Undertaking this challenge first required consideration of the current paradigm shift and AAMR's new conceptualization of mental retardation. It became apparent that a new vision of prevention was needed that incorporated these realities, a vision that I have described as an ecological approach to prevention. This now provides a basis for considering the articles in this special issue.

Crocker's (1992a) introduction to this symposium reflects his long-standing leadership in focusing attention on policies and programs to prevent mental retardation. He described the evolution of the current concepts and guidelines, including recognition of the "new morbidity" (Baumeister, 1991), the necessity for collaboration and for adoption of a more holistic approach, and the need for more research in the areas of causation and social dynamics. He defined current directions in the field that included consideration of multifactorial issues, family-focused early intervention, community involvement, and prevention of secondary conditions. Crocker's description of the current scene demonstrates that the stage is now set for adoption of an ecological approach to prevention that incorporates these new concepts and directions.

Table 1
**Etiology and Prevention of Mental Retardation:  A Multidemensional Model**

| Recipient of Service | Biomedical | Social | Behavioral | Educational |
|---|---|---|---|---|
| **Primary prevention**<br>**Parent of Person with MR[a] as:** | | | | |
| Child | 25. Lead screening<br>30.  Malnutrition | 32. Abuse & neglect | | |
| Teenager | 30. Malnutrition | | 8. Teenage births<br><br>12. Alcohol treatment | 1. Family planning<br>42. Family life curricula<br>43. Education of public |
| Parent to be | 3. Genetic carrier testing<br>4. Prenatal care available<br>5. Prenatal care received<br>6. MS/AFP use<br>7. Amniocentesis<br>10. Pregnancy complications<br>11. Pregnancy loss<br>30. Malnutrition | 9. Out of wedlock | 12. Alcohol treatment | 1. Family planning<br>2. Genetic counseling |
| **Primary and secondary prevention**<br>**Person with (or at risk for) MR as:** | | | | |
| Newborn | 13. Regional NICUs<br><br>15. Screening for metabolic disease<br>16.  HIV screening<br>18. Neonatal mortality<br>20. Low birthweight<br>21. Birth defects<br>22. Other diagnostic information | 14. Trained staff for birth certificate | | 17. High-risk tracking system |
| Child | 19. Infant mortality<br><br>25. Lead screening<br>26. Immunizations<br>27. Medical home<br>29. Childhood mortality<br>30 Malnutrition | 28. Family support<br><br>32. Abuse & Neglect<br>33. Out-of-home | 31. Accidents & injuries | 23. Developmental screening<br>24. Early intervention<br>35. Special Education |
| **Tertiary prevention**<br>**Person with MR as:** | | | | |
| Child or adult | Health care services | Environmental factors | Healthy behaviors | Assistive technologies |

*Note:  Numbers refer to Crocker's (1992) Fateful Forty-Three.* [a] *Mental Retardation*

The comprehensiveness of Crocker's vision is demonstrated by his description of the "Fateful Forty-Three" indicators of the effects of prevention efforts (Crocker, 1992b). These indicators include most of the risk factors that may interact to cause mental retardation. In the new AAMR manual of definition, classification, and systems of supports (Luckasson et al., 1992), the multifactorial and intergenerational aspects of causation, including the impact of risk factors present in one generation (parent) on the occurrence of mental retardation in the next generation (child), were discussed. Table 1 (adapted form Coulter, 1990) summarizes these aspects of causation. Most of Crocker's Fateful Forty-Three indicators have been charted on this table to demonstrate how well they measure all of the multiple risk factors that may be present. Crocker's indicators also include measures of basic demographic data, information about incidence and prevalence (Items 34 through 38), and other service indicators (Items 39 and 41) that could not be charted on Table 1. The only thing missing from Crocker's Fateful Forty-Three indicators is a measure of the impact of potential interactions among all of these risk factors. It may well be that available interaction measures might not meet Crocker's requirement that they be quantifiable and accessible. It is also possible that some interactions may be more important than others. A comprehensive prevention program should include activities that address all of the elements measured by Crocker's Fateful Forty-Three indicators, but this is not enough. The case study in the present paper illustrates the inadequacy of prevention programs that focus too narrowly on just one or a few of the risk factors measured by Crocker's indicators. In addition, adoption of an ecological approach to prevention will require development of new indicators that would measure the effects of potential interactions among risk factors and among prevention strategies that address only one or a few of these factors.

In his article in this symposium, Pope described the Institute of Medicine (IOM) model of the disabling process referred to previously. This model recognizes the importance of multiple risk factors and describes three categories of risk factors -- biological, environmental, and lifestyle/behavioral -- that correspond to three of those included in the new AAMR manual (depicted in Table 1). With respect to mental retardation, the IOM model is incomplete because it omits educational factors. Ramey and Ramey (1992) demonstrated in this symposium how the absence of adequate educational interventions may represent an important risk factor for mental retardation. Pope did make the very important point that attention must be paid to prevention of secondary conditions that can be as disabling as the primary condition or more so and that the IOM model can be adapted to enable people to understand how these secondary conditions might be prevented. The components of Pope's comprehensive program for prevention of secondary conditions include several that reflect an ecological approach: a focus on comprehensiveness in the organization and delivery of services and attention to environmental considerations that may have an impact on secondary conditions. The components of this program for prevention of secondary conditions are charted on Table 1 under *Tertiary Prevention* (an alternative term to describe strategies to improve functioning). Pope's proposal for a comprehensive, coordinated, and integrated service-delivery system deserves serious consideration.

Ramey and Ramey (1992) presented evidence that intensive early intervention is an effective strategy for prevention of mental retardation. They showed that it is particularly effective when certain risk factors are present. Their studies included children with multiple risk factors, including biomedical (low birthweight), social (maternal intelligence and socioeconomic status), behavioral (parenting skills), and educational risks (adequacy of educational programs). Intensive intervention included strategies to address all of these risk factors and focused on fostering growth in the individual as well as improving the child's environment. Their studies reflect an ecological approach to prevention and document clearly the benefits of this approach for children who are at risk for mental retardation. This ecological approach is evident in their understanding of how children at risk are affected by the environment in which they grow and develop, in their attention to interactions between various risk factors present in the lives of these children, and in the comprehensiveness of their intervention program that addressed these multiple risk factors and the interactions among them. Politicians and professionals can no longer question the benefit of early intervention for infants and children at risk. Ramey and Ramey presented convincing evidence that prevention strategies must include all of the elements of their comprehensive intervention program. Furthermore, their program is a model of how an ecological approach can be incorporated into a prevention program and challenges us to develop ecological strategies to address other causative factors that may result in mental retardation.

The other articles in this symposium provide important information about selected aspects of prevention. One must avoid the pitfall of focusing too narrowly on only one aspect of the overall program, however. For example, Keenan et al. (1992) focused on educating the public and professionals about fragile X syndrome. They recognized that there are many other genetic disorders associated with mental retardation and that educational programs must be developed to increase community awareness of all of these disorders. Even this would seem to perpetuate a "medical model" that localizes the causes of mental retardation only within the individual. The educational component of a comprehensive prevention program must be much broader than this and must also include information about environmental risk factors.

The President's Committee on Mental Retardation (PCMR) and the Centers for Disease Control (CDC) have a long history in the area of prevention. In the past, PCMR often emphasized prevention programs composed of multiple single projects that focused mainly on the individual rather than on environmental factors that also determine functioning. The PCMR and the CDC now appear to be moving toward recognition of the new paradigm of mental retardation, the new model of the disabling process, and the resulting need for an ecological approach to the design and stimulation of programs to prevent mental retardation. In their article in this special issue, Adams and Hollowell (1992) described the origin of the CDC Disabilities Prevention Program and some of the activities that it currently sponsors. They recognized the need for coordination and comprehensiveness within state prevention programs and that the collaboration between public and private agencies needed to achieve this goal is often absent. Their emphasis on community-based projects is particularly commendable because environmental risk factors may be best identified and addressed within the community.

## Conclusions:
## A New Vision of Prevention

The field of mental retardation is at a critical turning point. A new way of thinking about what mental retardation is requires a new way of thinking about how to prevent it. The field is turning to an ecological understanding of how the interaction between individuals and their environment results in mental retardation. Prevention efforts must also incorporate an ecological approach to understanding the interactions among all of the personal, social, and environmental factors that affect the disabling process and that may result in functioning within the range of mental retardation. This new vision of prevention has two separate but related components: (a) an ecological understanding of the interaction between individuals and their environment, and (b) an ecological understanding of how risk factors from multiple dimensions (biomedical, social, behavioral, and educational) interact across generations to result in mental retardation (as shown in Table 1).

The articles in this symposium demonstrate that the stage is set for adopting a new approach to prevention based on this vision. This approach will include greater attention to environmental variables that are critical modifiers of the impact of intellectual limitations on personal functioning. Prevention has the opportunity to interrupt or reverse the disabling process by altering the extent to which these functional limitations cause significant social disability. Our challenge for the 1990s and beyond is to realize a comprehensive, coordinated, and integrated strategy that reflects the ecology of prevention and will improve the lives of people at risk for mental retardation.

********

## REFERENCES

Adams, M. J., & Hollowell, J. G. (1992). Community-based projects for the prevention of developmental disabilities: Community involvement and evaluation of interventions. *Mental Retardation, 30*, 331-336.

Baumeister, A. (1991). A model for preventing the "New Morbidity": Implications for a national plan of action. In President's Committee on Mental Retardation, *Summit on the national effort to prevent mental retardation and related disabilities* (pp. 57-74). Washington, DC: U.S. Department of Health and Human Services.

Bradley, V. J., & Knoll, J. (1990). *Shifting paradigms in services to people with developmental disabilities.* Cambridge, MA: Human Services Research Institute.

Bronfenbrenner, U. (1979). *The ecology of human development.* Cambridge: Harvard University Press.

Coulter, D. L. (1990, Fall). Etiology, epidemiology and prevention of mental retardation. *Academy on Mental Retardation Newsletter*, 3-5.

Coulter, D. L. (1991). The failure of prevention. *Mental Retardation, 29*(6), iii-iv.

Crocker, A. C. (1992a). Introduction: Where is the prevention movement? *Mental Retardation, 30*(6), iii-v.

Crocker, A. C. (1992b). Data collection for the evaluation of mental retardation prevention activities: The fateful forty-three. *Mental Retardation, 30*, 303-317.

Institute of Medicine. (1991). A. M. Pope & A. R. Tarlov (Eds.). *Disability in America: Toward a national agenda for prevention.* Washington, DC: National Academy Press.

Keenan, J., Kastner, T., Nathanson, R., Richardson, N., Hinton, J., & Cress, D.A. (1992). A statewide public and professional education program on fragile X syndrome. *Mental Retardation, 30*, 355-361.

Luckasson, R., Coulter, D. L., Pollaway, E. A., Reiss, S., Schalock, R. L., Snell, m., Spitalnik, D., & Stark, J. A. (1992). *Mental retardation: Definition, classification, and systems of supports.* Washington, DC: American Association on Mental retardation.

Odom, E. P. (1959). *Fundamentals of ecology* (2nd ed.). Philadelphia: Saunders.

Pope, A. M. (1992). Preventing secondary conditions. *Mental Retardation, 30*, 347-354.

Ramey, C. T., & Ramey, S. L. (1992). Effective early intervention. *Mental Retardation, 30*, 337-345.

*Webster's new 20th century dictionary* (2nd ed.). (1979). New York: Simon & Shuster.

******

**About the Author:** David L. Coulter, MD., is an Associate Professor, Pediatrics and Neurology, Boston University School of Medicine, Division of Pediatric Neurology, Boston City Hospital, 818 Harrison Avenue, Boston, MA: 02118.

**Source:** Reprinted with permission from *Mental Retardation*, Vol. 30, No. 6, December 1992, pp. 363-369. Published by American Association of Mental Retardation, Washington, DC: 20009.

# 6 Education, Employment, Social Planning and Disability

Since World War II, and more particularly in the last two decades, people with disabilities have made viable advances into the mainstream of contemporary society. Of notable significance are the inroads which have been made in the areas of education and employment. In the past, people with disabilities, like other minority groups, found themselves banished from the labour market or barred from public educational institutions as a result of a value system that did not accept those who were not "normal". For people with disabilities, institutionalism, isolation and paternalism were perceived as the key means by which this group was "looked after". However, as we enter the 90s decade, people with disabilities no longer are prevented from experiencing all the opportunities that are available to mainstream society. The responsibility for this positive social change rests with two key factors: *advocacy* and *empowerment*. Through the considerable efforts of people with disabilities who have taken an activist approach to social change, through the people who have advocated on behalf of people with disabilities, and through the considerable new bodies of research and information gathering that is presently being conducted, society is now recognizing the vast human potential which exists within this community. Although change seems slow, there has never been a time when so much attention has been focused on the needs, rights, and inherent dignity of all those who experience disability of any kind.

As a result of this focus, barriers for people with disabilities are finally being removed or surmounted with new legislation ~ a significant step towards the changing of negative social attitudes and towards facilitating the integration of this group in all realms of society. Legislative frameworks, such as the Americans with Disabilities Act (1990) and the Canadian Charter of Rights and Freedoms, have evolved to guarantee that people who traditionally have been vulnerable to exclusion, now have access to the means whereby they can make choices for themselves, be able to speak for themselves, or where necessary, have an advocate who will support or speak for them. This is an important step in the process of assuming ownership and control of one's own life and the means for establishing or regaining self respect and autonomy through self empowerment.

Traditionally, people with disabilities have not been targeted as consumers, clients or professionals. The tendency has always been to regard this group as unimportant and not worthy of attention where products and services were designed, or where talent and skill was considered. Happily, these attitudes are changing through activism, advocacy and "being heard"; through hard work, determination, and awareness programs; and through research, development and the organization of community support groups. Today, a significant number of people with disabilities are enjoying a number of new products and assistive devices which have been developed to allow greater lifestyle enjoyment and comfort. As well, new services such as outpatient facilities, independent living centers, and sports and recreation programs add to the quality of life for many individuals with disabilities. People with disabilities are now entering advanced institutions of learning and are being included in the labor market in the blue collar, white collar, and professional categories at unprecedented levels. No longer are people allowed to be judged by what they look like or cannot do, but rather by what they can do, or what their abilities are.

For the majority of people with disabilities it is rewarding to know the trend has moved away from the "sheltered workshop" system, and the "nursing home" type of institution which created and maintained a negative and exclusionary image for individuals who had mental and physical disabilities. Many people with disabilities were "protected" and "looked after" in these environments because they traditionally lacked the educational background or support systems which would allow them to become independent and self-sufficient individuals. Fortunately, people with disabilities are finally becoming integrated into mainstream society. Educational facilities at all levels are not only becoming physically accessible, but they are also providing specialized programs which accommodate disabilities of all natures. Employers, while they are being mandated to do so, are also being encouraged to hire people with disabilities and are developing new and creative ways to accommodate this group with very positive and rewarding results. Of course, the critical consideration in all realms of society for integrating people with disabilities is cost. In fact, it has been proven that in most instances it is more cost-efficient to encourage people with disabilities to acquire the education and skills necessary to become functioning members of society, rather than to be dependent members of society.

Advocacy and empowerment are two powerful tools that can be used for the achievement of an enhanced quality of life for any minority group, but these tools are particularly important and necessary for people with disabilities. As people with disabilities continue to gain autonomy through education and employment opportunities, the rewards will be recognized by all segments of society. While there is still a great deal of work to do in surmounting existing barriers and negative attitudes for this group of individuals, the following articles illustrate the trend toward facilitating the integration of people with disabilities in two important social institutions: education and employment.

Pamela Gent and Mary Beth Mulhauser in, *Public Integration of Students with Handicaps: Where It's Been, Where it's Going, and How It's Getting There,* examine integrated public school education for students with disabilities from two perspectives: legal and educational. The authors are concerned with the "free and appropriate" and "least restrictive environment" provisions with the Education for All Handicapped Children Act of 1975, how these terms have been interpreted and what kinds of service delivery have resulted from this legislation. Unfortunately, their research findings have indicated that "the professional community and society at large have still not completely acceded to practical implementation" [of integrated public education]. There remains a need for increased awareness of placement options, legal courses of action, advocacy for eliminating media stereotypes of people with disabilities, and for parents and professionals in the field of special education to work together to promote a positive image and a "united, informed, and positive front."

Susan Hamre-Nietupski, John Nietupski and Steve Maurer also examine the integration of students in the education system in *A Comprehensive State Education Agency Plan to Promote the Integration of Students with Moderate/Severe Handicaps.* They propose that state education agencies (SEAs) take "a proactive, leadership role in promoting integration." From a case study conducted in the state of Iowa, the authors share the means by which successful integration of students with moderate/severe handicaps can be achieved. As well, the article provides strategies which can be used at various educational system levels which represent a combination of *directives* to change and *support* for change at these various levels.

Another approach to integration in education is through part-time programs where children with disabilities are mainstreamed for part of a day and spend the rest of the time in a self-contained special education classes. Roberta Schnorr studied a first-grade class in terms of what the school experience meant for both the regular students and a part-time mainstream student called Peter. Her article, *"Peter? He Comes and goes...". First Graders' Perspective on a Part-time Mainstream Student* suggests that it would be beneficial for all those concerned with integration efforts to seek and learn from students' perspectives and valuable insights. As Schnorr concludes, "Students are the only legitimate source for some of the answers we need for understanding and promoting school inclusion, because it is their world, not ours, that defines it."

Advocacy is the key theme in the article *Parent/Professional Partnerships in Advocacy: Developing Integrated Options within Resistive Systems,* by Susan Hamre-Nietupski, Lynn Krajewski, John Nietupski, Donna Ostercamp, Karen Sensor, and Barbara Opheim. The authors make the case for "parents and professionals working in concert" to achieve integrated educational options in school communities. After four years of first hand experience and devoting many hours to advocacy efforts, they are able to outline practical strategies for meeting and overcoming resistance to integrated options from the area educational system. Through a parent/professional advocacy partnership, it is possible to achieve a common goal of successful and positive integration and interaction of children with and without disabilities.

For the teaching professionals, Dianne Ferguson and Diane Baumgart re-examine the concept of partial participation in *Partial Participation Revisited.* Their goal is to assist teachers in implementing effective educational programming for students with severe disabilities, and to alleviate some of the frustrations encountered by teachers by outlining some of the error patterns that have lead to these difficulties as a result of the partial participation philosophy. From a perspective of "critical hindsight", the authors describe how the concept of partial participation and its 'mission of schooling' has been misunderstood and misused.

Jamie Satcher and Glenn Hendren launch the discussion for employment concerns with their article *Employer Agreement with the Americans with Disabilities Act of 1990: Implications for Rehabilitation Counseling.* As the authors state, the employment community is substantially impacted by this legislation. For the successful implementation of the ADA by employers, rehabilitation counselors and service providers should play a key role by "providing expertise to employers regarding how they may better serve workers with disabilities." There is a critical need for this assistance if employers are to meet their responsibilities under the ADA.

The next two articles, *Away with Barriers* by Mary Lord, and *Open Your Doors to Disabled Workers* by Elaine Johnson provide valuable and practical insights and methods by which employers can implement the legislative directives of the Americans with Disabilities Act. While employers may be intimidated by what they perceive are going to be costly accommodations if they are to incorporate people with disabilities into their firms, it is reassuring to know that there are many ways this can be done with minimum cost and maximum benefits to both employers and employees.

The new philosophies of advocacy and empowerment in the disabled community have become the foundation tools for future efforts in integrating people with disabilities into all realms of society. The work is not easy, and at many times advocacy efforts appear to be futile. Those who strive to change attitudes, open doors, and break down barriers know only too well that the process is slow and frustrating. Those people also know that it takes tenacity, courage and an unwavering belief in the ability of the human spirit to overcome the obstacles. For the basic tenet of equality for all to become a reality, it is necessary for all people with and without disabilities and from all disciplines to work together in a spirit of cooperative sharing and caring.

# Public Integration of Students with Handicaps: Where It's Been, Where It's Going, and How It's Getting There

Pamela J. Gent

Mary Beth Mulhauser

**Abstract** ~ *This article addresses integrated public school education for students with disabilities from both a legal and an educational perspective. Variables critical to public integration, including the influence of the media, the need for increased dissemination of legal and educational findings, the need for well-developed IEPs, and a critical examination of the existing data base are discussed.*

**Descriptors:** educational placement, integration, least restrictive environment, P.L. 94-142.

**Introduction:** Integration of students with disabilities into "regular" public education classrooms is a relatively new concept thrust into the public arena by the passage of the Education for All Handicapped Children Act of 1975. The "free and appropriate" education and the "least restrictive environment" provisions of the Act raise controversial legal and educational issues.

One of the primary difficulties with the interpretation (and, as a result, implementation) of integrated public education is the discrepancy between the educational concept of "mainstreaming" and the legal interpretation of "least restrictive environment." Coupled with the democratic and philosophical implications of civil rights legislation, what initially appeared as a panacea for students with disabilities all too often deteriorated into a legal and educational quagmire.

Although legal decisions dictate the immediate course of placement activity, it is essential to realize that the subsequent educational interpretations and service delivery determine the long-term ramifications and the ultimate success or failure of integrated public education for individuals with disabilities. This article addresses several critical factors involved in the acceptance of individuals with disabilities in integrated public school settings as well as in the community at large. The first section discusses integrated public school education for students with disabilities from a legal and educational perspective, followed by an examination of critical variables related to the promotion of integration, including (a) informed parental involvement in the educational and legal decision-making process with regard to students labeled handicapped, (b) the existing data base, and (c) media influence on public perceptions and attitudes.

## Legal and Educational Perspectives

The major support for placement of individuals with severe disabilities into integrated settings derives from the Education for All Handicapped Children Act (EAHCA). Historically in the United States, public education has been a matter delegated to individual states, and the impact of federal legislation of this nature was dramatic. Prior to the passage of the EAHCA, courts generally elected to answer only questions of law regarding the violation of individual rights and avoided making determinations regarding the content of educational programming (Burgdorf, 1980). Because the task of compliance with the federal mandate fell mainly to the states, the initial result was that services to the population labeled handicapped varied greatly on a state by state basis (McCarthy, 1983). When it became clear that local and state level due process hearings were not always sufficient to settle differences of opinion regarding the interpretation of the federal mandate, higher courts became involved in the determination of the intent, purpose, and definitions originally outlined by Congress.

The original funding allotted by Congress to accompany the EAHCA apparently left the courts little choice but to assume that the major concerns of Congress were in the areas of identification and inclusion in public education (O'Hara, 1985). Legal determinations with far-reaching implications for public school integration of students with disabilities involve the following areas:

1. The "least restrictive environment" clause and the intent to integrate to the maximum extent possible;

2. Interpretation of the "free and appropriate education" clause of the EAHCA, including (a) differentiation between best and appropriate practice and (b) appropriate as related to least restrictive environment;

3. Availability of related services and the implications thereof for integrated and segregated settings; and

4. The continuum of available placement options.

**The Least Restrictive Environment**

The EAHCA 612(5) (B) as amended by 20 U.S.C.A. 412(5)(B) states:

> The state has established procedures to assure that, to the maximum extent appropriate, handicapped children, including children in public or private institutions or other care facilities, are educated with children who are not handicapped, and that special classes, separate schooling, or other removal of handicapped children from the regular environment occurs only when the nature or severity of the handicap is such that education in regular classes with the use of supplemental aids and services cannot be achieved satisfactorily.

Although volumes have been devoted to defining the concept of "least restrictive environment" (LRE), several important issues

have remained relatively untouched throughout the reviews. Many supporters of the EAHCA have failed to differentiate between the legal doctrine of least restrictive and the educational concept of mainstreaming as described in some educational journals as well as in the popular press. In addition, with regard to the issue of segregated versus integrated schools, little mention has been made of the civil rights implications underlying the EAHCA.

Contrary to some of the information available since the passage of the EAHCA, the legal doctrine of least restrictive does not emanate from the 1975 federal mandate. Rather, as Zettel and Ballard (1982) indicate, "the concept of the right to education in the least restrictive environment undoubtedly has its origin in a fundamental ethos of the American people: stated quite simply, it is better to be with your peers than to be apart from them" (p. 17). Combined with the provisions of the Fourteenth Amendment, early litigation, and more recent civil rights litigation (*Brown v. Board of Education,* 1954), the infusion of a constitutional context for judicial decision making was clearly established (Gerry & Benton, 1982). The consent agreement in *Pennsylvania Association for Retarded Citizens v. Commonwealth of Pennsylvania* (1972) established the idea that it is highly desirable to educate children identified as mentally retarded in programs most like those provided for nonhandicapped children (Zettel & Ballard, 1982). The provision for children with disabilities to receive a "free public program of education and training appropriate to their capacity" lent further credence. The judgment in *Mills v. Board of Education* (1972) went even further in establishing the rights of children with disabilities by creating procedural guidelines to be followed *prior* to the exclusion of a student with disabilities from a publicly funded school. In retrospect, it is quite evident that the wording of EAHCA, 612(5) (B) as amended by 20 U.S.C.A. 1412(5) (b) evolved from the P.A.R.C. and *Mills* cases (Burgdorf, 1980; Herr, Arons, & Wallace, 1983; Phillips & Rosenberg, 1980; Woody, 1974; Ysseldyke & Algozzine, 1982).

Special education professionals may be well advised to consider several aspects of the LRE component of the EAHCA for future reference. The legal imperative for provision of services within the public domain was clearly established in *Brown v. Board of Education* (1954). In addition to stating that the doctrine of separate but equal has no place in public education, the court further stated:

> Today, education is perhaps the most important function of state and local government.... In these days it is doubtful that any child may reasonably be expected to succeed in life if he is denied the opportunity of an education. Such an opportunity, where the state has undertaken to provide it, is a right which *must be available to all on equal terms* [emphasis added] (Zettel & Ballard, 1982, p. 13).

The question of inclusion of children with disabilities in public education was answered, in theory, in 1954. Unfortunately, in the 30+ years which have since elapsed, several federal mandates have been issued specifically addressing the issues of integrated public education for students with disabilities. The professional community and society at large have still not completely acceded to practical implementation.

It is important to consider that in spite of what current or future efficacy studies indicate regarding the success or failure of integrating students with disabilities into the public schools, the argument is essentially already concluded; the courts have ruled it preferable to educate children with disabilities in integrated settings to the maximum extent possible (*Campbell v. Talladega County*, 1981; *In re* Holly S., 1986; In the matter of *Thomas and Jacqueline M. et al. v. the School District of Waukesha*, 1984; In the matter of the *School District of Marathon et al. v. Jennifer P.*, 1985; *Pennsylvania Association for Retarded Citizens v. Commonwealth of Pennsylvania*, 1972; *Roncker et al. v. Walter et al.*, 1983). Efficacy studies may be reasonable only as a means of determining more efficient, cost effective, and educationally sound methods for instructing students with disabilities within the continuum of least restrictive alternatives.

## Appropriate Education

"Free and appropriate public education" is defined in the EAHCA, section 1401 [18] as:

> Special education and related services which (A) have been provided at public expense, under public supervision and direction, and without charge, (B) meet the standards of the State educational agency, (C) include an appropriate preschool, elementary, or secondary school education in the State involved, and (D) are provided in conformity with the individualized education program required under section 1414(a) (5) of this title.

These parameters were slightly modified and adopted by the Supreme Court as a barometer for measuring "appropriateness" (Tucker, 1984) as follows:

1. Program must be provided with public funds and supervised by public personnel;

2. The state standards for public education must be adhered to;

3. The program must approximate grade levels according to state standards; and

4. The program must comport with the child's IEP.

In lieu of other guidelines, many lower courts have adopted this checklist for appropriateness and have used the components to determine appropriate placement for children with disabilities. From a professional standpoint, it is not difficult to surmise that such criteria may often be viewed as reflecting a more restrictive placement in the educational sense than in the legal sense.

It is also important to note that the judicial interpretations of the EAHCA to date contain no expressed or implied requirement that schools maximize the potential of children with disabilities. Rather, the provision of a basic "floor of opportunity" regarding equal access and related services is emphasized (Yanok, 1986). The question of determination of educational benefit as it relates to appropriateness was at issue in *Board of Education of the Henrick Hudson Central School District v. Rowley* (1982), where the court ruled that no single criterion could be applied to the wide range of actual and potential achievement needs among students with special needs. Consequently, each case must be reviewed on an individual basis (Yanok, 1986).

In addition to this emphasis on the individual, the determination of appropriate education must be made in interaction with the determination of placement in the least restrictive environment. *Springdale School District v. Grace et al.* (1982) established the fact that although the education Sherry Grace was receiving at the segregated Arkansas School for the Deaf was superior to the program available in the Springdale School District, Sherry could benefit from the education Springdale provided *and* have the opportunity to interact with nonhandicapped peers in an integrated setting. In *Mark A. et al. v. Grant Wood Area Education Agency et al.* (1986), an integrated preschool classroom was deemed the best educational setting for 5-year-old Alleah A. But the court surmised that Alleah could attend a segregated classroom in an integrated school and still accrue educational benefit. Clearly then, both the least restrictive and free appropriate education clauses were considered when deciding these cases.

**Related Services**

As the *Board of Education of Henrick Hudson Central School District v. Rowley* case demonstrated, the extent to which related services are provided should be decided on an individual basis with respect to the actual benefit the child will receive. Although the courts have not always ruled affirmatively with regard to related services, it is important to note that decisions have been rendered in the areas of psychological counseling (Cullinan & Epstein, 1986; *Piscataway Township Board of Education v. T. G.*, 1985), medical services (*Irving Independent School District v. Tatro*, 1984), integrated treatment (*Handicapped Students and Special Education*, 1985), and extended school year (*Battle v. Commonwealth of Pennsylvania*, 1980; *Georgia Association for Retarded Citizens v. McDaniel*, 1981). The critical factor here is that the courts have not uniformly denied a variety of related services

to students with disabilities, but rather have promoted the original intent of Congress and the EAHCA by insisting that each case be reviewed on individual merit. The emphasis on the individual child has dominated legal precedent if not public education service delivery.

The district court ruling in *Roncker et al. v. Walter et al.* (1983) outlined guidelines for the inclusion of special education students within integrated public schools. Although the court ruled that a placement may be deemed appropriate for academic reasons but inappropriate because of failure to provide for contact with nonhandicapped peers, it also pointed out that provision of related services within a segregated facility must be scrutinized to determine if their delivery within an integrated setting is feasible. If special services can be provided in an integrated facility, then placement in a segregated facility is deemed inappropriate. The court outlined *when* integration should occur and determined that whenever possible schooling, along with related services, should be provided in an integrated facility. These recommendations may be the basis for future litigation.

The involvement of parents informed of available placement options and provided with necessary information to construct an appropriate and legally compelling IEP is critical to the direction of integrated public education.

**Continuum of Available Placement Options**

The EAHCA requires the availability of a full continuum of service delivery systems for individuals with disabilities. This continuum of services has been described in detail and viewed as progressing from "less desirable" (more restrictive) to "more desirable" (less restrictive) in the educational literature ( e.g., Brown et al., 1977) and in the community habilitation literature (Elder, Conley, & Noble, 1986). In one case, *St. Louis Developmental Disabilities Treatment Center Parents' Association et al. v. Mallory et al.* (1984), the plaintiffs argued that denying students with disabilities the opportunity to interact with their nonhandicapped peers by affirming placement in a segregated facility did not comply with the provisions of the EAHCA. The plaintiffs therefore reasoned that all segregated schools should be closed. The court ruled that the wholesale closure of segregated schools would deny that potential placement option for students with disabilities.

Implications from the resolution of cases such as *St. Louis* on the continuum of services philosophy are important to parents, professionals, and legal representatives regarding future litigation. It is clear that the plaintiffs in the *St. Louis* case did not anticipate the outcome which occurred. However, if the case had not been presented as a type of modified class action suit, the results might have been different. Once again, the courts ruled that appropriateness of placement within a continuum of options must be made on an individual basis. The *Mark A..* (1986) case suggests an economically feasible alternative that many states have quickly adopted; states do not have to develop entire new levels of public education... integration *can* occur within the context of existing levels of public education.

The review of legal outcomes related to individuals with disabilities in recent years provides a valuable information base for parents and professionals in special education. Clearly, the key to improved public school integration and community-based education for people with disabilities from a legal perspective is the word *individual*. As outlined, legal reviews of the four areas of the EAHCA related to integrated programming (i.e., LRE, appropriate education, related services, and continuum of placement options) indicate that decisions rendered have been determined consistently on an individual basis.

Since the passage of EAHCA in 1975, it has become increasingly evident that legal decisions have necessitated a modification in the basic approach to American public education. Ironically, the alterations that have occurred are similar to the educational parameters outlined by Dewey in the early 1900s (e.g., *Democracy in Education,* 1916; *Experience in Education,* 1938). The implementation of the IEP is, in theory at least, the basis for true child-centered education. The IEP and the *emphasis on the individual* for the determination of educational

placement and "appropriate" service delivery within the context of the "least restrictive environment" provide the guidelines for present and future developments in public school education.

**Increased Accountability, Credibility, and Visibility among Parents and Professionals in Special Education:    Shaping Positive Public Attitudes**

Continued improvement in educational service delivery for individuals with disabilities is contingent upon the effective knowledge and use of past legal decisions, as well as the examination of current programming. From both educational and legal perspectives, it is critical that parents and professionals investigate the importance of improving current service delivery by:

1.  Placing educational emphasis on the unique needs of each *individual* student;

2.  Keeping abreast of relevant legal and educational developments and sharing information;

3.  Adopting/adapting plans for the creation and implementation of *working* IEPs, including (a) increased parent involvement and (b) collection of data on individual IEP goals specifically formulated to accommodate the use of continuous data as a method of ongoing evaluation;

4.  Advocating strongly for the individual rights and privileges of persons with disabilities including elimination of stereotypical media images; and

5.  Conducting data-based research for the purposes of determining more efficient, cost-effective, and educationally sound methods of instruction for students with disabilities *within* the context of integrated public school settings.

**Educational Emphasis on the Individual**

It is clear from legal precedent that individuals advocating the integration of persons with disabilities into schools must address both the educational system and the larger social structure.    Societal and educational "norms" that fail to consider the great diversities that exist throughout the physical-mental-cultural continuum do little to unite the culture as a whole. Rather, such narrow definitions tend to lead to continued perpetuation of the robotic middle class mystique, happy suburban families with annual incomes of $35,000 to $50,000 and 2.2 well-adjusted mobile children of "average" intelligence.

The calls for "functional" programming (Brown, Nietupski, & Hamre-Nietupski, 1976), "educational synthesizers" (D. Bricker, 1976), and "normalization" (Wolfensberger, 1972) carry an underlying theme of individuality too long ignored. But the recognition of individual differences is not in itself sufficient. The general public must come to realize that the promotion of individual differences with the accompanying modifications in teaching style and group integration of individual skills will produce the most positive outcome for *all* learners - not just learners with disabilities. As the public becomes increasingly aware of the positive tangible results that accompany emphasis on the individual, persons with and without disabilities will reap the benefits.

Parents and professionals must also understand the importance of the individual with respect to judicial proceedings. The EAHCA, by its very nature, forces individual rather than class suits. Since cases are decided on the basis of individual merit, it is *critical* that the case against segregated schools rests on the individual merit of a purposeful, well-constructed IEP that emphasized the acute need for integrated placement.

**Keeping Abreast of Relevant Legal and Educational Developments**

Although 12 years have passed since the original legislation designed to provide educational services for students with disabilities became law, it appears that with the exception of scattered and isolated instances, many professionals and parents of children with disabilities are often still unaware of placement options and legal courses of action. Although there is little question that the information is available, there appears to be a serious communication breakdown between service delivery agencies and parents of children with disabilities.

In order to continue to advocate for the rights of individuals with disabilities, it is imperative that parents and professionals keep abreast of current legal developments. In many instances, since either no legal precedent currently exists or the precedent has only recently been established, parents and professionals would be well advised to be aware of major developments in the area, so that in the event of legal proceedings the most plausible option may be chosen. Several national organizations provide information regarding legislation and legal updates (e.g., Association for Retarded Citizens, Children's Defense Fund, TASH *DC Update, Special Education Law Reporter*).

The current data base of legal and educational developments is informative both for researchers and teacher training facilities. Without an organized means of communicating such information to direct service providers, however, much of the information is unfortunately relegated to the bookshelves of university libraries. This is unfortunate, especially when direct service providers are most often called upon to provide testimony in cases undergoing litigation. These direct service providers have been judged credible, knowledgeable witnesses in spite of an apparent lack of familiarity with current special education best practices and literature. In the *St. Louis* case, for example, the judge placed more credence in the testimony of the direct service providers than in the testimony of expert witnesses (many of whom were well-read, well-published, well-known TASH members), since the teachers were familiar with the students and worked with them on a daily basis. Information on legal precedents and current research on integrated placements must be disseminated to these "front-line" members.

Legislative committees and teacher training facilities may be a source of assistance on information dissemination. As a result of recent technological advances in the field and the rapidly changing face of special education in general, it may be necessary for stringent federal and/or state mandates to be implemented which would dictate standards for continuing education for special education teachers, coordinators, and administrators. In addition, an organized state and local plan for provision of information updates to all participants at the annual IEP meeting may be a viable consideration.

## Creating and Implementing Working IEPs

As stated previously, it is *critical* that any case against segregated schools rests on the merit of a purposeful well-constructed IEP that emphasizes the need for integrated placement. Parents must be viewed as the originators of the long-term IEP goals, based on their experience, observation, and interactions with their children. Professionals, in turn, must learn to view their roles as creative implementors in their respective areas of expertise, often helping to devise short-term objectives. In addition, professionals must accept a guiding role in assisting parents to assess available options as well as introducing parents to the necessity for functional programming in the least restrictive environment. Finally, parents and professionals need to work together as the critical core members of the IEP team responsible for positive outcomes for the child.

Tindal (1985) offers an "alternative paradigm for conducting effectiveness research" (p. 105), which provides for the construction of the IEP based on a measurement system incorporating evaluation of both long and short-term goals. The goals are established on the basis of initial assessment information and include teacher expectations and the specific performance rate anticipated for the student (Deno, Mirkin, & Wesson, 1984). This method of ongoing evaluation is reminiscent of the test-teach strategy described by W. Bricker (1976) and includes four different metrics: (a) slope of improvement on the IEP, (b) mastery or nonmastery of the IEP goal, (c) absolute rate of improvement, and (d) relative rate of improvement on standard curriculum tasks administered three times a year (Tindal, 1985). Although this paradigm and others similar to it are in the developmental stages, the maintenance of consistent and continuous data

derived specifically from the IEP may provide the evidence necessary for securing appropriate placements in future litigation. Indeed, the availability of continuous, consistent data was the determining factor in several litigated cases concerning placement in integrated settings (*In re* South Bend Community School Corporation, 1982).

## Advocating for Individuals with Disabilities and Eliminating Media Stereotypes

Relatively little has been written in recent years regarding the image of persons with disabilities in the media (Bauer, 1985a, 1985b; Bauer, Campbell, & Troxel, 1985; Biklen, 1986; Longmore, 1985; Monson & Shurtleff, 1979; Zola, 1987). As individuals with disabilities, their parents, and related professionals are well aware, attempts to change public attitudes toward handicapping conditions are continuously undermined by media images, which present people with disabilities in a variety of unrealistic ways. The general public is unlikely to accept individuals with disabilities into the schools and the surrounding community and deal with them in a "normal" manner as long as the media is permitted to portray people with disabilities as either superhumans who have managed somehow to exist in the world and accomplish something "normal" by overcoming insurmountable odds, or as pitiful, helpless creatures doomed to a perpetual childhood. Clearly, neither of these stereotypes is acceptable. Yet, these characterizations continue to exist and are evident in the litigation. Indeed, in the *St. Louis* case, a teacher characterized her students as so disabled that they could not differentiate between themselves and the environment and could not hold their heads up. The immediate impression is that of the helpless, perpetual child. Additionally, several state level hearing officers have upheld placements in segregated settings on the basis that the child with disabilities needs to be "protected" (*In re* Marin County Office of Education, 1982; Michigan Case #H-487, 1979) and that the child with disabilities is simply "too" handicapped to function in less segregated settings (In the matter of the Application of a

Handicapped Child, 1980; *Tomika M. v. Jasper County Board of Education,* 1985).

As Turnbull (1985) has noted, it is difficult to uphold the law in its fullest measure unless the weight of public opinion is behind the law. As advocates for persons with disabilities, parents and professionals can take active steps to eradicate persistent media representation of "disabled" people as dependent and, consequently, allow public opinion to fully support integration. As Biklen (1986) indicates, the central issue deals specifically with society's perspective of the situation. As long as people with disabilities are described as *DISabled* rather than differently *abled* or capable in any manner, society is presented with the picture of an individual or group of individuals incapable of a productive contribution to the community at large. Advocates, individuals with disabilities, and media representatives must assume responsibility for more accurate representation of the positive contributions afforded society by people with disabilities. This may enable the societal perspective to shift from the view that people with disabilities *ought* to be dependent to the idea that they ought to be accorded the same rights, privileges, jobs, and responsibilities as other citizens.

Two means of accomplishing this seemingly formidable task are monitoring existing media presentations (e.g., Kansas Media Watch, journal articles, and newspaper editorial responses) and organizing efforts to present factual representations of individuals with disabilities. An excellent resource for the latter is a guide titled "How to Make Friends and Influence the Media" (1979).

## Data-Based Research within the Context of Integrated Public School Settings

The present data base may be loosely categorized into articles concerning the generic issue of mainstreaming (Atterbury, 1986; Gottlieb, 1981; Gresham, 1982; Gresham, Elliott, & Black, 1987; Gresham & Reschly, 1986; Knoff, 1985; Meisel, 1986; Ray, 1985; Sabornie, 1985; Sansone & Zigmond, 1986; Saur, Coggiola, Long, & Simonson, 1986; Silon & Harter, 1985; Travis, Thomas, & Fuller, 1985), the legal implications of least

restrictive environment (Cullinan & Epstein, 1986; Laski, 1985; Yanok, 1986), public school integration (Certo, Haring, & York, 1984; Colozzi et al., 1986; McGregor, Janssen, Larsen, & Tillery, 1986; Singer, Butler, Palfrey, & Walker, 1986; Stainback & Stainback, 1985), segregation (Brady & Cunningham, 1985; Silverstein, 1985), and the comparison between integrated and segregated settings (Beckman & Kohl, 1987; Brinker, 1985; Brinker & Thorpe, 1985, 1986; Gibb & Flavahan, 1987; Hunt, Goetz, & Anderson, 1986). In addition, the data base includes the related area of special education and school or social policy (Algozzine, Morsink, & Algozzine, 1986; Hersh & Walker, 1983; Reynolds & Wang, 1983) and the area of investigation involving social effects of interactions between persons with and without disabilities (Bak & Siperstein, 1986; Cole, Meyer, Vandercook, & McQuarter, 1986; Esposito & Reed, 1986; Jenkins, Speltz, & Odom, 1985; Odom, Hoyson, Jamieson, & Strain, 1985; Sasso & Rude, 1987; Van Bourgondien, 1987).

A brief review of the presently existing data base points to several areas of concern for professionals in the field:

1. No separate, substantial data base appears to exist which specifically addresses the *actual* population of children labeled profoundly or multiply handicapped;

2. A paucity of research in the area of school-age students with disabilities in integrated settings is a concern;

3. A marked discrepancy exists in the literature concerning the success of students with severe disabilities in integrated settings and the failure of students with mild disabilities in similar settings -- an apparent incongruent finding in need of explanation;

4. The lack of clear differentiation is evident among social aspects of integration as they apply in the lives of individuals with mild disabilities and individuals with severe disabilities;

5. The use of qualitative and descriptive research, while valuable in the broader context of special education, often seems to dominate the literature, whereas appropriate quantitative research might be

more beneficial to ascertain the strengths and weaknesses of current programming;

6. There is a lack of dissemination of pertinent, current information form the data base to parents, direct service providers, and the public at large.

An overview of research to date clearly delineates specific areas for additional/further research ( e.g., continued research in the area of data-based IEP management systems; attempts to explain the apparent discrepancies between students with mild and severe disabilities in integrated school settings; the distinction between social skills or social aspects as they apply to students with mild and severe disabilities; and the application of quantitative research paradigms to determine improved methods of programming and cost-effective teaching techniques). The need for specific research with children labeled profoundly or multiply handicapped in integrated settings is escalating. Only when the data base includes investigations of integrated placement for the students with the most severe impairments will the reluctance demonstrated by many parents, professionals, and judges to recommend integrated placements for students with less severe impairments begin to dissipate. Using the existing data base, one can only affirm Tindal's (1985) conclusion that "the only conclusion that can be made at this time is that no conclusion is yet available about special education efficacy" (p. 109). Future research in the area of placement of persons with disabilities in integrated settings must fill the "holes" in the existing data base. As W. Bricker (1976) indicated, isolated efforts and research conducted solely to promote the visibility of the researcher among one's colleagues can no longer be tolerated.

## CONCLUSION

Based on past legal decisions, one might surmise that the pivot variable for receiving appropriate services is the design, construction, and content of the IEP. In this respect, parents and professionals are often direct advocates for the person with disabilities. One major consideration for these

advocates is the increasing influence of legal decisions as they affect the educational process for students with disabilities (Cullinan & Epstein, 1986). Parents and professionals must stay informed of current legal developments and the implications for special education and work together to develop policies and procedures which either promote positive practice *without* legal intervention, or which form the basis for strong legal position in support of *educationally* appropriate programming for students with disabilities within the context of the least restrictive environment. Without such informed cooperation, there is a real danger that both parents and professionals may surrender one of the most valuable assets of students with disabilities -- expertise and understanding from a personal perspective (Kauffman, 1984).

Although there is little doubt that the P.A.R.C. and *Mills* cases laid the groundwork for the EAHCA, these cases also represent significant judicial rulings which appeared time and again as the basis for decisions in later litigation. The 1975 passage of the EAHCA coupled with the 1977 *Halderman v. Pennhurst (State Hospital and School)* case marked the end of an era of state-dominated discriminatory and exclusionary policies. However, attempts continue to view the education of children with disabilities outside of the multidimensional framework, which includes legal, educational, philosophical, and social domains. Such attempts can only be categorized as counterproductive to the continued promotion of the rights of individuals with disabilities and the development of future programs to accommodate the accompanying diverse needs of this portion of the population.

Awareness of the increasing presence of legal intervention in special education is only the first step. Professionals must present a united, informed, and positive front. National, regional, state, and local organization and interagency coordination are critical to the further development of positive programs and community integration. Parents and professionals in the field of special education must work together for the promotion of a positive image of the field. It is only through practical research, cooperation, and an informed and educated position *within* the field that a significant impact can be orchestrated .

\*\*\*\*\*\*\*\*

## REFERENCES

Algozzine, K. M., Morsink, C. V., & Algozzine, B. (1986). Classroom ecology in categorical special education classrooms: And so, they counted the teeth in the horse! *Journal of Special Education, 20*, 209-217.

Atterbury, B. (1986). A survey of present mainstreaming practices in the southern United States. *Journal of Music Therapy, 23*, 202-207.

Bak, J. J., & Siperstein, G. N. (1986). Protective effects of the label "mentally retarded" on children's attitudes toward mentally retarded peers. *American Journal of Mental Deficiency, 91*, 95-97.

Battle v. Commonwealth of Pennsylvania, 629 F. 2d 269 275 (3rd Cir. 1980).

Bauer, C. J. (1985a). Fostering positive attitudes toward the handicapped via the literature. *Middle School Journal, 16*, 19-22.

Bauer, C. J. (1985b). Books can break the attitudinal barriers toward the handicapped. *The School Counselor*, 302-306.

Bauer, C. J., Campbell, N. J., & Troxel, V. (1985). Altering attitudes toward the mentally handicapped through print and nonprint media. *School Library Media Quarterly, 13*, 110-114.

Beckman, P. J., & Koh, F. L. (1987). Interactions of preschoolers with and without handicaps in integrated and segregated settings: A longitudinal study. *Mental Retardation, 25*, 5-11.

Biklen, D. (1986, Winter). Framed: Journalism's treatment of disability. *Social Policy, 16*, 45-51.

Board of Education of Henrick Hudson Central School District v. Rowley, 458 U.S. 176, 102S. Ct. 3034, 73, 2d 690 (U.S.S. Ct. 1982).

Brady, M. P., & Cunningham, J. (1985). Living and learning in segregated environments: An ethnography of normalization outcomes. *Education and Training of the Mentally Retarded, 20*, 241-252.

Bricker, D. (1976). Educational synthesizer. In M. A. Thomas (Ed.), *Hey, don't forget about me! Education's investment in the severely, profoundly, and multiply handicapped* (pp. 84-97). Reston, VA: Council for Exceptional Children.

Bricker, D. (1976). The service of research. In M. A. Thomas (Ed.), *Hey, don't forget about me! Education's investment in the severely, profoundly, and multiply handicapped* (pp. 162-179). Reston, VA: Council for Exceptional Children.

Brinker, R. P. (1985). Interactions between severly mentally retarded students and other students in integrated and segregated public school settings. *American Journal of Mental Deficiency, 89*, 587-594.

Brinker, R. P., & Thorpe, M. E. (1985). Some empirically derived hypotheses about the influence of state policy on the degree of integration of severely handicapped students. *Remedial and Special Education, 6*(3), 18-26.

Brinker, R. P., & Thorpe, M. E. (1986). Features of integrated educational ecologies that predict social behavior among severely mentally retarded and nonretarded students. *American Journal of Mental Deficiency, 91*, 150-159.

Brown v. Board of Education, 347 US 483 (1954).

Brown, L., Nietupski, J., & Hamre-Nietupski, S. (1976). The criterion of ultimate functioning. In M. A. Thomas (ed.), *Hey don't forget about me! Education's investment in the severely, profoundly, and multiply handicapped.* (pp. 197-209). Reston, VA: Council for Exceptional Children.

Brown, L., Wilcox, B., Sontag, E., Vincent, B., Dodd, N., & Gruenewald, L. (1977). Toward the realization of the least restrictive environment for severely handicapped students. AAESPH Review, 2, 195-201.

Burgdorf, R. L., Jr. (1980). *Legal rights of handicapped persons: Cases, materials and texts.* Baltimore: Paul H. Brookes.

Campbell v. Talladega County Board of Education and the Board of Education of the State of Alabama. 518 F. Supp. 47 (N.D. Ala. 1981).

Certo, N., Haring, N., & York, R. (Eds). (1984). *Public school integration of severely handicapped students: Rational issues and progressive alternatives.* Baltimore: Paul H. Brookes.

Cole, D. A., Meyer, L. H., Vandercook, T., & McQuarter, R. J. (1986). Interactions between peers with and without severe handicaps: Dynamics of teacher intervention. *American Journal of Mental Deficiency, 91*, 160-169.

Colozzi, G. A., Coleman-Kennedy, M., Fay, R., Hurley, W., Magliozzi, M., Schackle, K., & Walsh, P. 1986). Data-based integration of a student with moderate special needs. *Education and Training of the Mentally Retarded, 21*,192-199.

Cullinan, D., & Epstein, M. H. (1986). Legal decisions and appropriate education of seriously emotionally disturbed (SED) students. *Journal of Special Education, 20*, 265-272.

Deno, S. L., Mirkin, P. K., & Wesson, C. (1984). Procedures for writing data based IEPs. *Teaching Exceptional Children, 16*(2), 94-104.

Dewey, J. (1916). *Democracy and education.* New York: The Free Press.

Dewey, J. (1938). *Experience and education.* New York: Macmillan.

Education for All Handicapped Children Act of 1975.

Elder, J. K., Conley, R. W., & Noble, J. H., Jr. (1986). The Service system. In W. E. Kiernan & J. A. Stark (Eds.), *Pathways to employment for adults with developmental disabilities* (pp. 53-66). Baltimore: Paul H. Brookes.

Esposito, B. G., & Reed, T. M. (1986). The effects of contact with handicapped persons on young children's attitudes. *Exceptional Children, 53,* 224-229.

Georgia Association for Retarded Citizens v. McDaniel, 511 F. Supp. 1263 .D. GA. 1981).

Gerry, M. H., & Benton, J. M. (1982). Section 504: The larger umbrella. In J. Ballard, B. A. Ramirez, & F. J. Weinntraub (Eds.), *Special education in America: Its legal and governmental foundations* (pp. 41-50). Reston, BA: Council for Exceptional Children.

Gibb, C. M., & Flavahan, H. P. (1987). What distinguishes integrated and segragated physically disabled pupils? *Educational Research, 29,* 3-11.

Gottlieb, J. (1981). Mainstreaming: Fulfilling the promise. *American Journal of Mental deficiency, 86,* 115-126.

Gresham, F. M. (1982). Misguided mainstreaming: The case for social skills training with handicapped children. *Exceptional Children, 48,* 422-433.

Gresham, F. M., Elliot, S. N., & Black, F. L. (1987). Teacher-rated social skills of mainstreamed mildly handicapped and nonhandicapped children. *School Psychology Review, 16,* 78-88.

Gresham, G. M., & Reschly, D. J. (1986). Social skill deficits and low peer acceptance of mainstreamed learning disabled children. *Learning Disabilities Quarterly, 9,* 23-32.

Halderman v. Pennhurst (State Hospital and School), 446 F. Supp. 1295 (E.D. Pa. 1977).

*Handicapped students and special education* (2nd ed.). (1985). Rosemount, MN: Data Research.

Herr, S., Arons, S., & Wallace, R. (1983). *Legal rights and mental health.* Lexington, MA: D.C. Health.

Hersch, R. H., & Walker, H. M. (1983). Great expectations: Making schools effective for all students. *Policy Studies Review, 2,* 147-187.

*How to make friends and influence the media. (1979).* Falls Church, VA: Institute for Information Studies.

Hunt, P., Goetz, L., & Anderson, J. (1986). The quality of IEP objectives associated with placement on integrated versus segregated school sites. *Journal of The Association for Persons with Severe Handicaps, 11,*125-130.

*In re* Holly S. (1986). 1986-1987 EHLR 508:140.

*In re* Marin County Office of Education (1982). 1982-1983 EHLR 504:103.

*In re* South Bend Community School Corporation (1982). 1982-1983 EHLR 503-309.

In the matter of the Application of a Handicapped Child by her Parents, for Review of a Determination of a Herarin Officer Relating to the Provision of Educational Services by the Niskayuna Central School District. (1980). 3 EHLR 501-405.

In the matter of the School District of Marathon and Marathon County Handicapped Board of Education v. Jennifer P. (1985). 1985-1986 EHLR 507-141.

In the matter of Thomas and Jacqueline M. and Larry Barthen and Carol Kay on behalf of Patrick v. The School District of Waukesha (1984). 1984-1985 EHLR 506:259.

Irving Independent School District v. Tatro, 104S. Ct. 3371, 82 L. Ed. 2d 664 (1984).

Jenkins, J. R., Speltz, M. L., & Odom, S. L. (1985). Integrating normal and handicapped preschoolers: Effects on child development and social interaction. *Exceptional Children, 52,* 7-17 Kauffman, J. M. (1984). Saving children in the age of Big Brother: Moral and ethical issues in the identification of deviance. *Behavioral Disorders, 10,* 60-70.

Knoff, H. M. (1985). Attitudes toward mainstreaming: At status report and comparison of regular and special educators in New York and Massachusetts. *Psychology in the Schools, 22,* 410-418.

Laski, F. J. (1985). Right to habilitation and right to education: The legal foundation. In R. H. Bruininks & K. C. Lakin (Eds.), *Living and learning in the least reestrictive environment* (pp. 67-79). Baltimore: Paul H. Brookes.

Longmore, P. K. (1985, Summer). Screening stereotypes: Images of disabled people. *Social Policy, 15,* 31-37.

Mark A. et al. v Grant Wood Area Education Agency et al. 795 F. 2d 52 (8th Cir. 1986).

McCarthy, M. M. (1983). The Pennhurst and Rowley decisions: Issues and implications. *Exceptional Children, 49,* 517-522.

McGregor, G., Janssen, C. M., Larsen, L. A., & Tiller, W. F. (1986). Philadelphia's urban model project: A system-wide effort to integrate students with severe handicaps. *Journal of The Association for Persons with Severe Handicaps, 11,* 61-67.

Meisel, C. J. (1986). *Mainstreaming handicapped children: Outcomes, controversies, and new directions.* Hillsdale, NJ: Lawrence Erlbaum.

Michigan Case #H-487. (1979). 1978-1979 EHLR 501:174.

Mills v. Board of Education, 348 F. Supp. 866 (D.D.C. 1972).

Monson, D., & Shurtleff, C. (1979). Altering attitudes toward the physically handicapped through print and non-print media. *Language Arts, 56,*163-170.

Odom, S. L., Hoyson, M., Jamieson, B., & Strain, P. (1985). Increasing handicapped preschoolers' peer social interactions: Cross setting and component analysis. *Journal of Applied Behavior Analysis, 18,* 3-16.

O'Hara, J. U. (1985). Determinants of an "appropriate" education under 94-142. *Education Law Reporter,* 1037-1045.

Pennsylvania Association for Retarded Citizens v. Commonwealth of Pennsylvania, 334 F. Supp. 1257(E.D. PA 1971) and 343 F. Supp. 279 (E.D. PA 1972).

Phillips, W., & Rosenberg, J. (Eds.). (1980). *Changing patterns of law, the courts, and the handicapped.* New York: Arno Press.

Piscataway Township Board of Education v T. G., 53 LW 3429 (1985).

Ray, B. M. (1985). Measuring the social position of the mainstreamed handicapped child. *Exceptional Children, 52,* 57-62.

Reynolds, M. C., & Wang, M. C. (1983). Restructuring "special" school programs: A position paper. *Policy Studies Review, 2,* 189-212.

Roncker et al. v. Walter et a., 700 F. 2d 1058 (6th Cir. 1981), cert. denied S. Ct. 81 (1983).

Sabornie, E. J. (1985). Social mainstreaming of Handicapped students: Facing an unpleasant reality. *RASE, 6,*12-16.

Sansone, J., & Zigmond, N. (1986). Evaluating mainstreaming through an analysis of students' schedules. *Exceptional Children, 52,*452-458.

Sasso, G. M., & Rude, H. A. (1987). Unprogrammed effects of training high-status peers to interact with severely handicpped children. *Journal of Applied Behavior Analysis, 20,* 35-44.

Saur, R., Coggiola, D., Long, G., & Simonson, J. (1986). Educational mainstreaming and the career development of hearing-impaired students: A longitudinal analysis. *The Volta Review, 88,* 79-89.

Silon, E. L., & Harter, S. (1985). assessment of perceived competence, motivational orientation, and anxiety in segregated and mainstreamed educable mentally retarded children. *Journal of Educational Psychology, 77,* 217-230.

Silverstein, R. (1985). The legal necessity for residential schools serving deaf, blind, and multiply impaired children. *Journal of Visual Impairment and Blindness, 12,* 145-149.

Singer, J. D., Butler, J. A., Palfrey, J. S., & Walker, D. K. (1986). Characteristics of special education placements: Findings form probability samples in five metropolitan school districts. *Journal of Special Education, 20,* 319-337.

Springdale School District #50 of Washington Co. V. Sherry Grace et al., 693 F. 2d 41 (1982).

St. Louis Developmental Disabilities Treatment Center Parents' Association et al. v. Mallory et al. 591 F. Supp. 14116 (W.D. Mo. 1984).

Stainback, S., & Stainback, W. (Eds.). (1985). *Integration of students with severe handicaps into regular public schools.* Reston, VA: Council for Exceptional Children.

Tindal, G. (1985). Investigating the effectiveness of special education: An analysis of methodology. *Journal of Learning Disabilities, 18,* 101-112.

Tomika M. V. Jasper County Board of Education. (1985). 1984-1985 EHLR 507-180.

Travis, L. W., Thomas, A. R., & Fuller, G. B. (1985). Handicapped students in the least restrictive environment: A longitudinal study. *School Psychology Review, 14,* 521-530.

Tucker, B. P. (1984). Legal aspects of education in the mainstream: The current picture. *The Volta Review, 86,* 53-70.

Turnbull, H. R. (1985). *Jay's story.* In R. Turnbull & A. P. Turnbull (Eds.), *Parents speak out: Then and now* (2nd ed.). (pp. 109-118). Columbus, OH: Charles E. Merrill.

Van Bourgondien, M. E. (1987). Children's responses to retarded peers as a function of social behaviors, labelling, and age. *Exceptional Children, 53,* 432-439.

Wolfensberger, W. (1972). *The principle of normalization in human services.* Toronto: National Institute on Mental Retardation, York University Campus.

Woody, R. (1974). *Legal aspects of mental retardation.* Springfield, IL: Charles C. Thomas.

Yanok, J. (1986). Free appropriate public education for handicapped children: congressional intent and judicial interpretation. *Remedial and Special Education, 7,* 49-53.

**Ysseldyke, J., & Algozzine, R. (1982).** *Critical issues in special and remedial education.* Boston: Houghton Mifflin.

**Zettel, J. J., & Ballard, J. (1982).** The Education for All handicapped Children Act of 1975 (P.L. 94-142): Its history, origins, and concepts. In J. Ballard, B. A. Ramirez, & F. J. Weintraub (Eds.), *Special education in America: Its legal and governmental foundations* pp. 10-22). Reston, VA: Council for Exceptional Children.

**Zola, I. K. (1987, Spring).** The portrayal of disability in the crime mystery genre. *Social Policy, 17,* 34-39.

\*\*\*\*\*\*\*\*

**About the Authors:** Pamela Gent is now affiliated with the Special Education Center, Clarion University of Pennsylvania, Clarion, PA: 16214
Mary Beth Mulhauser is now associated with MSG Associates, 1062 West Market, Akron, OH 44313

**Source:** Reprinted with permission from the authors and *JASH,* Vol. 13, No. 3, 1988, pp. 188-196. Published by The Association of Persons with Severe Handicaps, Seattle Washington: 98133-8612

# A Comprehensive State Education Agency Plan to Promote the Integration of Students with Moderate/Severe Handicaps

Susan Hamre-Nietupski
John Nietupski
Steve Maurer

**Abstract** ~ *Attempts to achieve integrated education for students with moderate/severe handicaps have grown considerably over the last 15 years. however, despite increased integrated educational opportunities for these students, wide variations in placement options continue to exist within and across states. We propose that state education agencies (SEAs) must take a proactive, leadership role in promoting integration. A case study illustrating comprehensive systems-change integration strategies employed by the Iowa Department of Education over the past 6 years and the results of those efforts are presented. Implications for other states are discussed.*

***Descriptors:*** educational placement, integration, least restrictive environment, placement, public policy, public schools, school age, segregation, service delivery, special education

In 1978, Kenowitz, Zweibel, and Edgar estimated that approximately 70% of all students with moderate/severe handicaps were served by segregated facilities. More recent reports suggest that progress has been made toward integration of these students into regular schools. The percentage of students with moderate/severe handicaps who are served in regular schools has been reported to range from less than 50% in some states to more than 90% in others (Fredericks, 1987).

These data are cause for both optimism and concern. Apparently, while some states and districts have made considerable progress, others continue to rely on segregated school models (McDonnel & Hardman, 1989). Indeed, the gap between what is considered "best practice," with regard to integration, and the status quo seems to be widening. Not long ago, "state-of-the-art" integration was considered to be self-contained special education classes in regular schools

with ongoing opportunities for interaction with nonhandicapped peers (Brown, Nietupski & Hamre-Nietupski, 1976; Hamre-Nietupski, Nietupski, Stainback & Stainback, 1984; Stainback & Stainback, 1985; Taylor, 1982). Today, however, attendance at neighborhood schools (Brown et al., 1989a) and full- or part-time placement in regular classes with support are cited as the preferred educational options for students with severe disabilities (Brown et al., 1989b; Ford & Davern, 1989; Sailor, 1989; Sailor et al., 1989; Stainback, Stainback & Forest, 1989; Vandercook, York & Forest, 1989). Yet, despite the call for increasingly integrated options, segregated schools that deprive students of any meaningful interaction opportunities continue to exist.

A current critical issue in the education of learners with severe disabilities is the reduction of the gap between "what is" and what is considered "best practice" (Horner, 1987). The continued widespread existence of segregated schools suggests that they will not simply fade away. Clearly, proactive efforts are needed to secure the rights of students to regular school placement (McDonnel & Hardman, 1989). Energy must be expended to move students from segregated schools to regular campuses and to develop more fully integrated models. In particular, systems-change strategies need to be developed and implemented to move students from increasingly entrenched segregated schools to options that allow for ongoing interactions on regular campuses (Haring & Billingsley, 1984). Bronfenbrenner has offered a broad-based perspective (1977, 1979; 1986; Bronfenbrenner & Weiss, 1983) that can be a guide for systems-change efforts in special education. He suggests that social systems are comprised of a number of levels, including individuals, their families, and external agencies (e.g., schools, human service systems) at local, state, and national/international levels. These systems can be depicted visually as being nested, with the individual and his/her family representing the smaller nests or inner core of the system. Public agencies and their social policies on local, state, and national levels represent considerably larger encircling systems. Bronfenbrenner (1986) and Marfo (1988) suggest that interrelationships exist between the various system levels such that changes within one level affect other levels in the system. For example, families who want their child integrated into regular schools or classes may find that local or state policies regarding integration need to be changed. Likewise, state or local districts that promote integration may encounter parental concerns that must be addressed. Because of the interrelationships of system levels, Bronfenbrenner suggests that support must be available at various levels of the system in order for changes in the system to be sustained.

Applying these concepts to promoting integration would suggest that a multi-level systems-change effort is necessary. specifically, any efforts to integrate students with moderate/severe handicaps into regular schools within a state will require strategies directed toward students, their families, local communities and state-level agencies and policies. Without strategies directed at all these levels, achieving or maintaining systems-change may be extremely difficult (Bronfenbrenner, 1986).

The racial desegregation literature (Chesler, Bryant and Crowfoot, 1981; Smith, Downs and Lachman, 1973) as well as recent writings on the desegregation of students with handicaps (McDonnel & Hardman, 1989; Williams et al., 1986) can provide direction for integration-related systems-change. Several guiding principles have been suggested. First, numerous researchers have emphasized the need for top-level administrative leadership in promoting integration (Haring & Billingsley, 1984; Harris, 1975; McDonnel & Hardman, 1989; Piuma, Halvorsen, Murray, Beckstead & Sailor, 1983; Stetson, 1984; Toews, Moore, Brodsky & Brostrom, 1984). State leadership can develop policies that direct attention away from nonproductive debates on the merits of

integration, and toward examination of how to develop quality integration options (Noel, 1984; Smith et al., 1973). Second, while promoting integration in a top-down fashion, care must be taken to cultivate broad-based support from parents and advocacy organizations (Hamre-Nietupski, et al., 1988). Such support can serve to validate the direction in which leaders wish to move. Third, policy makers must provide organizational and interpersonal support to sustain change (Chesler et al., 1981). That is, dictates to change are not as effective longitudinally as dictates accompanied by assistance in planning and executing change. Fourth, while change efforts should acknowledge the barriers/obstacles to change faced by districts (Stetson, 1984), they should also provide examples of successful change (Haring & Billingsley, 1984). Such examples can provide a vision as well as encourage parents and professionals to "take a chance" on a new service delivery model (Noel, 1984). Finally, effective systems change efforts should foster collaboration on the local level (Noel, 1984; Stetson, 1984; Stetson et al., 1981). Parents, teachers, and administrators need to be actively involved in developing integrated service delivery models to ensure both local commitment to the integration process and goals and to ensure that students actually benefit from integration.

State Education Agencies (SEAs) represent a logical source of leadership in promoting integrated educational opportunities. SEAs are mandated by PL 94-142 to develop plans showing how the state proposes to meet the least restrictive environment (LRE) requirement of the law. Since SEAs develop plans and monitor compliance, they are in a powerful position to influence the degree of integration experienced within local districts by students with moderate/severe handicaps. Given this potential for leadership, and the fact that wide variation in the degree of integration exists within and across states (Biklen, 1985), it would seem critical that SEAs take a leadership role in promoting integrated education.

With the exception of Williams et al. (1986), no examples of efforts for statewide systems change concerning integration have appeared in the literature. Further, that report did not specifically address the move from segregated schools to regular campuses. The purpose of this paper is to illustrate the efforts of Iowa's Department of Education (subsequently referred to as the "Department") to promote integrated educational options for all students with moderate/severe handicaps. General recommendations will be provided for other SEAs seeking to take a proactive, longitudinal approach to promote integrated educational opportunities.

## Iowa Case Study

### Background

Iowa is a predominantly rural state with a population of approximately 2.8 million people. In 1974, the Iowa legislature revised the Iowa Code, extending the benefits of a public school education to all students with handicaps. This legislation created 15 geographically based intermediate units, termed Area Education Agencies (AEAs) across the state. These AEAs provided support services (e.g., psychologists and occupational and physical therapists) to local education agencies (LEAs). In some instances, AEAs also operated programs, particularly for low-incidence populations such as students with moderate/severe handicaps.

Iowa classifies students with moderate/severe handicaps into two subcategories: Moderate mental disabilities and severe/profound disabilities. The former group consists of pupils who in other states may be referred to as "trainable mentally retarded." The latter group consists of students with severe or profound mental disabilities and /or multiple impairments. Integration efforts in Iowa were directed toward both these groups, and the generic term" moderate/severe handicaps" will be used to refer to students from both groups throughout this paper.

In the 10 years following the revision of Iowa statutes pertaining to education, the Department focused on assisting AEAs and LEAs in developing quality educational programs for students with moderate/severe handicaps. Initial efforts were mainly on

curriculum and instructional technology. The Department organized extensive inservice training efforts, developed training and certification programs in collaboration with universities, secured outside consultation, and supported site visits by LEA and AEA staff to exemplary programs. Project AMES, conducted in Ames, Iowa (Teas, Maurer & Bates, 1980), a nationally recognized community-based training program, is one example of the Iowa Department's commitment to AEAs and districts. Project AMES was initiated in one district in 1979 and was extended to over 22 districts in a 4-year period.

Although direct Departmental efforts to promote integration were limited, increasing numbers of students moved to regular school programs. For example, some 60 segregated schools existed within the state in 1976, serving almost 100% of the students with moderate/severe handicaps. By 1984, the number of segregated facilities had been reduced to 43. These schools served approximately 83% of the population of students with moderate mental disabilities and 94% of the students with severe/profound handicaps.

Beginning in 1984, the Department began to examine integration more systematically. Impetus for this change came from a growing recognition by Departmental staff of the benefits of integration and parents were provided with only segregated options in many areas of the state. Staff also believed that, without direction from the Department, parents and advocates seeking integration in these areas would be faced with the difficult task of changing increasingly entrenched service systems. Finally, it was felt that Departmental involvement in a proactive, carefully planned and supportive manner was essential to promote integrated programs that, in fact, benefited students. The following section describes the statewide integration efforts initiated by the Department from 1984 to 1989.

### Statewide Integration Strategies Employed in Iowa

Six strategies were employed to facilitate regular school integration. These strategies were designed to promote integration in the form of placing students with moderate/severe handicaps in self-contained classes within age-appropriate regular schools, with ongoing interactions with nonhandicapped peers and community-based instruction. While there was some awareness at that time of efforts to integrate regular classrooms, the initial focus was on promoting quality interactions for students placed in special classes.

**Department position statement on integration developed.** Staff members of the Department's Bureau of Special Education developed a position statement on integration of students with moderate/severe handicaps (Iowa Department of Public Instruction, 1984a). This document outlines a public policy in support of integration with the expectation that such a policy would provide direction to AEAs and LEAs throughout the state in developing integrated options.

The position statement contained a definition of, and rationale for, integration. Integration was defined as including four components: (a) *physical integration* -- the placement of students in age-appropriate regular school campuses; (b) *functional integration* -- the maximized use of school resources and areas in the manner and times in which such resources are used by nonhandicapped students; (c) *social integration* -- the provision of community-based instruction that prepares students to function in integrated, adult environments (Biklen, 1985). The rationale focused on (a) the research base, (b) successes already evident in Iowa, and (c) the legal basis for integration.

**Support for the integration position statement obtained.** The first step in developing support for the position statement was to secure the endorsement of the Superintendent of Public Instruction. This individual had served as superintendent for 12 years and was widely respected by the State Board of Education, the legislature, and professionals throughout the state. Discussions were held with him about the need for the Department to take a leadership role in promoting integration. Evidence of positive integration experiences within Iowa, research findings, and legal opinions in this area were shared. Staff also sought his counsel as to how

best to build support for integrated educational options.

Probably because of these activities, the superintendent concluded that the Department should actively promote integration. He recommended that staff obtain broad-based support for the position statement as well as formal Board approval. He also agreed to work with the State Board of Education to develop its awareness and gain approval for a public policy promoting integration.

The second step in obtaining support was to secure the active involvement of key organizations and individuals within the state. The Iowa chapter of The Association for Retarded Citizens (ARC) and the Iowa chapter of The Association for Persons with Severe Handicaps (TASH) were the most active advocacy organizations in the state. Both had been on record in support of integrated education. Since the Iowa chapters of The Council for Exceptional Children and The American Association on Mental Retardation were viewed as neutral on this issue, a decision was made to collaborate with state ARC and TASH chapters. Department staff shared drafts of the position statement with the leadership of these two organizations. Staff also sought their advice and assistance in heightening public awareness of the need for integrated options.

As a result of discussions with Department staff, ARC and TASH actively worked to develop community support for the position statement. For example, ARC/Iowa and Iowa TASH sponsored presentations throughout the state on integration, many of which included Department representatives. These presentations focused on the steps that could be taken to insure positive integration experiences and examples of success stories across a range of communities and students.

While support was being sought from groups such as Iowa TASH and ARC/Iowa, the draft position statement was disseminated to the 15 AEA Directors of Special Education. This diverse group of individuals reflected a range of positions on integration. The Department chose to share the draft document with the directors and ask for their input prior to developing a final statement that would be submitted for approval to the Board of Education. Staff members and advocates urged the directors to support the position statement. Such lobbying resulted in a key vote by directors to support the position statement. This action was considered pivotal in that the directors had considerable influence with the Board.

Additional support was sought from the community at large, primarily through work with local media around the state. At this point, the Department worked both directly and in concert with advocacy groups. When the position statement was made public, reports began appearing in local newspapers and on television and radio stations throughout the state. Often, these reports contained inaccuracies and /or were openly critical of the intent of the proposal. When these misrepresentations occurred, integration proponents responded directly, alerting Department staff to the reports or referring media representatives to Department staff for more accurate information. Proactive media efforts were initiated by Department staff and advocacy group members. Discussions with media representatives led to newspaper and television pieces favorable to integration across the state.

Finally, in several communities, support was sought from local school boards. The Department could not realistically work with each school board. However, working through advocate organizations enhanced and encouraged local support. For example, advocates made presentations at a local school board hearing on a motion critical of the position statement. Their action resulted in the Board passing a motion *supporting* the development of integrated options.

**Obtaining state Board of Education approval.** Once the draft position statement had been circulated and input received, a modified proposal was developed for Board approval. Prior to acting on the position statement, the Board requested public comment. Again, the grassroots constituency mobilized to secure Board member approval. For example, letters were sent to members of the Board urging their support. One teacher of students with moderate handicaps asked her students to write to the Board member in their

area about their positive experience in a regular high school. The Board member subsequently visited the high school and adopted a favorable position on integration. As another example, petitions supporting the position statement were circulated at the Iowa TASH conference and were forwarded to the Board President.

In November of 1984, the Board convened to act on the position statement. Department staff, parents, teachers at integrated sites, the ARC/Iowa Executive director and the Iowa TASH president spoke on behalf of the proposal. At that time the Board unanimously voted to approve the integration position statement and directed each district and AEA to develop a model outlining integration plans within their catchment areas.

**Integration materials developed and disseminated.** With passage of the position statement, the Department began assisting LEAs and AEAs. Materials development was one facilitation strategy employed.

The first set of materials was an integration manual (Iowa Department of Public Instruction, 1984b). This 180-page publication contained the position statement on integration and its rationale, journal articles discussing integration, materials describing strategies to promote integration and positive interaction opportunities, as well as integration checklists and comprehensive bibliographies of print and audio visual media for use with parents, school staff and nondisabled students. Copies of the handbook were distributed at no cost to each LEA and AEA, with suggestions for its use in integration planning and implementation.

A second set of materials involved two videotapes on integration. The first videotape was designed to defuse staff and general population fears/myths about integration by presenting accurate information. It illustrated strategies for making integration a positive experience for all students. A second videotape was targeted to parents to ease their concerns over integration. Both videotapes were disseminated at no cost to each AEA, to university faculty, and to others throughout the state.

**Integration technical assistance team.** To assist districts and AEAs in the development and implementation of integration plans, a Statewide Integration Technical Assistance Team was formed. This team consisted of nine or more members representing parents, special educators at preschool, elementary, middle/junior high and high school levels, regular educators, AEA consultants, school principals, and university faculty members. The Department made arrangements with districts/agencies for these individuals to provide up to 12 consultation days per year, with the Department either paying a consultation fee to the individual or to the agency when substitutes were necessary. The Department covered all team expenses and charged no consultation fees to requesting LEAs/AEAs.

Information on the availability of team services was disseminated to all districts/AEAs in the state through memoranda, direct contact by staff, Departmental newsletters, and the *Iowa TASH Newsletter.* Any LEA or AEA interested in assistance in integration planning or implementation could request team services by contacting the Department, explaining the nature of their needs and indicating a time frame for the services. Based on that information, team members were selected and consultation provided. Since 1985, the team has received over 265 requests for its services and has provided 300 consultation days of technical assistance.

The team has assisted agencies in many ways. It has reviewed district plans and made recommendations. It has held discussions with concerned staff and parents on integration strategies and the benefits of integration. The team has helped agencies plan and implement the systematic transition of students from segregated schools to regular campuses that afforded interaction opportunities. The only restriction on team involvement was that members would not engage in debates over the merits of integration. This, coupled with an explanation that the team only made recommendations, which agencies could accept, modify, or reject, set the stage for collaborative, nonadversarial relationships.

**Integration workshops were conducted.** The Department sponsored a number of workshops on integration. In 1985, separate week-long workshops for principals and counselors were developed in collaboration with educational administration and counseling faculty from a state university. The workshop focused on the role of principals and counselors in developing quality integration programs.

In both 1986 and 1988, the Department and a state university special education program jointly sponsored a series of no-cost workshops across the state. Individuals attending these workshops were grouped in teams to include principals and other administrators, special and regular education teachers, and parents and/or support staff (e.g., counselors, therapists, social workers, psychologists). Their focus was on forming partnerships to develop quality integrated services. Specific information on integration IEP goals, peer interaction programs, and regular class integration strategies was presented.

At the conclusion of these workshops, participants identified integration goals for the school or district. For example, a team might agree to develop a building level integration planning committee to assist in promoting interactions or to develop peer partner programs. The summer 1988 workshop extended this commitment one step further by requiring participants to develop a detailed work plan for accomplishing their stated goals (activities, responsible parties, timeline). They also were to write a report detailing integration progress and received follow-up visits by the Statewide Technical Assistance Team.

In addition to these training workshops, Department staff and Technical Assistance Team members made presentations at state conferences and workshops. Most were to organizations whose members were less familiar with integration, but who were critical to its success: associations of principals, superintendents, regular educators, parents. Generally, at least one member of the panel had special education background, and one had membership in the sponsoring organization.

## Results of Iowa Department of Education Efforts

The results of the Department's efforts to promote regular school integration have been quite remarkable. From 1976 to 1989, departmental records indicate that 60 segregated public schools existed in 1976, and 43 segregated public schools operated in 1984, immediately prior to the Department's integration initiative. As of June 1989, 10 such schools continue to operate.

Data also taken from past Departmental records, indicate that approximately 17 and 6% of students with moderate and severe/profound handicaps, respectively, attended regular schools in 1984. During 1988, the last school year for which complete attendance figures are available, approximately 71 and 37%, respectively, attended regular schools.

It should be noted that the data presented only reflect progress in *physical integration*. While more difficult to quantify, our observations across the state indicate that most integrated sites have developed functional, social, and societal integration opportunities as well.

In addition to the increased placement in regular schools, several districts recently have developed regular class options (Forest, 1987; Stainback et al., 1989; Strully & Strully, 1989). The Department has designated two pilot sites to study strategies for integrating students into regular classes with support. Further, a workshop on regular class integration strategies was offered in 1989.

Finally, Departmental efforts to integrate students with moderate/severe handicaps has spawned a statewide initiative to promote closer collaboration between special and regular education. The Department is studying the feasibility of a renewed/revised service delivery system that reallocates support resources to the regular classroom so that specialized services are provided in the mainstream. Such a system is being piloted in four AEAs during the 1989/90 school year. The results of the pilot programs will provide future directions to the state.

**Table 1**
**Strategies to Promote Integration at Various System Levels**

| System Level | Change Strategies |
|---|---|
| State Level | - Approve policy, strongly encouraging integrated options throughout the state.<br>- Build coalition with key dicision makers and advocacy/parent groups<br>- Eliminate financial disincentives for integration (Sailor, et. al., 1989)<br>- Monitor progress toward integrated options |
| District Level | - Require collaborative local planning regarding the manner in which integrated options will be developed.<br>- Provide information/materials and training to assist districts in integration planning<br>- Provide technical assistance during integration planning and implementation<br>- Support visits to integrated programs and/or presentations from integrated programs to district staff. |
| Family Level | - Provide opportunities for families to express integration concerns<br>- Provide specific examples of successfully integrated programs in similar communities<br>- Support visits to integrated programs and/or presentations by parents from integrated programs |

| Student Level | - Develop resource materials on facilitating specific interactions (e.g., circle of friends)<br>- Provide technical assistance to insure student opportunities for functionl, social, and societal integration |
|---|---|

While the above findings are positive, some areas still need to be addressed. Specifically, SEA leadership efforts are needed to broaden the integration options available in the areas served by the remaining segregated schools. Actions thus far taken by the Department have focused on *encouraging* districts/AEAs to provide integrated education. Most AEAs/LEAs have developed integrated programs on a broad scale basis. However, progress has been exceedingly slow in areas served by several of the largest segregated schools.

At least two strategies are open to the Department in these highly segregated pockets of the state. The Department could use its compliance review process to *mandate* further integration as appropriate to the individual needs of students. A second, less confrontational strategy, would be to encourage LEAs currently sending students to segregated schools to develop integrated options in the resident district. This strategy could result in the gradual reduction in segregated programs without direct confrontation with districts/AEAs operating the segregated schools. While the Department's posture generally has been facilitative, action clearly is needed in those areas where minimal movement toward integration has been made. Further, most integrated students in Iowa do not attend neighborhood schools. Clearly, this issue will need to be addressed as integration progress continues.

## Implications for Other States

Applying Bronfenbrenner's system-change model to integration, and using Iowa's experience as an example, SEAs should plan and execute strategies at various system levels. Table 1 presents a summary of strategies that could be employed at the following levels: (a) state, (b) local district, (c) family, and (d) student. These strategies, most of which were used in Iowa, are based on the professional literature. In essence, they represent a combination of *directives* to change and *support* for change at various system levels. At a state level, policies that encourage integration are needed. Such policies must be strong enough to produce action, but not so extreme as to result in backlash against integration efforts. Further, coalitions need to be formed within the SEA and with outside organizations. Internal coalitions allow agencies to speak with one voice. External coalitions provide community validation for SEA efforts.

SEAs also should build district-level capacity to carry out quality integrated programs by providing directives for change, a vision of how integration can be successful, and resources to assist districts in integration planning. In promoting integration, SEAs must be sensitive to family concerns. Strong parental objections to integration can thwart state department change efforts. ESAs need to acknowledge parental concerns while still presenting a vision of what can be accomplished in integrated programs. Having parents from integrated programs share their initial apprehensions and their subsequent positive integration experiences can convince parents to take and attempt integration.

At the student level, change efforts must be focused on enhancing opportunities for functional, social and societal integration. State level policy directives and support for districts and families clearly are important. However, if students do not, in fact, benefit from integrated opportunities, broad-scale systems change efforts ultimately may not be successful. Thus, SEAs must devote resources and energies to ensure that integrated programs do result in students being integrally involved in regular school life.

As SEAs attempt to effect change at each system level, it is essential to monitor progress. In many cases, monitoring can be accomplished in a supportive/facilitative manner. That is, SEAs can review plans, make recommendations, provide technical assistance, and so forth. Should progress not occur, however, SEAs must be willing to use monitoring to *require* specific changes. While this form of monitoring can be adversarial, it may be necessary if agencies resist movement to integrated education or do not promote functional, social, and societal integration.

## Summary and Conclusion

State education agencies are in a unique position to provide leadership in promoting integrated education for students with moderate/severe handicaps. This paper has described the effects of strategies employed by Iowa's Department of Education. Certainly, Iowa's unique characteristics have contributed to this progress: its historic commitment to high quality educational services; its relatively sparse population and lack of large urban communities; its history of collaboration between state, area, and local education agencies, its relatively collaborative union-management relationship; and its openness to change. While other states may face unique challenges in promoting integration, proactive SEA leadership can result in significant progress toward integrated education. SEAs that are committed to integration as a key component of quality educational services and that are willing to formulate state level integration policies, and to support change efforts on a district, family, and student level can have a substantial positive impact on the nature of services in their states.

\*\*\*\*\*\*\*\*

**Acknowledgements:** The authors wish to express their deepest appreciation to Mr. Frank Vance both for the leadership he has shown in promoting integrated services and for his insightful comments and suggestions regarding this manuscript. The relative contributions of the authors to the preparation of this manuscript are considered equal.

\*\*\*\*\*\*\*\*

## REFERENCES

Biklen, D. (1985). *Achieving the complete school: Strategies for mainstreaming.* New York: Teachers College Press.

Bronfenbrenner, U. (1977). Toward an experimental ecology of human development. *American Psychologist, 32,* 513-531.

Bronfenbrenner, U. (1979). *The ecology of human development.* Cambridge, MA: Harvard University Press.

Bronfenbrenner, U. (1986). Ecology of the family as a context for human development: Research perspectives. *Developmental Psychology, 22,* 723-742.

Bronfenbrenner, U., & Weiss, H. (1983). Beyond policies without people. In E. Zigler, S. Kagan, & E. Klugman (Eds.), *Children, families and government: Perspectives on American social policy.* (pp. 373-394). New York: Cambridge University Press.

Brown, L., Long, E., Udvari-Solner, A., Davis, L., VanDeventer, P., Algren, C., Johnson, F., Gruenewald, L., & Jorgensen, J. (1989a). The home school: Why students with severe intellectual disabilities must attend the schools of their brothers, sisters, friends, and neighbors. *Journal of The Association for Persons with Severe Handicaps, 14,* 1-7.

Brown, L., Long, E., Udvari-Solner, A., Davis, L., VanDeventer, P., Algren, C., Johnson, F., Gruenewald, L., & Jorgensen, J. (1989b). Should students with severe intellectual disabilities be based in regular or in special education classrooms, in home schools? *Journal of The Association for Persons with Severe Handicaps, 14,* 8-12.

Brown, L., Nietupski, J., & Hamre-Nietupski, S. (1976). The criterion of ultimate functioning and public school services for severely handicapped students. In M. A. Thomas (Ed.), *Hey, don't forget about me: Education's investment in the severely and profoundly handicapped.* (pp. 2-15). Reston, VA: The Council for Exceptional Children.

Chesler, M., Bryant, B., & Crowfoot, J. (1981). *Making desegregation work: A professional guide to effecting change.* Beverly Hills: Sage.

Ford, A., & Davern, L. (1989). Moving forward with school integration: Strategies for involving students with severe handicaps in the life of the school. In R. Gaylord-Ross (Ed.), *Integration strategies for students with handicaps* (pp. 11-31). Baltimore: Paul H. Brookes.

Forest, M. (Ed.) (1987). *More education/integration.* Downsview, Ontario: G. Allan Roeher Institute.

**Fredericks, B. (1987, June).** Back to the future: Integration revisited. *The Association for Persons with Severe Handicaps Newsletter,* p. 1.

**Hamre-Nietupski, S., Krajewski, L., Nietupski, J., Sensor, K., Ostercamp, D., & Opheim, B. (1988).** Parent/professional partnerships in advocacy: Developing integrated options within resistive systems. *Journal of The Association for Persons with Severe Handicaps, 13* 251-259.

**Hamre-Nietupski, S., Nietupski, J., Stainback, W., & Stainback, S. (1984).** Preparing a school system for longitudinal integration efforts. In N. Certo, N. Haring, & R. York (Eds.), *Public school integration of the severely handicapped: Rational issues and progressive alternatives,* (pp. 107-141). Baltimore: Paul H. Brookes.

**Haring, N., & Billingsley, F. (1984).** Systems-change strategies to ensure the future of integration. In N. Certo, N. Haring, and R. York, (Eds.), *Public school integration of the severely handicapped: Rational issues and progressive alternative* (pp. 83-106). Baltimore: Paul H. Brookes.

**Harris, B. (1975).** *Supervisory behavior in education.* Englewood Cliffs, NJ: Prentice-Hall.

**Horner, R. (1987).** Editorial. *Journal of The Association for Persons with Severe Handicaps, 12,* 1.

**Iowa Department of Public Instruction (1984a).** *The rationale for integration of moderately and severely handicapped students.* Des Moines, IA: author.

**Iowa Department of Public Instruction (1984b).** *Integration strategies for students with moderate and severe handicaps.* Des Moines, IA: Author.

**Kenowitz, L., Zweibel, S., & Edgar, E. (1978).** Determining the least restrictive educational opportunity for the severely and profoundly handicapped. In N. Haring & D. Bricker, (Eds.), *Teaching the severely handicapped* (vol. 3). Seattle: AAESPH.

**Marfo, K. (1988).** *Parent-child interaction and developmental disabilities: Theory, research and intervention.* New York: Praeger.

**McDonnel, A., & Hardman, M. (1989).** The desegregation of America's special schools: Strategies for change. *Journal of The Association for Persons with Severe Handicaps, 14,* 68-74.

**Noel, M. (1984).** Securing integrated services: Four histories. In N. Certo, N. Haring, & R. York, (Eds.), *Public school integration of the severely handicapped : Rational issues and progressive alternatives.* (pp. 43-63). Baltimore: Paul H. Brookes.

**Piuma, C., Halvorsen, A., Murray, C., Beckstead, S., & Sailor, W. (1983).** *Project REACH administrator's manual.* San Francisco:

San Francisco State University and San Francisco Unified School District.

**Sailor, W. (1989).** The educational, social and vocational integration of students with the most severe disabilities. In D. Lipsky & A. Gartner (Eds.), *Beyond separate education: Quality education for all* (pp. 53-74). Baltimore: Paul H. Brookes.

**Sailor, W., Anderson, J. L., Halvorsen, A. T., Doering, K., Filler, J., & Goetz, L. (1989).** *The comprehensive local school: Regular education for all students with disabilities.* Baltimore: Paul H. Brookes.

**Smith A., Downs, A., & Lachman, M. L. (1973).** *Achieving effective desegregation.* Lexington, MA: Lexington Books.

**Stainback, S., & Stainback, W. (1985).** *Integration of students with severe handicaps into regular schools.* Reston, VA: Council for Exceptional Children.

**Stainback, S., Stainback, W., & Forest, M. (1989).** *Educating all students in the mainstream of regular education.* Baltimore: Paul H. Brookes.

**Stetson, F. (1984).** Critical factors that facilitate integration: A theory of administrative responsibility. In N. Certo, N. Haring, & R. York, (Eds.), *Public school integration of the severely handicapped: Rational issues and progressive alternatives.* (pp. 65-81). Baltimore: Paul H. Brookes.

**Stetson, F. E., Elting, S. E., Biggs, L. K., Raimondi, S. L., Burnette, J., & Scheffter, A. (1981).** *Options: A training program to present administrative options for implementing the least restrictive environment (LRE) mandate.* Annandale, BA: JWK International Corporation.

**Strully, J. & Strully, C. (1989).** Friendships as an educational goal. In S. Stainback, W. Stainback & M. Forest (Eds.), *Educating all students in the mainstream of regular education* (pp. 59-68). Baltimore: Paul H. Brookes.

**Taylor, S. J. (1982).** From segregation to integration: Strategies for integrating severely handicapped students in normal school and community settings. *Journal of The Association for Persons with Severe Handicaps, 8,* 42-49.

**Teas, S., Maurer, S., & Bates, P. (1980).** *Project AMES.* Des Moines: Iowa Department of Public Instruction.

**Toews, J., Moore, W. G., Brodsky, M. & Brostrom, G. (1984).** *Implementation strategies for integration: An administrator's manual.* Monmouth, OR: Teaching Research.

**Vandercook, T., York, J., & Forest, M. (1989).** The McGill Action Planning System (MAPS): A strategy for building the vision. *Journal of The*

*Association for Persons with Severe Handicaps, 14,* 205-215.

**Williams, W., Fox, W., Christie, L., Thousand, J., Conn-Powers, M., Carmichel, L., Vogelsberg, R. T., & Hull, M. (1986).** Community integration in Vermont. *Journal of   The Association for Persons with Severe Handicaps, 11,* 294-299.

******

**About the Authors:**   Susan Hamre-Nietupski is with the Division of Curriculum & Instruction, University of Iowa, Iowa City, IA 52242

John Nietupski is with the Division of Developmental Disabilities, Department of Pediatrics, University Hospital School, Univeristy of Iowa, Iowa City, IA 52242

Steve Maurer is a Consultant, Severe and Profound Handicaps, Iowa Department of Education, Bureau of Special Education, Grimes State Office Building, Des Moines, IA 50319: (Phone: 515-281-3176)

**Source:**   Reprinted with permission from the authors and *JASH* , Vol. 15, No. 2, 1990,pp. 106-113. Published by The Association of Persons with Severe Handicaps, Seattle, Washington. 98133.

# "Peter?  He comes and goes ...":  First Graders' Perspective on a Part-time Mainstream Student

## Roberta F. Schnorr

*Part-time integration of students with moderate and severe disabilities into regular classes has become a common feature of special education programs.  How regular education students think about their school experience, including part-time mainstreaming, can be a source of information for integration efforts, but these perceptions have received little attention in the special education literature.  Participant observation and in-depth interviews were employed over a 7 month period to study a first grade class in which a student described as "moderately mentally retarded" participated on a part-time basis.  This student spent most of his school day in a self-contained special education class.*

*The findings reveal that these first graders had a common framework for defining their school experience.  Their descriptions centered around themes of "where you belong", what you do," and "with whom you play".  Data collected about Peter, the part-time mainstream student, are interpreted according to this student framework. Findings indicate significant discrepancies between the students' definitions of what it means to be part of first grade and the focus of the teacher's efforts to include Peter and present him as a member of the class.*

**Descriptors:**. educational placement, ethno-graphic research, integration, mainstreaming, mental retardation, nonhandicapped peers, participant observation, peer relationships, qualitative research, school age.

In recent years there has been a growing movement to include all students regardless of the level of disability in the life of the school, including regular classes (Lipsky & Gartner, 1987, 1989; Stainback & Stainback, 1984; Stainback, Stainback & Forest, 1989).  The emerging literature on how to achieve this goal has focused on issues of placement (Brown et al., 1989), classroom organization (Davern & Ford, 1989; Stainback, Stainback & Slavin, 1989), and instruction (Davern & Ford, 1989).

There is also increasing recognition of the importance of social relationships between students labeled disabled and their nondisabled peers as a fundamental goal of inclusive education (Forest & Lusthaus, 1989; Strully & Strully, 1985, 1989; Vandercook, York, & Forest, 1989).  However, only a few recent studies consider the perspectives of those students without disabilities who make up the social fabric of the regular classes we seek to understand.  One study of full-time elementary students in regular classes reported on relations between class members with and without disabilities (Biklen, Corrigan, & Quick, 1989).  Another study reported on the social relations between high school students who had severe disabilities and a sample of nondisabled students in the same school (Murray-Seegert, 1989).  The perspectives of the nondisabled peers in these studies suggested that students with disabilities were often viewed just as "students" or "friends" ...disability was not central to how he thought about his friend ..." (Bilklen, et al., 1989, p.208).  Some students described their classmates (with disabilities) as people who have rights, interests and abilities.  These studies also indicate that peer interactions are influenced by a number of factors beyond the characteristics associated with disability, such as the social and cultural experiences of nonlabeled students, ongoing opportunities for students with and without disabilities to spend time together, and strategies used by teachers to share information and promote positive images of students who have disabilities.

This article describes a study on part-time mainstreaming and how it is understood by a class of first grade students.  The situation represents a common arrangement.  Peter (a pseudonym) a 7 year old student who is assigned to a self-contained special education class, joins a first grade class for a period each morning as well as for daily "special" (i.e. art, music, physical education, library). Several questions are examined in the present study:

What is the *meaning* of first grade for these regular class students?

How might this meaning shape their understanding of Peter, the part-time mainstream student?

What are the implications of the ways children define their school experience for facilitating the inclusion of a student who has disabilities?

## Method

Qualitative or ethnographic research techniques were used to gather data about the setting and the participants over a 7-month period. Some of the theoretical assumptions of qualitative research were described by Bogdan and Biklen (1982):

...that meaning and process are crucial to understanding human behavior; that descriptive data is what is important to collect; and that analysis is best done inductively.

Qualitative research methods call for the investigator to enter the lives of the persons being studied as fully as possible (Edgerton, 1984) and often require a long term involvement to allow the investigator to become a natural part of the setting (Stainback and Stainback, 1989).

Two methods of data collection were used, participant observation and interviewing (Bogdan and Biklen, 1982; Stainback & Stainback, 1989). The researcher's role in this study could best be described as moderate to active participation. As an adult, the researcher could not become a full participant in the first grade class. However, conscious efforts were made to assume a role that was distant from that of a teacher or typical adult (e.g. refusing to monitor children's behaviors or assist with "work"). Whenever appropriate, the researcher joined the children as an active participant (e.g. playing with board games or puzzles, conversation). Qualitative interviews

may also vary, particularly in the degree to which they are structured. In this case, informal conversations during participant observations as well as scheduled individual interviews with students and the teacher contributed to the data. The scheduled interviews were relatively open-ended, but focused around particular topics, such as "first grade" and impressions of classmates.

## Participants and Setting

The study involved 23 students from one first grade class, their teacher, and a 7 year old mainstream student who was assigned to a self-contained special education class. The setting was an elementary school located in a middle class neighborhood on the outskirts of a small city. The school enrolls about 500 students in kindergarten through fifth grade. The first grade class was a heterogeneous group of 6 and 7 year old students, including five students who were repeaters. All first graders in this class received exactly the same content and used the same materials, except for small group reading instruction. Three homogeneous reading groups used different level materials from the same basal series in daily, teacher-directed small group instruction. A typical day began with individual seat work, followed by opening exercises, full group practice of phonics skills, and students reading along as the teacher printed a brief story on the board for them to copy. For the remainder of the morning, students worked quietly on "folder work" at their desks while the teacher led instruction in each reading group. After lunch and recess, the class had several full group lessons in math and language arts (sometimes followed by seat work), a "special" (e.g., art), and free time to play with friends (for those who were finished with work).

Peter, the mainstream student, was assigned to a special class for students who have moderate and severe disabilities. The class was part of a regional school district that rents classroom space in this school. At least three of the students in the special class were described as having "severe and profound" cognitive disabilities. Peter, who has Down syndrome, was described as "trainable or moderately mentally retarded." He spoke in single words and short phrases and was difficult to understand unless one was familiar with him and the context of the conversation. Peter tended to talk in response to adults, or occasionally to greet familiar students ("Hi, Lisa"). He did not initiate many verbal interactions with first graders. Physically, he had a healthy appearance and was about the same size as many of the other children in the class. Peter dressed much like other students his age. He followed the cues of the first graders quite well in routine situations (e.g., walking in line, waiting for directions, playing a game in gym, or performing with a small group in music.) In unstructured situations, Peter sometimes left his seat, climbed on desks, or took other children's crayons or papers. Individual activities (e.g. coloring at his desk) did not hold his interest for very long. Peter did show interest in the first grade teacher as well as many of the students and used their names frequently as he pointed to them or to their photos, which were posted in the hall.

Peter was scheduled to join this first grade class every morning from 8:30 to 9:00 and for all "specials" (e.g. music, physical education, art). One of the teacher assistants from the special class joined him for art class, which was taught in the first grade classroom. Two other students from the special class also attended these music and physical education classes with Peter, along with a teacher assistant. The first graders would stop at the special education classroom on the way to physical education or music to pick up Peter. He would join their line and walk with them.

## Data Collection Procedures

Participant observations began in mid-October and took place about once a week through mid-May. Visits generally lasted from 1.5 to 2.5 hr. and included times that Peter was participating as well as many hours when he was not present. Observations were conducted primarily in the first grade classroom but also included the specials (e.g. music, physical education), lunch, outdoor recess, and two field trips. Detailed field notes were written immediately after each participant observation session to reconstruct the experiences as accurately as possible. Beginning in March, unstructured, open-ended interviews (Bogdan

& Biklen, 1982) were conducted with 22 of the 23 first graders, Peter, and the participating first grade teacher. By this point in the school year, the investigator's frequent visits had contributed to a strong rapport with both children and adults. Guiding questions for the interviews focused on themes that were emerging from the data, but the informants provided the direction and content as they talked about their interests. Each interview was tape recorded with the permission of the informant, and later transcribed verbatim. In all, approximately 300 pages of field notes were generated, based on about 50 hours in the setting.

## Data Analysis

In qualitative research, data analysis is inductive and ongoing throughout the study. As data were collected, field notes (detailed written descriptions of participant observations and interview transcripts) were examined, and memos or observer comments were written discussing emerging themes, possible relationships, and reflections on the researcher's role in the setting (Bogdan & Biklen, 1982; Taylor & Bogdan, 1984). Symbolic interactionism provided the theoretical frame work for data interpretation. According to this framework, meaning is constructed by individuals through their interactions and experiences with other people (Blumer, 1969).

## Process

Although analysis was a continuous process, it was divided into roughly three stages during the study. The first stage, which could be described as "choosing a focus", took place over the first 2 to 3 months of participant observation. A variety of themes and potential studies were noted as the researcher became more familiar with the participants and the context. At this time, a decision was made to look beyond the formal activities and plans determined by adults and focus on how students define their school experience. There were already emerging themes, such as students' use of free time, comments on what is *not* first grade, types of students, and class membership. The second stage, which continued through later participant observations and individual interviews, explored student participation and perspectives on first grade. Data were sorted and re-sorted into categories such as "work", "fun", "friends", "rules", "rewards", "types of kids" and "teachers". The final stage of intensive analysis occurred after data collection was completed. Analysis related to student perspectives on first grade continued, and data on Peter's participation were analyzed according to the perspectives generated by the first graders. At this final stage, interview data were coded into 31 different categories related to student activities, student definitions/impressions, or "our class". Codes were designed to "fit the data" (Taylor & Bogdan, 1984), with categories emerging from themes in the field notes, recurring conversation topics and the vocabulary of the informants, typologies (e.g. types of activities, types of students), and "concrete" concepts derived from the participants' culture (e.g. first grade "work", "friends", "teams"). Coding categories were not predetermined or created de novo by the investigator, but were grounded in the data (field notes and interview transcripts). From these, the most frequently occurring themes in the students' responses were identified, and coding categories were refined further. A three-part framework emerged that was common to the student descriptions of first grade. Next all data from both participant observations and interviews that included Peter or referred to him were re-examined and interpreted according to the students' framework of "What first grade is ...".

*Validity and credibility.* Lincoln and Guba (1985) remind us that naturalistic inquiry methods are based on an assumption that there are multiple constructed realities rather than a single "true" reality. Because of this fundamental difference in perspectives, procedures used to ensure validity and reliability in other research methodologies are not appropriate for qualitative approaches. However, alternative techniques do exist to increase the probability that credible findings will be produced by qualitative research methods. A number of strategies were used to maximize the validity and credibility of this study, including prolonged engagement, persistent observation, triangulation, peer debriefing (Lincoln & Guba, 1985; Stainback, 1988) use of observer comments and memos, and ongoing use of an experienced outside reader (Bogdan & Biklen, 1982; Taylor & Bogdan, 1984). Prolonged engagement (7 consecutive months of fieldwork during one school year) allowed sufficient time to learn about the classroom and school culture, experience that provided insight into the context necessary for accurate interpretation of the data. Prolonged engagement also contributes to trust-building. It is a time-consuming, developmental process that is fundamental to naturalistic research (Lincoln & Guba, 1985). Persistent observation requires the identification of those characteristics of the situation that are most relevant to the issue (i.e. the issue of Peter's inclusion, students' perspectives) and focusing on these aspects in depth. Triangulation was employed by using different sources (interviewing numbers of students and the teacher; observing in different places and situations) and methods (participant-observation as well as individual interviews). To acknowledge and maintain awareness of personal biases and perspectives, the investigator recorded her own feelings and assumptions in observer's comments and memos throughout the study, and referred to these as a check during various stages of analysis. Throughout all stages of data collection and analysis, a researcher experienced in qualitative methodology collaborated as an independent reader and debriefer. The reader reacted to field notes, observer comments, and memos written by the investigator, suggested considerations for directions the study was taking, and commented on emerging themes, categories, and hypotheses. Regular debriefing sessions helped to keep the investigator honest by probing possible biases, exploring meanings, and clarifying interpretations and findings. Differences between the researchers were resolved by seeking examples in the data to support or eliminate possible interpretations. The same reader read all draft stages of this report and found the analysis was consistent with the data.

## Findings

*What is First Grade?*

During the unstructured interviews, students were asked to "Tell me about first grade." A number of recurring themes in their responses suggested a fairly common framework for how this group of students defined their first grade experience. The predominant themes fit three major categories: *where* you belong (your class assignment), *what* you do (structured and unstructured activities) and *with whom* you play (peer networks). Table 1 lists common features for each of the three categories.

*Where you belong.* The two features of "where you belong" had to do with the teacher (and grade) to whom a student was assigned and the physical space associated with their class. The importance of the teacher to one's school identity was evident in student comments. One girl responded to the question "Are all first graders the same?" in this way: "No - 'cause all the first graders gots different *teachers*." The teacher also defined and maintained class rules and rewards that differed from class to class.

*What you do.* "Work," "play" "projects" and "specials" were reflected in many students' descriptions. "Work" was closely related to formal materials:

Hmmm...It's like you have to do math ...red book ...writing paper. Like word papers.

The amount of play, materials, and activities help to determine if something "is" or "is not" first grade.

Kindergarten all we did was played.
(In kindergarten) we get playtime more often than work ... (in first grade) we have to get finished. We can't monkey around.

What first graders "do" became part of the way they came to define first grade.

*With whom you play.* During the interviews, many first graders shared detailed information about one another, and their interactions and relationships. Students in this class consistently reported friends and relationships based on "with whom one played" during classroom free times and outdoor recess. Nearly all of those mentioned were in the same first grade class. "With whom a person played" became part of that person's identity:

She plays a lot with Susie and Melanie.
They're always hanging around together ... I hang around with Kristen.

Another factor in friendship-building was the status of individual students. Students were influenced by how they felt the teacher acted toward particular classmates. Students were aware of "who got hollered at" and to whom the teacher gave special responsibilities. Well-liked students were often described by their classmates as "good". Being good was also offered as a desirable quality in friends. One student, Kristen, described her friends:

Anna, Amy ...Todd. I like a lot of people. Everybody that's good.

Gender was another distinguishable feature of friendship. Girls were most likely to report other girls as their friends and boys to report other boys. Those who reported both girls and boys as their friends reported several same gender friends before mentioning the others.

Another type of peer network evolved during outdoor recess. Many students were on "teams". Teams were initiated and led by students. Participants played a kind of a tag game in which team members chased and "captured" students from the other teams. By March, there were at least two distinct teams consisting of boys and girls, both led by girls. According to many students, Kristen and Susie (the leaders) had started these teams. When they were outdoors, they pretended not to like each other because their teams competed against each other. Although they determined team membership and participation for the majority of first graders in this class during daily recess, Kristen and Susie were not the students identified by the first grade teacher as "leaders" or those to whom other students "looked up".

*Summary: What is first grade?* From the perspective of the students in this class, first grade is a complex world created through a variety of experiences that are shaped by their class assignment and grade (where you belong), activities (what one does), and classmates (with whom one spends his/her days, and especially free time). Members of the group describe a fairly consistent definition of what is, and what is not, first grade. These first graders seem to use this framework to think about school and the other students they come to know.

---

### Table 1
### First Graders' Framework: "What is First Grade?"

| "Where you Belong" | "What you do" | "With whom you play" |
|---|---|---|
| Class assignment: teacher class rules routines | Work: assigned papers books | Free time playmates: class free time recess playmates (team members) |
| Physical Space: classroom ("Room 19") lockers our "hall space" | Free time activities: (examples) drawing puzzles chess | Types: same gender have same teacher "good" (liked by teacher) |
| | Projects: class individual | |
| | Specials: art music physical education library | |

---

*How Do First Graders Think About a Part-Time Mainstream Student?*

What do these first graders think about Peter, a student who is assigned to a special education class but who spends part of each day with this first grade class? Early in the observations, Nate (a first grader) clarified Peter's status within the first grade class.

(Who's desk is this?)
Oh, that's Peter's desk.
(Who's Peter?)
He comes here in the morning. He's not in our class. He doesn't ever stay. He comes in the morning when we have seat work. Then he leaves to go back to his room.

Nate's comments reflected several common themes. Peter was viewed as an outsider, someone who is not "in our class", a visitor who "comes and goes". Nate's impressions were confirmed later. How might these and other impressions of Peter have been influenced by the students' own understanding of first grade? How might the framework that emerged from the students affect Peter's status and participation in his mainstream activities?

*Where You Belong*

When they spoke of Peter, the first graders commented in two ways: He was *not* in *their* class (Mrs. T's First grade), and was in *his class - Room 10".*

He comes in the classroom when we get to school ... and when it's after 9, then he goes up to his classroom. Sometimes he's in this class and the other time he goes down to his room - his class in Room 10.

Unlike themselves or other students they knew, the first graders did not seem to be able to understand or describe Peter's place in the school in the usual way, by his teacher and grade. They did refer to his physical place in the school, but described it only by the room number - Room 10. Other students' classrooms were always designated by their teachers' names.

Mrs. T. made efforts to help Peter appear to be part of the class. For example, he had his own desk, which was situated among the other student desks. Just like the others, it had his name printed on the tag board sign. However, as the year wore on, Peter's desk was not respected as "his space" in the same way as that of the other students. For example, by spring, Peter's desk was often used to store a stack of completed worksheets.  One afternoon Teri was coloring at Peter's desk during free time:

> Teri needed a pink crayon.  She decided to borrow one from a classmate, Josh.  Geri walked over to his desk, but Josh was a few feet away, playing a game.  She called over to him, "Josh, may I borrow your pink crayon?"
> He said, "Sure.  It's in my desk."
> Teri removed the crayon from his desk and thanked him.
> Josh replied. "Anytime".
> When it was time to clean up, I saw Teri stuff her coloring paper inside of Peter's desk.  I asked her if that was okay.  She replied. "yeah, he doesn't ever notice."

There were also other discrepancies relating to classroom assignment.  Peter did not have a locker near the first grade room, and, as one girl reported, he operated under a different reward system:

> Peter - he gives a sticker book to his teacher, because if he behaves very well, she gives him a sticker.
> (Does anyone else get stickers?)
> No ... 'cause Peter's in Room 10.

Peter's name was not on the various reward charts in the first grade classroom for happygrams, homework, and other accomplishments.

How could these first graders think about Peter, someone who has no grade, no teacher to speak of, someone whose desk is empty most of the day, someone who is not eligible for happygrams and homework rewards, but instead gets his own stickers?  It was obvious that he didn't fit what they knew about first grade based on the "where you belong" test.  Many of the differences first graders reported had nothing to do with Peter's individual characteristics, but related instead to "where he went" and the amount of time he spent in first grade or other places.  As one student, George, explained:

> (Is he in your class?)
> Who?
> (Peter)
> Yeah - he's *really* in Room 10.  'Cause he stays in Room 10 most.
> (And when is he in your class?)
> In the morning.  And then he leaves when one of the teachers come down or otherwise he can leave whenever he wants.

George saw Peter as someone who could "leave whenever he wanted," which is quite different from the first graders who spent all but a 40-min lunch/recess period and a 40-minute special in their room.  He was also aware of how little time Peter actually spent in the first grade room (20 to 30 min each morning before instruction began and 20 min for a special at the end of the day, which was usually in another room).  In this class there were about eight first graders who left the room for some kind of extra service (e.g. remedial reading, speech).  Most of them left for no more than 30 min a day, and the student who was gone the most was out for no more than 60 min on any given day.  George and others came to the conclusion that "where Peter belongs" is the place where he spends most of his time.

*What You Do*

Another way that first graders defined their experience was based on "what you do": work, play, projects, and specials.  How did this aspect of their definition color their impressions of Peter?  Some of the students' comments, like Nate's, suggested that Peter did not participate in "work" activities.

> He comes in the morning when we have math.
> (So, Peter has math with you?)
> No.  He comes here then, but he doesn't have math.  We do math, but he doesn't.
> (What does he do?)
> Colors.  We do math and he colors.

(What do you think of him coloring? Is it okay if sometimes kids have different things to do?)

Yeah, if they're littler.

(What do you mean, "littler"?)

Littler -- not as old.

(How old is Peter?)

I think he's about 4.

(Where does he go when he leaves here?)

He goes to his room. He's in pre-school.

Later in the year, Nate told me this about Peter:

(How's Peter doing?)

Doin' good. His coloring - he's doin' his best coloring.

(And what do you do then?)

I just do my morning *work*.

Nate's explanation was consistent with other comments made by his classmates, who defined first grade work as "papers and books," and described the difference between kindergarten and first grade as "mostly play" versus distinct playtimes or free times that were contingent upon work completion. Actually, coloring was something that many of the first graders reported as an activity they enjoyed during free time. Peter, however, was coloring during a work time. In fact, Peter was not scheduled to participate in the first grade classroom during the regular free times. The longest first grade free time, when students got to play with one another, occurred during the last half hour of the day, after Peter's special bus had departed. I asked one student, Robert, about Peter's participation in recess, the time when first graders played with their teams.

(Tell me about Peter.)

He does Art.

(Does he ever do anything with you and        Nate?)

Uh uh. He don't go outside.

Like other students' comments, Robert's remarks didn't focus on Peter's individual characteristics, but rather on what he *does* (e.g. art) or *does not do* (e.g. go outside) with the first grade class. Jennifer expressed a similar theme as she recalled Peter's participation in her kindergarten class.

...and when I was in kindergarten there was Peggy and Peter and Joey came.

(Peggy was your teacher?)

Miss C. was my  real teacher. Peggy just came sometimes with Peter and Joey.

(And they came to your kindergarten class?)

Uh huh .. but he ... we just liked played around and stuff.

(How?)

In kindergarten we used to play with blocks ... but when they came we didn't really do our work, because they didn't know how really to do it.

(They came during playtime?)

Yeah. But not work time.

Jennifer's comments suggest a complication if a student with a disability is perceived to participate only during playtime.

Other discrepancies in "what you do" became apparent when some first graders compared the materials and activities associated with Room 10 (Peter's room) with those in first grade. Megan, a first grader who went to Room 10 for an extra reading session each day, offered these comments:

They play more. They sit at tables ... They do circles and stuff. They put their chairs in a circle to talk about the weather and stuff ...and, well, it's a little different there.

(How?)

Because it's very, very different. They have a playhouse in there and we don't. It's fun in there. We get to play with a giant beach ball.

Megan's impressions of Peter's room highlighted how different it was from first grade: it was all play.

Peter was scheduled to participate in specials, another activity that some first graders brought up in their descriptions of school life. One or two other students from the special class attended music and physical education with this first grade.  Peter was accompanied to art and music class by a teacher assistant from the special class.  He sat next to this adult and had little interaction with other students.  However, Peter participated actively in physical education, and classmates tended  to offer natural support to him by redirecting him or assisting him only when necessary.

First grade specials were scheduled from 1:45 to 2:25 in the afternoon on 5 of 6 days, but Peter left at 2:10.  Although first graders acknowledged Peter's participation in specials, the fact that he always left early highlighted differences.

They're leaving.  They always leave early. They come for one game and then they go. They get a different bus. They have to wait for it back there [pointing].  They don't get the bus where we do.  We get it down there [pointing to opposite end of the building].

He comes for half and half ...Half of gym and half of art and half of music.

Again Peter's schedule confirmed his image as an outsider who "comes and goes".

Another part of "what do you do" was participating in special events (e.g. parties) and projects that were unique to your class. Valentine's Day was revealing in terms of Peter's participation.  All of the first graders had large, identical envelopes on the front of their desks.  These were made of white construction paper and decorated with red paper hearts.  One was also taped to Peter's desk, and like the others it was stuffed with valentines.  As a surprise, several students had made an envelope filled with cards for the researcher.

The party was held after gym, during the last half hour of the school day.  Peter was not there.  He never attended holiday or birthday parties in first grade because they were always held at the end of the day, after his special bus had left.  Mrs. T. had a student take Peter's valentines down to "his" room.

Some of the first graders described how they decided to whom they would write their cards.

Mrs. T. gave us all a list.
(What names were on the list?)
Everybody's.
(Was anybody else's name on it besides the kids in your class?)
Different voices responded:
Yours!
Mrs. T's!
And Peter's!
(Did Peter make his big envelope?)
No, he wasn't here.  Somebody made his for him.

Peter did not experience this first grade ritual as the others did.  As if he were a visitor, his name had been added to the list by the teacher, and someone else had made the envelope in an effort toward symbolic inclusion.

When one considers Peter's participation using the second part of the first grader's framework, "what you do," more discrepancies arise.  The differences that students cited often focused not on Peter, but what he didn't do with them.  He didn't do work (papers and books), he didn't play when they played (he was not around for free time or recess), he didn't stay for all of specials, he didn't come to parties or work on class projects.  Many of these activity gaps seem to have more to do with Peter's class assignment and schedule than  his individual abilities. Students noticed and saw him as someone who didn't fit what they knew about "what we do."

*With Whom You Play*

The final theme of the students' descriptions of first grade had to do with their relationships with one another:  "with whom you play."  Peer networks were reported to be an integral part of daily free times.  What did this mean for how students came to know and understand Peter, who did not participate during the all-important free times?  The first concern might be that his opportunities to develop and sustain relationships were severely limited.  (It should be noted that

Peter's special education teacher reported that his goals in the mainstream situation were "all social.") Second, there were limitations on the assumptions the first grade students could make or other indirect sources that they could use to determine Peter's identity as it related to a peer group.

Of the 23 students in the first grade class, each was mentioned by at least one classmate as a friend or playmate. Peter was mentioned by no one. Perhaps because he had no friends or playmates during first grade free times, Peter was associated with two other boys (Joey and Jessie) from the special education class who usually attended first grade specials with him.

I help Peter and he has his friend, Joey.

Yeah. Because Peter is only a little, little guy ... like Joey ... and Jessie's even smaller.

Peter's image as a "little guy" seemed to be influenced by Mrs. T., the first grade teacher. Students were aware of how she thought about Peter. Mrs. T. enjoyed Peter, but often described him as being "like a little kid," or "like a 3-year-old" when she talked about him to the researcher. This message was frequently passed on to the first graders.

When the class lined up for special, Mrs. T. said, "Who is my line leader?" Jim answered, "Me". She said, "Don't forget to stop at Room 10. It's your responsibility to pick up our two little guys" [referring to Peter and his classmate].

For Peter, the issue of "with whom you play" was, at best, unknown, because he shared no free time with the first graders. This left him outside of the class social networks, and gave him an identity that was based on certain assumptions. The major assumptions seemed to be his association with other outsiders, the students in Room 10, and Mrs. T.'s "little guy" image.

Seven months of participant observation suggested that Peter was viewed by the first graders as an outsider, someone who "comes and goes". They clearly did not

think of him as a peer. By examining the data concerning Peter according to the students' framework of "what first grade is," we get a picture of why this may be so.

## Discussion

For this particular group of elementary students, the meaning of school goes far beyond curriculum. Their perspectives raise several issues that may help us to understand and support the inclusion of a student who has significant disabilities as a member of a regular elementary class.

First, *part-time is different, not just less.* These first graders had great difficulty sorting aspects of their definition of school life into discrete parts. Based on students' perspectives, Peter's experience differed in kind as well as amount. Although he visited for part of each day, he did not share in the first grade experience as defined by the students. Peter's different class assignment and his "coming and going" were highlighted by a number of students as prominent discrepancies between him and other first graders. In fact, these discrepancies were reported much more frequently than any of Peter's individual characteristics (e.g. academic abilities, or behavior). This study raises questions about part-time placements: Is the difference only quantitative, one that can be measured in hours and minutes? Or, does it in fact redefine the experience for both the individual and the regular class members?

Another factor to be considered is the notion of *belonging.* These first graders talked about their school lives in ways that reflected their strong sense of belonging to a clearly defined group - their class. In comparing and contrasting their life in Mrs. T.'s class with past situations (e.g. kindergarten) and other classes (e.g. other first grade classes, special education classes), they often described their situations in terms of "we" and "they" or "us" and "them". Class members reported a number of shared experiences that made up a general definition of first grade. However, based on interview themes, two of these factors seemed most related to belonging to their class. These were: (a) the teacher and class to whom a student was assigned, and (b) shared daily experiences (e.g. common schedules, rules and rewards, activities).

Differences in *methods and materials* colored student descriptions of what was, and was not, first grade. Most learning activities (work) centered around papers and books, creating a narrow view of first grade work. Doing papers and books ( the same papers and books for all members) and working individually became part of the definition of being a first grader in this setting. By this definition, someone like Peter is at risk of exclusion because he does different activities, needs help, or uses materials associated with play. On the other hand, if teachers can provide a balance of learning activities (e.g. projects, themes, hands-on materials, cooperative groups, role playing) in addition to individual paper and pencil activities, first grade (or any class) might be redefined in a broader way. Methods and materials that promote active, experiential learning in meaningful contexts benefit all students, and may facilitate planning for a wider range of student abilities and learning styles (Bredekamp, 1987).

There was also evidence that the *teacher can have a powerful influence on the status of individual students* as valued members of the class. Todd, a first grader in this class, was a "repeater" and very withdrawn. However, Todd was mentioned by a number of students as a friend or as a popular student. His teacher described promoting Todd's image by giving him valued roles and responsibilities and "talking up his strengths in front of his classmates." Another student, Jim, had difficulty making friends. Students said some people didn't want to be his friend because "he's bad - always getting in trouble and getting hollered at by the teacher." Similarly, a number of students reflected the first grade teacher's view of Peter as a younger child rather than a respected peer.

*Relationships* between individual class members emerged as a fundamental part of these students' definition of first grade. Those described as one's friends were almost exclusively members of the same class. Although class assignment does not ensure friendships, it may preclude the development of relationships between students. This is an important factor to consider when facilitating relationships between individuals who have disabilities and those who do not.

According to this study, class membership also plays an important role in maintaining friendships. Some students reported that they had been friends for "a long time - ever since kindergarten!" For some students, maintaining existing relationships might become a priority when planning for transition to the next grade or setting.

For these first graders, friendships were developed and maintained during free times. Identifying when and how students interact with their classmates is the first step. Ensuring that a student with a disability has access to these important times, as well as meaningful ways to participate, may be a prerequisite to developing relationships with classmates.

*Future Research Considerations*

Because this was a case study, the findings may reflect features that are unique to this particular situation. Future research efforts might focus on understanding aspects of classrooms and schools that shape their meaning for all members, such as organization, instructional practices, grouping patterns, teacher's beliefs, local policies and student diversity. These features differ from classroom to classroom and from school to school. Research that investigates such characteristics will contribute to a broader understanding of how meanings are shaped by student experiences. Other aspects of schools and classrooms that relate more directly to the participation of students who have disabilities also need further study. These include the proportion of students with and without labels, the class to which students are assigned (or "based" in), the amount of time students with disabilities spend in regular classes, the activities and routines that are shared, the role of support staff, and how different students participate in regular routines deserve more in-depth investigation.

In this first grade classroom, for example, learning activities and rewards were usually organized according to individualistic or competitive goal structures, rather than through a cooperative approach. Opportunities for students to interact were limited to non work times, which may have had an impact on relationship patterns that were strongly tied to freetime. Students were rewarded for their individual accomplishments. How did these practices influence the student definition of their experience? Would the definitions of these students differ significantly from those of first graders whose classroom is organized according to more cooperative goal structures?

There is evidence that Peter was viewed as an outsider because of the limited amount of time and number of activities he shared with the first graders. Future studies should explore issues of time and participation related to where a student who has disabilities is placed (regular or special class), the amount of time in the regular class, and perhaps just as important, what those shared times mean to other students. Should students begin and end their day together? Is the shared preparation for a holiday party as important as the actual event? What are the times and activities that students associate with friendship-building?

Research must also focus on the perspectives of regular class teachers whose classes have part-time or full-time students who have significant disabilities. How do regular class teachers think about a student who has different abilities and characteristics? Are their perceptions and beliefs reflected by their other students? Although the teacher in this study made some effort to present Peter as a member of the class, she herself clearly viewed him as a visitor who was not part of her teaching responsibilities. In many ways, the students' comments and beliefs were closely aligned with her views about Peter's membership in the class. How is membership among classmates the same or different in cases where teachers have more ownership and responsibility for a student with disabilities?

Similarities and differences according to student age and grade level also may be of interest to future researchers. For instance, are there other primary age students who think about school in ways that are similar to the first graders in this study? Do student perspectives change as children get older?

## Conclusion

Attention to formal and informal aspects of classrooms as social settings can contribute much to the successful inclusion of students who have disabilities. This study points out the value of seeking and learning from student perspectives. Even very young students, such as these first graders, have important insights that are different from those of the adult members in their setting. Students are the only legitimate source for some of the answers we need for understanding and promoting school inclusion, because it is their world, not ours, that defines it.

**Acknowledgements:** I would like to express my sincere appreciation to Dr. Steven J. Taylor for his collaboration as a reader throughout the research process and suggestions in the preparation of this manuscript.

\*\*\*\*\*\*

## REFERENCES

**Biklen, D.,** Corrigan, C., & Quick, D. (1989). Beyond obligation: Students' relations with each other in integrated classes. In D.K.Lipsky & A. Gartner (Eds.) *Beyond separate education: Quality education for all.* Baltimore: Paul H. Brookes

**Blumer, H.** (1986) *Symbolic interactionism: Perspective and Method.* Englewood Cliffs, NJ: Prentice Hall.

**Bogdan, R.C.** & Biklen, S.K. (1982). *Qualitative research for education: An introduction to theory and methods.* Boston: Allyn and Bacon.

**Bredekamp, S.** (Ed.) (1987). *Developmentally appropriate practice in early childhood programs serving children from birth through age 8.* Washington DC: National Association for the Education of Young Children.

**Brown, L.,** Long, E., Udvari-Solner, A., Davis, L., Van Deventer, P., Ahlgren, C., Johnson, F., Gruenewald, L. & Jorgenson, J. (1989). The home school: Why students with severe intellectual disabilities must attend the schools of their brothers, sisters, friends, and neighbors. *Journal of The Association for Persons with Severe Handicaps. 14,* 1-7.

**Davern, L.** & Ford, A. (1989). Managing classroom operations. In A. Ford, R. Schnorr, L. Meyer, L. Davern, J. Black, & P. Dempsey (Eds.) *The Syracuse community-referenced curriculum*

*guide for students with moderate and severe disabilities.* Baltimore: Paul H. Brookes.

**Edgerton, R.** (1984) The participant-observer approach in research in mental retardation. *American Journal of Mental Deficiency, 88,* 345-351.

**Ford, A.** & Davern, L. (1989) Moving forward with school integration: Strategies for involving students with severe handicaps in the life of the school. In R. Gaylord-Ross (Ed.) *Integration strategies for persons with disabilities.* Baltimore: Paul H. Brookes.

**Forest, M.,** & Lusthaus, E. (1989) Circles and maps: Promoting educational equality for all students. In S. Stainback, W. Stainback, & M. Forest (Eds.) *Educating all students in the mainstream of regular education.* Baltimore: Paul H. Brookes.

**Lincoln, Y.S.** & Guba, E.G. (1985). Establishing trustworthiness, in Y.S.Lincoln & E.G.Guba, *Naturalistic inquiry.* Beverly Hills, CA: Sage.

**Lipsky, D.K.** & Gartner, A. (1987). Capable of achievement and worthy of respect: Education for handicapped students as if they were full-fledged human beings. *Exceptional Children, 54,* 60-74.

**Lipsky, D.K.** & Gartner, A. (1989) *Beyond separate education: Quality education for all.* Baltimore: Paul H. Brookes.

**Murray-Seegert, C.** (1989) *Nasty girls, thugs, and humans like us: Social relations between severely disabled and nondisabled students in high school.* Baltimore: Paul H. Brookes.

**Stainback, S.** (1988) *Understanding and conducting qualitative research.* Dubuque, IA: Kendall Hunt.

**Stainback, S.** & Stainback, W. (1984). A rationale for the merger of special and regular education. *Exceptional Children, 51* , 102-111.

**Stainback, S.,** Stainback, W., & Forest, M. (1989) *Educating all students in the mainstream of regular education.* Baltimore: Paul H. Brookes.

**Stainback, S.,** Stainback, W. & Slavin, R. (1989) Classroom organization for diversity among students. In S. Stainback, W. Stainback, & M. Forest (Eds.) *Educating all students in the mainstream of regular education.* Baltimore: Paul H. Brookes.

**Stainback, W.,** & Stainback, S. (1989) Using qualitative data collection procedures to investigate supported education issues. *Journal of the Association for Persons with Severe Handicaps, 14,* 271-277.

**Strully, J.** & Strully, C. (1989). Friendships as an educational goal. In S. Stainback, W. Stainback, & M. Forest (Eds.) *Educating all students in the mainstream of regular education.* Baltimore: Paul H. Brookes.

**Taylor, S.J.** & Bogdan, R. (1984). *An introduction to qualitative research methods (2nd ed.)* New York: Wiley

**Vandercook, T.,** York, J. & Forest, M. (1989) The McGill action planning system (MAPS): A strategy for building the vision. *Journal of The Association for Persons with Severe Handicaps, 14,* 205-215.

******

**About the Author:** Robert F. Schnorr, Ph.D. is an Assistant Professor, Elementary Education, State University of New York, 109 Poucher Hall, SUNY, Oswego, Oswego, NY: 13126.

**Source:** Reprinted with permission from the author and *Jash,* Vol. 15, No. 4, 1990, pp. 231-240. Published by The Association of Persons with Severe Handicaps, Seattle, Washington 98133-8612.

# Parent/Professional Partnerships in Advocacy: Developing Integrated Options within Resistive Systems

Susan Hamre-Nietupski, Lynn Krajewski, John Nietupski,
Donna Ostercamp and Karen Sensor
Barbara Opheim

**Abstract** ~ *The lack of integrated educational options in many communities suggests the need for continued advocacy efforts with local school districts. The case is made here that parents and professionals working in concert can form a more effective advocacy partnership, particularly when districts present resistance to integrated options. Strategies for obtaining integrated options through advocacy partnerships are suggested, with examples provided. The strategies are drawn from direct experience as well as from recommendations in the professional literature.*

**Descriptors:** advocacy, educational placement, families, integration, least restrictive environment, parent-professional relations, placement, public schools, segregation

-----------

Last year a TASH Newsletter contained an article written by a parent sharing her frustrations with having to continually "fight the system" in order to gain an integrated placement for her son with severe disabilities (Roots, 1987). Not only was she frustrated that legal mandates apparently were insufficient to convince the school district of her son's right to integration, but also with the knowledge that she lived only 20 miles away from one of the most fully integrated school districts in the country. Her story motivated us to share our experiences as parents and professionals who were faced with a similarly frustrating lack of integrated options and our subsequent efforts as partners in advocacy. The frustration is a common one: the reality of what *is* versus what we know is *"supposed to be."* Horner (1987, p.1), in a recent JASH editorial, succinctly stated this frustration

when he said, "The values and dreams of our field all too often stand in stark contrast to the reality of available educational and service systems."

Parents and professionals are aware of the substantial impact of laws such as P.L. 94-142 and its state counterparts on the provision of appropriate educational programs for students with severe disabilities (Turnbull, 1986). They also are aware of recent progress in the provision of integrated educational services in many parts of this country and Canada. To illustrate this progress, compare the 30% integration figure reported in 1978 (Kenowitz, Zweibel, & Edger, 1978) to current reports that the percentage of students with moderate to severe disabilities who are being served in integrated settings ranges from less than 50% to almost 90% across the 50 states (Fredericks, 1987; Meyer & Putnam, in press). Although students with severe disabilities increasingly are being served in regular public school settings (Biklen, 1985; Certo, Haring, & York, 1984; Stainback & Stainback, 1985), the reality for too many families is that substantial discrepancies remain between federal/state laws and policies, the lofty goals and policy statements of advocate organizations, and what actually exists in far too many school districts in the nation (Meyer & Putnam, in press).

Parents and professionals advocating for students with severe disabilities often find that if a student lives in City A, or District B, or State C, it is assumed and practiced that the student will have the option of an integrated placement in a regular class for all or portions of the day, or in a self-contained class in a regular school with efforts made to maximize interactions with nondisabled peers. However, not every student with severe disabilities has an equal opportunity. As the Roots (1987) article indicates, if that student happens to live 20 miles away from City A, the only "option" currently in existence or readily made available may be a segregated facility. Biklen (1985, p.14) has referred to this variability in practices of integration from state to state as "...nothing less than extraordinary."

The frustration over lack of widespread availability of integrated options in regular *schools* comes at a time when more fully integrated options are being developed in some districts. In both Canada and the United States, a growing number of professionals and parents are encouraging regular *class* placement for students with severe disabilities (Forest, 1984, 1987; Ruttiman & Forest, 1986; Stainback & Stainback, 1987; Strully, 1986, 1987). In other words, at a time when some are urging us to accept nothing less than "a whole loaf" (Strully, 1986), many families and professionals find that they must "fight the system" in order to even get a foot in the door by securing self-contained class options in regular schools.

It is precisely when systems are extremely resistive to change that strong parent/professional advocacy partnerships must be formed. The growth in integrated opportunities observed thus far has occurred primarily within districts that experts in the marketing field might term "innovators" "early adopters," and "early majority" - that is, those more open to change (McCarthy & Perrealt, 1987). The remaining districts, those who are most resistive to the integration concept and who in marketing jargon might be termed "late majority" and "nonadaptors" (McCarthy & Perrealt, 1987), may never integrate without sustained, powerful advocacy efforts. Undoubtedly, parent advocacy over the past 40 years has resulted in improved educational services for students with disabilities (Berres & Knoblock, 1987). However, when faced with the challenge of extremely resistive systems, parental advocacy must be combined with that of professionals in the field who support integration to forge an even more powerful systems-change alliance.

Parent/professional partnerships bring the particular strengths of each group to the advocacy process. Many writers have observed that parents can be the *most effective* long-term advocates for their children with disabilities (Des Jardins, 1971; Donnellan & Mirenda, 1984; Vincent, Laten, Salisbury, Brown & Baumgart, 1981). Parents can bring (a) an intense, energetic commitment to their children and a strong desire for a better life in the community; (b) intimate knowledge of their children's needs and the ability to articulate those needs to the general community; and (c) the ability to network with other parents and influence community leaders through the advocacy process.

Parental efforts, however, can be strengthened significantly through sustained assistance from professionals in the community who support integrated services. Professionals can add the following to the partnership: (a) experience with "the system" ; an understanding of how it works, who to contact, and strategies for overcoming system-imposed obstacles; (b) access to professional literature/research to support family contentions that integration is feasible and in the best interest of all children; and (c) knowledge of strategies to make integration work and resources to implement such strategies.

Many examples of successful parent/professional partnerships exist. In a recent situation in a neighboring state, parents of a child with severe disabilities attending a segregated school sought a regular class placement in their neighborhood elementary school. Upon being informed by the district that such options were not available, they sought advocacy assistance from an area university professional. This individual assisted the parents in obtaining an appeal, strategized with them in building their case, developed a system for documenting what parents believed were the child's needs that could only be met through integrated placement, and connected them with a professional of international reputation whose strong testimony contributed to a ruling that upheld the parents' request. In this example, the parents' commitment to meeting their child's needs and their ability to articulate those needs, combined with the support of professionals, brought about an integration decision that, in our view, neither parents nor professionals alone would have obtained.

The purpose of this article is to describe a parent/professional advocacy partnership. Specifically, we will delineate practical strategies based on 4 years of our own experience and upon the writings of others (Bilken, 1974; Des Jardins, 1971; Taylor & Bilken, 1980). This advocacy partnership evolved due to the lack of integrated options in our area and the resistance of the area educational system to the provisions of integrated services. Although, ideally, parent/professional advocacy partnerships should include administrative leadership within the system, substantial opposition to integration from within our area educational system caused us to select the methods described here. Thus, the strategies we describe are offered when systems indicate an unwillingness to work collaboratively to develop integrated programs.

## Strategies for Securing Integrated Options

Eleven strategies suggested for use in advocating for integrated services are presented in Table 1. Discussion of each of the strategies follows:

### Table 1
### Strategies for Securing Integrated Options

1. Organize an advocacy group
2. Become better informed on integration issues
3. Inform others of integration benefits and strategies
4. Work to influence policies on integration
5. Work with the media
6. Meet frequently with influential school administrators
7. Influence others in the school system
8. Work within other advocacy organizations
9. Consult with a legal advisor
10. Bring advocates to IEP conferences and placement staffings
11. Contact other parents and advocates

## Organize an Advocacy Group

An important initial step in advocating change is to form a group with similar concerns. Seek group members with a strong commitment to integration, since advocacy for change can be time-consuming and frustrating. Group size can vary. In our view it is better to have a smaller group comprised of truly committed members than a larger group that includes less committed participants. Select an organized leader or rotate leadership. The leader should develop a specific agenda for group meetings. Plan to meet on a regular basis, possibly every 2 weeks as the group gets started. In order to keep meetings on track, set a specific time period to cover agenda items and stick to it.

Select a group name which describes your common interest (e.g., "Advocates for Integrated Options"). This presents the appearance of a more highly organized effort. Consider purchasing letterhead stationery with the group name. The costs are minimal and the stationery provides a useful means of communicating organized responses to school district administration, media, other parents, and interested citizens.

Concentrate initially on a small number of common goals to complete within a foreseeable, specified time period. It is helpful periodically to review progress toward these goals. When initial goals are met, set new or revised goals in order to continue momentum. When sufficiently organized and operating, the group should continue to meet possibly every 3 to 4 weeks.

Our initial focus was to establish integrated options within one regular elementary school. When an integrated option was implemented successfully in one regular elementary school, we began to focus on securing integrated preschool options. Over time we also changed our elementary school focus from simply securing integrated options to ensuring that quality integrated services were being provided, as well as expanding to an additional elementary school. More recently, our focus has been on securing integrated summer school options at the preschool and elementary levels. A goal for the near future includes securing integrated middle/junior high school options.

Expand the group to include other interested persons. For example, if the group is comprised primarily of parents, consider asking university faculty, educators, community leaders, interested relatives, and other interested citizens. Such persons may offer a slightly different perspective, serve as resources, and also may be important connections for communicating the issue to others.

Ideally, such a group eventually should include administrators and teachers within the system who have come to support integration. The professionals in our group, for example, initially included only university faculty members but eventually included teachers who supported us and who in turn found our group support very beneficial. These individuals can exert considerable influence upon their peers as well as district policy. Furthermore, the involvement of such persons may reduce the adversarial climate surrounding advocacy efforts.

## Become Better Informed on Integration Issues

If advocacy efforts are to succeed, advocates in the group must be better informed than those who oppose integration. It is essential that the group obtain accurate information on a variety of issues. One particularly important area concerns the legal rights of students with disabilities and their parents. Possible sources include advocacy organizations such as the Association for Retarded Citizens (ARC) or TASH, from a legal advisor with expertise in the area of disability rights, or from university personnel in education or related areas. Also obtain accurate information about successful methods of integrating children with severe disabilities through updated journal articles, handbooks, and monographs now available (Biklen, 1985; Certo, Haring, & York, 1984; Forest, 1984, 1987; Hamre-Nietupski & Nietupski; Hamre-Nietupski, Berger, & Erickson 1987; Nietupski, Hamre-Nietupski, Schuetz, & Ockwood, 1980; Stainback and Stainback, 1985), or by observing successful integrated programs when possible. In our group members obtained copies of summaries of laws and an integration position paper which had been drafted recently by our state Department of Public Instruction. Members of the university faculty supplied copies of journal articles and handbooks, which were shared with all members of the group.

## Inform Others of Integration Benefits and Strategies

After obtaining accurate information, that information should be provided to others in an easy-to-read form. Persons benefiting from this information may include other parents, regular and special education school principals and staff, local and regional education agency administrators, board of education members, influential persons in the media, and other interested citizens.

Consider writing a group position paper on why integrated options should be provided, including examples of how integrated options can and do work successfully and can be beneficial to all involved. Such a paper should be brief, easy to read, and accurate. After our group members had gathered considerable accurate information from journals, monographs, and handbooks, we also wrote a position paper clarifying what constituted integration and several reasons why integrated options should be provided in our area. This information was shared in person or by mail with the above mentioned individuals.

At times, incomplete or inaccurate information regarding integration is provided to parents, school staff, the media, and other citizens by those opposed to integration. In one community, for example, the administrator of a segregated school informed parents that the push for integration would result in the immediate closure of the school, loss of ancillary services, and the likely teasing and physical abuse by nondisabled students upon placement of their children in regular schools. In such cases, be prepared to provide more complete, accurate information to the same consumers through a letter on the group stationery, letters to the editor of the local newspaper, comments on call-in radio shows, radio or television public information spots, news releases to media, and/or personal visits and/or phone contacts to other parents. Over time, the group will be viewed by others as a credible source of information.

Consider presentations to other related groups such as local and state chapters of ARC, TASH, or preschool parent groups at their general meetings, committee meetings (e.g. ARC Education Committee), or conventions. By working with local chapters of these groups, we organized slide presentations about the potential benefits of integration for all students. Consider organizing materials to present to local civic groups such as the Kiwanis, Lions, or Rotary clubs or church groups. Presentations can focus on what integration is and is not, successful integration strategies, and on present and future goals. Visual aids such as slides or a videotape of students with severe disabilities interacting with nondisabled peers can be very effective in generating community awareness and support.

### Work to Influence Policies on Integration (Local, Regional, State, National)

Key change agents such as board of education members often have scant accurate information on the issue of integration of students with severe disabilities. Increase board member awareness by personally contacting them and providing verbal as well as written information. Encourage them to visit existing programs and to talk to involved staff, principals, parents, nondisabled students, and with students with disabilities themselves.

Some boards of education have only recently begun to draft integration policies. Know when the board of education in your area meets and what agenda items are scheduled. Be prepared to present your position at any meetings relating to the integration issue. Offer to work cooperatively with them. Often it is possible to influence the early drafts of written board policies by providing input during hearings or meetings. Frequently it is necessary to sign up in advance to speak at such meetings, especially above the local level. When boards of education are writing or rewriting policies, they often form committees to draft policies for full board consideration. Advocates might volunteer to

serve on such committees to ensure that a pro-integration position is considered.

Several of our group members spoke in favor of integrated options at local and state board of education meetings. Some volunteered to help rewrite a first draft of the local district integration policy so that our views were included. As a result of similar efforts throughout the state, our state board adopted an "integration imperative" directing local and area education agencies to provide integrated options for students with severe disabilities.

### Work with the Media

Persons in the media frequently present traditional "status quo" information about persons with disabilities and issues related to integration unless they are informed of more current, accurate information and alternatives. Influence media presentations on an ongoing basis by visiting influential persons such as television and radio station managers and newspaper executive editors to share information about the integration issue. One or two members can make personal contacts together, providing both verbal and written information.

Provide media representatives with a list of resource persons who are both knowledgeable and supportive of integration to serve as "sources" of accurate information about the integration issue. Since others, such as school officials or board of education members, often have a more established route to the media, it is crucial that the media also listen to your position.

Provide feedback on any media efforts. Good efforts should be praised promptly by a letter on your stationery to the editor or station manager and to the reporter. Any inaccurate information should be corrected as soon as possible through phone contacts as well as letters. Again, a letter to the editor will let many other readers or viewers know of the need for corrected information. At a later time, make personal contacts with media representatives to suggest possible follow-up stories (e.g. "Integration:

One Year Later") and additional sources to interview.

The efforts of our group in working with the media resulted in a very positive two-part story about integration on a local television station and additional articles in two area newspapers.  In both television and newspaper stories, parent and professional members of our group were interviewed and then featured.  Follow-up contact was made, praising the efforts and encouraging similar features.  On another occasion when a local radio news report referred to integration as "mainlining" of students with severe disabilities and implied that they would be "dumped" into regular classes with no support services, group members called immediately to suggest a correction; a more accurate version of the story was broadcast on the next edition of the news.

## Meet Frequently with Influential School Administrators

Initiate meetings with influential administrators from the local school district and/or regional education agency, preferably those who actually make policy and programming decisions.  Constructively and firmly present the group goals for integrated options and then cooperatively discuss the most effective ways to meet those goals. Continue to initiate contacts in order to keep communication lines open and to keep the program working well.  Help evaluate and encourage more integration when appropriate.

Early in our advocacy efforts, several of our group members periodically began to request meetings with local and regional school administrators responsible for programming and placement.  We often found this to be one of the more frustrating aspects of our advocacy work, since group members frequently believed that these were many attempts to make us feel that we were too demanding and unappreciative of the fact that students with severe disabilities already were provided quality services, particularly in the one large segregated school in the area.  We persisted by stating and restating our goals and offering to work cooperatively with

administration to establish integrated options. The group members' mutual encouragement and support of each other's efforts were crucial in these difficult situations.

## Influence Others in the School System

Many school districts have advisory boards composed of a variety of educational service "consumers," including parents and other advocates.  One or more group members could volunteer to serve on such a board.  For example, some of our group members volunteered and were placed on a district-wide consumer advocacy board.  These members then provided input on the positive aspects of integration and helped to keep integration issues at the forefront.

Work also to inform and influence other persons who actually report to influential administrators; for example, the school-to-parent liaison coordinator(s) or area supervisor(s).  It can be helpful to meet with persons in similar positions to positively present the group goals and discuss ways of working cooperatively with the school system on a long-term basis to meet those goals.  Our consumer advocacy board members find that they do, in fact, have opportunities to work periodically with the educational agency's school-to-home liaison coordinator. Encourage these people to visit integrated programs to observe how they work and the positive outcomes of such efforts.

## Work within Other Advocacy Associations

Group members already may be involved in organizations such as ARC, TASH, or other specific disability support groups that also advocate for rights for persons with disabilities.  Group members might volunteer to serve as officers in these organizations.  Also, consider volunteering to serve on committees that may be influential on issues related to integration.  It is common, for example, for a local or regional ARC chapter to have an "education committee."  We found that having one or more members of our group on such a committee can help to influence the chapter's position and action on issues,

Additionally, a member of your group might serve on the newsletter staff of these organizations. Having group members serve as editors or frequent article contributors has been useful in our advocacy efforts. In our group, all parent and professional members also were members of other advocate groups such as TASH, ARC, and a local preschool parent group. All group members believed it necessary to form a less formal advocacy group whose sole purpose was to develop integrated options, due to the perceived difficulty of this task within a particularly resistive system. In addition, group members were all members of different advocacy organizations and did not all share membership in one common organization.

**Consult with a Legal Advisor**

Contact a lawyer knowledgeable on integration who can fully explain to the group the legal rights afforded children and their parents under applicable federal and state statutes. Such a legal advisor may be available free of charge through organizations such as ARC, state Developmental Disabilities Council, or state Legal Services agencies. Be certain to find a legal advisor who is informed about disability rights, since all lawyers do not possess the necessary expertise to assist effectively in integration issues.

Our group obtained the services of a lawyer free of charge through the state ARC. After he met with our group for an informal question-and-answer session, we organized a presentation on legal rights of children with disabilities and their parents in conjunction with a preschool parent group meeting. This lawyer also agreed to serve as an advocate, along with members of our group, for individual IEP and placement conferences.

**Bring Advocates to IEP Conferences and Placement Staffings**

Parents often find themselves greatly outnumbered by "experts" when they attend IEP conferences and placement staffings. Although parents have the right to bring advocates, many have not been informed of this right. We suggest that parents use advocates--one or more persons sufficiently informed of legal rights and integration issues. We have effectively included parents and university faculty members from our group and/or a legal advisor as advocates in both IEP and placement staffings.

Parents frequently are not encouraged to be involved in developing the IEP of their son or daughter. Instead, they receive a completed IEP at their parent/teacher conference. If this occurs, parents and their advocates should study the IEP carefully, requesting IEP goals and objectives relating to integration and interactions on a daily basis with nondisabled peers. Request such goals and objectives even when a student currently is located in a segregated placement, since this could further encourage school district personnel to provide an integrated option. Parents and their advocates should be aware that the IEP does not have to be signed "on the spot" at the conference; instead, consider taking the IEP home to read more thoroughly; discuss it with others, add objectives, and consider appropriate options carefully. The document can then be signed at a future date when appropriate integration aspects have been included.

In placement staffings, parents often are told their son or daughter would best be served in an existing segregated program and are given little or no information about possible integrated options. Instead, they may be told that numerous "options," which range from least to most restrictive, are being considered. However, when those options are examined, they may be simply variations on segregated placements. When this happens, parents need to be aware that they can request an integrated option, even if such a program does not currently exist. Offer to work cooperatively with school district personnel to establish integrated options, including selecting a school site, principal, and teacher(s). Provide accurate information about integration to all who will be involved in the process.

In one placement staffing situation involving parents from our group with a preschool child, the family was offered seven options said to be arranged according to the degree of restrictiveness. The options included several variations of home instruction coupled with placement in a segregated preschool center, or placement in a large segregated school serving students through age 21. Agency staff then told the parents that the segregated school option actually could be considered "least restrictive" because it offered services not usually available in regular schools such as occupation/physical/speech therapy, a low pupil/teacher ratio, and a functional life skills curriculum. With the combined efforts of the parents and the advocates who had accompanied them, the point was made that for a quality education, those services provided in the segregated school should also be provided in an integrated regular school environment. In other words, parents should not be forced to choose between integration and necessary services; both are critical to an appropriate education. An integrated option for younger students, including this preschool student, was developed due to continued advocacy partnership efforts.

## Contact Other Parents and Advocates

For integrated options truly to become established for all students with disabilities, it is crucial that other parents indicate their desire for integrated options for their son or daughter as well. Personally contact other parents and potential advocates to encourage them to consider integration, visit an integrated classroom, and perhaps join in the advocacy efforts of the group. Our group continues to accomplish this by phone, home visits, hosting informal social gatherings in our own homes, and/or by letter. Work to inform the community of the benefits of integration for all students, with and without disabilities. Some parents/professionals may be fearful of integration, afraid to let go of what they have, afraid of moving from a known service to an unknown one. Do not become discouraged. Our experience has been that some people require continued encouragement, support, and advocacy to consider integrated options for their children.

## Results of Advocacy Efforts

It is difficult to evaluate the results of advocacy efforts. Although systems change can be noted, it is difficult to specify the precise cause of that change. However, in seeking to determine the outcomes of our partnership, we examined five specific areas. First, we documented the number of integrated programs that were developed. Prior to the formation of our group, all classrooms for students with severe disabilities were located in a segregated school serving a seven-county area or in a segregated preschool program. Since formation of our group, two elementary schools have established integrated programs with an additional option for preschool students in a third elementary building.

Second, we looked at the number of students participating in integrated programs. Ten students with severe disabilities ages 6 to 12 have been served in the elementary program initially established, and seven students ages 4 to 12 have been served in the second elementary site. One 4-year-old student with severe disabilities (his peers had mild to moderate disabilities) has attended the site established for preschool students within a third elementary building. For at least one semester, two of those students were integrated full time into a regular half-day kindergarten, and one 12-year-old has spent increasing parts of his day in a regular sixth grade class. Furthermore, additional students considered to have moderate disabilities have been transferred from the segregated school to existing classes for students with mild to moderate disabilities in a middle school and a high school within the past 2 years.

Third, we noted other opportunities for integration spawned by integration advocacy efforts. Parents in our group who obtained integrated school year programs were not interested in the segregated extended year program offered during the summer and helped to develop an integrated summer program offered jointly through the schools, the YMCA, and the community recreation department (Hamre-Nietupski, Nietupski, Moravec, Cantine-Stull, & Riehle, in preparation). Now in its second year of operation, this program has served 18 students with disabilities each summer and has become a budgeted item within the YMCA program.

A fourth index of success might be the level of parent involvement in the advocacy process. Our group started with three parents. In the 4 years since its inception, the group has maintained two of the three original representatives, one family having moved to another state, and has expanded to include as many as 13 additional families. The group has maintained a high activity level, working to interest other families in obtaining integrated options and continuing to advocate for options at the middle and high school level.

Finally, we have attempted to evaluate effects on the school system itself. A logical outcome of establishing successfully integrated programs is that the local and/or area educational system becomes more supportive of integration. Eventually, such support should come not only from building level staff but from top administrative levels as well.

Given this criterion, only partial success can be claimed at this time. On the building level we have observed considerable enthusiasm for the integrated programs. The teachers have developed a variety of interaction opportunities, including peer tutor and partner programs and integration into regular classes for all or part of the day. Two elementary school principals have become outstanding advocates for integration with their regular and special education staff, with other parents, and with their administrative peers in the local and area educational systems. In fact, both were asked to serve on the Iowa State Department of Education Integration Technical Assistance Team, established to assist districts across the state in planning and implementing quality integrated programs. In addition to administrative support, several curriculum/program support consultants within the area educational system have begun to view integration as a positive option. They have become a valuable resource in establishing interaction opportunities in schools, in raising the possibility of integration with parents at staffings, and referring parent questions to staff at integrated sites or to members of our group.

Unfortunately, our efforts have not been as successful in engendering upper level administrative support in our area educational system and in some local districts. Perhaps this was inevitable, given the perceived adversarial nature of our advocacy efforts. The advocacy group, after all, was formed due to frustration over lack of administrative support for integration. In all likelihood, mistrust still exists and positions have perhaps even hardened as administrators have perceived themselves to be pushed and pulled reluctantly to create integrated options. Undoubtedly, a change in strategy is called for as integrated options are established across the full age spectrum. At some point, we must develop advocates within the system if integration is to be adopted by local or area education systems.

## Critical Features of Advocacy Partnerships

What are the critical features of the advocacy partnership described here? In our view, the most critical feature was the organized nature of the group: We met on a regular basis, an agenda was developed and adhered to, goals and objectives were established, and each member of the group contributed to the attainment of those goals and objectives. The group focused on problem solving and goal attainment, rather that simply complaining about resistance encountered to integration.

The second critical aspect of this partnership was the sustained commitment and involvement over the past 4 years. Resistive systems often attempt to "wait out the storm" of initial system-change efforts. Had our group not continued to set goals and move forward toward a variety of integrated opportunities, we doubt whether much progress would have been made or maintained. It would appear that advocacy in resistive systems requires longitudinal involvement for substantial change to occur.

A third critical aspect was the sustained effort to inform others of the benefits of integration and integration strategies. Members of our group worked with other parents, spoke at board meetings, spoke on television and radio programs, suggested integration feature ideas to members of the local media, and provided inservice opportunities for principals, teachers, and other staff. These efforts kept integration visible, facilitating further growth, and appeared to influence other families in integrated options and to generate support from principals and teachers at integrated sites.

## Future Policy and Research Directions

Several policy directions may be posed as a result of our experience. First, if the effort required in our area to obtain integrated options is reflective of what others experience with resistive systems, assistance is needed. Specifically, federal or state education agencies should mandate the provision of integrated options regardless of severity of disability. Far too many districts continue to offer only segregated programs to students with severe disabilities because no pressure is being placed on them to integrate. Second, substantive training on conflict resolution needs to be an integral component of any parent/professional partnership grant program. Parents need to know that it is "okay" to disagree with professionals and should be taught strategies for successfully presenting their disagreements. Specific training through role playing would be helpful in preparing parents for the difficult negotiations that often ensue. Third, federal or state partnership grants should require the inclusion of integration experts (parents or professionals) *outside* the local area educational system. Within-system advocacy, as seen in district-sponsored parent/professional partnership programs, may be effective when systems are open to change. When systems are resistive, however, they frequently place pressure on their staff members to not promote the integration concept--at least not to the point where changes need to be made.

Several research questions regarding parent/professional advocacy partnerships may be posed. First, how may the results of advocacy efforts be measured? Should one consider outcomes in terms of (a) changes in the type/location of services? (b) changes in parent advocacy behavior? (c) responsiveness of school personnel? Second, do parent/professional partnerships represent the most effective means of creating change in resistive systems? Third, which partnership model (i.e., a within-the-system or, as in our case, and outside-the-system model) is most effective in creating change in resistive systems? Fourth, if advocacy partnerships engender increased hostility to the integration concept, what strategies might ultimately engender more support? An examination of these and other research questions should allow for more information of effective advocacy strategies.

## Summary

As in most advocacy efforts, the task of securing quality integrated options for children with severe disabilities is a lengthy process and can be frustrating and discouraging at times. It is essential for parents and professionals to continue working as partners in advocacy, using planned strategies such as those suggested here to ensure the provision of quality integrated services. It should be noted that although the issue being advocated for here is integration, similar strategies can be employed when advocating for more appropriate IEP content, architectural accessibility, alternatives to transporting students long distances to segregated facilities (Taylor & Biklen, 1980), and extended school year services.

The members of our advocacy group realize that the task is not completed. Although school year and summer integrated options for preschool and elementary age students have been secured, no such options exist at the middle/junior high and high school levels. We also recognize that more advocate partnerships within the system must be developed.

Our advocacy work has taken countless hours of "free time" that none of us really had. However, as we see children with and without disabilities interacting positively together, we know that it is well worth the investment of time. We are confident that the potential long-term results of adults with severe disabilities living, working, and recreating in an integrated manner in their own communities as an outcome of integrated education will justify the time and the efforts of parents and professional working together in advocacy partnerships.

\*\*\*\*\*\*\*\*

## REFERENCES

Berres, M., & Knoblock, P. (1987). Introduction and perspective. In M. Berres & P. Knoblock (Eds.), *Program models for mainstreaming: Integrating students with moderate to severe disabilities* (pp. 1-18). Rockville, MA: Aspen

Biklen, D. (1974). *Let our children go: An organizing manual for advocates and parents.* Syracuse, NY: Human Policy Press.

Biklen, D. (1985). *Achieving the complete school: Strategies for effective mainstreaming.* New York: Teachers College Press.

Certo, N., Haring, N., & York, R. (Eds.). (1984). *Public school integration of severely handicapped students: Rational issues and progressive alternatives.* Baltimore: Paul H. Brookes.

Des Jardins, C. (1971). *How to organize an effective parent/advocacy group and move bureaucracies.* Chicago: Coordinating Council for Handicapped Children.

Donnellan, A., & Mirenda, P. (1984). Issues related to professional involvement with families of individuals with autism and other severe handicaps. *Journal of The Association for Persons with Severe Handicaps, 9*, 16-25.

Forest, M. (Ed) (1987). *Education/integration.* Downsview, Ontario: G. Alan Roeher Institute.

Forest, M. (Ed). (1987). *More integration/education.* Downsview, Ontario: G. Alan Roeher Institute.

Fredericks, B. (1987, June). Back to the future: Integration revisited. *The Association for Persons with Severe Handicaps Newsletter*, p. 1.

Hamre-Nietupski, S., & Nietupski J. (1981). Integral involvement of severely handicapped students within regular public schools. *Journal of The Association for the Severely Handicapped, 6*(2), 30-39.

Hamre-Nietupski, S., & Nietupski, J. (1985). Taking full advantage of interaction opportunities. In W. Stainback and S. Stainback (Eds.), *Integration of students with severe handicaps into regular schools* (pp. 98-112). Reston, VA: Council for Exceptional Children.

Hamre-Nietupski, S., Nietupski, J., Moravec, J., Cantine-Stull, P., & Riehle, R. (In preparation). Summer integration: Community recreation integration opportunities for students with moderate/severe disabilities.

Horner, R. (1987). Editorial. *Journal of The Association for Persons with Severe Handicaps,* 12, 1.

Iowa Department of Public Instruction (1984). *Integration strategies for students with moderate and severe handicaps.* Des Moines, IA: Author.

Kenowitz, L., Zweibel, S., & Edgar, E. (1978). determining the least restrictive educational opportunity for the severely and profoundly handicapped. In N. G. Haring & D. Bricker (Eds.), *Teaching the severely handicapped* (Vol. 3). Seattle: AAESPH.

McCarthy, E., & Perrealt, W., Jr. (1987). *Basic marketing* (9th ed.). Homewood, IL: Richard D. Irwin.

Meyer, L., & Putnam, J. (in press). Social integration. In V. Van Hasselt, P. Strain, & M. Hersen (Eds.), *Handbook of developmental and physical disabilities.* New York: Pergamon.

Nietupski, J., Hamre-Nietupski, S., Burger, P., & Erickson, K. (1987). A principal's role in integrating students with severe handicaps into regular schools. *The Illinois Principal, 18,* 14-16.

Nietupski, J., Hamre-Nietupski, S., Schuetz, G., & Ockwood, L. (Eds.). (1980). *Severly handicappped students in regular schools.* Milwaukee, WI: Milwaukee Public Schools.

Roots, A. (1987, February). Where are the services? *The Association for Persons with Severe Handicaps Newsletter*, p.2.

Ruttiman, A., & Forest, M. (1986). With a little help from my friends: The integration facilitator at work. *Entourage, 1,* 24-33.

Stainback, S., & Stainback, W. (1985). *Integration of students with severe handicaps into regular schools.* Reston, VA: Council for Exceptional Children.

Stainback, W., & Stainback, S. (1987, April). Educating all students in regular education. *The Association for Persons with Severe Handicaps Newsletter,* p. 7.

Strully, J. (1986, November). Our children and the regular education classroom: Or why settle for anything less than the best? Paper presented at the convention of The Association for Persons with Severe Handicaps, San Francisco, CA.

Strully, J. (1987, October). All children can learn together: No more segregation of any kind. Paper presented at the convention of the Iowa Chapter of The Association for Persons with Severe Handicaps, Ames, IA.

Taylor, S., & Biklen, D. (1980). *Understanding the law: An advocate's guide to the lay and developmental disabilities.* Syracuse, NY: Developmental Disability Rights Center of the Mental Health Law Project and the Center on Human Policy.

Turnbull, H. R. (1986). *Free appropriate public education: The law and children with disabilities* (pp. 127-174). Denver, CO: Love.

Vincent, L., Laten, S., Salisbury, C., Brown, P., Baumgart, D. (1981). Family involvement in the educational process of severely handicapped students: State of the art and directions for the future. In B. Wilcox & R. York (Eds.), *Quality educational services for the severely handicapped: The federal investment* (pp. 164-179). Washington, DC: U.S. Department of Education, Office of Special Education.

********

**About the Authors:** Susan Hamre-Nietupski is with the Division of Curriculum & Instruction, The University of Iowa, N270 Lindquist Center, Iowa City IA: 52242

Information about the other authors at the time of writing of this article is as follows: Lynn Krajewski, Cedar Falls, Iowa, John Nietupski, University of Northern Iowa, Donna Ostercamp and Karen sensor, Cedar Falls, Iowa, Barbara Opheim, Waterloo, Iowa.

**Source:** Reprinted with permission from the first author and *JASH*, Vol. 13, No. 4, pp. 251-259. Published by The Association of Persons with Severe Handicaps, Seattle, Washington. 98133-8612

# Partial Participation Revisited
Dianne L. Ferguson
Diane Baumgart

**Abstract** ~ *This article reanalyzes the principle of partial participation, which was introduced in 1982 to support educational programming for students with the most severe and profound disabilities. The article presents four "error patterns" in how the concept has been used, some reasons why such error patterns have occurred, and strategies for avoiding these errors.*

**Descriptors:** profound disability, curriculum development, schooling outcomes, partial participation, adaptations, family-referenced, community-referenced

As the 1990s begin, it seems appropriate to reflect on the reforms of the recent past. In a scant 15 years the changes in how we think about all aspects of educational experiences for students with severe disabilities have been dramatic, forceful, and controversial. Indeed many of our current reforms seek to modify the most progressive innovations of only a few years ago. This article proposes just such a reanalysis of the notion of the principle of partial participation, which was introduced in 1982 (Baumgart et al.). We begin by reminding the reader what occasioned the original article with a brief review of the curricular issues, and the students that it sought to address. We then describe four ways we believe the notion has been misunderstood, and even misused, in the ensuing years. Finally, we offer an explanation for the source of these "error patterns" and briefly describe four strategies for avoiding them.

We revisit the notion of partial participation in this way because we believe it continues to be an important idea for helping teachers conceptualize and implement effective educational programming for some students with very severe disabilities. We further believe that some of the frustrations felt by teachers of students with very severe

disabilities and their parents can be traced to the effects of the four error patterns we describe. We hope that revisiting the notion of partial participation with all the advantages of critical hindsight, will help.

## Why We Needed Partial Participation

The increasingly sophisticated behavioral technology available in the mid-1970s allowed teachers and researchers to confirm quickly that students previously excluded as too severely disabled to be "educable" could indeed learn. This confirmation underscored the appropriateness of the insistence in the Education of the Handicapped Act that *all* students, regardless of the type and degree of their disability, should participate in public schooling. What our field continued to debate was *what* to teach and for what purpose. Each successive reform of our curricular logic seemed driven by our dissatisfaction with the impact our teaching was having on students' lives, especially those students with the most extreme disabilities. Did what students learn make any substantive difference in their lives? Early efforts to use the prevailing developmental logic certainly gave teachers a place to start (Baldwin, 1976; Cohen, Gross, & Haring, 1976; Haring & Bricker, 1978; Haring & Brown, 1976), but the shortcomings were all too quickly obvious (Barrett, 1979; Shane, 1979; Switzkey, Rotatori, Miller, & Freagon, 1979). even when students eventually mastered the developmental skills, teachers and families were left wondering if learning would ever really make a difference. The common use of chronologically age inappropriate materials damaged students' already tarnished social images, encouraging more, not less, stigma. Teachers and students were left with little guidance from the developmental sequences when physical and sensory impairments made some skills simply unattainable.

The developmental logic for curricular decision making was quickly replaced by a functional logic (Brown, Nietupski, & Hamre-Nietupski, 1976); that is, teach only those items from developmental or other schedules that are useful in the student's life either immediately or some time in the future. This logic certainly helped teachers narrow the field of teaching choices from that previously offered by the more commonly used developmental sequences, or other compendia of functional skills, but it did not narrow it enough. Still too many things might be functionally worthy. Families and teachers still struggled to see the effects of students' learning on those students' lives outside, as well as inside, the classroom. An unclear, and often much too distant, future was simply not enough promise.

It was in this climate of a rejected developmental logic, but a still unsatisfying conceptualization of a functional alternative, that the ecological domain strategy for selecting curricular content emerged to shift teachers from lists of developmental skills to examining students lives as the most appropriate source for curriculum content (Brown et al. 1979a, 1979b). Teachers were advised to examine students' homes and neighborhoods to discover actual activity patterns that might be shared by students' nondisabled peers, and then teach those activities and functional skills that would directly support students' performance of the activities in their naturally occurring environments. Teachers were encouraged to teach the resulting functional skills in the context of the actual activities in order to maximize the likelihood that their students would use their learning (Belmore & Brown, 1978; Brown et al., 1980; Falvey, Brown, Lyon, Baumgart, & Schroeder, 1978; Hamre-Nietupski, Nietupski, Bates, & Maurer, 1982).

Several flaws still remained in the curricular reform logic. The newly elaborated curricular decision-making logic still depended, at least implicitly, on the assumption that students would achieve independence in the elected functional activity or skill. Being able to improve our curricular focus, we seemed to believe, would result in students actually becoming independent in the performance of those skills and activities most needed in their lives. Although effective for many students, the underlying assumption of independence seemed to exclude those students with the most severe disabilities. The principle of partial participation was proposed to ensure that even those students who might never be able to acquire a full enough complement of functional skills to *completely* participate in the activities of their peers would still be able to learn enough to *partially* participate. That is, the principle of partial participation was generated in order to make our curriculum and programming reforms also "work" for students with very severe cognitive and multiple disabilities.

Taken together, the activity-based curriculum, buttressed by the notions of partial participation and functional outcomes, was meant to assure that school would cater to all students in some very direct and visible ways. What had not changed was the still firm rejection of a developmental logic for curriculum decision making. Consequently, teachers had no means for integrating developmental and other existing decision-making approaches with other aspects of the teaching and learning process. Unfortunately, we also may not have fully appreciated the complexity and challenge presented by those students with the most extreme disabilities. The new curricular approach, which included the principle of partial participation, still relied on a behaviorally oriented instructional technology and a student's repertoire for deciding what to teach. As a field, special education is only now beginning to discover the need to reconsider instructional as well as curricular approaches, very likely expanding instructional capacity to embrace other understandings of teaching and learning in addition to a behavioral approach (Baumgart, Johnson, & Helmstetter, 1990; Brown, Helmstetter, & Guess, 1986; Ferguson & juniper, 1990; Guess & Thompson, 1991; Meyer, 1991).

## Patterns of Error in Using Partial Participation

As the special education field has tried to use the notion of partial participation, the concept has acquired many new interpretations. It is certainly true that for many students the notion has provided a way to expand their participation and learning in a variety of more natural settings; for other students, however, the notion has reaped much less positive results. Indeed, it seems as if the concept of partial participation was adopted only partially. We believe this partial application has resulted in renewed confusion and frustration for students, families, and teachers. This section briefly describes four error patterns we find in the current use of partial participation. In each case, it is the kind of participation that students achieve that betrays the misunderstanding.

## Passive Participation

*An illustrative vignette*. John's IEP calls for him to participate in daily activities in the fourth grade class. Because John seems to be calmed by music, his teacher has decided that he should go to music class with the fourth graders three times a week, and participate in the after lunch group reading activity every day. When it is music time, John and a classroom assistant meet the fourth graders at the music room. John and his assistant usually position themselves on the side of the room. The assistant participates in the singing and instrument playing, touching John often to encourage his listening. After lunch, another assistant drops John off in the fourth grade classroom on his way to his own lunch break. for the next half hour different students take turns reading their library books aloud to John.

*The error pattern*. This error results from defining participation as presence. Students who formerly experienced a fairly narrow range of environments and instructional activities now find themselves merely present in more natural community and school environments. Typically this presence involves only the opportunity to observe others engage in activity or, at best, to receive the benefits of the completed activity. Thus, using the school library might only mean that you are present while someone else selects a book and carries it back to the classroom for you. Being out and about in the community and school as a passive spectator becomes the point--substituting both for more active participation and for systematic instruction.

Of course, not all examples of passive participation necessarily constitute an error. As in the example of John, sometimes being read to by your classmates might be appropriate and image enhancing. It is when passive participation is the dominant form of participation that the practice becomes problematic.

## Myopic Participation

*An illustrative vignette.* Maria's IEP meeting is scheduled to occur in 2 weeks. Lori, Maria's teacher, has already talked with Maria's mother and knows that she really wants Maria to participate more in community training, especially different kinds of shopping. Because Maria's mother doesn't drive, they shop together almost every day at the small comer grocer, bakery, and other stores in their neighborhood. Maria's mother would like Maria to act better in the stores and maybe even help more. Lori has taken Maria to the grocery store she uses for all her community training to assess her shopping skills. Lori discovered that Maria seems to enjoy pushing the cart but, about halfway through shopping, sits down in the aisle. Sometimes she screams. Lori has decided to have her use picture cards to find a drink and a snack and then have her sit on the bench outside the store to eat while the other students finish their shopping.

*The error pattern.* Myopic participation results when teachers select a student's involvement in potential learning activities using only one, or just a few, of the relevant perspectives. Lori has included shopping in Marie's instructional agenda but only in a manner that fits within her own established teaching format. That is, the basis for choosing some parts of an activity over others fails to include consideration of the full range of variable that should enter into curricular and programming decisions. Another teacher might select the first part of an activity for participation, the easiest part for the teacher or student, the parts that most frequently recur, or those that seem to take the least amount of time. Often, the resulting instruction fails to support family goals and needs, as in this example about Maria. While any components taken alone might be appropriate for a student to learn, the error lies in not considering the student's current and potential skill repertoire, the student's preferences, long-term learning needs, family priorities, reactions of peers, and other socially validated, community-reference guidelines.

## Piecemeal Participation

*An illustrative vignette.* Mark has devised a 25-minute lesson format, with 5 minutes for transitions throughout the morning. He and his two staff take small groups of two to four students for each lesson. After lunch, the class is divided into three groups, and each staff person takes three or four students out for community training at either the public library, a nearby grocery store, or the city park. Larry, one of the 11-year-old students in Mark's class, has the following schedule of lessons and activities on Mondays, Wednesdays, and Fridays: (a) play skills, (b) object discrimination and labeling, (c) snack/bathroom/recess, (d) language group, (e) physical therapy, (f) lunch/bathroom, recess, (g) checking out a story tape at the public library, (h) art or music, and (i) bathroom/departure. Every day Mark reminds Larry's parents to play the story tape at home so he can be sure that Larry will understand why he is going to the library.

*The error pattern.* It seems that some teachers only use the notion of partial participation, and the accompanying ideas of functional, activity-based, age-appropriate instructional curricular content, *some of the time*. These ideas are not combined with other, more familiar ways of deciding what to teach to create an integrated curricular logic. Instead, it seems that partial participation in real activities of life only occurs during an "activity" or "community" time, carefully scheduled opposite lessons derived using a totally separate, often developmental, curricular logic. In essence, the student experiences a piecemeal approach to partial participation, curriculum, and involvement in life. Classroom-based instruction, while it may succeed, fails to connect with the student's out-of-class, functional curriculum times. Instead of using classroom instruction to prepare a student for out-of-class, activity-based instruction classroom learning may even compete. The relevance of both in- and out-of class instruction can be lost for the student. This lack of coherence in the student's curriculum can slow a student's understanding of and competence in real, functional, meaningful activities clearly minimizing the impact of schooling on the student's life outside of school.

Of course, the power of piecemeal participation will vary somewhat with a student's age; there is simply more time to build connections for students who are quite young. Nevertheless, even very young students need to have some understanding of why they are learning what they are learning and how their time in school relates to the rest of their lives.

## Missed Participation

*An illustrative vignette.* Sarah is 16 and has just started attending Acres High School. About 10 minutes before the bell for first lunch, Sarah leaves ceramics class to head for the lunch room. Walking is difficult for Sarah and she needs to stop frequently to rest. Despite the extra time it takes Sarah to get to the lunch room, her teacher and therapist think it is a good opportunity to work on walking, especially because they know she is usually eager to eat lunch. Her teacher has identified enough handy rest stops along the way so Sarah doesn't get too frustrated and still gets to the cafeteria line before the lunch bell. Once in the cafeteria, Sarah pushes her tray along the hot lunch line. The teacher helps Sarah to choose each item, holding up a picture card so the cafeteria worker knows what Sarah wants and then assisting Sarah to grasp each item and place it carefully on her tray. At the end of the line, the teacher has arranged for a cart where Sarah can put her tray because it is still too hard for her to carry the whole tray to a table. Instead, the tray waits on the cart while Sarah carries one or two items at a time to a seat of her choice. When Sarah is able to carry a whole tray of food she will be able to choose a fast food lunch. (The fast food area doesn't have a shelf for sliding the tray.)

***The error pattern.*** This vignette illustrates that, in a few instances, it seems that the point of partial participation is missed altogether. Our overarching commitment to helping students "be independent" encourages us to try to teach or involve a student in *all* the parts of an activity. We also seem to interpret "doing things independently" as doing them alone, or "all by yourself," which can result in too narrow a prescription for performance. The standard of "all by yourself" might mean that a student can only reasonably attempt a very small amount of the whole activity (only buying one thing in a grocery store, or just pushing the switch to turn on the appliance). "All by yourself" can also take a very long time, require burdensome accommodations and adaptations, or restrict the interactions between teacher and student to formal instruction. As a consequence, the implicit expectation of "all by yourself" can limit rather than expand participation.

When first considered, it might seem too restrictive to ever decide that a student will always have another person present for some activities. On further consideration, the needed presence of another person offers teachers and students the opportunity to enhance participation by having the other person perform those parts of the activity that are burdensome, time consuming, or image damaging for the student. The resulting shared participation might truly enhance the person's enjoyment at finally *doing* the activity rather than spending years laboriously trying to learn to do it, and does not necessarily prevent later acquisition (even if partial) of previously supported components. As noted for an earlier "error," the age of the student should influence this instructional emphasis, but not so much that natural, shared and enjoyable participation is prevented.

## Sources of Errors

One of the reasons it is so hard to think about active participation for students

with extremely severe and multiple disabilities (the very group the principle was created to better include) is that these students are often unavailable for learning, providing teachers with very narrow windows of teaching opportunity. Students' complex and multiple disabilities may cause them to be asleep or drowsy, agitated or crying, or even awake and seemingly alert but not "connecting to the environment in any recognizable way" (Ferguson & Juniper, 1990, p. 4; Guess et al., 1988). When for noticeable proportions of students' days they are unavailable for learning, active and contributory participation becomes not only difficult to accomplish but increasingly difficult for teachers to imagine.

A second reason active participation is difficult to think about for students with very extreme disabilities is that they may have very few behaviors (e.g., orienting to some sight or sound, assisted movement of a hand or arm, a few nonsymbolic vocalizations). Most teachers, however, depend upon a behaviorally grounded instructional approach that seeks to expand a student's behavioral repertoire -- that is , to *add* behaviors by building on what students can already do, thereby remediating the performance discrepancies between students with disabilities and their nondisabled peers. While this instructional approach serves us well with many students, the very few behaviors that some students possess are so small and fragile that teachers struggle to shape tiny additional pieces of behavior or perhaps just to improve the consistency with which a student responds. Too often these instructional beginnings become the sum total of instruction because the student fails to respond either quickly or consistently. Teachers are left feeling unsatisfied that they are meeting the curricular challenge of making enough of a difference in students' lives. Indeed, those skills that it seems most appropriate to *teach* some very complex and disabled students may more nearly resemble the developmental skills our curricular reforms have rejected than the functional, activity-based outcomes being achieved with other, more able students (Ferguson & Juniper, 1990). Having moved away from reliance on a deficit-remediation model for some learners with severe disabilities (Meyer, 1991), we seem to retreat to it for those students who experience the most extreme disabilities. Certainly these students spend their school days more passively than actively engaged in learning (Downing, 1988).

In sum, we think partial participation is *not:*

1. Meant to be used alone for deciding what to teach. The concept depends upon, and is grounded within, notions of teaching students how to participate in the real activities of their age peers that occur routinely in life both in and out of school. This requires attention to student and family preferences, family activities, the ideas and reactions of peers, and the ethos of the community, to mention just a few.

2. Meant to be used in alternation with a developmental logic for deciding what to teach. As we will explain in more detail later, developmental information is not only useful, but is necessary to effective educational programming for students with severe disabilities, but it is not a useful curriculum decision-making logic. Activity-based curriculum with its attendant dimensions, including partial participation, is the most effective way to decide *what* to teach. More traditional developmental information can greatly assist teachers' decisions about *how* to teach.

3. A way of achieving social inclusion at the cost of instruction and growth. Schooling is about learning. Passive participation in the hopes of social acceptance is a poor substitute for growth in functional competence, even when the increments of growth are small and fragile.

### Avoiding Errors In the Application of Partial Participation

We believe that the notion of partial participation is still quite valuable. Originally, it served to affirm that functional, age-appropriate, community-based and community-referenced, student- and family-referenced programming did indeed apply to even those students with the most severe disabilities. Despite the errors of interpretation and application we have described, we believe

it still has this power. Even students with very extreme and complex disabilities, who seem to "do" very little, can be supported to participate actively in the life of their communities in ways that help others view them as contributing members.

The concept of partial participation supports a mission of schooling based on the concept that, whatever any student learns, that learning should allow him or her to participate actively in the community so that others come to care enough about what happens to that student to look out for him or her (Ferguson & Jeanchild, 1992). This section very briefly describes four strategies that might help teachers rediscover this essential spirit of partial participation.

### Strategy 1: Achieving *Active* Instead of Passive Partial Participation

One strategy for avoiding dependence upon teaching isolated skills and reliance on passive presence is to think less about adding to students' behavioral repertoires and more about increasing opportunities for students to practice their admittedly small and tenuous current behaviors in real school and community activities. Let us hasten to add that we are not arguing that increasing students' behavioral repertoires is not a good idea. However, we agree with Meyer (1991) that to "set that goal as the *only* thing to do is problematic" (p. 633), perhaps especially so for students with the most extreme disabilities. We simply do not have the medical and educational ability to remediate the very large performance discrepancies experienced by students with the most severe disabilities. Yet if schooling is to produce meaningful outcomes, we cannot afford to wait to acquire this technical expertise.

Table 1 illustrates how a focus on practicing ability instead of adding behaviors might occur for one student in just four different school activities. A variety of curricular planning approaches (e.g., Baumgart et al., 1990; Falvey, 1989; Ferguson & Wilcox, 1987; Ford, et al., 1989; Guess & Helmstetter, 1986; Sailor et al., 1989) contain the specific planning tools that teachers can use to first establish a routine of real, age-appropriate activities, and then determine how to maximize students opportunities for practicing the behaviors they currently possess, even if small and inconsistent.

Using a "practice abilities" logic rather than an "add behaviors" logic for instruction does not mean that teachers will not be building students' skills. Rather, it is a matter of how teachers frame their efforts. Practicing abilities within a context is more likely to result in building skills for students with extreme disabilities, if skills are to be built at all. Although students may never complete a movement entirely alone, they may begin to actively contribute to a movement, or continue a movement they have been assisted to begin.

In some situations a student's few behaviors might not substantially change, but physically supported *active* participation in real settings can still result in two important benefits. First, the student's physical condition and health might be better maintained as a consequence of physically supported active participation (increasing joint flexibility and range of motion, for example). Second, well-constructed and supported active participation is more likely to enhance the image of the student in the eyes of nondisabled peers, encouraging peer interest and even involvement. It is this interest and involvement of peers that will support the continued community presence of students with very severe multiple disabilities. Ferguson and Juniper (1990) provided a more detailed description of how one teacher used this practice abilities strategy and developed a data management system to support it.

**Strategy 2:**
**Avoiding Myopic Participation by**
**Attending To Multiple Perspectives**

There are good reasons why teachers often lose track of some of the important perspectives needed for functional curriculum planning. The work of creating effective educational experiences for a student with severe disabilities, indeed, for any student, is exceedingly complex. First, many teachers do

not receive specific preparation in how to access and use multiple perspectives. Indeed, their own experience of learning how to teach may not have been well informed by multiple perspectives. Second, teachers rarely have all the time and resources required to meet the challenge. Daily they must make hundreds of decisions, very rapidly, under conditions of ambiguity, instability, and value conflict. Given such conditions, it is hardly surprising that some of their curricular and instructional decisions are affected more by convenience, efficiency, and ease than by carefully articulated preferred practice ideals. Too often our field's new practice recommendations fail to adequately respect the complexity of teachers' work, making it difficult for them to change their practices or adopt new ones. We offer three suggestions that can help teachers to access some often overlooked perspectives.

**Use family- and community-referenced assessment strategies.**

Traditional approaches to assessment for students with severe disabilities have proved inadequate for three reasons. First, students with severe disabilities need to formally learn things their nondisabled peers acquire informally, and second, students with severe disabilities cannot always "use" what they have learned when it is needed. Third, these students will simply not learn all the things, either formally or informally, that their nondisabled peers learn in roughly the same period of time. Given these basic learning challenges, it makes the best sense for teachers to select those "things" to teach that will have the greatest impact on helping students become as competent as possible in their everyday lives.

There are several available strategies for doing activity-based and family-referenced assessment (Baumgart et al., 1990; Falvey, 1989; Ferguson & Wilcox, 1987; Ford et al., 1989; Guess & Helmstetter, 19866; Sailor et al., 1989). Activity-based, family-referenced assessment is particularly critical to curriculum planning for students with the most severe disabilities because it focuses on a student's *abilities*. As we argued above, improving the consistency and quality of a student's existing abilities, even when very small, is the key to achieving active partial participation. The *activity* focus of such assessments helps teachers design learning experiences that will more easily transfer to a student's flow of experience. Activities, not skills, are the real building blocks of life for all of us: yet the overwhelming disabilities of some students can encourage a focus on skill building in preparation for eventual activity participation.

## Use ongoing instructional information systems.

Meyer and Janney (1989) recommended that teachers move away from collecting trial-by-trial data, a strategy that more nearly resembles that of single-subject design research, toward data collection strategies that are formative, easy, and reflective of multiple outcomes. To this we would add that teachers should collect data that also reflect multiple perspectives. For example, existing data-collection strategies can be expanded to encourage instructional staff to rate their perception of the student's reaction to and enjoyment of the learning activity and invite their suggestions for improving both the process and the outcomes of the learning activity. The simplest version of this strategy is a blank piece of paper that prompts the instructor to briefly describe what occurred in the lesson, with an analysis of the lesson's appropriateness, effectiveness, and need for change.

Table 1
"Practicing Abilities" Examples

Student: Julie
Age: 10
Abilities Targeted for Practice: *reach/touch/push/pass; grasp/hold/release*

| Activity | Opportunity for Practice |
|---|---|
| Activity: Making fruit salad for lunch/snack | The teacher assists Julie to pick up a banana and pass it to Clark, who peels it and passes it to Dana, who begins to slice it. With support, Julie picks up and passes another banana to Clark, who peels and slices. While Clark is slicing, Dana passes his slices back to Julie, who is assisted to reach/touch/push them into a bowl held at the edge of the work surface. Julie passes an apple to Clark to slice and add to the bowl, and another to Dana, who receives insstruction on proper slicing from the teacher. Dana returns his apple slices to Julie, who is supported to reach/touch/push them into the bowl. The activity continues with additional fruits |
| Activity: Library Assistant Job | Julie and Lisa check in for their library job by signing the student assistant attendance sheet. After Lisa prints her name, Julie is assisted to reach/touch/push a name stamp. Today's assignment is to reshelve books. The teacher piles books from the cart on Julie's tray and assists her to grasp/hold/release each one as she passes it to Lisa, who reads the letter on the spine and puts it on the shelf with the same letter. Later another student assistant will insert the books in their appropriate alphabetical location on the shelf. |

| | |
|---|---|
| Activity: Math Drill | Julie is in the second grade. Tony and Clark, two of her classmates, are working on an addition and subtraction facts drill during small group time. Julie participates as the teacher's assistant. Sitting next to Julie and facing Tony and Clark, the teacher assists Julie to grasp and hold each math fact card for Tony and Clark to solve. Julie releases the cards into a box on her wheelchair tray, which she then helps the teacher put away on the shelf under the windows. |
| Activity: Cafeteria Helper | The cafeteria server places half pints of milk on Julie's tray. As primary-age students come through the line, the cafeteria server receives his/her tray from another server, adds the dessert, and assists Julie to reach/touch/push/pass the milk into the remaining square on the combination plate/tray before handing it to the student. |

**Use ongoing outcome information systems.**

No matter how well conceived and planned our educational programs may be, teachers know that things always change, usually rather quickly. Anticipated outcomes may simply not result. Because teachers rarely have the luxury of being closely involved in all instruction, they may not realize that things have changed quickly enough to make the necessary changes to maximize student learning. A simple form that collects ongoing information from employers, regular classroom teachers, and other community members might help teachers anticipate problems and needs before big issues arise while confirming that planned learning outcomes are occurring from others' points of view.

Another version of this strategy is the use of simple student and family questionnaires that generate information about family and student satisfaction with the current educational program as well as suggestions for improvements that might more closely meet family and student needs. An entire program or school might then share the information summarized from such questionnaires with families, allowing each parent to compare his/her opinions and reactions to those of other parents responding to the survey. This comparison can sometimes help parents to think in a different way about their involvement with school. Of course, a teacher can also use this concept, either in the form of a paper questionnaire or a phone interview, to access parents' perspective several times a year.

**Strategy 3: Avoiding Piecemeal Participation by Using Information from Multiple Sources for Ongoing Curricular Planning and Program Development**

The error of piecemeal participation seems to occur when teachers try to shift their program orientation to encompass an ecological/activity-based approach. Many teachers begin this change in orientation by designating one part of the school day for community instruction. This gradual approach is certainly a good strategy for beginning a programmatic revision, but too often teachers never completely revise their curriculum decision-making logic. Instead, the initial strategy of "adding on" a period of community-based instruction becomes permanently institutionalized. During the remaining periods of the day, teachers continue to teach the same developmentally derived curriculum content. The result for students is piecemeal participation.

Piecemeal participation can also occur when the different activities and routines of a student's day, however derived, are not organized to lead from one to another in a way that is sensible and meaningful to the student. Even well-conceived activity routines can be experienced by a student in a fragmented, piecemeal way. Students may not understand changes from one activity or location to the next or how instructional experiences within and outside of school are supposed to relate to each other. Instructional transitions can seem to occur out of context and routine, leaving students confused about "what's next" and "why." For students with very severe disabilities, this discontinuity may be particularly troublesome. Recognition of familiar, meaningful routines can hardly occur if such routines do not really exist. We propose two strategies: (a) merging an ecological/activity-based perspective with developmental, behavioral, adaptive, communicative, and biobehavioral perspectives, and (b) using ongoing planning and program improvement processes to help keep students' school experiences and schooling outcomes in sync.

**Merging "competing" perspectives.**

Unfortunately, traditional, developmental, and ecological/activity-based approaches to assessment and curriculum development have come to be viewed by many teachers as mutually exclusive. We believe that a strategy of careful synthesis of these "competing" perspectives both makes good educational sense and will respond to the "error" of piecemeal participation. This synthesis strategy involves two phases: (a) determining what and where to teach, and (b) determining how to teach. Decisions about what and where to teach must identify the environments and activities within which a student does or can participate in order to achieve greater actual and/or perceived competence as a consequence of instruction. That is, figuring out what to teach means identifying the ways a student's life will change from the points of view of students (where possible) and families. Procedures for identifying environmental contexts and activities are available from a number of sources (e.g., Falvey, 1989; Ferguson & Wilcox, 1987; Ford et al., 1984; Guess & Helmstetter, 1986; Sailor et al., 1989). In general, they all assist teachers to solicit information from students, families, the life-styles of nondisabled peers, community resources, and other socially significant sources to identify both a fairly extensive list of possible environments and activities within which to target instruction. This initial list is then reviewed in more detail, and a smaller priority list is selected based on additional practical realities (places and activities

logistically, temporally, and financially feasible for the program to access) and the student's repertoire (learning rate, physical and sensory abilities, understanding of events and objects, learning characteristics and needs).

Completing this selection of what and where to teach, which is grounded more in the perspectives of students and families than in that of the teachers, sets the stage for phase two: deciding how to teach, or how to implement these curricular decisions. At this point, sources of information teachers have traditionally used for deciding what and where to teach are more appropriately used. Teachers should generate and consider a variety of additional information from at least developmental, behavioral, adaptive, communicative, and biobehavioral sources for deciding how to teach. Finally, all curricular and program decision making--what, where, and how to teach--should be guided by an effort to maximize both the amount of learning that will result and the image produced by the process of instruction.

**Ongoing planning and program improvement.**

While teachers typically receive preparation in evaluation and management skills as they pertain to student progress, rarely do they also receive preparation in overall program evaluation, management, and improvement strategies. Yet being able to see and evaluate your efforts in terms of the "bigger picture" of broad schooling outcomes for students is especially effective with students who are especially difficult to teach. Some materials and professional support are emerging that address these needs for teachers (Ferguson, Flennery, & Parker, 1988; Ferguson & Parker, 1988; Fredericks & Piazza-Templeman, 1990: Goodlad, 19990; Helmstetter et al., 1987). Although strategies vary in their specifics, most involve at least the following components.

First, this kind of teacher-managed program development requires that teachers use some strategy for articulating a mission or describing the things they wish their program to accomplish. Second, teachers need a way to identify things to work on in addition to their usual duties and tasks that will move them toward attainment of at least some aspect of their mission. Often this second step results in the identification of program development goals and objectives. Third, teachers must develop some kind of practicable action plan that will prioritize and guide activity. Finally, teachers must annually reflect upon their mission or descriptions of desired program accomplishments in order to revise mission, accomplishments, goals, and action plans in response to the year's efforts and other new information or values. Whether teachers use this four-step process or some other ongoing planning procedure, the work of program management and program improvement is usually easier and more productive when done in the context of teacher work groups (Ferguson, in press) or in-service workshops and consultations (Ford et., 1984; Fredericks & Piazza-Templeman, 1990; Helmstetter et al., 1987).

### Strategy 4: Avoiding Missed Participation by Enhancing Image and Achieving Interdependence

The error of missed participation seems to occur because of an underlying confusion about the meaning of independence. Teachers design instruction to fade the person providing instructional support. Of course, this is precisely what a logic of stimulus control requires. Good instructors are always seeking to minimize their own role as the student's ability to respond to naturally occurring cues increases. It is this notion of fading the person, however, that also leads to missed participation.

There are two reasons why another person might always be present with individuals who are extremely disabled. One reason has to do with the functional impact of the person's impairments, the other with lifestyle. For example, a person who cannot see well enough to identify curb cuts or make safe judgments about when to cross a street will always need another person to accompany him or her in the community. Someone whose limbs cannot reach out far enough to open doors or select items in the cafeteria line will

also require another individual to perform these critical skills. If a person lives with family or housemates, the sharing of domestic responsibilities may require at least two members of the household to shop for weekly groceries. Shared shopping offers the opportunity for a person with very severe disabilities to depend upon their more able shopping partner to do those parts of shopping that are particularly difficult, time-consuming, or burdensome.

In situations in which the student's abilities, impairments, and life situation suggest that some performance gaps will simply not change or not need to change, teachers should shift their instructional choices to emphasize interdependence and image. Consider the following example:

Paul and his mother always do the family grocery shopping together. Since they live close to the store, they typically walk. Paul carries the two-wheel grocery cart on the back of the motorized wheelchair he is just learning to use. Paul's mother stops before crossing streets, naturally cueing Paul to stop and wait for her to begin to cross. He then follows closely alongside her to drive himself across the street. Once inside the grocery store, Paul heads for the produce section, where they always begin their 'nopping. While his mom selects other fruit, Paul selects the bananas he eats with his cereal most mornings. His mom turns the grocery cart so he can easily put the bananas in the cart. As she selects other produce, she hands it to Paul, who drops it in the baby seat section of the cart. As Paul and his mom progress through each aisle, Paul selects some items (cat food, toilet paper, ice cream, oatmeal, soup, tuna fish, cookies) and is handed others (things they need that are on high or low shelves he cannot reach, or that are too heavy), which he then drops or throws into the cart. Paul's mom selects his participation on each aisle according to three rules:
1. Paul should select items he directly uses (the cat food, ice cream, juice, soup).
2. Paul should have at least one thing on each aisle that he directly selects, and two or three he is handed to put in the cart.
3. Paul should not have to ask for help unless something unexpected occurs

(he drops something on the floor instead of in the cart).

When Paul and his mom get to the checkout line, she positions the cart so that Paul can reach the items in the baby seat part of the cart and hand them to her to put on the counter. Paul's mom usually pays for the groceries with a check while Paul holds the two-wheel cart for the person who is bagging their groceries.

Paul's teacher could arrive at the same approach to teaching grocery shopping if she had begun with the strategies already discussed. Had she completed some kind of activity-based, family-referenced assessment, she would have learned that Paul and his mom live close to a large grocery store and shop together most weeks. Careful attention to the information about Paul's motor, visual, and communication skills might have encouraged the teacher to target driving safely in the store and maximizing opportunities to practice reach/grasp/hold/release with his one "good" hand and arm. If these skills begin to improve or change, there are a variety of ways that Paul's participation might be expanded either within the context of grocery shopping or in other kinds of shopping.

Avoiding missed participation simply requires that teacher think through the following questions:

1. Is this student likely to have a person present for this activity either because of disabilities that cannot be remediated or accommodated, or because of some life-style preference?

2. What abilities can this student practice in each component of this activity?

3. How can this practice be maximized through all activity components?

4. If we maximize practice in this way, what skills might be developed that could expand this student's participation?

5. How can we maximize image, helping the student to appear, and perhaps feel less dependent and more competent?

6. How can we expand this student's cooperative and supportive relationships with others in this, and similar, settings and activities?

## Concluding Remarks

One of the lessons of the last 15 years seems to be that there are rarely single correct approaches, always correct strategies, or even useful ideas that can endure both the passage of time and the challenges posed by students with severe disabilities. It is for this reason that we have revisited the concept of partial participation 8 years after it was first advanced. Our analysis described four ways we think the notion has been misunderstood and misused, and some of the reasons this occurred. In fact, we argue that it is the very complexity of students' impairments that is the greatest source of these misunderstandings. Until we better understand the nature and meaning of teaching and learning, of inclusion and contribution for such very complicated students, we expect that these and other errors of practice will continue to occur. Nevertheless, we identify and describe strategies for responding to these error patterns that might support teachers and families as we all continue to discover the meaning of effective educational programming for these most vulnerable of our students.

\*\*\*\*\*\*\*\*

**Note:** Preparation of this manual was supported in part by grants GOO8730420 and GOO8730403 to the University of Oregon's Specialized Training Program, and grant HO 29A0039 to the University of Idaho from the U.S. Department of Education, Office of Special Education and Rehabilitative Services. However, the opinions expressed therein do not necessarily reflect the position or policy of the U.S. Department of Education and no official endorsement by the Department should be inferred.

An expanded version of this article with more specific examples and resources is available from the first author at the Specialized Training Program, University of Oregon, Eugene, OR 97403.

\*\*\*\*\*\*\*\*

# REFERENCES

Baldwin, V.I. (1976). Curriculum concerns. In M. A. Thomas (Ed.) *Hey, don't forget about me!* (pp. 64-73). Reston, VA: Council for Exceptional Children.

Barrett, B. (1979). Communitization and the measured message of normal behavior. In R. York & E. Edgar (Eds.). *Teaching the severely handicapped* (Vol. IV, pp. 301-318). Columbus, OH: Special Press.

Baumgart, D., Brown, L., Pumpian, I., Nisbet, J., Ford, A., Sweet, M., Messina, R., & Schroeder, J. (1982). Principle of partial participation and individualized adaptions in education programs for severely handicapped students. *The Journal of the Association for Persons with Severe Handicaps,* 7(2), 17-27.

Baumgart, D., Johnson, J., & Helmstetter, E., (1990). *Augmentative and alternative communication systems for persons with moderate and severe disabilities.* Baltimore: Paul Brooks Publishing Company.

Belmore, K., & Brown, I., (1978) A job skill inventory strategy designed for severely handicapped potential workers. In N. Haring & D. Bricker (Eds.) *Teaching the severely handicapped,* Vol. III (pp. 223-262). Columbus, OH: Special Press.

Brown, F., Helmstetter, E., & Guess, D. (1986). *Current best practices with students with profound disability: Are there any?* Unpublished manuscript, University Center at Binghampton, Binghampton, NY.

Brown, L., Branston, M., Hamre-Nietupski, S., Pumpian, I., Certo, N., & Gruenewald, L., (1979a) A strategy for developing chronological age-appropriate and functional curricular content for severely handicapped adolescents and young adults. *Journal of Special Education,* 13, 81-90.

Brown, L., Branston-McLean, M., Baumgart, D., Vincent, L., Falvey, M., & Schroder, J. (1979b). Using the characteristics of current and subsequent least restrictive environments in the development of content for severely handicapped students. *AAESPH Review,* 4, 407-424.

Brown, L., Falvey, M., Vincent, L., Kaye, N., Johnson, F., Ferrara-Parrish, P., & Gruenewald, I., (1980). Strategies for generating comprehensive, longitudinal, and chronological age-appropriate individualized education programs for adolescent and young adult severely handicapped students. *Journal of Special Education,* 14, 199-215.

Brown, L., Nietupski, J., & Hamre-Nietupski, S., (1976). Criterion of ultimate functioning. In M. A. Thomas (Ed.), *Hey, don't forget about me!* (pp. 2-15). Reston, VA: Council for Exceptional Children.

Cohen, M., Gross, P., & Haring, N. G. (1976). Developmental pinpoints. In N. Haring & L. Brown (Eds.), *Teaching the severely handicapped* (Vol. l, pp. 35-110). New York: Grune & Stratton.

Downing, J. (1988). Active versus passive programming: A Critique of IEP objectives for students with the most severe disabilities. *The Journal of The Association for Persons with Severe Handicaps,* 13, 197-201.

Falvey, M. A., (1989) *Community-based curriculum: Instructional strategies for students with severe handicaps* (2nd Ed.). Baltimore: Paul H. Brookes.

Falvey, M., Brown, L., Lyon, S., Baumgart, D., & Schroeder, J. (1978). Strategies for using cues and correction procedures. In W. Sailor, B. Wilcox, & L. Brown (Eds.). *Methods of instruction for severely handicapped students (pp. 109-135).* Baltimore: Paul H. Brookes Publishing Company.

Ferguson, D. L., (in press). Teacher work groups: Getting a little help from your friends. *Teaching Exceptional Children.*

Ferguson, D. L., Flannery, K. B., & Parker, R. (1988). *The elementary/secondary system: Supportive education for students with severe handicaps. Module 6a: Program and teacher development system.* Eugene, OR: Specialized Training Program, University of Oregon.

Ferguson, D. L., & Jeanchild, L. (1992). It's not a matter of method: Thinking about how to implement curricular decisions. In S. Stainback & W. Stainback (Eds.), *Adapting the regular class curriculum: Enhancing student success in inclusive classrooms (*pp. 159-174). Baltimore: Paul H. Brookes.

Ferguson, D. L., & Juniper, L. (1990). *A data-based programming approach for students with the most severe disabilities: An applied case study report.* Eugene, OR: Specialized Training Program, University of Oregon.

Ferguson, D. L., & Parker. (1988). *The Elementary/secondary system: Supportive education for students with severe handicaps. Module 3: The Classroom Management information system.* Eugene, OR: Specialized Training Program, University of Oregon (submitted).

Ferguson, D. L., & Wilcox, B. (1987). *The elementary secondary system: Supportive education for students with severe handicaps. Module I: The activity-based IEP.* Eugene, OR: Specialized Training Program, University of Oregon.

Ford, A., Brown, L., Pumpian, I., Baumgart, D., Nisbet, J., Schroeder, J., & Loomis, R. (1984). Strategies for developing individualized recreation and leisure programs for severely handicapped students. In N. Certo, N. Haring, & R. York (Eds.), *Public school integration of severely handicapped students* (pp. 245-276). Baltimore: Paul Brookes Publishing Company.

Ford, A., Schnorr, R., Meyer, L., Davern, L., Black, J., & Dempsey, P. (1989). *The Syracuse community-referenced curriculum guide for students with moderate and severe disabilities.* Baltimore: Paul H. Brookes.

Fredericks, H. D., & Piazza-Templeman, T. (1990). A generic in-service training model. In a. Kaiser & C. M. McWhorter (Eds.), *Preparing personnel to work with persons with severe disabilities* (pp. 301-317). Baltimore: Paul Brookes Publishing Company.

Goodlad, J. I. (1990). The occupation of teaching in schools. In J. I. Goodlad, R. Soder, & K. A. Sirotnik (Eds.), *The moral dimensions of teaching* (pp. 3-34). San Francisco: Jossey-Bass, Inc.

Guess, D. & Helmstetter, E. (1986). Skill cluster instruction and the individualized curriculum sequencing model. In R. H. Horner, L. H. Meyer, & H. D. Fredericks (Eds.), *Education of learners with severe handicaps: Exemplary service strategies* (pp. 221-248). Baltimore: Paul H. Brookes.

Guess, D., Mulligan-Ault, M., Roberts, S., Struth, J., Siegel-Causey, E., Thompson, B., Bronicki, G. J. & Guy, B. (1988). Implications of biobehavioral states for the education and treatment of students with the most profoundly handicapped conditions. *The Journal of the Association of Persons with Severe Handicaps,* 13, 163-174.

Hamre-Nietupski, S., Nietupski, J., Bates, P., & Maurer, S. (1982). Implementing a community-based educational model for moderately/severely handicapped students: Common problems and suggested solutions. *The Journal of the Association for the Severely Handicapped,* 7(4), 38-43.

Haring, N., & Brown, L., (1976). *Teaching the severely handicapped* (Vol. 1). New York: Grune & Stratton.

Helmstetter, E., Baumgart, D., Curry, C., Donaldson, B., Lynch, V., & Peck, C. (1987). *The Inland Northwest Consortium for severely handicapped/deaf-blind inservice training: final report.* Pullman: Washington State University.

Meyer, L., & Janney, R. (1989). User-friendly measures of meaningful outcomes: Evaluating behavioral interventions. *The Journal of the Association for Persons with Severe Handicaps, 14,* 263-270.

Meyer, L. H. (1991). Advocacy, research and typical practices: A call for the reduction of discrepancies between what is and what ought to be and how to get there. In L. H. Meyer, C. A. Peck, & L. Brown (Eds.), *Critical issues in the levels of people with severe disabilities* (pp. 629-649). Baltimore: Paul H. Brookes.

Sailor, W., Anderson, J., Halvorsen, A., Doering, K., Filler, J., & Goetz, L. (1989)*The Comprehensive local school: Regular education for all children with disabilities.* Baltimore: Paul H. Brookes.

Shane, H. C. (1979). Approaches to communication training with the severely handicapped. In R. York & E. Edgar (Eds.), *Teaching the severely handicapped* (Vol. IV, pp. 155-179). Columbus, OH: Special Press.

Switzky, H., Rotatori, A., Miller, T., & Freagon, S. (1979). The developmental model and its implications for assessment and instruction for the severely/profoundly handicapped. *Mental Retardation,* 17, 167-170.

\*\*\*\*\*\*

**About the Author:** Dianne L. Ferguson is with the Specialized Training Program, University of Oregon, Eugene, OR 97403.

Diane Baumgart is with the University of Idaho

**Source:** Reprinted with permission from the authors and from the *Journal of the Association of Persons with Severe Handicaps,* Vol. 16, No. 4, 1991, pp. 218-227. Published by The Association of Persons with Severe Handicaps, Seattle, Washington 98133-8612.

# Employer Agreement with the Americans with Disabilities Act of 1990: Implications for Rehabilitation Counseling

Jamie Satcher
Glen R. Hendren

**Abstract** ~ *Agreement with the Americans with Disabilities Act of 1990 (ADA) by the employment community may have a substantial impact on the successful implementation of this legislation. This article describes a study investigating the extent to which employers agree with this legislation and examines possible predictors of their agreement. Recommendations are provided describing how rehabilitation counselors can help employers to learn about, understand, and comply with this legislation.*

Persons with disabilities are substantially under-represented in the United States' labor force. For example, the Bureau of the Census (1987) reported that, of the 13.3 million persons with disabilities of working age in the United States, only 33.6% were participating in the labor force. For nondisabled persons between the ages of 16 and 65, the labor force participation rate was 78%. Discriminatory attitudes held by employers toward persons with disabilities have often been described as contributing to the difficulties that members of this population have experienced in achieving equal employment opportunities (Bolton & Roessler, 1985; Carrell & Heavrin, 1987; DeJong & Lifchez, 1983; Houck, 1987; Jamero, 1979; Lobed, 1985; Pati & Hilton, 1980).

Although Sections 503 and 504 of the Rehabilitation Act of 1973 mandated that agencies and businesses receiving federal funds not discriminate against qualified persons with disabilities in their employment practices and policies (Album, 1988; Susser & Jett, 1988), this legislation did not affect private-sector employers who received no federal funds. Therefore, persons with disabilities have often had no legal protection when confronted with discriminatory employment practices.

The Americans with Disabilities Act of 1990 (ADA), P. L. 101-336, is designed to ensure the integration of persons with disabilities into the mainstream of American society. This legislation prohibits discrimination against persons with disabilities in four major areas affecting the private sector: (a) employment, (b) telecommunications, (C) transportation, and (d) public services and accommodations. The employment provisions of this legislation, which will become fully effective in July, 1994, will require all employers who have more than 15 employees to provide reasonable accommodation for the known limitations of qualified persons with disabilities and to ensure that their hiring policies and practices are nondiscriminatory (Rovner, 1990).

The ADA promises an unprecedented initiative for providing equal employment opportunity for qualified persons with disabilities in private-sector employment (Doyon, 1990). Implementation of this legislation may be problematic, however, if employers do not agree with its employment provisions. According to Mithaug (1979), disability legislation does not, of itself, change responses to the efforts of persons with disabilities to achieve equal opportunity. Attitude theory indicates that, by understanding an individual's attitudes, information is gained which will help to predict that individual's behavior (Yuker, 1965). If employers do not agree with this legislation, then compliance at more than a minimal level may not be readily achieved without litigation, a process that could prove costly for both employers and persons with disabilities.

The employment community appears to be aware of the ADA and its provisions and concerned about the potential impact of litigation on their business practices (Darkery, 1990; Mandel, 1989; Millar, 1990; Murphy, Barlow, & Hatch, 1990). Knowing employers' agreement with the ADA and identifying employer characteristics predictive of their agreement may help rehabilitation counselors and persons with disabilities develop cooperative, facilitative relationships with employers as implementation of the ADA becomes a reality. The primary purpose of this study was to investigate the extent to which employers agree with the ADA and to identify possible predictors of their agreement. A secondary purpose was to determine if employers differ in their agreement with the four areas of the legislation affecting the private sector: (a) employment, (b) transportation, (c) telecommunications, and (d) public services and accommodations.

### Identification of Predictor Variables

A review of the business and human-services literature was conducted to identify variables that have been shown to affect attitudes towards and/or employment of persons with disabilities. Variables selected as predictor variables for the present study were gender (Deck, 1986; Krauft, Rubin, Cook, & Bozarth, 1976; Martin, Scalia, Gay, & Wolfe, 1982; Fonosch & Schwab, 1981; Smith, Edwards, Heinemann, & Geist, 1985), subject disability (Elston & Snow, 1986; Fish & Smith, 1983) and contact with persons who have disabilities (Antonak, 1981; Darnell, 1981; Florian, 1978; Fonosch & Schwab, 1981; Holmes & McWilliams, 1981). In this study, contact was defined as having a friend, relative, or close acquaintance with a disability.

Other variables included in the study were type of occupation, size of occupational setting, and the highest level of education of the employer. Harris and Associates 91987), Gade and Toutges (1983), and Combs (1983) found that businesses employing more than 50 employees were more likely to hire workers with disabilities than those having less than 50 employees. In this study, size of occupational setting was defined as small (less than 49

employees), medium (50-999 employees), and large (over 1000 employees). Greenwood and Johnson (1985) and Harris and Associates (1987) found that manufacturing firms were more likely to hire workers with disabilities than businesses engaged in other work activities. For this study, types of occupations were categorized as manufacturing, service, sales, or other, which included occupations not falling into the other three categories. Gade and Toutges (1983) found that college educated employers were significantly more favorable in their attitudes toward persons with disabilities than were employers having a high school diploma. In this study, educational status was defined as (a) having a high school diploma or less, or (b) having at least a four-year college degree.

### FIGURE I

### SURVEY ITEMS

1. People with physical or mental disabilities should have legal protection from discrimination when applying for jobs in private businesses.

2. Private employers should be required to make existing facilities used by employees accessible to persons with physical or mental disabilities.

3. Private employers should be required to restructure jobs, modify work schedules, or modify equipment for persons with physical or mental disabilities who are otherwise qualified.

4. Persons with physical or mental disabilities should have legal protection from discrimination by private providers of public transportation.

5. Private providers of public transportation should be required to make their facilities accessible to persons with disabilities, including those in wheelchairs.

6. Private providers of public transportation should be required to purchase only vehicles that are accessible to persons with disabilities, including those in wheelchairs.

7. Restaurants should be required to serve persons with physical or mental disabilities, regardless of disability.

8. All new office buildings should be accessible to persons with physical or mental disabilities, regardless of disability.

9. Recreational facilities should be accessible to persons with physical or mental disabilities, regardless of disability.

10. Persons with disabilities should have legal protection from discrimination when using telephone services.

11. Telephone companies should be required to pay fines if they do not make their services available for persons who use telecommunications devices for the deaf (TDD). *

12. Persons who use TDDs* should be given the same opportunities for telephone communication as persons who use voice telephones.

*A telecommunications device for the deaf (TDD) is a machine that allows persons with hearing impairments to communicate over the telephone by visual display of typed words, rather than spoken language.*

## METHODS

### Subjects

The population for this study was employers belonging to the Chambers of Commerce in three counties in the state of Mississippi. From this population, 250 employers were randomly selected for participation in the study. A survey instrument and a demographic information sheet were mailed to the employers in October, 1990. Nonrespondents were mailed a second survey after two weeks. Eighty-five (85) employers responded to the survey for a response rate of 34%.

The majority of the employers were male (89%) and more than one-half (55%) had at least a four-year college degree. A large percentage of the employers (73%) indicated that their businesses employed less than 49 employees. The overwhelming majority (96%) reported having no disability although over one-half (53%) indicated having a friend or relative with a disability. Almost one-half (49%) indicated that their primary business activity was sales whereas 13% were engaged in service occupations and 20% were engaged in manufacturing. Eighteen percent reported that their occupation did not belong to any of these categories.

### Instrumentation

Data for this study was collected using the Americans with Disabilities Act (ADA) Survey developed by Satcher and Hendren (1991). This instrument contains twelve statements about the ADA with every three statements, or subscales, representing a different area of the legislation. Participants are asked to indicate the extent to which they agree or disagree with these twelve statements using a Likert-type scale, with a rating of 1 = "Strongly Disagree" to a rating of 5 = "Strongly Agree." This instrument is scored by summing the responses to all 12 items, with the highest possible total score being 60. Scores approaching 60 indicate greater agreement with the ADA while lower scores indicate a lesser degree of agreement.

A pilot study using this instrument indicated a Cronbach's alpha reliability coefficient of .85. Subsequent factor analysis indicated that the subscales of this instrument loaded on one factor, with each subscale having a loading value of .60 or grater (Satcher & Hendren, 1991). This instrument appears to adequately measure agreement with the ADA.

### Results

In comparison to possible total scores, it appears that the employers participating in this study were relatively moderate in their agreement with this legislation ($M$ = 40.193, $SD$ = 9.348, Maximum Possible Score = 60). Determining whether gender, size of occupational setting, type of occupation, existence of subject disability, contact with persons who have disabilities, and highest level of educational attainment predicted agreement with the ADA was investigated through stepwise multiple regression analysis. Using forced entry, all of the independent variables were entered into the regression equation in six steps. The results of the regression analysis indicated that none of the independent variables accounted for a significant amount of variance in agreement with the ADA. As a group, the independent variables accounted for less than 4% of the variance in agreement with this legislation, leaving 96% of the variance unexplained.

Determining whether the employers differed in their agreement depending on the area of the legislation was answered using t-test comparisons among all possible combinations of the four major areas of the ADA. The results of this analysis are presented in Table 1.

The employment area of the ADA was agreed with significantly less than the transportation, telecommunications, and public services and accommodations areas. Both the transportation and telecommunications areas were agreed with significantly less than the public services and accommodations area.

## Discussion

The finding that the employers were only moderate in their agreement with the ADA may mean that greater efforts need to be given to disseminating information about this legislation within the employment community. Public awareness activities may be needed if both employers and the general public are to learn about, understand, and actively support the provisions of the ADA. Rehabilitation counselors can assist in promoting public awareness of this legislation by working with television and radio stations, local chambers of commerce, city and local governments, and newspapers to disseminate information about the ADA. Furthermore, rehabilitation counselors can develop informational packages describing the ADA for dissemination to employers. This means that rehabilitation counselors must become familiar with the provisions of the ADA so that they can serve as resource persons for employers and community members wanting information about this legislation.

## Table 1
## Multiple Comparisons Among ADA Areas

| Areas | N | M | SD | t | p |
|---|---|---|---|---|---|
| Emptot | 85 | 8.777 | 2.958 | | |
| Transtot | 85 | 10.376 | 2.712 | -5.94 | .000** |
| Emptot | 85 | 8.777 | 2.958 | | |
| Pubtot | 85 | 11.012 | 2.675 | -8.74 | .000** |
| Emptot | 85 | 8.777 | 2.958 | | |
| Teltot | 85 | 10.224 | 2.762 | -4.91 | .000** |
| Transtot | 85 | 10.376 | 2.712 | | |
| Pubtot | 85 | 11.012 | 2.675 | -2.49 | .015* |
| Transtot | 85 | 10.376 | 2.712 | .53 | .596 |
| Teltot | 85 | 10.224 | 2.762 | | |
| Pubtot | 85 | 11.012 | 2.675 | 3.27 | .002** |
| Teltot | 85 | 10.224 | 2.224 | | |

* p < .05        ** p < .01

| Note: | | |
|---|---|---|
| Emptot | = | Employment Total |
| Transtot | = | Transportation Total |
| Pubtot | = | Public Services and Accommodations Total |
| Teltot | = | Telecomunications Total |

Possible Total Score for Each Area = 15

It appears that many of the variables that have been shown to influence attitude toward and/or employment of persons with disabilities did not predict agreement with the ADA. This finding supports the previous work of Satcher and Hendren (1991), who found a lack of significance among predictor variables in a study of personnel management students' acceptance of the ADA and indicates that whatever agreement employers have of the ADA cannot be accounted for by the variables previously studied in acceptance of persons with disabilities. Further research is needed to identify employer characteristics which predict agreement with this legislation. As Martin & Vieceli (1988) indicated, understanding employers is critical if the rehabilitation profession is to enhance the employment of persons with disabilities in the private sector. Understanding employer characteristics which predict agreement with the ADA could help rehabilitation counselors develop and implement educational programs and job placement strategies targeting those employers most likely to be receptive to hiring, or maintaining in employment, workers with disabilities.

The finding that the employers agreed less with the employment area of the ADA than of the transportation, telecommunications, and public services and accommodations areas may mean that employers believe that persons with disabilities should have legal protection from discrimination as long as this protection does not extend to the employment community. If the rehabilitation profession is to help employers learn about, understand, and comply with the employment provisions of the ADA, it appears that educational programs specifically targeting employers need to be developed. Information that might be provided in an educational program includes: (a) definitions of disability, reasonable accommodation, qualified person with a disability, and undue hardship; (b) ADA requirements and compliance; (c) how to conduct job analysis and write accurate job descriptions; (d) costs and resources for job accommodation; (e) the impact of the ADA on preemployment medical and other screening examinations, (f) advantages of hiring persons who have disabilities, and (g) myths and facts about workers with disabilities. All of these topics fall within the expertise of rehabilitation counselors. Rehabilitation counselors and rehabilitation agencies can market this expertise to employers in the form of workshops and staff development programs. Rehabilitation counselors could also market their availability to employers as resource persons through direct marketing tactics, such as brochures mailed to employers and personal visits with employers.

## Conclusions

The Americans with Disabilities Act of 1990 is now a reality. As federal legislation protecting persons with disabilities from discrimination in private-sector employment, this legislation is enforceable and compliance will be expected of the employment community. However, compliance with the employment provisions of this legislation may likely be only at a minimally required level unless employers agree with and endorse the intent of the ADA. It appears that much is yet to be accomplished if the employment community is to agree with this legislation. With improved understanding and agreement, it is possible that implementation of the legislation will occur through cooperative planning among the rehabilitation profession, persons with disabilities, and employers.

The ADA is not rehabilitation legislation; rather, it insures the civil rights of persons with disabilities. The rehabilitation profession has, however, a responsibility to both the employment community and persons with disabilities to play a primary role in facilitating the successful implementation of this legislation by providing expertise to employers regarding how they may better serve workers with disabilities.

Further study with larger sample sizes is needed to assist the rehabilitation profession in gaining a greater understanding of employer agreement with the ADA. Also, the present study was conducted in one geographic location, limiting generalizability of the results. The present study does, however, provide an indication that the employment community may be resistant to the intent and provisions of the ADA and points out a need for developing strategies for providing information to employers about this legislation and the availability of rehabilitation counselors to assist them in meeting their responsibilities under the ADA.

\*\*\*\*\*\*\*\*

## REFERENCES

**Album, M. J. (1988).** Affirmative action and the handicapped. *Employment Relations Today, 15,* 99-106.

**Antonak, R. F. (1981).** Prediction of attitudes toward disabled persons: A multivariate analysis. *The Journal of General Psychology, 104,* 119-123.

**Bolton, B., & Roessler, R. (1985).** After the interview: How employers rate handicapped employees. *Personnel, 62*(7), 38-39.

**Bureau of the Census (1987).** Unpublished tables from March 1987 Current Population Survey. In *Chartbook on disability in the United States.* Washington, DC: National Institute on Disability and Rehabilitation Research.

**Carrell, M. R., & Heavrin, W. T. (1987).** The "handicapable" employee: An untapped potential. *Personnel, 64*(18), 40-45.

**Combs, I. H. (1983).** Hiring practices and attitudes toward handicapped individuals of companies covered under Public Law 93-112 and companies not covered under this law. *Dissertation Abstracts International, 44*(6), 1768A.

**Darkery, P. M. (1990).** The Americans with Disabilities Act: Its impact on small business. *The National Public Accountant, 35,* 42-50.

**Darnell, R. (1981).** Attitudinal dimensions of rehabilitation professionals toward disabled persons. *Dissertation Abstract International, 42,* 4210A.

**Deck, M. (1986).** Attitudes of school counselors toward the handicapped and mainstreaming. *Dissertation Abstracts International, 42,* 4804A.

**DeJong, C., & Lifchez, R. (1983).** Physical disability and public policy. *Scientific American, 248*(6), 40-49.

**Doyon, M. (1990).** The practical impact of the Americans with Disabilities Act. *Rehab* USA, (2), 14.

**Elston, R., & Snow, B. (1986).** Attitudes toward people with disabilities as expressed by rehabilitation professionals. *Rehabilitation Counseling Bulletin, 29*(4), 284-286.

**Fish, D., & Smith, S. (1983).** Disability: A variable in counselor effectiveness and attitudes toward disabled persons. *Rehabilitation Counseling Bulletin, 27*(2), 120-123.

**Florian, B. (1978).** Employers' opinions of the disabled person as a worker. *Rehabilitation counseling Bulletin, 22*(1), 38-43.

**Fonosch, G., & Schwab, L. (1981).** Attitudes of selected university faculty members toward disabled students. *Journal of College Student Personnel, 22,* 229-235.

**Gade, E., & Toutges, G. (1983).** Employers' attitudes toward hiring epileptics: Implications for job placement. *Rehabilitation Counseling Bulletin, 26*(5), 353-356.

**Greenwood, R., & Johnson, V. A. (1985).** *Employer concerns regarding workers with disabilities.* Hot Springs: Arkansas University, Arkansas Rehabilitation and Research Center.

**Harris and Associates (1987).** *The ICD survey II: Employing disabled Americans: A nationwide survey of 920 employers.* New York: Author.

**Holmes, D. A., & McWilliams, J. H. (1981).** employers' attitudes toward hiring epileptics. *Journal of Rehabilitation, 47*(2), 20-21.

**Houck, C. K. (1987).** Education and employment for the handicapped: Attitudes in the eighties. *Educational Research Quarterly, 11*(4), 23-28.

**Jamero, P. M. (1979).** Handicapped individuals in the changing work force. *Journal of Contemporary Business, 8*(4), 33-42.

**Krauft, C., Rubin, S., Cook, D., & Bozarth, D. (1976).** Counselor attitudes toward disabled persons and client program completion: A pilot study. *Journal of Applied Rehabilitation Counseling, 7*(1), 50-54.

**Lobed, H. Z. (1985).** Employing the disabled is good business. *Industry Week, 227*(2), 14.

**Mandel, S. (1989).** Disabling America. *National Review, 41*(18), 23-24.

**Martin, T. N., Scalia, V., Gay, D., & Wolfe, R. (1982).** Beginning counselors' attitudes toward disabled persons. *Journal of Rehabilitation, 13*(2), 14-16.

**Martin, T. N., & Vieceli, L. (1988).** The business of rehabilitation placement: What to understand about private employers before approaching them. *Journal of Rehabilitation, 54*(4), 49-55.

**Millar, W. H. (1990).** Lawyers' delight: Fast moving disability rights bills threaten industry with wave of litigation. Industry Week, 239, 2-3.

**Mithaug, D. E. (1979).** Negative attitudes toward hiring the handicapped: Fact or fiction? *Journal of Contemporary Business, 8*(4), 19-26.

**Murphy, B. S., Barlow, W. C., & Hatch, D. D. (1990).** ADA signed into law. *Personnel Journal, 69,* 18-20.

Pati, G. C., & Hilton, E. F. (1980). A comprehensive model for a handicapped affirmative action program. *Personnel Journal, 59*(2), 99-108.

Rovner, J. (1990). Provisions: Americans with Disabilities Act. *Congressional Quarterly,* July, 2437-2444.

Satcher, J. F., & Hendren, G. R. (1991). Acceptance of the Americans with Disabilities Act of 1990 by persons preparing to enter the business field. *Journal of Applied Rehabilitation Counseling, 22*(2), 15-18.

Smith, C., Edwards, J., Heinemann, A., & Geist, C. (1985). Attitudes toward and performance evaluations of workers with disabilities. *Journal of Applied Rehabilitation Counseling, 16*(1), 39-41.

Susser, P. A., & Jett, D. A. (1988). Accommodating handicapped workers: The extent of the employer's obligation. *Employment Relations Today, 15*, 113-120.

Yuker, H. E. (1965). Attitudes as determinants of behavior. *Journal of Rehabilitation, 31*(6), 15-16.

****** 

**About the Author:** The first author, Dr. Jamie Satcher, is currently an assistant professor of rehabilitaiton counseling at the University of Alabama. He also serves as project director of the LD career project, a program to provide career planning and placement services for college students with learning disabilities. Dr. Satcher received his doctorate from Mississippi State University. He has previously worked as a rehabilitation counselor, vocational evaluator, and rehabilitation administrator. Correspondence may be directed to University of Alabama, Box 870231, Tuscaloosa, AL 35487-0231

**Source:** Reprinted with permission from *The Journal of Rehabilitation*, Vol. 58, No. 3, Jul/Aug/Sep/ 1992, pp. 13-17. Published by National Rehabilitation Association, Alexandria, Virgina.

# Away With Barriers
Mary Lord

**Employers can satisfy the new disabilities act without spending a mint. Here's a guide:**

Business owners from beauticians to restauranteurs are in a sweat. On July 26, the provisions of the Americans with Disabilities Act kick in, and federal hot lines are being swamped by calls from concerned managers.

While few employers quarrel with the ADA's aim of integrating some 43 million disabled Americans into the workplace, many are uncertain about their precise obligations in achieving it. Can companies be sued if they fail to install elevators or undertake other costly renovations? What if reassigning a disabled employee violates union seniority rules? To anxious retailers like Mike Madison, who is trying to determine whether he must build ramps and new restrooms in his Madison's Home Furnishings stores, in Boise and Nampa, Idaho, the law seems maddeningly vague. "I'd like to accommodate everyone," he says, "but not to the detriment of my business."

**No sweat.** Phil Kosak, co-founder of Carolina Fine Snack Foods in Greensboro, N.C., isn't worried. Four years ago, chronic absenteeism and carelessness nearly destroyed the firm just as it landed a lucrative contract to supply gourmet pork skins for the Republican National Convention. Instead of closing shop, Kosak hired a disabled man whose exemplary performance inspired the rest of the work force into shaping up. Today, half the firm's 18 employees have impairments - a track record that helped Carolina Fine Snack Foods earlier this year become the first small business to win accolades from the President's Committee on Employment of People with Disabilities. "Any manager who does not look first for a disabled person," says Kosak, "is leaving gold sitting on the back porch."

When it comes to complying with the ADA, most employers expect to pay a fortune, not find one. Passed virtually unopposed in 1990 over the protests of small business, the law prohibits discrimination against individuals with infirmities ranging from AIDS and epilepsy to paraplegia and schizophrenia. It also compels companies with 25 or more employees to make "reasonable accommodations" for qualified workers and job applicants with impairments. (Firms with 15 to 24 employees have until 1994 to comply.) Another set of provisions, which took effect in January, requires any enterprise that serves the public to improve the accessibility of such areas as store aisles, health clubs, even doctors' waiting rooms.

ADA experts argue that employers actually have great flexibility because of the statute's ambiguities. "I tell businesses they've got to use common sense," says Liz Savage, a sight-impaired attorney and training director for the Disability Rights Education and Defense Fund in Washington, D.C. "If I sued every hotel that didn't have a large-print phone list in the room, I'd be spending all my time in litigation. Life is tough enough."

Contrary to their worst fears, business owners find that compliance can prove cheap and easy. For Sally Tholl, owner of the Step Five Design beauty salon in Ballston Spa, N.Y., it means sending someone out to assist cancer patients into the shop. Instead of splurging on Braille menus, which fewer than 20 percent of all sight-impaired Americans can read, restaurants can have a waiter read the menu aloud. Cup dispensers provide an inexpensive alternative to lowering drinking fountains for wheelchair-bound employees, while simply insulating exposed hot-water pipes under bathroom sinks allows paraplegics to wash up without scalding their legs. Indeed, according to a survey by the Job Accommodation Network, one of several federally funded ADA clearinghouses, 31 percent of all modifications cost nothing and two thirds can be done for under $500.

Of course, many businesses spend more - a lot more. Alan Armstrong, owner of the Tiffany Dining Place Restaurant in Blue Bell, Pa., has hired architects to devise ways of improving accessibility. Modifications include, widened doors in the newly renovated $13,000 powder room, plus a grab bar in the men's toilet. But because the corridors are too short and the ceilings too low, building a ramp into the dining room seems infeasible. For now, customers are wheeled through the kitchen. "We've tried to do everything as environmentally and as politically correct as we can," says Armstrong. "But in this market, you can't afford everything."

Nor does the law demand it. The ADA explicitly makes exceptions for "undue hardship", for instance, while tax credits and deductions are available to help defray costs. Employers need not compromise safety standards either - or even give preference to a job candidate with a disability. "This is not a quota statute or an affirmative-action statute" assures Jonathan Mook, a law partner at Ogletree, Deakins, Nash, Smoak & Stewart in Washington, D.C. and author of a new ADA litigation guide. "It's a totally interactive process between people with disabilities, employers and employees."

Carolina Fine Snack Foods' experience demonstrates just how profitable that dialogue can prove. Before owner Kosak hired David Bruton, a sight-impaired man with severe learning disabilities who showed up at a local job fair, personnel problems were sapping the bottom line. Employees sometimes showed up drunk - if at all. Kosak found himself replacing warehouse hands every three weeks. Productivity was dismal, with miscounts and sloppy shipments the norm. "We were at our wits' end just trying to maintain a basic, semi-skilled work force," recalls Kosak.

David Bruton changed all that. Armed with a large-number calculator, which he brought himself, he kept track of outbound freight more accurately than had any previous able-bodied monitor. He greeted customers, established rapport and improved the customers' view of the company. Such diligence prompted other employees to spruce up their performance. Efficiency zoomed. Absenteeism plunged to almost zero as morale soared; the personnel director even taught herself sign language.

**Creativity counts.** The bottom-line lesson was not lost on Kosak, who subsequently hired eight other disabled individuals. "There are still problems, but they are trivial compared with what I had before." he says.

As Carolina Fine Snack Foods learned, adjustments need not prove burdensome. Most simply entailed a little ingenuity and some extra training time. For instance, Kosak's learning-impaired employees have difficulty counting. To enable such workers to load the proper number of snack packs into a carton, Kosak simply shows them how a carton full of bags looks, and they are able to learn by imitation. Forms are simplified so that mentally disabled workers can keep track of inventory. "Employers are just afraid of taking the time to be a little bit creative," says Kosak.

Several recent surveys bear that out. A study conducted last month by the labor-law firm Jackson, Lewis, Schnitzler & Krupman found that 71 percent of the companies polled had set aside no funds for compliance. Of firms with more than 500 employees contacted in April by Buck Consultants, the New York-based benefits experts, just slightly more than half had reviewed or modified such personnel-selection criteria as employment tests.

To assuage corporate concerns and ease compliance, the government has earmarked more than $8 million to establish training programs, hot lines and information clearinghouses (see "Common Sense Changes" at end of article) Response time may be slow, however. The Equal Employment Opportunity Commission, the lead enforcer of the ADA workplace provisions, currently fields more than 1,000 requests a day for publications (compared with 55 each day last year), and is struggling to whittle down its response time to four days.

Community groups that represent the disabled and trade associations also can provide a wealth of ideas on modifications. The Building Owners and Managers Association International in Washington, D.C. for example, has boiled 315 pages of regulations into a 325 item checklist of physical alterations. The Council of Better Business Bureaus in Arlington, Va., in addition to tracking down scammers who charge high fees for phony ADA certification, recently developed inexpensive compliance tip sheets for six industries, including retail outlets and fitness clubs.  The Council also plans to offer mediation services to give employers and disabled employees an alternative means of settling discrimination complaints.

Though the law does not require them to go out and recruit, business owners can tap local agencies for talent as well.  Many of the 6,000 disabled individuals hired by Pizza Hut over the last seven years were aggressively recruited at vocational and rehabilitation centers.

For all the  brouhaha over physical modifications, it is the psychological adjustments required under the ADA - from application procedures to employment practices - that could prove the bigger legal challenge.  For instance,  simply giving a telephone number  to call in a want ad may discriminate against individuals with hearing or speech impairments;  ADA experts advise giving applicants the option to write for interview.  Du Pont, considered one of the country's most sensitive employers, changed its rules to allow new hires to use any photo identification instead of a driver's license, since that would exclude people with sight impairments, cerebral palsy or a host of other disabilities.

**Snack breaks.**  Many adjustments are less obvious.  Under the ADA, a boss who tries to fire a diabetic for eating on the job risks trouble;  if food poses a health or safety problem, the company can allow for breaks and offer a separate room for snacking. Employers cannot inquire into an applicant's past treatment for alcohol abuse - although drug testing remains permissible.  Even the legal profession has had its fingers rapped; recently, a lawyer with learning disabilities won the right to take the New York bar examination in a separate room and over four days instead of two.

Business owners may have a thorny time trying to determine whether a job applicant's health can keep him from performing essential tasks.  The ADA forbids employers from asking about a job applicant's disabilities - even if they are germane to the job.  Thus, a warehouse operator would be on safer legal ground to inquire if a prospective stevedore can lift 100 pounds rather than

quizzing him on back problems.  Companies also cannot refuse to hire an individual for fear his disability, or a family member's will boost the cost of the firm's health insurance. However, an employer need not bolster that individual's benefits package or make special allowances for someone caring for a sick spouse.

Ultimately, the courts will have to settle many of the compliance questions now troubling employers.  But if Carolina Fine Snack Food's experience is any indication, lawyers don't have to be the only group to profit.

********

## COMMON -SENSE CHANGES

The Americans with Disabilities Act asks firms to treat the disabled fairly.  That doesn't mean spending a bundle, as these examples show.

### Water fountains:

*Conventional wisdom:  Lower the fountains so they are accessible to people in wheelchairs.  Simple solution:  Put cup dispensers at waist level.*

### Want ads:

*Conventional wisdom:  Help-wanted ads that list only phone numbers discriminate against the hearing impaired, so companies should buy special telecommunications devices for the deaf (TDD).  Simple solution: Rephrase the ad to tell applicants they can also write to request an interview.*

### Manuals and menus:

*Conventional wisdom:  Publish Braille editions of, say, menus or company handbooks. Simple solution: Ask a staffer to read to blind customers or colleagues, or put information on audio cassettes.*

**Doors:**

*Conventional wisdom: Make employment offices accessible by installing automatic doors. Simple solution: Install a doorbell and make a staffer responsible for answering.*

## WHERE TO GO FOR HELP

Business owners seeking information on the Americans with Disabilities Act can check these free resources:

**Department of Justice.**

*Fields questions on compliance, 11 a.m. to 5.p.m. weekdays, P.O.Box 66118, Washington, DC 20035; (202) 514-0301; (202) 514-0383 (TDD)*

**Equal Employment Opportunity Commission.**

*Provides hot-line assistance, employer manuals and posters. 1801 L Street N.W., Washington, DC 20507; (800) 669-3362; (800) 800-3302 (TDD)*

**Jobs Accommodation Network.**

*Experts on call 8 a.m. to 8 p.m. Monday-Thursday (to 5 p.m. Fridays) for advice on workplace modifications. West Virginia University, Morgantown, WV 26506; (800) 232-9675*

**Council of Better Business Bureaus.**

*Easy ideas for auto dealers, retailers and other enterprises. Write to 4200 Wilson Boulevard, Suite 800, Arlington, VA 22203, or call local chapter*

**Disability Rights Education and Defense Fund.**

*Advice on training programs, 1633 Q Street N.W.; Washington, DC 20009; (800) 466-4232.*

********

**Source:** Reprinted with permission from *US News and World Report,* July 20, 1992, pp.60-63. Copyright © July 20, 1992, U.S. News & World Report, Washington, DC 20037-1196.

# Open Your Doors to Disabled Workers
Elaine Johnson

*Here's how to revamp your hiring practices to meet ADA guidelines:*

Vincent Fogarty's company, Project Design Inc. in Conyers, GA., makes rough-textured tiles used in access ramps and other safety devices mandated by the Americans with Disabilities Act. However, not only does Fogarty make products that help persons with disabilities; he wants to hire them as well.

Project Design is looking for workers with disabilities to fit all job categories; machine operators, shipping and handling, materials handling, assembly and packing, and secretarial and reception, Fogarty says. "I would like to hire disabled people," he says. "I would like to give them a chance."

By actively recruiting workers with disabilities, Fogarty goes above and beyond the requirements of the ADA, the sweeping legislation that went into effect in July 1992. Project Design represents "the first case I've seen of total compliance from the ground up," says Wesley A. Godwin, president of the Deventer Group, and ADA-consulting firm that worked with Fogarty to set up hiring procedures and identify physical accommodations required by the law.

## Most Employers Affected by ADA
While some employers might not respond to the ADA with Fogarty's zeal, the vast majority are required to comply with its mandates. Yet, months after the law went into effect, many businesses remain confused about its implications for the hiring and accommodation of employees with disabilities.

Simply put, the ADA requires employers with 25 or more employees (the law will extend to companies with 15 or more employees in 1994) to make reasonable accommodations for qualified applicants or employees with disabilities. Contrary to a widespread misunderstanding, the law does not compel businesses to hire or accommodate someone who can't do the job.

"The ADA is not an affirmative-action law," says Theodore J. Ronca, president and CEO of Workers' Compensation Claims Control Co., New York. "People with disabilities are allowed to compete on equal footing, but not preferred footing. It's not true that you have to hire people who can't perform."

In barring discrimination against the estimated 43 million Americans with physical or mental disabilities, the ADA has obligated employers to carefully reevaluate long-held hiring and employment practices.

## Reconsider Hiring Criteria
Job-application forms, interview questions, selection criteria, testing procedures, medical-examination policies, disability and retirement plans all are seen in a new way in light of the ADA. Under its stiff mandates, even a written job application can be discriminatory.

"If the job doesn't require reading, a written job application discriminates against dyslexics," explains John N. Shanks II, an attorney with Buschmann, Carr and Shanks, PC. To comply with the ADA, an employer would have to allow applicants with dyslexia to fill out the form verbally or make some other accommodations.

Mine-field navigation may seem easier than avoiding these missteps. Consultants and lawyers agree that employers can go a long way toward ADA compliance merely by establishing some basic procedures for the hiring and employment of persons with disabilities.

## Start With the Written Job Description
"Most employers can comply with minimal effort, particularly those with extensive safety programs," says Thomas D. Schneid, an attorney and associate professor in the Department of Loss Prevention and Safety at Eastern Kentucky University. "The key is for employers to identify essential elements.

If they've already done a job-hazard analysis, they aren't starting from scratch. There's a lot of the same information on both."

Written job descriptions that outline both the essential and marginal functions of each position are a key first step, since the ADA states that a person with disabilities must be able to perform only the essential functions of a job, with or without reasonable accommodations. "There's no requirement that the job functions be written - it's simply the first line of defense and a wise practice," says Schneid.

Because many employers have never considered jobs in terms of essential and marginal functions," I strongly advise employers to base their job descriptions on what they actually see," says Ronca. "Take video cameras and photograph workers on busy shifts. Employers should make sure that they observe workers really performing a function on the job." Once the job descriptions are written, employers may want to ask agencies that train the disabled for their input.

A team approach, similar to that used to involve workers in plant safety programs, also can gather information about job functions, Schneid says. "Companies can use the same [safety] teams for writing job descriptions. The key is to use what you have and modify it."

Software programs can help smaller companies with limited personnel and resources. The Deventer Group, for example, worked with Knowledge Point, a software company, to develop a package of 2,400 canned job descriptions that can be written or modified according to a company's particular needs.

Employers should provide written descriptions of every job - from chief executive to the lowliest mailroom attendant, advises Godwin of Deventer. "In Chicago, there was a recent lawsuit filed by an executive of a company when the board let him go after he got cancer. It's very important to have a description for every job, even the higher positions."

In the event of such a lawsuit, a written job description helps determine whether or not an employee can continue to perform the essentials of the job.

## Treat Interviews with Kid Gloves

Similarly, the job description can serve as the basis for evaluating an applicant's abilities during the sensitive application and interview process - a process fraught with the potential for discrimination.

"Where employers are getting into problems is when someone walks in with a visible disability and the employer asks the interviewee about it," Schneid says. "That in and of itself could be discriminatory. It shouldn't be part of the hiring criteria. You can only ask if the applicant can perform essential functions of the job."

## Questions to Avoid at All Costs

Other questions, including many that were once standard on job applications and during interviews for years, could similarly leave a company vulnerable to a discrimination suit:

- Have you ever had or been treated for any of the following diseases or conditions?
- Please list any conditions or diseases you've been treated for in the last three years.
- Have you ever been hospitalized and if so, why?
- Have you ever been treated by a psychiatrist or psychologist?
- Have you been treated for a mental condition?
- How many days are you absent due to illness?
- do you have any physical defects that might preclude you from performing certain jobs?
- Have you ever filed a workers compensation claim?
- Have you ever been treated for drug addiction or alcoholism?

To stay within the letter of the law, Schneid recommends that employers draw up a series of interview questions - carefully screened to be nondiscriminatory - that are posed to all applicants.

"If you limit yourself to asking people what they *can* do, you've gone a long way to show you're not discriminatory," Ronca says.

Employers may ask applicants to demonstrate their abilities - typing proficiency, for example. "Employers are permitted to see if a person can perform an essential function, as long as the applicants aren't [asked to submit to] medical tests," Ronca says. "Asking someone to take a job test is not asking them about disability. It's asking about ability."

## Auxiliary Aids Lend a Hand

Some applicants with disabilities may require an auxiliary aid in order to perform an aptitude test - a so-called "reasonable accommodation" which the ADA mandates employers to provide.

Many employers handle this requirement by help-wanted ads or applications that state that applicants who require an aid should contact the employer in advance, Schneid says.

"They don't necessarily have to have this equipment on hand - the employer can borrow it." The Equal Employment Opportunity Commission's technical-assistance manual tells where to find this equipment.

## Hold Off on Medical Examinations

Unlike aptitude tests and drug testing (which is also allowed under the ADA), medical examinations aren't permitted until after the employer makes a formal job offer, and then only to determine whether a person can perform the essential functions of the job.

"The job of the doctor who performs the post-hire physical is limited to advising the employer about the individual's abilities and limitations as they relate to a specific job, and whether the individual meets health-and-safety requirements," says Shanks. "This isn't a fishing expedition. The doctor must know about the essential functions of the job."

Once again, a written job description can provide a basis for the physician's assessment of whether or not a candidate is medically capable of performing the job.

"There are computer programs that will help the physician and managers determine which jobs a person can do and what restrictions there are," says Dr. Howard Sandler, president of Sandler Occupational Medical Associates Inc. "The physician must be the ultimate decision-maker, recommending whether a person can do a job with or without

accommodation. Then it's up to the employer to take that information and sit down with the employee."

If the results of the medical exam are unfavorable, employers must give candidates an opportunity to answer the concerns raised by the exam, and to suggest a "reasonable" accommodation that would allow them to perform the job.

Unfortunately, the ADA doesn't give employers definitive guidelines to determine whether an accommodation is reasonable, other than to state that it shouldn't impose an "undue hardship."

Employers have to be sure that if they deny employment, they can document their reasons, based on 'reasonable business necessity,' " Godwin says. "What is 'undue hardship' is a gray area. It depends on the size of the employer, the history of the job and the incumbents who have held it."

Schneid notes that "the burden of proof is on the employer to prove that it costs too much. You must document all bids and assessments and document all accommodations requested by applicants or current employees. You should also document what's provided or why you failed to accommodate them."

## What's Reasonable in Accommodations

The concept of "reasonable accommodations" strikes fear in the hearts of many employers, who envision a potentially devastating impact on the bottom line. Godwin points out that ADA allows more latitude than many employers might suspect.

"The government says that the priorities are parking places, access to the building including a curb ramp and wide doorways, and the use of the facilities, goods and services," Godwin says. He cites an example of a small, privately held clothing store for which installing restroom facilities for persons with disabilities would be an economic hardship.

"If there isn't enough money or space to bring the bathroom up to code, the store owner can go back to his or her policies and procedures and state that no client or customer is allowed to use the bathroom, that it's for employees only," Godwin says.

Even if the store then hires an employee with disabilities, it may not be necessary to bring the restroom up to code, he says. "The law states that if the employee is able to negotiate the barrier and says that he or she doesn't need an accommodation, it's okay."

## Identify a Direct Threat

Apart from undue hardship, the only other acceptable grounds for withdrawing an offer of employment, under the ADA, is if the employment of a candidate with disabilities would result in a significant material risk of harm to the candidate, co-workers or the community, which can't be accommodated by some type of protective equipment.

"If you, as an employer, evaluate a person as a direct threat to him or herself or fellow workers, you're not obligated to hire that person," Shanks says. "A doctor who informs you of this must show that the exclusion is based on 'the most current medical knowledge and the best available objective evidence about this individual.' It's very touchy."

In this regard, the ADA exacts a narrower test than the traditional legal grounds of increased risk of injury. "The test isn't increased risk of harm, it's a direct threat of injury, which is defined as a high probability of imminent harm in the immediate future," says Jeffrey C. Napolitano, an attorney with Sutherland, Juge, Horack & Dwyer, P.L.C.

## Keep Medical Info Under Wraps

No matter what the medical examination reveals, employers must take care to keep the information confidential. This means that medical information should be separated from the personnel file and kept under lock and key. Only those employees identified by the EEOC - first-aid personnel, supervisors and those dealing with workers' compensation claims - should be allowed access.

As a further safeguard against leaks of confidential information, Shanks advises employers to keep a log of who has access to the company's medical files.

Careful maintenance and control of medical files, in addition to other recommendations for ADA implementation,

will hold to a minimum an employer's exposure to the lawsuits and claims that have mushroomed since the law went into effect.

Statistics for the fiscal year that ended September 30, 1992 - comprising only the first three months of the ADA - indicate the EEOC recorded 774 ADA - related claims. "The EEOC takes the lead in investigating allegations," explains Napolitano. "If the organization feels the claim has merit, it will prosecute."

## The Cost of Noncompliance

Decisions against employers who run afoul of the ADA range from reinstatement with back pay or rehiring to compensatory and punitive damages. Depending on the employer's size, damages can range from $50,000 to $300,000, although word on the street indicates that the range will soon reach "unlimited" status, Napolitano says.

How can you be certain that your company won't get stung? "People can spend a fortune on this when they really don't have to," says Sandler. "If you try to do the right thing and have laid out a written program and document what you're doing, you'll be okay. Big companies have to be very careful to stay consistent. Human resources personnel, all managers and health care professionals all have to sing from the same hymnal."

Schneid recommends that employers establish an audit mechanism by which they examine their compliance efforts on a periodic basis. Changes in company personnel and interpretations of the ADA could have a significant impact.

"Employers should acquire and read the ADA and interpretations by the EEOC and other agencies," he says. "Since this is a growing area of case law, watch for those decisions. A lot of employers are naming an individual to identify these areas of interest and follow developments. You may want to designate an individual as your own ADA expert. This could be someone from the safety or human resources departments, or legal counsel."

Experts also recommend companies analyze their operations and identify applicable areas - such as parking lots and access ways - as well as practices, policies and procedures that might require modification under the ADA.

Document all analysis in detail. While not required by the ADA, a plan of action for personnel evaluation and bringing the physical plant up to code, complete with completion dates for each phase, is a start. Also, the EEOC would see these actions as indications of good faith, Schneid says. "If someone files a claim against you, this gives you a game plan to work from."

Schneid also recommends that employers review collective bargaining agreements, employment agency contracts and other contractual agreements to make sure that they comply with the ADA and to document any modifications required.

"If you can show you're making a good faith effort to comply by reviewing and creating job descriptions, and involving medical, human resources and legal experts, it would go a long way in the eyes of the EEOC, " Shanks says. "In my conversations with the EEOC, they're more interested in getting compliance than in filing lawsuits."

Yet, Sandler cautions employers against getting so caught up in the letter of the law that they forget the spirit of it. "Treat people with respect, look at what they can do, offer them jobs and discuss reasonable accommodations," he says. "People with disabilities don't want a job where they'll hurt themselves or someone else. They'll work with you."

Godwin ran across one of the best examples of this in southern Georgia, at a small country store that had no resources or funds to implement a sophisticated ADA program.

"The store had a cardboard sign out front that said, 'If you need help, honk,' " he says. "That's equivalent facilitation, because they're saying, 'We recognize you can't get in here, that we have a problem, but we'll help you.' "

## List of Sources:
Vincent Fogarty, vice-president and CEO, Project Design Inc. (USA); Wesley A. Godwin, president, The Deventer Group; Jeffrey Napolitano, attorney, Sutherland, Juge, Horack & Dwyer P.L.C.: Theodore J. Ronca, president and CEO, Workers' Compensation Claims Control Co. of New York; Dr. Howard M. Sandler, president, Sandler Occupational Medical Associates Inc.: Thomas D. Schneid, associate professor/attorney, department of loss prevention and safety, Eastern Kentucky University; John N. Shanks II, attorney, Buschmann, Carr & Shanks P.C.

********

**Source:** Reprinted with permission from *Safety and Health,* December 1991, pp. 30-34. Published by National Safety Council, Chicago, IL. 60611

# 7 Legal and Ethical Issues and Disability

In the second chapter of this edition, professor Bryant outlined the religious concerns pertinent to the study of disability. From our major religious traditions, attitudes emerged which define people with disabilities in a condescending perspective. People with disabilities were traditionally viewed as being associated with sin and at best were entitled to "charity". The concepts of integration, empowerment, and advocacy were foreign to the way this group was viewed or treated.

Since the 50s and particularly since the late 80s people with disabilities have accomplished major strides in many segments of society. Motivated by the accomplishments of Helen Keller and Franklin D. Roosevelt, a major change in orientation has evolved which affects people with disabilities and most segments of society. As mentioned before, George Bush took advantage of the concerns of people with disabilities by promising them the Americans with Disabilities Act - a document which legislated the integration of 34 million Americans with disabilities into American society. This adopted legislative document defines what is *supposed* to happen but it is the adaptation of documents by people in society in terms of the value system that lays the ground work for legitimate integration of people with disabilities.

George Bush in his first presidential election was successful in garnering the majority of support from the American disabled population. The election of the president illustrated the potential for the use of power by people with disabilities. Traditionally this power had not been harnessed as most people with disabilities focused primarily on their own individual disabilities. Therefore, this group tended to neglect the power potential that could be used by uniting and organizing in large numbers to obtain the social change they sought. Under the direction of Evan Kemp and the Equal Employment Opportunity Commission (EEOC), the emergence of the ADA signified to the disabled, not only in the US but in many other jurisdictions, that legitimate integration of people with disabilities in all aspects of society was not only a dream which became a goal, but also a legitimate document of public policy that could be translated into reality. The ADA continues to be the cornerstone of disability related legislation that will bring about the future integration of people with disabilities in all societies.

The ADA and other legislative initiatives serve to establish human rights for persons with disabilities. However, the establishment of these legal requirements is only a first, although major step. The translation of policy into public will is the vital goal. People with disabilities in many societies continue to encounter barriers as a result of the consequences of diseases such as AIDS, traditional patterns of prejudice and discrimination which have stifled the acceptance and integration of people with disabilities, and economic recessions and depressions which have limited the access of this group into many realms of society.

In his article *Human Rights for Persons with Disabilities*, David Baker illustrates that "While the initiatives of local, national, and international cross-disability consumer organizations and other advocacy groups have clearly had an impact in recent years, North America's poor legislative record stands as a grim reminder of how much more remains to be done by disabled people in the legislatures and in the courts." In the last two decades people with disabilities have made substantial gains in all segments of society and "it is to be hoped that positive change will accelerate as the consumer movement of disabled persons becomes stronger and more effective."

Jerome Bickenbach in the article, *AIDS as Disability,* confirms that the most dramatic concerns about disability in contemporary society have evolved since the late 70s with the emergence and ramifications of Acquired Immune Deficiency (AIDS). The myths that have emerged concerning this twentieth century plague have evolved patterns of prejudice and discrimination in the treatment of people with AIDS bearing marked similarity to the treatment of lepers in the Biblical tradition. As Bickenbach demonstrates, AIDS "...is a handicap that results from a life-threatening, as yet incurable, and contagious disease syndrome. The concerns for public health and safety for all and the issues of equality are at the forefront of discussions for social policy planning. "When the stakes are high," the author states, "...we cannot afford our cherished political values: short of medical certainty, as a matter of policy, we should always err on the side of caution and put considerations of equality in abeyance. The dilemma that a widespread, contagious disease poses for all of society is frightening and leaves many challenging questions unanswered in the growing body of law surrounding disability.

David Coulter in his article *Beyond Baby Doe: Does Infant Transplantation Justify Euthanasia?* explores the ramifications of the advancement of medical technology and its potential ability to save the lives of some individuals through fetal tissue transplantation by terminating the lives of infants born with severe disabilities. He effectively raises the ethical concerns of the medicalized killing which developed in the era of Nazi Germany and he maintains that the ultimate resolution of the question posed by this article requires that "continued vigilance and advocacy for fulfillment of defined requirements are the challenges that must be met by those who seek to protect the rights and interests of persons with severe disabilities."

Marcia Rioux's three-part synopsis, *Rights, Justice, Power* is based on a model for justice leading to community living and inclusion and is adapted from her forthcoming book, *The Equality-Disability Nexus.* Rioux maintains "It is impossible to win battles and lose wars. One of the great challenges of social movements is to recognize that incremental reforms are not ends in themselves. They are simply part of a continuum of change that leads to a broader objective of the movement." This author concludes the first segment of her analysis by stating that "this new agenda (the inclusion of those with disabilities in all activities) based on the equality-disability nexus and promoting the goals of rights, justice and power provides a set of guidelines against which change can be evaluated over the next few years. In Part II, Rioux points out that not only is it a moral imperative to ensure that all people are fully participating citizens in society, but it is now a legal imperative as well. The difficulty is the time it takes society to alter ways of thinking so that social, legal and economic benefits are provided in reality, not just in principle. And in Part III, Rioux challenges the uses and context of technological developments which create special problems for the ideology of "respect for persons". The author feels that new developments in behaviour modification technology and reproductive technology need a great deal more scrutiny and regulation where the rights of people with disabilities are concerned.

Sonja Feist examines the ethical and legal concerns around confidentiality issues that arise for service providers who work with and assist people with AIDS in the article, *Ethical and Legal Rights of Persons with AIDS: Confidentiality Issues.* Since there are no clear guidelines for determining whether confidentiality should be breached and at present, there are no legal cases to define or guide the service provider in this dilemma, it remains that the two principles of beneficence and nonmaleficence are the only two ways the industry might consider ethical decision-making in this area.

Further discussion of appropriate ethical decision-making for rehabilitation counselors is presented in the article *Applying Ethical Principles in Rehabilitation Counseling,* by authors John Howie, Eugenie Gatens-Robinson, and Stanford E. Rubin. Five ethical principles are outlined and discussed in an effort to promote greater understanding of the job activity of rehabilitation counselors. As the authors conclude, "The ethical principles of beneficence, nonmaleficence, autonomy, fidelity, and justice are general guidelines that arise from our experience of trying to live well together."

Legal and ethical issues concerning disability will continue to emerge as a consequence of the changing values and laws that are adapted by society. Inevitably the disabled like other dispossessed minorities before them will encounter and surmount the barriers that have frustrated and continue to frustrate their integration into their respective societies. People and groups who advocate for change leading to greater equality for all, no doubt often feel justifiably hampered and challenged to their limits when confronting long held traditional values and beliefs which are exclusionary. However, as we can see by the articles in this chapter, and indeed throughout the book, great achievements and gains have been made because of the determination of people from all walks of life who have been touched by some form of disability and who have worked to achieve a proper place in society for this previously disadvantaged group.

# Human Rights For Persons With Disabilities
David Baker

For many years, persons with disabilities have been regarded as objects of pity whose needs would be met out of acts of individual charity. While charity remained a pervasive factor in their lives, the rise of the modern welfare state led to the introduction of publicly funded health, welfare and social services. The emphasis remained upon the incapacity and dependence of persons with disabilities.

Most recently, members of disadvantaged groups, such as members of visible minorities, women and the disabled community, have demanded and won legal recognition of their human rights. In practice, this has meant the legally mandated removal of barriers which have the effect of preventing members of these groups from pursuing their ambitions and their potential. Within a pluralistic society, the emphasis shifted to recognizing disabled people's capacity and encouraging their independence.

The shift has been reflected in the growing influence of law on the day to day life of disabled persons. In Canada, this movement is most clearly symbolized by the inclusion of equality guarantees for persons with disabilities in its Constitution: the first country in the world to do so. More recently, the *Americans with Disabilities Act* was signed into law by former President George Bush. It provides a number of systemic reforms in areas such as accessible transportation and telephone message relay systems for the deaf. It has also given individuals the right to demand that accommodations be made to their particular circumstances in important areas such as employment and access to public services. In countries such as Germany and Japan, disabled people have a systemic right to a significant number of jobs, high quality job training, and public support for job accommodations.

These laws reflect how the new found political muscle of the disabled community has been effective in changing public attitudes.

One should never underestimate the importance of what a well organized consumer movement can achieve at the ballot box. Take the 1988 United States Presidential election as an example. Early in the campaign Vice-President George Bush trailed Governor Dukakis in the polls. Bush announced his support for the *Americans with Disabilities Act*. According to pollster Louis Harris, between 40 and 60 percent of his eventual margin of victory was due to the changed voting patterns of the disabled electorate, attributable to this announcement. Not surprisingly, following his election, President Bush moved promptly to deliver on a campaign promise which figured so prominently in the outcome of the election.

Traditional legal analyses have tended to view disabled persons' rights as subsets of generic areas of law, e.g., criminal, tax and family. In order to emphasize the functional impact of the law on the lives of disabled people, I have chosen to cross these boundaries by reviewing rights issues which have been designated "universal", and applying them to rights issues which have arisen for persons with disabilities.

Canada and the United States became members of the United Nations in 1945. In doing so, they pledged to follow article 55(1) of the U.N. Charter whereby "...the U.N. shall promote: universal respect for an observance of human rights and fundamental freedoms for all ..." The foundation document for the international protection of human rights is the *Universal Declaration of Human Rights* (1948). While "disabled people" are not specifically listed as a protected class, under Article 2 it states "everyone is entitled to all rights and freedoms set forth in this Declaration without discrimination of any kind, such as race, colour ... birth or other status". The International Commission on Human Rights has interpreted the open ended category of "other status" to include "the disabled". The subsequent passage of the

*Declaration on the Rights of Mentally Retarded Persons* (1971), and the *Declaration on the Rights of Disabled Persons* (1975 and the appointment of a Special Rapporteur (Leandro Despouy) by the U.N.Commission on Human Rights, further substantiate this position. The following Articles are contained in the *Universal Declaration.*

## 1. Life

### Article 2 - Everyone has the right to life, liberty and security of the person

In most industrialized countries, recent developments in medical technology and the emergence of the welfare state have raised the issue of whether severely handicapped people have the right to live. This is not to suggest that overt genocide is taking place against disabled persons, as was practiced by the Nazis in the thirties and forties. At this point, the debate appears to be confined to the questions of whether "heroic" medical procedures can be withdrawn or whether life saving medical procedures can be refused. Nevertheless, it is safe to predict that economic downturns resulting in decreased availability of medical or social services, or the rationing of highly expensive new medical technologies will broaden the debate.

One developmentally handicapped child who resided in an institution required the surgical implantation of a shunt in his brain (a routine medical procedure) if he was to survive. His parents refused to give the consent necessary for the operation, and the Public Guardian brought an application in court to allow a substituted consent to be given. The first court to hear the case refused to interfere with the parents' decision. The evidence accepted by the court indicated that the child was in constant pain and lived a "vegetative existence". The second court hearing the matter, heard evidence which suggested that he was severely handicapped, but happy, and responded in his own way to his environment. This court gave the authority necessary for the operation to be performed.

The two cases suggest courts may permit a person to die based on quality of life criteria. The criteria which would be applied have not been clearly articulated and raise troubling ethical issues.

Many countries have comprehensive Medicare systems which ensure that procedures of a life sustaining nature are generally available, irrespective of a person's disability. While there are those who have recommended cost containment by allocating services to those who are most fit, this attitude is not reflected in the law. There are, of course, countries where persons die for lack of adequate medical care. In others, mechanisms are being discussed for rationing care on a basis other than need. In these countries, the lives of persons with rare or severe disabilities or with high health care costs may be in jeopardy.

Disabled people who are financially unable to support themselves are often eligible for a subsistence level of welfare. Many persons on welfare find it impossible to locate minimally decent housing, and have minimally adequate diets. At some point, the situation could be characterized as having reached the point of being life threatening. There are countries which offer no welfare safety net. In these countries, a disabled person's survival may depend upon their family or private charity. When these prove inadequate, the most vulnerable die.

## 2. Liberty

Many disabled people are institutionalized against their will. This result is achieved through indirect and direct means. At one point, this was viewed as the hallmark of a generous society: seeking to care for those who were considered unable to care for themselves. Many physically disabled people reside in institutions which restrict or eliminate contacts with the outside world, all the while knowing they could be living in the community enjoying their freedom, often at considerably less cost to the state. This thinking is changing.

Persons with mental or emotional handicaps have their liberty restricted in an additional way. Virtually all countries have guardianship and mental health legislation. A guardian is someone who makes decisions on behalf of an adult deemed by a court to be incapable of making those decisions. Normally the guardian is the next of kin. A general lack of standards suggests substitute decision making is quite arbitrary. Recently, there have been long overdue efforts made in developing guardianship models which view people as interdependent. By providing them with appropriate support, it may be possible to enable people to retain control over their lives.

Mental health legislation is used in acute cases where a period of involuntary institutionalization in a psychiatric facility is deemed necessary by a court or physician. In contrast to guardianship legislation which has not been fundamentally altered for hundreds of years, changing treatment modalities and an aggressive "inmates rights" movement has led to many recent changes. Balancing the wider application of these laws have been legislative and judicial efforts intended to enhance the rights of "involuntary patients".

## 3. Security of the Person

A fundamental premise of natural law is the sanctity of the human body from unconsented to interference. The violation of this principle constitutes a battery and can result in criminal prosecution and a civil suit for damages. Clearly, exceptions to this rule must be made in the case of communicable diseases where the public interest is at risk. Nevertheless, treatment without consent in what are perceived to be the person's best interests for social control is constantly being suggested to be of predominant concern.

Persons with mental handicaps, particularly mental illnesses, are routinely subjected to treatment against their will. The first problem, once again a product of technological developments, is the question of defining procedures for which a consent is required in law. Many psychoanalytic and behaviour modification techniques do not involve either direct or indirect touching. Instead, they involve psychological interaction or deprivation techniques which are known to be as potent as surgical or chemical procedures for which consent is acknowledged as a prerequisite. The law in this area requires clarification.

Secondly, there is a mistaken assumption that persons who are confined against their will in psychiatric hospitals are incapable of making treatment decisions on their own behalf. This "wholesale" approach is being replaced by a process of individualized assessments of capacity, backed up by a right to appeal a doctor's decision to treat without consent.

The security of a mentally handicapped person, incapable in law of providing a consent to certain non-therapeutic procedures raises special issues. For example, a medical doctor who instructed at a university medical school used developmentally handicapped adolescents in an institution to teach her students how to perform rectal examinations. A court rejected her contention that the 'unconsented to' procedures served a larger good and convicted her of assault.

The sterilization of developmentally handicapped women was recently reviewed by the Supreme Court of Canada. Many states and provinces had eugenic sterilization laws which were repealed in the 1920's. Since then no overt legal authority has existed for discriminatory sterilization practices. Nevertheless, a report in Ontario demonstrated that as late as 1978, developmentally handicapped women and girls were being routinely sterilized. In a strongly worded decision, the Supreme Court ruled that a guardian can never give a valid substitute consent to a "non-therapeutic" sterilization.

Another issue which has arisen concerns the personal dignity of persons with disabilities in custodial settings or who are dependent upon attendant or other care services. This group has their liberty restricted, but must their personhood be compromised as well? Those outside these settings would never consider it routine to be viewed bathing or toiletting by members of the opposite sex. The interests of staff persons (in this case the understandable desire to be able to work irrespective of a person's gender) are often seen as predominating over those of residents who are vulnerable, disempowered and dehumanized as a result.

**Article 4** - No one shall be held in slavery or servitude; slavery and the slave trade shall be prohibited in all forms.

Political status of slave no longer exists.  Having said that, it is clear that disabled people, if they choose to work, are exposed to exploitation.

Often, a disabled person can be paid less than minimum wage. Proponents of this discriminatory provision point to the high rates of unemployment amongst disabled people and suggest this will give them a competitive advantage on the labour market.  They overlook the purpose of a minimum wage, (i.e., to raise standards of living above the barest level of subsistence and to allow everyone to enjoy a standard of living deemed socially acceptable).

A substantial number of disabled people work in sheltered workshops for which they are paid a pittance.  While not forced into workshops, disabled persons who wish to supplement their meager welfare cheques or who seek to enter the competitive  labour market  (for whom sheltered workshops represent the only "rehabilitation" program available) must accept these conditions.  The rehabilitative  results  of workshops are acknowledged to be very poor.  Many people work full-time in workshops for their entire lives.  Others are placed by workshops in competitive businesses for extended periods of time without the benefit of  labour law protections.

**Article 5** - No one shall be subjected to torture or to cruel inhuman or degrading treatment or punishment.

Many  constitutions  provide guarantees that a country's citizens will be free from cruel and unusual punishment.

This provision has been used as the basis for challenging the provisions governing the treatment of persons found "not guilty" of a criminal offence by reason of their mental incapacity at the time the offence was committed.

Offering this defence represents no special favour to an individual if he/she is held in a maximum security institution, with minimal therapeutic opportunities for an indefinite period. A person with a developmental disability was charged with the minor criminal offence of purse snatching.  He was being held indefinitely until found to have been "cured". Since his disability was a permanent one, his incarceration clearly was unfair.  Recently, courts have linked the maximum period of incarceration to the length of time the person could have been imprisoned if convicted of the offence.

**Article 6** - Everyone has the right to recognition everywhere as a person before the law.

Everyone upon reaching the age of majority  (the age varies from province to province) is considered a person, in the sense of being able to freely enjoy full rights of citizenship.  These rights are to be enjoyed unless removed by process of law.

A  major exception to this rule involves residents in various institutions for the care of the disabled. Here, for example, as a condition of receiving the services of a nursing home or home for the aged, a disabled person is required to sign over management of his or her affairs to the administrator of the facility.  Thus, the coercive effect of withholding essential services routinely results in the compromising of the individual's rights.

The primary method for removing a person's rights as an adult in a plenary fashion is pursuant to mental incompetency legislation of one form or another.  In a case which received international public attention, a non-verbal young man with cerebral palsy battled in court for the right to decide where he would live.  His parents, who had placed him in an institution and who had not come to visit him for many years, sought to prevent him from leaving the institution by having him declared mentally incompetent.  He testified using a system of picture symbols called blissymbolics.  In the end, the court declared him mentally competent despite his severe physical handicaps and his lack of experience outside the institution.

### Article 7 - All are equal before the law and are entitled without any discrimination to the equal protection of the law.

Over the last ten years, Canadians have been repeatedly shocked to learn of the widespread abuse of handicapped and elderly persons who were institutionalized for their own protection. Grisly details of torture and abuse of persons in institutions for the mentally handicapped have been revealed and numerous inquests into deaths in nursing homes in Ontario have resulted in widespread calls for reforms.

In a rare case where criminal charges were laid against a staff member for physical abuse, important law was made. The staff member, who admitted striking the resident with a heavy spoon on the head, sought the protection of a section of the *Criminal Code* which permitted a parent or person *in loco parentis* to use reasonable force to discipline a child. It was argued that the developmentally handicapped adult had the mental age of a child and that the staff member should therefore be given the benefit of his defence. After finding the force used was unreasonable and that the staff member was not *in loco parentis*, the court went on at length to state that handicapped people should not be denied equal protection of the law by being subjected to perpetual childhood.

### 4. Arrest and Detention

### Article 9 - No one shall be subjected to arbitrary arrest, detention or exile.

Persons with a mental disorder have long been detained like accused criminals, but have enjoyed few of the procedural safeguards guaranteed to the accused. This situation has been changing over the last thirty years. For example, in Ontario two medical doctors were authorized to order the detention of persons they believed required psychiatric treatment up until 1967. At that time, the *Mental Health Act* was amended to provide criteria based on protecting the "safety of the person or the safety of others". It also created an administrative tribunal to review whether involuntary admission is justifiable in light of new criteria.

The 1967 *Act* was soon duplicated across Canada. Its introduction paralleled the emergence of psychotropic drugs which in turn resulted in shorter periods of hospitalization and a trend towards deinstitutionalization.

In 1978, Ontario again amended its *Mental Health Act*. Almost simultaneously, a large number of beds in the large provincial psychiatric hospitals were closed. The revised *Act* further narrowed the criteria for involuntary detention and afforded a due process hearing before a mental health review board. Perhaps sensing the revisions were collateral to the increase of community care for the mentally ill, the amendments were strongly opposed by the medical establishment. Interestingly, the new Ontario model still leaves the power of arrest and detention up to one doctor. The doctor's decision will be over turned if serious and imminent risk of danger to the person or others cannot be demonstrated.

### 5. Exile

No citizen is ejected from their homeland because of disability. Nevertheless, disability plays a significant part in immigration policy, and is the cause of much hardship.

Immigration policy is usually designed with three objectives in mind: (1) supply of labour which would be otherwise unavailable; (2) reunification of families; and (3) providing a safe haven for refugees.

Most immigration legislation prohibits the admission of persons with communicable diseases with which it is difficult to find fault, provided diseases such as AIDS which cannot be passively transmitted and against which precautions can be taken, are not included.  Where a disease requires quarantine it is probably advisable that this be done in the country of origin.  It also restricts potential refugees and relatives from sponsoring for permanent admission, otherwise eligible disabled persons who might be a drain upon a country's health or social services.  As a result, many families are living in North American with one disabled family member obliged to remain in the country of origin.  This discriminatory policy is being challenged.

**Article 12** - **No one shall be subjected to arbitrary interference with his privacy, family, home or correspondence, nor to attacks upon his honour and reputation.**

Consistent with most jurisdiction's endorsement of deinstitutionalization of disabled people, a patchwork of community support services is slowly emerging.  Generally speaking, it can be said that a spectrum of support services is not available, the services are uncoordinated, and demand hopelessly exceeds supply.  One mechanism used to deinstitutionalize disabled people is called a group home, where 3-10 disabled people live together in a normal residence, indistinguishable from others in the community.

In most jurisdictions, there exists zoning legislation designed to prevent socially incompatible uses (i.e. heavy industry and residential housing) from being proximately located.

While logic would suggest all people should be treated equally under zoning legislation, group homes have been treated as non-residential uses.  As a result, when a group of disabled people wish to live together in order to share common support services, they must apply for a spot-rezoning.  This involves notifying all one's neighbours of the proposed use (i.e., as a residence for disabled people) and inviting them to attend before the municipal council to state why no exception to the general zoning rule should be made.

From coast to coast such meetings before municipal councils have resulted in the

clearest expressions of hatred and fear of disabled people.  Local ratepayers have articulated concerns that group homes will bring dangerous and unsightly people into their neighbourhood which, in turn, will result in reduced property values for their house.

Some municipalities have decided to avoid the heat of spot-rezonings (i.e., dealing with cases on an individual basis) by passing by-laws which permit group homes, provided they are not concentrated in any one area.  These "as of right" by-laws have involved lengthy debates and expensive legal challenges.  It should also be noted that the end result is far from satisfactory, in that group homes are not treated as normal residential uses but rather as nuisances which must be separated and endured.

Courts are now starting to adopt the view that there is no justifiable reason for treating housing differently, because the residents happen to have disabilities.  The United States Supreme Court has made a clear statement on this issue.

Obviously, hospitals and nursing homes are different from residential homes.  At some point, the size of the operation and the medical or commercial nature of the services provided, requires special attention.

Sometimes that line has not been crossed, but the fact that residents are dependent upon care, e.g., attendant care, supervision of medication, etc., is used as a justification to deny them the protection of landlord-tenant legislation.

Most residential options for disabled people involve far more interference with a person's lifestyle than is necessary.  Many institutions following the "medical model" treat disabled people as if they are ill.  This involves serious infringements of privacy and little attention being paid to people's dignity.  In one case, a disabled man successfully challenged having care of his genital area attended to by a female.  Most residential programs for physically disabled people interfere in a paternalistic way with an individuals's lifestyle decisions, (e.g. dating a member of the opposite sex, consumption of alcohol).  There is no separation of the privacy one expects in one's own home from the rehabilitative function over which the disabled person has no control.

### Article 13 - Everyone has the right to freedom of movement and residence within the borders of each state.

There are no laws which state that disabled people may not travel or enter buildings freely. Because most countries' architectural and transportation systems were built on the premise that disabled people need not enter, no law was necessary.

Only very recently have there been the first fledgling efforts to make mainline buses, subways and street cars accessible to mobility handicapped people. Instead, municipalities have developed a variety of "parallel" transportation systems, usually built around a fleet of lift and radio equipped vans which provide a "door to door" service. Due to underfunding, it would be fair to characterize these systems as undependable, inflexible and dangerous. Some municipalities provide no service or restrict access very tightly. Others depend upon the services of charities.

Accessible regional transportation is extremely rare. Thus, persons who live in rural areas or satellite communities around larger communities have no means of getting into the larger centres of commerce and government.

In what stands as the most important transportation decision to date involving a disabled person, it was decided that it would be in the public interest to require the passenger rail service to significantly improve its accessibility. The order had four major components:

1.  Disabled people were given a right of self-determination, i.e., the right to decide whether or not they required an attendant.
2.  The principle of "one-person-one-fare" was adopted, i.e., the attendant was perceived alternatively as an extension of the disabled person or of the services provided by the railway, but in either event would be permitted to travel on the disabled person's ticket.
3.  Despite being presented with a plan by the railway to install mechanical lifting devices over time in all major rail stations, the railway was required to immediately provide manual boarding assistance at its 52 largest stations, i.e., equality of access.
4.  While aware of the additional risks faced by disabled people when traveling, they were not found to be so substantial as to justify denial of carriage, i.e. dignity of risk. Also, the railway was not permitted to extract waivers of liability from such passengers. To allow waivers would have exposed them to undue danger and reduced the incentive for improved safety procedures reflecting the special needs of disabled passengers.

As important as these principles have been, the overall impact of this decision is restricted by the inaccessible design of the aging passenger rolling stock which is still in operation. Thus, while the train has become a preferred inter-city transportation system for many disabled people, the environment within most railway cars remains quite inhospitable.

Inter-city buses had escaped regulatory attention because the bus industry is not subject to a high degree of public regulation. Most private bus companies have implemented the principles of self-determination, one-person one-fare and the dignity of risk: the big problem remains equality of access. The technology now exists to provide mechanical lifts and specially designed seating to accommodate the disabled passenger. In the United States there are new guarantees that this technology will be in operation starting in 1995. In Canada the issue has not been resolved.

Despite the limitations of all the foregoing modes, it is in air travel that the greatest frustration is experienced. This is because most of the high cost renovations allowing accessibility are in place both in airports and on board planes, and yet progress towards full accessibility remains slow.

Repeated government reports and complaints by representatives of the disabled have gone unheeded.  Hard won gains of the four standards referred to above have been lost by disabled air passengers as a result of deregulation.  Some standards are emerging but much more needs to be done.

## 6. Residence

Each jurisdiction is responsible for prescribing its own building standards, including standards of accessibility for disabled people.

Governments are responsible for the accessibility of their own buildings.  Most governments are to be praised for the manner in which they have made their buildings accessible whether old or new, and wherever they are located.  Shockingly, public schools and universities are amongst the least accessible public buildings.

Governments have also used their financial leverage with the private sector to influence residential construction.  It is commonly required when seeking public mortgages or loan guarantees that a specified number of units will be designed with interests of persons with disabilities in mind.

Unfortunately, building codes have not always gone so far.  Most codes apply only to new construction or major renovations, (i.e. no requirement to retrofit) of certain public or quasi-public buildings (i.e. no application to single family housing), are of minimal benefit (i.e., do not deal with design features outside the building such as approaches to the building or major interior features) and can be easily avoided (i.e., by adjusting level of grade or applying for exemption).

Even with major improvements, the overall progress to be achieved with such laws would be incremental and leave existing buildings permanently inaccessible.  For this reason, a recent decision of the application of human and civil rights legislation to this problem signals a major shift in judicial attitudes.  In one case, a young man in a wheelchair entered a movie theater with a friend.  Because there were no spaces available in the body of the theater from which a person in a wheelchair could view the movie, he was wheeled down to the front of

the theater where he viewed the movie separated from his friend and segregated for all to see.  The court  ruled that the threatre must provide several spots from which a person in a wheelchair could view the movie.  The decision signals that renovations to provide accessibility will be required for existing structures.

**Article 16 - Men and women of full age have the right to marry and found a family.  They are entitled to equal rights as to marriage, during marriage, and at its dissolution.**

A paternalistic system would deny a disabled person normal healthy sexual outlets and restrict the possibility of marriage and raising a family.

There exist a  number of laws which have such a stifling effect on disabled people.  For example, until recently, it was a criminal offence to have sexual relations with a "feeble-minded" person.  This prohibition made anyone, including a mentally handicapped person who was engaging in healthy, consensual sexual relations with another mentally handicapped person, liable to prosecution.  The purpose of the law was clearly to prevent mentally handicapped people from engaging in sexual activity of any type, and only secondarily to protect the person from exploitation.

If there are children, law requires that the child's "best interests" prevail over those of the parent.  Obviously, the natural parents enjoy the advantage of the "bonding" which exists between the parent and child.  Just as obviously, the courts, when considering whether to remove a child from a disabled parent or parents, consider the degree to which the disability impairs a person's child raising capacity.  Until very recently, children were routinely removed from their disabled parents.  Discriminatory attitudes have moderated somewhat recently to the point where a court will consider whether the state can assist disabled parents by providing them with the "tools necessary to care for their child."  Special training, supports and technical aids appear to be contemplated by this decision.

Another area where society's discriminatory attitudes are apparent is adoption. Governmental agencies interpret their discretion to match orphan children with the best available parents. Physically disabled people have been precluded from adopting on the basis that their disability disqualified them from ever being considered suitable. In a recent case, a woman in a wheelchair successfully challenged her disqualification.

**Article 21 - Everyone has the right to take part in the government of his country, directly or through freely chosen representatives.**

Remunerative employment is probably the ultimate human right because the salary and status which it provides ensure that other rights are guaranteed.

North America has a very high rate of unemployment amongst its disabled citizens relative to industrialized countries. The reasons for this poor record are numerous and complex.

The most readily apparent is that neither the United States nor Canada, unlike the rest of the industrialized world, has either an affirmative action or quota scheme guaranteeing acceptable levels of employment amongst disabled workers. A Royal Commission Report recommended Canada adopt a mandatory affirmative action program; however, the government introduced a voluntary program. During the first two years of the voluntary program, employment of disabled people actually decreased.

A second reason for the rate of unemployment is the woefully inadequate system of vocational rehabilitation available to disabled people. Unlike in Europe where rehabilitation has been integrated into active job training and apprenticeship programs, North America relies upon passive and segregated rehabilitation programs. As well, insufficient attention is paid to the accommodations required by persons with

disabilities within such job training programs as are available.

Finally, there is a provision in the *Income Tax Act* prohibiting the deduction of disability related expenses of earning employment income (except for a limited deduction for on-the-job attendant care introduced in 1989). As a result, disabled people must bear the cost of making the accommodations which will make them employable, and yet they are required to pay for these expenditures of after-tax rather than before-tax income. Many disabled people are financially further ahead remaining on welfare than accepting low paying jobs or jobs that require substantial job related expenditures. It is increasingly being recognized that these disincentives must be removed.

Human rights legislation requires that employers accommodate the special needs of disabled people. Administrative problems have resulted in this obligation being inadequately enforced.

The most important accommodations involve job restructuring. In a recent case, an employer was required to re-allocate heavy lifting from the job description of an employee with a bad back and replace it with additional light duties. Other accommodations would include use of special technologies, support services and modified training. Time will tell whether this *ad hoc* kind of decision-making is administratively more feasible and effective at securing employment for disabled people than providing quotas or mandatory affirmative action. The two methods are clearly compatible and disabled advocates are seeking reforms which would include both strategies.

**Article 25 - Everyone has the right to a standard of living adequate for the health and well-being of himself and of his family, including food, clothing, housing and medical care and necessary social services and the right to security in the event of unemployment, sickness, disability, widowhood, old age or other lack of livelihood in circumstances beyond his control.**

Disability is the least well provided for of the catastrophic circumstances enumerated in Article 25. Generally speaking, disabled people who are "unemployable" are eligible for welfare. In fact, disability is a major reason for receiving welfare in North America. Such payments carry with them the stigma of being labeled "unemployable", together with the intrusive consequence that they will be terminated in the event of cohabitation with another person whose income need be no higher than minimum wage.

Some disabled people do reasonably well. For example, persons injured in the course of their employment are relatively well provided for and are given both a strong financial incentive to return to work and high quality professional assistance in the rehabilitation process. Disabled veterans of the armed forces are also treated relatively generously.

At the other end of the scale are the minimal payments from Criminal Injuries Compensation Funds, out of which the victims of crime who are injured or disabled may claim benefits. These benefits are allocated according to highly subjective standards and, in any event, they rarely exceed what welfare would provide.

Most other persons who become disabled must look to the courts for compensation which is only available if the disabled person can demonstrate that the other party was negligent (i.e. was at "fault"). A great deal of money is spent on negligence insurance or motor vehicle owners, doctors, property owners and businesses. Unfortunately, a very large percentage of the premiums paid for this insurance never reaches the disabled people but instead, goes into the administration and profits of the insurance industry, and to defray the costs of the litigation process. The worker's compensation scheme is far more cost efficient in the sense of translating premiums into payments to disabled people. While a strong lawyers lobby urges that jurisdiction retain "fault" as the basis of compensation, Quebec, and some American states, have recently introduced "no fault" systems.

Another factor in the income redistribution scheme is the *Income Tax Act*. Most tax systems are basically neutral in terms of their redistributive effect. There are two major provisions in the *Act* itself dealing with disability.

The first is the handicapped person credit which is available to persons with a severe disability. Secondly, a credit is provided for "medical expenses" (i.e., including many disability-related costs) not subsidized by the government or private insurance schemes.

A minority of workers in Canada, primarily those who are members of trade unions, are eligible for private disability insurance benefits. Unfortunately, most workers eligible for these benefits find out after they become disabled that they will have to pay tax on their benefits. The result is that many are only slightly better off than they would have been on welfare. Moreover, most policies terminate the benefits after two years if the recipient is capable of any type of remunerative employment whatsoever.

Canada's largest social program is its fully government funded Medicare scheme. At the present time, the last vestiges of two-tier medicine have been removed. Thus, while low income people still do not get equal benefit from Medicare, the financial deterrents have virtually all been removed. Ironically, 100% funding for all necessary medical services co-exists in many parts of the country with totally unsubsidized dental care, drugs and prosthetics. This raises important questions about "universality" of services, and whether it is sustainable now that the welfare safety net has stopped expanding. In some provinces, these are only provided by municipalities to persons on welfare. Even then, these benefits are totally discretionary. Similar discretion is exercised in the case of persons who require special clothing, diets or medical accessories. Thus many of Canada's lowest income disabled people are dependent upon private charities for these essential services or devices, or go without if charity doesn't meet the need.

Another result of the generous funding of the medical system is that it encourages the medicalization of what would normally be considered non-medical problems. For example, many physically handicapped people are given the option of having their attendant care needs met in a nursing home where their food and shelter costs are met by the state along with unnecessary medical care, or receiving no support whatsoever. Under such circumstances, it is hardly surprising that people reluctantly accept a life of dependence on the medical system. A major battle is shaping up around the world with disabled persons' demanding control over the resources allocated for their care (i.e. direct funding). Service providers find this threatening but appear to have few methods of rebutting this demand outside of the medical area where specialized expertise justifies professionalization.

**Article 26 - Everyone has the right to an education. Education shall be free, at least in the elementary and fundamental stages. Elementary education shall be compulsory. Technical and professional education shall be compulsory. Technical and professional education shall be made generally available and higher education shall be equally accessible to all on the basis of merit. Education shall be directed to the full development of the human personality ... Parents have a prior right to choose the kind of education that shall be given to their children.**

Education is a state or provincial responsibility, although services are typically delivered by municipally elected school boards.

Nowhere can it be said that official policy is to meet the individual educational needs of children, whether or not they are disabled. In Canada, most provinces have not changed their policies since the Supreme Court of Canada held in 1950 that educators could decide whether or not a child had the mental or physical qualifications for admission to school. Thus, educators were free to refuse to serve children who did not fit the norm. This remains the law to this day, and many disabled children in Canada go without any formal education as a result.

The broad discretion left with school boards to define who will be educated also extends to their right to set standards for the quality of education they provide in general, and more particularly, to the quality of education they provide to disabled children. Not surprisingly, the educational levels achieved by disabled Canadians are far below average.

Some parents have sought integrated placements in regular classrooms. They reason that segregation has the same socially debilitating consequences for mentally or physically handicapped children that it does on racial or ethnic minorities. The results of these cases are not yet conclusive.

Ontario amended its *Education Act to* 1989 to guarantee every child an "appropriate education". To emphasize this focus on the individual, every parent of an "exceptional child" may appeal the placement of their child in a particular special education program to a Provincial Tribunal. Initial indications are that appropriateness may be subordinated to the availability of programs which the board of education is prepared to offer. The Ontario model was patterned after the American *Education of Handicapped Children Act*, although its enforcement provisions were intentionally weakened so that families could not endorse their rights in as effective a fashion. Post-secondary education for disabled students is very uneven. For example, virtually no deaf students attend university in Canada. On the other hand, a group of blind and learning disabled students recently succeeded in a human rights complaint to prompt the government to fund an audio reading service which transcribes books onto tape. This gave the students equal access to materials generally available to non-print handicapped students. Much remains to be done in this area.

## Conclusion

While the initiatives of local, national and international cross-disability consumer organizations and other advocacy groups have clearly had an impact in recent years, North America's poor legislative record stands as a grim reminder of how much more remains to be done by disabled people in the legislatures and in the courts. Legislators have been very slow to move from exclusion to equality in their attitudes towards disabled people. It is to be hoped that positive change will accelerate as the consumer movement of disabled persons becomes stronger and more effective.

********

**About the Author:** J. David Baker is a Toronto lawyer and the Executive Director of the Advocacy Resource Centre for the Handicaped (ARCH), 40 Orchardview Blvd., #255, Toronto, Ontario, Canada M4R 1B9 (Phone: 4416-482-8255)

**Source:** Reprinted with permission from the author who wrote this article specifically for the second edition of *Perspectives on Disability.*

# AIDS as Disability
Jerome E. Bickenbach

## The Social Perception of AIDS

Acquired Immune Deficiency Syndrome (AIDS) is a contagious, viral disease syndrome that impairs the body's immune system, making it vulnerable to opportunistic infections and malignancies. AIDS is caused by a fluid-borne retrovirus called Human Immunodeficiency Virus, or HIV. The virus is spread when infected blood, semen, and (possibly) other bodily fluids enter into another person's bloodstream. Outside the body and bloodstream, HIV is extremely fragile and can be easily killed. Although there are now indications that the progress of the disease can be slowed somewhat in the early stages by means of pharmaceutical agents such as azidothymidine (AZT), there is as yet no cure, or vaccine. AIDS victims face the horror of disfigurement, emaciation, and an inevitable, and painful death, usually within two years. More recently, public health officials have also noticed that the increased vulnerability of AIDS victims to drug-resistant forms of tuberculosis bacterium has raised the prospect of that scourge becoming epidemic as well.

In North America, the AIDS epidemic has entered into what epidemiologists call the 'mature' phase, in which the explosive rate of growth characteristic of the early 1980s has slowed so that our ability to predict long-term consequences has improved somewhat. Significantly, the rate of increase in spending on prevention has also leveled off in recent years, in part because, unlike other historic epidemics such as bubonic plague, AIDS in North America is concentrated among socially marginalized groups with little economic, political and social power. Even though more public money is spent on AIDS-related research than on any other disease except cancer, there remain major gaps in our knowledge of AIDS, including how long it may take for someone infected, and so contagious, to become symptomatic. This means that prognoses are both speculative, and frightening. In the United States, for example, while there have been over 200,000 deaths so far, the estimate of the number of those who are infected but asymptomatic is over two million.

On the African continent, the situation is far worse. The World Health Organization estimates that by 1994, Africa will have ten million HIV cases. and in the next 25 years perhaps as many as 37 million Africans will die of AIDS. Currently, in some of the larger cities such as Kampala in Uganda and Kilgali in Rwanda, as many as one in three adults are likely infected; and in rural areas, where preventive measures are far more difficult to put into place, the infection rate is increasing rapidly. There is hope, but not much more, that the AIDS epidemic in Africa will level off by the end of the first decade of the next century.

From the outset of the disease, at least in North America and Europe, the social perception of AIDS, and the metaphors that have influenced the public discourse about it, [1] have been shaped by the fact that it is a sexually transmitted disease the greatest burden of which has been borne by the gay community. It is common knowledge that the disease can also be transmitted non-sexually -- directly from contaminated needles and syringes, from the transfusion of infected blood or blood products, or perinatally from infected mother to unborn child. It is also commonly known that there are victims of the disease other than homosexual males; indeed, in Africa more than 80 percent of infection is caused by heterosexual intercourse and, increasingly, far more women are being infected than men. Nonetheless, the perception persists, and is daily reinforced by the media, that the AIDS epidemic principally raises questions of sexual morality or lifestyle-created vulnerability.

We know from other epidemics that it is the social perception of a contagious disease, rather than its medical and epidemological profile, that sets the tone for the public debate over the kinds of social measures required to alter its course.  Since in our political culture we are committed to the protection both of individual rights and general welfare, this debate needs to resolve tensions between starkly conflicting interests.  In particular, our social response to the AIDS epidemic must weigh the rights of those already infected against the rights of those who are not, and must balance the effectiveness of public health measures in checking the epidemic against the sacrifices those measures demand of individual citizens.

There is no doubt that the sexual imagery of AIDS has profoundly distorted this social debate.  Attitudes about sexuality have hampered the planning and implementation of 'safe sex' campaigns, even though these are by far the least intrusive of the traditional repertoire of public health measures.  Health officials have had to contend, not only with delicate sensibilities, but with the widely held belief that by encouraging the use of condoms, they are condoning promiscuity.  Far more damaging, though, has been the belief that AIDS is the result of a blameworthy failure of sexual self-restraint, a moral lapse that calls forth its own punishment.

These distortions have only been worsened by the association of AIDS and male homosexuality.  This linkage endures even though the factual basis for it has been misinterpreted.  For the claim that gays constitute a high risk population does not mean that AIDS has, somehow, targeted gays, or that heterosexuality is proof against infection -- two myths that have had a surprisingly long life.  Rather, at best, the statistical correlation connects the risk of HIV-infection with certain kinds of sexual activity.

There has been in North America, in short, a partial fusion of issues of health policy and the politics of sexual orientation, drug abuse and other perceived sins.[2]  As we struggle to confront and deal with the epidemic, these social perceptions will continue to prejudice the interests of the AIDS victim, aligned with socially vulnerable, high risk populations and stigmatized by a vague,

but powerful, image of sexual or moral impropriety.

Many diseases, contagious and otherwise, have acquired a social perception at variance with medical fact and sound public health policy.  With AIDS, though, powerful images of impurity, pollution and deviance have been responsible for much of the fear that the disease has created.[3]  This raises the question whether politicians and public health officials should make the effort to alter the social perception of AIDS by de-emphasizing its association with sexual morality.  It is now clear that this tactic is not worth the massive cost of public re-education it would require, and that it would be far more sensible to revise existing frameworks for social policy development, since these are more flexible and can be explicitly altered by legislation, enforceable regulations, and policy guidelines.  The question then becomes, what aspects of the disease should be emphasized for public health purposes?

Ironically, the most obvious dimension of AIDS is only beginning to receive the attention it deserves:  AIDS is a disease syndrome, brought about by viral infection, that involves impairments of organic functioning that restrict normal activities.  In other words, AIDS qualifies, not only as an *impairment*, but also as a *disability*, as those terms are defined by the World Health Organization 1980 document, *The International Classification of Impairment, Disability and Handicap (ICIDH)*[4].  Moreover, the fact that AIDS is a physical (and mental) [5] disability is an intrinsic feature of the disease, since if it had had no disabling consequences, public health officials could safely ignore it.  By contrast, though foremost in the public's mind, the connection between AIDS and sexual conduct or drug use has never been more than an epidemiological accident, as the case of Africa makes clear.

Intuitively too, AIDS is also a *handicap*, once again as that term is characterized in the ICIDH, and refined in later documents.[6]  That is, having AIDS is the basis for a variety of social disadvantages such as stigmatization and discrimination.  Although it is not always the case that being disabled by virtue of a disease means that one is also handicapped, the social perception of AIDS is such that it invariably attracts handicapping responses from others.

To be sure, it is not beyond dispute that diseases -- especially contagious or infectious ones -- should come within the purview of social policy for people with disabilities. It might be argued, for example, that for acute illnesses, which, even if life-threatening, are intrinsically self-limiting, the social programs designed for people with disabilities are not appropriate. Disability, we tend to believe, is a chronic or permanent state. And although specific diseases may yield chronic conditions, it is these conditions, rather than the acute and episodic diseases that produce them, that are more likely candidates for social policy.

If these conceptual issues can be dismissed as unimportant, another worry looms larger. Emphasizing this dimension of AIDS may not be welcome to people who have the disease, since, from their perspective, all that is involved is a shift from one form of stigmatization to another. Although people with disabilities are rarely perceived as sexual deviants, they often face denial of equal access to services and opportunities, assumptions of inferiority and failure, and paternalistic treatment that undermines autonomy and self-respect. To make matters worse, those whose disabilities are viewed as self-inflicted -- which is often how AIDS is perceived -- may have to bear the additional burden of moral blame or sanctimonious aversion.

There is no doubt that people with disabilities who are thereby handicapped face these and other forms of oppression in our culture. But the fact remains that people with AIDS must bear most of this burden already, and could only benefit from a closer affiliation with people with disabilities. Furthermore, the two groups have much in common: both regularly confront discrimination in employment, public accommodation, and education. Both must contend with institutionalization, quarantine, guardianship, and other restrictions on their liberty. And both share the frustrations of trying to obtain information about, and input into, medical research. If nothing else, by joining in the cause of people with disabilities, people with AIDS might lose their isolation -- a precondition to the long-range goal of increased self-empowerment[7].

Most importantly, though, a shift from the domain of sexual morality, or the social deviance associated with drug use, to that of entitlements for people with disabilities is an important step in developing a sane social response to the disease. In the absence of clearly articulated policy, it is inevitable that courts of law, human-rights tribunals and other administrative adjudicators will be called upon to resolve specific disputes raised by the AIDS epidemic. The law with respect to the rights of people with disabilities, although far from a panacea for handicapping, can assist us in resolving both of the tensions created by the AIDS epidemic -- that of weighing the rights of those infected against the rights of those who are not, and that of balancing the effectiveness of public health measures against the sacrifices they entail.

### AIDS As Disability and Handicap

Does AIDS pose a challenge to the concepts of *impairment, disability, and handicap?* Inasmuch as AIDS is a disease syndrome, it is obviously an impairment. Moreover, people with AIDS have a variety of disabilities, not just immunodeficiency itself, but those associated with opportunistic diseases such as Pneumocystis Carinii Pneumonia, Kaposi's Sarcoma, malignant lymphomas, and others. Finally, people with AIDS daily encounter stigma, discrimination, and other social disadvantages of the sort we would otherwise unhesitantly call forms of handicapping.

Though these connections seem obvious, two objections with treating AIDS as a disability come to mind. First, unlike blindness, deafness, epilepsy, cerebral palsy and other disabilities, AIDS is a contagious disease. Second, it is not entirely clear what it means to 'have AIDS'. That is, because AIDS is a complex medical syndrome, involving a spectrum of disease conditions, there are at least three categories of AIDS victims: those with full-blown AIDS; those with symptoms of persistent lymphadenopathy syndrome or a milder form of immunodeficiency called AIDS-Related Complex (ARC); and those who have tested HIV-seropositive but are asymptomatic.[8]

In addition to these two issues, it should be added, it is sometimes argued that AIDS cannot be a disability because it is a 'voluntary' or self-inflicted disease. To this there is the obvious response that, even if some cases of infection have been negligently (or even intentionally) acquired, that is not true of the vast majority of cases. In addition, as I have argued elsewhere, the question of **how** an impairment is acquired should be completely irrelevant to **whether** the impairment causes a disability or not.[9]. Unfortunately, at least according to a recent U.S.Supreme Court decision, the issue of voluntarinress may indeed be relevant to whether or not an individual is, in the appropriate legal sense, handicapped. [10] The disqualification of people with a history of alcoholism or drug abuse from the anti-discrimination provisions of the *Americans with Disabilities Act of 1991* [11] reflects a similar attitude.

Despite this, I will ignore the issue of voluntariness here. To be sure, public health officers would be wise to worry about reckless or negligent individuals who are HIV-seropositive; but this concern has nothing to do with the prior conceptual issue of whether AIDS is a disability or a handicap. What this latter concern rests upon is not voluntariness at all, but the fact that AIDS is a contagious disease.

Contagiousness is a public health concern. Still, although not a common feature of disabilities, contagiousness is not fundamentally different from any other of a variety of dangers that disabilities create. After all people who are blind should not drive cars because they would pose an obvious threat to the safety of others. That is why, absent feasible accommodation, we are justified in discriminating against them when we issue drivers licenses. Yet, no one would ever argue that this fact about blindness disqualifies it as a disability or a handicap. So, who should contagiousness of AIDS make any difference?

A brief history of the legal reaction to this issue is instructive. In June 1986, U. S. Assistant Attorney General Charles J. Cooper issued a memorandum concerning the interpretation of the anti-discrimination provision of the *Rehabilitation Act of 1973* [12]. The definition of handicap in that act has a minimal threshold -- only those with impairments that 'substantially limit' major life activities are defined by the act to be handicapped. Granting that people with full-blown AIDS are handicapped in this sense, Mr. Cooper denied that someone who was asymptomatic but contagious should be viewed as handicapped:

"To be sure, a carrier of a contagious disease may suffer adverse social and professional consequences. Persons susceptive to the disease may be reluctant to be associated with him, but a person cannot be regarded as handicapped simply because others shun his company. Otherwise, a host of personal traits -- from ill-temper to poor personal hygiene -- would constitute handicaps, a conclusion [that would be] untenable." [13].

Advocates for the disabled community quickly pointed out that the Cooper memorandum had dire legal consequences. If contagiousness is not the basis for a handicap, they argued, then it is always open to someone, charged with discriminating on the basis of a contagious disease, to argue that it was not the disease, but only its contagiousness, that motivated their discriminatory behaviour. This concern was soon borne out when the U. S. Supreme Court was asked to consider the case of Gene Arlene, an elementary school teacher for 13 years who had been discharged because, after 20 years of remission, her tuberculosis became active again. [14]

The school board conceded that if Arlene had been dismissed because of her diminished physical capabilities, that would have violated the *Rehabilitation Act* since tuberculosis is obviously a disability. Having made this concession, they could have then argued that dismissal was justified because Arlene's active tuberculosis posed a plausible threat to the health of others. In light of the Cooper memorandum, they chose instead to make the much stronger argument that dismissal on grounds of contagiousness is not a case of discrimination at all since contagiousness (unlike tuberculosis) cannot be a handicap.

The Supreme Court soundly rejected this argument, remarking that it requires us to draw a spurious distinction between an impairment (the disease) and one of its salient features (contagiousness), and then prohibiting discrimination for the former but allowing it for the latter. Moreover, the court argued that such a distinction betrays a fundamental confusion about the nature of handicaps. Handicaps arise because of society's accumulated myths and fears about diseases, and no feature of diseases is more productive of these fears than contagiousness. Therefore, to protect Ms Arlene against discrimination, the school board must be prohibited from dismissing her from her job on the basis of fears, rather than facts.

It is important to be clear about what the court decided in the Arlene case. The court was not claiming that a medically proven threat to the health and safety of others is not a legitimate ground for dismissing an employee. Quite the contrary, had there been such evidence, dismissal might have been warranted. What the court insisted was that it is discriminatory to dismiss an employee on the basis of irrational and medically groundless fears and assumptions about the contagiousness of a disease, since, those fears and assumptions partly constitute the handicap.

Following this decision, other legal cases involving AIDS came to the conclusion that contagiousness is only a relevant consideration when it can be shown that the individual with AIDS poses a genuine, medically supportable threat to the health of others. Because of this trend, in September 1988, the U. S. Department of Justice abandoned its pre-*Arlene* stand on AIDS and held that : "...the symptomatic or asymptomatic HIV-infected individual is protected against discrimination if he or she is able to perform the duties of the job and does not constitute a direct threat to the health or safety of others."[15]. This approach was then built into the *Americans with Disabilities Act of 1991* which characterizes contagiousness merely as a defense to an allegation of discrimination on the basis of handicap.

So, legally speaking, in the United States and Canada [16] little controversy remains about whether the contagiousness of AIDS challenges the status of AIDS as a disability or a handicap. The resolution of this issue also underscores an important lesson for resolving the social tensions created by the AIDS epidemic: however we balance the rights of the infected against those of the healthy, we can only in fairness rely on proven scientific information about the actual, not the merely perceived, health risks posed by the contagiousness of AIDS. If someone with AIDS is asked to make a sacrifice for the health and safety of others, that sacrifice must not be founded on fear-induced assumptions but on facts.

This leads, though, to the second concern about treating AIDS as a disability. Does someone who is HIV-seropositive and contagious but otherwise asymptomatic have a disability? Plainly, HIV infection, even if asymptomatic, is a physiological abnormality: the body's lymphatic system is producing antibodies detectable through standard diagnostic techniques, and the presence of the virus, though not active, is responsible for a structural abnormality of the immune system. But even if the infection is an impairment, need it always be a disability? For if one is asymptomatic, what ordinarily expected, functional abilities does the infected individual lack?

What is at issue here can best be put in somewhat different language: In order to qualify for the social programs, benefits, accommodations and other privileges associated with disability policy, must an individual actually experience the disfunctional consequences of a disease condition or impairment? To be sure, if we discover that **everyone** who is HIV-seropositive will eventually develop full-blown AIDS, then this question will become irrelevant. Until then, should we be wary using the label "disability" for someone who is HIV-seropositive but asymptomatic?

Intuitively, it seems both fair and reasonable to require, as a condition of eligibility for disability benefits, that one actually have -- that is, experience -- a disability. It is easy enough to imagine someone acquiring mental or emotional disabilities upon learning they are seropositive. But what need would they have for vocational or occupational therapy, or any other response to physical disability, if indeed they are not physically disabled?

It should be noted that the challenge posed here involves the concept of disability, not handicap. There is no doubt whatsoever that someone who is HIV-seropositive but asymptomatic could experience the complete range of stereotyping stigmatizing and discriminatory reactions that are associated with handicaps. Conceptually, one can meaningfully and justifiably complain of being handicapped without actually having any disability (or, for that matter, any impairment): being handicapped is entirely a function of how one is perceived by others, since **handicap** is not a medical or rehabilitative notion at all, but a sociological or political one.[17]

Legally speaking, the asymptomatic carrier has sometimes posed a problem since definitions of "handicap" in anti-discrimination legislation reflect the rehabilitative ancestry of those statutes. So, although discrimination against the asymptomatic carrier has regularly been found to violate the legislation, courts have occasionally thought it necessary to invent disabilities that the carrier suffers from. One U. S. court , for example, argued that the disability of seropositivity is that procreation and childbirth, should it ever be attempted, would be dangerous to others. [18] And two Canadian commentators have argued that seropositivity is a disability with respect to those activities that pose a risk of infection to others since "the condition ought to prevent sero-positive individuals from engaging in those activities."[19]

These definitional maneuvers are nonsensical: what limits the activities of an asymptomatic carrier is not a physical inability, it is rather the moral and legal obligation not to harm others. Fortunately, it is no longer necessary to invent disabilities in this manner since, in both the United States and Canada, the legal definitions of handicap are interpreted very broadly, so broadly, indeed, as to include not only asymptomatic HIV carriers, but also anyone who may be incorrectly perceived to be impaired or disabled.

Legal definitions aside, the concern about the status of the asymptomatic HIV carrier is really a worry about threshold requirements for the administrative category of disability. How one deals with this problem depends entirely upon one's understanding of what disability policy is. If it is understood as policy providing employment-based rehabilitative services to those who really need them, then the category of disability needs threshold requirements. On the other hand, if disability policy is understood as society's response to the social phenomena of handicapping, then any medically-based threshold requirement is irrelevant and socially pernicious. In any event, this debate has nothing to do with the status of AIDS as a disability.

In short, neither the fact of contagiousness nor the case of the asymptomatic HIV-seropositive individual poses a serious problem for the overall project of bringing AIDS within the reach of disability policy, as long as we understand that policy in suitable broad terms. That said, though, it still must be shown why the perspective of disability is the most appropriate social response to the AIDS epidemic. How does this perspective assist us in weighing the rights of those infected against the rights of those who are not?

**The AIDS Epidemic and Disability**

As mentioned, there are more than two million North Americans who are HIV-seropositive. Of these, only a small proportion are significantly disabled or make extensive use of the health care system. And many individuals with AIDS are able to carry on with their lives. But, since they are contagious the question arises whether it is, as a matter of social policy, fair to expose others to the risk of infection in order to allow those who are infected to lead a relatively normal life.

One context in which this issue has been repeatedly raised is the workplace.[20] Here the tensions between equally legitimate interests is often dramatic. Persons with AIDS call for equal treatment and the right to carry on with jobs they are qualified and fit to perform. Their co-workers, however, insist that they have a right to a safe and healthy working environment, a concern also shared by customers and clients. How might such disputes be fairly resolved?

For concreteness, suppose a qualified primary school teacher who is HIV-infected, but otherwise healthy, is fired from a teaching job because of fear of contagion -- a fear voiced by both co-workers and parents. The teacher brings an action under a state or federal anti-discrimination statute, or in Canada, under one of the provincial Human Rights Codes, charging discrimination on the basis of physical handicap. [21]

Given the very broad legal definition, the adjudicator would have no trouble finding that the teacher was handicapped. Nor could there be much dispute that the teacher had been fired because of that handicap. So the onus would shift to the school board, as employer, to justify its actions. In particular, the school board would be called upon to convince the adjudicator that, in the circumstances, and taking into consideration the interests of all people involved, outright dismissal was both the appropriate, and the only feasible course of action open to it.

The school board would undoubtedly begin by pointing to its legal duties to provide a safe workplace, duties arising from occupational health and safety legislation, collective agreements, and government policy. It would then argue that the dismissal was justified inasmuch as the nature and extent of the disability made the teacher "incapable of performing or fulfilling the essential duties or requirements" of the job. [22] In effect, that is, the employer would argue that being free of HIV infection is a reasonable and legitimate precondition to employment as a teacher. Insisting that this precondition be met, the board would conclude, is the only feasible way of satisfying their legal duties and protecting all the interests involved.

In both the United States and Canada, the adjudicator would rely on a two-stage legal analysis to make sense of this argument. It would first ask whether the continued presence of the teacher on the job would pose a "sufficient risk" to the health and safety of others. To make this judgment it would ask for evidence of the realistic likelihood of HIV transmission in the school environment. Public perceptions of the risk, or commonly held but unsupportable fears about modes of transmission, are of no interest to the adjudicator: the issue before it is a purely factual one. As well, what is required is medical evidence with respect to the risk actually posed by **this** teacher in **this** working environment. In other words, our law incorporates the insight mentioned earlier that fairness requires, when balancing the rights of the infected against those of the healthy, that we rely on proven scientific information about the actual, not the merely perceived, health risks posed by the disease.

Given our current knowledge of the AIDS virus, the risk of infection from a teacher in the school environment is so minimal as to count, at best, as a theoretical possibility.[23] But a theoretical risk is not a "sufficient risk" in law since the latter level of risk incorporates and recognizes the legitimacy of the competing interests at stake. So, the school board would likely be unable to show that the teacher was, by virtue of HIV-positivity, unqualified to hold the job. In the result, dismissal being neither appropriate nor necessary, the school board would be asked to reinstate the teacher.

Suppose, though, the situation was different, and, instead of being a teacher, the complainant was a medical technician regularly exposed to transfusable blood, or an emergency room nurse, or an osteophathic surgeon. In these cases, the likelihood of transmission is significantly increased and the risk of infection no longer "theoretical". In these employment circumstances, an adjudicator might well be convinced that the risk was sufficient to warrant dismissal. If it does, however, that is not the end of the matter in our law. For now the adjudicator must determine whether the dismissal was the only feasible course of action open to the employer.

In this second stage of the analysis, the adjudicator asks whether "reasonable accom-modation" would enable the HIV-infected em-ployee to continue working without exposing others to unacceptable levels of risk. What is reasonable accommodation?

In the employment context, accommodation involves job restructuring or reassignment, the acquisition of new equipment and special aids, or the adoption or modification of appropriate procedures and protocols.[24] And accommodation is reasonable, according to the current legal test, if it would not unduly burden the employer.

In order to make the argument that she or he will be burdened unduly, the employer could raise considerations of cost, technical feasibility, the requirements imposed by health and safety regulations, inconvenience, and the like. The adjudicator's job will then be to look at this evidence, assess it, and reach a judgment. Should it decide that reasonable means for accommodating the HIV-infected employee do exist, then it might order that these be put into place. Otherwise, the employee with AIDS will have to look for other employment.

Of course, the law in this area is not as clear cut as this outline might suggest. Still, it is perfectly possible to detach the "sufficient risk"/"reasonable accommodation" analysis from its legal moorings and assess it as a model for public health policy -- as a method, that is, for setting out, and resolving, conflicts of interest created by the AIDS epidemic. And viewed as a general framework for making decisions about health measures, the analysis has much to recommend it.

First of all, the analysis is easily applicable to other AIDS-related conflicts. It would be appropriate, for example, to apply both the sufficient risk and the reasonable accommodation tests to the dilemma of whether to allow HIV-infected children to continue in the normal school programme. The analysis could also be used to resolve the conflict between a person with AIDS needing medical, dental, or psychiatric care and a health care worker who, fearing infection, refused to provide that care. It might also help to settle disputes between people with AIDS and their landlords.

In addition, the "sufficient risk/"reasonable accommodation" analysis places the onus of proof on those who would limit the rights of people with AIDS. This is appropriate because people with AIDS constitute (and hopefully will continue to constitute) a minority whose voice can be easily drowned out by the demands of an apprehensive majority. The analysis also requires a realistic and scientifically accurate determination of risk of infection, an important safeguard against the distortive effects of misinformation and misperception. As well, the analysis insists upon a case-by-case determination of both the risks to others and the ways of accommodating those who are HIV-infected, the two most salient aspects of conflicts between those who have a contagious disease and those who do not.

Finally, the analysis is founded, implicitly, on the premise that people with disabilities must be treated as equals, with a right to equal participation in all facets of society. Because of this focus, the issue of sexual morality need never be raised when the analysis is applied to AIDS. Instead, HIV-infection can be viewed as a handicap that results from a life-threatening, as yet incurable, and contagious disease syndrome. The analysis proceeds on the assumption that risks to others can be realistically assessed, and, in the usual instance, accommodated without imposing an undue burden on the healthy, or resorting to the drastic measure of preventing people with AIDS from engaging in the normal, social activities of living.

Despite all these virtues, there is a popular objection to this, or any other policy model that seeks to balance interests. We have only two options, the objector will insist. Either we try to secure the greatest health benefit for all, and ignore considerations of equality, or else we accept the cost in public health that the protection of equality might entail. Though we may be tempted by the second, only the first option is socially acceptable, for the simple reason that we can never be certain of the actual health risks posed by an epidemic. When the stakes are high, the argument goes, we cannot afford our cherished political values; short of medical certainty, as a matter of policy, we should always err on the side of caution and put considerations of equality in abeyance.

In effect, this objection suggests that our standard for "sufficient risk" should be set as low as possible, so that the merest possibility of a risk will be viewed as sufficient to justify unequal treatment. But the point of the objection is quite general and applies to any public health measure thought to be of assistance in dealing with AIDS. Compulsory testing and reporting, involuntary contact tracing, forced quarantine of non-compliant positives, criminal restrictions on forms of sexual conduct -- these and other intrusive measures could easily be justified as having potential -- which is say, merely possible -- epidemiological benefits.

This objection, therefore, leads us to the second tension created by the AIDS epidemic, that of balancing the effectiveness of public health measures against the sacrifices those measures require of everyone, healthy and ill alike. How can the law's approach to the rights and interests of people with disabilities assist us here?

In both Canada and the United States, the state has the constitutional authority to enact emergency health measures of the sort required in an epidemic. Yet, though courts of law have been reluctant to question the rationale or necessity of public health measures, they have always insisted that the state's authority in this regard is not unlimited. Quarantining or compulsory vaccination may be justifiable even though they involve sacrifices in individual rights; but the state must have a legitimate purpose in mind.

One facet of legitimacy has been the product of developments in the law regarding the rights of minorities, such as people with disabilities. It is now generally believed that legitimacy is undermined if the state shows a disregard for the political commitments that underwrite a free and democratic society. In particular, a disregard for equality, especially when manifested by arbitrary, irrational, or discriminatory policies prejudicing the interests of an identifiable group of people, undermines the legitimacy of the state's authority.

This basic doctrine is reflected in the legal principles that could be called upon to assess the constitutionality of invasive AIDS measures. In the United States, any social response to the AIDS epidemic that infringed the guarantee of "equal protection" would be subjected to strict judicial scrutiny.[25] The court would demand evidence that preserving public health was the real goal of the proposed measures, rather than, say, quieting the unsupportable fears of the electorate, or pursuing a policy of harassing gays. The state would also be obliged to show, both that there is a rational connection between the policy's objective and the means proposed to achieve it, and as well that there are no other, less intrusive means available for achieving that end.

In Canada, the governing law is the *Charter of Rights and Freedoms*, section 15 of which guarantees equality before the law, and prohibits discrimination on various grounds, including mental and physical handicap. Since public health measures have the effect of disproportionately burdening people with AIDS, they would be constitutionally suspect. The *Charter* provides as well, though, that infringements of individual rights can be justified if, on the evidence, the rights-infringing policies are themselves consistent with the values that allow all individuals to live their lives as free and equal citizens.

From a legal point of view, then, if AIDS is understood as a handicapping condition, the social response to the AIDS epidemic must embody a rational respect for medical and other scientific evidence, possess a clearly enunciated purpose, be open to public scrutiny and debate, and show a commitment to avoiding unnecessary restrictions on the rights and interests of those with the disease. In effect, these are the law's guidelines for assessing the legitimacy of the use of the state's authority to deal with the AIDS epidemic.

The rationale of these legal guidelines is not to outlaw all public health measures, reasonably believed to be necessary to meet a health emergency, which happen to infringe on the rights of people with disabilities. Rather, they ensure that attempts to respond to genuine and serious public health threats are medically necessary and do not needlessly violate the core political values that underwrite a free and democratic community.

Consider how the guidelines might help to resolve the tension between the effectiveness of health measures and the sacrifices they demand. Because of our political commitment to equality, the goal of our social response to AIDS must be to protect the legitimate interests of **everyone.** Thus people who have AIDS are protected from unwarranted infringements of equal protection, as well as from ill-conceived measures motivated by misinformation or fear. At the same time, as individuals with a contagious disease, people with AIDS do not have a legitimate interest in preventing any measure that is medically necessary to prevent the spread of AIDS. That is, as a rule, duties as well as rights are tied to disabilities.

Plainly, the interests of healthy people are also best protected by a medically sound response to the disease. It is also in their interest, however, to ensure that the rights of people with AIDS are protected, since, given the nature of the disease, there is no guarantee that they will not find themselves a member of that handicapped minority. And, more fundamentally, it is not a legitimate interest of this majority that the social response to the AIDS epidemic be irrational, duplicitous, discriminatory or otherwise undermine the political values of equality and liberty.

It is now easy to see why the objection mentioned earlier is mistaken. A social response to AIDS that sets its standard of medical rationality at the level of medical certainty undermines our commitment to equality, as it utterly pre-empts consideration of the interests of a specific minority. Refusing to allow any level of risk, whatever the consequences, is at odds with our political values; so, such a response to the AIDS epidemic would be outside of the state's legitimate authority. More concretely too, a zero-risk policy would be irrational and imprudent; it would cater to biases and fuel paranoia, greatly increase the likelihood of stigmatization, and make every unfounded fear a potential basis for a health measure.

**Conclusion**

Emphasizing the dimension of AIDS as a disability and handicap is thus helpful, not merely because it avoids the distortions raised when issues of sexual morality dominate, but also because it enables us to tap the resources of the growing body of law involving disability. Care must be taken in applying these legal principles as guidelines for policy formation, since they have evolved as devices for resolving interpersonal, rather than intrasocietal, conflicts of interest. And, it is true, these principles leave many questions unanswered: What level of risk is "sufficient"? When are accommodations unreasonable? What state goals and purposes are proper? How do we determine the least restrictive alternative means? Still, it is often the case for policy issues of the complexity of those raised by AIDS that any assistance in knowing where to begin, what questions to ask and what is really at stake, is a great assistance indeed.

**REFERENCES**

[1] For the metaphoric development of diseases see Susan Sontag *Illness and Metaphor* (New York, Vintage Books, 1979) and *AIDS and Its Metaphors* (New York, Farrar, Straus and Giroud, 1988).
[2] This perception is mirrored in many academic treatments of AIDS. The recent collection *AIDS: Ethics and Public Policy* edited by Christine Pierce and Donald Vandeveer (Belmont, California, Wadsworth Publishing Company. 1988), for example, is almost entirely devoted to a discussion of sexual autonomy and related issues.
[3] See L. Eisenberg "The Gensis of Fear: AIDS and the Public's Response to Science" (1986) 14 *Law, Medicine and Health Care* , 243.
[4] *International Classification of Impairments, Disabilities, and Handicaps: A Manual of Classification Relating to the Consequences of Diseases* (World Health Organization, Geneva, 1980). **Impairment** is defined here as "any loss or abnormality of psychological, physiological, or anatomical structure or function" (27) and **disability** as any restriction or lack ( resulting from an impairment) of ability to perform an activity in the manner or within the range considered normal for a human being."
[5] American studies suggest that between 30 and 60% of AIDS patients develop a syndrome of dementia, characterized by cognitive and behavioural changes including memory loss, inability to concentrate, and lethargy.
[6] The most recent version of the definition of **handicap** has been proposed by the Canadian Section of the ICIDH in order to more clearly highlight what the original drafters of the ICIDH had in mind. This definition focuses on the social

context in which the handicaps arise, and so defines a **handicap situation** as "a disruption in the accomplishment of a person's life habits, taking into account age, sex and socio-cultural identity, resulting, on the one hand, from impairments or disabilities and, on the other hand, from obstacles caused by environmental factors."

[7] See *Denver Principles"* the statement of the aims of the People with AIDS empowerment movement, set out in William B. Rubenstein in "Law and Empowerment: The Idea of Order in the Time of AIDS" (1989) 98 *Yale Law Journal,* 975, 990-4.

[8] That a category approach might be a convenient way of analysing anti-discrimination law as it applies to AIDS was suggested first by A. Leonard in "Employment Discrimination Against Persons with AIDS," (1985) 10 *University of Dayton Law Review* 681.

[9] See my discussion of etiological neutrality in *Physical Disability and Social Policy,.* The University of Toronto Press, forthcoming, June 1993.

[10] *Traynor v. Turnage,* Administrator, Veterans' Administration, e t al. 485US 535, (1988).

[11] The *Americans with Disabilities Act, 1991* Title 1 section 101: "For the purposes of this title, the term 'qualified individual with a disability' shall not include any employee or applicant who is currently engaging in the illegal use of drugs ..."

[12] 29 U.S.C. article 794

[13] Memorandum from Assistant Attorney General Cooper on Application of Section 504 of the *Rehabilitation Act* to Persons with AIDS is reprinted in *Aids and the Workplace* second edition (Rockville, Maryland, The Bureau of National Affairs, Inc. 1987) 137-85.

[14] School Board of Nassau County, Florida, et al v. Arlene 480 U.S.273 (1987)

[15] U.S.Justice Department, Office of Legal Counsel, application of Section 504 of the *Rehabilitation Act* to HIV-infected Individuals (September, 1988).

[16] See, for example, "Acquired Immune Deficiency Syndrome (AIDS): Policy Adopted by the Canadian Human Rights Commission "(May 25, 1988) and Ontario Human Rights Commission Policy on AIDS (November 1985) and the human rights case Biggs v Hudson (1988) 9 C.H.R.R. D/5391 for the Canadian approach.

[17] See my discussion of the dimension of handicap in *Physical Disability and Social Policy, The University of Toronto Press,* forthcoming June 1993.

[18] Thomas v Atascadero United School District 662 F. Supp. 376, 379 (C.D.Cal. 1987). For the claim that one can be presently disabled even if the disabling effects of an impairment are all in the future see *Department of Fair Employment and Housing v Raytheon Co* 56 U.S.L.W. 2637 (1988) and Local 1812, American Federation of Government Employees v United States Department of State, 662 F. Supp. 50 (D.D.C.1987). A similar argument was made for asymptomatic hepatitis B infection in *Kohl v Woodhaven Learning Center* 672 F. Supp. 1226 (W..D.Mo., 1987). And compare the argument of Robert A. Kushen in "Asymptomatic Infection with the AIDS Virus as a Handicap under the Rehabilitation Act of 1973" (1988) 88 *Columbia Law Review,* 563, 574.

[19] Philip N. Bryden and Brian N. Jarrett "AIDS, Employment Discrimination and the B.C.Human Rights Act" (1988) 9 *Canadian Human Rights Reporter* C/88-7, C/88-13.

[20] Another troubling situation involves HIV-infected children who have been removed from school because of fears of contagion. In the United States, the *Education for All Handicapped Children Act,* 20, U.S.C. (1986) provides parents and educators with fairly clear guidelines for dealing with these troubling cases. In Canada, no such legislation exists and the situation is legally unclear.

[21] My scenario roughly follows the case of Eric Smith, a Shelburne County, Nova Scotia teacher who was removed from the classroom and reassigned to non-teaching duties when a medical secretary disclosed that he had tested positive for the AIDS virus; the case was never litigated. (cf. The U.S. case of *Chalk v. U.S.District Court Central California* 840 F. 2d. 701 (9th Cir. 1988) .) I am following here the analysis provided by Derek J. Jones and N. Colleen Sheppard in "AIDS and Disability Employment Discrimination in and Beyond the Classroom" (1989) 12 *Dalhousie Law Journal 103* .

[22] See Royal Society of Canada, "AIDS: A perspective for Canadians (Summary Report and Recommendations) (1988), David Spurgeon *Understanding AIDS: A Canadian Strategy* (Toronto, Key Porter Books, 1988), and Canadian Medical Association, "ACMA Position: Acquired Immunodeficiency Syndrome" (1989) 140 *Canadian Medical Association Journal 64A).*

[24] See the U.S. Public Health Service, Centers for Disease Control "Guidelines for Prevention of Transmission of Human Immunodeficiency Virus and Hepatitis B Virus to Health Care and Public Safety Workers" (Feb.1989) and Canadian Federal Centre for AIDS "Occupational Exposure to the Human Immunodeficiency Virus Among Health Care Workers in Canada" (1 March 1989), 140 *Canadian Medical Association Journal* 503.

[25]  See the discussion of U.S. equal protection law in Note, "The Constitutional Rights of AIDS Carriers" (1987) 99 *Harvard Law Review* 1274.

[26]  An earlier version of this paper was published as "AIDS  and Disability" in Christine Overall and William P. Zion  (Editors) *Perspectives on AIDS* (Toronto:  Oxford University Press, 1991,) 13-26

\*\*\*\*\*\*\*\*

**About the Author:**  Jerome E. Bickenbach is with the Department of Philosophy , Queen's University, Kingston, Ontario, Canada. K7L 3N6 (Phone:  613-545-2182: FAX 613-545-6611

**Source:**  Reprinted with permission from the author who re-wrote this article specifically for the second edition of *Perspectives on Disability*.

# Beyond Baby Doe: Does Infant Transplantation Justify Euthanasia?
## David L. Coulter

*Recent advances in medical technology have made it possible to transplant organs into infants with severe heart and kidney disease, but the need for these organs exceeds the presently available supply. Some have suggested that infants born with the severe neurological defect of anencephaly might be used as organ donors, even if these infants do not meet the criteria for brain death. Current criteria for brain death are reviewed and it is concluded that this proposal represents active euthanasia or medical killing of infants with anencephaly. Justification of active euthanasia is discussed in medical, ethical, and historical terms. Recently developed protocols to obtain organs for transplantation from infants with anencephaly after brain death has been determined are described and their ethical implications are discussed. It is argued that active euthanasia of infants with anencephaly is undesirable and should be prohibited in order to safeguard the rights of all persons with severe neurological disabilities.*

**DESCRIPTORS:** advocacy, "Baby Doe," bioethics, euthanasia, medical treatment, public policy, seriously ill newborns

Professionals who work with people with mental retardation have a long-standing and legitimate interest in protecting the rights of infants born with neurological disorders who are at risk for developmental disabilities. In what became known as the "Baby Doe" issue, a certain measure of success was achieved in assuring that medical treatment is not denied to these infants (U.S. Department of Health and Human Services, 1985). Recently, however, there is an issue that goes beyond "Baby Doe," because it involves consideration of the active termination of the lives of infants with the most severe disabilities (Capron, 1987). This active euthanasia is being proposed so that organs may be removed for transplantation into other neurologically intact

infants. This article considers the arguments for and against such a proposal within the general context of safeguarding the rights of persons with developmental disabilities.

## Nature of the Problem

The past 20 years have witnessed increased success in transplanting organs into adults with end-stage kidney disease and, more recently, with end-stage heart disease. Until recently, however, organ transplantation was not generally available for young infants (Moskop, 1987). Nevertheless, 1,000 to 1,500 infants are born every year in the United States who might benefit if organ transplantation were available (Capron, 1987). This includes approximately 500 infants born with hypoplastic left heart syndrome, an abnormal development of the side of the heart that pumps blood to the body. This condition does not cause any problems prior to birth, but immediately after birth the heart is unable to circulate blood to the body adequately, and the infant invariably dies. There is no currently accepted or effective medical or surgical treatment for this condition. Recently, surgeons at Loma Linda University Hospital in California transplanted a heart from a young baboon into a baby with the hypoplastic left heart syndrome (Bailey, Nehlsen-Cannarella, Concepcion, & Jolley, 1985). The baboon heart was rejected by "Baby Fae". It is worth noting that babies with hypoplastic left heart respect except for the heart defect. If the heart defect could be corrected by successful heart transplantation, these babies would likely survive and live normal lives. Their long-term survival would be limited only by the (as yet unknown) life expectancy of recipients of heart transplantation in infancy.

Another group of infants who might benefit from organ transplantation are those who are born with severe kidney malformations or without any kidneys at all (Lum, 1985). The annual incidence of these kidney malformations is 3 to 5 cases per

10,000 births in the United States (National Institute of Handicapped Research, 1985). Some of these infants have other malformations, such as severely undeveloped lungs, which may affect their survival after birth. For the most part, very little treatment is available for these infants. Sometimes dialysis can control the problem until kidney transplantation is performed at a later date, and several efforts have been made to transplant kidneys into young children who have been maintained on dialysis. Transplant kidneys have functioned reasonably well despite several (Reversible) rejection crises (Holzgreve, Beller, Buchholz, Hansmann & Kohler, 1987).

Although many newborns might benefit from organ transplantation, the pool of available organs is quite limited (The Hastings Center, 1985). Generally speaking, hearts and kidneys for transplantation are available only from infants who suffer brain death as a result of birth asphyxia, sudden infant death syndrome, head trauma or battering, near-drowning episodes, or other severe injuries. However, organs from these infants are often unsatisfactory for transplantation due to anoxic injury to the heart and kidney as well as to the brain.

Recently, attention has focused on another potential source of hearts and kidneys for transplantation: infants born with the severe brain malformation known as anencephaly (Caplan, in press). Anencephaly is defined as "partial or complete absence of the cranial vault (skull) as well as absence of overlying tissues (scalp), and varying degrees of malformation and destruction of the exposed brain structures" (Lemire, Beckwith, & Warkany, 1978, p.8). At birth, an observer is able to look directly at the exposed rudimentary brain tissue, since the scalp and skull are missing. Generally speaking, the cerebral hemispheres are completely absent. All that is present is the brainstem, and even this residual brainstem tissue is malformed or incomplete. Infants with anencephaly may survive for a few days or weeks, but the residual brainstem tissue does not sustain breathing beyond that point and the infant invariably dies (Baird & Sadovnick, 1984).

Anencephaly occurs in approximately 3 of 10,000 births per year in the United States (National Institute of Handicapped Research, 1985), or 2,000 to 3,000 cases per year (Elwood & Elwood, 1980). Since anencephaly can be diagnosed before birth using $\alpha x$-fetoprotein screening or ultrasound examination, therapeutic abortion is an option that would prevent the live birth of these infants. The number of live-born infants with anencephaly who could become organ donors may also be reduced because of the existence of other malformations. In one study of 56 cases of anencephaly, 6 had major congenital heart defects and 7 had major kidney malformations (Lemire et al., 1978). Nonetheless, the number of infants born with anencephaly whose hearts and kidneys are normal is sufficient to permit transplantation of these organs into many infants and children who would otherwise die from heart or kidney disease.

Infants who present the appearance of anencephaly described above are easily diagnosed. Unfortunately, the diagnosis of anencephaly is sometimes made in infants who do not fit this description (Baird & Sadovick, 1984). During a presentation on this subject, the author was informed by a pediatrician of a patient with "anencephaly" who had survived for 10 months. Further discussion clarified that this infant had an intact scalp and skull and thus was not anencephalic at all.

What this infant most likely had was a very different condition called hydranencephaly. Instead of failure of brain development, as in anencephaly, the brain develops normally in hydranencephaly until some time late in gestation, at which point the cerebral hemispheres are completely destroyed by a mechanism that is not yet known (Fried, 1975). Infants with hydranencephaly appear to be normal at birth, since the scalp and skull are normally formed. Later, when the infant fails to develop any mental or motor skills, investigation demonstrates the severe brain defect. Infants with hydranencephaly may live for months or years in a vegetative state.

Hydranencephaly in turn can be confused with severe hydrocephalus, in which the cerebral hemispheres are present but pressed very thin against the inside of the skull by increased pressure and volume of cerebrospinal fluid. In the extreme situation, when the cerebral tissue is compressed to only 1- to 2-mm thickness, it is not hard to consider (erroneously) that there is no cerebral tissue. Relieving the pressure and drainage or shunting of the excess cerebrospinal fluid may allow some re-expansion of the compressed cerebral tissue in severe hydrocephalus. Hydrocephalus is treatable, while hydranencephaly is not.

Assuming that anencephaly has been diagnosed accurately, should organ removal for the purpose of transplantation be permitted? If so, at what point after birth should the organs be removed? This is the problem to be considered. In order to address these questions, one must first understand the current procedures for determining brain death prior to removing organs for transplantation.

## Brain Death

Brain death is defined as irreversible cessation of all brain function due to a known cause. The definition comprises cessation of all cerebral function as well as all brainstem function (President's Commission, 1981). The recently published guidelines for determining brain death in infants and children also incorporate this definition (Task Force on Brain Death in Children, 1987). Special emphasis is placed on the absence of all brain-stem function, including the absence of any spontaneous respiratory effort. A patient who makes any attempt to breathe is not brain-dead, even if this respiratory effort is inadequate. This is the currently accepted medical standard (Capron, 1987) and applies to infants with anencephaly. According to this standard, infants with anencephaly who are capable of breathing spontaneously are not brain-dead. Since the cerebral hemispheres are absent and there is no possibility of conscious awareness or social interaction, these infants are best described as being in a permanent vegetative state (Coulter, 1987).

Removal of organs for the purpose of transplantation from an individual who still has some brainstem function (such as spontaneous breathing) would be a form of active euthanasia. However, when the brainstem stops functioning and the infant does in fact fulfill the criteria for brain death (Task Force on Brain Death in Children, 1987), the infant could be pronounced dead and organs removed without controversy.

Some have argued that anencephaly is a unique situation because the brain is "absent". An "absent" organ has never been alive, so "death" is not a relevant concept. According to this argument, the "brain-absent" state is equivalent to brain death, so infants with anencephaly are by definition brain-dead (Holzgreve et al., 1987). One problem with this argument is that the *entire* brain is not absent in anencephaly, because some brainstem tissue is still present. Since brain death includes brainstem tissue death, "brain absence" would have to include absence of the brainstem if the terms are to be considered equivalent. Others have argued against defining infants with anencephaly as brain-dead because of uncertainty about the diagnosis of anencephaly (as described about) and because of confusion about the prognostic implications of the diagnosis of brain death if it were applied to infants who were actually in a vegetative state (Capron, 1987).

Ultimately, determining criteria for brain death is a medical responsibility (Task Force on Brain Death in Children, 1987) and not the province of law or philosophy. As of this date, the definition of brain death has not changed and still requires the irreversible cessation of all cerebral and brainstem functions, including complete absence of any respiratory effort. No exception has been made for infants with anencephaly.

This, then, is the dilemma facing transplant surgeons, parents of infants with anencephaly, and those who are concerned with protecting the rights of persons with severe disabilities. If live-born infants with anencephaly are not brain-dead, then they must be alive. Therefore, removal of their organs for the purpose of transplantation prior to the cessation of all brainstem function would have to be considered medical killing or active euthanasia. The result, however, may save another infant's life. Can this be justified? Can this dilemma be resolved?

## Ethical Issues

One source of guidance in approaching this dilemma is provided by ethics. The ethical principle of *justice* instructs us to treat all persons fairly. A person with a disability has at least an equal claim to a just distribution of the goods of society as anyone else and may have a greater claim because of society's duty to provide compensatory resources (Veatch, 1986). The question becomes whether an infant with anencephaly is a person. If such an infant is not a person, then there is no obligation to treat, and active euthanasia may be permitted (Weir, 1984). If (as the law recognizes) all live-born infants are persons, then active euthanasia is prohibited. Ethics cannot answer the question of the personhood of infants with severe disabilities, which reflects other philosophical and theological arguments and social values (Coulter, 1988; Lusthaus, 1985; Nelson, 1984). In any event, Weir (1984) argues that active euthanasia is justified only to prevent prolonged suffering when there is no interest in continued life. Active euthanasia to benefit another requires consideration of other ethical principles.

The principle of *beneficence* instructs to do good and *nonmaleficence* to avoid doing harm to others (Jonsen, Siegler, & Winslade, 1986. According to this standard, the good of each person deserves equal respect and protection, regardless of the interests of society as a whole. In medical treatment situations, this has become identified as the "best interests" standard and is the prevailing standard embodied in the "Baby Doe" rules of the U.S. Department of Health and Human Services (1985). According to those rules, continued medical treatment is not required if the infant is chronically and irreversibly comatose or if the treatment is virtually futile because it would only prolong the act of dying. Life-saving medical treatment may be withheld or withdrawn from such infants. Certainly this policy would justify withholding or withdrawing treatments from infants with anencephaly. There is nothing in this approach, however, which justifies the initiation of actions which would actually terminate life. In other words, the approach allows nature to take its course. Since infants with anencephaly are unconscious and will die within a few days or weeks if treatment is withheld, there is no necessity for active euthanasia to prevent prolonged suffering or harm to the person.

If an infant can be said to have no interests in continued life, then it is reasonable to consider the interests of the family and society in continuing the infant's life (Coulter, Murray, & Cerreto, 1988). Parents of infants with anencephaly often express the desire to see that some good comes from the experience (Gorman, 1986; Robinson-Haynes, 1987) and find some comfort in the knowledge that their tragedy has helped someone else's child. Society would likely benefit from using infants with anencephaly as organ donors, since it would save the lives of other infants who could become productive citizens. This utilitarian approach, which recognizes the possibility that the expected benefit to society may be more important than the potential harm to the individual, might permit active euthanasia. However, if a policy of active euthanasia actually represented a greater threat to society than the social benefit which it sought to provide, utilitarian considerations would oppose such a policy.

Western civilization does in fact have a long-standing tradition of respect for all human life. An extensive philosophical and theological literature exists that attempts to define human life in physical, mental, and spiritual terms (Nelson, 1984). The physical brain is not identical to the spiritual "soul" or mind, so the brain may be damaged while the soul is intact (Coulter, 1988). Judeo-Christian tradition prohibits killing in the fifth commandment (Exodus 20:13), which states simply "Thou shalt not kill." Active euthanasia would violate this commandment and thus represent a significant deviation from this traditional respect for human life. In this respect, a policy of active euthanasia might be a threat to society.

Perhaps an even greater threat to society is represented by the "slippery slope" scenario, in which once a process is started, a chain of events is set in motion which cannot be reversed. It is not hard to see that infants with anencephaly, hydranencephaly, or a permanent vegetative state have few, if any, interests in continued life. Thus, active euthanasia could be justified in all these situations as a potential benefit to society. Capron (1987) has pointed out how allowing persons in all of these conditions to serve as organ donors might actually represent a significant threat to society and undermine the benefit of transplantation. A more extreme extension of the "slippery slope" scenario occurred in Nazi Germany and is worth examining to see the effects of the absence of adequate societal controls.

## Medicalized Killing

Reviewing the experience of Nazi Germany in discussions of active euthanasia is sometimes regarded as inflammatory rhetoric that is irrelevant to the current time. Certainly those events occurred in a very different society, and current procedures would likely prevent a similar outcome today. Nevertheless, persons interested in safeguarding the rights of persons with disabilities should read Lifton's book, *The Nazi Doctors* (1986), particularly Chapters 1 to 6, and draw their own conclusions.

Lifton describes the "medicalized killing" program that ultimately led to the Holocaust, emphasizing "[A]t the heart of the Nazi enterprise was the destruction of the boundary between healing and killing (Lifton, 1986, p.14). The justification for this process was that killing "defective" persons would heal or benefit society. The concept of "life unworthy of life" was developed to describe such persons, and thus their killing was considered to be therapeutic and for the greater good of society.

The medicalized killing program began very modestly. Initially it involved only the killing of "severely defective" newborns. It was then expanded to include killing of children with severe mental retardation or cerebral palsy, and subsequently to include killing of persons with Down syndrome. Finally, medicalized killing was permitted for juvenile delinquents and adults with "schizophrenia, epilepsy, mental retardation, dementia, severe paralysis, syphilis, and persons who were chronically institutionalized or criminally insane" (Lifton, 1986, p.65)

The relevance of the Nazi experience to this consideration of active euthanasia for infants with anencephaly consists of the premise for the Nazi program, the concept of "life unworthy of life." Modern society must reject this concept outright. The life of an infant with anencephaly (even though brief) is worth something, as much as the life of an infant with severe heart or kidney disease. This worth must be recognized by those who are willing to end that life (through transplantation) in order to save the life of another. In this regard, it is worth noting that the recent report from Germany of organ removal from infants with anencephaly who were not brain-dead emphasized the need for "respect toward the fetal donor" and explicitly objected to "relaxing the protection of fetuses or newborns with anomalies less devastating than anencephaly" (Holzgreve et al., 1987, p.1070). Only through such vigilance will a "slippery slope" to more extreme situations be avoided.

## Resolution

The arguments in support of using infants with anencephaly as organ donors to save the lives of other infants with severe heart or kidney disease are indeed powerful and compelling. Yet, it must be clear that removing organs from an infant with anencephaly who is not brain-dead is a form of active euthanasia or medical killing. Those who seek to permit this active euthanasia must recognize the significant ethical, legal, and historical risks inherent in such a policy. On the other hand, those whose concern for safeguarding the rights of persons with severe disabilities leads them to oppose active euthanasia must acknowledge the suffering of infants who might benefit from organ transplantation as well as their families. Perhaps some way can be found to provide these organs without the necessity of active euthanasia.

The resolution of this situation involves the determination of brain death. As noted earlier, there must be irreversible cessation of all cerebral and brainstem functions due to a known cause. The recent guidelines for determining brain death in newborns suggest waiting until 7 days after the "insult" before considering brain death, in order to minimize any uncertainty about irreversibility (Task Force on Brain Death in Children, 1987). With anencephaly, the "insult" or cause of the life-threatening situation is anencephaly itself, a process that begins in the second month of gestation. Furthermore, there is no doubt about the irreversibility of the condition, since all infants with true anencephaly (as defined earlier) die within a few days or weeks. Thus, it may not be necessary to wait for 7 days to determine irreversibility. It may be reasonable to diagnose brain death as soon as the brainstem ceases to function.

If one simply waits for the infant to stop breathing and then declares brain death, the heart and kidneys will have been damaged by the progressive respiratory failure and consequent lack of oxygen to the point that they are no longer viable organs for transplantation. To preserve these organs in a transplantable condition, one must support respiration with a mechanical ventilator. Turning off the ventilator from time to time would permit assessment of brainstem function (i.e., spontaneous respiratory effort). If the infant no longer made any effort to breathe spontaneously, and if there was no other evidence of cerebral or brainstem function, a diagnosis of brain death could be made. Organs could then be removed without controversy, as with other persons who suffer brain death (Annas, 1987).

The practicality of this approach is demonstrated by the recent "Baby Gabriel" case, in which a Canadian infant with anencephaly was determined to be brain-dead according to these procedures and flown to Loma Linda University Hospital, where the heart was removed and transplanted successfully into an infant with the hypoplastic left heart syndrome (Anna, 1987). Replication of this result and confirmation of the success of these procedures would make the whole question of active euthanasia unnecessary.

One persisting ethical question, however, remains. According to this protocol, the infant with anencephaly is placed on a ventilator to preserve the organs for the benefit of another. There is clearly no intent or desire to preserve the life of the infant with anencephaly. If the ventilator is construed as harmful to the dying infant with anencephaly, then this procedure would seem to violate the principles of beneficence and nonmaleficence. If the risk of harm is minimal compared with the enormous benefit to the potential organ recipient, however, then this procedure may be justifiable (Annas, 1987).

The ultimate resolution of the question posed by this article would require that (a) society respect the worth of the infant with anencephaly; (b) all active euthanasia be prohibited; (c) mechanical ventilation be permitted only if adequate steps are taken to minimize harm and prevent suffering; (d) brain death is diagnosed according to currently accepted medical criteria (i.e., irreversible cessation of all cerebral and brainstem function, including spontaneous respiratory effort); and (e) removal of organs for transplantation is permitted only after a diagnosis of brain death has been made according to these criteria. Continued vigilance and advocacy for fulfillment of these requirements are the challenges that must be met by those who seek to protect the rights and interests of persons with severe disabilities.

\*\*\*\*\*\*

## REFERENCES

Abbas, G.J. (1987). From Canada with love: Anencephalic newborns as organ donors? *Hastings Center Report, 17,* 36-38.

Baily, L.L., Nehlsen-Cannarella, S.L., Concepcion, W., & Jolley, W.B. (1985). Baboon to human cardiac transplantation in a neonate. *Journal of American Medical Association, 254,* 3321-3329.

Baird, P.A. & Sadovinick, A.D. (1984). Survival in infants with anencephaly. *Clinical Pediatrics, 23,* 268-272.

Caplan, A.L. (in press). Should fetuses or infants be utilized as organ donors? *Bioethics*

Capron, A.M. (1978) Anencephalic donors: Separate the dead from the dying. *Hastings Center Report, 17,* 5-9.

Coulter, D.L. (1987) Neurologic uncertainty in newborn intensive care. *New England Journal of Medicine, 316,* 840-844.

**Coulter, D.L.** (1988) *Ethical Issues in the treatment of persons with mental retardation.* Manuscript submitted for publication.

**Coulter, D.L.,** Murray, T.H. & Cerreto, M.C. (1988). Particle Ethics in pediatrics. *Current Problems in Pediatrics, 18,* 137-195.

**Elwood, J.M.** & Elwood, J.H. (1980). *Epidemiology of anencephalus and spina bifida.* New York: Oxford University Press.

**Friede, R.L.** (1975). *Developmental neuropathology.* New York: Springer-Verlag.

**Gorman, C.** (1988, February 1). A balancing act of life and death. *Time Magazine,* p.49.

**Holzgreve, W.,** Beller, F.K., Buchholz, B., Hansmann, M. & Kohler, K. (1987). Kidney transplantation from anencephalic donors. *New England Journal of Medicine, 316,* 1069-1070.

**Jonsen, A.R.,** Seigler, M., & Winslade, W.J. (1986). *Clinical ethics* (2nd ed.) New York: Macmillan.

**Lemire, R.J.,** Beckwith, J.B. & Warkany, J. (1978). *Anencephaly.* New York: Basic Books.

**Lum, C.T.** (1985). Current thinking in transplantation in infants and children. *Pediatric Clinics of North America, 32,* 1203-1232.

**Lusthaus, E.W.,** (1985). Involuntary euthanasia and current attempts to define persons with mental retardation as less than human. *Mental Retardation, 23,* 148-154.

**Moskop, J.C.** (1987). Organ transplantation in children: Ethical issues. *Journal of Pediatrics, 110,* 175-180.

**National Institute of Handicapped Research** (1985). *Summary of data on handicapped children and youth* (Department of Education Publication No. ED 395). Washington, DC: U.S. Government Printing Office.

**Nelson, J.R.** (1984). *Human Life: A biblical perspective for bioethics.* Philadelphia: Fortress Press.

**President's** Commission for the Study of Ethical Problems in Medicine and Biomedical and Behavioral Research. (1981). Guidelines for the determination of death. *Journal of the American Medical Association, 246,* 2184-2186.

**Robinson-Haynes, E.** (1987, July 28). Parents of dying babies can't help others. *Sacramento Bee,* pp.A1, A8.

**Task Force** on Brain Death in Children. (1987). Guidelines for the determination of brain death in children. *Pediatrics, 80,* 298-300.

**The Hastings Center** (1985). *Ethical, legal and policy issues pertaining to solid organ procurement.* Hastings, NY: Author.

**United States** Department of Health and Human Services. (1985, April 15). Child abuse and neglect prevention and treatment program: Final rules. 45 CFR, Part 1340. *Federal Register, 50 (72),* 14878-14901.

**Veatch, R.M.** (1986. *The foundations of justice: Why the retarded and the rest of us have claims to equality.* New York: Oxford University Press.

**Weir, R.F.** (1984). *Selective nontreatment of handicapped newborns: Moral dilemmas in neonatal medicine.* New York: Oxford University Press.

*******

**About the Author:** Davod L. Coulter, MD., is an Associate Professor, Pediatrics and Neurology, Boston University School of Medicine, Division of Pediatric Neurology, Boston City Hospital, 818 Harrison Avenue, Boston, MA: 02118

**Source:** Reprinted with permission from the author and *JASH,* Vol. 13, No. 2, 1988, pp. 71-75. Published by The Association for Persons with Severe Handicaps, Seattle Washington. USA 98133-8612

# Rights, Justice, Power: An Agenda for Change
## Marcia H. Rioux

### PART I

It is possible to win battles and lose wars. One of the great challenges of social movements is to recognize that incremental reforms are not ends in themselves. They are simply part of a continuum of change that leads to the broader objectives of the movement. For example, an organization wanting education for all people with disabilities could find policy-makers putting in place a nation-wide network of segregated schools which they claim would provide the education demanded. This solution would not, however, meet the target of an equal education - one which could only be attained within the regular school system. Neither would the target of equal education be met by placing students with disabilities in the regular school system without the supports needed to accommodate their particular needs. Similarly if an organization were working to ensure that all people with disabilities had adequate medical treatment, placing all people with disabilities in institutions with medical care would achieve that particular objective. It would, however, defeat the overall goal of the movement to achieve integration and citizenship. Social change, in itself, does not necessarily lead to the results that are being demanded

Within the disability movement we have, for the past few years, been going through a period of transition. During this time we have been developing a new agenda for social change - based on the link between equality and difference. To understand that agenda, and to find new ways of achieving the changes it calls for, we have to review previous agendas. We have to learn from the past and understand the limitations of the work we have done. We have to examine the present and to fit our existing goals with the directions in which Canada is changing and with what we want to achieve. And, we have to look to the future in the hope of fulfilling our wishes and dreams.

Learning from the past is usually the starting point for a new agenda. This does not mean that we reject what has been done before, but instead come to an understanding of why we did what we did, how we benefited from it, in what way it did not lead us to where we wanted to go and how we can use this information to move in new directions. To build a new agenda for social change that recognizes the equality-disability nexus, we must recognize opportunities that exist now which did not exist at other times.

For most of this century, people with disabilities were considered unfortunate, pitiable people who were given things because others felt sorry for them. They were the recipients of charity from people who were being kind. This was fortunate for them because if they were not cared for by their families or were not given charity they would have had nothing. They were not considered productive members of society, so no one considered that the state or anyone else had any obligation to give them the services and money they needed.

Since the 1950s there have been a number of changes in the way issues of disability have been addressed. First, the social movement and concerned professionals concentrated their efforts on establishing the means and the financial support to habilate or rehabilitate the individual. The primary motivation behind changes to programs and policies was the objective of "fixing" the person so that he or she could fit into society. This objective became the focus of programs and of reform lobbying.

There followed a period during which reformers wanted to ensure that an overall set of services was available to people with disabilities to meet their needs for rehabilitation. Energies were devoted to providing the best possible disability services. Most of these services were more or less segregated and were designed to give the person with a disability the greatest opportunity to fit into existing social structures. There was an ongoing effort to tinker with these services, to make them better and better - to ensure that service providers valued their "clients", to make services individually tailored, and to design services which would enable individuals to move into the mainstream.

Over the past 10 years a new agenda for social change was evolved. It was triggered in part by the enactment of the Charter of Rights and Freedoms and in part by reformers who recognized the kind of change needed to ensure social integration and citizenship. Rehabilitation in itself, no matter how effective , will not lead to fulfilling the goals that are now being demanded. Neither will a better system of services on its own achieve these new goals. While rehabilitation and services are necessary to achieve these goals, they are not enough to ensure justice and inclusion for people with disabilities.

The new goals for social change, which have evolved over the past few years, begin from a different premise. They recognize that the society, the "social system", has to change if people with disabilities are to be fully participating members. These goals are best characterized by three words:

## RIGHTS , JUSTICE, POWER.

What do these words mean?

*Rights* are entitlements. They are owed to a person, not bestowed because someone is kind enough to respond to a need. People who can demand their rights no longer have to wait for attitudes to change to get what they may rightfully claim as human beings, as citizens of Canada and as members of their communities. They do not have to wait until the rest of society is educated enough to accept them.

*Justice* is equality in its broadest sense, that is, equality of outcome. People with disabilities are entitled to the social and economic support they need to accommodate their differences in education, work and leisure to ensure that they end up with the same benefits as their fellow citizens. People with disabilities must be assured not only procedural equality (that the rules applied are the same), not only equality of opportunity to

compete, they must also be assured a portion of the pie that is equal to everyone else's.

*The third goal, *power*, involves having the ability and the will to bring about changes on one's own behalf for oneself. Power means being able to make one's own decisions and having the support, either financial or otherwise, which makes that possible.

In specific terms, the goals of *rights, justice* and *power* lead to a new agenda for social change which recognizes the inextricable link between equality and difference. This affects both the kind of changes demanded and the way society has to respond to these demands. The demands have switched: from charity to rights; from best interests to choice; from paternalism to self-determination; from disempowerment to empowerment; from professional control to self-advocate control; from cost-effectiveness to output effectiveness; from fixing a weakness (rehabilitation) to developing a strength; from expedient categorization to individual need; from service to support. What is this new agenda with its basis in the goals of rights, justice and power?

First, the new agenda is a political agenda. The traditional charity model, caring for the "deserving" poor, has created sympathy. Consequently the accompanying benefits for people with disabilities has come as a response to that sympathy. But sympathy is apolitical. A political agenda calls for a change in the nature of the interaction between society and people with disabilities, to a politicized relationship in which both parties have power. Political demands would replace requests based on the powerlessness or the weakness of one group. Second, the new agenda calls for services to be addressed in a different way. The old agenda dictated that people should receive the "best" services that the deliverers could conjure up. Services were in place to make sure that people were clothed and housed and looked after. But the notion of "best" changed over time. It used to be that a 12-bed group home was considered the best; now we think in terms of four person group homes or shared apartments or living on one's own. "Best" has gone from living on the outskirts of town or on a farm to living in desirable downtown residential areas. Best has changed from segregated pre-school programs to supporting children as students in their neighbourhood schools.

Third, the new agenda calls for an end to the notion that people with disabilities have needs and desires to participate that are different from those of other Canadians. The new agenda is about giving people autonomy, self-determination and power to make decisions for themselves and look after their own needs. It advocates for the citizenship, self-determination and equality of people with disabilities - basic benefits and rights that the rest of society already has. On behalf of people with disabilities the new agenda claims their right to entitlement to participate.

Fourth, the new agenda makes demands on the non-handicapped to share their power. It involves giving over the power of the service provider, the medical professional, the health care worker, the social worker to the person with a disability. At the community level, this means ensuring that persons with disabilities have enough money and contractual status to decide the type and scope of services that will meet their needs. For those without disabilities it means giving up their position of power and authority, and recognizing that the expertise lies in the hands of the consumer of services. It means changing the traditional platform of government agendas which have been cost controlled and accepting only output controlled agendas.

Fifth, the new agenda calls for the recognition of the impact that people with disabilities in our communities will have on us all. It is often easier for people to understand the unfairness of excluding people from our environments than to understand the benefits that result from their inclusion. Having children with disabilities in the neighbourhood schools, in the regular labour force, in the community recreational facilities, in the movie theaters changes the quality of all those places, and changes what takes place there. It fosters a spirit of acceptance, a sense of community, a re-evaluation of basic values and a creative diversity. The education system is better overall for everyone when it has to recognize individual needs. The labour force has to set different priorities when people who were traditionally excluded are included in jobs, in boardrooms, and in policy setting activities. The experience of women entering the labour force showed us that. As cultural and arts communities have begun to include aboriginal art and theatre and the work of other cultures, they have become richer sources of education and enjoyment for all audiences. And so arts and culture will be richer for all consumers when people with disabilities are both producers and audiences. The benefits of inclusion of those with disabilities in all activities will be experienced by everyone in society.

This new agenda based on the equality-disability nexus and promoting the goals of rights, justice and power provides a set of guidelines against which change can be evaluated over the next few years. In the following three parts of this series of articles the specific implications of this new agenda will be considered.

\*\*\*\*

PART II

# Rights, Justice, Power: A Culture of Diversity

The special well-being of a society requires that people of all kinds are included and accepted as equals.

It means finding ways of ensuring that everyone is a fully participating citizen, without being penalized because of race, sex, ethnicity, religion, or physical or mental ability. This is not only a moral imperative but a social and legal requirement in Canada under the Charter of Rights and Freedoms, as well as Provincial/Territorial and Federal human rights legislation.

It seems, however, to be taking some time for us to alter our way of providing social, legal and economic benefits so that we can truly say - in reality, not just in principle - that all Canadians have equal rights and that differences are respected and taken into account.

Traditionally, social programmes and laws were established to "protect" those too infirm or too inarticulate to protest their fundamental deprivations. However, most of the laws and programmes established for this purpose have acted as a means of protecting certain classes of people in exchange for the waiver of other fundamental rights, such as liberty, property, self-determination, reputation and even life.

These laws have put people with disabilities into the position of having to prove that they are entitled to goods and services which have become "privileges" rather than rights.

Many of the laws and social programmes in place establish and reinforce a social order that involves exclusion or paternalistic protections - and emphasize the inabilities rather than the abilities of people with a disability. The law continues to allocate rights on the basis of social contribution.

As a result, the contributions of people with disabilities have been unjustly undervalued or, worse, gone unnoticed because of their traditional segregation. People with disabilities have, consequently, had difficulty justifying their claim to the rights normally accorded with citizenship.

This is, in part, a result of a complex "labelling" process which, by permitting ignorance and fear of persons with disabilities to persist, has reduced their societal influence and credibility.

The history of the treatment of people with disabilities reflects two distinct ways of thinking.

The first was the idea that people with disabilities were dangerous and disruptive to society and, therefore, society should protect itself from their impact. The resulting policy was one of confinement and control. This led to laws and policy such as guardianship, institutional isolation and other forms of restraint. It also resulted in restrictions on certain people's rights to vote, to immigrate, to marry, to procreate and to own property.

Arguments in favour of such restrictions, and acceptance of them, were based on a perceived need to protect society from the assumed incompetencies and incapacities of persons with disabilities. In other words, people with disabilities were judged against incapacity, inability and difference from others. The differences were viewed as being negative, disruptive and dangerous.

The second wave of thinking, and of ensuing policy and programmes for people with disabilities, was to view people with disabilities as "pitiable" but deserving of charity and benevolence.

The resulting policy was one of control, exercised through medical decision-making, and provision of services through local authority and charity. The need to isolate people was no longer a need to protect society at large but to protect the individual with the disability - and to provide "special" services for these "special" people.

Within this framework, institutionalization and segregation were seen as beneficial to the individual. Therapy became the central reason for - and purpose of - treatment, programme and policy. The financial resources available were generally provided to the service, rather than the individual. This was based on the premise that a service provider was in the best position to determine the needs of the individual. The assumption that people with disabilities were being helped by special programmes in institutions or other segregated settings resulted in a failure to evaluate their benefits critically.

The impact of the programmes was viewed in isolation and, consequently, benefits considered fundamental to the well-being of other citizens were ignored in deciding the criteria of people with disabilities. The individuality and self-determination of people with disabilities is secondary - within a paternalistic, protectionist framework in which habilitation and rehabilitation are the primary goals of care, treatment, and programming.

This, once again, reflects the notion that difference is problematic and must be addressed and eliminated - or ameliorated.

In both these ways of thinking about disability - the protection/containment model and the charitable privilege model - the "problem" of disability has been presumed to reside in the individual. It was the individual who was out of step with the world.

Once labelled as "different", the individual did not fit into the labour market, did not fit into the educational system, did not fit into recreational and social programmes, and did not fit into the community.

The presumption then was that the individual had to be changed, somehow, to conform to the social, professional, and political structures in place. Consequently, the professional community and service providers in the field tended to focus on ways to "fix" the individual. The difference of disability was the problem, and it had to be remedied if people were to be able to exercise their right to equality.

The focus on "fixing" the problem was initially seen as a strategy of prevention. In some cases, this translated into "preventing" life - through sterilization, through withholding life supports or surgical procedures, or through genetic engineering. In other cases, prevention is interpreted to mean therapy or habilitation to make the individual fit into an existing environment and social structure created to meet the needs of those without a disability.

As a medical problem, specialists applied the medical model and sought medical solutions for what was accepted as an "organic" disease. Doctors diagnosed and treated those people with disabilities as patients, and the latter assumed the role of invalids. Much of the current literature on disability still reflects this model, with its emphasis on classification systems, diagnostic systems, criteria for evaluating disabilities, drugs administered and so on.

As a therapeutic problem, the individual was still seen as the locus of the problem, but the focus was not so much organic as therapeutic and educational. Specialists concentrated on teaching those in need the skills to adjust to their milieu. With the shift from medicine to therapy came a focus on effective service delivery. Social workers, therapists and non-profit organizations providing services increasingly came to believe the solution to the "problem" of disability was to ensure good services.

This was supposedly ensured by closely monitoring their benefits and appropriateness. Was the actual service benefiting the individual? Did the service enable the individual to learn and grow? In other words, specialists placed a strong emphasis on services and delivery mechanisms, rather than analyzing the services in a larger social context.

If the services were good enough, the "problem" would be solved. The issue was seen as one of appropriate service design and delivery.

Recently, there have been attempts to reframe the disability issue as a "rights and equality" issue.

This has important and significant implications for the way in which services, programmes, policies and laws are formulated. The way questions are framed is fundamentally altered from this perspective. A number of recent events has shaped this development.

Over the past 15 years, provincial and federal human rights laws have been amended to include persons with mental and physical disabilities. The Canadian Charter of Rights and Freedoms was introduced in 1982 and, among other disadvantaged groups, it extends rights to people with physical and mental disabilities. It recognizes that affirmative action is necessary to redress discrimination against all Canadians. Employment equity legislation is being introduced. These developments have, and continue to have, an important impact on people with disabilities - and on discussions concerning their rights and citizenship and the place and design of social services and income programmes.

Viewing people with disabilities as social units in need of repair or rehabilitation before being elevated to the status of "real" persons or citizens seems now to be outmoded, both legally and socially. Fitting in with the social structure has become much less important than changing the system to fit the individual.

The locus of the problem has shifted from the individual to the system, and this has had repercussions on generic and specialized service systems and on the work of advocates, governments, families and individuals with disabilities.

Examples of the strides that have been made in Canada to advance citizenship of people with disabilities in recent years are numerous. They include the recently won right to vote for persons residing in mental-health and other specialized institutions, and the precedent-setting right to integrated education for all children in their neighbourhood schools in New Brunswick.

The Supreme Court of Canada decision Re Eve has limited the power of the state and other third parties to perform intrusive medical procedures on non-consenting adults with mental disabilities.

These developments, along with a federally supported programme of deinstitutionalization, broad and ongoing reviews of guardianship and competency, new employment equity measures, and government implementation of special task forces on disability, are all indicators of a new perspective on disability.

Re-thinking what is needed to ensure the real participation and involvement in society by people with disabilities involves much more than figuring out how to rehabilitate people so that they are like others. It involves reorganizing the contribution of people with disabilities, not despite of, but because of their differences.

We have to recognize what we gain by the inclusion of people with disabilities and how changes in structures and services designed to include those with differences improve the quality of life and well-being of everyone.

Difference is not a problem. It is a solution to the narrow-minded, bigoted attitudes that have hampered our ability to make real progress in achieving the national goals of collective well-being.

Rights, justice and power can then be claimed by those with disabilities.

*****

## PART III

# Rights, Justice, Power : Rights-Based Technology

Starting with a view of the world that assumes that all people are equally valuable

and equally entitled to rights, justice and power has an important effect on the way an issue is addressed. The development of technology is an example. To address the ethical, social and legal debates surrounding the uses of technology from this perspective requires us to focus on the ways in which technologies can enhance and expand values that respect people's rights and increase social well-being. The uses and context of technological developments which create special problems from the perspective of respect for persons, beneficence, justice and the allocation of resources have then to be identified and eliminated.

Two specific examples provide illustrations of what a rights-based approach to technological development might look like. Both of these are currently recipients of large financial and scientific investment and too little scrutiny and regulation.

One is the issue of behaviour modification technology widely developed and practised with people who are said to have "severe behavioural problems" - including both self-injurious behaviour and aggressive behaviour. The other is the issue of new reproductive technologies. These two types of technological development are of particular concern to people with disabilities. Although they raise different sets of concerns in each case, people with disabilities are particularly vulnerable to the adverse consequences of their use.

Within the past few years, a number of technologies have been developed to control self-injurious and aggressive behaviour. There are people-prodding electrical shock systems, there are full body suits with computer-controlled electrical shock systems, there are electronically-controlled shock helmet systems, there are electronic white noise generators, and a whole myriad of drug therapies. This is the dark side of technological development. Such technology particularly affects people with developmental or psychiatric disabilities. It is qualitatively different from the technological development that makes computers accessible to people who have little use of the upper part of their body, advanced motorized wheelchairs that enable greater mobility for those who have limited use of their legs and arms or the development of accessible buses.

But the development of therapeutic technology affects other types of disability as well. One of the major concerns is that the decision to undertake technological and drug research and development fails to take into consideration the views of the people whom it will supposedly benefit. Some of the developments are simply benign (or irrelevant) in terms of their impact, interesting from the scientific perspective but of limited use to the consumer. Some are beneficial in a real sense, and some are detrimental. It is critical that there be consultation before funds are allocated to the development of technology and there be an evaluation of the potential for benign or discriminatory legal or ethical distinctions.

The development and use of behaviour modification technology is rationalized as a means to control behaviours which are determined to be so severe, self-injurious or aggressive that no other technique for controlling these behaviours will work. While they are claimed to be measures of "last resort", once developed they are marketed and used. There are a number of critical questions this raises. What does society and what do the developers of technology mean by "success" when they say these work? Why do non-technological - that is, social and environmental - solutions receive so little research attention? At what point does an action cease to be an ethical good, regardless of efficacy? What is the nature of treatment or therapy? How does one determine that a person has indeed consented to the use of the latest technology on themselves? At what point is it just to use technological solutions because they are in a persons's best interests? How can we ensure that individuals can refuse a treatment and still receive the care and services they need?

The starting point for discussions about the use of technology is unfortunately often made after it has already been developed. Waiting until then to initiate the debate is in itself problematic. Research and development cost a great deal and individuals become committed to the technological solution in the earliest stages. The conceptualization of the problem as one that

has a solution found in technology often precludes research and development in other areas. It assumes that the problem rests within the individual, rather than placing the emphasis of the research question on other causes and needs. For example, people who exhibit challenging behaviours typically do so in environments where they are subject to continuous management and control, where they are deprived of ordinary human interactions and where they have few opportunities to experience life in the community in ways that others do. It is scientifically imprudent and against common sense to assume that the individual's challenging behaviours have no relation to this controlling environment, to the techniques of control or to the people who are using those techniques. Consideration of environmental factors, such as the longitudinal effects of certain kinds of control and power, is frequently left out of the analysis of the behaviour of the person. In the absence of knowledge about where the real problem lies, it is questionable to proceed with the development of behavioural control technology/treatment that is predicated on the individual being the principal source of the problem.

The use of aversive technology raises ethical issues as well. At a very general level, the point at which an action ceases to be an ethical good regardless of its efficacy must be clarified. A decision has to be made whether technology that is ethically unacceptable is ever permissible, and if so, under what circumstances. In other words, where should society draw the line between what it knows is expedient, on the one hand, and what it believes is just, on the other? Things that are legally permissible may be ethically objectionable or prohibited. The use of depo-provera as an alternative to sterilization is a case in point.

Aversive technology also raises more general questions about society's obligations to the individual citizen. What, for example, are society's obligations to ensure that forms of "care" other than the use of behavioural management and punishment are made available in meaningful ways to individuals who have a disability and who need service or support? Is technology to be a substitute for the changes necessary to enable a citizen to integrate into the social and economic structures? Does this mean that whatever is the easiest and least costly solution is to be the end goal of the development of technology? And if so, is this to be generally applicable in society or only where the population in question is considered less worthy?

The lines between punishing technology, discriminatory technology and liberating technology must be carefully drawn and socially and legally regulated to ensure that some groups in society, particularly those with disabilities, are not disproportionately affected.

The case of new reproductive technologies again raises scientific, social, ethical and legal issues. New reproductive technologies include such procedures as in-vitro fertilization, genetic engineering and prenatal screening, which again raise questions about the impact of technology on people with disabilities. All of these procedures focus to some degree on enhancing the chances of producing healthy, able-bodied babies. The technological agenda in these areas risks the ethical and social transformation of the technological advances from a central concern for the well-being and potential of all people into an imperative to reduce or eliminate birth disability from the population. Because it is possible to change the nature of the fetus or eliminate it, there is a potential for people to feel they have to use that more intrusive technology. In this way, there is a dangerous tendency towards the normalization of procreative and genetic technologies.

The very emergence of research and development in this area has triggered within the disability community a sense of outrage, insecurity and inequality. Designating a class of people who are insinuated, through the research and development of reproductive technology, to be unnecessary and undesirable is questionable by any standard. It is also inconsistent with the principles of equality and justice which underpin civilized society.

The disability movement has faced an uphill battle in its attempts to become recognized as a disadvantaged group which deserves, indeed mandates, an equal share of well-being and social justice. To the already disproportionate liability that people with disabilities have had to bear, because of the lack of resources and services to support their participation, in order to participate in society, is added the further implication that technology ought to be developed which would encourage their elimination at the reproductive stages.

As a start, this is based on a false presumption. Even if genetic diagnosis were perfected so it could be carried out early and non-invasively, it could never be effective in eliminating disability. Eighty-five per cent of adult disability is caused after the age of 13 and more than 90% of infant disability is due to social, not genetic, causes. What is really troubling about this over-medicalization and geneticization of disability, besides its injustice, is that it obscures the basic socio-economic contributors to disability (including malnutrition, physical abuse, stress, exhaustion, and toxicity from environmental pollution). By obscuring these causes in over-emphasizing the genetic causes, social attention and resources are deflected into medical technology and professional salaries rather than into providing the nutrition, social support and other low-tech, non-medical measures designed to minimize infant disability or to counter its impact. Once again, technology is suggested as an easy solution to our problems - a vision of a technological utopia is proffered.

In other words, even if we thought it desirable, disability could not be prevented by genetic means. The idea of valuing the perfect able-bodied human is both irrational and a dangerous eugenic premise.

We are already seeing some of the negative repercussions of genetic monitoring and selection. In some countries, national and state governments are already compelling doctors to urge genetic counselling and abortion for fetuses which they believe will be costly if allowed to come to term. DNA databanks are already in use in criminology and being proposed as a mechanism to predict suitability for employment. The possibility of whole new forms of discrimination are raised by this technology. These include pressures for sterilization, threats to remove medical insurance coverage unless one aborts a fetus with a disabling condition (cases have already apparently been documented of such an occurrence) or the denial of employment based on genetic susceptibility to hazardous work place substances.

There must be a comprehensive review of what forms of distinction in recourse to new reproductive technologies, and in support of reproductive health research, may constitute discrimination on grounds of disability.

People with disabilities have the right to receive the full benefits of technological research, development and scientific progress. However, technological research and development is not a value-free enterprise, as it is so often held to be by the scientific community and by those who have been convinced that science is an objective enterprise. Science is not pre-eminent to these other issues. Without recognizing this fact, science threatens to mask the need to examine technology within a social, moral, cultural and legal context. It is imperative that social controls operate to restrict the real and potential hazards of technology and the biorevolution and to stop the legitimization of research and development which operates to obfuscate the advances that are being made towards greater equality and rights for those with disabilities. Wariness is in order wherever technological advances and scientific reconstruction of problems threaten to victimize less advantaged persons and fails to take into account their experience. Scientists and those who apply technology have no legitimate claim to be the moral gatekeepers of society - to enforce their standards, values and interests, like any form of moral gatekeeping, is only another form of discrimination based on social prejudices. If the principles of justice, respect for persons and nondiscrimination are to be upheld, then the development and use of technology must be subjected to the same legal and social scrutiny as housing, employment and educational opportunity receive. Further, the social and human impact of the proliferation of technological development must be evaluated, based on the *experience* of those who are at the receiving end of technology. The control of technology ought not to be left in the hands of doctors and hospitals, medical, industrial and military laboratories, and pharmaceutical and chemical companies.

Taking into account the values and interests of all groups in society, especially those who will be disproportionately affected by its use, has to be the minimum obligation in the funding, research and development of technology.

\*\*\*\*\*\*

**About the Author:** Marcia Rioux is Director of the Roeher Institute, 4700 Keele Street, Kinsmen Building, York University, North York, Ontario, Canada. M3J 1P3. She is an active advocate for equal rights for Canadians with a disability. Part IV of this series will be published in *Abilities Magazine* in the Fall 1993 issue. This four-part series of articles are from Ms Rioux's forthcoming book *The Equality-Disability Nexus.*

**Source:** Reprinted with permission from the author and *Abilities Magazine,* Autumn 1991, pp. 58-59: Spring 1992, pp. 60-61: Fall/Winter 1992, pp. 49.51. Published by Canadian Abilities Foundation, Box 527, Station P, Toronto, Ontario Canada. M5S 2T1.

# Ethical and Legal Rights of Persons with AIDS: Confidentiality Issues

## Sonja M. Feist

**Abstract** ~ *More and more health and human service providers are faced with assisting people with AIDS. Often they are faced with an ethical dilemma when clients refuse to inform those with whom they come in contact of their disease. Although confidentiality is crucial in the codes of ethics for health and human service providers, many practitioners are unsure of when confidentiality should be breached. This paper provides important ethical and legal guidelines that are helpful in making this decision.*

Confidentiality between the client and counselor is of major significance to the helping professions through their respective codes of ethics. The original intent of confidentiality was to promote full client disclosure during therapy and to protect clients from stigmatization (Gray & Harding, 1988). However, the recent development of the acquired immune deficiency syndrome (AIDS) epidemic has stimulated concern among health and human service providers. The main question often considered by practitioners is: At what time, if any, should a practitioner breach confidentiality with a client who has the AIDS virus to preserve the health and safety of society? Many practitioners emphasize the confusion felt by their duty to respect confidentiality when told that their clients refuse to share their HIV-positive status with their sex partners, or they share needles with other non-AIDS infected persons. This paper attempts to address the dilemma. First, it will define AIDS and confidentiality; and second, it will attempt to discuss legal cases and issues important in answering the very critical question--breach or fail to breach confidentiality.

### AIDS Defined

AIDS is a highly contagious, fatal disease primarily associated with, but not limited to, homosexuality and intravenous drug use. Since it was fist reported in the United States in 1981, AIDS has occurred predominantly in the homosexual and bisexual male populations. Other groups who are also at risk are current or former intravenous drug users, recipients of transfuse blood, heterosexual partners of AIDS-diagnosed and seropositive persons, male and female prostitutes and their sexual partners, and infants born to seropositive mothers (Center for Disease Control [CDC], 1986a). This disease is impartial to social, cultural, economic, ethnic, and religious groups and crosses all walks of life. AIDS is a virus that inhibits the body's immune system through the destruction of white blood cells, i.e., T4 lymphocytes (CDC, 1986b). This allows opportunistic infections to develop, such as dementia and pneumocystic carcimi pneumonia, a type of cancer known as Kaposi's Sarcoma.

In the United States alone, 38,312 cases were reported by the end of July, 1987 (CDC, 1987), and the cumulative case total by 1991 is conservatively projected at 270,000 (Morgan & Curran, 1986). As many as 25-50% of these HIV (human immunodeficiency virus) infected individuals may develop the full blown disease within 5 to 10 years after exposure to the virus (Oregon State Health Division [OSHD], 1987). Because there is no cure, the disease ranks as the most serious epidemic of the past 50 years (Quinn, Mann, Curran, & Piot, 1986). The severity and incurable nature of this disease poses the following professional question: At what point, if any, should a health or human service provider breach confidentiality in an attempt to preserve society's goal of health and human safety?

### Confidentiality Defined

Confidentiality is a very important aspect of all health and human service programs. In fact, it is the foundation of most, if not all, ethical and legal codes for such programs (Melton, 1988). Confidentiality is one of the assurances by which many service providers encourage clients or patients to disclose freely and honestly. Without confidentiality, many clients might be reluctant to self-disclose or avoid confiding in the service providers, consequently not seeking necessary medical or social services in fear of the repercussions.

Hansen, Stevic, and Warner (1986) defined counselor-client confidentiality as the retention of information received in a personal interaction with a client, which is composed of several levels. The first involves professional use of information. All discussion at this level occurs with others who have a degree of understanding of the meaning of the information. Information at this level would include test data, records, and other information about the client. A second level involves information that is transmitted by the client on a personal basis in the counseling interview. At the third level of confidentiality, the counselor does not divulge any material given by the client. However, there are four exceptions to this rule: (a) when a client presents a serious danger of violence to another, (b) when the client consents to divulging the information, (c) suspected or known instance of child abuse or neglect, and (d) when ordered to disclose by the court where no statute exists (Hansen, Stevic, & Warner, 1986; *Tarasoff v. the Regents of the University of California*, 1976).

Posey (1988) indicated that confidentiality is a question of responsibility: Who is responsible for protecting whom? Because AIDS has social, political, health, and moral implications, breaching confidentiality is often contemplated when health and human service providers consider the health and well being of others. Kain (1988) suggested that health and human service providers should protect the client since not all sexual relations are danger provoking. However, is this a risk worth taking?

Confidentiality has been noted specifically as the ethical standard which protects the client from unauthorized disclosures of any sort by the professional

without the informed consent of the client (Shah, 1969). The American Psychological Association (1981) and American Association of Counseling and Development (1981) define the limits of confidentiality as the point that a client or other persons are thought to be in clear and imminent danger. When this situation occurs, it is the duty of the service provider to inform the appropriate authorities. The American Nurses' Association Code of Ethics 91985) states that the "nurse must safeguard the client's right to privacy by judiciously protecting information of a confidential nature" (p. 40. The Code of Professional Ethics for rehabilitation counselors (Commission on Rehabilitation Counselor Certification, 1987) states that "a rehabilitation counselor will take reasonable personal action or inform responsible authorities, or inform those persons at risk, when the conditions or actions of clients indicate that there is clear and imminent danger to clients or others after advising clients that this must be done" (p. 30). The American Medical Association states that a "physician shall respect the rights of patients, of colleagues, and of other health professionals, and shall safeguard patient confidences within the constraints of the law" (Mappes & Zembaty, 1986, p. 148).

Many service providers confront ethical dilemmas whose resolution may result in an action which breaches confidentiality. An ethical dilemma occurs when a difficult problem exists that is seemingly incapable of satisfactory resolution, or when a choice is required between equally unsatisfactory alternatives (Davis & Aroskar, 1983). Indeed, breaching confidentiality can be an action taken to resolve an ethical dilemma. also, breaching confidentiality may provoke another problem with many consequences. When choosing between diametrically opposed solutions to ethical dilemmas, various ethical principles such as beneficence, nonmaleficence, autonomy, justice, and fidelity may be compromised.

Beneficence (to do only good) and nonmaleficence (to do no harm) are very critical aspects of dealing with persons with AIDS. Herrick and Smith (1989) indicated that although confidentiality is a weighty issue concerning persons with AIDS, beneficence versus nonmaleficence are two principles which may guide decisions regarding confidentiality, i.e., to do only good and to do no harm. Yet many argue that protecting the health and human safety of those persons not infected with AIDS supercedes the benefits of client confidentiality (Melton, 1988). This is especially important for persons with AIDS who deny that the disease exists and infect those with whom they may come in sexual contact. Herrick and Smith (1989) suggested that because some patients come from outside the mainstream of society (homosexual, bisexual, or intravenous drug users), breach of confidentiality can have catastrophic effects. Potential losses include jobs, insurance, friends, lovers, and relatives. Therefore the health and human service provider is working contrary to the ethical principles of beneficence and nonmaleficence. The Institute of Medicine, National Academy of Sciences (1986), informs that concern over possible breaches in confidentiality may promote patients to conceal their HIV positive diagnosis rather than to seek the medical treatment and human services needed.

Respect for autonomy, as it is manifested in the process of informed consent, is a very important guideline for health and human service providers who assist people with AIDS. Autonomy is based on self-governance, liberty rights, privacy, and individual choice (Beauchamp & Childress, 1989). Informed consent deals with the right to truthful information and the obligation of the health and human service professional to provide that information to their clients/patients. Hence, informed consent addresses the patient's right to information (Herrick & Smith, 1989). Cassidy and Oddi (1986) have pointed out that the process of informed consent involves the capacity of consent, disclosure of information, and the freedom to decide. Kjervik (1987) reported that the patient should be given the opportunity for meaningful informed consent based upon justice, according to what is fair, due, or owed to the patient. Laufman (1989) described the dilemma involved with the AIDS patient as a conflict between patient rights to confidentiality with the family's right to

information in order to protect themselves from possible infection, plus the patient's need to do some anticipatory grief work with his or her family.

When contemplating breaching confidentiality, justice and fidelity are ethical principles that are the most complicated to determine. Justice implies fairness and equitable treatment to all persons regardless of disease or economic status (Rawls, 1971). Fidelity implies the obligation to be loyal to the patient, community, and the profession (American Nurses Association, 1985). One's greatest uncertainty in making the decision to breach or not to breach is determining to whom one's fidelity should be strongest, the client with AIDS or society as a whole.

As a health and/or human service provider, imagine the scenario depicted below:

James is a 29 year old male who has been referred to your agency. After informing him of his limits of confidentiality, he confides in you. He indicates that he had been involved in a homosexual relationship for three years until he met Marsha, a young lady who works with him. Marsha, who has no idea of James' previous sexual history, has also become interested in him. Though James and Marsha have been intimate, they have not had sexual intercourse.

James has recently been informed by his previous homosexual lover that he has tested positive for the AIDS virus. James, after being tested, was also informed that he has tested positive to the AIDS virus. However, he has refused to inform Marsha of his condition. James is still determined to continue his relationship with Marsha, with the intention of having sexual intercourse without informing her of his HIV status.

As a service provider, you have tried repeatedly to encourage James to inform Marsha of his infection with AIDS, but to no avail. James refuses and indicates that this may be his only opportunity to have a heterosexual relationship, and Marsha is the "girl of his dreams." He also indicates that if Marsha is informed, she will end their relationship. As a service provider, what do you do?

Cohen (1990) provides an ethical theory and model rule that may assist health and human service providers determine their limits of confidentiality when faced with a scenario similar to the one mentioned above. This ethical theory and model rule defines a counselor's obligations involving sexually active clients who have AIDS and their sexual partners. Service providers should recognize a bond of confidentiality through utilitarianism and Kantian ethics. Utilitarianism provides a warrant for recognizing a professional rule under which providers are obligated, other things being equal, to respect client confidentiality. Kantian ethics suggest that providers never treat their clients as objects to be manipulated or used.

The model rule that defines a counselor's obligations is based on the ethical principles of nonmaleficence versus autonomy. It is Cohen's (1990) belief that the health and safety of society is more important than the clients' choice(s) and self-governance behavior. The model rule indicates that a health and/or human service provider should breach confidentiality when the following occur:

(a) Service providers who receive confidential information from a client suggesting that the client may have a disease commonly known to be both communicable and fatal must disclose pertinent information to a relevant third party(ies) if, and only if:

(1) There is medical evidence (e.g., a lab report) establishing that the client has the disease.
(2) The client is in a specific relation (e.g., a sexual relation) with a third party(ies) that, on the basis of current medical authority, places the third party(ies) at high risk of contracting the disease from the client.
(3) The client has not already informed the third party(ies) about his or her disease, nor is the client likely to make such disclosure, in any timely fashion, in the future.

(b) When the above-mentioned conditions exist, Cohen (1990) related that the service provider should follow these guidelines for third party disclosures:

(1) The service provider must make all reasonable effort to educate and encourage the client to make the disclosure on his own.
(2) The service provider must inform third party(ies) in a timely fashion.
(3) The service provider must inform the clients of her/his intentions to inform the third party(ies) before doing so.
(4) The counselor must disclose the information only to the party(ies) at risk or the legal guardian(s) (in the case of minors).
(5) The service provider must limit third party disclosure to general medical information regarding the client's disease.
(6) The service provider must provide counseling or an appropriate referral (if needed) to the party(ies) at risk.

### Community and Societal Rights

Many health and human service providers fear possible consequences of law suits and losing their job if confidentiality is breached. However, the rights of the community and society as a whole must be considered. Levine and Bayer (1985) ask the question, "To what extent should the identification of carriers...be a matter of public health responsibility?" (p. 10). Herrick and Smith (1989) question whether health professionals ensure confidentiality at a time when the public health is at risk. The answer to these questions will have varied effects on the rights of the AIDS person and the community as well. Davis and Aroskar (1983) identify altruism or the obligation to protect the welfare of the community as taking precedence based upon the utilitarianism. This position suggests that in serving AIDS patients the need to produce the greatest good for the greatest number should be adhered to. Herrick and Smith (1989) indicated that it is the health care worker's ethical and legal obligation to breach confidentiality in order to protect the public. This is based on the court decision of Tarasoff v. the Regents of the University of California (1976). Therefore, protection of community and society has been seen as taking precedence over maintaining confidentiality of information concerning the person with AIDS, if the situation is life threatening. However, Dean Guido Calabresis of the Yale law school (cited in Belitsky & Solomon, 1987) stated that since the repercussions of disclosure of AIDS are so great, the need for confidentiality arguably outweighs even the potential death of third party individuals who might contract AIDS. In fact, in California there is the risk of a fine and a jail sentence if harm results from disclosure of HIV test results (Melton, 1988).

### Legal Issues

The legal aspect of confidentiality is a very crucial and intricate part of the guidelines of health and human service providers in dealing with persons with AIDS. It has priority over other ethical concerns because there are no clear-cut federal court precedents in determining whether the University of California (1976) has become a legal reference for the helping professions in establishing one aspect of the limits of confidentiality. In the Tarasoff case, if was held that a psychotherapist was civilly responsible for failure to directly warn the intended murder victim of one of his/her clients when it was known or "should have been known" that the threat was real (*Tarasoff v. the Regents of the University of California*, 1976, p. 353). The court was vague in defining when a therapist "should know" that the client poses a real threat to another but concluded that "the protective privilege ends where the public peril begins" (*Tarasoff v. the Regents of the University of California,* 1976, p. 337).

The court found that although there is generally no legal duty imposed on one person to control the conduct of another, there is duty to warn if three factual conditions exist: 1) a special relationship; 2) a reasonable prediction of conduct that constitutes a threat; and 3) a foreseeable victim (Gehring, 1982).

Following the Tarasoff case, *Gammill v. United States* (1984) is another case that follows similar legalities and may assist health and human service providers in solving the dilemma of breaching confidentiality. In this case the Tenth Circuit Court of Appeals considered whether a military physician was liable for failing to report a case promptly to public health authorities of a patient under his care who had infectious hepatitis. The plaintiff became ill with hepatitis after babysitting a child with the disease. Interpreting Colorado law, the circuit court found that no special relationship existed between the physician and the plaintiff, whom the physician did not know. The court reflected the argument that a professional position by itself creates a duty of care.

The concept of duty to warn was initially developed in California and has since been variously applied in other states, depending upon the state's statutory and court-made law on confidentiality (Denkowski & Denkowski, 1982). For example, the civil statute in Texas does not require a therapist to warn potential victims of their clients' AIDS status, and, inadvertently, prevents them legally from doing so. In Maryland, confidentiality may not be breached even when the lives of others are at risk (Mappes, Robb, & Engels, 1985). In Illinois, however, the privileged communication act permits therapists/counselors to break confidentiality without concern for their own civil liability, in order to save lives (Mappes et al., 1985). Inconsistencies in state statutes are to be expected, in part, because the Tarasoff case only specifically addressed a unique set of circumstances in one state from which inferences about confidentiality are made to others. Furthermore, because a case involving a person with the AIDS virus has not actually been litigated, the precedent settling these kinds of confidentiality issues is not predictable (Gray & Harding, 1988).

### Conclusion

There are no clear guidelines for determining whether confidentiality should be breached. It is often difficult to determine a course of action if a client who is carrying the deadly AIDS disease refuses to inform his or her sexual partner of that fact. Yet another difficult situation exists when a client, who is an HIV infected intravenous drug user, fails to inform someone with whom he or she is sharing a needle. At present, there are no legal cases pertaining to breaching confidentiality with persons with AIDS that can be used as a guide for communication with their peers/sex partners. Tarasoff v. the Regents of the University of California case may be used as a guide, but there may be legal obstacles in one's own state that would supercede this decision. In essence, to breach or not to breach is a very important question and should be weighed very carefully, taking into consideration the potential ethical and legal outcomes.

When faced with an ethical dilemma with a person who has the AIDS virus, one should first determine statutes in their particular state that would govern breaching confidentiality. Second, it is necessary to obtain their agency's policy and procedure for breaching confidentiality if such a situation should arise. If there are no clear-cut guidelines, it is necessary to rely on their own ethical views.

The information provided in this paper can be used to assist present and future rehabilitation practitioners, and other health and human service providers when faced with a dilemma assisting persons with AIDS. It is important to carefully assess this dilemma prior to making any type of decision.

********

## REFERENCES

American Association for Counseling and Development. (1981). *Ethical standards.* Alexandria, VA: Author

American Nurses Association. (1985). *Code for nurses with interpretive statements.* Kansas City, MO: Author.

American Psychological Association. (1981). *Ethical principles of psychology* (rev.ed.). Washington, DC: Author.

Beauchamp. T., & Childress, J. (1989). *Principle of biomedical ethics* (3rd ed. pp. 3-67). New York: Oxford University Press.

Belitsky, R., & Solomon, A. (1987). Doctors and patients: Responsibilities in a confidential relationship. In H. Dalton, S. Burris, & the Yale AIDS Law Project (Eds.). *AIDS and the law: A guide for the public* (pp. 201-204). New Haven: Yale University Press.

Cassidy, V., & Oddi, L. (1986). Legal and ethical aspects of informed consent: A nursing research perspective. *Journal of Professional Nursing, 2,* 343-349.

Center for Disease Control. (1986a). Additional recommendations to reduce sexual and drug abuse related transmission of human T-lymphotropic virus type III/lymphadenopathy-associated virus. *Morbidity and Mortality Weekly Report, 35,* 152-155.

Center for Disease Control. (1986b). Update: Acquired immunodeficiency syndrome - United States. *Morbidity and Mortality Weekly Report, 35,* 17-21.

Center for Disease Control. (1987). *AIDS weekly surveillance report* (Report No. FTS 236-2472). Atlanta, GA: Author.

Cohen, E. D. (1990). Confidentiality, counseling, and clients who have AIDS: Ethical foundations of a model rule. *Journal of Applied Rehabilitation Counselors.*

Commission on Rehabilitation Counselor Certification. (1987). Code of professional ethics for rehabilitation counselors. *Journal of Applied Rehabilitation Counselors, 18*(4). 26-31.

Davis, A., & Aroskar, M. (1983). *Ethical dilemmas and nursing practice* (2nd ed.). Norwalk, CT: Appleton-Century-Crofts.

Denkowski, D. M., & Denkowski, G. C. (1982). Client-counselor confidentiality: An update of rationale, legal status, and implications. *Personnel and Guidance Journal, 60,* 371-375.

*Gammiff v. United States.* 727 F. 2nd 950 (10th Cir. 1984).

Gehring, D. D. (1982). The counselors duty to warn. *Personnel and Guidance Journal, 61,* 209-210.

Gray, L. A., & Harding, A. D. (1988). Confidentiality limits with clients who have the AIDS virus. *Counseling and Development, 66,* 219-222.

Hansen, J. C., Stevic, R. R., & Warner, R. W. (1986). *Counseling: Theory and process* (4th ed. ). Boston: Allyn & Bacon.

Herrick, C. A., & Smith, J. E. (1989). Ethical dilemmas and AIDS: Nursing issues regarding rights and obligations. *Nursing Forum, 24,* 35-45.

Institute of Medicine, National Academy of Sciences. (1986). *Confronting AIDS: Directions for public health, health care, and research.* Washington, DC: National Academy Press.

Kain, C. D. (1988). To breach or not to breach: Is that the question? *Journal of Counseling and Development, 66,* 224-225.

Kjervik, D. (1987). Consent and unequal power relationships. *Journal of Professional Nursing, 3*(3), 81-124.

Laufman, L. (1989). AIDS and the truth. *American Journal of Nursing, 89,* 924-930.

Levine, D., & Bayer, R. (1985). Screening blood: Public health and medical uncertainty. *Hastings Center Report, 15,* 8-11.

Mappes, D. C., Robb, G. P., & Engels, O. W. (1985). Conflicts between ethics and law in counseling and psychotherapy. *Journal of Counseling and Development, 64,* 246-252.

Mappes. T., & Zembaty, J. (1986). *Biomedical ethics.* New York: McGraw Hill.

Melton, G. D. (1988). Ethical and legal issues in AIDS related practice. *American Psychologist, 43,* 911.

Morgan, W. M., & Curran, J. W. (1986). Acquired immunodeficiency syndrome: Current and future trends. *Public Health Reports, 101,* 459-465.

Oregon State Health Division. (1987). *AIDS: Epidemiology and control information for Oregon physicians.* Portland: Department of Human Resources.

Posey, E. C. (1988). Confidentiality in an AIDS support group. *Journal of Counseling and Development, 66,* 226-227.

Quinn, T. C., Mann, J. M., Curran, J. W., & Piot, P. (1986). AIDS in Africa: An epidemiologic paradigm. *Science, 234,* 955-962.

Rawls, J. (1971). *A theory of justice.* Cambridge, MA: Harvard University Press.

Shah, S. A. (1969). Privileged communication, confidentiality and privacy: Privileged communication. *Professional Psychology, 1,* 56-59.

*Tarasoff v. the Regents of the University of California,* 17 Cal. 3rd 424, 551 P. 2d (1976).

\*\*\*\*\*\*

About the Author: Dr. Sonja M. Feist is an Assistant Professor in the Graduate Program in Rehabilitation Counseling at the University of Kentucky, Lexington, KY: 40506-0001. Her doctoral degree is in Rehabilitation from Southern Illinois University at Carbondale. In the past, she has specialized in gerontological research and is still pursuing research interests that include investigating the ways to enhance the lives of elderly individuals. Her present research interests include investigating the effectiveness of Federal-State Vocational Rehabilitation Services in assisting various disability and ethnic groups, especially visually impaired, African-American and Hispanic-Americans. She has begun a comparative analysis among African-American and White Kentuckians with disabilities to assess successful rehabilitation services.

Source: Reprinted with permission from the author and *Rehabilitation Education,* Vol. 5, 1992, pp. 225-231. Published by the National Council on Rehabilitation Education.

# Applying Ethical Principles in Rehabilitation Counseling

John Howie,
Eugenie Gatens-Robinson,
Stanford E. Rubin

**Abstract** ~ *Five ethical principles are considered to provide appropriate guidance for the behavior of rehabilitation counselors. These are the ethical principles of beneficence, nonmaleficence, autonomy, justice, and fidelity. Although they have been addressed in the rehabilitation literature, that discussion has been brief. This article is directed at providing a more in-depth discussion of the five ethical principles to promote an understanding of how they relate to the job activity of rehabilitation counselors.*

The relevance of the ethical principles of beneficence, nonmaleficence, autonomy, justice, and fidelity for guiding the behavior of professionals who provide services to persons with disabilities has been stressed in medical ethics (Beauchamp & Childress, 1989), psychology (Kitchener, 1984) and rehabilitation (Patterson, Buckley, & Smull, 1989; Rubin & Millard, 1991; Rubin, Millard, Wilson, & Wong, 1991; Tarvydas, 1987; Welfel, 1987; Wilson, Rubin, & Millard, 1991; Wong, Rubin, & Millard, 1991) literature. In the rehabilitation literature, they have been discussed as the theoretical foundation: (a) for the canons and rules in the Code of Professional Ethics for Rehabilitation Counselors, and (b) for the resolution of ethical dilemmas (Rubin et al., 1991). The ability to understand the importance of the content of the Code beyond the "I was told that this is how an ethical professional behaves" level is greatly dependent on a clear understanding of the ethical principles. Because previous discussions of these ethical principles in the rehabilitation literature have been brief, the purpose of this article is to provide rehabilitation counselors with a more in-depth discussion of them to promote an understanding of how they impact on their job performance.

In their daily work, rehabilitation counselors face decision-making situations involving conflicts between these ethical principles. They also have disagreements with others concerning what actions are in the best interests of particular clients. It is important, therefore, to understand the complex nature of these principles so they may serve as functional guides for the resolution of ethical dilemmas and disagreements with others. The way in which these varied conflicts are resolved will clearly affect one or more individuals with disabilities.

## THE PRINCIPLE OF BENEFICENCE

The Code of Professional Ethics for Rehabilitation Counselors (1987) states, in both its Canons and Rules, that the counselor must hold the interest of clients as primary and act in ways that promote their welfare. Therefore, it is quite clear that actions that would be classified as beneficent (i.e., doing good for or helping others) are central to the practice of rehabilitation counseling. The principle of beneficence defines an obligation to help others to "further their important and legitimate interests" (Beauchamp & Childress, 1989, p. 194).

Since an obligation to act in the interest of the client is central to the ethical context of rehabilitation counseling, both the general obligations to the principle of beneficence and the role-specific duty to beneficence within rehabilitation counseling will be discussed. Several problems associated with beneficent action, which may put such action in conflict with duties defined by other principles, such as duties to respect autonomy or duties not to harm (nonmaleficence) are also noted.

### The General Obligation to Beneficence

The extent to which people are obligated to actively promote the welfare of others is often difficult to define. In most circumstances, we clearly know that we ought not actively bring harm to another. But how far ought we to go in actively helping another? All things being equal, there seems to be some obligation to what philosophers have called "mutual aid" (Rawls, 1971, p. 114; Reeder, 1982, p. 84). Beneficence, defined as mutual aid, presumes that I should legitimately expect that another will come to my assistance or further my welfare if the situation is serious (e.g., if I were about to drown or starve), and if the action required to help me would require minimal sacrifice of the assisting person. The philosopher John Rawls (1971) asked what a society would be like where this duty to assist, which he classified as a natural duty, was rejected. In such a society, the individual members would be totally indifferent to each other's needs. Knowing that their own welfare had little significance in the eyes of others, they would have a difficult time in establishing or maintaining a sense of their own worth. In such a situation, the idea of the "common good" or the "general welfare" would make very little sense.

The strength of the duty to mutual aid is open to a wide range of interpretations. Singer (1972) suggested that when it is in our power to do so without risking anything of comparable worth, we have a moral duty to prevent harm or loss to others. But, how do we assess what counts as "comparable worth?" Ought I risk my livelihood, which is required to sustain and care for my own children, in order to remove a stranger from life-threatening harm? Or in the case of rehabilitation counselors, should they sacrifice much of their free time, during which they might meet the needs of their own children or other family members, in order to meet personally some of the social or personal care needs of their clients with disabilities?

Several elements are involved in assessing the strength of our general duty to beneficence. Following Beauchamp and Childress (1989), these might be summarized in the following way:

1. How significant is the need that is to be met, or how serious is the risk of loss or injury to the person to be aided?

2. Am I particularly qualified to meet the need? That is, am I in a privileged position in terms of either knowledge or skill to act in the interest of another?

3. Does my action have a high probability of actually achieving the desired end?

4. How much of a risk or burden to myself, or to those for whom I am responsible, does the action entail? Will the benefit to the person outweigh any harm or burden to me or mine?

The scenario often used to illustrate the weighing of these factors is that of someone witnessing a stranger about to drown. Such factors as one's swimming ability, whether one is the only one present who can help, whether the individual about to drown is an adult or a child, will amplify or diminish one's obligation to jump in and swim to the person's aid. A healthy adult with life-saving training, faced with the possibility of aiding a drowning child, seems morally bound to do so. It could be argued that a weak swimmer faced with the situation of a drowning adult has no obligation to dive in to save the individual in distress. Less effective, but less risky alternatives would be called for, such as yelling or running for help or throwing a limb or rope to the person. Just walking away, however, would be moral negligence, in light of the general expectation of mutual aid and the gravity of the situation.

In addition, the duty to help seems to be strengthened significantly if the person called upon to help is in some way responsible for the situation in question (i.e., for generating the need). If one's behavior has put another at risk or caused injury to that person, then a stronger obligation to act to assist that person exists. For example, if circumstances that I have created for my own benefit, directly result in serious risk or injury (or loss of livelihood) to another, I would have a stronger than ordinary obligation to help that individual even at some risk or burden to me. That individual's difficulty is, in a significant sense, my affair.

Such circumstances could be encountered in the rehabilitation process. For instance, a counselor has jointly developed an Individual Written Rehabilitation Plan (IWRP) with a client. The IWRP calls for getting the client off the SSDI roles and into competitive employment. If after a year of successful employment the client is about to lose her job and is no longer an SSDI recipient, the counselor would have a stronger than ordinary obligation to help her through the situation.

The obligation to mutual aid can function to establish a general societal obligation to provide services and facilitate the restoration of people with disabilities to a level of self-sufficiency and a reasonable quality of life. For instance, from the general obligation of mutual aid, interest can emerge in the welfare of those among us who require assistance in performing the basic activities of daily living, while maintaining a reasonable quality of life. This obligation to benefit others exists because of our mutual dependence upon one another and our basic respect for human beings. It is a duty which is mitigated by the limits of our ability to provide that assistance without seriously damaging the general welfare.

The obligation to aid one another should not be seen as something totally separate from and in competition with the general welfare. It is a mistake to see the resources of a community that go to aid those in need as a drain on the common welfare. Rather, acting on the obligation to help those in serious need of assistance contributes to the general welfare itself. Therefore, rather than viewing rehabilitation services as a publicly supported charitable venture, they can be viewed as a necessary component in any description of a "good" society.

Secondly, since the design of our social and physical environment is primarily aimed at furthering the interests and preferences of people without disabilities, many of the barriers, risks, and handicaps encountered by people with disabilities are relative to a certain environment (e.g., inaccessible public buildings or public transportation). A world designed for people who use wheelchairs or are blind would be a structurally different world. Thus, at least to the extent that these arrangements are arbitrary, society is involved in unnecessarily creating and sustaining conditions that put people with disabilities at risk and in various states of isolation, thereby increasing the level of dependence. Therefore, to the extent it can be accomplished without seriously hindering the important activities of others within the society, there is a general responsibility to eliminate any environmental barriers, risks and handicaps that specifically affect the quality of life of people with disabilities.

How a balance is to be achieved between the general welfare and the specific interests of people with disabilities is an ongoing debate. DeJong and Lifchez (1983) pointed out that given our aging population and the prevalence of disabilities in the older group, more and more of us will experience the onset of disability during part of our life time. It appears that the general welfare and the specific welfare of the population of people with disabilities will, in time, converge.

### Role Related Duty to Beneficence

The role-based obligation to beneficence can present a much stronger claim than that supported by the general obligation to beneficence. It is clear that within the context of certain roles such as parent, the obligation to assist and rescue from harm is very strong indeed, and the risk tolerated in fulfilling that obligation may be quite high. For instance, if the potential rescuer in the scenario referred to above is a parent, and the drowning person is her child, her view of her responsibility will not be as strongly influenced by lack of training or by putting her life at risk.

The Code of Professional Ethics for Rehabilitation Counselors, Canon 2 states: "Rehabilitation counselors shall endeavor at all times to place their clients' interests above their own" (p. 27). This is a very strong statement of a role-based obligation to beneficence which goes beyond any general obligation. The reasons behind this strengthened obligation to act in the interest of another in arenas like rehabilitation counseling include:

1. *Special knowledge.* Through training, education, and practical experience, the counselor has acquired a well-developed

knowledge of the special needs and risk conditions of a certain group of individuals. Therefore, they are in a unique position to help and to be able to assess the risk and benefits associated with different client actions.

2. *Control of Benefits.* The counselor has power to dispense or withhold resources and/or information that could promote the welfare of the client. Indeed, the counselor may at times be the client's sole access to needed information and resources.

3. *Societal Expectations of the Profession.* There is an implicit covenant within the client/counselor relationship that the counselor will act to promote the interests of the client. By entering the relationship, the counselor has given the client reason to have this expectation. Furthermore, the nature of the relationship allows the counselor special access to the intimate details of the client's life. The client provides the counselor with a picture of his/her needs and desires, strengths and weaknesses, with the understanding that appropriate help can be given. This access to private information not only increases the counselor's ability to help, it also increases his/her obligation to use this information in the helping process. The fact that the counselor is paid to help the client in specific ways further adds to the obligation.

These three conditions considerably strengthen the obligation to actively promote the interest of the client even at some burden or risk to the counselor. For example, the rehabilitation counselor may have to disagree respectfully with the other members of the treatment team in order to promote the interests of a particular client. Such disagreements with the majority of the team can be very stressful for the counselor. The counselor may be labeled as uncooperative, difficult, or even naively wrong.

### Problems with Beneficence

There are specific problems that relate to beneficent actions. First, there is a risk of undermining the dignity of those who require help, with the possibility of fostering a prolonged or dysfunctional dependency. Second, there is the danger that, while seeking to act in the interests of the client (as the counselor sees them), he/she will either

override or ignore the client's own judgment about what ought to be done (viz., paternalism). Thus beneficent actions may lead to conflict with other duties, such as those to nonmaleficence or the autonomy of the client (Beauchamp & Childress, 1989). One such conflict can be seen in the case of Jake, a client with a head injury. He has been on medication to control seizures, and has not had one in five months. Jake wants to take a job that involves considerable driving. The earnings associated with the job will restore him and his family to their pre-accident level of financial security. The counselor wants to help Jake become self-sufficient and does not want to interfere with his decisions. However, Jake's driving may pose a serious danger to himself and others. Here respect for autonomy and beneficence are in conflict with nonmaleficence. To forbid Jake to take the job involving driving would be to act paternalistically and to compromise Jake's autonomy. Not to intervene would place Jack and others at risk of harm.

Doing good for others is complicated. Rarely can we significantly change the circumstance of another for the better, without introducing new risks. Acting for another's interest involves assessing as competently as possible how that action might also put the person or others at risk. A good example is the situation of an individual with chronic schizophrenia who seems to be stabilized on medication. The individual has trained for a job in computer sales. There is an open computer sales position in the community for which the individual wants to apply. However, the psychiatrist believes that the client cannot handle the stress of the job. This case obviously contains a question of a balance of risks and benefits which must be evaluated in determining how best to promote the client's interests.

When a counselor succeeds in helping a client find desired employment, there is always the risk that the situation may prove too challenging or stressful. There are many types of challenging employment that would appeal to the client in terms of earnings, but might present a risk. Some clients might fail at these desired jobs and lose confidence and incentive. However, trying less risky situations might not allow clients to obtain a valid picture of their skills, and may result in some clients achieving a lower level of independence and financial security.

The counselor-client relationship is asymmetrical because of differences in power and expertise. If the course of action chosen is to be more than merely superficially beneficial, the help must be provided in a manner that does not undermine the client's sense of self worth.  By doing so, the counselor encourages a desirable level of independence rather than reinforcing unwarranted dependence.

At the same time, it is vital that the need to rely upon others when help is genuinely needed  is not construed as a failing by either the client or the counselor.  The pairing of a responsibility to provide help with societal ambivalence about dependency and the high value placed upon individual autonomy creates a tension that pervades the role of the rehabilitation counselor.  The tension is also there for the client faced with risking his or her autonomy in order to reach a higher level of self-sufficiency in the future.

Through education and experience, the counselor has a generally greater ability to assess the risks and benefits of various courses of action open to the client.  The client may have a decreased level of competence in some areas, or he or she may be socially naive due to educational isolation or parental over-protection.  There may be valid reasons to question the client's ability to make good judgments concerning personal interests.  It may be the counselor's best judgment that certain courses of action are far too risky or have a high probability of failing, and therefore, are inappropriate for the client.  If the client (for his or her own reasons) chooses the risky course, the counselor may have a very difficult dilemma.  This type of conflict can arise in a variety of ways.  A client with a chronic condition may choose employment which is ill advised (e.g., a person with asthma who wants to work in a coal mine or a client with a history of epilepsy who wants to drive a truck).  Or, the client may be strongly inclined to pursue a course of training which, given all the evidence, he or she will not complete (e. g., to start a four year college degree when, due to

depression, the client has never been able to complete even one semester in a junior college).  In such circumstances the counselor has the delicate task of helping clients pursue their genuine interests, which may involve helping them change their mind, while not overriding their autonomy.

Mature people with normal faculties are typically allowed to make their own mistakes.   In fact, freedom to err and experience the consequences of one's actions is essential to developing maturity and independence.  Therefore, we do not interfere, except perhaps verbally, with a friend who has decided to climb Everest or race cars although the level of mortal risk is very high.  On the other hand, we do restrain an intoxicated friend from swimming across a lake, and we do not knowingly allow a depressed person access to a gun.

To treat people paternalistically is to treat them like children.  This sort of treatment stands in serious tension with the primary goal of rehabilitation to foster growth and independence.   To justify paternalistic beneficent action, the current authors believe that certain conditions must be present.  They would include the following:

1. The client is *actually* limited in his or her ability to act autonomously and to adequately assess personal interests.  (The client is seriously depressed, mentally ill, uninformed, coerced, drugged, etc.).

2. The authority to act in the interest of another is based on a knowledge of the conditions promoting the client's *real* interests that is superior to the client's own knowledge.

3. A serious effort has been made to know the particular personal interests of the client and to take those interests as primary.

4. The risk to the client is real and significant, making the subsequent loss of autonomy the minimum necessary to promote the well-being of the client.

These conditions are not easily met. It should be emphasized that the factual authority possessed by various kinds of experts does not automatically confer the moral authority required for legitimate paternalistic action. Sennet (1980) called paternalism based only on expertise, and not in the intimate and attentive knowledge required to understand the welfare of another, "the authority of false love" (p. 50).

## THE PRINCIPLE OF NONMALEFICENCE

The principle of nonmaleficence requires that one neither inflict harm nor impose risk of harm upon another. Since beneficence requires one to do something actively for another, it is more discretionary than nonmaleficence, which requires only that one refrain from harming. Therefore, there is a sense that beneficence is more action-oriented, whereas nonmaleficence requires refraining from certain actions. The level of risk that an individual ought to incur in order to help another is usually of a lesser degree than the risk that ought be endured not to harm another seriously. For example, if a person has a serious communicable disease that might be passed to co-workers or even strangers, he or she has a strong obligation to avoid infecting those co-workers even if it means losing his or her job in the process. In a moral and a legal sense, it seems much clearer that nonmaleficence is required in most circumstances.

The situations that actually require beneficence are harder to define. For this reason, nonmaleficence is often viewed as always taking precedence over beneficence. For example, based upon nonmaleficence, a rehabilitation counselor might discourage a client from seeking certain placements, which involve both risks of harm and desirable benefits for the client. In a sense, a permanent hierarchical relationship can be hypothesized between the two principles so that one must always choose nonmaleficence over beneficence. This relationship does not always hold however. In the area of health care or rehabilitation, it sometimes is best to tolerate a rather high level of risk, or even to do a certain amount of harm in order to achieve a future benefit. Nevertheless, in order not to violate the principle of nonmaleficence, the level of acceptable risk must be carefully determined (Kitchener, 1984).

The codes of ethics of most helping professions include admonitions against doing harm. This admonition is a recognition of the special situation of the physician and patient or the client and counselor. Counselors are in a position to either help or harm clients by virtue of their authority. They may be in the morally troubling position of doing harm, while being undetected. Thus they must always consciously avoid any opportunity to use the power given by either access to confidential knowledge or expertise to do harm.

A counselor cannot be expected to like or get along well with every client. The possibility of acting in ways that undermine the client's best interest might be at times quite real, but the counselor has a strong role-related obligation never to act on that possibility.

Not only is the counselor in the position to harm the client deliberately, but also through negligence. The latter could involve a careless imposition of unnecessary risk, or it might stem from the lack of knowledge or skill which a professional should have acquired.

Kitchener (1984) pointed out that misdiagnosis by the counselor can be a significant harm to a client. This is especially true when judgments about a client's competency can determine the extent to which that individual will have control over his or her life. She also indicated that risk is involved when diagnostic labels, such as mental retardation or autism, are used. Individuals who are labeled incorrectly may not have access to the services that they actually need.

It is difficult to assess what may count as culpable ignorance on the part of the rehabilitation counselor. That determination requires an understanding of what knowledge and skills are sufficient for performing specific counselor tasks. It also requires an understanding of those special circumstances, such as excessive stress on the counselor or severe depression experienced by the counselor, that can lead to neglect of the client's needs. Therefore, it would be in keeping with the principle of nonmaleficence for the counselor to take steps to remedy such a situation before it adversely affects clients' care. It would also be reasonable for those in supervisory positions to take responsibility for maintaining an environment where the counselor's capacities to focus on the client's welfare are not impaired by excessive stress, uncertainties or lack of access to needed training.

## THE PRINCIPLE OF AUTONOMY

Autonomy refers to self-rule or self-governance. In an ethical context, autonomous choices require that an individual be free from the control of others. A rehabilitation counselor, in attitudes and actions, shows respect for the self-rule of clients by recognizing their diverse abilities and viewpoints, while respecting their perogatives to make independent decisions and take actions accordingly. Their respect for autonomy is expressed by the counselor's refusal to pressure the client toward specific vocational choices, and avoidance of withholding or distorting information crucial to the client's independent decision-making in regard to independent living or vocational goals.

In the rehabilitation process, client autonomy (as manifested in freedom of choice) is dependent on the presence of three conditions: (a) having a counselor who refrains from unnecessary interference in the client's independence in choice-making and action; (b) the client having relevant knowledge upon which necessary choices can reasonably be made; and (c) the client having the competence to use that knowledge to assess a situation, plan an action, and act in accordance with that plan. If any one of these three necessary conditions is not present, the client's autonomy is abridged (Beauchamp & Childress, 1989). The three conditions are elaborated upon below.

### *Voluntariness*

In order for the client to give voluntary consent to a rehabilitation plan, coercion must be absent and the client must have and understand information relevant to the decision to be made. Consent of the client obtained through coercion, undue pressure or through ignorance is a moral travesty against the client's autonomy.

In the rehabilitation context, authorization or consent means far more than it does in the medical context because of radical differences between the relationship of

doctor to patient and rehabilitation counselor to client. Generally speaking, in rehabilitation counseling, the relationship is an open-ended one that requires more discipline and action on the part of the client in the cooperative task.

### *Competence*

A person who is competent is capable of adequate decision-making. Such decision-making is presupposed for autonomy. In the absence of the ability to make adequate decisions, a person will not be deemed competent whether in law, medicine, psychiatry, philosophy or rehabilitations.

The boundary between competence and incompetence in decision-making is often difficult to determine. Perhaps, a wise approach would be to consider an individual competent to make his/her own decisions until the courts explicitly establish specific incompetencies of the client. Even then the counselor must be cautious because of the limitations of such court assessments. The law has often assumed that a person "...incompetent to manage his or her estate is also incompetent to vote, to make medical decisions about their own care, and get married, and so on" (Beauchamp & Childress, 1989, p. 81). The rehabilitation counselor dare not make such generalizations without sufficient supporting data.

In part, the sort of client competence needed for success in the counseling situation is the ability of the client to assess major risks and benefits and to make decisions based on such assessments. Some clients (such as people with traumatic brain-injuries, people with addictions, and people with psychosis) may, temporarily or permanently, lack such ability. Clients who cannot utilize relevant knowledge to make reasonable choices, or who lack understanding of the knowledge needed to assess a situation and to plan and execute an action, are incapable of autonomous decision-making. On the grounds of beneficence or nonmaleficence, the autonomy of such persons may be restricted. If beneficence is the ground, then their autonomy is restricted to choices among actions from which they can benefit. If nonmaleficence is the ground, their autonomy can be restricted to keep them from harming themselves or others. For example, when there are deficiencies in the independent living skills of a client and correlated risks of serious injury, then the counselor may refuse to support the client's desire for an independent living placement until the client has completed necessary independent living skills training.

For medical practice or research, competence might be restricted to giving consent to surgery or an experiment. However, for the rehabilitation counseling situation, competence means much more (e.g., the ability to assess critically various job possibilities and prospects, to work cooperatively to develop necessary skills for a more independent living situation, or to resolve affective problems under the sensitive guidance of a counselor).

## Full Disclosure of Relevant Information to Clients

Because of a special trust relationship with their clients, rehabilitation counselors have unusual responsibilities. For a client capable of competent decision-making, these responsibilities involve full disclosure of relevant information to the client. Disclosure of such information serves to empower the client for autonomous action. Similarly, this information enables the client and counselor to formulate jointly rehabilitation plans, including vocational objectives.

What information, generally speaking, ought the counselor to share with a client? Certainly the counselor should inform the client of the limits of confidentiality. The counselor is obliged to tell the client that whatever information the client shares will be kept confidential, except when the counselor is legally required to disclose such information or when its disclosure becomes necessary to reduce or to eliminate a "clear and imminent danger" to clients or to others (Code of Professional Ethics for Rehabilitation Counselors, 1987, Rule 6.2).

Most important for the rehabilitation counseling situation is the client's having relevant information to make wise decisions. For example, by denying relevant information to the client the rehabilitation counselor can limit the client's choice and thereby, effectively restrict the client's autonomy. Providing relevant information helps the client reach a decision and shows respect for the client's autonomy. For example, in vocational counseling, providing the

client with comprehensive information about job opportunities to facilitate client selection of a suitable vocational training program demonstrates in action respect for the client's autonomy.

Disclosure in rehabilitation counseling is more complicated than merely stating the facts. The relevance of the information and its use ought to be indicated for client decision-making. In addition, the disclosure of information, however crucial or important, cannot be counted as successful unless the client understands its bearing on his/her actual decisions. Understanding the relevance of the disclosed information is crucial for the client. For example, how does the counselor decide if a client truly understands, let us say, the job possibilities and prospects? If the client can offer a reasoned justification of a choice, the counselor may assume that the client has understood.

Directly connected with the issue of disclosure of information to clients is the concept of informed consent. Informed consent is inextricably related to information disclosure because what the counselor tells the client often is the basis of the client's consent. Informed consent serves a number of important functions, including: (a) enabling clients to make autonomous choices (e.g., in choosing a vocational training program to help achieve vocational goals); (b) minimizing the harms and risks to which clients are exposed by increasing their ability to protect themselves against unsuitable rehabilitation plans; and (c) encouraging the counselor and client to discuss matters in a fully informed way which will help in formulating plans that promote client success. This sort of discussion and planning puts the counselor and client on a more nearly equal footing.

## THE PRINCIPLE OF JUSTICE

Justice is another useful principle for guiding actions of the rehabilitation counselor. Distributive justice is especially relevant to the job of a rehabilitation counselor because it considers fairness in relation to distribution or allocation (who gets what) of resources and services.

In situations of abundance and cooperation, it is difficult to imagine any ethical problem of distribution or allocation. However, scarcity and competition make justice a troublesome ethical problem. Either of these conditions, taken by itself, would exacerbate ethical conflicts. Scarcity means that a resource or service is in short-supply. Only some needs, for example, rather than all, can be met. In such a situation, who gets what and why is a lingering ethical issue. Similarly, in a competitive situation, some demands can be met while others must remain unmet or perhaps even deferred. Who gets what, when, and why is a tangled problem. Taken together, scarcity and competition make distributive justice as a positive goal difficult to achieve.

For the rehabilitation counselor, scarcity means a *limited* amount of money and time to be allocated to meet the many and various demands inseparable from the job. Similarly, competition means that time and money allocated for one activity or goal cannot also be allocated for another activity or goal.. What is clearly immoral, in view of scarcity and competition, is waste.

Justice requires employing a relevant criterion as the basis of warranted differential treatment. For example, justice may require that one treats each client in relation to her/his needs, although those needs may vary from one client to another. In rehabilitation counseling, the principle of justice generally applies to the fair allocation of caseload monies to clients, as well as the fair allocation of the counselor's limited time for direct client services and the completion of other job tasks.

### Criteria of Justice

To understand the variety of just actions, one must consider the criteria used to determine a fair distribution of society's resources and services. These criteria that form the basis for distributing or allocating resources, indicated a property or characteristic that an individual must have to be a recipient. In each situation, a just action is one in which the resource or service is distributed on the basis of the relevant property or characteristic.

Consider a list of six (of a much longer possible list of such properties): to each person

an *equal* share, to each person according to *need*, to each person according to *motivational effort*, to each person according to *free-market exchanges*, and to each person according to *fair opportunity.* Each of these bases or properties may function as a criterion for distribution or allocation of time, resources, and service.

These criteria for distribution are sometimes thought of as rival approaches, or as alternative approaches for public and institutional policies. They offer different approaches for allocating scarce rehabilitation resources. However, there seems to be no obvious objection to accepting more than one of these criteria as useful. Indeed, any of these criteria might be accepted as useful once judged relevant for a specific situation. Deciding which criteria to employ in a particular situation and why is not easy.

Suppose, however, that, of these six, the criterion of need is chosen. If this is the choice, then distribution based on need is just. To say that a person needs something implies that without it a person will be harmed (or at least affected adversely). What needs will one choose? Fundamental needs would be a logical choice. If a person has a fundamental need, then the person will be harmed or affected in an undesirable way if that need is not met. For example, a person with a disability may be harmed by the inability to acquire an income sufficient to meet basic needs such as food, shelter, health care, or by an inaccessible environment that may prevent participation in many community activities.

A brief list of examples of these six criteria applied to rehabilitation counseling may be helpful:

1. *Equal shares*: Utilization of this criterion can be observed in keeping individual case service costs down in order to provide equal access to rehabilitation services to a larger number of eligible persons with disabilities or by limiting the amount of time spent with any one client in order to provide equal access to services for a larger number of clients.

2. *Need:* The counselor may give (or allocate) more case service time to a person with a severe spinal cord injury than to one with an amputated hand. The warrant for this discrepancy in case service time allocation is

that the person with the amputated hand might be more capable of finding needed services without the counselor's assistance.

3. *Motivation/effort:* A counselor would allocate more time and funds to clients with demonstrated high motivation (usually thorough effort required to accomplish tasks) than to clients not so highly motivated. A counselor might simply refuse to spend time attempting to assist an unmotivated client who is not working toward independent living or vocational goals. A wise counselor, rather than abandoning such a client, would likely suggest alternative avenues of help and enhancement or renewal of client motivation.

4. *Contribution:* More services would be made available to veterans with disabilities in recognition of their service, at no cost to them, than to civilians with similar disabilities, regardless of their financial state.

5. *Free-market exchanges:* The counselor could provide the client with those needed services that the client is willing to purchase. Laws of supply and demand are allowed to operate in an unimpeded manner.

6. *Fair Opportunity:* More services would be made available free of charge to persons with disadvantages resulting from congenital, disease, or accident related disabilities. This criterion is employed to equalize the opportunities of two groups, those disadvantaged persons and those not affected in that way, in order to provide the former with equal access to opportunities in a competitive society.

The last criterion, the fair opportunity criterion, can be seen as an application of the Fair Opportunity Rule. This rule functions in two ways. It prevents persons from being granted social benefits on the basis of undeserved advantaging properties and insists that persons should not be denied social benefits on the basis of undeserved disadvantaging properties (Beauchamp & Childress, 1989). In effect, this rule requires that people with mental retardation, individuals with reading difficulties, or individuals with low IQ's should receive more of society's resources and services to offset their disadvantaging properties. For these persons to have fair opportunities, in competition with those not disadvantaged, the disadvantages

they have received in the lottery of life must be counterbalanced. Not to correct (within the limits of our resources) or to ignore these disadvantages (while being aware of their presence) is to lend them our approval.

In addition to the aforementioned criteria of distributive justice, indices of economic efficiency can be used as gauges of justice. One such index is cost effective analysis (CEA) which may be used to bring about a just allocation of rehabilitation resources. It has the advantage over some schemes of subjective weighing of choices since it involves a quantitative analysis directed at identifying the means of securing the most benefits for the least cost. It is generally formulated in terms of dollars spent for resulting benefits, although it could be formulated (still in a quantitative manner) in terms of time and energy. A just distribution, taking CEA as a guide, would be achieved if the counselor undertook whatever action necessary to produce the greater benefit (or, stated differently, a benefit equal to the best possible) for each cost dollar. With this quantitative gauge of justice, just expenditure would be one that brings about more benefits per unit of cost than other possible alternatives.

Although there is nothing wrong with economic analysis per se, when taken to be the *sole* or *determinative* element, humane considerations seem to be minimized. Since human dignity and worth obviously cannot be quantified, the impact of a purely quantitative economic criterion in rehabilitation policy and practice would be devastating. Often actions are morally appropriate because they express important values of society, even though they are not economically efficient. For example, efforts in terms of expenditure of time, energy, or money to habilitate or rehabilitate some individuals with severe disabilities are quite often not cost efficient. But such efforts are nonetheless morally appropriate because they symbolize the value of the lives of people with severe disabilities within our society.

### Unjust Criteria for the Distribution of Resources

Justice stresses the avoidance of discrimination, exploitation, and judgmental bias. Rehabilitation counselors, as a part of their client advocacy, are to eliminate "stereotyping and discrimination" toward persons with disabilities (Code of Professional Ethics, 1987, Rule 3.4). Much discrimination involves allocating or distributing resources or services on inappropriate bases such as sex, race, religion, IQ, national origin, and social status. To make these properties or criteria the basis for distribution is to act in a discriminatory manner. It makes difficulties resulting from luck or "life's lotteries" the basis for distribution rather than the defensible criteria of dessert or responsibility. When these properties or conditions are taken as the basis for allocating or distributing rehabilitation resources or service *injustice* has been perpetrated.

## THE PRINCIPLE OF FIDELITY

The principle of fidelity requires keeping the promises or commitments that have either been explicitly made or that others have been given good reason to believe have been made. Obligations to fidelity focus upon conceptions of loyalty and honesty. Ramsey (1970) considered the principle of fidelity to be the fundamental ethical principle, since it is basic to all sound human relationships. He viewed loyalty as a basic requirement for all good.

Obligations of fidelity are most clearly defined in certain voluntary relationships, such as marriage, friendship, or counselor/client relationships. The health and very existence of such relationships depend upon the trust that participants can place in each other, and the skill with which each person performs his or her role within the relationship. Kitchener 91984) pointed out that the quality of relationships like that between the counselor and client greatly depends upon the presence of honest communication and trust. To remove that trust would be to destroy the counselor's capacity to help and the client's capacity to receive that help.

Beauchamp and Childress (1989) claimed that the content of specific obligations to fidelity is dependent "on promises that were made, the expectations that were legitimately engendered, the nature of the special relationship and the like" (p. 342). The

tendency to reduce matters of fidelity to merely contractual considerations must be resisted. Although acting against fidelity may often be seen as a breach of contract or breaking of a promise, it is surely a mistake to reduce *all* types of ethical relationships to contractual ones. The character of the counselor/client relationship does not fit the contractual model for three reasons. First, there is asymmetry between the client (the one in need of assistance) and the counselor (the expert) who has the knowledge and power to assist. Second, it is not at all clear that the association is freely chosen or self interested in the symmetrical way that classical contract theory assumes. Third, since people have many relationships, they also have many correlated loyalties, some of which can conflict.

The kind of fidelity required from the care giver can be defined as the propensity to believe in the personal worth of the others and to have a serious and focused interest in furthering that person's welfare. Obviously, there cannot be an obligation to like another. However, one might argue that within the counselor/client relationship, the rehabilitation counselor ought to try to understand the client and to behave toward that client in a way that expresses this attitude of commitment to the client's good. This would actually create a situation in which the client responds to the counselor in an open and trusting manner. Examples of betrayal might involve gossiping and careless breaches of confidentiality (i.e., asking for personal information on the client from across a reception area).

Nodding (1984), in giving a phenomenological analysis of the caring relationship, defined different roles for the caregiver and the one to whom care is being provided. She claimed that there is not only an ethics of care but of being cared for. Nodding claimed the primary obligation of the one giving care is a certain kind of responsiveness, the cultivation of an ability to "feel with the other" (p. 30). The one caring, whether parent, teacher, or counselor, has a dual perspective in that they see from both their own position and from the position of the one receiving care. Since to be that well understood can be threatening, the opportunity for safe self-disclosure in an atmosphere of confidentiality is essential. Only then will those cared for be free to be themselves and not feel vulnerable. Indeed, it is being oneself, the "willing and unselfconscious revealing of self" (Nodding, 1984, p. 73), that is the major contribution of the person cared for to the relationship. Nodding claimed further that, "To behave ethically in the potential caring relation, the cared-for must turn freely toward his[sic] own projects, pursue them vigorously and share his [sic] accounts of them spontaneously. This is what the one genuinely caring wants but never demands" (p. 75).

Nodding (1984) made an important point concerning the difference in the role of the care giver and the cared-for individual. The care giver must see the cared-for as he or she is, or may become (i.e., "as he envisions his best self," p. 67). But the one cared for need not see the care giver in the same way. The cared-for can pursue his/her projects without considering their significance for the personal development of the counselor. The situation is what she calls "generously unequal," and involves what was earlier called the "asymmetrical" aspect of the relationship. If it becomes more mutually inclusive, it is no longer a relationship of counselor and client but of friends, where the concern for the well-being of the other is entirely mutual. Therefore, one can understand the prohibitions against special friendships or sexual relationships between the counselor and client, not only in terms of nonmaleficence, but also in light of analysis of the character of the relationship itself.

## Confidentiality

The place of confidentiality within the counselor/client relationship follows from the above discussion. Within this relationship, the counselor has a clear obligation to maintain honesty and the client's confidentiality, to keep the client adequately informed of his or her circumstances and options, and to support as much as possible the interests of the client.

There are arguments that justify the breaking of client confidentiality under certain circumstances. These circumstances are usually seen as involving high probability of major harm to the client or to others (Beauchamp & Childress, 1989). Tarasoff v. Regents of the University of California (1976) is a dramatic example of such a situation. In that case, a patient told a psychologist that he planned to kill a woman named Tatiana Tarasoff. The man was briefly detained, then released because he appeared rational. Neither the police nor the hospital informed the woman or her family of his repeated threats. The man carried out his threat and her family sued the hospital. Here the obligation to preserve the confidentiality of the patient was in very serious conflict with the welfare of others. The Code of Professional Ethics for Rehabilitation Counselors (1987) recognizes this sort of conflict in Canon 6, Rule 6.2, by stating that counselors have an obligation to notify authorities or the person at risk if "the actions of the clients indicated that there is clear and imminent danger to clients or others" (p. 29). There are also legal requirements for breaking confidentiality in order to avoid harm to a specific individual or the public. Examples of these situations would involve the threat of communicable disease, child abuse, or illegal activities, such as drug dealing.

It is very important to the integrity of the relationship that the client be aware beforehand of the conditions under which confidentiality cannot be maintained. In some instances, this client awareness can produce a tension that will reduce that client's willingness to be optimally forthcoming in informing the counselor of his or her real situation, and thus may impede the counselor's ability to help. The obvious tension here is between trust and betrayal. Nonetheless, openness in spelling out the limitations of the relationship in advance seem to be in keeping with the level of honesty required to maintain a functional relationship of this sort.

## Conflicts of Interests

The counselor is also involved in professional and institutional relationships that call for loyalty and honesty. It is clear that colleagues have expectations of one another based upon their relationships. Gossiping about or criticizing a colleague's abilities to clients is damaging to the community within which the counselor and clients function.

There should be some appropriate and easily accessible channels for review if the ability of a counselor is seriously in question. Bringing clients into such a discussion is potentially damaging to them, and should be avoided if possible. The conflicts may be very difficult if a counselor believes that a client is in danger of being harmed by a colleague's actions. It would seem that supervisors of counseling situations have strong obligations to ensure that mechanisms are in place to minimize such conflicts.

There is also the consideration of obligations which arise from team decisions. Canon 4 of the Code addresses professional relationships. It encourages rehabilitation counselors to promote the effective functioning of the treatment team in the interest of clients served. That effective functioning depends on the presence of mutual respect, trust and cooperation within the team. Rule 4.2 specifically states that rehabilitation counselors should abide by team decisions, even if they personally disagree, *unless there is a breach of ethical rules.* This, of course, involves a difficult judgment. What if a rehabilitation counselor is convinced that a team directed action is not a benefit or is even a harm to a client, and views it as a violation of the ethical rules? Perhaps a difficult conflict such as this ought to be addressed at the level of the community. An institutional structure that frequently places the judgments of rehabilitation counselors and other professionals at odds with one another, without an appropriate outlet for expression of difference and negotiation, can put counselors in very difficult positions in terms of both their professional and their moral integrity.

## CONCLUDING COMMENTS

The ethical principles of beneficence, nonmaleficence, autonomy, fidelity, and justice are general guidelines that arise from our experience of trying to live well together. They serve as general guides to our behavior. The common moral sense that this experience gives has been incorporated, sometimes awkwardly and not without contradictions, into our social and cultural structures and habits. Both our experience, as part of a public world and our more private individual experience, have lead most of us to understand that the viability of our shared life together, in any community from family to nation, depends on an acknowledgment of the kinds of basic shared values contained in these principles. This means we ought to promote each other's welfare. We ought not to harm one another. We ought to respect each other's freedom of choice. We ought to be faithful to our promises. We ought to be fair.

But, for any general principles, even scientific laws, the difficulty comes in the application to particular and often ambiguous cases. Rehabilitation counselors may agree that they ought to be fair to their clients. But how is fairness determined in situations where a rehabilitation counselor does not have enough time or resources to go around? Or how can a rehabilitation counselor benefit a client where the client's view of what is most urgently needed differs radically from that of the counselor?

The personal values rehabilitation counselors hold arise from their own personal interactions in the world and are bound to influence their interpretation of these ethical principles that have been examined. Those perceptions tend to create a predisposition to rank some principles as having precedence over others. For example, rehabilitation counselors who have personally had to struggle to achieve and maintain financial and personal autonomy may see the value of independence as being primary in almost all cases. Consequently, it may be difficult to believe that a person with cerebral palsy, for example, might not want to acquire the very time consuming skills of dressing herself/himself because she/he chooses to expend the energy elsewhere, and does not mind relying on a personal attendant. Rehabilitation counselors who place a strong value on autonomy, may personally tend to override other kinds of values such as safety (nonmaleficence) in order to promote the independence of their clients. They may be more likely to see fewer possibilities for clients as unrealistic and be more likely to support client risk-taking behavior in an attempt to maximize rehabilitation benefits. On the other hand, if through their personal experiences they developed a strong desire to help and protect those in need, rehabilitation counselors may have a strong tendency to foster the dependence of clients and to override clients' attempts at self-determination in order to "care" for clients in ways that minimize risk. Thus, rehabilitation counselors would have a strong tendency to favor behaviors that are beneficent and nonmaleficent over those that foster autonomy.

It is not necessary to view these tendencies to value one principle over another in a totally negative light. Strong commitments to all of these ethical principles are part of the very practice of rehabilitation counseling. Furthermore, it is natural that in the course of our individual lives we have come to see the importance of one or several of these values very vividly. For example, if one is a member of a social group that is frequently discriminated against, justice may take on a pervasive importance. In a sense, such a person may *know* more about justice than someone who has never had to be concerned about it. However, these priorities and unexamined strong commitments must be open to continual critical examination by rehabilitation counselors so that they do not close their minds to alternative points of view that might be more appropriate in particular situations involving clients with different, but equally valid experience.

********

## REFERENCES

Beauchamp, T., & Childress, J. (1989). *Principles of biomedical ethics* (3rd. ed). New York: Oxford University Press.

Code of Professional Ethics for Rehabilitation Counselors. (1987). *Journal of Applied Rehabilitation Counseling, 18,* (4), 26-31.

DeJong, G., & Lifchez, R. 91983). Physical disability and public policy. *Scientific American, 248*(6), 41-49.

Kitchener, K. 91984). Intuition, critical evaluation, and ethical principles: The foundation for ethical decisions in counselor's psychology. *Counseling Psychologist, 12*(3), 43-55.

Nodding, N. (1984). *Caring, a feminine approach to ethics and moral education.* Berkeley: University of California Press.

Patterson, J., Buckley, J., & Smull, M. (1989). Ethics in supported employment. *Journal of Applied Rehabilitation Counseling, 20*(3), 12-20.

Ramsey, P. (1970). *The patient as person.* New Haven: Yale University Press.

Rawls, J. (1971). *A theory of justice.* Boston: Harvard University Press.

Reeder, J. P. (1982). Beneficence, supererogation, and role duty. In E. Shelp (Ed.), *Beneficence and health care* (pp. 83-108). Dordrecht, Holland: D. Reidel Publishing.

Rubin, S. E., & Millard, R. P. (1991). Ethical principles and American public policy on disability. *Journal of Rehabilitation, 57*(1), 13-16.

Rubin, S. E., Millard, R. P., Wilson, C. A., & Wong, H. D. (1991). An introduction to the Ethical Case Management Training Program. *Rehabilitation Education, 5,* 113-120.

Sennet, R. (1980). *Authority.* New York: Alfred J. Knopf.

Singer, P. (1972). Famine, affluence, and morality. *Philosophy and Public Affairs, 2*(1), 229-243.

Tarasoff v. Regents of the University of California, 17 Calif. 42 (1976).

Tarvydas, V. (1987). Decision-making models in ethics: Models for increased clarity & wisdom. *Journal of Applied Rehabilitation Counseling, 18*(4), 50-52.

Welfel, E. 91987). A new code of ethics for rehabilitation counselors. *Journal of Applied Rehabilitation Counseling, 18*(4), 9-11.

Wilson, C. A., Rubin, S. E., & Millard, R. P. (1991). Preparing rehabilitation counselors to deal with ethical dilemmas. *Journal of Applied Rehabilitation Counseling, 22*(1), 30-33.

Wong, H. D., Rubin, S. E., & Millard, R. P. (1991). Ethical dilemmas frequently encountered by rehabilitation counselors. *Rehabilitation Education, 5,* 19-23.

********

**About the Authors:** **John Howie**, Professor of Philosophy at Southern Illinois University, Carbondale, received his Ph.D. degree from Boston University. He is the author of *Perspectives for Moral Decision,* editor of *Ethical Principles for Social Policy,* and co-editor of *Contemporary Studies in Philosophical Idealism* and *The Wisdom of William Ernest Hocking.* He has published articles in *The Philosophical Forum, Stylus, Educational Theory, The Calcutta Review, Darshana International, Idealistic Studies, Religious Studies, Bulletin of Bibliography and Magazine Notes,* and *Indian Philosophical Quarterly.*
**Stanford E. Rubin** is with the Rehabilitation Institute, Southern Illinois University, Carbondale, IL: 62901.

**Source:** Reprinted with permission from the authors and *Rehabilitation Education*, Vol. 6, 1992, pp. 41-55. Published by the National Council on Rehabilitation Education.